ITALY

Football League

Tables and Results

1898 to 2012

Alex Graham

INTRODUCTION

This book features a statistical history of football in Italy from 1898 when a national championship first began. Initially this was played in a knockout format, but as the years went by, some regional qualifying rounds and even the final itself took place on a League basis. The National League, known to this day as "Serie A", commenced in the 1929-30 season.

The national cup competition, the Coppa Italia, was first contested in 1922 and then, after a 14-year hiatus ran from 1936 to 1943. The Coppa Italia was finally reinstated as a regular event in 1958 and has run annually since then.

Between 1925 and 1944 a period of "Italianisation" was ordered by the fascist government led by Benito Mussolini. This meant that clubs whose names had "foreign" origins were forced to change in order to become more Italian. However, after World War II ended in 1945 and the fascist government was overthrown, many of the clubs reverted to their traditional names.

In addition to the results of all League matches and Final League tables for Serie "A" and Serie "B", a list of the top goal-scorers and results of the latter stages of the national Cup competition are also included in this book.

Most of the information in this book is taken from the now defunct "Statistical History of Football" series which were published by Skye Soccer Books. As in the original series, the full names of clubs are used whenever possible with name-changes, mergers etc. shown as and when they occur. The club names are listed in the following format: Club Name (Home Town/City/Village).

The information contained in this book has been gathered over a number of years and has come from myriad sources although most was collected through personal contacts. Other sources of information include newspapers, magazines, books etc. and in more recent times the internet. I would like to extend my thanks to all those who helped with the collection of this information. In an attempt to ensure accuracy, the information has been checked and collated. However, if any errors are found, readers are invited to notify the author care of the address below and if possible provide the corrected information.

Alex Graham

British Library Cataloguing in Publication Data

A catalogue record for this book is available from the British Library

ISBN 978-1-86223-255-6

72 St. Peter's Avenue, Cleethorpes, N.E. Lincolnshire, DN35 8HU, England

Printed by 4edge Ltd.

1898

Final (Torino - 08/05/1898)

GENOA CRICKET & ATHLETIC CLUB	2-1 (aet)	FBC Internazionale (Torino)
Spensley 1-0, Leaver 2-1	(90 minutes - 0-0)	*Unknown 1-1*

Genoa: J.R. Spensley, R. Leaver, Bocciardo, E. Dapples, Bertolio, Le Pelley, E. Ghiglione, Ernesto Pasteur, F.Ghigliotti, E. De Galleani, W.Baird.

Qualifying Round (Torino - 08/05/1898)

Genoa Cricket & Athletic Club (Genova)	2-1	Società di Ginnastica Torinese (Torino)
FBC Internazionale (Torino)	1-0	FBC Torinese (Torino)

1899

Final (Genova - 16/04/1899)

GENOA CRICKET & ATHLETIC CLUB	2-0	FBC Internazionale (Torino)

Genoa: J.R. Spensley, R. Leaver, F. Ghigliotti, E. Dapples, Edoardo Pasteur, I. Arkless, F. Passadoro, Ernesto Pasteur, Detaindre, E. De Galleani, Agar.

Qualifying Round (Torino - 09/04/1899)

FBC Internazionale (Torino)	2-0	Società di Ginnastica Torinese (Torino)

Preliminary Round (Torino - 02/03/1899)

Società di Ginnastica Torinese (Torino)	2-0	FBC Torinese (Torino)

Genoa Cricket & Athletic Club (Genova) received a bye to the Final as defending champions

Genoa Cricket & Athletic Club (Genova) changed to Genoa Cricket & Football Club (Genova), commonly abbreviated to Genoa CFC.
FBC Internazionale (Torino) merged with FBC Torinese (Torino) under FBC Torinese (Torino).

1900

Final (Torino - 22/04/1900)

GENOA CFC (GENOVA)	1-0	FBC Torinese (Torino)

Genoa: J.R. Spensley, P. Rossi, F. Ghigliotti, E. Dapples, Edoardo Pasteur, F. Passadoro, B. Hermann, Bocciardo, Agar, E. Ghiglione, G.C. Fakus.

Torino: G. Beaton, Franz, E. Bosio, Nasi, E.D. Dobbie, G. Lubatti, A. Weber, U. Cagnassi, M. Colongo, G. Beltrami, E. Verdan.

Qualifying Round

15/04/1900	FBC Torinese (Torino)	3-0	Milan Cricket & FBC (Milano)
11/03/1900	FBC Torinese (Torino)	1-0	FBC Juventus (Torino)
04/03/1900	FBC Torinese (Torino)	3-1	Società de Ginnastica Torinese (Torino)

1901

Final (Genova - 05/05/1901)

MILAN CRICKET & FBC (MILANO)	1-0	Genoa CFC (Genova)

Milan: Hoode, Sutter, Gadda, Lees, Kilpin, D. Angeloni, Recalcati, Davies, Negretti, Allison, G. Colombo.

Semi-Finals (Torino - 28/04/1901)

Milan Cricket & FBC (Milano)	3-2	FBC Juventus (Torino)

Qualifying Round (14/04/1901)

FBC Juventus (Torino)	5-0	Società di Ginnastica Torinese (Torino)
Milan Cricket & FBC (Milano)	2-0	SG Mediolanum (Milano)

1902

Final (Genova - 13/04/1902)

GENOA CFC (GENOVA)	2-0	Milan Cricket & FBC (Milano)

Genoa: J.R. Spensley, P. Rossi, F. Ghigliotti, Pasteur 1, Senft, F. Passadoro, Agar, Salvadé, E. Dapples, Cartier, Pasteur 2.

Semi-Finals (Torino - 06/04/1902)

Genoa CFC (Genova)	4-3 (aet)	FBC Torinese (Torino)

Preliminary Round (Ligure - Lombardo)

16/03/1902	Genoa CFC (Genova)	1-0	SG Mediolanum (Milano)
09/03/1902	Genoa CFC (Genova)	3-2	SG Andrea Doria (Genova)

Preliminary Round (Piemontese)

23//03/1902	FBC Torinese (Torino)	4-1	FBC Juventus (Torino)

1902 Qualifying Group Piemontese	FBC Juventus	FBC Torinese	FBC Audace	Società di Gin. Torinese
FBC Juventus		1-1	6-0	1-0
FBC Torinese			2-0	1-0
FBC Audace				5-2
Società di Ginnastica Torinese				

	Piemontese	Pd	Wn	Dw	Ls	GF	GA	Pts
1.	FBC Juventus (Torino)	3	2	1	-	8	1	5
1.	FBC Torinese (Torino)	3	2	1	-	4	1	5
3.	FBC Audace (Torino)	3	1	-	2	5	10	2
4.	Società di Ginnastica Torinese (Torino)	3	-	-	3	2	7	-
		12	5	2	5	19	19	12

After losing 2-5 to FBC Audace, Società di Ginnastica Torinese withdrew and their remaining fixtures were awarded to their opponents with a 0-1 scoreline.

1903

Final (Genova - 29/04/1903)

GENOA CFC (GENOVA)	3-0	FBC Juventus (Torino)

Genoa: J.R. Spensley, P. Rossi, F. Ghigliotti, Pasteur 1, Senft, Cartier, Agar, Foffani, E. Dapples, Montaldi, Pasteur 2.

Qualifying Round

22/03/1903	Milan Cricket & FBC (Milano)	0-2	FBC Juventus (Torino)
15/03/1903	FBC Juventus (Torino)	7-1	SG Andrea Doria (Genova)
08/03/1903	FBC Audace (Torino)	1-2	FBC Juventus (Torino)
01/03/1903	FBC Juventus (Torino)	5-0	FBC Torinese (Torino)

1904

Final (Genova - 27/03/1904)

GENOA CFC (GENOVA)	1-0	FBC Juventus (Torino)

Genoa: J.R. Spensley, Bugnion, P. Rossi, Schoeller, Senft, Pasteur 1, Salvadé, Goetzlof, Agar, Pasteur 2, Pellerani.

Qualifying Round

20/03/1904	Milan Cricket & FBC (Milano)	0-1	FBC Juventus (Torino)
13/03/1904	FBC Juventus (Torino)	1-1 (aet)	Milan Cricket & FBC (Milano)
06/03/1904	FBC Juventus (Torino)	1-0	FBC Torinese (Torino)
	Milan Cricket & FBC (Milano)	1-0	SG Andrea Doria (Genova)

1905

1905 Final	FBC Juventus	Genoa CFC	US Milanese
FBC Juventus		1-1	3-0
Genoa CFC	1-1		2-2
US Milanese	1-4	2-3	

	Final (05/03/05 – 09/04/05)	Pd	Wn	Dw	Ls	GF	GA	Pts
1.	FBC JUVENTUS (TORINO)	4	2	2	-	9	3	6
2.	Genoa CFC (Genova)	4	1	3	-	7	6	5
3.	US Milanese (Milano)	4	-	1	3	5	12	1
		12	3	6	3	21	21	12

Qualifying Round (Ligure - 05/02/05 + 12/02/05 + 19/02/05)

Genoa CFC (Genova)	0-0, 1-1, 1-0	SG Andrea Doria (Genova)

Qualifying Round (Lombardo - 12/02/05 + 19/02/05)

Milan FBC (Milano)	3-3, 6-7	US Milanese (Milano)

Qualifying Round (Piemontese - 19/02/05)

FBC Juventus (Torino)	3-0	FBC Torinese (Torino)

Note: SS Vigor (Ascoli (Piceno) changed their club name to CS Vigor (Ascoli Piceno) (Circolo Sportivo)

1906

Play-off (Torino – 29/04/06)

FBC Juventus (Torino) 0-0, 0-2 MILAN FBC (MILANO)
(Juventus protested at the replay venue being in Milano then withdrew when their protest was overruled. As a result of this Milan FBC were awarded a 2-0 forfeit win).

1906 Final	FBC Juventus	Milan FBC	Genoa CFC
FBC Juventus		2-1	2-0
Milan FBC	1-0		2-0
Genoa CFC	1-1	2-2	

	Final (21/01/06 – 22/04/06)	Pd	Wn	Dw	Ls	GF	GA	Pts
1.	FBC Juventus (Torino)	4	2	1	1	5	3	5
1.	Milan FBC (Milano)	4	2	1	1	6	4	5
3.	Genoa CFC (Genova)	4	-	2	2	3	7	2
		12	4	4	4	14	14	12

Juventus 1-0 Genoa on 18/03/06 was abandoned and replayed in Milano on 01/04/06. Juventus won 2-0.
Milan – Genoa on 08/04/06 was awarded as a 2-0 (underlined) forfeit win to Milan.
Juventus were awarded home venue in the play-off as they had scored more goals than Milan whose 2-0 win by forfeit (underlined) over Genoa was not counted in the decision.

Qualifying Round (07/01/06 + 14/01/06)

Ligure:	Genoa CFC (Genova)	3-1, 1-0	SG Andrea Doria (Genova)
Lombardo:	Milan FBC (Milano)	4-3, 2-1	US Milanese (Milano)
Piemontese:	FBC Juventus (Torino) were the only entrants.		

FBC Torinese (Torino) merged on 03/12/06 with a break-away group from FBC Juventus (Torino) and founded a new club under the name of FBC Torino (Torino).

1907

1907 Final	Milan FBC	FBC Torino	SG Andrea Doria
Milan FBC		2-2	5-0
FBC Torino	1-1		2-0
SG Andrea Doria	0-2	0-0	

	Final (10/02/07 – 14/04/07)	Pd	Wn	Dw	Ls	GF	GA	Pts
1.	MILAN FBC (MILANO)	4	2	2	-	10	3	6
2.	FBC Torino (Torino)	4	1	3	-	5	3	5
3.	SG Andrea Doria (Genova)	4	-	1	3	-	9	1
		12	3	6	3	15	15	12

FBC Torino 2-0 SG Andrea Doria was awarded as a forfeit win after SG Andrea Doria withdrew from the Final.

Qualifying Round (13/01/07 + 03/02/07)

Ligure:	Genoa CFC (Genova)	1-1, 1-3	SG Andrea Doria (Genova)
Lombardo:	Milan FBC (Milano)	6-0, 1-0	US Milanese (Milano)
Piemontese:	FBC Torino (Torino)	2-1, 4-1	FBC Juventus (Torino)

1908

1908 Final	US Pro Vercelli	US Milanese	SG Andrea Doria	FBC Juventus
US Pro Vercelli		0-0	1-1	1-1
US Milanese	1-2		5-1	
SG Andrea Doria	1-2	1-2		
FBC Juventus	0-2			

	Final (01/03/08 – 17/05/08)	Pd	Wn	Dw	Ls	GF	GA	Pts
1.	US PRO VERCELLI (VERCELLI)	4	2	2	-	5	3	6
2.	US Milanese (Milano)	4	2	1	1	8	4	5
3.	SG Andrea Doria (Genova)	4	-	1	3	4	10	1
-.	FBC Juventus (Torino)	2	-	1	1	1	3	1
		12	4	4	4	17	17	12

FBC Juventus resigned after losing to Pro Vercelli. Their record was deleted and is not included in the above totals.

1909

Final (Vercelli – 04/04/09 + Milano – 28/04/09)

US PRO VERCELLI (VERCELLI) 2-0, 1-1 US Milanese (Milano)

Vercelli: Innocenti, Binaschi, Servetto, Ara, Milano 1, Leone, Milano 2, Visconti, Fresia, Rampini 1, Corna.

Semi-Finals (Ligure – Piemontese) / (Lombardo – Veneta)

US Pro Vercelli (Vercelli)	3-2, 1-1	Genoa CFC (Genova)
Venezia FC (Venezia)	1-7, 2-11	US Milanese (Milano)

Qualifying Round

Ligure:	SG Andrea Doria (Genova)	1-1, 3-3, 1-2	Genoa CFC (Genova)
Piemontese:	US Pro Vercelli (Vercelli)	2-1, 1-0	FBC Torino (Torino)
	FBC Torino (Torino)	1-0, 1-3, 1-0	FBC Juventus (Torino)
Veneto:	Venezia FC (Venezia) were the only entrants.		

1909 Lombardo	US Milanese	Milan FBC	FBC Internazionale
US Milanese		3-1	2-0
Milan FBC			3-2
FBC Internazionale			

	Lombardo	Pd	Wn	Dw	Ls	GF	GA	Pts
1.	US Milanese (Milano)	2	2	-	-	5	1	4
2.	Milan FBC (Milano)	2	1	-	1	4	5	2
3.	FBC Internazionale (Milano)	2	-	-	2	2	5	-
		6	3	-	3	11	11	6

1909-10

Play-off (Vercelli – 24/04/10)

US Pro Vercelli (Vercelli) 3-10 FBC INTERNAZIONALE (MILANO)

Pro Vercelli considered themselves as champions due to better goal-difference but the FA ordered a play-off. However, the Vercelli players were involved in a military competition, and as an alternative date could not be agreed upon Pro Vercelli fielded their 4th XI which included some 11 year-olds!).

	Championship	Pd	Wn	Dw	Ls	GF	GA	Pts
1.	US Pro Vercelli (Vercelli)	16	12	1	3	46	15	25
1.	FBC Internazionale (Milano)	16	12	1	3	55	26	25
3.	FBC Juventus (Torino)	16	9	2	5	30	18	20
4.	FBC Torino (Torino)	16	8	1	7	43	30	17
5.	Genoa CFC (Genova)	16	6	3	7	28	25	15
6.	US Milanese (Milano)	16	6	1	9	34	54	13
7.	Milan FBC (Milano)	16	5	2	9	25	40	12
7.	SG Andrea Doria (Genova)	16	5	2	9	22	40	12
9.	FBC Ausonia (Milano)	16	-	5	11	17	52	5
		144	63	18	63	300	300	144

1910-11

Play-off (Vercelli – 11/06/11 + Vicenza – 18/06/11)

US PRO VERCELLI (VERCELLI) 3-0, 2-1 AC Vicenza (Vicenza)

Vercelli: Innocenti, Binaschi, Valle, Ara, Milano 1, Leone, Milano 2, Berardo, Ferraro, Rampini 1, Corna.

	Ligure-Lombardo-Piemontese	Pd	Wn	Dw	Ls	GF	GA	Pts
1.	US Pro Vercelli (Vercelli)	16	12	3	1	44	6	27
2.	Milan FBC (Milano)	16	10	2	4	44	19	22
3.	FBC Torino (Torino)	16	9	-	7	29	27	18
4.	SG Andrea Doria (Genova)	16	8	-	8	28	30	16
5.	Genoa CFC (Genova)	16	7	-	9	25	29	14
6.	FBC Internazionale (Milano)	16	6	1	9	26	34	13
7.	FBC Piemonte (Torino)	16	4	4	8	21	35	12
7.	US Milanese (Milano)	16	6	-	10	19	43	12
9.	FBC Juventus (Torino)	16	3	4	9	16	29	10
		144	65	14	65	252	252	144

FBC Torino 5-0 US Milanese was later awarded by the FIGC as a win to US Milanese

Veneto-Emilia	Pd	Wn	Dw	Ls	GF	GA	Pts
1. AC Vicenza (Vicenza)	6	6	-	-	12	1	12
2. Hellas (Verona)	6	3	1	2	10	5	7
3. Bologna FBC (Bologna)	6	2	-	4	11	20	4
4. Venezia FC (Venezia)	6	-	1	5	2	9	1
	24	11	2	11	35	35	24

Note: CS Vigor (Ascoli Piceno) changed their club name to SS Ascoli (Ascoli Piceno).

1911-12

Final (Venezia – 28/04/12 + Vercelli – 05/05/12)

Venezia FC (Venezia) 0-6, 0-7 US PRO VERCELLI (VERCELLI)

Vercelli: Innocent, Binaschi, Valle, Ara, Milano 1, Leone, Milano 2, Berardo, Ferraro, Rampini 1, Corna.

Ligure-Lombardo-Piemontese	Pd	Wn	Dw	Ls	GF	GA	Pts
1. US Pro Vercelli (Vercelli)	18	15	2	1	50	12	32
2. Milan FBC (Milano)	18	14	3	1	60	10	31
3. Genoa CFC (Genova)	18	10	4	4	35	21	24
4. FBC Internazionale (Milano)	18	10	1	7	42	21	21
4. FBC Torino (Torino)	18	8	5	5	31	31	21
6. Casale FBC (Casale Monferrato)	18	6	3	9	20	28	15
6. SG Andrea Doria (Genova)	18	7	1	10	26	38	15
8. FBC Juventus (Torino)	18	3	3	12	22	47	9
9. US Milanese (Milano)	18	3	2	13	12	52	8
10. FBC Piemonte (Torino)	18	1	2	15	15	57	4
	180	77	26	77	313	317	180

Veneto-Emiliano	Pd	Wn	Dw	Ls	GF	GA	Pts
1. Venezia FC (Venezia)	6	3	1	2	8	12	7
2. AC Vicenza (Vicenza)	6	3	-	3	10	5	6
2. Hellas (Verona)	6	2	2	2	9	9	6
4. Bologna FBC (Bologna)	6	2	1	3	10	9	5
	24	10	4	10	37	35	24

Note: FBC Como (Como) merged with Club Studentesc Minerva (Como) and kept the name FBC Como (Como). FBC Audax (Modena) merged with Associazione Studentesca del Calcio (Modena) and became Modena FBC (Modena).

1912-13

Final (Genova – 01/06/13)

US PRO VERCELLI (VERCELLI) 6-0 SP Lazio (Roma)

Vercelli: Innocenti, Binaschi, Valle, Ara, Milano 1, Leone, Milano 2, Berardo, Ferraro, Rampini 1, Corna.

North Play-off	Pd	Pts
1. US Pro Vercelli (Vercelli)	10	18
2. Casale FBC (Casale Monferrato)	10	11
2. Genoa CFC (Genova)	10	11
4. Milan FBC (Milano)	10	10
5. AC Vicenza (Vicenza)	10	6
6. Hellas (Verona)	10	4
	60	60

South/Centre Play-Offs

Naples FC (Napoli)	1-2, 1-1	SP Lazio (Roma)
FBC Virtus Juventusque (Livorno)	1-3, 0-3	SP Lazio (Roma)

Qualifying Round (North)

Ligure-Lombardo

		Pd	Wn	Dw	Ls	GF	GA	Pts	
1.	Milan FBC (Milano)	10	9	-	1	30	8	18	PO
2.	Genoa CFC (Genova)	10	8	-	2	33	12	16	PO
3.	FBC Internazionale (Milano)	10	6	-	4	24	14	12	
4.	SG Andrea Doria (Genova)	10	4	1	5	20	30	9	
5.	US Milanese (Milano)	10	1	2	7	8	25	4	
6.	Racing Club Libertas (Milano)	10	-	1	9	8	34	1	
		60	28	4	28	123	123	60	

Piemonte

		Pd	Wn	Dw	Ls	GF	GA	Pts	
1.	US Pro Vercelli (Vercelli)	10	9	1	-	38	2	19	PO
2.	Casale FBC (Casale (Monferrato)	10	5	3	2	15	8	13	PO
3.	FBC Torino (Torino)	10	5	1	4	35	21	11	
4.	FBC Piemonte (Torino)	10	5	-	5	17	37	10	
5.	FBC Novara (Novara)	10	1	2	7	13	29	4	
6.	FBC Juventus (Torino)	10	1	1	8	14	35	3	
		60	26	8	26	132	132	60	

Group Play-Off

AC Vicenza (Vicenza)	2-1	Hellas (Verona)

Veneto-Emilia

		Pd	Wn	Dw	Ls	GF	GA	Pts	
1.	Hellas (Verona)	10	8	-	2	28	10	16	PO
1.	AC Vicenza (Vicenza)	10	7	2	1	32	10	16	PO
3.	Venezia FC (Venezia)	10	6	2	2	28	6	14	
4.	FBC Volontari (Venezia)	10	3	2	5	19	29	8	
5.	Bologna FBC (Bologna)	10	2	-	8	14	30	4	
6.	Modena FBC (Modena)	10	1	-	9	6	42	2	
		60	27	6	27	127	127	60	

Qualifying Round (South/Centre)

Campania

		Pd	Wn	Dw	Ls	GF	GA	Pts	
1.	Naples FC (Napoli)	2	2	-	-			4	PO
2.	Internazionale FC (Napoli)	2	-	-	2	_	_	-	
		4	2	-	2	_	_	4	

Lazio

		Pd	Pts	
1.	SP Lazio (Roma)	10	18	PO
2.	FBC Juventus Audax (Roma)	10	14	
3.	FBC Esperia (Roma)	10	13	
4.	Roman FC (Roma)	10	11	
5.	US Pro Roma (Roma)	10	4	
6.	SS Alba (Roma)	10	-	
		60	60	

	Toscana	Pd	Pts	
1.	FBC Virtus Juventusque (Livorno)	6	9	PO
2.	FBC Spes (Livorno)	6	7	
3.	CS Firenze (Firenze)	6	4	
3.	SC Pisa (Pisa)	6	4	
		24	24	

Note: FC Bergamo (Bergamo) merged with Società Bergamasce di ginnastica e scherma (Bergamo) to become Società sportiva di Bergamo (Bergamo).
AC Cremona (Cremona) changed their club name to US Cremonese (Cremona).

1913-14

Final (C. Monferrato – 05/07/14 + Roma – 12/07/14)

CASALE FBC (CASALE MONFERRATO)	7-1, 2-0	SP Lazio (Roma)

Casale: Gallina 1, Maggiani, Serivano, Rosa, Barbesino, Parodi, Caire, Mattea, Gallina 2, Varese, Bertinotti.

	North Play-off	Pd	Wn	Dw	Ls	GF	GA	Pts
1.	Casale FBC (Casale Monferrato)	10	9	-	1	15	4	18
2.	Genoa CFC (Genova)	10	6	2	2	21	10	14
3.	FBC Internazionale (Milano)	10	4	3	3	22	16	11
4.	FBC Juventus (Torino)	10	4	2	4	18	18	10
5.	AC Vicenza (Vicenza)	10	3	1	6	13	18	7
6.	Hellas (Verona)	10	-	-	10	6	28	-
		60	26	8	26	95	94	60

South/Centre Play-Offs

SP Lazio (Roma)	1-0, 8-0	Internazionale FC (Napoli)
SP Lazio (Roma)	1-0, 3-0	FBC Spes (Livorno)

Qualifying Round (North)

	Ligure-Piemontese	Pd	Wn	Dw	Ls	GF	GA	Pts	
1.	Casale FBC (Casale Monferrato)	18	14	3	1			31	PO
1.	Genoa CFC (Genova)	18	14	3	1			31	PO
3.	US Pro Vercelli (Vercelli)	18	13	4	1			30	
4.	FBC Torino (Torino)	18	12	2	4			26	
5.	US Alessandria (Alessandria)	18	8	3	7			19	
6.	SG Andrea Doria (Genova)	18	5	2	11			12	
7.	FBC Vigor (Torino)	18	3	4	11			10	
7.	Piemontese (Torino)	18	4	2	12			10	
9.	Savona FBC (Savona)	18	3	3	12			9	
10.	FBC Liguria (Genova)	18	-	2	16			2	
		180	76	28	76			180	

Lombardo-Piemontese		Pd	Wn	Dw	Ls	GF	GA	Pts	
1.	FBC Internazionale ((Milano)	18	15	1	2			31	PO
2.	FBC Juventus (Torino)	18	13	2	3			28	PO
3.	Milan FBC (Milano)	18	11	4	3			26	
4.	US Milanese (Milano)	18	9	5	4			23	
5.	FBC Novara (Novara)	18	9	1	8			19	
6.	Nazionale Lombardia (Milano)	18	7	2	9			16	
7.	Racing Club Libertas (Milano)	18	6	2	10			14	
8.	FBC Juventus Italia (Milano)	18	4	3	11			11	
9.	FBC Como (Como)	18	2	3	13			7	
10.	AC Milanese (Milano)	18	1	3	14			5	
		180	77	26	77			180	

Veneto-Emiliano		Pd	Pts	
1.	AC Vicenza (Vicenza)	16	27	PO
2.	Hellas (Verona)	16	25	PO
3.	Venezia FC (Venezia)	16	18	
4.	Modena FBC (Modena)	16	17	
5.	FBC Brescia (Brescia)	16	16	
5.	Bologna FBC (Bologna)	16	16	
7.	Petrarca GC (Padova)	16	15	
8.	SG Udinese (Udine)	16	6	
9.	FBC Volontari (Venezia)	16	4	
		144	144	

Qualifying Round (South/Centre)

Campano		Pd	Wn	Dw	Ls	GF	GA	Pts	
1.	Internazionale FC (Napoli)	2	1	1	-			3	PO
2.	Naples FC (Napoli)	2	-	1	1			1	
		4	1	2	1			4	

Lazio		Pd	Wn	Dw	Ls	GF	GA	Pts	
1.	SP Lazio (Roma)	10	10	-	-			20	PO
2.	Roman FC (Roma)	10						15	
3.	FBC Juventus Audax (Roma)	10						9	
4.	SGS Fortitudo (Roma)	10						6	
4.	FBC Audace (Roma)	10						6	
6.	US Pro Roma (Roma)	10						4	
		60						60	

Toscano		Pd	Pts	
1.	FBC Spes (Livorno)	14	26	PO
2.	CS Firenze (Firenze)	14	20	
3.	FBC Virtus Juventusque (Livorno)	14	19	
4.	Fiorentina Libertas	14	16	
5.	SS Italia (Firenze)	14	13	
6.	SC Pisa (Pisa)	14	8	
7.	FBC Lucca (Lucca)	14	5	
7.	AC Prato (Prato)	14	5	
		112	112	

Note: SS Ascoli (Ascoli Piceno) dissolved.

1914-15

GENOA CFC (GENOVA)

Genoa CFC were awarded the championship by the FIGC after the competition was suspended because of World War 1 (1914-18). The competition did not resume until the 1919-20 season.

	North Play-off	Pd	Wn	Dw	Ls	GF	GA	Pts
1.	Genoa CFC (Genova)	5	3	1	1	13	11	7
2.	FBC Torino (Torino)	5	1	3	1	11	7	5
2.	FBC Internazionale (Milano)	5	2	1	1	11	12	5
4.	Milan FBC (Milano)	5	-	3	3	4	9	3
		20	6	8	6	39	39	20

	Centre Play-off	Pd	Wn	Dw	Ls	GF	GA	Pts
1.	SP Lazio (Roma)	5	4	-	1			8
2.	Roman FC (Roma)	5	3	-	2			6
2.	SC Pisa (Pisa)	5	3	-	2			6
4.	FBC Lucca (Lucca)	5	-	-	5			-
		20	10	-	10			20

	North (Semi-Final Group "A")	Pd	Wn	Dw	Ls	GF	GA	Pts	
1.	Genoa CFC (Genova)	6	5	-	1	25	5	10	PO
2.	FBC Juventus (Torino)	6	4	-	2	15	13	8	
3.	Casale FBC (Casale Monferrato)	6	3	-	3	8	11	6	
4.	Venezia FC (Venezia)	6	-	-	6	3	22	-	
		24	12	-	12	51	51	24	

	North (Semi-Final Group "B")	Pd	Wn	Dw	Ls	GF	GA	Pts	
1.	Milan FBC (Milano)	6	4	1	1	9	6	9	PO
2.	US Alessandria (Alessandria)	6	3	1	2	11	8	7	
3.	FBC Vigor (Torino)	6	2	-	4	9	10	4	
3.	FBC Novara (Novara)	6	2	-	4	8	13	4	
		24	11	2	11	37	37	24	

	North (Semi-Final Group "C")	Pd	Wn	Dw	Ls	GF	GA	Pts	
1.	FBC Torino (Torino)	6	6	-	-	18	3	12	PO
2.	US Pro Vercelli (Vercelli)	6	4	-	2	12	6	8	
3.	Hellas (Verona)	6	1	-	5	10	16	2	
3.	FBC Como (Como)	6	1	-	5	4	19	2	
		24	12	-	12	44	44	24	

	North (Semi-Final Group "D")	Pd	Wn	Dw	Ls	GF	GA	Pts	
1.	FBC Internazionale (Milano)	6	4	1	1	27	2	9	PO
2.	SG Andrea Doria (Genova)	6	3	1	2	11	10	7	
3.	AC Vicenza (Vicenza)	6	2	1	3	8	23	5	
4.	FBC Juventus Italia (Milano)	6	1	1	4	6	17	3	
		24	10	4	10	52	52	24	

Qualifying Round (South – Campano)

		Pd	Wn	Dw	Ls	GF	GA	Pts
1.	Internazionale FC (Napoli)	2	1	1	-	4	1	3
2.	Naples FC (Napoli)	2	-	1	1	1	4	1
		4	1	2	1	5	5	4

Qualifying Round (North)

Group "A"

		Pd	Wn	Dw	Ls	GF	GA	Pts	
1.	Genoa CFC (Genova)	10	9	-	1	63	5	18	SF
2.	US Alessandria (Alessandria)	10	6	2	2	36	7	14	SF
3.	SG Andrea Doria (Genova)	10	6	1	3	20	18	13	SF
4.	Savona FBC (Savona)	10	4	2	4	17	32	10	
5.	US Acqui (Acqui Terme)	10	-	3	7	7	29	3	
6.	FBC Liguria (Genova)	10	-	2	8	2	52	2	
		60	25	10	25	145	143	60	

Group "B"

		Pd	Wn	Dw	Ls	GF	GA	Pts	
1.	FBC Torino (Torino)	10	9	1	-	37	9	19	SF
2.	FBC Juventus (Torino)	10	7	1	2	46	14	15	SF
3.	FBC Vigor (Torino)	10	7	-	3	27	20	14	
4.	FBC Valenzana (Valenza)	10	2	2	6	12	30	6	
5.	Piemontese (Torino)	10	2	1	7	12	33	5	
6.	FBC Veloce (Biella)	10	-	1	9	8	35	1	
		60	27	6	27	142	141	60	

Group "C"

		Pd	Wn	Dw	Ls	GF	GA	Pts	
1.	US Pro Vercelli (Vercelli)	10	8	1	1	28	11	17	SF
2.	Casale FBC (Casale Monferrato)	10	7	2	1	22	11	16	SF
3.	FBC Novara (Novara)	10	6	-	4	24	9	12	SF
4.	Nazionale Lombardia (Milano)	10	5	1	4	13	22	11	
5.	Racing Club Libertas (Milano)	10	2	-	8	7	21	4	
6.	FBC Savoia (Milano)	10	-	-	10	4	24	-	
		60	28	4	28	98	98	60	

Group "D"

		Pd	Wn	Dw	Ls	GF	GA	Pts	
1.	Milan FBC (Milano)	10	10	-	-	51	3	20	SF
2.	FBC Juventus Italia (Milano)	10	4	4	2	27	16	12	SF
3.	Bologna FBC (Bologna)	10	2	5	3	15	24	9	
4.	AC Milanese (Milano)	10	3	2	5	26	19	8	
5.	FC Chiasso (Chiasso)	10	2	3	5	24	37	7	
6.	FBC Audax (Modena)	10	2	-	8	14	58	4	
		60	23	14	23	157	157	60	

Group "E"

		Pd	Wn	Dw	Ls	GF	GA	Pts	
1.	FBC Internazionale (Milano)	10	9	-	1	50	8	18	SF
2.	FBC Como (Como)	10	5	2	3	22	20	12	SF
3.	FBC Brescia (Brescia)	10	3	3	4	18	19	9	
4.	US Milanese (Milano)	10	2	5	3	12	20	9	
5.	US Cremonese (Cremona)	10	4	-	6	15	25	8	
6.	Modena FBC (Modena)	10	1	2	7	13	38	4	
		60	24	12	24	140	130	60	

Group "F"

		Pd	Wn	Dw	Ls	GF	GA	Pts	
1.	AC Vicenza (Vicenza)	10	8	-	2	38	13	16	SF
2.	Hellas (Verona)	10	7	1	2	29	16	15	SF
3.	Venezia FC (Venezia)	10	4	4	2	22	18	12	SF
4.	AC Padova (Padova)	10	3	1	6	23	27	7	
5.	SG Udinese (Udine)	10	2	2	6	14	24	6	
6.	Petrarca GC Padova)	10	2	-	8	11	38	4	
		60	26	8	26	136	136	60	

Qualifying Round (Centre)

Lazio

		Pd	Pts	
1.	Roman FC (Roma)	10	18	PO
2.	SP Lazio (Roma)	10	15	PO
3.	FBC Audace (Roma)	10	11	
4.	SGS Fortitudo (Roma)	10	6	
5.	US Pro Roma (Roma)	10	5	
5.	FBC Juventus Audax (Roma)	10	5	
		60	60	

Toscano

		Pd	Pts	
1.	SC Pisa (Pisa)	12	20	PO
2.	FBC Lucca (Lucca)	12	18	PO
3.	PG Libertas (Firenze)	12	15	
4.	CS Firenze (Firenze)	12	12	
5.	FBC Spes (Livorno)	12	11	
6.	FBC Virtus Juventusque (Livorno)	12	6	
7.	AC Prato (Prato)	12	2	
		84	84	

Note: FBC Spes (Livorno) merged with FBC Virtus Juventusque (Livorno) to become US Livorno (Livorno). The championship was abandoned due to the conditions incurred by World War 1. Regional competitions were contested prior to the resumption of the championship for the 1919-20 season.

1915-16

1915-1916 Romano	SG Fortitudo	FBC Juventus Audax	Pro Roma	FBC Audace
SG Fortitudo		2-1	1-1	*2-0*
FBC Juventus Audax	0-1		2-1	5-0
Pro Roma	3-2	2-2		3-1
FBC Audace	*0-2*	*0-2*	1-4	

FBC Audace 2-1 FBC Juventus Audax was abandoned after 65 minutes. The match was later awarded 2-0 to FBC Juventus Audax.
SG Fortitudo vs FBC Audace and FBC Audace vs SG Fortitudo – both matches were awarded 2-0 to SG Fortitudo.

Romano	Pd	Wn	Dw	Ls	GF	GA	Pts
1. SG Fortitudo (Roma)	6	4	1	1	10	5	9
2. FBC Juventus Audax	6	4	-	2	13	6	8
3. Pro Roma (Roma)	6	3	1	2	14	10	7
4. FBC Audace (Roma)	6	-	-	6	2	18	-
	24	11	2	11	39	39	24

1915-1916 Milano	Milan FBC	FBC Internazionale	US Milanese	FC Nazionale Lomb.
Milan FBC		1-1	2-1	5-0
FBC Internazionale	0-1		3-1	1-0
US Milanese	0-3	1-2		3-0
FC Nazionale Lombardia	0-5	0-8		

Milano	Pd	Wn	Dw	Ls	GF	GA	Pts
1. Milan FBC (Milano)	6	5	1	-	17	2	11
2. FBC Internazionale (Milano)	6	4	1	1	15	4	9
3. US Milanese (Milano)	5	1	-	4	6	10	2
4. FC Nazionale Lombardia	5	-	-	5	-	22	-
	22	10	2	10	38	38	22

Copa Gazzetta Sport Final

FC Nazionale Lombardia	2-1	AC Stelvio

Semi-Finals

FC Nazionale Lombardia	1-0	AC Milanese (Milano)
AC Stelvio	2-1	Enotria

Quarter-Finals

Enotria	1-0	FBC Juventus Italia
AC Milanese (Milano)	1-0	Racing Club Libertas
FC Nazionale Lombardia	3-1	Olona
AC Stelvio	2-0	Ausonia *(withdrew)*

1916-17

1916-1917 Coppa Emilia	Bologna FBC	Modena FBC	Fortitudo Bologna	Audax Modena	Nazionale Emilia	Audace Bologna
Bologna FBC		5-2	8-1	3-0	9-1	10-1
Modena FBC	3-2		7-1	11-0	13-0	13-0
Fortitudo Bologna	2-5	0-5		5-1	6-1	*2-0*
Audax Modena	1-5	0-9	*0-2*		6-0	*2-0*
Nazionale Emilia	1-13	0-1	0-6	*2-0*		1-1
Audace Bologna	*0-2*	0-15	1-5	*0-2*	2-0	

Scores of 2-0 or 0-2 in Italics were awarded.

Coppa Emilia Play-off (Mantova)

Modena FBC (Modena) 5-1 Bologna FBC (Bologna)

Fresia 37', Albertoni 39', 42', Leone 86' — *Badini I 05'*

Modena: Borgetti, Benassati, Ara, Fresia, Leone, Barbieri, Albertoni, Gay, Perin, Forlivesi, Massari.

Bologna: Santoni, Miano, Vicini, Sala, Badini I, Ghiselli, Alberti, Della Valle III, Badini II, Pifferi, Della Valle II.

	Coppa Emilia	Pd	Wn	Dw	Ls	GF	GA	Pts
1.	Bologna FBC (Bologna)	10	9	-	1	62	12	18
1.	Modena FBC (Modena)	10	9	-	1	79	8	18
3.	Fortitudo (Bologna)	10	6	-	4	30	28	12
4.	Audax (Modena)	10	3	-	7	12	37	6
5.	Nazionale Emilia	10	1	1	8	6	57	3
6.	Audace (Bologna)	10	1	1	8	5	52	3
		60	29	2	29	194	194	60

1916-1917 Coppa Lazio	Pro Roma	SG Fortitudo	FBC Juventus Audax	SP Lazio
Pro Roma		3-1	5-1	9-2
SG Fortitudo			2-1	1-0
FBC Juventus Audax				2-1
SP Lazio				

	Coppa Lazio	Pd	Wn	Dw	Ls	GF	GA	Pts
1.	Pro Roma (Roma)	3	3	-	-	17	4	6
2.	SG Fortitudo (Roma)	3	2	-	1	4	4	4
3.	FBC Juventus Audax	3	1	-	2	4	8	2
4.	SP Lazio (Roma)	3	-	-	3	3	12	-
		12	6	-	6	28	28	12

1916-1917 Coppa Liguria	Genoa CFC	SG Andrea Doria Genova	Varazze	Giovani Calciatori Genova	Savona FBC	Libertas Savona
Genoa CFC		4-0	8-0	6-0	7-0	5-0
SG Andrea Doria Genova	*2-0*		5-0	1-3	6-3	1-2
Varazze	1-3	3-1		0-0	2-3	1-0
Giovani Calciatori Genova	0-6	1-2	1-1		3-1	3-0
Savona FBC	*2-0*	2-1	1-2	1-1		1-2
Libertas Savona	0-5	1-5	1-2	3-1	2-2	

Scores of 2-0 or 0-2 in Italics were awarded.

Coppa Liguria

		Pd	Wn	Dw	Ls	GF	GA	Pts
1.	Genoa CFC (Genova)	10	8	-	2	44	5	16
2.	SG Andrea Doria (Genova)	10	5	-	5	24	19	10
3.	Varazze	10	4	2	4	12	23	10
4.	Giovani Calciatore (Genova)	10	3	3	4	13	21	9
5.	Savona FBC (Savona)	10	3	2	5	16	26	8
6.	Libertas (Savona)	10	3	1	6	11	26	7
		60	26	8	26	120	120	60

1916-1917 Coppa Piemont	FBC Juventus	FBC Torino	US Torinese	Amatori GC
FBC Juventus		3-1	6-1	7-2
FBC Torino	5-0		3-2	5-1
US Torinese	2-3	1-3		2-4
Amatori GC	2-4	2-4	2-3	

Coppa Piemont

		Pd	Wn	Dw	Ls	GF	GA	Pts
1.	FBC Juventus (Torino)	6	5	-	1	23	13	10
2.	FBC Torino (Torino)	6	5	-	1	21	9	10
3.	US Torinese (Torino)	6	1	-	5	11	21	2
4.	Amatori GC (Torino)	6	1	-	5	13	25	2
		24	12	-	12	68	68	24

1916-1917 Campionato Lombardia Final	Milan FBC	FBC Internazionale	AC Legnano	US Milanese
Milan FBC		4-0	5-2	*2-0*
FBC Internazionale	1-1		2-3	2-0
AC Legnano	1-0	2-3		1-1
US Milanese	1-2	0-1	*2-0*	

1916-1917 Campionato Lombardia Group "A"	Milan FBC	US Milanese	US Cremonese	Enotria
Milan FBC		4-1	8-2	3-1
US Milanese	0-2		4-1	4-0
US Cremonese	3-5	1-1		4-0
Enotria	0-9	0-2	2-1	

1916-1917 Campionato Lombardia Group "B"	AC Legnano	FBC Internazionale	Saronno FC
AC Legnano		4-3	1-1
FBC Internazionale	0-3		6-0
Saronno FC	3-4	2-7	

Scores of 2-0 or 0-2 in Italics were awarded.

Campionato Lombardia (Final)

		Pd	Wn	Dw	Ls	GF	GA	Pts
1.	Milan FBC (Milano)	6	4	1	1	14	5	9
2.	FBC Internazionale (Milano)	6	3	1	2	9	10	7
3.	AC Legnano (Legnano)	6	2	1	3	9	13	5
4.	US Milanese (Milano)	6	1	1	4	4	8	3
		24	10	4	10	36	36	24

Campionato Lombardia (Group "A")

		Pd	Wn	Dw	Ls	GF	GA	Pts
1.	Milan FBC (Milano)	6	6	-	-	31	7	12
2.	US Milanese (Milano)	6	3	1	2	12	8	7
3.	US Cremonese (Cremona)	6	1	1	4	12	20	3
4.	Enotria	6	1	-	5	3	23	2
		24	11	2	11	58	58	24

Campionato Lombardia (Group "B")

		Pd	Wn	Dw	Ls	GF	GA	Pts
1.	AC Legnano (Legnano)	4	3	1	-	12	7	7
2.	FBC Internazionale (Milano)	4	2	-	2	16	9	4
3.	Saronno FC (Saronno)	4	-	1	3	6	18	1
		12	5	2	5	34	34	12

1916-1917 Coppa Romano	SG Fortitudo Roma	Pro Roma	SP Lazio Roma	FBC Juventus Audax	Tiberis
SG Fortitudo Roma		1-0	6-0	4-0	12-0
Pro Roma	1-0		2-0	4-1	8-0
SP Lazio Roma	*0-2*	*2-0*		*0-2*	*2-0*
FBC Juventus Audax	2-4	1-2	2-2		1-0
Tiberis	*0-2*	*0-2*	0-7	*0-2*	

Scores of 2-0 or 0-2 in Italics were awarded.

SP Lazio 2-2 Pro Roma was abandoned after 68 minutes and was later awarded 2-0 to SP Lazio.

Coppa Romano

		Pd	Wn	Dw	Ls	GF	GA	Pts
1.	SG Fortitudo (Roma)	8	7	-	1	31	3	14
2.	Pro Roma (Roma)	8	6	-	2	19	5	12
3.	SP Lazio (Roma)	8	3	1	4	13	14	7
4.	FBC Juventus Audax	8	3	1	4	11	16	7
5.	Tiberis	8	-	-	8	-	36	-
		40	19	2	19	74	74	40

1916-1917 Coppa Toscana	US Livorno	Libertas Firenze	SC Pisa	Esperia Firenze	Virtus Firenze
US Livorno		0-0	3-0	*2-0*	6-0
Libertas Firenze	4-0		*2-0*	1-0	1-0
SC Pisa	0-1	4-0		3-0	3-1
Esperia Firenze	0-1	0-2	*2-0*		*2-0*
Virtus Firenze	1-3	*0-2*	*0-2*	*0-2*	

Scores of 2-0 or 0-2 in Italics were awarded.

Coppa Toscana

		Pd	Wn	Dw	Ls	GF	GA	Pts
1.	US Livorno (Livorno)	8	6	1	1	16	5	13
2.	Libertas (Firenze)	8	6	1	1	12	4	13
3.	SC Pisa (Pisa)	8	4	-	4	12	9	8
4.	Esperia (Firenze)	8	3	-	5	6	9	6
5.	Virtus (Firenze)	8	-	-	8	2	21	-
		40	19	2	19	48	48	40

1917-18

1917-1918 Campionato Lombardo	FBC Internazionale	Milan FBC	AC Legnano	FC Nazionale Lombardia	US Milanese	Saronno FC	Enotria Goliardo
FBC Internazionale		1-0	2-0	*2-0*	2-1	4-1	4-0
Milan FBC	1-0		1-2	4-0	3-0	2-1	*2-0*
AC Legnano	*0-2*	*0-2*		3-2	6-1	*0-2*	3-0
FC Nazionale Lombardia	3-2	2-4	*2-0*		3-0	1-1	1-0
US Milanese	0-2	0-2	2-4	3-0		3-1	2-2
Saronno FC	0-9	*0-2*	*0-2*	*2-0*	1-2		3-1
Enotria Goliardo	2-3	1-3	0-8	1-1		1-0	

Scores of 2-0 or 0-2 in Italics were awarded by forfeit.

	Campionato Lombardo	Pd	Wn	Dw	Ls	GF	GA	Pts
1.	FBC Internazionale (Milano)	12	10	-	2	33	8	20
2.	Milan FBC (Milano)	12	10	-	2	26	7	20
3.	AC Legnano (Legnano)	12	7	-	5	28	16	14
4.	FC Nazionale Lombardia	12	4	2	6	15	22	10
5.	US Milanese (Milano)	11	3	1	7	14	26	7
6.	Saronno FC (Saronno)	12	3	1	8	12	27	7
7.	Enotria Goliardo	11	1	2	8	8	30	4
		82	38	6	38	136	136	82

1918-19

1918-1919 Coppa Biffi	US Milanese	FBC Internazionale	Milan FBC	AC Legnano	Saronno FC	Enotria Goliardo
US Milanese		7-3		1-1		
FBC Internazionale			2-1		8-0	9-2
Milan FBC	1-3			1-0		
AC Legnano		1-5			7-3	4-0
Saronno FC	3-5		1-5			*2-0*
Enotria Goliardo	0-2		1-4			

Scores of 2-0 or 0-2 in Italics were awarded by forfeit.

	Coppa Biffi	Pd	Wn	Dw	Ls	GF	GA	Pts
1.	US Milanese (Milano)	5	4	1	-	18	8	9
2.	FBC Internazionale (Milano)	5	4	-	1	27	11	8
3.	Milan FBC (Milano)	5	3	-	2	12	7	6
4.	AC Legnano (Legnano)	5	2	1	2	13	10	5
5.	Saronno FC (Saronno)	5	1	-	4	9	25	2
6.	Enotria Goliardo	5	-	-	5	3	21	-
		30	14	2	14	82	82	30

1918-1919 Campionata Lombardo	AC Legnano	Milan FBC	US Milanese	FBC Internazionale	Saronno FC	Enotria Goliardo
AC Legnano		6-2	0-1	5-2	3-0	3-1
Milan FBC	0-0		1-2	4-3	2-0	6-1
US Milanese	0-2	2-2		1-1	2-1	3-1
FBC Internazionale	2-2	2-5	1-0		4-0	4-3
Saronno FC	0-5	1-3		1-2		1-1
Enotria Goliardo	2-8	0-3	1-5	0-2	*0-2*	

Scores of 2-0 or 0-2 in Italics were awarded by forfeit.

	Campionata Lombardo	Pd	Wn	Dw	Ls	GF	GA	Pts
1.	AC Legnano (Legnano)	10	7	2	1	34	10	16
2.	Milan FBC (Milano)	10	6	2	2	28	17	14
3.	US Milanese (Milano)	9	5	2	2	16	10	12
4.	FBC Internazionale (Milano)	10	5	2	3	23	21	12
5.	Saronno FC (Saronno)	9	1	1	7	6	22	3
6.	Enotria Goliardo	10	-	1	9	10	37	1
		58	24	10	24	117	117	58

1918-1919 Campionata Romano Group "A"	FBC Juventus Audax	SP Lazio	US Romana
FBC Juventus Audax		1-0	2-0
SP Lazio	0-1		4-0
US Romana	1-2	1-1	

1918-1919 Campionata Romano Group "B"	SG Fortitudo	Pro Roma	FBC Audace
SG Fortitudo		2-1	2-0
Pro Roma	0-2		2-1
FBC Audace	0-1	0-4	

1918-1919 Campionata Toscano	SC Pisa	CS Firenze	US Livorno	Libertas
SC Pisa		3-0	5-1	7-1
CS Firenze	1-1		*2-0*	3-2
US Livorno	0-2	4-0		4-1
Libertas	1-5	0-0	1-0	

Scores of 2-0 or 0-2 in Italics were awarded by forfeit.

Campionata Romano (Final – Roma)

FBC Juventus Audax 3-0 SG Fortitudo (Roma)

De Giuli II 19', 90, Meille 32'

	Campionata Romano (Group "A")	Pd	Wn	Dw	Ls	GF	GA	Pts
1.	FBC Juventus Audax	4	4	-	-	6	1	8
2.	SP Lazio (Roma)	4	1	1	2	5	3	3
3.	US Romana (Roma)	4	-	1	3	2	9	1
		12	5	2	5	13	13	12

	Campionata Romano (Group "B")	Pd	Wn	Dw	Ls	GF	GA	Pts
1.	SG Fortitudo (Roma)	4	4	-	-	7	1	8
2.	Pro Roma (Roma)	4	2	-	2	7	5	4
3.	FBC Audace (Roma)	4	-	-	4	1	9	-
		12	6	-	6	15	15	12

Campionata Toscano		Pd	Wn	Dw	Ls	GF	GA	Pts
1.	SC Pisa (Pisa)	6	5	1	-	23	4	11
2.	CS Firenze (Firenze)	6	2	2	2	6	10	6
3.	US Livorno (Livorno)	6	2	-	4	9	11	4
4.	Libertas (Firenze)	6	1	1	4	6	19	3
		24	10	4	10	44	44	24

1919-20

National Final (Bologna - 20/06/20)

FBC INTERNAZIONALE (MILANO) 3-2 US Livorno (Livorno)

Internazionale: Campelli, Francesconi, Beltrami, Milesi, Pino Fossati 1, Scheidler, Conti, Aebi, Agradi, Cevenini 3, Asti.

1919-1920 North Play-off	FBC Internazionale	FBC Juventus	Genoa CFC
FBC Internazionale		1-0	
FBC Juventus			3-2
Genoa CFC	1-1		

North Play-off		Pd	Wn	Dw	Ls	GF	GA	Pts
1.	FBC Internazionale (Milano)	2	1	1	-	2	1	3
2.	FBC Juventus (Torino)	2	1	-	1	3	3	2
3.	Genoa CFC (Genova)	2	-	1	1	3	4	1
		6	2	2	2	8	8	6

South/Centre (Play-off)

US Livorno (Livorno) 3-2 SGS Fortitudo (Roma)

North (Semi-Finals Group "A")		Pd	Pts	
1.	Genoa CFC (Genova)	10	19	PO
2.	US Pro Vercelli (Vercelli)	10	14	
3.	US Alessandria (Alessandria)	10	9	
3.	Milan FBC (Milano)	10	9	
5.	FBC Legnano (Legnano)	10	7	
6.	Venezia FC (Venezia)	10	2	
		60	60	

North (Semi-Finals Group "B")		Pd	Pts	
1.	FBC Juventus (Torino)	10	17	PO
2.	US Milanese (Milano)	10	15	
3.	Modena FBC (Modena)	10	9	
4.	Casale FBC (Casale Monferrato)	10	8	
5.	AC Brescia (Brescia)	10	6	
6.	AC Padova (Padova)	10	5	
		60	60	

	North (Semi-Finals Group "C")	Pd	Wn	Dw	Ls	GF	GA	Pts	
1.	FBC Internazionale (Milano)	10	7	2	1	37	13	16	PO
2.	FBA Novara (Novara)	10	6	1	3	22	15	13	
2.	Bologna FBC (Bologna)	10	6	1	3	20	14	13	
4.	FBC Torino (Torino)	10	4	1	5	17	21	9	
5.	SG Andrea Doria (Genova)	10	2	1	7	14	21	5	
6.	FBC Enotria (Goliardo)	10	2	-	8	11	37	4	
		60	27	6	27	121	121	60	

	South/Centre (Semi-Finals Group "A")	Pd	Wn	Dw	Ls	GF	GA	Pts	
1.	SGS Fortitudo (Roma)	4	4	-	-			8	PO
2.	SC Pisa (Pisa)	4						2	
2.	Puteolana US (Pozzuoli)	4						2	
		12	12						

	South/Centre (Semi-Finals Group "B")	Pd	Wn	Dw	Ls	GF	GA	Pts	
1.	US Livorno (Livorno)	4	4	-	-			8	PO
2.	FBC Audace (Roma)	4						2	
2.	Internazionale FC (Napoli)	4						2	
		12	12						

North Qualifying Round

	Emilia	Pd	Pts	
1.	Bologna FBC (Bologna)	10	18	SF
2.	Modena FBC (Modena)	10	15	SF
3.	AC Mantova (Mantova)	10	10	
4.	AC Carpi (Carpi)	10	7	
5.	FBC Nazionale Emilia (Bologna)	10	6	
6.	GS Bolognese (Bologna)	10	4	
		60	60	

	Liguria	Pd	Pts	
1.	Genoa CFC (Genova)	10	19	SF
2.	SG Andrea Doria (Genova)	10	15	SF
3.	Grifone e Giovani Calciatori (Genova)	10	8	
4.	SG Sampierdarenese (Genova)	10	7	
4.	FBC Spes (Genova)	10	7	
6.	Savona FBC (Savona)	10	4	
		60	60	

	Lombardo (Group "A")	Pd	Pts	
1.	FBC Internazionale (Milano)	10	18	SF
2.	AC Brescia (Brescia)	10	14	SF
3.	FBC Juventus Italia (Milano)	10	9	
3.	CS Trevigliese (Treviglio)	10	9	
5.	US Cremonese (Cremona)	10	5	
5.	FBC Libertas (Milano)	10	5	
		60	60	

Lombardo (Group "B")

		Pd	Pts	
1.	Milan FBC (Milano)	10	20	SF
2.	FBC Enotria (Goliardo)	10	14	SF
3.	Atalanta BC (Bergamo)	10	11	
4.	FC Chiasso (Chiasso)	10	8	
5.	FBC Pavia (Pavia)	10	5	
6.	FBC Ausonia (Milano)	10	2	
		60	60	

Lombardo (Group "C")

		Pd	Pts	
1.	US Milanese (Milano)	10	18	SF
2.	FBC Legnano (Legnano)	10	17	SF
3.	FBC Saronno (Saronno)	10	10	
4.	Nazionale Lombardia (Milano)	10	7	
5.	FBC Varese (Varese)	10	4	
5.	FBC Como (Como)	10	4	
		60	60	

Piemonte (Group "A")

		Pd	Wn	Dw	Ls	GF	GA	Pts	
1.	FBC Juventus (Torino)	10	7	2	1	29	7	16	SF
1.	US Pro Vercelli (Vercelli)	10	6	4	-	25	5	16	SF
3.	FBC Torino (Torino)	10	6	3	1	27	10	15	SF
4.	AS Biellese (Biella)	10	2	1	7	12	34	5	
5.	Amatori Giuoco Calcio (Torino)	10	1	2	7	12	32	4	
5.	US Alessandrina (Alessandria)	10	1	2	7	7	24	4	
		60	23	14	23	112	112	60	

Piemonte (Group "B")

		Pd	Pts	
1.	US Alessandria (Alessandria)	10	19	SF
2.	Casale FBC (Casale Monferrato)	10	12	SF
3.	FBA Novara (Novara)	10	11	SF
4.	US Torinese (Torino)	10	8	
5.	FBC Pastore (Torino)	10	7	
6.	US Valenzana (Valenza)	10	3	
		60	60	

Veneto

		Pd	Pts	
1.	AC Padova (Padova)	10	17	SF
2.	Venezia FC (Venezia)	10	13	SF
3.	Petrarca GC (Padova)	10	11	
4.	AC Vicenza (Vicenza)	10	7	
5.	SG Udinese (Udine)	10	6	
5.	Hellas AC (Verona)	10	6	
		60	60	

South/Centre Qualifying Round

	Campano	Pd	Pts	
1.	Internazionale FC (Napoli)	8	14	SF
2.	Puteolana US (Pozzuoli)	8	11	SF
3.	Pro Napoli (Napoli)	8	9	
4.	Naples FC (Napoli)	8	6	
5.	Pro Caserta (Caserta)	8	-	
		40	40	

	Lazio	Pd	Pts	
1.	SGS Fortitudo (Roma)	12	21	SF
2.	FBC Audace (Roma)	12	16	
3.	SP Lazio (Roma)	12	14	
4.	FBC Juventus Audax (Roma)	12	12	
5.	US Pro Roma (Roma)	12	8	
6.	Roman FC (Roma)	12	7	
7.	US Romana (Roma)	12	6	
		84	84	

	Toscana	Pd	Pts	
1.	SC Pisa (Pisa)	10	16	SF
1.	US Livorno (Livorno)	10	16	
3.	PG Libertas (Firenze)	10	10	
4.	CS Firenze (Firenze)	10	9	
5.	CS Gerbi (Pisa)	10	7	
6.	AC Prato (Prato)	10	2	
		60	60	

1920-21

Final (Torino)

US PRO VERCELLI (VERCELLI) 2-1 SC Pisa (Pisa)

Vercelli: Curti, Rosetta, Bossola, Ara, Parodi, Perino, Ceria, Ardissone, Gay, Rampini 2, Borello.

North Play-off

US Pro Vercelli (Vercelli) 2-0 Bologna FBC (Bologna)

US Pro Vercelli (Vercelli) 4-0 US Alessandria (Alessandria)

South/Centre Play-off

SC Pisa (Pisa) 1-0 US Livorno (Livorno)

	North (Semi-Finals Group "A")	Pd	Wn	Dw	Ls	GF	GA	Pts	
1.	Bologna FBC (Bologna)	6	4	2	-	13	4	10	PO
2.	Genoa CFC (Genova)	6	2	3	1	10	9	7	
3.	FBA Novara (Novara)	6	2	2	2	7	7	6	
4.	Milan FBC (Milano)	6	-	1	5	8	18	1	
		24	8	8	8	38	38	24	

Group "B" Play-Off

US Alessandria (Alessandria) 4-0 Modena FBC (Modena)

(Alessandria qualified for the North play-offs)

	North (Semi-Finals Group "B")	Pd	Wn	Dw	Ls	GF	GA	Pts
1.	US Alessandria (Alessandria)	6	4	-	2	17	5	8
1.	Modena FBC (Modena)	6	4	-	2	12	10	8
3.	SG Andrea Doria (Genova)	6	3	-	3	9	11	6
4.	US Milanese (Milano)	6	1	-	5	4	16	2
		24	12	-	12	42	42	24

Group "C" Play-Off

FBC Torino (Torino) 1-1 AC Legnano (Legnano)

(the tie was not replayed and both clubs renounced a place in the play-offs)

	North (Semi-Finals Group "C")	Pd	Wn	Dw	Ls	GF	GA	Pts
1.	FBC Torino (Torino)	6	4	-	2	13	10	8
1.	AC Legnano (Legnano)	6	4	-	2	10	8	8
3.	AC Padova (Padova)	6	2	-	4	9	10	4
3.	AC Mantova (Mantova)	6	2	-	4	7	11	4
		24	12	-	12	39	39	24

	North (Semi-Finals Group "D")	Pd	Wn	Dw	Ls	GF	GA	Pts	
1.	US Pro Vercelli (Vercelli)	6	5	-	1	13	4	10	PO
2.	US Torinese (Torino)	6	4	1	1	14	6	9	
3.	FBC Internazionale (Milano)	6	1	1	4	8	13	3	
4.	Bentegodi SC (Verona)	6	1	-	5	4	16	2	
		24	11	2	11	39	39	24	

	South/Centre (Semi-Finals Group "A")	Pd	Wn	Dw	Ls	GF	GA	Pts	
1.	US Livorno (Livorno)	4	4	-	-			8	PO
2.	Naples FC (Napoli)	4	1	1	2			3	
3.	SP Lazio (Roma)	4	-	1	3			1	
		12	5	2	5			12	

	South/Centre (Semi-Finals Group "B")	Pd	Wn	Dw	Ls	GF	GA	Pts	
1.	SC Pisa (Pisa)	4	3	1	-			7	PO
2.	SGS Fortitudo (Roma)	4	2	1	1			5	
3.	US Bagnolese (Bagnoli)	4	-	-	4			-	
		12	5	2	5			12	

North Qualifying Round

	Emilia (Play-off)	Pd	Pts	
1.	Bologna FBC (Bologna)	6		SF
2.	Modena FBC (Modena)	6		SF
3.	AC Mantova (Mantova)	6		SF
4.	Parma FBC (Parma)	6		
		24		

Emilia (Group "A")

		Pd	Pts	
1.	Modena FBC (Modena)	8	13	PO
2.	Parma FBC (Parma)	8	11	PO
3.	CC Piacenza (Piacenza)	8	9	
4.	US Reggiana (Reggio Emilia)	8	6	
5.	AC Carpi (Carpi)	8	1	
		40	40	

Emilia (Group "B")

		Pd	Pts	
1.	Bologna FBC (Bologna)	8	15	PO
2.	AC Mantova (Mantova)	8	10	PO
3.	S.P.A.L. (Ferrara)	8	7	
4.	FBC Virtus (Bologna)	8	5	
5.	FBC Nazionale Emilia (Bologna)	8	3	
		40	40	

Liguria

		Pd	Pts	
1.	SG Andrea Doria (Genova)	14	20	SF
2.	Genoa CFC (Genova)	14	19	SF
3.	FBC Spezia (La Spezia)	14	18	
4.	SG Sampierdarenese (Genova)	14	17	
4.	Savona FBC (Savona)	14	17	
6.	FS Sestrese (Sesto Fiorentino)	14	11	
7.	FBC Spes (Genova)	14	10	
8.	US Rivarolese (Rivarolo Canavese)	14	-	
		112	112	

Lombardo (Play-off)

		Pd	Pts	
1.	FBC Internazionale (Milano)	10	16	SF
2.	FBC Legnano (Legnano)	10	15	SF
3.	US Milanese (Milano)	10	13	SF
4.	Milan FBC (Milano)	10	10	
5.	FBC Saronno (Saronno)	10	6	
6.	CS Trevigliese (Treviglio)	10	-	
		60	60	

Lombardo (Group "A")

		Pd	Pts	
1.	FBC Internazionale (Milano)	6	12	PO
2.	FBC Casteggio (Casteggio)	6	7	
3.	Giovanni Calcio Legnanese (Legnano)	6	5	
4.	Ausonia Pro Garlo	6	-	
		24	24	

Lombardo (Group "B")

		Pd	Pts	
1.	Milan FBC (Milano)	6	11	PO
2.	Pro Patria (Busto Arsizio)	6	8	
3.	US Cremonese (Cremona)	6	5	
4.	AC Monza (Monza)	6	-	
		24	24	

Lombardo (Group "C")

		Pd	Pts	
1.	US Milanese (Milano)	6	12	PO
2.	FBC Pavia (Pavia)	6	8	
3.	FBC Varese (Varese)	6	2	
3.	AC Sesto (Sesto San Giovanni)	6	2	
		24	24	

Lombardo (Group "D")

		Pd	Pts	
1.	FBC Legnano (Legnano)	6	10	PO
2.	FC Chiasso (Chiasso)	6	6	
2.	FBC Como (Como)	6	6	
4.	AC Stelvio	6	2	
		24	24	

Lombardo (Group "E")

		Pd	Pts	
1.	FBC Saronno (Saronno)	6	9	PO
2.	FBC Libertas (Milano)	6	6	
2.	AC Brescia (Brescia)	6	6	
4.	Atalanta BC (Bergamo)	6	3	
		24	24	

Lombardo (Group "F")

		Pd	Pts	
1.	CS Trevigliese (Treviglio)	6	10	PO
2.	FBC Juventus Italia (Milano)	6	8	
3.	Nazionale Lombardia (Milano)	6	4	
4.	FBC Enotria (Goliardo)	6	2	
		24	24	

Piemonte (Group "A")

		Pd	Wn	Dw	Ls	GF	GA	Pts	
1.	FBA Novara (Novara)	10	7	2	1			16	SF
1.	FBC Torino (Torino)	10	7	2	1			16	SF
3.	US Torinese (Torino)	10	6	1	3			13	SF
4.	FBC Juventus (Torino)	10	4	3	3			11	
5.	FBC Pastore (Torino)	10	1	1	8			3	
6.	FBC Carignano (Carignano)	10	-	1	9			1	
		60	25	10	25			60	

Piemonte (Group "B")

		Pd	Pts	
1.	US Alessandria (Alessandria)	10	17	SF
2.	US Pro Vercelli (Vercelli)	10	15	SF
3.	Casale FBC (Casale Monferrato)	10	14	
4.	AS Biellese (Biella)	10	7	
5.	US Valenzana (Valenza)	10	5	
6.	Amatori Giuoco Calcio (Torino)	10	2	
		60	60	

Veneto (Play-off)	**Pd**	**Pts**	
1. AC Padova (Padova)	6	8	SF
2. Bentegodi SC (Verona)	6	7	
3. Hellas AC (Verona)	6	6	SF
4. Petrarca GC (Padova)	6	3	
	24	24	

Veneto (Group "A")	**Pd**	**Pts**	
1. Petrarca GC (Padova)	8	13	PO
2. Bentegodi SC (Verona)	8	12	PO
3. Venezia FC (Venezia)	8	10	
4. SG Udinese (Udine)	8	4	
5. FC Treviso (Treviso)	8	1	
	40	40	

Veneto (Group "B")	**Pd**	**Pts**	
1. AC Padova (Padova)	8	13	PO
1. Hellas AC (Verona)	8	13	PO
3. AC Vicenza (Vicenza)	8	9	
4. Lanerossi Schio (Vicenza)	8	4	
5. CS Dolo (Dolo)	8	1	
	40	40	

South/Centre Qualifying Round

Campania (Play-off)	**Pd**	**Pts**	
1. Puteolana US (Pozzuoli)	6	10	disq.
2. US Bagnolese (Bagnoli)	6	7	SF
3. Naples FC (Napoli)	6	5	SF
4. Internazionale FC (Napoli)	6	2	
	24	24	

Campania (Group "A")	**Pd**	**Pts**	
1. Puteolana US (Pozzuoli)	6	11	PO
2. Naples FBC (Napoli)	6	8	PO
3. AC Savoia (Torre Annunziata)	6	5	
4. US Salernitana Audax (Salerno)	6	-	
	24	24	

Campania (Group "B")	**Pd**	**Pts**	
1. Internazionale FC (Napoli)	6	9	PO
2. US Bagnolese (Bagnoli)	6	8	PO
3. US Pro Napoli (Napoli)	6	7	
4. FBC Audace	6	-	
	24	24	

Lazio

		Pd	Pts	
1.	SGS Fortitudo (Roma)	14	27	SF
2.	SP Lazio (Roma)	14	22	SF
3.	FBC Juventus Audax (Roma)	14	15	
4.	FBC Audace (Roma)	14	13	
5.	US Pro Roma (Roma)	14	12	
6.	PS Romana 9Roma)	14	10	
7.	FBC Vittoria (Roma)	14	7	
8.	US Romana (Roma)	14	6	
		112	112	

Toscana

		Pd	Pts	
1.	SC Pisa (Pisa)	14	23	SF
2.	US Livorno (Livorno)	14	22	SF
3.	US Lucchese Libertas (Lucca)	14	18	
4.	AC Prato (Prato)	14	14	
5.	CS Firenze (Firenze)	14	10	
6.	AC Viareggio (Viareggio)	14	9	
6.	CS Gerbi (Pisa)	14	9	
8.	PG Libertas (Firenze)	14	7	
		112	112	

1921-22 F.I.G.C. Championship

F.I.G.C. Final (Genova – 07/05/22 + Novi Ligure – 14/05/22 + Cremona – 21/05/22)

SG Sampierdarenese (Genova) 0-0, 0-0 1-2 US NOVESE (NOVI LIGURE)

Novese: Stritzel, Vercelli, Grippi, Bonato, Bertucci, Toselli, Gambarotta, Neri, Cevenini 2, Santamaria, Parodi.

Semi-Final (Group "A")

		Pd	Wn	Dw	Ls	GF	GA	Pts
1.	US Novese (Novi Ligure)	4	3	1	-	9	3	7
2.	Petrarca GC (Padova)	4	1	2	1	4	2	4
3.	US Livorno (Livorno)	4	-	1	3	3	11	1
		12	4	4	4	16	16	12

Semi-Final (Group "B")

		Pd	Wn	Dw	Ls	GF	GA	Pts
1.	SG Sampierdarenese (Genova)	4	2	1	1	8	7	5
1.	S.P.A.L. (Ferrara)	4	2	1	1	4	3	5
3.	Esperia FC (Como)	4	-	2	2	6	8	2
		12	4	4	4	18	18	12

Play-off

SG Sampierdarenese (Genova) 2-1 S.P.A.L. (Ferrara)

Qualifying Round

Emilia (Play-off)

		Pd	Pts	
1.	S.P.A.L. (Ferrara)	6	9	SF
2.	FBC Virtus (Bologna)	6	8	
3.	Parma FBC (Parma)	6	4	
4.	CC Piacenza (Piacenza)	6	3	
		24	24	

Emilia (Group "A")

	Team	Pd	Wn	Dw	Ls	GF	GA	Pts	
1.	CC Piacenza (Piacenza)	4	2	2	-	10	4	6	PO
2.	Parma FBC (Parma)	4	2	1	1	6	4	5	PO
3.	Mantovana (Mantova)	4	-	1	3	3	11	1	
		12	4	4	4	19	19	12	

Emilia (Group "B")

	Team	Pd	Wn	Dw	Ls	GF	GA	Pts	
1.	FBC Virtus (Bologna)	6	2	3	1	8	4	7	PO
2.	S.P.A.L. (Ferrara)	6	1	4	1	5	2	6	PO
2.	AC Carpi (Carpi)	6	2	2	2	5	4	6	
4.	US Reggiana (Reggio Emilia)	6	2	1	3	5	13	5	
		24	7	10	7	23	23	24	

Liguria

	Team	Pd	Wn	Dw	Ls	GF	GA	Pts	
1.	SG Sampierdarenese (Genova)	10	8	2	-	25	7	18	SF
2.	FBC Speranza (Savona)	10	5	2	3	17	17	12	
3.	US Rivarolese (Rivarolo Canavese)	10	5	1	4	14	13	11	
4.	FS Sestrese (Sesto Fiorentino)	10	3	1	6	17	14	7	
4.	FBC Spes (Genova)	10	3	1	6	11	20	7	
6.	Grifone Giovanni Calciatori (Genova)	10	2	1	7	9	22	5	
		60	26	8	26	93	93	60	

Lombardo (Play-off)

	Team	Pd	Pts	
1.	Esperia FC (Como)	6	9	SF
2.	US Cremonese (Cremona)	6	6	
3.	FBC Como (Como)	6	5	
4.	FBC Enotria (Goliardo)	6	4	
		24	24	

Lombardo (Group "A")

	Team	Pd	Wn	Dw	Ls	GF	GA	Pts	
1.	FBC Como (Como)	6	4	1	1	20	8	9	PO
2.	FC Chiasso (Chiasso)	6	2	4	-	11	5	8	
3.	FBC Saronno (Saronno)	6	2	2	2	7	8	6	
4.	FBC Varese (Varese)	6	-	1	5	7	23	1	
		24	8	8	8	45	44	24	

Lombardo (Group "B")

	Team	Pd	Wn	Dw	Ls	GF	GA	Pts	
1.	US Cremonese (Cremona)	6	4	2	-	18	4	10	PO
2.	CS Trevigliese (Treviglio)	6	3	1	2	9	10	7	
3.	Atalanta BC (Bergamo)	6	3	-	3	9	14	6	
4.	AC Stelvio	6	-	1	5	6	14	1	
		24	10	4	10	42	42	24	

Lombardo (Group "C")

	Team	Pd	Wn	Dw	Ls	GF	GA	Pts	
1.	FBC Enotria (Goliardo)	6	4	2	-	12	7	10	PO
2.	FBC Juventus Italia (Milano)	6	2	1	3	9	12	5	
2.	AC Monza (Monza)	6	2	1	3	10	11	5	
4.	FBC Casteggio (Casteggio)	6	2	-	4	8	9	4	
		24	10	4	10	39	39	24	

Lombardo (Group "D")	Pd	Wn	Dw	Ls	GF	GA	Pts	
1. Esperia FC (Como)	6	3	1	2	8	4	7	PO
2. FBC Pavia (Pavia)	6	2	2	2	6	6	6	
2. Pro Patria (Busto Arsizio)	6	2	2	2	5	7	6	
4. FBC Libertas (Milano)	6	2	1	3	5	7	5	
	24	9	6	9	24	24	24	

Piemonte	Pd	Wn	Dw	Ls	GF	GA	Pts	
1. US Novese (Novi Ligure)	8	5	3	-	16	1	13	SF
2. US Torinese (Torino)	8	3	3	2	7	9	9	
3. FBC Pastore (Torino)	8	2	4	2	7	10	8	
4. US Valenzana (Valenza)	8	2	1	5	8	12	5	
4. Giovani Calciatori Cappuccini (Vercelli)	8	1	3	4	6	12	5	
	40	13	14	13	44	44	40	

Toscana	Pd	Wn	Dw	Ls	GF	GA	Pts	
1. Pro Livorno (Livorno)	10	7	1	2	20	8	15	SF
2. US Lucchese Libertas (Lucca)	10	5	3	2	25	10	13	
3. PG Libertas (Firenze)	10	5	2	3	11	15	12	
4. AS Viareggio (Viareggio)	10	5	1	4	16	16	11	
5. AC Prato (Prato)	10	1	3	6	11	18	5	
6. CS Firenze (Firenze)	10	1	2	7	8	24	4	
	60	24	12	24	91	91	60	

Veneto	Pd	Pts	
1. Petrarca GC (Padova)	10	14	SF
2. SG Udinese (Udine)	10	12	
3. Bentegodi SC (Verona)	10	9	
3. AC Treviso (Treviso)	10	9	
5. FBC Legnano (Legnano)	10	8	
5. Lanerossi Schio (Vicenza)	10	8	
	60	60	

Note: Internazionale FC (Napoli) merged with Naples FBC (Napoli) to become Internaples FC (Napoli). Messinese (Messina) merged with SC Messina (Messina) to become FBC Messina (Messina).

1921-22 C.C.I. CHAMPIONSHIP

C.C.I. Final (Roma – 11/06/22 + Vercelli – 18/06/22)

SGS Fortitudo (Roma) 0-3, 2-5 US PRO VERCELLI (VERCELLI)

Vercelli: Curti, Rosetta, Bossola, Milano 4, Parodi, Perino, Ceria, Ardissone, Gay, Rampini 2, Borello.

North Semi-Final

US Pro Vercelli (Vercelli) 0-0, 2-1 Genoa CFC (Genova)

South Semi-Final

SGS Fortitudo (Roma)	2-0	Puteolana US (Pozzuoli)
SGS Fortitudo (Roma)	4-1	FBC Audace (Taranto)
FBC Audace (Taranto)	1-0	US Palermo (Palermo)
Puteolana US (Pozzuoli)	3-0	US Anconitana (Ancona)

1921-1922 North Qualifiers Group "A"	US Pro Vercelli	AC Novara	Bologna FBC	FBC Juventus	SG Andrea Doria	AC Mantova	Hellas-Verona	Milan FBC	US Milanese	US Livorno	Specia FBC	AC Vicenza
US Pro Vercelli	■	2-1	4-0	1-1	3-0	2-1	3-2	5-0	3-0	5-1	3-1	10-0
AC Novara	0-1	■	1-1	0-0	4-0	3-1	2-0	5-0	1-1	1-0	1-0	4-2
Bologna FBC	2-1	2-1	■	1-1	0-1	2-0	4-1	4-0	1-0	5-0	2-0	11-1
FBC Juventus	1-7		1-1	■	2-0	1-2	2-1	1-1	0-2	3-1	2-2	1-0
SG Andrea Doria	1-0	1-2	1-2	6-2	■	4-2	5-2	1-2	1-0	3-1	1-0	3-0
AC Mantova	0-5	2-2	1-0	0-1	1-0	■	3-0	1-1	2-0	2-1	4-0	6-2
Hellas-Verona	0-1	0-4	0-2	0-2	2-0	2-1	■	2-1	2-1	3-0	2-1	3-1
Milan FBC	1-0	2-3	2-1	1-3	0-0	2-2	0-1	■	2-0	1-2	0-1	7-0
US Milanese	1-2	2-2	1-1	2-1	2-4	2-0	0-0	0-0	■	2-1	2-1	2-1
US Livorno	1-2	2-1	2-0	0-0	3-1	1-5	1-0	3-1	1-1	■	0-0	2-1
Specia FBC	0-1	0-0	1-0	1-1	2-0	3-2	2-3	1-2	1-1	1-0	■	1-2
AC Vicenza	1-1	0-6	1-2	1-1	0-3	0-1	0-1	0-3	2-1	1-2	2-2	■

	North Qualifiers (Group "A")	Pd	Wn	Dw	Ls	GF	GA	Pts	
1.	US Pro Vercelli (Vercelli)	22	17	2	3	62	15	36	SF
2.	FBA Novara (Novara)	21	11	6	4	44	19	28	
2.	Bologna FBC (Bologna)	22	12	4	6	44	21	28	
4.	FBC Juventus (Torino)	21	7	9	5	27	30	23	
4.	SG Andrea Doria (Genova)	22	11	1	10	36	32	23	
4.	AC Mantova (Mantova)	22	10	3	9	39	34	23	
7.	Hellas AC (Verona)	22	10	1	11	27	36	21	
8.	Milan FBC (Milano)	22	7	5	10	30	36	19	
8.	US Milanese (Milano)	22	6	7	9	23	29	19	
8.	US Livorno (Livorno)	22	8	3	11	25	40	19	
11.	Spezia FBC (La Spezia)	22	5	6	11	21	31	16	
12.	AC Vicenza (Vicenza)	22	2	3	17	18	73	7	
		262	106	50	106	396	396	262	

1921-1922 North Qualifiers Group "B"	Genoa CFC	US Alessandria	SC Pisa	Modena FBC	AC Padova	FBC Torino	Casale FBC	AC Legnano	Savona FBC	AC Venezia	AC Brescia	FBC Internazionale
Genoa CFC	■	2-2	2-0	7-0	7-1	2-0	5-0	2-0	2-0	7-0	1-0	2-0
US Alessandria	1-1	■	3-0	1-0	3-1	2-0	1-1	3-1	3-0	5-2	1-0	5-0
SC Pisa	1-1	3-2	■	4-1	3-1	4-1	2-0	4-0	4-0	5-1	5-0	7-2
Modena FBC	1-1	2-0	2-1	■	2-1	1-2	2-1	2-0	2-0	4-1	1-0	5-1
AC Padova	0-1	2-1	2-1	2-1	■	1-1	1-1	2-1	3-1	1-0	2-0	2-
FBC Torino	0-2	1-1	0-2	3-2	2-0	■	1-1	2-0	2-0	1-1	1-0	2-2
Casale FBC	3-2	0-0	0-0	6-0	0-2	1-1	■	0-1	2-1	3-0	4-0	7-0
AC Legnano	0-5	0-0	4-2	0-0	3-1	1-1	1-0	■	2-1	3-0	0-0	6-0
Savona FBC	1-1	1-1	2-1	2-0	2-0	3-1	2-0	2-1	■	3-0	2-3	3-1
AC Venezia	1-5	2-2	2-0	0-2	0-1	0-0	1-0	2-0	2-1	■	2-0	1-0
AC Brescia	0-1	0-1	0-2	1-0	2-0	2-0	4-0	1-1	3-0	0-3	■	3-1
FBC Internazionale	1-4	2-2	2-2	1-2	3-4	0-1	1-3	2-2	2-0	2-1	2-1	■

North Qualifiers (Group "B")		Pd	Wn	Dw	Ls	GF	GA	Pts	
1.	Genoa CFC (Genova)	22	16	5	1	63	12	37	SF
2.	US Alessandria (Alessandria)	22	10	9	3	40	21	29	
3.	SC Pisa (Pisa)	22	12	3	7	53	28	27	
4.	Modena FBC (Modena)	22	11	2	9	32	35	24	
5.	AC Padova (Padova)	22	10	3	9	30	37	23	
6.	FBC Torino (Torino)	22	7	8	7	23	28	22	
7.	Casale FBC (Casale Monferrato)	22	7	6	9	33	28	20	
7.	FBC Legnano (Legnano)	22	7	6	9	27	32	20	
9.	Savona FBC (Savona)	22	8	2	12	27	36	18	
10.	Venezia FC (Venezia)	22	7	3	12	22	45	17	
11.	AC Brescia (Brescia)	22	7	2	13	20	30	16	
12.	FBC Internazionale (Milano)	22	3	5	14	27	65	11	
		264	105	54	105	397	397	264	

South Qualifying Round

Campania		Pd	Pts	
1.	Puteolana US (Pozzuoli)	12	24	SF
2.	AC Savoia (Torre Annunziata)	12	16	
3.	Juventus Stabia SC (Castellammare di Stabia)	12	13	
4.	Internazionale FC (Napoli)	12	12	
5.	US Bagnolese (Bagnoli)	12	10	
6.	Naples FC (Napoli)	12	9	
7.	US Salernitana Audax (Salerno)	12	-	
		84	84	

Lazio		Pd	Pts	
1.	SGS Fortitudo (Roma)	16	26	SF
2.	FBC Juventus Audax (Roma)	16	22	
2.	SP Lazio (Roma)	16	22	
4.	SS Alba (Roma)	16	21	
5.	Roman FC (Roma)	16	16	
6.	US Romana (Roma)	16	15	
7.	FBC Audace (Roma)	16	10	
8.	US Pro Roma (Roma)	16	8	
9.	Roma Tivoli SS (Roma)	16	4	
		144	144	

Marche (Play-off)		Pd	Wn	Dw	Ls	GF	GA	Pts	
1.	US Anconitana (Ancona)	6	6	-	-	17	3	12	SF
2.	US Vigor (Senigallia)	6	3	1	2	13	12	7	
3.	FBC Helvia Recina (Macerata)	6	2	-	4	8	13	4	
4.	FBC Macerata (Macerata)	6	-	1	5	9	21	1	
		24	11	2	11	47	49	24	

Marche (Group "A")		Pd	Wn	Dw	Ls	GF	GA	Pts	
1.	FBC Helvia Recina (Macerata)	4	4	-	-	16	5	8	PO
2.	FBC Macerata (Macerata)	4	2	-	2	8	8	4	PO
3.	FBC Virtus	4	-	-	4	3	14	-	
		12	6	-	6	27	27	12	

Marche (Group "B")

		Pd	Pts						
1.	US Anconitana (Ancona)	4	4	-	-	18	2	8	PO
2.	US Vigor (Senigallia)	4	2	-	2	4	8	4	PO
3.	FBC Folgore (Folgore)	4	-	-	4	4	16	-	
		12	6	-	6	26	26	12	

Puglie

		Pd	Pts	
1.	FBC Audace (Taranto)	6	9	SF
2.	SS Pro Italia (Taranto)	6	8	
3.	FBC Liberty (Bari)	6	6	
4.	FBC Veloce	6	1	
		24	24	

Sicilia

		Pd	Pts	
1.	FBC Palermo (Palermo)	8		SF
2.	US Messinese (Messina)	8		
3.	FBC Libertas (Messina)	8		
4.	SS Umberto 1 (Messina)	8		
5.	FBC Vigor (Palermo)	8		
		40		

Due to a dispute among the clubs 2 championships were contested this season, the "official" championship run under the auspices of the F.I.G.C. and an "unofficial" championship which was under the control of the break-away group, the C.C.I.. However differences were resolved and the break-away club returned to the F.I.G.C. in time for the start of the 1922-23 season.

Coppa Italia Final (Vado Ligure – 16/07/22)

AC VADO (VADO LIGURE)	1-0 (aet)	SG Udinese (Udine)

Levratto 118'

Vado: A.Babboni, L.Babboni, Raimondi, Masio, Romano, Cabiati, Roletti, G.Babboni, Marchese, Esposto, Levratto.

Udinese: Lodolo, Bertoldi, Schifio, Dal Dan, Barbieri, Gerace, Tosolini, Melchior, Moretti, Semintendi, Ligugnana.

Semi-Finals

SG Udinese (Udine)	4-3 (aet), 1-0	US Lucchese Libertas (Lucca)
AC Vado (Vado Ligure)	1-0	PG Libertas (Firenze)

Quarter-Finals

PG Libertas (Firenze)	+:-	US Valenzana (Valenza)

The match was awarded as a forfeit win to PG Libertas (Firenze)

US Novese (Novi Ligure)	0-2	SG Udinese (Udine)
Pro Livorno (Livorno)	0-1	AC Vado (Vado Ligure)
FBC Speranza (Savona)	1-2	US Lucchese Libertas (Lucca)

Final (Genova – 15/07/23 + Roma – 22/07/23)

GENOA CFC (GENOVA) 4-1, 2-0 SP Lazio (Roma)

Genoa: De Prà, Bellini, De Vecchi, Barbieri, Burlando, Leale, Neri, Moruzzi, Catto, Santamaria, Bergamino.

	Semi-Finals (North)	Pd	Wn	Dw	Ls	GF	GA	Pts
1.	Genoa CFC (Genova)	4	3	1	-			7
2.	US Pro Vercelli (Vercelli)	4	1	1	2			3
3.	AC Padova (Padova)	4	1	-	3			2
		12	5	2	5			12

Semi-Finals (South)

AC Savoia (Torre Annunziata)) 3-3, 1-4 SP Lazio (Roma)

1922-1923 North Group "A"	US Pro Vercelli	FBC Torino	SG Sampierdarenese	SC Pisa	Hellas-Verona	Casale FBC	FBC Internazionale	FBC Virtus	AC Mantova	US Torinese	FBC Petrarca	SC Speranze
US Pro Vercelli		0-2	2-3	1-2	0-0	3-0	1-0	1-1	2-1	3-1	2-0	3-0
FBC Torino	1-2		2-0	6-1	0-1	1-1	2-2	3-0	2-0	6-0	8-0	8-0
SG Sampierdarenese	0-1	1-0		2-0	1-1	0-0	3-1	1-1	3-1	2-0	0-0	2-0
SC Pisa	1-3	2-1	5-0		2-1	2-2	0-2	1-0	4-1	2-0	2-0	4-2
Hellas-Verona	1-2	1-1	0-2	2-0		1-1	2-3	1-0	2-0	1-1	3-2	3-1
Casale FBC	0-1	0-1	0-2	0-0	3-0		1-1	2-0	0-0	1-0	2-2	3-0
FBC Internazionale	1-5	0-6	4-2	2-2	2-0	0-1		1-0	1-1	2-3	4-0	3-0
FBC Virtus	0-2	0-1	1-3	2-1	2-0	1-0	2-0		0-0	1-0	0-0	1-0
AC Mantova	0-1	0-3	1-0	3-1	1-1	0-1	3-2	0-1		1-1	0-1	1-0
US Torinese	0-5	1-1	1-0	0-3	0-3	2-1	0-1	4-0	0-1		1-3	3-2
FBC Petrarca	0-6	0-2	1-4	1-2	1-2	0-4	3-1	1-2	0-2	1-4		2-1
SC Speranze	0-3	0-2	0-6	1-7	1-3	0-0	0-0	0-0	1-1	1-1	0-1	

	North (Group "A")	Pd	Wn	Dw	Ls	GF	GA	Pts	
1.	US Pro Vercelli (Vercelli)	22	17	2	3	49	14	36	SF
2.	FBC Torino (Torino)	22	14	4	4	59	12	32	
3.	SG Sampierdarenese (Genova)	22	12	4	6	37	22	28	
4.	SC Pisa (Pisa)	22	12	3	7	44	32	27	
5.	Hellas AC (Verona)	22	9	6	7	29	26	24	
6.	Casale FBC (Casale Monferrato)	22	7	9	6	23	17	23	
7.	FBC Internazionale (Milano)	22	8	5	9	33	37	21	
7.	FBC Virtus (Bologna)	22	8	5	9	15	22	21	
9.	AC Mantova (Mantova)	22	6	6	10	18	27	18	
10.	US Torinese (Torino)	22	6	4	12	23	41	16	
11.	Petrarca GC (Padova)	22	5	3	14	19	52	13	
12.	FC Speranza (Savona)	22	-	5	17	10	57	5	
		264	104	56	104	359	359	264	

1922-1923 North Group "B"	Genoa CFC	AC Legnano	Bologna FBC	Milan FBC	FBC Juventus	US Cremonese	Modena FBC	Derthona FBC	Spezia FBC	FBC Rivarolese	Esperia Como	SC Udinese
Genoa CFC		1-1	2-1	4-1	2-1	2-1	2-1	3-1	4-0	5-1	0-0	1-0
AC Legnano	1-1		1-0	1-1	0-1	4-0	0-0	1-1	2-1	3-2	1-0	3-1
Bologna FBC	1-2	5-1		8-0	4-1	3-0	2-0	1-1	1-2	6-0	4-2	1-0
Milan FBC	1-3	1-0	2-0		2-2	2-1	1-1	0-0	0-0	4-0	4-1	1-1
FBC Juventus	1-1	2-3	2-2	0-0		3-1	4-2	2-1	0-0	0-2	1-0	1-0
US Cremonese	0-2	0-2	1-1	0-1	1-0		1-1	2-0	2-0	4-0	2-0	2-2
Modena FBC	2-3	0-3	2-0	0-1	1-0	0-0		1-0	3-2	0-2	2-0	2-0
Derthona FBC	1-4	1-1	2-2	1-1	0-2	0-2	1-0		1-1	1-4	4-0	5-0
Spezia FBC	1-1	0-2	0-5	2-1	1-0	0-1	0-2	1-0		2-2	0-0	2-2
FBC Rivarolese	0-4	0-2	0-0	1-1	0-5	2-3	1-3	1-3	0-0		2-1	3-1
Esperia Como	2-8	0-2	0-5	1-1	0-1	0-3	0-2	1-3	0-0	0-2		3-2
SC Udinese	0-6	1-3	0-14	1-6	0-2	0-1	0-2	1-2	0-5	1-3	1-0	

	North (Group "B")	Pd	Wn	Dw	Ls	GF	GA	Pts	
1.	Genoa CFC (Genova)	22	17	5	-	61	18	39	SF
2.	FBC Legnano (Legnano)	22	13	6	3	37	19	32	
3.	Bologna FBC (Bologna)	22	11	5	6	66	21	27	
4.	Milan FBC (Milan)	22	8	10	4	32	28	26	
5.	FBC Juventus (Torino)	22	10	5	7	31	23	25	
6.	US Cremonese (Cremona)	22	10	4	8	28	25	24	
6.	Modena FBC (Modena)	22	10	4	8	27	23	24	
8.	Derthona FBC (Tortona)	22	6	7	9	29	31	19	
8.	Spezia FBC (La Spezia)	22	5	9	8	20	29	19	
10.	US Rivarolese (Rivarolo Canavese)	22	7	4	11	28	49	18	
11.	Esperia FC (Como)	22	1	4	17	11	50	6	
12.	AC Udinese (Udine)	22	1	3	18	14	68	5	*
		264	99	66	99	384	384	264	

	North (Group "C")	Pd	Wn	Dw	Ls	GF	GA	Pts	
1.	AC Padova (Padova)	22	14	4	4	47	20	32	SF
1.	US Alessandria (Alessandria)	22	14	4	4	34	14	32	
3.	US Livorno (Livorno)	22	13	4	5	43	19	30	
3.	S.P.A.L. (Ferrara)	22	12	6	4	37	15	30	
5.	FBA Novara (Novara)	22	12	2	8	42	24	26	
6.	SG Andrea Doria (Genova)	22	8	5	9	32	28	21	
7.	US Novese (Novi Ligure)	22	5	8	9	23	34	18	
8.	AC Brescia (Brescia)	20	6	4	10	23	27	16	
9.	US Lucchese Libertas (Lucca)	21	6	3	12	20	53	15	
10.	US Milanese (Milano)	21	3	7	11	22	40	13	
11.	FBC Pastore (Torino)	22	5	3	14	17	45	13	
12.	Savona FBC (Savona)	20	5	2	13	16	37	12	
		258	103	52	103	356	356	258	

Group "C" Play-Off

AC Padova (Padova) 2-1 US Alessandria (Alessandria)

South (Play-off Group "A")

		Pd	Pts	
1.	AC Savoia (Torre Annunziata)	6	10	SF
2.	SS Alba (Roma)	6	7	
2.	US Anconitana (Ancona)	6	7	
4.	SS Pro Italia (Taranto)	6	-	
		24	24	

South (Play-off Group "B")

		Pd	Wn	Dw	Ls	GF	GA	Pts	
1.	SP Lazio (Roma)	6	6	-	-			12	SF
2.	US Ideale (Bari)	6	4	-	2			8	
3.	FBC Libertas (Palermo)	6	2	-	4			4	
4.	Internaples FBC (Napoli)	6	-	-	6			-	
		24	12	-	12			24	

South (Campania)

		Pd	Pts	
1.	AC Savoia (Torre Annunziata)	8	15	PO
2.	Internaples FBC (Napoli)	8	11	PO
3.	SC Juventus Stabia (Castellammare di Stabia)	8	8	
4.	FBC Cavese (Cava dei Tirreni)	8	6	
5.	US Bagnolese (Bagnoli)	8	-	
		40	40	

South (Lazio)

		Pd	Pts	
1.	SP Lazio (Roma)	10	17	PO
2.	SS Alba (Roma)	10	13	PO
3.	SGS Fortitudo (Roma)	10	11	
4.	US Romana (Roma)	10	9	
5.	FBC Juventus Audax (Roma)	10	6	
6.	Roman FC (Roma)	10	4	
		60	60	

South (Puglie)

		Pd	Pts	
1.	SS Pro Italia (Taranto)	8	13	PO
2.	US Ideale (Bari)	8	12	PO
3.	FBC Audace (Taranto)	8	8	
4.	FBC Liberty (Bari)	8	4	
5.	SC Lecce (Lecce)	8	3	
		40	40	

South (Sicilia – Play-off)

		Pd	Wn	Dw	Ls	GF	GA	Pts	
1.	FBC Libertas (Palermo)	2	2	-	-			4	PO
2.	FBC Messina (Messina)	2	1	-	1			2	
3.	FBC Palermo (Palermo)	2	-	-	2			-	
		6	3	-	3			6	

South (Sicilia)

		Pd	Pts	
1.	FBC Libertas (Palermo)	4	4	
1.	FBC Messina (Messina)	4	4	*
1.	FBC Palermo (Palermo)	4	4	
		12	12	

* FBC Messina (Messina) reverted to Messinese (Messina) and SC Messina (Messina) for the next season.

1923-24

Final (Genova – 31/08/24 + Torre Annunziata – 07/09/24)

GENOA CFC (GENOVA) 3-1, 1-1 AC Savoia (Torre Annunziata)

Genoa: De Prà, Bellini, De Vecchi, Barbieri, Burlando, Leale, Neri, Moruzzi, Catto, Santamaria, Bergamino.

Semi-Final (North)

Genoa CFC (Genova) 1-0, 2-0 Bologna FBC (Bologna)

The second game was abandoned after 39 minutes with the score at 1-1 and was awarded 2-0 to Genoa by the FIGC.

Semi-Final (South)

AC Savoia (Torre Annunziata) 2-0, 0-1, 2-0 SS Alba (Roma)

The third game in Livorno was awarded 2-0 to AC Savoia as SS Alba did not show for the match.

1923-1924 North Group "A"	Genoa CFC	AC Padova	FBC Juventus	FBC Internazionale	US Livorno	US Alessandria	Modena FBC	Casale FBC	SG Sampierdarenese	AC Novara	AC Brescia	FBC Virtus
Genoa CFC		1-2	1-1	5-1	2-0	2-0	4-1	6-1	4-0	4-0	1-0	5-0
AC Padova	0-1		1-2	1-2	2-0	1-1	3-1	3-0	5-0	3-1	4-2	3-0
FBC Juventus	0-2	3-0		2-0	1-1	3-1	0-2	3-2	4-1	2-0	0-1	1-0
FBC Internazionale	1-2	2-1	2-2		4-0	1-0	1-1	3-0	1-0	1-1	3-0	2-0
US Livorno	3-1	1-1	3-2	3-0		2-1	3-1	0-0	2-0	3-1	3-2	4-1
US Alessandria	1-1	2-2	3-1	3-1	0-1		5-0	5-1	3-0	0-0	4-0	4-0
Modena FBC	0-0	0-0	2-0	1-2	3-0	5-1		2-0	2-1	7-2	2-0	2-1
Casale FBC	0-0	1-0	2-3	1-0	2-0	0-1	1-0		1-0	1-0	0-3	4-0
SG Sampierdarenese	1-0	0-1	2-3	2-1	0-1	1-2	1-0	2-0		1-0	1-0	4-0
AC Novara	1-2	0-0	1-0	1-2	3-0	1-2	2-2	2-3	0-2		2-1	2-1
AC Brescia	0-5	0-1	0-2	1-1		0-0	1-1	1-4	0-2			1-0
FBC Virtus	1-1	0-1	0-3	0-1	2-3	0-1	1-1	0-1	2-0	2-1	1-2	

	North (Group "A")	Pd	Wn	Dw	Ls	GF	GA	Pts	
1.	Genoa CFC (Genova)	22	14	5	3	50	14	33	SF
2.	AC Padova (Padova)	22	11	5	6	35	20	27	
2.	FBC Juventus (Torino)	22	12	3	7	38	27	27	
2.	FBC Internazionale (Milano)	22	11	5	6	32	25	27	
2.	US Livorno (Livorno)	21	12	3	6	33	29	27	
6.	US Alessandria (Alessandria)	22	10	6	6	38	23	26	
7.	Modena FBC (Modena)	22	9	6	7	36	29	24	
8.	Casale FBC (Casale Monferrato)	22	10	2	10	25	34	22	
9.	SG Sampierdarenese (Genova)	22	9	-	13	21	32	18	
10.	FBA Novara (Novara)	21	4	4	13	21	39	12	
11.	AC Brescia (Brescia)	20	4	3	13	15	37	11	
12.	FBC Virtus (Bologna)	22	2	2	18	12	47	6	
		260	108	44	108	356	356	260	

1923-1924 North Group "B"	Bologna FBC	FBC Torino	US Pro Vercelli	Hellas-Verona	AC Legnano	US Cremonese	SC Pisa	SG Andrea Doria	Milan FBC	SPAL Ferrara	Spezia FBC	US Novese
Bologna FBC		0-1	3-3	3-1	3-2	2-0	5-0	3-0	4-0	2-1	5-0	2-0
FBC Torino	4-1		1-2	1-1	1-2	4-1	1-1	3-1	3-3	3-1	2-1	4-1
US Pro Vercelli	0-1	0-0		3-0	1-0	4-1	4-1	2-2	2-1	6-0	4-0	3-1
Hellas-Verona	2-2	1-2	1-0		3-1	2-0	2-1	2-2	5-1	8-1	2-2	5-2
AC Legnano	1-1	3-1	1-0	1-0		1-2	3-0	3-0	2-2	4-0	2-0	1-0
US Cremonese	0-0	0-0	2-1	1-1	0-1		2-0	2-0	4-1	1-1	3-1	2-1
SC Pisa	2-1	1-1	1-0	1-1	1-1	2-1		0-0	2-2	2-1	2-0	1-0
SG Andrea Doria	0-1	2-1	1-1	4-2	4-0	4-0	1-1		1-1	0-1	1-0	0-2
Milan FBC	1-0	0-3	1-3	2-1	2-1	0-1	5-1	1-2		3-4	3-1	5-0
SPAL Ferrara	0-1	1-2	4-4	1-1	1-1	2-1	1-0	1-1	1-1		0-1	2-0
Spezia FBC	0-0	1-0	0-5	1-2	1-0	1-0	1-4	1-0	2-1	0-1		1-1
US Novese	0-1	0-5	1-1	3-0	1-1	1-2	2-2	1-0	1-2	2-1	0-1	

	North (Group "B")	Pd	Wn	Dw	Ls	GF	GA	Pts	
1.	Bologna FBC (Bologna)	22	13	5	4	41	18	31	SF
2.	FBC Torino (Torino)	22	12	6	4	43	22	30	
3.	US Pro Vercelli (Vercelli)	22	11	6	5	46	23	28	
4.	Hellas AC (Verona)	22	8	7	7	43	35	23	
4.	FBC Legnano (Legnano)	22	9	5	8	30	24	23	
6.	US Cremonese (Cremona)	22	9	4	9	26	30	22	
6.	SC Pisa (Pisa)	22	7	8	7	26	35	22	
8.	SG Andrea Doria (Genova)	22	6	7	9	26	29	19	
8.	Milan FBC (Milano)	22	7	5	10	38	44	19	
10.	S.P.A.L. (Ferrara)	22	6	6	10	26	44	18	
11.	Spezia FBC (La Spezia)	22	7	3	12	16	35	17	
12.	US Novese (Novi Ligure)	22	4	4	14	20	42	12	
		264	99	66	99	381	381	264	

	South Play-off (Group "A")	Pd	Pts	
1.	AC Savoia (Torre Annunziata)	6	8	SF
2.	SP Lazio (Roma)	6	7	
3.	US Ideale (Bari)	6	5	
4.	US Anconitana (Ancona)	6	4	
		24	24	

	South Play-off (Group "B")	Pd	Pts	
1.	SS Alba (Roma)	6	8	SF
1.	FBC Audace (Taranto)	6	8	
3.	Internaples FBC (Napoli)	6	5	
4.	FBC Palermo (Palermo)	6	3	
		24	24	

Play-off

SS Alba (Roma) 2-0 FBC Audace (Taranto)

South Qualifying Round

	Campania	Pd	Pts	
1.	AC Savoia (Torre Annunziata)	10	19	PO
2.	Internaples FBC (Napoli)	10	11	PO
3.	SS Cavese (Cava dei Tirreni)	10	10	
4.	US Bagnolese (Bagnoli)	10	9	
5.	SC Juventus Stabia (Castellammare di Stabia)	10	6	
6.	US Salernitana Audax (Salerno)	10	5	
		60	60	

	Lazio	Pd	Pts	
1.	SS Alba (Roma)	10	16	PO
2.	SP Lazio (Roma)	10	15	PO
2.	SGS Fortitudo (Roma)	10	15	
4.	SS Roma Tivoli (Roma)	10	8	
5.	US Romana (Roma)	10	6	
6.	FBC Juventus Audax (Roma)	10	-	
		60	60	

Play-off SP Lazio (Roma) 2-0 SGS Fortitudo (Roma)

Marche: US Anconitana (Ancona) received a bye directly to the Semi-Final stage.

	Puglie	Pd	Pts	
1.	FBC Audace (Taranto)	10	15	PO
2.	US Ideale (Bari)	10	13	PO
3.	SS Pro Italia (Taranto)	10	11	
4.	FBC Liberty (Bari)	10	10	
5.	FBC Enotria (Empoli)	10	7	
6.	US Foggia (Foggia)	10	4	
		60	60	

Sicilia

SC Messina (Messina) 1-1, 2-3 FBC Palermo (Palermo)

Note: Cagliari FBC (Cagliari) merged with US Italia (Cagliari) to become CS Cagliari (Cagliari) for the next season.
Foggia SC (Foggia) merged with Velo Club (Foggia) to become US Foggia (Foggia) for the next season.
SP Lazio (Roma) changed their name to SS Lazio (Roma) for the next season.

1924-25

Final (Bologna – 16/08/25 + Roma – 23/08/25)

BOLOGNA FBC (BOLOGNA) 4-0, 2-0 SS Alba (Roma)

Bologna: Gianni, Borgato, Gasperi, Genovesi, Baldi, Giordani, Pozzi, Schiavio, Della Valle, Perin, Muzzioli.

Semi-Final (North)

Bologna FBC (Bologna) 1-2, 2-1, 2-2, 1-1, 2-0 Genoa CFC (Genova)

Semi-Final (South)

US Anconitana (Ancona) 1-3, 0-1 SS Alba (Roma)

1924-1925 North Group "A"	Genoa CFC	Modena FBC	Casale FBC	FBC Internaz.	SC Pisa	FBC Torino	US Cremon.	AC Reggiana	Hellas-Verona	AC Brescia	AC Legnano	Spezia FBC
Genoa CFC		2-0	4-1	2-1	1-1	0-0	4-0	4-1	3-0	2-0	6-3	3-2
Modena FBC	1-0		3-0	5-0	4-0	0-1	0-1	2-1	1-0	2-0	3-1	2-0
Casale FBC	2-1	4-0		2-1	3-1	0-0	3-0	2-0	2-0	2-1	1-0	6-3
FBC Internazionale	2-1	4-1	4-0		1-2	2-5	4-2	3-0	3-1	1-0	1-2	5-2
SC Pisa	1-2	0-1	2-2	3-1		1-0	3-0	2-0	2-0	6-1	1-0	3-2
FBC Torino	1-1	2-2	1-2	1-2	3-1		1-0	3-1	3-1	0-0	0-1	2-1
US Cremonese	2-0	0-3	2-1	1-1	1-0	0-1		1-1	2-2	3-0	3-0	6-0
AC Reggiana	2-4	1-4	1-0	4-2	3-1	2-1	4-1		6-2	2-1	3-1	2-0
Hellas-Verona	2-2	3-3	2-1	2-3	3-0	2-2	1-2	3-0		2-0	2-1	3-0
AC Brescia	0-5	4-1	3-1	1-0	0-1	1-2	5-0	1-1	4-0		1-0	4-2
AC Legnano	1-0	0-0	0-1	0-2	0-0	4-1	0-1	2-0	1-1	0-0		1-1
Spezia FBC	0-1	0-3	1-1	0-1	0-1	1-0	0-0	2-1	1-1	1-0	1-0	

	North (Group "A")	Pd	Wn	Dw	Ls	GF	GA	Pts	
1.	Genoa CFC (Genova)	22	13	4	5	48	23	30	SF
2.	Modena FBC (Modena)	22	13	3	6	41	24	29	
3.	Casale FBC (Casale Monferrato)	22	12	3	7	37	30	27	
4.	FBC Internazionale (Milano)	22	12	1	9	44	37	25	
4.	SC Pisa (Pisa)	22	11	3	8	32	28	25	
6.	FBC Torino (Torino)	22	9	6	7	30	25	24	
7.	US Cremonese (Cremona)	22	9	4	9	28	34	22	
8.	US Reggiana (Reggio Emilia)	22	9	2	11	36	42	20	
9.	Hellas AC (Verona)	22	6	6	10	33	42	18	
10.	AC Brescia (Brescia)	22	7	3	12	27	34	17	
11.	FBC Legnano (Legnano)	22	5	5	12	18	29	15	
12.	Spezia FBC (La Spezia)	22	4	4	14	20	46	12	
		264	110	44	110	394	394	264	

1924-1925 North Group "B"	Bologna FBC	FBC Juventus	US Pro Vercelli	AC Padova	US Alessandria	US Livorno	Milan FBC	SG Andrea Doria	AC Novara	SG Sampierdar.	AC Mantova	Derthona FBC	SPAL Ferrara
Bologna FBC		2-1	3-0	3-0	3-1	2-1	2-0	5-0	0-0	4-0	5-0	4-1	3-1
FBC Juventus	2-1		0-0	0-2	3-0	2-0	5-3	1-0	1-1	4-1	3-0	2-1	2-1
US Pro Vercelli	3-0	2-1		6-0	2-0	6-1	3-2	2-0	5-1	2-0	5-3	5-0	5-0
AC Padova	3-2	2-1	0-0		4-0	5-1	4-0	6-1	1-1	2-0	1-2	2-1	9-0
US Alessandria	1-0	2-2	1-0	1-1		2-3	3-1	2-1	1-0	1-0	6-1	0-0	2-1
US Livorno	2-2	2-2	4-1	2-0	1-1		4-0	0-1	1-1	2-0	4-1	6-2	4-0
Milan FBC	3-1	0-0	1-2	1-3	3-0	4-2		2-0	3-1	2-0	2-1	3-2	3-1
SG Andrea Doria	0-1	0-2	1-1	4-0	0-0	0-0	3-2		2-0	2-1	3-1	4-1	1-0
AC Novara	1-2	1-1	1-1	1-1	0-0	1-1	4-2	1-0		0-2	3-1	0-2	4-1
SG Sampierdarenese	0-0	0-0	2-2	2-3	1-0	1-1	3-2	2-0	1-0		4-1	1-0	0-0
AC Mantova	0-0	0-1	4-2	2-1	1-1	4-0	4-2	1-0	0-1	1-1		5-1	4-0
Derthona FBC	2-4	0-2	1-1	2-0	1-1	2-1	0-3	0-3	1-1	1-0	3-0		2-0
SPAL Ferrara	0-4	0-2	3-0	1-1	1-1	0-0	3-1	2-0	1-0	2-1	4-1	2-2	

North (Group "B")		Pd	Wn	Dw	Ls	GF	GA	Pts	
1.	Bologna FBC (Bologna)	24	15	4	5	53	22	34	SF
2.	FBC Juventus (Torino)	24	13	7	4	40	21	33	
3.	US Pro Vercelli (Vercelli)	24	13	6	5	56	29	32	
4.	AC Padova (Padova)	24	12	5	7	51	34	29	
5.	US Alessandria (Alessandria)	24	8	9	7	27	30	25	
6.	US Livorno (Livorno)	24	8	8	8	43	40	24	
7.	Milan FBC (Milano)	24	10	1	13	45	51	21	
7.	SG Andrea Doria (Genova)	24	9	3	12	26	33	21	
9.	FBA Novara (Novara)	24	5	10	9	24	31	20	
9.	SG Sampierdarenese (Genova)	24	7	6	11	23	32	20	
11.	AC Mantova (Mantova)	24	8	3	13	38	53	19	
12.	Derthona FBC (Tortona)	24	6	5	13	28	50	17	
12.	S.P.A.L. (Ferrara)	24	6	5	13	24	52	17	
		312	120	72	120	478	478	312	

South Play-off (Group "A")		Pd	Pts	
1.	US Anconitana (Ancona)	6	8	SF
1.	SS Lazio (Roma)	6	8	
3.	AC Savoia (Torre Annunziata)	6	5	
4.	SS Pro Italia (Taranto)	6	3	
		24	24	

Play-off

US Anconitana (Ancona) 1-0 SS Lazio (Roma)

South Play-off (Group "B")		Pd	Pts	
1.	SS Alba (Roma)	6	11	SF
2.	SS Cavese (Cava dei Terrini)	6	8	
3.	FBC Liberty (Bari)	6	3	
4.	SC Messina (Messina)	6	2	
		24	24	

South Qualifying Round

Campania		Pd	Pts	
1.	AC Savoia (Torre Annunziata)	6	9	PO
2.	SS Cavese (Cava dei Terrini)	6	8	PO
3.	Internaples FBC (Napoli)	6	7	
4.	US Salernitana Audax (Salerno)	6	-	
		24	24	

Lazio		Pd	Pts	
1.	SS Alba (Roma)	8	12	PO
2.	SS Lazio (Roma)	8	11	PO
3.	SGS Fortitudo (Roma)	8	10	
4.	CS Audace (Roma)	8	5	
5.	US Pro Roma (Roma)	8	2	
		40	40	

Marche US Anconitana (Ancona) received a bye directly to the Semi-Final stage.

Puglie	Pd	Pts	
1. SS Pro Italia (Taranto)	10	16	PO
2. FBC Liberty (Bari)	10	14	PO
3. US Ideale (Bari)	10	11	
4. FBC Audace (Taranto)	10	9	
5. FBC Tarantino (Taranto)	10	7	
6. FBC Bari (Bari)	10	3	
	60	60	

Sicilia

SC Messina (Messina) 2-2, 1-0 FBC Palermo (Palermo)
SC Messina qualified for the play-off stage.

Note: Esperia FC (Como) merged with FBC Como (Como) to become AC Comense (Como) for the next season.

1925-26

Final (Torino – 08/08/26 + Roma – 22/08/26)

FBC JUVENTUS (TORINO) 7-1, 5-0 SS Alba (Roma)

Juventus: Combi, Rosetta, Allemandi, Grabbi, Viola, Bigatto, Munerati, Vojak, Pastore, Hirzer, Torriani.

Semi-Final (North)

Bologna FBC (Bologna) 2-2, 0-0, 1-2 FBC Juventus (Torino)
(the third match was played in Milano)

Semi-Final (South)

SS Alba (Roma) 6-1, 1-1 Internaples FBC (Napoli)

1925-1926 North Group "A"	Bologna FBC	FBC Torino	Modena FBC	Hellas-Verona	FBC Internazionale	Casale FBC	SG Andrea Doria	AC Brescia	AC Novara	AC Udinese	SC Pisa	AC Legnano
Bologna FBC		3-2	1-0	7-0	4-1	1-0	3-0	6-0	4-1	4-0	7-0	6-0
FBC Torino	6-2		3-1	5-2	2-1	2-0	4-0	5-0	2-1	7-0	4-1	4-1
Modena FBC	0-0	1-1		3-2	3-0	2-3	6-0	3-2	4-1	5-1	6-2	2-0
Hellas-Verona	2-2	1-1	0-2		1-0	4-3	5-1	4-2	2-2	4-0	7-1	4-1
FBC Internazionale	1-1	3-4	2-1	3-3		4-1	0-1	4-0	5-4	4-2	1-0	2-0
Casale FBC	0-1	2-3	4-0	3-2	3-3		2-0	2-0	1-1	2-1	4-0	5-0
SG Andrea Doria	3-3	0-0	2-1	3-2	2-0	3-2		4-1	2-2	3-2	5-1	3-1
AC Brescia	1-2	3-4	2-2	3-2	0-1	2-1	5-0		4-1	3-1	2-0	1-0
AC Novara	1-2	0-2	0-1	1-2	1-1	0-0	3-1	5-1		6-3	2-0	3-1
AC Udinese	1-7	4-3	3-1	3-3	3-4	2-1	3-2	3-3	0-2		1-2	2-2
SC Pisa	0-6	1-1	1-0	1-3	1-3	1-1	3-2	0-1	4-3	1-2		2-0
AC Legnano	1-2	1-2	0-1	1-3	1-1	0-2	1-0	1-1	0-0	6-1	4-1	

North (Group "A")

		Pd	Wn	Dw	Ls	GF	GA	Pts	
1.	Bologna FBC (Bologna)	22	17	4	1	74	20	38	SF
2.	FBC Torino (Torino)	22	16	4	2	67	28	36	
3.	Modena FBC (Modena)	22	11	3	8	45	30	25	
3.	Hellas AC (Verona)	22	10	5	7	58	48	25	
3.	FBC Internazionale (Milano)	22	10	5	7	44	38	25	
6.	Casale FBC (Casale Monferrato)	22	9	4	9	42	32	22	
7.	SG Andrea Doria (Genova)	22	9	3	10	37	50	21	
8.	AC Brescia (Brescia)	22	8	3	11	37	51	19	
9.	FBA Novara (Novara)	22	6	6	10	40	42	18	
10.	AC Udinese (Udine)	22	5	3	14	38	75	13	
11.	SC Pisa (Pisa)	22	5	2	15	23	65	12	
12.	FBC Legnano (Legnano)	22	3	4	15	22	48	10	
		264	109	46	109	527	527	264	

1925-1926 North Group "B"	FBC Juventus	US Cremonese	Genoa CFC	AC Padova	US Livorno	SG Sampierdarenese	US Pro Vercelli	Milan FBC	AC Reggiana	US Alessandria	Parma FBC	AC Mantova
FBC Juventus		4-0	2-0	3-2	3-0	4-0	2-1	6-0	5-0	4-0	6-0	8-1
US Cremonese	0-0		1-0	2-1	8-0	2-1	4-2	1-0	1-0	3-0	3-0	2-0
Genoa CFC	1-3	2-1		2-0	0-0	3-1	2-1	2-1	3-0	7-2	3-0	3-1
AC Padova	2-2	1-1	2-0		6-1	3-0	5-2	4-2	6-2	1-0	6-1	9-0
US Livorno	1-1	2-1	3-2	3-0		5-1	2-0	1-1	2-0	6-2	4-0	6-1
SG Sampierdarenese	2-1	2-1	2-3	2-1	2-1		1-0	2-1	3-3	2-1	4-1	8-1
US Pro Vercelli	0-1	4-0	2-0	1-1	7-0	2-0		3-1	3-0	1-0	2-2	3-0
Milan FBC	1-2	1-4	1-3	3-0	4-1	2-0	4-0		4-0	2-2	4-2	3-1
AC Reggiana	2-0	0-2	2-2	4-1	5-2	1-1	3-2	0-1		2-1	2-0	4-0
US Alessandria	1-3	2-3	1-0	0-2	1-0	5-0	1-1	4-3	6-0		2-0	9-0
Parma FBC	0-3	3-1	1-5	2-0	0-1	1-3	0-3	1-2	2-0	1-0		5-3
AC Mantova	0-5	0-0	2-5	0-2	0-2	1-1	2-2	0-2	3-0	7-1	1-1	

North (Group "B")

		Pd	Wn	Dw	Ls	GF	GA	Pts	
1.	FBC Juventus (Torino)	22	17	3	2	68	14	37	SF
2.	US Cremonese (Cremona)	22	13	3	6	41	25	29	
3.	Genoa CFC (Genova)	22	13	2	7	48	29	28	
4.	AC Padova (Padova)	22	11	3	8	55	33	25	
4.	US Livorno (Livorno)	22	11	3	8	43	45	25	
6.	SG Sampierdarenese (Genova)	22	10	3	9	38	43	23	
7.	US Pro Vercelli (Vercelli)	22	9	4	9	42	31	22	
7.	Milan FBC (Milano)	22	10	2	10	43	39	22	
9.	US Reggiana (Reggio Emilia)	22	7	3	12	30	50	17	
10.	US Alessandria (Alessandria)	22	7	2	13	41	48	16	
11.	Parma FBC (Parma)	22	5	2	15	23	58	12	
12.	AC Mantova (Mantova)	22	2	4	16	24	81	8	
		264	115	34	115	496	496	264	

South Play-off (Group "A")		Pd	Wn	Dw	Ls	GF	GA	Pts	
1.	Internaples FBC (Napoli)	8	5	3	-	23	5	13	SF
2.	SGS Fortitudo (Roma)	8	4	3	1	15	9	11	
3.	US Anconitana (Ancona)	8	4	1	3	16	13	9	
4.	FBC Liberty (Bari)	8	2	3	3	18	18	7	
5.	US Messinese (Messina)	8	-	-	8	2	29	-	
		40	15	10	15	74	74	40	

South Play-off (Group "B")		Pd	Wn	Dw	Ls	GF	GA	Pts	
1.	SS Alba (Roma)	8	6	2	-	19	8	14	SF
2.	US Bagnolese (Bagnoli)	8	5	2	1	22	8	12	
3.	SS Pro Italia (Taranto)	8	4	2	2	15	11	10	
4.	FBC Palermo (Palermo)	8	1	-	7	10	15	2	
4.	SS Maceratese (Macerata)	8	1	-	7	5	29	2	
		40	17	6	17	71	71	40	

South Qualifying Round

Campania		Pd	Wn	Dw	Ls	GF	GA	Pts	
1.	Internaples FBC (Napoli)	8	7	1	-	35	4	15	PO*
2.	US Bagnolese (Bagnoli)	8	5	1	2	20	8	11	PO
3.	US Casertana (Caserta)	8	4	-	4	11	21	8	
4.	SC Stabia (Castellammare di Stabia)	8	3	-	5	13	22	6	
5.	Puteolana US (Pozzuoli)	8	-	-	8	5	29	-	
		40	19	2	19	84	84	40	

Lazio		Pd	Wn	Dw	Ls	GF	GA	Pts	
1.	SS Alba (Roma)	10	8	1	1	41	13	17	PO*
2.	SGS Fortitudo (Roma)	10	8	-	2	35	13	16	PO*
3.	SS Lazio (Roma)	10	6	2	2	45	27	14	
4.	CS Audace (Roma)	10	3	1	6	27	42	7	*
5.	Roman FC (Roma)	10	2	2	6	14	28	6	
6.	US Pro Roma (Roma)	10	-	-	10	5	44	-	*
		60	27	6	27	167	167	60	

Marche		Pd	Wn	Dw	Ls	GF	GA	Pts	
1.	US Anconitana (Ancona)	2	2	-	-	9	3	4	PO
2.	SS Maceratese (Macerata)	2	-	-	2	3	9	-	PO
		4	2	-	2	12	12	6	

Puglie		Pd	Wn	Dw	Ls	GF	GA	Pts	
1.	SS Pro Italia (Taranto)	8	6	2	-	14	4	14	PO
2.	FBC Liberty (Bari)	8	5	-	3	11	8	10	PO
3.	FBC Audace (Taranto)	8	4	1	3	11	9	9	
4.	US Ideale (Bari)	8	-	5	3	6	9	5	
5.	US Foggia (Foggia)	8	-	2	6	1	13	2	
		40	15	10	15	43	43	40	

Sicilia

		Pd	Wn	Dw	Ls	GF	GA	Pts	
1.	FBC Palermo (Palermo)	2	1	-	1	7	1	2	PO
1.	US Messinese (Messina)	2	1	-	1	1	7	2	PO
		4	2	-	2	8	8	4	

* SS Alba (Roma) merged with CS Audace (Roma) to become Alba Audace FC (Roma) for the next season.
SG Fortitudo (Roma) merged with US Pro Roma (Roma) to become SGS Fortitudo (Roma) for the next season.
AC Napoli (Napoli) (founded 01/08/26) absorbed Internaples FBC (Napoli) under AC Napoli (Napoli).

Note: SS Ascoli (Ascoli Piceno) re-formed as Vigor GS (Ascoli Piceno).
CS Firenze (Firenze) merged with PG Libertas (Firenze) to become Associazione Fiorentina del Calcio (Firenze).
US Romana (Roma) merged with US Carlo Oriano (Roma) to become US Roma (Roma) for the next season.
SS Roma Tivoli (Roma) merged with SS Andrea Doria (Roma) to become Tivoli Roma (Roma) for the next season.
AS Varesina (Varese) changed their name to Varese Sportiva (Varese) for the next season.

1926-27

1926-27 Final	Bologna FBC	Genoa CFC	FBC Internazionale	FBC Juventus	Milan FBC	FBC Torino
Bologna FBC		1-0	3-0	1-0	2-1	5-0
Genoa CFC	1-0		1-1	2-3	2-0	3-1
FBC Internazionale	1-0	2-3		2-1	1-1	1-2
FBC Juventus	1-1	6-0	1-3		2-0	1-0
Milan FBC	1-1	4-2	2-1	2-8		2-3
FBC Torino	1-0	3-1	2-1	2-1	3-0	

Final

		Pd	Wn	Dw	Ls	GF	GA	Pts	
1.	FBC Torino (Torino)	10	7	-	3	17	15	14	**
2.	Bologna FBC (Bologna)	10	5	2	3	14	6	12	
3.	FBC Juventus (Torino)	10	5	1	4	24	13	11	
4.	Genoa CFC (Genova)	10	4	1	5	15	21	9	
5.	FBC Internazionale (Milano)	10	3	2	5	13	16	8	
6.	Milan FBC (Milano)	10	2	2	6	13	25	6	
		60	26	8	26	96	96	60	

** The title was later revoked by the F.I.G.C. after a bribery trial in which FBC Torino were found guilty of paying Juventus full-back, Luigi Allemandi to "play badly" in the derby match versus FBC Juventus (Torino).

1926-27 Group "A"	Alba Audace FC	AC Brescia	Casale FBC	Genoa CFC	Hellas AC	FBC Internazionale	FBC Juventus	Modena FBC	AC Napoli	US Pro Vercelli
Alba Audace FC		5-2	0-1	1-3	3-0	1-1	0-2	1-2	5-2	3-0
AC Brescia	4-0		3-1	1-0	4-2	0-3	0-2	2-2	5-1	0-0
Casale FBC	3-1	3-0		2-1	2-0	1-1	0-2	3-0	3-0	1-1
Genoa CFC	2-0	4-1	4-0		2-0	4-0	1-2	2-1	4-1	3-0
Hellas AC	2-0	1-4	1-2	1-1		1-1	1-0	1-0	5-0	2-1
FBC Internazionale	2-1	4-1	3-0	2-1	5-0		3-0	2-1	9-2	2-0
FBC Juventus	1-0	2-0	4-0	0-0	6-0	4-1		7-2	8-0	0-1
Modena FBC	2-2	2-0	1-0	1-1	0-0	1-4	1-1		1-0	3-1
AC Napoli	0-2	0-0	0-2	0-2	0-1	0-3	0-3	0-1		0-3
US Pro Vercelli	3-0	3-1	0-0	2-2	4-1	4-3	0-0	0-0	4-1	

	Group "A"	Pd	Wn	Dw	Ls	GF	GA	Pts	
1.	FBC Juventus (Torino)	18	12	3	3	44	10	27	
1.	FBC Internazionale (Milano)	18	12	3	3	49	22	27	
3.	Genoa CFC (Genova)	18	10	4	4	37	15	24	
—	—	—	—	—	—	—	—	—	—
4.	Casale FBC (Casale Monferrato)	18	9	3	6	24	22	21	
5.	US Pro Vercelli (Vercelli)	18	7	6	5	27	22	20	
6.	Modena FBC (Modena)	18	6	6	6	21	27	18	
7.	AC Brescia (Brescia)	18	6	3	9	28	35	15	
7.	Hellas AC (Verona)	18	6	3	9	19	35	15	
9.	Alba Audace FC (Roma)	18	5	2	11	25	32	12	**
10.	AC Napoli (Napoli)	18	-	1	17	7	61	1	#
		180	73	34	73	281	281	180	

** Alba Audace FC (Roma) and SGS Fortitudo (Roma) were both relegated but on 22 July 1927 they merged with US Pro Roma (Roma) and Romana FC (Roma) to become AS Roma (Roma) and were re-admitted to the league under that name.

1926-27 Group "B"	US Alessandria	SG Andrea Doria	Bologna FBC	US Cremonese	SGS Fortitudo	US Livorno	Milan FBC	AC Padova	SG Sampierdarenese	FBC Torino
US Alessandria		5-0	5-1	2-1	3-1	0-0	3-1	6-1	6-1	1-3
SG Andrea Doria	1-2		0-1	2-1	1-2	2-1	1-0	1-0	1-1	1-2
Bologna FBC	2-0	0-0		4-2	2-1	3-2	4-1	5-1	4-2	1-1
US Cremonese	1-0	3-1	1-0		1-0	0-1	1-2	0-2	4-0	0-1
SGS Fortitudo	1-1	0-1	0-2	1-2		0-2	2-3	1-2	0-1	4-2
US Livorno	1-2	2-1	3-1	4-0	3-1		1-2	5-0	3-0	2-1
Milan FBC	1-1	4-1	4-2	1-0	4-0	3-0		5-2	1-2	3-1
AC Padova	3-2	1-1	0-2	4-1	5-3	3-1	1-3		3-1	0-1
SG Sampierdarenese	2-1	3-0	1-3	2-0	3-1	1-1	3-1	3-0		4-1
FBC Torino	3-2	3-1	2-1	8-1	4-0	8-0	2-2	3-1	6-1	

	Group "B"	Pd	Wn	Dw	Ls	GF	GA	Pts	
1.	FBC Torino (Torino)	18	12	2	4	52	25	26	
2.	Milan FBC (Milano)	18	11	2	5	41	27	24	
2.	Bologna FBC (Bologna)	18	11	2	5	38	26	25	
4.	US Alessandria (Alessandria)	18	9	3	6	42	24	21	
5.	US Livorno (Livorno)	18	9	2	7	32	28	20	
5.	SG Sampierdarenese (Genova)	18	9	2	7	31	36	20	*
7.	AC Padova (Padova)	18	7	1	10	29	44	15	
8.	SG Andrea Doria (Genova)	18	5	3	10	16	31	13	*
9.	US Cremonese (Cremona)	18	6	-	12	19	35	12	#
10.	SGS Fortitudo (Roma)	18	2	1	15	18	42	5	**
		180	81	18	81	318	318	180	

Promoted: SS Lazio (Roma), FBA Novara (Novara), Pro Patria et Libertate (Busto Arsizio) and US Reggiana (Reggio Emilia).

AC Napoli (Napoli) and US Cremonese (Cremona) were both relegated and then re-instated for the next season.
* SG Andrea Doria (Genova) merged with SG Sampierdarenese (Genova) to become AC La Dominante (Genova) for the next season.
Casale FBC (Casale Monferrato) changed their name to US Casale FBC X1 Legione (Casale Monferrato).

FBC Audace (Taranto) merged with US Pro Italia (Taranto) to become AS Taranto (Taranto) for the next season.
US Foggia (Foggia) merged with Daunia FC 1909 (Foggia) and US Savoia (Foggia) under the name of US Foggia.
FBC Liberty (Bari) changed their name to FBC Bari (Bari) for the next season.
FBC Palermo (Palermo) merged with FBC Vigor (Palermo) to become AC Palermo (Palermo) for the next season.
US Salernitana Audax (Salerno) merged with FC Libertas (Salerno) and Compania FC (Salerno) to become US Salernitana Fascista (Salerno) for the next season.
Savona FBC (Savona) merged with Speranza FBC (Savona) to become Associazione Savona (Savona).
AC Venezia (Venezia) absorbed US Virtus Rialta (Venezia) and played under the name of AC Venezia next season.

1927-28

1927-28 Final	US Alessandria	Bologna FBC	US Casale FBC XI Leg.	Genoa CFC	FBC Internazionale	FBC Juventus	Milan FBC	FBC Torino
US Alessandria		1-1	5-1	6-1	6-3	2-0	2-0	2-1
Bologna FBC	1-1		7-0	3-1	3-1	0-2	5-0	1-1
US Casale FBC XI Legione	5-0	3-4		0-4	1-3	0-2	2-2	0-3
Genoa CFC	2-0	2-0	1-1		6-0	3-0	2-2	2-1
FBC Internazionale	4-3	3-1	3-0	2-2		1-4	2-3	1-3
FBC Juventus	0-0	1-1	3-0	6-1	1-0		0-1	1-4
Milan FBC	3-0	1-1	2-0	1-2	1-2	3-1		2-2
FBC Torino	3-3	1-0	2-1	5-1	3-2	1-2	3-0	

Final		Pd	Wn	Dw	Ls	GF	GA	Pts	
1.	FBC TORINO (TORINO)	14	8	3	3	33	18	19	
2.	Genoa CFC (Genova)	14	7	3	4	30	27	17	
3.	US Alessandria (Alessandria)	14	6	4	4	31	25	16	
4.	Bologna FBC (Bologna)	14	5	5	4	28	18	15	
5.	FBC Juventus (Torino)	14	6	2	6	21	18	14	
5.	Milan FBC (Milano)	14	5	4	5	21	24	14	
7.	FBC Internazionale (Milano)	14	5	1	8	27	37	11	*
8.	US Casale FBC X1 Legione (Casale Monferrato)	14	2	2	10	15	39	6	
		112	44	24	44	206	206	112	

1927-28 Group "A"	US Alessandria	AC Brescia	US Cremonese	Genoa CFC	SS Lazio	Milan FBC	AC Napoli	AC Padova	US Pro Vercelli	US Reggiana	FBC Torino
US Alessandria		4-1	5-0	4-0	6-0	0-0	11-1	3-1	0-0	11-0	3-1
AC Brescia	0-1		3-2	0-1	4-3	1-3	2-0	1-0	2-1	5-2	3-1
US Cremonese	4-1	0-1		1-2	2-0	0-1	5-0	3-0	3-1	1-1	2-2
Genoa CFC	2-0	0-0	4-1		4-0	1-1	3-0	4-1	5-0	5-2	2-1
SS Lazio	0-1	2-1	2-1	1-2		3-1	0-2	0-3	1-1	1-1	0-2
Milan FBC	2-2	4-1	2-1	1-1	2-1		5-1	3-0	1-0	2-2	1-3
AC Napoli	1-1	0-4	3-1	2-1	0-0	1-2		2-2	2-0	4-0	0-1
AC Padova	2-1	1-1	0-2	1-2	2-0	2-1	2-1		1-0	2-0	0-4
US Pro Vercelli	0-1	1-0	3-0	3-0	6-0	1-1	1-1	3-1		4-0	0-3
US Reggiana	1-3	0-0	1-2	0-3	1-3	0-2	2-2	2-2	5-3		3-8
FBC Torino	4-1	11-0	2-2	2-0	3-0	2-0	11-0	3-1	0-1	14-0	

Group "A"		Pd	Wn	Dw	Ls	GF	GA	Pts	
1.	FBC Torino (Torino)	20	14	2	4	77	19	30	
2.	US Alessandria (Alessandria)	20	13	3	4	64	20	29	
2.	Genoa CFC (Genova)	20	13	3	4	42	21	29	
4.	Milan FBC (Milano)	20	10	6	4	35	22	26	
5.	AC Brescia (Brescia)	20	9	3	8	30	37	21	
6.	US Cremonese (Cremona)	20	7	3	10	33	34	17	
6.	US Pro Vercelli (Vercelli)	20	7	3	10	29	32	17	
6.	AC Padova (Padova)	20	7	3	10	24	36	17	
9.	AC Napoli (Napoli)	20	5	5	10	23	54	15	
10.	SS Lazio (Roma)	20	4	3	13	17	45	11	#
11.	US Reggiana (Reggio Emilia)	20	1	6	13	23	77	8	#
		220	90	40	90	397	397	220	

SS Lazio (Roma) and AC Reggiana (Reggio Emilia) were both relegated but then later re-instated in league for the next season.

1927-28 Group 'B'	Bologna FBC	US Casale XI Legione	Hellas AC	FBC Internazionale	FBC Juventus	AC La Dominante	US Livorno	Modena FBC	FBA Novara	Pro Patria et Libertate	AS Roma
Bologna FBC		4-1	10-1	1-1	2-0	7-0	3-0	1-1	1-0	1-1	3-0
US Casale XI Legione	0-0		8-1	2-2	2-0	4-1	2-1	2-5	0-0	3-2	3-2
Hellas AC	0-1	1-1		1-2	1-2	1-1	1-1	2-2	1-3	2-1	2-0
FBC Internazionale	2-4	3-2	4-1		1-0	6-1	3-2	2-1	3-0	5-2	3-3
FBC Juventus	1-0	1-2	5-1	1-1		3-1	2-1	1-1	4-3	6-2	3-0
AC La Dominante	0-0	0-0	7-0	2-0	1-1		1-1	1-0	1-2	2-3	0-0
US Livorno	0-3	1-2	5-2	2-1	0-3	4-2		5-3	2-1	4-1	2-1
Modena FBC	2-1	0-0	5-1	0-0	1-1	3-1	1-1		5-1	1-2	2-0
FBA Novara	4-0	0-0	1-1	3-0	2-2	0-2	1-0	2-1		1-0	2-1
Pro Patria et Libertate	1-1	2-0	4-0	1-1	2-1	1-0	2-0	1-2	1-1		0-3
AS Roma	1-1	1-1	3-1	3-0	0-0	4-2	2-0	3-3	4-1	0-1	

	Group "B"	Pd	Wn	Dw	Ls	GF	GA	Pts	
1.	Bologna FBC (Bologna)	20	10	7	3	44	16	27	
2.	FBC Juventus (Torino)	20	9	6	5	37	24	24	
2.	US Casale FBC X1 Legione (Casale Monferrato)	20	8	8	4	35	27	24	
4.	FBC Internazionale (Milano)	20	9	5	6	39	32	23	
—	—	—	—	—	—	—	—	—	—
5.	Modena FBC (Modena)	20	7	8	5	39	28	22	
6.	FBA Novara (Novara)	20	8	5	7	28	29	21	
7.	Pro Patria et Libertate (Busto Arsizio)	20	8	4	8	30	34	20	
8.	AS Roma (Roma)	20	7	5	8	31	29	19	
9.	US Livorno (Livorno)	20	7	3	10	32	37	17	
10.	AC La Dominante (Genova)	20	4	6	10	26	40	14	#
11.	Hellas AC (Verona)	20	2	5	13	21	66	8	#
		220	79	62	79	362	362	220	

AC La Dominante (Genova) and Hellas AC (Verona) were both relegated but later re-instated to the league for the next season.

Promoted: Atalanta BC (Bergamo), US Bari (Bari), AC Biellese (Biella), Assoc. Fiorentina del Calcio (Firenze), US Fiumana (Fiume), AC Legnano (Legnano), US Pistoiese (Pistoia), AC Prato (Prato), US Triestina (Trieste), AC Venezia (Venezia).

The League was extended to two groups of 16 clubs for the next season.

* FBC Bari (Bari) merged with US Ideale (Bari) as US Bari (Bari) for the next season.
Hellas AC (Verona) merged with Bentegodi SC (Verona) and Scaligera AC (Verona) to become AC Verona.
FBC Internazionale (Milano) were forced to merge with US Milanese (Milano) and became Ambrosiana SS.
US Messinese (Messina) changed their club name to AC Messina (Messina) for the next season.
Associazione Fiorentina del Calcio (Firenze) merged with US Fiorenza (Firenze) and SS Italia (Firenze) to become AC Fiorentina (Firenze) for the next season.

Note: SS Roma Tivoli (Roma) merged with 114th Legione MVSN GS Tivoli (Roma) to become Tivoli 114th Legione MVSN (Roma) for the next season.

Final 1st Leg (Bologna - 23/06/29)

BOLOGNA FBC (BOLOGNA) 3-1 FBC Torino (Torino)

Della Valle 31', Schiavio 41', 58' *Libonatti 86'*

Bologna: Gianni, Monzeglio, Gasperi, Genovesi, Baldi, Pitto, Busini 1, Della Valle, Schiavio, Busini 2, Muzzioli.

Torino: Bosia, Vincenzi, Martin 2, Martin 3, Colombari, Speroni, Vezzani, Baloncieri, Libonatti, Rossetti 2, Franzoni.

Final 2nd Leg (Torino - 30/06/29)

BOLOGNA FBC (BOLOGNA) 0-1 FBC Torino (Torino)

Libonatti 65'

Bologna: Gianni, Monzeglio, Gasperi, Genovesi, Baldi, Pitto, Busini 1, Della Valle, Schiavio, Busini 2, Muzzioli.

Torino: Bosia, Monti 3, Martin 2, Martin 3, Colombari, Aliberti, Vezzani, Baloncieri, Libonatti, Rossetti 2, Franzoni.

Final Play-Off (Roma - 07/07/29)

BOLOGNA FBC (BOLOGNA) 1-0 FBC Torino (Torino)

Muzzioli 82'

Bologna: Gianni, Monzeglio, Gasperi, Genovesi, Baldi, Pitto, Martelli, Della Valle, Schiavio, Busini 2, Muzzioli.

Torino: Bosia, Janni, Martin 2, Martin 3, Colombari, Monti 3, Vezzani, Baloncieri, Libonatti, Rossetti 2, Franzoni.

1928-1929 Group "A"	US Alessandria	Atalanta BC	US Bari	US Casale FBC	AC La Dominante	AC Legnano	US Livorno	Milan FBC	Modena FBC	FBA Novara	AC Padova	AC Prato	Pro Patria et Libertate	AS Roma	FBC Torino	US Triestina
US Alessandria		3-2	6-3	1-1	4-0	2-0	5-1	1-0	3-1	3-0	2-1	2-1	4-1	0-2	3-3	2-0
Atalanta BC	0-2		0-0	2-0	2-0	2-0	0-3	0-1	0-0	2-0	2-2	2-0	0-0	1-3	0-1	4-1
US Bari	4-1	1-1		1-4	3-2	2-0	1-1	2-2	2-3	3-3	4-1	0-3	0-0	2-1	0-2	4-2
US Casale FBC	1-4	1-0	0-0		1-1	6-0	7-2	3-3	5-2	6-2	3-0	4-2	3-3	1-5	0-1	1-4
AC La Dominante	0-1	2-2	1-0	2-2		3-2	2-0	0-2	0-0	4-2	0-3	3-2	3-5	1-2	1-1	2-0
AC Legnano	1-1	1-1	2-1	5-2	0-1		1-0	1-5	0-3	0-0	1-0	2-0	1-0	1-2	1-2	2-3
US Livorno	2-2	3-2	1-1	5-0	8-1	4-1		1-0	2-0	5-3	2-0	2-1	2-2	1-0	1-3	1-1
Milan FBC	2-2	5-1	5-1	3-1	5-2	6-1	2-1		1-1	7-0	1-2	4-0	3-2	0-1	3-1	2-1
Modena FBC	1-1	4-0	2-1	4-0	1-0	3-2	5-1	3-0		1-1	5-1	0-0	1-1	3-1	1-5	4-2
FBA Novara	0-1	5-1	2-0	2-0	0-0	1-1	0-2	1-4	4-2		1-1	2-1	3-2	1-3	0-5	2-1
AC Padova	3-3	1-0	5-0	3-3	0-0	3-1	4-3	1-2	2-3	2-2		2-1	4-3	4-3	0-0	2-2
AC Prato	3-1	0-0	2-0	3-0	2-1	1-0	2-3	0-2	2-3	1-2	1-3		2-2	0-0	0-2	2-1
Pro Patria et Libertate	4-0	2-0	2-1	2-1	2-3	2-1	2-1	0-4	3-1	7-0	3-0	5-1		4-3	1-3	2-1
AS Roma	2-2	3-0	0-0	2-1	3-1	4-1	0-0	1-1	5-0	4-0	1-2	4-0	3-0		6-1	4-0
FBC Torino	6-1	7-0	0-0	4-0	8-1	7-0	10-1	2-2	3-1	5-0	3-1	9-1	2-3	3-0		12-0
US Triestina	2-1	2-0	7-1	4-2	5-1	1-4	4-2	1-0	3-1	1-0	3-0	2-2	1-3	3-3	2-2	

Group "A"		Pd	Wn	Dw	Ls	GF	GA	Pts
1.	FBC Torino (Torino)	30	21	6	3	115	31	48
2.	Milan FBC (Milano)	30	18	6	6	77	34	42
3.	AS Roma (Roma)	30	17	6	7	71	34	40
3.	US Alessandria (Alessandria)	30	16	8	6	64	47	40
5.	Pro Patria et Libertate (Busto Arsizio)	30	15	6	9	68	52	36
6.	Modena FBC (Modena)	30	14	7	9	59	51	35
7.	US Livorno (Livorno)	30	13	6	11	61	62	32
8.	AC Padova (Padova)	30	11	8	11	53	58	30
9.	US Triestina (Trieste)	30	12	5	13	60	68	29
10.	US Casale FBC X1 Legione (Casale Monferrato)	30	8	7	15	59	72	23
10.	AC La Dominante (Genova)	30	8	7	15	38	68	23
10.	FBA Novara (Novara)	30	8	7	15	40	77	23
13.	US Bari (Bari)	30	6	10	14	38	61	22
14.	Atalanta BC (Bergamo)	30	6	8	16	27	53	20
15.	AC Prato (Prato)	30	7	5	18	36	63	19
16.	AC Legnano (Legnano)	30	7	4	19	33	68	18
		480	187	106	187	899	899	480

The top 9 clubs of each Group formed a new 18 club National League (Serie "A") for the next season with the remaining 7 clubs from each Group plus US Lecce (Lecce), AC Monfalcone (Monfalcone), Parma FBC (Parma) and Spezia FBC (La Spezia) forming an 18 club 2nd division of the National League (Serie "B").

1928-29 Group "B"	Ambrosiana SS	AC Biellese	Bologna FBC	AC Brescia	US Cremonese	AC Fiorentina	US Fiumana	Genoa CFC	FBC Juventus	SS Lazio	AC Napoli	US Pistoiese	US Pro Vercelli	AC Reggiana	AC Venezia	AC Verona
Ambrosiana SS		7-0	1-1	5-1	0-1	3-0	8-1	0-1	4-2	3-1	8-1	9-1	3-0	5-1	10-2	9-0
AC Biellese	2-1		1-1	0-2	2-1	3-1	1-0	2-1	1-3	2-0	3-2	1-0	1-2	3-0	2-1	3-0
Bologna FBC	3-1	3-0		1-0	6-0	3-0	2-0	3-1	0-0	6-2	5-1	5-0	3-0	5-1	3-0	4-1
AC Brescia	0-0	1-0	10-0		0-0	5-0	3-2	5-0	1-1	4-2	2-0	3-0	0-0	5-1	3-1	2-1
US Cremonese	0-2	3-1	0-2	2-1		6-0	4-1	3-2	0-0	4-2	5-1	1-0	0-2	3-0	2-1	1-0
AC Fiorentina	0-3	2-0	2-3	2-3	2-1		3-0	1-2	0-4	0-4	1-1	0-1	0-1	2-0	0-2	1-1
US Fiumana	1-2	2-1	0-2	0-2	1-1	4-2		0-0	1-3	0-2	1-1	2-2	2-2	4-0	1-1	2-1
Genoa CFC	6-1	5-0	3-0	1-1	2-0	7-0	4-2		3-3	1-0	2-1	2-1	2-0	2-2	1-0	11-0
FBC Juventus	0-0	0-0	1-1	0-1	3-0	11-0	11-0	2-0		0-1	3-1	4-0	1-3	2-0	4-0	4-0
SS Lazio	1-0	2-0	0-1	0-1	3-0	5-1	2-0	0-2	1-2		0-0	4-0	1-1	4-0	1-0	3-0
AC Napoli	4-1	5-0	0-4	4-0	1-1	7-2	2-1	1-2	1-0	1-2		4-1	3-3	6-2	4-1	3-0
US Pistoiese	1-0	1-1	0-0	2-3	2-0	2-0	1-1	1-0	0-4	2-1	0-1		2-1	8-2	3-1	1-1
US Pro Vercelli	4-1	5-1	2-0	3-0	2-1	5-0	4-1	1-1	3-4	3-1	4-1	9-0		4-0	3-0	1-1
AC Reggiana	1-4	2-2	3-9	1-4	3-4	2-3	1-1	2-1	2-2	1-1	8-2	2-2	3-0		4-5	3-4
AC Venezia	1-4	3-1	1-2	3-2	1-1	3-1	3-1	3-1	1-1	2-0	2-2	1-1	5-2	3-3		5-0
AC Verona	1-0	0-0	1-6	3-2	0-1	4-0	2-0	0-5	0-1	2-1	0-0	2-1	2-1	3-1	2-1	

Group "B"		Pd	Wn	Dw	Ls	GF	GA	Pts	
1.	Bologna FBC (Bologna)	30	22	5	3	84	32	49	*
2.	FBC Juventus (Torino)	30	16	9	5	76	25	41	
2.	AC Brescia (Brescia)	30	18	5	7	67	35	41	
4.	Genoa CFC (Genova)	30	17	5	8	71	35	39	*
5.	US Pro Vercelli (Vercelli)	30	16	6	8	71	40	38	
6.	Ambrosiana SS (Milano)	30	17	3	10	95	38	37	
7.	US Cremonese (Cremona)	30	14	5	11	46	43	33	
8.	SS Lazio (Roma)	30	13	3	14	47	39	29	
8.	AC Napoli (Napoli)	30	11	7	12	61	64	29	
10.	AC Biellese (Biella)	30	11	5	14	34	56	27	
11.	AC Venezia (Venezia)	30	10	6	14	53	65	26	
12.	US Pistoiese (Pistoia)	30	9	7	14	36	65	25	
12.	AC Verona (Verona)	30	10	5	15	32	73	25	
14.	US Fiumana (Fiume)	30	4	8	18	32	73	16	
15.	AC Reggiana (Reggio Emilia)	30	3	7	20	51	103	13	
16.	AC Fiorentina (Firenze)	30	5	2	23	26	96	12	
		480	196	88	196	882	882	480	

* Bologna FBC (Bologna) changed their club name to Bologna FC (Bologna) for the next season.
Genoa CFC (Genova) changed their club name to Genova 1893 AC (Genova) for the next season.
FBC Juventus (Torino) changed their club name to FC Juventus (Torino) for the next season.
AC Padova (Padova) changed their club name to Associazione Fascista Calcio (Padova) for the next season.

Note: US Catanese (Catania) changed their club name to SS Catania (Catania) for the next season.

1929-30

1929-1930 Serie "A"	US Alessandria	Ambrosiana SS	Bologna FC	AC Brescia	US Cremonese	Genova 1893 AC	FC Juventus	SS Lazio	US Livorno	Milan FBC	Modena FBC	AC Napoli	AFC Padova	Pro Patria et Lib.	US Pro Vercelli	AS Roma	FBC Torino	US Triestina
US Alessandria		1-2	2-3	4-0	3-0	0-2	1-0	4-2	3-2	2-1	1-1	2-1	4-2	0-0	0-2	3-1	3-3	4-1
Ambrosiana SS	2-0		2-1	5-1	3-2	3-3	2-0	4-2	6-2	2-0	5-1	2-1	6-1	8-0	4-0	6-0	3-0	1-2
Bologna FC	1-2	2-2		0-0	4-1	0-1	0-1	3-2	6-1	1-1	2-1	3-1	1-2	2-0	2-2	5-2	0-1	2-2
AC Brescia	2-1	0-0	2-0		4-3	4-1	2-2	3-2	2-0	4-1	3-2	2-1	3-2	2-1	1-0	1-1	0-2	0-1
US Cremonese	1-1	0-0	0-3	0-1		1-2	0-0	1-3	1-2	0-2	2-2	0-0	1-1	1-2	0-0	1-0	0-1	2-1
Genova 1893 AC	2-1	1-4	2-0	1-0	2-1		2-0	2-0	2-0	2-2	2-2	2-2	8-0	6-2	1-0	3-1	1-0	2-1
FC Juventus	2-1	1-2	2-0	0-0	4-1	0-0		3-1	4-1	3-1	1-0	3-2	3-1	1-0	6-1	2-1	2-0	0-1
SS Lazio	0-0	1-1	3-0	0-0	6-0	3-0	0-1		3-1	0-0	4-0	0-2	4-0	2-1	3-2	0-1	1-0	0-0
US Livorno	2-1	1-2	0-2	5-3	1-1	3-1	1-5	4-0		4-1	2-2	3-0	4-3	2-1	1-1	1-0	1-0	2-0
Milan FBC	0-1	1-2	0-1	4-1	5-2	0-2	1-1	2-1	2-2		1-0	2-2	6-0	3-2	3-0	3-1	1-2	2-1
Modena FBC	0-1	2-0	1-2	2-1	5-1	2-1	2-1	0-0	6-0	1-1		0-5	0-2	2-1	1-1	1-2	2-1	2-1
AC Napoli	3-1	3-1	2-1	1-1	3-0	1-2	2-2	3-0	1-1	2-1	2-1		1-0	4-2	1-1	1-1	2-0	4-1
AFC Padova	1-3	1-2	2-3	2-1	0-1	0-0	2-1	2-1	3-1	1-1	1-3	3-0		7-0	5-0	3-0	1-0	1-2
Pro Patria et Libertate	4-0	0-0	2-1	2-0	4-2	0-1	0-1	0-0	5-0	2-1	2-0	3-2	0-0		1-0	6-1	1-0	1-1
US Pro Vercelli	2-2	1-0	2-2	2-0	3-2	3-3	1-0	3-1	4-1	0-1	2-1	4-0	5-1	0-0		2-0	0-2	6-0
AS Roma	1-1	2-0	2-2	2-1	9-0	2-0	2-3	3-1	2-0	1-0	4-2	2-2	8-0	5-0	7-0		3-0	5-0
FBC Torino	2-2	4-1	0-0	5-0	2-3	1-1	0-0	1-0	3-0	0-0	0-0	1-0	3-1	7-0	5-1	1-0		4-1
US Triestina	1-0	1-2	0-1	1-0	4-0	0-2	0-1	3-3	3-0	2-2	0-1	3-4	2-1	2-1	3-1	1-1	0-1	

Serie "A"

	Club	Pd	Wn	Dw	Ls	GF	GA	Pts	
1.	AMBROSIANA SS (MILANO)	34	22	6	6	85	38	50	*
2.	Genova 1893 AC (Genova)	34	20	8	6	63	39	48	
3.	FC Juventus (Torino)	34	19	7	8	56	31	45	
4.	FBC Torino (Torino)	34	16	7	11	52	31	39	
5.	AC Napoli (Napoli)	34	14	9	11	61	51	37	
6.	AS Roma (Roma)	34	15	6	13	73	52	36	
6.	Bologna FC (Bologna)	34	14	8	12	56	46	36	
6.	US Alessandria (Alessandria)	34	14	8	12	55	49	36	
9.	US Pro Vercelli (Vercelli)	34	12	9	13	52	60	33	
9.	AC Brescia (Brescia)	34	13	7	14	45	56	33	
11.	Milan FBC (Milano)	34	11	10	13	52	48	32	
12.	Modena FBC (Modena)	34	11	8	15	48	55	30	
12.	Pro Patria et Libertate (Busto Arsizio)	34	12	6	16	46	64	30	
14.	US Livorno (Livorno)	34	12	5	17	51	79	29	
15.	SS Lazio (Roma)	34	10	8	16	49	50	28	
15.	US Triestina (Trieste)	34	11	6	17	42	59	28	
17.	AFC Padova (Padova)	34	11	4	19	52	78	26	R
18.	US Cremonese (Cremona)	34	4	8	22	31	83	16	R
		612	241	130	241	969	969	612	

Top goalscorers

1)	Giuseppe MEAZZA	(Ambrosiana SS)	31
2)	Rodolfo VOLK	(AS Roma)	21
3)	Giovanni FERRARI	(US Alessandria)	19
	MAINI	(Bologna FC)	19
	Antonio VOJAK	(AC Napoli)	19

* Ambrosiana SS (Milano) changed their club name to AS Ambrosiana (Milano) for the next season.
AC La Dominante (Genova) changed their club name to FC Liguria (Genova) for the next season.
Parma AS (Parma) changed their club name from Parma FBC (Parma) from this season.
AC Venezia (Venezia) changed their club name to SS Serenissima (Venezia) for the next season.

Serie "B"

	Club	Pd	Wn	Dw	Ls	GF	GA	Pts	
1.	Casale FBC (Casale Monferrato)	34	22	5	7	85	39	49	P
2.	AC Legnano (Legnano)	34	19	8	7	56	31	46	P
3.	AC La Dominante (Genova)	34	18	6	10	53	53	42	*
4.	US Pistoiese (Pistoia)	34	17	6	11	46	36	40	
4.	AC Fiorentina (Firenze)	34	16	8	10	64	39	40	
6.	AC Verona (Verona)	34	17	5	12	48	47	39	
7.	AC Venezia (Venezia)	34	17	4	13	60	58	38	*
8.	Atalanta BC (Bergamo)	34	11	15	8	37	26	37	
9.	FBA Novara (Novara)	34	15	6	13	63	41	36	
9.	US Bari (Bari)	34	16	4	14	72	40	36	
11.	AC Monfalcone (Monfalcone)	34	16	3	15	58	44	35	
12.	Parma AS (Parma)	34	12	8	14	38	57	32	*
13.	Spezia FBC (La Spezia)	34	12	6	16	36	54	30	
13.	US Lecce (Lecce)	34	11	8	15	39	44	30	
15.	AC Biellese (Biella)	34	11	3	20	34	58	25	R
16.	AC Reggiana (Reggio Emilia)	34	8	7	19	45	75	23	R
17.	AC Prato (Prato)	34	5	7	22	27	72	17	R
18.	US Fiumana (Fiume)	34	6	5	23	26	73	16	R-1
		612	249	114	249	887	887	611	

US Fiumana (Fiume) had 1 point deducted by the F.I.G.C. Committee.

Note: SS Catania (Catania) changed their club name to AFC Catania (Catania).

Promoted to Serie "B": Derthona FBC (Tortona), US Lucchese Libertas (Lucca), AC Palermo and AC Udinese.

1930-31

1930-1931 Serie "A"	US Alessandria	AS Ambrosiana	Bologna FC	AC Brescia	Casale FBC	Genova 1893 AC	FC Juventus	SS Lazio	AC Legnano	US Livorno	Milan FBC	Modena FBC	AC Napoli	Pro Patria et Lib.	US Pro Vercelli	AS Roma	FBC Torino	US Triestina
US Alessandria		2-0	1-6	4-0	2-0	0-1	2-3	1-3	5-0	2-2	3-0	1-1	4-3	4-1	0-1	0-2	1-1	4-1
AS Ambrosiana	2-0		0-1	3-3	5-1	2-0	2-3	3-2	3-0	1-1	1-1	0-0	2-1	2-1	6-1	5-0	3-0	1-0
Bologna FC	0-0	4-1		7-1	6-1	1-1	4-0	4-0	2-1	5-0	2-2	2-0	2-0	4-1	3-0	3-3	3-0	6-1
AC Brescia	7-3	0-0	2-0		2-0	1-2	1-1	2-0	2-1	1-1	3-0	1-2	0-1	3-1	2-2	3-2	2-1	1-0
Casale FBC	0-0	1-0	1-2	0-0		1-0	0-1	0-2	1-1	3-2	3-2	3-1	0-2	4-0	2-2	0-3	3-1	2-3
Genova 1893 AC	5-1	1-0	3-1	1-2	1-0		0-3	2-0	5-0	3-2	2-1	5-3	4-2	1-0	1-0	0-0	3-2	1-0
FC Juventus	4-1	1-0	2-0	3-0	2-0	4-1		3-1	1-0	4-1	3-3	4-1	1-2	4-1	5-1	3-2	2-0	4-0
SS Lazio	3-1	1-0	2-0	2-1	1-0	5-0	2-1		4-0	3-2	1-2	2-0	0-1	1-1	1-2	2-2	0-0	1-0
AC Legnano	1-0	2-2	0-2	2-2	1-0	2-1	1-2	0-2		3-0	1-2	6-2	2-0	0-0	2-2	0-0	0-1	1-1
US Livorno	1-0	0-2	0-2	0-1	5-0	1-2	1-1	0-0	2-1		0-0	0-2	1-2	1-0	3-1	1-3	1-1	3-2
Milan FBC	1-1	1-4	1-2	1-0	4-0	1-2	0-3	0-1	2-0	5-0		3-1	2-3	1-1	2-1	0-2	1-1	2-0
Modena FBC	3-2	2-5	0-2	3-2	5-1	4-2	1-2	3-0	4-1	4-1	3-0		2-0	3-1	1-3	1-1	2-0	2-0
AC Napoli	3-2	0-2	2-0	3-1	1-0	0-1	1-2	2-0	2-1	2-0	0-1	4-1		1-0	1-0	3-0	0-2	5-1
Pro Patria et Libertate	0-1	1-1	1-2	3-0	1-0	2-3	1-3	3-1	2-0	0-0	2-1	3-2	3-2		2-2	0-4	1-2	2-1
US Pro Vercelli	6-2	1-1	2-0	2-0	1-1	0-1	1-3	3-0	8-0	3-1	0-2	3-0	6-3	2-1		0-3	1-0	2-2
AS Roma	2-0	2-1	2-1	3-0	3-1	5-0	5-0	1-1	3-0	7-1	1-2	4-0	3-1	2-0	5-0		5-1	3-0
FBC Torino	4-1	6-0	1-1	1-1	1-0	0-2	1-1	2-0	5-0	4-0	3-1	1-1	3-1	3-1	1-0	1-4		2-0
US Triestina	0-1	5-0	1-1	0-4	1-2	1-1	0-0	2-1	1-0	1-0	3-1	1-1	0-0	0-0	3-1	0-0	1-0	

	Serie "A"	Pd	Wn	Dw	Ls	GF	GA	Pts	
1.	FC JUVENTUS (TORINO)	34	25	5	4	79	37	55	
2.	AS Roma (Roma)	34	22	7	5	87	31	51	
3.	Bologna FC (Bologna)	34	21	6	7	81	33	48	
4.	Genova 1893 AC (Genova)	34	22	3	9	58	47	47	
5.	AS Ambrosiana (Milano)	34	15	8	11	60	45	38	
6.	AC Napoli (Napoli)	34	18	1	15	54	49	37	
7.	FBC Torino (Torino)	34	14	8	12	52	43	36	
8.	SS Lazio (Roma)	34	15	5	14	45	44	35	
9.	AC Brescia (Brescia)	34	13	8	13	51	55	34	
10.	US Pro Vercelli (Vercelli)	34	13	7	14	60	60	33	
10.	Modena FBC (Modena)	34	14	5	15	61	66	33	
12.	Milan FBC (Milano)	34	12	7	15	48	53	31	
13.	US Alessandria (Alessandria)	34	10	6	18	52	67	26	
14.	US Triestina (Trieste)	34	8	9	17	32	55	25	
15.	Pro Patria et Libertate (Busto Arsizio)	34	8	7	19	37	61	23	
16.	Casale FBC (Casale Monferrato)	34	8	5	21	31	64	21	
17.	US Livorno (Livorno)	34	6	8	20	34	71	20	R
18.	AC Legnano (Legnano)	34	6	7	21	30	71	19	R
		612	250	112	250	952	952	612	

Top goalscorers

1)	Rodolfo VOLK	(AS Roma)	29
2)	Giuseppe MEAZZA	(AS Ambrosiana)	25
3)	Antonio VOJAK	(AC Napoli)	20
4)	Raimondo ORSI	(FC Juventus)	18
	Carlo REGUZZONI	(Bologna FC)	18

Note: SC Pisa (Pisa) changed their club name to AC Pisa (Pisa) for the next season.

	Serie "B"	Pd	Wn	Dw	Ls	GF	GA	Pts	
1.	AC Fiorentina (Firenze)	34	18	10	6	54	27	46	P
1.	US Bari (Bari)	34	18	10	6	57	33	46	P
3.	AC Palermo (Palermo)	34	18	8	8	54	31	44	
4.	AFC Padova (Padova)	34	18	7	9	77	51	43	
5.	AC Verona (Verona)	34	19	4	11	68	43	42	
6.	Atalanta BC (Bergamo)	34	15	11	8	62	35	41	
6.	US Cremonese (Cremona)	34	16	9	9	68	46	41	
8.	FBA Novara (Novara)	34	17	5	12	52	48	39	
9.	SS Serenissima (Venezia)	34	13	10	11	49	50	36	
10.	US Pistoiese (Pistoia)	34	14	7	13	54	42	35	
11.	AC Monfalcone (Monfalcone)	34	9	10	15	34	51	28	
11.	Spezia FBC (La Spezia)	34	10	8	16	35	54	28	
13.	Parma AS (Parma)	34	10	7	17	45	64	27	
14.	US Lecce (Lecce)	34	10	6	18	44	53	26	
15.	AC Udinese (Udine)	34	7	11	16	58	78	25	
15.	US Lucchese Libertas (Lucca)	34	9	7	18	33	70	25	R
17.	Derthona FBC (Tortona)	34	7	7	20	43	65	21	R
18.	FC Liguria (Genova)	34	6	7	21	33	79	19	R
		612	234	144	234	920	920	612	

Relegation Play-off

AC Udinese (Udine)	7-0	US Lucchese Libertas (Lucca)

Promoted: CS Cagliari (Cagliari), AC Comense (Como) and AC Vigevanese (Vigevano).

1931-32

1931-1932 Serie "A"	US Alessandria	AS Ambrosiana	US Bari	Bologna FC	AC Brescia	Casale FBC	AC Fiorentina	Genova 1893 AC	FC Juventus	SS Lazio	Milan FBC	Modena FBC	AC Napoli	Pro Patria et Libertate	US Pro Vercelli	AS Roma	FBC Torino	US Triestina
US Alessandria		2-1	3-0	3-3	3-2	1-4	1-0	2-2	2-3	2-1	2-1	5-0	3-1	6-1	4-5	0-1	1-1	4-0
AS Ambrosiana	4-0		0-0	4-3	5-0	4-0	1-1	3-1	2-4	2-0	0-0	4-2	6-1	3-1	4-1	2-1	1-1	4-4
US Bari	1-0	0-0		1-2	1-1	0-1	3-0	4-2	0-1	1-0	2-5	1-0	0-2	2-1	1-0	1-2	3-2	3-2
Bologna FC	3-1	2-0	2-0		6-1	4-2	2-1	2-0	1-1	5-1	3-0	4-0	2-0	4-0	1-0	3-0	4-2	8-0
AC Brescia	1-0	0-2	0-0	0-1		1-0	0-1	4-2	0-4	1-0	2-3	2-1	1-0	0-0	2-0	1-1	1-2	2-1
Casale FBC	2-2	3-1	6-2	1-5	2-1		3-2	2-0	1-1	0-1	0-1	4-0	1-0	1-2	0-1	1-0	1-1	0-1
AC Fiorentina	0-1	3-0	2-1	1-3	2-1	4-1		2-2	1-2	2-0	3-0	5-0	2-0	1-0	1-0	3-1	4-2	1-0
Genova 1893 AC	1-2	0-1	3-0	3-2	4-0	3-1	1-1		2-0	1-0	1-2	3-0	1-0	4-1	2-1	1-1	2-2	2-0
FC Juventus	3-0	6-2	7-3	3-2	3-0	3-2	2-2	2-1		1-2	2-0	3-0	5-3	7-2	4-1	7-1	3-0	4-2
SS Lazio	2-2	2-2	3-2	2-1	2-0	1-3	1-0	0-0	0-3		0-0	9-1	0-2	1-2	5-0	1-4	2-0	2-0
Milan FBC	1-1	2-3	2-1	1-0	2-2	4-2	1-1	3-0	0-0	2-0		5-0	3-1	1-1	3-0	1-2	6-1	1-1
Modena FBC	2-1	3-1	0-0	0-0	2-2	4-1	1-1	0-0	0-1	3-1	2-1		2-2	1-1	2-0	2-3	5-2	1-1
AC Napoli	1-1	1-0	3-0	1-1	1-1	5-1	0-2	3-1	2-0	0-0	3-1	4-1		1-1	2-1	1-0	0-0	4-2
Pro Patria et Libertate	2-1	1-1	2-2	0-2	0-0	3-1	0-3	2-0	1-1	1-1	2-0	3-1	0-0		2-1	2-2	2-1	0-2
US Pro Vercelli	1-1	2-0	2-0	1-1	1-0	0-1	1-0	4-2	1-2	2-2	0-2	2-1	1-1	1-0		0-0	2-0	1-1
AS Roma	1-2	2-1	0-0	1-1	3-1	4-0	1-1	6-0	2-0	2-0	1-0	4-2	1-0	0-0	2-1		2-3	1-0
FBC Torino	1-3	2-1	6-1	1-1	4-0	3-1	1-0	3-1	0-0	3-1	0-0	6-0	4-1	3-1	4-0	2-1		1-1
US Triestina	1-4	2-2	2-0	1-1	1-1	2-2	2-1	0-0	0-1	3-2	1-3	5-2	1-2	0-0	1-1	2-0	1-0	

	Serie "A"	Pd	Wn	Dw	Ls	GF	GA	Pts	
1.	FC JUVENTUS (TORINO)	34	24	6	4	89	38	54	
2.	Bologna FC (Bologna)	34	21	8	5	85	33	50	
3.	AS Roma (Roma)	34	16	8	10	53	42	40	
4.	AC Fiorentina (Firenze)	34	16	7	11	54	35	39	
4.	Milan FBC (Milano)	34	15	9	10	57	40	39	
6.	AS Ambrosiana (Milano)	34	15	8	11	67	52	38	*
6.	US Alessandria (Alessandria)	34	15	8	11	66	53	38	
8.	FBC Torino (Torino)	34	14	9	11	64	53	37	
9.	AC Napoli (Napoli)	34	13	9	12	48	46	35	
10.	Pro Patria et Libertate (Busto Arsizio)	34	9	13	12	37	55	31	
11.	Genova 1893 AC (Genova)	34	11	8	15	48	56	30	
12.	Casale FBC (Casale Monferrato)	34	12	4	18	51	67	28	
13.	SS Lazio (Roma)	34	10	7	17	45	53	27	
13.	US Triestina (Trieste)	34	8	11	15	42	61	27	
13.	US Pro Vercelli (Vercelli)	34	10	7	17	35	54	27	
16.	US Bari (Bari)	34	9	7	18	36	64	25	
16.	AC Brescia (Brescia)	34	8	9	17	31	60	25	R
18.	Modena FBC (Modena)	34	7	8	19	41	87	22	R
		612	233	146	233	949	949	612	

Top goalscorers

1)	Pablo PETRONE	(AC Fiorentina)	25
	Angelo SCHIAVIO	(Bologna FC)	25
3)	Giuseppe MEAZZA	(AS Ambrosiana)	22
4)	MAINI	(Bologna FC)	21
	MARCHINI	(US Alessandria)	21
	Raimondo ORSI	(FC Juventus)	21

Relegation Play-off

US Bari (Bari) 2-1 AC Brescia (Brescia)

* AS Ambrosiana (Milano) changed their club name to AS Ambrosiana "Inter" (Milano) for the next season.

Note: SS Ancona (Ancona) changed their club name to US Anconitana Bianchi (Ancona) for the next season.
FC Liguria (Genova) changed their club name to SG Sampierdarenese (Genova).

	Serie "B"	Pd	Wn	Dw	Ls	GF	GA	Pts	
1.	AC Palermo (Palermo)	34	21	8	5	80	35	50	P
2.	AFC Padova (Padova)	34	19	9	6	79	26	47	P
3.	AC Verona (Verona)	34	17	7	10	61	50	41	
4.	AC Vigevanese (Vigevano)	34	16	7	11	57	46	39	
4.	Atalanta BC (Bergamo)	34	13	13	8	57	42	39	
6.	US Cremonese (Cremona)	34	13	11	10	43	43	37	
7.	US Livorno (Livorno)	34	13	10	11	54	43	36	
7.	Spezia FBC (La Spezia)	34	13	10	11	53	36	36	
9.	AC Monfalcone (Monfalcone)	34	13	9	12	42	50	35	
9.	AC Comense (Como)	34	13	9	12	47	49	35	
11.	AC Legnano (Legnano)	34	14	6	14	50	54	34	
11.	US Pistoiese (Pistoia)	34	13	8	13	49	50	34	
13.	CS Cagliari (Cagliari)	34	12	8	14	42	39	31	-1
14.	FBA Novara (Novara)	34	12	6	16	40	54	30	
15.	SS Serenissima (Venezia)	34	10	10	14	43	56	30	
16.	AC Udinese (Udine)	34	9	7	18	44	67	25	R
17.	US Lecce (Lecce)	34	8	7	19	23	51	23	R
18.	Parma AS (Parma)	34	3	3	28	25	98	9	R
		612	232	148	232	889	889	611	

CS Cagliari (Cagliari) had 1 point deducted by the F.I.G.C. Committee.

Promoted to Serie "B": Grion (Pola), AC Messina (Messina) and SG Sampierdarenese (Genova).

1932-33

1932-1933 Serie "A"	US Alessandria	Ambrosiana "Inter'	US Bari	Bologna FC	Casale FBC	AC Fiorentina	Genova 1893 AC	FC Juventus	SS Lazio	Milan FBC	AC Napoli	AFC Padova	AC Palermo	Pro Patria et Libertate	US Pro Vercelli	AS Roma	FBC Torino	US Triestina
US Alessandria		2-3	1-0	2-0	1-1	0-3	3-1	3-2	0-1	0-2	3-2	4-1	0-0	1-0	0-0	2-2	1-1	4-1
Ambrosiana "Inter'	1-0		5-1	1-1	4-2	3-1	0-2	2-2	1-2	5-4	3-5	3-2	5-1	6-2	3-0	3-2	5-1	2-1
US Bari	1-2	2-3		1-1	3-3	1-0	4-2	0-4	2-3	2-2	2-4	1-0	1-1	2-0	2-0	0-2	3-1	2-1
Bologna FC	4-0	2-1	3-0		7-0	1-1	0-0	1-2	4-1	2-2	3-1	1-0	3-0	6-1	2-0	2-2	1-1	5-0
Casale FBC	0-0	2-2	5-1	3-4		1-0	2-3	1-2	1-0	0-0	1-0	1-0	2-1	3-2	0-1	1-1	1-0	2-0
AC Fiorentina	3-1	0-0	1-0	1-0	3-0		2-0	1-0	3-1	5-1	1-0	2-2	1-0	1-0	2-0	0-0	0-1	0-1
Genova 1893 AC	2-3	2-2	3-1	1-0	2-0	2-4		3-2	2-1	2-2	2-2	1-1	7-2	1-1	0-2	2-1	2-0	4-0
FC Juventus	3-0	3-0	2-0	2-2	6-0	5-0	4-1		4-0	3-0	3-0	3-1	5-0	2-0	4-2	1-0	2-1	6-1
SS Lazio	6-0	0-0	0-0	0-2	1-0	0-0	0-0	1-0		2-0	0-1	4-0	1-1	2-1	2-1	2-1	0-0	1-2
Milan FBC	3-3	1-3	2-0	0-3	3-0	2-2	4-2	1-1	0-0		0-3	6-2	2-1	5-0	2-1	2-1	4-3	2-2
AC Napoli	4-1	3-0	2-0	2-1	4-0	2-1	3-0	1-0	3-1	0-1		1-1	5-0	2-1	3-0	1-2	1-1	2-0
AFC Padova	2-1	1-1	1-2	0-0	2-1	1-1	3-0	1-1	1-1	2-1	2-2		3-0	4-1	2-1	1-1	3-1	0-1
AC Palermo	1-1	0-2	1-0	0-0	1-0	1-3	1-1	0-2	2-1	1-0	1-0	3-0		2-1	1-1	0-2	1-0	1-0
Pro Patria et Libertate	2-1	0-0	2-1	3-3	5-1	1-2	3-4	0-2	2-3	3-1	2-0	1-0	2-3		1-0	1-3	1-1	1-2
US Pro Vercelli	3-2	2-4	4-2	1-3	2-1	1-0	1-0	0-2	1-1	2-1	2-1	3-1	2-0	0-2		3-1	2-3	3-2
AS Roma	1-0	0-1	1-0	0-0	2-0	4-2	1-3	0-1	3-1	4-0	1-1	1-1	3-0	1-1	2-0		7-1	4-0
FBC Torino	3-0	3-2	6-3	3-2	9-0	3-2	3-0	0-1	4-2	0-0	0-1	4-2	0-1	3-1	4-0	1-1		1-0
US Triestina	1-0	1-4	0-0	1-0	3-0	3-0	2-1	0-1	2-1	2-1	2-2	0-0	2-0	3-2	2-1	1-1	2-2	

	Serie "A"	Pd	Wn	Dw	Ls	GF	GA	Pts	
1.	FC JUVENTUS (TORINO)	34	25	4	5	83	23	54	
2.	AS Ambrosiana "Inter" (Milano)	34	19	8	7	80	53	46	
3.	Bologna FC (Bologna)	34	15	12	7	69	33	42	
3.	AC Napoli (Napoli)	34	18	6	10	64	38	42	
5.	AS Roma (Roma)	34	14	11	9	58	35	39	
5.	AC Fiorentina (Firenze)	34	16	7	11	48	38	39	
7.	FBC Torino (Torino)	34	14	8	12	65	54	36	
8.	Genova 1893 AC (Genova)	34	13	8	13	58	60	34	
8.	US Triestina (Trieste)	34	14	6	14	41	56	34	
10.	SS Lazio (Roma)	34	12	9	13	42	44	33	
11.	Milan FBC (Milano)	34	11	10	13	57	62	32	
12.	US Pro Vercelli (Vercelli)	34	13	3	18	42	58	29	
12.	AC Palermo (Palermo)	34	11	7	16	28	58	29	
14.	AFC Padova (Padova)	34	8	12	14	43	55	28	
14.	US Alessandria (Alessandria)	34	10	8	16	42	60	28	
16.	Casale FBC (Casale Monferrato)	34	9	6	19	35	75	24	
17.	US Bari (Bari)	34	8	6	20	40	68	22	R
18.	Pro Patria et Libertate (Busto Arsizio)	34	8	5	21	46	71	21	R
		612	238	136	238	941	941	612	

Top goalscorers

1)	Felice Placido BOREL	(FC Juventus)	29
2)	Angelo SCHIAVIO	(Bologna FC)	28
3)	Antonio VOJAK	(AC Napoli)	22
4)	Giuseppe MEAZZA	(AS Ambrosiana)	20

Serie "B" was extended to two groups of 13 clubs each for the next season, with the top 3 of each group entering promotion play-offs.

	Serie "B"	Pd	Wn	Dw	Ls	GF	GA	Pts	
1.	US Livorno (Livorno)	32	22	7	3	72	23	51	P
2.	AC Brescia (Brescia)	32	23	4	5	54	19	50	P
3.	Modena FBC (Modena)	32	17	4	11	58	41	38	
4.	Spezia FBC (La Spezia)	32	14	9	9	46	47	37	
5.	FBA Novara (Novara)	32	13	9	10	59	50	35	
6.	AC Verona (Verona)	32	12	10	10	47	45	34	
6.	AC Comense (Como)	32	15	4	13	51	53	34	
8.	SG Sampierdarenese (Genova)	32	13	7	12	55	47	33	
9.	AC Vigevanese (Vigevano)	32	13	6	13	42	49	32	
10.	AC Messina (Messina)	32	11	8	13	49	53	30	
11.	SS Serenissima (Venezia)	32	11	5	16	41	41	27	
12.	US Cremonese (Cremona)	32	9	8	15	48	59	26	
12.	AC Legnano (Legnano)	32	9	8	15	40	53	26	
14.	CS Cagliari (Cagliari)	32	9	6	17	37	60	24	
14.	Grion (Pola)	32	9	6	17	38	72	24	
16.	Atalanta BC (Bergamo)	32	9	5	18	52	60	23	
17.	US Pistoiese (Pistoia)	32	7	6	19	29	46	20	
---.	AC Monfalcone (Monfalcone)	6	-	1	5	4	16	1	#
		544	216	112	216	818	818	544	

AC Monfalcone (Monfalcone) resigned from the league after only 6 matches, their record was deleted and is not included in the above totals.

Promoted to Serie "B": Catanzarese (Catanzaro), Derthona FBC (Tortona), US Foggia (Foggia), AC Pavia (Pavia), AC Perugia (Perugia), Seregno FBC (Seregno), S.P.A.L. (Ferraro), ASC Viareggio (Viareggio) and AC Vicenza (Vicenza).

1933-34

1933-1934 Serie "A"	US Alessandria	Ambrosiana 'Inter'	Bologna FC	AC Brescia	Casale FBC	AC Fiorentina	Genova 1893 AC	FC Juventus	SS Lazio	US Livorno	Milan FBC	AC Napoli	AFC Padova	AC Palermo	US Pro Vercelli	AS Roma	FBC Torino	US Triestina
US Alessandria		9-2	2-2	1-0	4-1	3-1	3-1	2-1	3-2	2-1	1-1	1-0	3-0	2-1	0-1	1-1	3-1	1-0
Ambrosiana 'Inter'	4-1		2-0	1-0	9-0	2-4	5-0	3-2	8-1	1-2	3-0	2-1	1-0	3-1	2-0	0-0	0-0	2-1
Bologna FC	4-1	0-1		4-1	2-0	0-0	3-0	2-2	0-0	1-0	2-1	3-0	3-0	4-1	4-1	1-0	2-2	2-0
AC Brescia	2-1	1-1	1-2		3-1	4-0	3-1	1-2	0-0	1-1	3-0	1-1	1-0	1-1	1-0	1-0	1-0	3-2
Casale FBC	2-1	0-1	0-3	1-0		2-2	2-1	0-3	1-1	4-4	0-0	1-4	0-0	2-2	1-1	0-2	3-2	1-1
AC Fiorentina	0-0	1-0	3-0	2-0	2-2		2-1	2-2	2-0	1-0	1-0	0-1	3-0	4-1	1-1	1-3	1-1	1-1
Genova 1893 AC	1-0	0-0	1-0	3-1	5-0	1-2		0-2	1-2	2-0	2-2	1-1	1-0	1-1	3-0	1-0	2-2	0-1
FC Juventus	3-1	0-0	4-1	5-1	6-1	5-0	8-1		2-2	4-1	4-0	2-0	5-1	1-1	3-0	3-1	4-0	1-1
SS Lazio	1-0	1-4	3-3	3-2	2-1	2-2	3-2	0-2		3-0	4-0	0-2	3-2	1-0	1-1	3-3	1-0	2-0
US Livorno	3-2	2-2	0-0	0-0	5-0	3-0	0-0	0-0	4-1		4-0	0-1	3-1	3-2	1-1	1-3	2-0	2-1
Milan FBC	3-0	1-2	1-1	4-0	6-2	2-0	1-0	3-1	4-2	3-1		0-2	2-2	1-0	2-0	1-0	4-0	0-1
AC Napoli	2-1	2-1	1-0	1-0	2-1	1-1	0-0	2-0	2-1	0-0	1-0		1-1	3-0	1-0	1-2	5-2	2-0
AFC Padova	1-0	1-2	0-0	2-1	2-0	0-0	0-0	1-2	2-0	1-1	0-0	3-1		3-1	1-1	1-0	1-0	2-0
AC Palermo	2-1	1-1	2-1	2-2	3-0	0-0	2-0	0-1	1-0	3-2	2-1	1-2	2-1		2-1	0-0	0-0	2-1
US Pro Vercelli	1-0	0-0	2-0	2-1	4-1	7-2	2-0	0-2	2-0	0-0	2-1	0-0	4-0	3-0		1-2	1-0	1-1
AS Roma	5-1	0-1	0-1	2-1	1-0	2-1	3-0	2-3	5-0	0-0	1-1	1-2	2-0	2-1	2-0		4-0	0-0
FBC Torino	1-1	1-0	0-1	1-0	5-2	4-1	3-1	1-2	1-1	5-0	3-3	0-0	4-2	2-1	0-0	3-6		2-1
US Triestina	3-0	0-0	1-1	0-1	2-0	2-3	1-0	0-1	4-2	0-1	2-2	4-1	2-1	1-0	2-1	1-1	1-1	

	Serie "A"	Pd	Wn	Dw	Ls	GF	GA	Pts	
1.	FC JUVENTUS (TORINO)	34	23	7	4	88	31	53	
2.	AS Ambrosiana "Inter" (Milano)	34	20	9	5	66	24	49	
3.	AC Napoli (Napoli)	34	19	8	7	46	30	46	
4.	Bologna FC (Bologna)	34	16	10	8	53	33	42	
5.	AS Roma (Roma)	34	16	8	10	56	32	40	
6.	AC Fiorentina (Firenze)	34	12	12	10	46	53	36	
7.	US Pro Vercelli (Vercelli)	34	12	10	12	41	37	34	
7.	US Livorno (Livorno)	34	11	12	11	47	45	34	
9.	Milan FBC (Milano)	34	12	9	13	50	49	33	
10.	SS Lazio (Roma)	34	11	9	14	48	66	31	
11.	US Triestina (Trieste)	34	10	10	14	38	40	30	
12.	AC Brescia (Brescia)	34	11	7	16	39	47	29	
12.	FBC Torino (Torino)	34	9	11	14	47	57	29	
12.	US Alessandria (Alessandria)	34	12	5	17	43	54	29	
12.	AC Palermo (Palermo)	34	10	9	15	39	51	29	
16.	AFC Padova (Padova)	34	9	9	16	32	49	27	R*
17.	Genova 1893 AC (Genova)	34	8	8	18	33	55	24	R
18.	Casale FBC (Casale (Monferrato)	34	4	9	21	32	91	17	R
		612	225	162	225	844	844	612	

Top goalscorers

1)	Felice Placido BOREL	(FC Juventus)	32
2)	Giovanni BUSONI	(US Livorno)	26
3)	Giuseppe MEAZZA	(AS Ambrosiana)	21
	Antonio VOJAK	(AC Napoli)	21

* CS Cagliari (Cagliari) dissolved but then re-formed immediately as a new club US Cagliari (Cagliari) with the same players and coaches etc.
FBA Novara (Novara) (Foot Ball Associazione) changed to AC Novara (Novara) (Associazione Calcio).
AFC Padova (Padova) (Associazione Fascista Calcio) changed to AC Padova (Padova) (Associazione Calcio).
SS Serenissima (Venezia) changed their club name to Associazione Fascista Calcio Venezia (Venezia).

Note: SS Robur (Siena) changed their club name to AC Siena (Siena) for the next season.

Serie "A" was reduced to 16 clubs for the next season

Promotion Play-off

SG Sampierdarenese (Genova) 1-0 US Bari (Bari)

	Serie "B" (Play-off)	Pd	Wn	Dw	Ls	GF	GA	Pts
1.	SG Sampierdarenese (Genova)	10	5	4	1	14	9	14
1.	US Bari (Bari)	10	6	2	2	17	9	14
3.	Modena FBC (Modena)	10	4	3	3	13	7	11
4.	Pro Patria et Libertate (Busto Arsizio)	10	2	5	3	8	10	9
5.	AC Vigevanese (Vigevano)	10	3	2	5	8	10	8
6.	AC Perugia (Perugia)	10	1	2	7	5	20	4
		60	21	18	21	65	65	60

	Serie "B" (Group "A")	Pd	Wn	Dw	Ls	GF	GA	Pts	
1.	SG Sampierdarenese (Genova)	24	16	4	4	42	16	36	
2.	AC Vigevanese (Vigevano)	24	12	9	3	45	22	33	
3.	Pro Patria et Libertate (Busto Arsizio)	24	13	4	7	49	25	30	
4.	FBA Novara (Novara)	24	13	2	9	53	30	28	*
5.	AC Messina (Messina)	24	11	5	8	38	28	27	
6.	ASC Viareggio (Viareggio)	24	11	4	9	30	32	26	
7.	Catanzarese (Catanzaro)	24	8	9	7	39	31	25	
7.	Spezia FBC (La Spezia)	24	7	11	6	24	26	25	
9.	Seregno FBC (Seregno)	24	8	8	8	33	31	24	
10.	AC Pavia (Pavia)	24	6	6	12	21	44	18	
11.	AC Legnano (Legnano)	24	5	6	13	20	38	16	
12.	CS Cagliari (Cagliari)	24	6	3	15	22	61	14	-1*
13.	Derthona FBC (Tortona)	24	2	5	17	17	49	9	
		312	118	76	118	433	433	311	

CS Cagliari (Cagliari) had 1 point deducted by the F.I.G.C. Committee.

	Serie "B" (Group "B")	Pd	Wn	Dw	Ls	GF	GA	Pts	
1.	AC Perugia (Perugia)	24	14	5	5	46	32	33	
2.	Modena FBC (Modena)	24	13	6	5	44	19	32	
3.	US Bari (Bari)	24	12	6	6	41	25	30	
4.	AC Comense (Como)	24	12	4	8	38	29	28	
5.	Atalanta BC (Bergamo)	24	9	8	7	31	24	26	
6.	Grion (Pola)	24	10	5	9	41	34	25	
7.	US Foggia (Foggia)	24	9	6	9	39	40	24	
8.	US Cremonese (Cremona)	24	7	6	11	26	32	20	
8.	S.P.A.L. (Ferrara)	24	6	8	10	34	43	20	
8.	US Pistoiese (Pistoia)	24	6	8	10	33	44	20	
11.	AC Verona (Verona)	24	6	6	12	25	47	18	
11.	AC Vicenza (Vicenza)	24	7	4	13	31	42	18	
11.	SS Serenissima (Venezia)	24	6	6	12	28	46	18	*
		312	117	78	117	457	457	312	

Promoted to Serie "B": AFC Catania (Catania), ASC L'Aquila (L'Aquila), US Lucchese Libertas (Lucca) and AC Pisa (Pisa).

Serie "B" was extended to two groups of 16 clubs each for the next season.

1934-35

1934-1935 Serie "A"	US Alessandria	Ambrosiana 'Inter'	Bologna FC	AC Brescia	AC Fiorentina	FC Juventus	SS Lazio	US Livorno	Milan FBC	AC Napoli	AC Palermo	US Pro Vercelli	AS Roma	Sampierdarenese	FBC Torino	US Triestina
US Alessandria		1-3	2-0	1-0	2-0	0-0	1-2	4-1	2-1	4-2	4-2	2-1	1-6	2-2	3-0	3-0
Ambrosiana 'Inter'	0-0		1-0	5-1	1-1	0-0	1-0	5-1	2-0	2-1	3-0	1-0	0-1	6-1	4-0	7-0
Bologna FC	3-3	0-0		3-0	2-1	2-0	1-2	4-0	6-3	3-0	0-0	5-0	1-1	0-1	3-1	1-3
AC Brescia	1-0	1-1	1-1		1-1	0-2	1-0	4-0	2-0	0-1	2-2	3-0	2-1	1-0	2-1	2-1
AC Fiorentina	4-1	1-1	1-0	1-0		0-1	2-1	0-1	1-0	3-2	2-0	1-0	4-1	0-0	4-0	1-0
FC Juventus	4-1	1-0	1-0	0-0	0-0		6-1	2-1	1-0	2-1	2-1	3-0	2-1	4-0	1-1	0-0
SS Lazio	0-1	4-2	2-1	4-0	3-5	5-3		6-1	1-4	3-1	1-0	6-0	0-0	2-1	1-1	0-0
US Livorno	1-0	1-1	4-1	3-1	1-2	1-2	0-1		0-2	0-2	0-3	1-0	1-1	0-0	1-1	1-0
Milan FBC	2-2	2-2	0-0	0-1	1-1	3-0	1-1	1-1		2-2	2-1	1-0	4-4	2-1	0-0	0-1
AC Napoli	0-1	0-1	1-1	2-0	1-1	0-0	3-0	1-1	0-1		6-0	1-0	3-2	1-1	2-1	2-1
AC Palermo	2-0	1-1	0-1	0-0	0-0	0-0	2-1	2-2	1-0	2-0		2-0	1-0	1-0	0-0	2-0
US Pro Vercelli	1-0	1-1	2-1	1-1	2-0	0-1	1-0	0-1	1-2	1-1	0-0		1-4	2-3	0-3	4-2
AS Roma	3-0	3-4	1-1	4-0	0-0	1-2	1-1	5-1	1-0	4-0	5-1	3-2		2-0	2-1	1-2
Sampierdarenese	2-1	0-0	2-1	3-0	0-1	0-1	2-3	0-0	0-0	1-3	1-0	0-0	1-0		3-2	1-0
FBC Torino	2-1	1-2	0-1	4-2	1-0	1-3	2-2	1-0	1-1	0-0	0-0	2-0	2-3	5-2		3-1
US Triestina	3-1	1-1	1-3	3-0	0-1	2-1	2-1	1-2	2-1	0-0	1-1	3-1	0-2	2-1	1-0	

	Serie "A"	Pd	Wn	Dw	Ls	GF	GA	Pts	
1.	FC JUVENTUS (TORINO)	30	18	8	4	45	22	44	
2.	AS Ambrosiana "Inter" (Milano)	30	15	12	3	58	24	42	
3.	AC Fiorentina (Firenze)	30	15	9	6	39	23	39	
4.	AS Roma (Roma)	30	14	7	9	63	38	35	
5.	SS Lazio (Roma)	30	13	6	11	55	46	32	
6.	Bologna FC (Bologna)	30	11	8	11	46	34	30	
7.	AC Napoli (Napoli)	30	10	9	11	39	38	29	
7.	US Alessandria (Alessandria)	30	12	5	13	44	48	29	
7.	AC Palermo (Palermo)	30	9	11	10	27	34	29	
10.	Milan FBC (Milan)	30	8	11	11	36	38	27	
10.	US Triestina (Trieste)	30	11	5	14	33	44	27	
10.	AC Brescia (Brescia)	30	10	7	13	29	45	27	
13.	SG Sampierdarenese (Genova)	30	9	8	13	29	42	26	
14.	FBC Torino (Torino)	30	8	9	13	37	45	25	
15.	US Livorno (Livorno)	30	8	8	14	28	54	24	R
16.	US Pro Vercelli (Vercelli)	30	5	5	20	21	54	15	R
		480	176	128	176	629	629	480	

Top goalscorers

1)	Enrico GUAITA	(AS Roma)	28
2)	Silvio PIOLA	(SS Lazio)	21
3)	Giuseppe MEAZZA	(AS Ambrosiana)	19
4)	Renato CATTANEO	(US Alessandria)	16
5)	Felice Placido BOREL	(FC Juventus)	13

Promotion Play-off

US Bari (Bari) 1-0, 0-4 Genova 1893 AC (Genova)

	Serie "B" (Group "A")	Pd	Wn	Dw	Ls	GF	GA	Pts	
1.	Genova 1893 AC (Genova)	29	18	6	5	48	23	42	P
2.	AC Novara (Novara)	29	17	5	7	61	34	39	
3.	SC Pisa (Pisa)	29	15	7	7	51	33	37	
3.	AFC Catania (Catania)	29	16	5	8	45	35	37	
5.	AC Vigevanese (Vigevano)	29	15	5	9	67	34	35	
5.	AC Viareggio (Viareggio)	29	15	5	9	43	32	35	
7.	US Lucchese Libertas (Lucca)	29	13	8	8	40	31	34	
8.	AC Messina (Messina)	29	12	8	9	52	45	32	
9.	US Cagliari (Cagliari)	29	12	6	11	45	40	30	R
10.	Seregno FBC (Seregno)	29	9	10	10	42	41	28	R
11.	Spezia FBC (La Spezia)	29	10	4	15	37	41	24	R
12.	Casale FBC (Casale Monferrato)	29	7	9	13	28	53	23	R
13.	AC Legnano (Legnano)	29	9	4	16	30	51	22	R
14.	Pro Patria et Libertate (Busto Arsizio)	29	4	8	17	22	45	16	R
15.	Derthona FBC (Tortona)	29	3	7	19	23	74	13	R
---.	AC Pavia (Pavia)	15	-	3	12	7	29	3	#
	AC Pavia (Pavia)	5	2	-	3	7	8	4	
		450	175	100	175	641	641	450	

AC Pavia (Pavia) resigned after 20 games, the results of their first 15 games (½ season) were allowed to stand.

Serie "B" (Group "B")		Pd	Wn	Dw	Ls	GF	GA	Pts	
1.	US Bari (Bari)	28	14	9	9	48	24	37	P
2.	Modena FBC (Modena)	28	17	2	9	43	31	36	
3.	US Pistoiese (Pistoia)	28	15	4	9	47	27	34	
4.	ASC L'Aquila (L'Aquila)	28	12	8	8	48	36	32	
4.	AC Verona (Verona)	28	12	8	8	36	32	32	
6.	S.P.A.L. (Ferrara)	28	13	5	10	45	42	31	
7.	Atalanta BC (Bergamo)	28	12	6	10	38	35	30	
8.	US Foggia (Foggia)	28	12	5	11	45	37	29	PO
8.	US Cremonese (Cremona)	28	11	7	10	34	35	29	R
10.	AC Padova (Padova)	28	10	7	11	45	35	27	R
11.	Catanzarese (Catanzaro)	28	9	4	15	33	41	22	R
11.	AC Vicenza (Vicenza)	28	8	6	14	27	40	22	R
11.	AFC Venezia (Venezia)	28	9	4	15	25	47	22	R
14.	AC Comense (Como)	28	7	6	15	27	55	20	R
15.	AC Perugia (Perugia)	28	6	5	17	25	49	17	R
---.	Grion (Pola)	15	4	1	10	14	28	9	#
		420	167	86	167	566	566	420	

Grion (Pola) resigned after only 15 games, their record was deleted and is not included in the above totals.

Relegation Play-off

US Foggia (Foggia) 1-1, 1-0 US Cremonese (Cremona)

Promoted to Serie "B": AC Siena (Siena) and AS Taranto (Taranto).

Serie "B" was reduced to one group of 18 clubs for the next season.

1935-36

1935-1936 Serie "A"	US Alessandria	Ambrosiana	US Bari	Bologna FC	AC Brescia	AC Fiorentina	Genova 1893 AC	FC Juventus	SS Lazio	Milan FBC	AC Napoli	AC Palermo	AS Roma	Sampierdare.	FBC Torino	US Triestina
US Alessandria		2-2	2-0	1-1	5-0	2-1	1-0	3-2	2-0	6-1	2-3	1-0	1-0	1-1	0-2	0-0
Ambrosiana 'Inter'	2-1		2-0	3-1	1-0	0-2	3-0	4-0	3-1	1-1	4-2	4-0	5-1	3-0	4-0	5-0
US Bari	4-0	2-1		0-0	1-1	0-0	3-2	1-1	1-1	0-2	0-0	1-0	0-1	1-1	2-0	0-0
Bologna FC	1-1	3-0	0-2		1-0	1-0	4-1	2-1	2-0	4-1	2-1	1-0	2-0	0-0	2-0	3-0
AC Brescia	1-1	1-0	1-2	2-1		2-0	0-0	0-1	3-1	1-2	2-0	0-1	1-1	1-2	2-2	0-0
AC Fiorentina	0-0	2-3	2-2	0-1	1-0		2-1	1-1	2-1	3-1	2-0	2-1	1-2	1-1	0-2	3-1
Genova 1893 AC	0-0	2-2	0-0	1-1	2-0	2-2		1-1	3-2	3-3	2-2	2-0	2-1	3-0	0-2	2-2
FC Juventus	4-0	1-0	0-0	0-0	1-0	0-0	4-0		2-1	3-1	2-2	3-1	1-3	7-2	2-1	3-0
SS Lazio	3-0	0-0	2-1	1-1	3-0	1-0	1-1	3-0		2-2	3-1	3-0	0-1	5-0	1-1	3-2
Milan FBC	2-0	2-2	4-0	1-2	2-1	1-0	1-0	2-1	5-0		0-1	3-1	0-0	1-2	0-1	0-0
AC Napoli	1-0	3-2	2-0	0-1	1-0	4-0	2-1	0-1	1-2	1-0		3-0	1-2	4-2	0-1	2-2
AC Palermo	1-0	1-1	2-1	2-0	3-2	1-3	0-1	1-0	2-1	0-0	2-2		1-3	2-0	0-1	1-0
AS Roma	3-1	0-0	3-0	1-0	1-0	0-1	0-0	1-1	1-0	0-0	1-0	0-1		2-0	1-0	1-0
Sampierdarenese	1-1	1-0	2-1	0-0	2-0	1-0	1-2	0-1	2-2	3-1	2-2	2-0	0-2		2-0	2-2
FBC Torino	1-0	3-3	2-0	0-0	2-0	5-0	4-4	2-2	0-2	2-1	1-0	5-0	1-0	3-0		5-3
US Triestina	0-0	2-1	4-1	2-2	2-0	5-1	0-0	1-0	3-3	1-0	6-1	5-0	0-0	1-0	2-0	

	Serie "A"	Pd	Wn	Dw	Ls	GF	GA	Pts	
1.	BOLOGNA FC (BOLOGNA)	30	15	10	5	39	21	40	
2.	AS Roma (Roma)	30	16	7	7	32	20	39	
3.	FBC Torino (Torino)	30	16	6	8	49	33	38	*
4.	AS Ambrosiana "Inter" (Milano)	30	14	8	8	61	34	36	
5.	FC Juventus (Torino)	30	13	9	8	46	33	35	
6.	US Triestina (Trieste)	30	10	12	8	46	39	32	
7.	SS Lazio (Roma)	30	11	8	11	48	42	30	
8.	Milan FBC (Milano)	30	10	8	12	40	41	28	
8.	AC Napoli (Napoli)	30	11	6	13	42	45	28	
8.	US Alessandria (Alessandria)	30	9	10	11	34	37	28	
8.	Genova 1893 AC (Genova)	30	7	14	9	38	44	28	
12.	AC Fiorentina (Firenze)	30	10	7	13	32	42	27	
12.	SG Sampierdarenese (Genova)	30	9	9	12	32	49	27	
14.	US Bari (Bari)	30	7	11	12	26	38	25	
15.	AC Palermo (Palermo)	30	10	3	17	24	50	23	R
16.	AC Brescia (Brescia)	30	5	6	19	21	42	16	R
		480	173	134	173	610	610	480	

Top goalscorers

1)	Giuseppe MEAZZA	(AS Ambrosiana)	25
2)	Guglielmo GABETTO	(FC Juventus)	20
3)	Silvio PIOLA	(SS Lazio)	19
4)	Giovanni BUSONI	(AC Napoli)	12

* AFC Catania (Catania) changed their club name to AC Catania (Catania) for the next season.
FBC Torino (Torino) changed their club name to AC Torino (Torino) for the next season.

Note: AC Comense (Como) merged with AS Ardita Rebbio (Como) to become AC Como (Como) the next season.
AS Fascista Empoli (Empoli) changed their name to Dopolavoro Empolese (Empoli) in September 1936.

	Serie "B"	Pd	Wn	Dw	Ls	GF	GA	Pts	
1.	US Lucchese Libertas (Lucca)	34	21	6	7	75	33	48	P
2.	AC Novara (Novara)	34	21	6	7	61	33	48	P
3.	US Livorno (Livorno)	34	19	9	6	73	30	47	
4.	AC Messina (Messina)	34	19	6	9	59	52	44	
5.	AC Pisa (Pisa)	34	14	9	11	52	45	37	
5.	US Pro Vercelli (Vercelli)	34	15	7	12	44	40	37	
5.	AC Verona (Verona)	34	14	9	11	48	45	37	
8.	AFC Catania (Catania)	34	16	1	17	45	47	33	*
8.	ASC L'Aquila (L'Aquila)	34	14	5	15	43	46	33	
10.	Atalanta BC (Bergamo)	34	13	6	5	25	50	32	
11.	Modena FBC (Modena)	34	13	5	16	43	50	31	
12.	ASC Viareggio (Viareggio)	34	8	12	14	43	53	28	PO
12.	S.P.A.L. (Ferrara)	34	11	6	17	48	59	28	R
12.	US Pistoiese (Pistoia)	34	12	4	18	28	44	28	R
12.	US Foggia (Foggia)	34	11	6	17	39	51	28	R
16.	AC Siena (Siena)	34	9	9	16	39	52	27	R
16.	AC Vigevanese (Vigevano)	34	10	7	17	34	51	27	R
18.	AS Taranto (Taranto)	34	5	9	20	20	38	19	R
		612	245	122	245	819	819	612	

2nd Relegation Play-off:

ASC Viareggio (Viareggio)	2-0	US Pistoiese (Pistoia)

	Relegation Play-Off (12th-15th places)	Pd	Wn	Dw	Ls	GF	GA	Pts
1.	ASC Viareggio (Viareggio)	3	2	1	-	9	2	5
1.	US Pistoiese (Pistoia)	3	2	1	-	8	1	5
3.	S.P.A.L. (Ferrara)	3	-	1	2	2	8	1
3.	US Foggia (Foggia)	3	-	1	2	1	9	1
		12	4	4	4	20	20	12

Promoted to Serie "B": Catanzarese (Catanzaro), US Cremonese (Cremona), Spezia FBC (La Spezia) and AFC Venezia (Venezia).

Serie "B" was reduced to 16 clubs for the next season

Coppa Italia Final (Genova – 11/06/36)

FBC TORINO (TORINO)	5-1	US Alessandria (Alessandria)
Galli 2, Silano 2, Buscaglia	*(H.T. 2-1)*	*Riccardi*

Torino: Maina, Brunella, O.Ferrini, Gallea, Janni, Prato, Bo, Baldi, Galli, Buscaglia, Silano.

Alessandria: Ceresa, Lombardo, Turino, Barale, Parodi, Milano, Busani, Riccardi, Noti, Robotti, Croce.

Semi-Finals

US Alessandria (Alessandria)	1-0	Milan FBC (Milano)
FBC Torino (Torino)	2-0	AC Fiorentina (Firenze)

Quarter-Finals

US Alessandria (Alessandria)	1-0	SS Lazio (Roma)
FC Juventus (Torino)	1-3	AC Fiorentina (Firenze)
AC Napoli (Napoli)	1-2	Milan FBC (Milano)
FBC Torino (Torino)	4-2	US Livorno (Livorno)

1936-37

1936-1937 Serie "A"	US Alessandria	Ambrosiana 'Inter'	US Bari	Bologna FC	AC Fiorentina	Genova 1893 AC	FC Juventus	SS Lazio	Lucchese Libertas	Milan FBC	AC Napoli	AC Novara	AS Roma	Sampierdarenese	AC Torino	US Triestina
US Alessandria		0-3	0-2	0-1	1-0	2-1	1-0	1-5	1-0	1-3	2-0	1-3	5-3	1-0	0-0	0-0
Ambrosiana 'Inter'	3-0		2-2	0-1	2-2	0-1	2-0	2-2	2-2	1-1	2-2	3-1	2-1	1-1	1-0	1-2
US Bari	2-1	1-1		0-1	1-1	1-0	1-1	0-2	2-0	2-0	3-1	4-1	1-0	0-1	0-0	4-0
Bologna FC	4-0	1-0	2-2		1-1	4-4	1-1	1-1	0-0	2-0	2-1	5-1	1-0	4-1	0-1	2-0
AC Fiorentina	1-0	1-0	1-0	0-0		1-2	2-2	5-1	2-2	1-2	1-1	1-0	2-0	2-1	1-0	2-1
Genova 1893 AC	4-0	1-2	3-1	0-1	1-1		1-1	4-1	1-1	0-1	0-1	5-1	3-1	1-1	2-2	4-3
FC Juventus	4-1	1-1	2-0	0-0	3-0	2-2		6-1	1-1	2-0	2-0	1-1	5-1	3-1	0-1	0-0
SS Lazio	4-0	1-0	3-1	0-0	2-1	2-1	1-0		2-1	3-0	4-0	1-0	0-1	1-0	0-0	2-1
Lucchese Libertas	1-0	1-0	0-0	2-2	1-1	2-2	1-1	1-0		0-0	3-2	3-1	5-1	1-0	3-1	1-1
Milan FBC	4-1	1-1	4-0	1-0	1-0	2-2	3-4	5-3	3-0		1-0	2-0	1-0	2-2	0-0	0-0
AC Napoli	2-0	2-1	3-0	0-1	1-0	0-0	0-1	3-5	4-2	0-1		4-0	0-0	0-2	1-1	0-0
AC Novara	3-4	3-5	1-1	4-0	2-1	1-0	0-2	2-4	1-2	1-0	0-0		5-1	3-3	0-0	2-1
AS Roma	1-0	0-0	5-2	0-1	2-2	0-0	3-1	3-1	3-0	0-0	1-0	1-0		3-0	1-1	1-3
Sampierdarenese	5-0	2-2	2-0	2-2	1-1	0-2	2-6	0-2	3-0	0-0	0-2	2-1	0-1		0-1	0-0
AC Torino	5-0	1-2	6-1	3-3	0-0	1-3	2-1	2-2	2-2	3-1	3-0	4-1	2-0	4-0		2-0
US Triestina	3-0	1-1	1-1	1-2	1-0	0-1	1-0	1-0	4-1	0-0	1-1	1-4	2-2	0-0	0-2	

	Serie "A"	Pd	Wn	Dw	Ls	GF	GA	Pts	
1.	BOLOGNA FC (BOLOGNA)	30	15	12	3	45	26	42	
2.	SS Lazio (Roma)	30	17	5	8	56	42	39	
3.	AC Torino (Torino)	30	13	12	5	50	25	38	
4.	Milan FBC (Milano)	30	13	10	7	39	29	36	*
5.	FC Juventus FC (Torino)	30	12	11	7	53	31	35	
6.	Genova 1893 AC (Genova)	30	11	11	8	51	36	33	
7.	AS Ambrosiana "Inter" (Milano)	30	9	13	8	43	35	31	
7.	US Lucchese Libertas (Lucca)	30	9	13	8	39	43	31	
9.	AC Fiorentina (Firenze)	30	9	12	9	34	32	30	
10.	AS Roma (Roma)	30	10	7	13	36	45	27	
10.	US Bari (Bari)	30	9	9	12	35	45	27	
12.	US Triestina (Trieste)	30	7	12	11	29	36	26	
13.	AC Napoli (Napoli)	30	8	8	14	31	39	24	
14.	SG Sampierdarenese (Genova)	30	6	10	14	32	46	22	*
15.	AC Novara (Novara)	30	8	5	17	43	62	21	R
16.	US Alessandria (Alessandria)	30	8	2	20	23	67	18	R
		480	164	152	164	639	639	480	

Top goalscorers

1)	Silvio PIOLA	(SS Lazio)	21
2)	Guglielmo GABETTO	(FC Juventus)	18
3)	Pietro BUSCAGLIA	(AC Torino)	17
4)	Felice Placido BOREL	(FC Juventus)	16
	MARCHIONNESCHI	(Genova 1893 AC)	16

* Milan FBC (Milano) changed their club name to AC Milano (Milano) for the next season.
SG Sampierdarenese (Genova) merged with Rivarolese Nazionale Liguria (Genova) and Polisportiva Cornigliianese (Genova) to become AC Liguria (Genova) for the next season.

Note: US Pistoiese (Pistoia) changed their club name to AC Pistoia (Pistoia) for the next season.

	Serie "B"	Pd	Wn	Dw	Ls	GF	GA	Pts	
1.	US Livorno (Livorno)	30	17	8	5	66	20	42	P
2.	Atalanta BC (Bergamo)	30	14	11	5	48	25	39	P
3.	Modena FBC (Modena)	30	12	11	7	46	33	35	
4.	Spezia FBC (La Spezia)	30	10	14	6	35	23	34	
5.	AC Pisa (Pisa)	30	13	7	10	40	36	33	
5.	US Cremonese (Cremona)	30	13	7	10	40	42	33	
7.	AC Palermo (Palermo)	30	9	12	9	43	32	30	
7.	AC Brescia (Brescia)	30	10	10	10	33	34	30	
9.	AC Verona (Verona)	30	8	13	9	33	36	29	
10.	AFC Venezia (Venezia)	30	9	10	11	35	35	28	
10.	US Pro Vercelli (Vercelli)	30	9	10	11	40	45	28	
10.	AC Messina (Messina)	30	11	6	13	39	52	28	
10.	AC Catania (Catania)	30	9	1-	11	35	42	28	R
14.	ASC L'Aquila (L'Aquila)	30	8	8	14	36	51	24	R
14.	Catanzarese (Catanzaro)	30	8	8	14	32	56	24	R
16.	ASC Viareggio (Viareggio)	30	5	5	20	21	60	14	R-1
		480	165	150	165	622	622	479	

Note: ASC Viareggio (Viareggio) had 1 point deducted by the F.I.G.C. Committee.
AC Catania (Catania) were relegated after play-offs against AFC Venezia, US Pro Vercelli and AC Messina.

Promoted to Serie "B": US Anconitana Bianchi (Ancona), AC Padova (Padova), US Sanremese (San Remo), AS Taranto (Taranto) and AC Vigevano (Vigevano).

Coppa Italia Final (Firenze – 06/06/37)

GENOVA 1893 AC (GENOVA)	1-0	AS Roma (Roma)
Torti	*(H.T. 0-0)*	

Genova: Bacigalupo, Agosteo, Genta, Pastorino, Bigogno, Figliola, Arcari, Perazzolo, Torti, Scarabello, Marchionneschi.

Roma: Valinasso, Monzeglio, Allemandi, Frisoni, Bernardini, Gadaldi, Amadei, Serantoni, Di Benedetto, Mazzoni, Tomasi.

Semi-Finals

AS Ambrosiana "Inter" (Milano)	0-2	AS Roma (Roma)
Milan FBC (Milano)	1-1 (aet), 1-2 (aet)	Genova 1893 AC (Genova)

Quarter-Finals

AS Ambrosiana "Inter" (Roma)	7-1	Spezia FBC (La Spezia)
US Bari (Bari)	2-2 (aet), 1-3	Milan FBC (Milano)
Genova 1893 AC (Genova)	4-0	AC Catania (Catania)
AC Napoli (Napoli)	0-1	AS Roma (Roma)

1937-38

1937-1938 Serie "A"	Ambrosiana 'Inter'	Atalanta BC	US Bari	Bologna FC	AC Fiorentina	Genova 1893 AC	FC Juventus	SS Lazio	AC Liguria	US Livorno	Lucchese Libertas	AC Milano	AC Napoli	AS Roma	AC Torino	US Triestina
Ambrosiana 'Inter'		1-0	9-2	2-0	5-1	0-0	2-1	3-1	2-1	3-1	4-0	2-1	2-1	1-0	1-0	1-2
Atalanta BC	1-1		0-0	1-2	1-1	3-4	0-1	0-0	2-0	1-3	1-0	0-0	2-0	0-2	2-1	0-3
US Bari	0-2	2-1		0-1	1-0	2-0	0-0	5-1	0-0	1-1	2-1	2-3	3-1	2-0	0-0	0-0
Bologna FC	1-0	2-1	4-1		0-0	2-2	0-0	0-2	3-2	5-1	3-0	2-2	3-2	2-0	2-0	0-0
AC Fiorentina	0-3	4-1	1-1	2-1		1-2	1-1	1-1	3-1	1-2	0-0	0-1	1-3	1-4	1-2	2-2
Genova 1893 AC	1-1	0-0	4-1	1-3	1-0		1-2	2-1	0-2	4-1	3-0	0-1	2-1	1-1	2-1	2-2
FC Juventus	2-1	5-0	3-1	0-0	5-2	1-2		1-1	0-1	2-0	1-0	2-0	2-1	0-0	3-0	2-0
SS Lazio	1-3	4-0	3-1	2-0	5-0	2-1	1-1		3-0	3-0	3-0	1-1	0-0	1-1	6-0	2-1
AC Liguria	3-1	2-1	5-0	0-0	1-1	0-1	1-3	2-1		1-1	2-1	1-1	0-0	1-1	0-3	1-2
US Livorno	0-0	1-1	1-0	3-2	1-1	0-1	0-1	1-0	2-3		2-1	1-2	1-0	0-2	1-1	0-1
Lucchese Libertas	3-3	3-2	2-1	3-3	2-1	0-4	0-0	0-0	0-0	1-1		1-1	2-2	2-0	2-2	1-0
AC Milano	1-0	3-0	5-1	0-1	3-1	2-2	1-1	2-2	2-1	1-0	4-0		3-1	1-0	0-1	0-0
AC Napoli	1-1	1-0	1-0	1-1	3-0	2-2	1-1	1-0	3-2	1-1	2-1	1-1		2-2	1-1	3-0
AS Roma	1-1	2-1	3-2	0-1	4-0	1-3	2-1	2-1	1-0	1-0	5-0	3-1	2-1		2-1	1-1
AC Torino	1-1	2-1	2-4	3-1	2-0	0-1	1-1	1-0	3-0	4-1	3-2	0-0	0-0	3-1		1-0
US Triestina	1-1	0-0	6-0	3-1	2-1	2-1	2-0	0-0	1-0	0-2	0-0	0-0	3-0	0-0	1-0	

	Serie "A"	Pd	Wn	Dw	Ls	GF	GA	Pts	
1.	AS AMBROSIANA "INTER" (MILANO)	30	16	9	5	57	28	41	
2.	FC Juventus (Torino)	30	14	11	5	43	22	39	
3.	AC Milano (Milano)	30	13	12	5	43	27	38	
3.	Genova 1893 AC (Genova)	30	15	8	7	50	35	38	
5.	Bologna FC (Bologna)	30	14	9	7	46	34	37	
6.	US Triestina (Trieste)	30	12	12	6	35	22	36	
6.	AS Roma (Roma)	30	14	8	8	44	31	36	
8.	SS Lazio (Roma)	30	11	10	9	48	30	32	
8.	AC Torino (Torino)	30	12	8	10	39	37	32	
10.	AC Napoli (Napoli)	30	8	12	10	37	39	28	
11.	AC Liguria (Genova)	30	8	8	14	33	42	24	
11.	US Livorno (Livorno)	30	8	8	14	29	45	24	
13.	US Bari (Bari)	30	8	7	15	35	60	23	
14.	US Lucchese Libertas (Lucca)	30	5	11	14	28	55	21	
15.	Atalanta BC (Bergamo)	30	4	8	18	22	50	16	R
16.	AC Fiorentina (Firenze)	30	3	9	18	28	60	15	R
		480	165	150	165	617	617	480	

Top goalscorers

1)	Giuseppe MEAZZA	(AS Ambrosiana)	20
2)	Guglielmo TREVISAN	(US Triestina)	18
3)	Aldo BOFFI	(AC Milano)	16
	Danilo MICHELINI	(AS Roma)	16
5)	Silvio PIOLA	(SS Lazio)	15
	Carlo REGUZZONI	(Bologna FC)	15

From the next season "goal-average" decided the positions of teams level on points at the end of the season.

Note: Dopolavoro Empolese (Empoli) changed their name to Dopolavoro Interaziendale Italo Gambacciani Sezione Calcio (Empoli) for the next season.

Promotion Play-offs

In Milano:	Modena FBC (Modena)	3-0	US Alessandria (Alessandria)
In Torino:	AC Novara (Novara)	3-2	US Alessandria (Alessandria)

(there was no need for a Novara vs Modena match to be played)

	Serie "B"	Pd	Wn	Dw	Ls	GF	GA	Pts	
1.	AC Novara (Novara)	32	16	11	5	57	23	43	P
1.	Modena FBC (Modena)	32	18	7	7	53	32	43	P
1.	US Alessandria (Alessandria)	32	18	7	7	62	34	43	
4.	AC Padova (Padova)	32	18	4	10	49	32	40	
5.	US Anconitana Bianchi (Ancona)	32	15	8	9	44	31	38	
6.	AC Pisa (Pisa)	32	15	7	10	54	51	37	
7.	AC Palermo (Palermo)	32	15	5	12	46	43	35	
7.	AFC Venezia (Venezia)	32	13	9	10	49	47	35	
9.	US Sanremese (San Remo)	32	13	8	11	42	37	34	
10.	AC Verona (Verona)	32	12	9	11	37	31	33	
11.	US Pro Vercelli (Vercelli)	32	13	6	13	54	40	32	
12.	AC Vigevano (Vigevano)	32	9	12	11	33	39	30	
13.	Spezia FBC (La Spezia)	32	9	8	15	34	47	26	
14.	AC Brescia (Brescia)	32	7	7	18	30	47	21	R
14.	US Cremonese (Cremona)	32	6	9	17	28	50	21	R
16.	AS Taranto (Taranto)	32	6	6	20	24	64	18	R
17.	AC Messina (Messina)	32	4	7	21	27	75	14	R-1
		544	207	130	207	723	723	543	

Note: AC Messina (Messina) had 1 point deducted by the F.I.G.C. Committee.

Promoted to Serie "B": Casale FBC (Casale Monferrato), AC Fanfulla (Lodi), US Salernitana Fascista (Salerno), AC Siena (Siena) and S.P.A.L. (Ferrara).

Coppa Italia Final (1st Leg) (Torino – 01/05/38)

AC Torino (Torino)	1-3	FC JUVENTUS (TORINO)
D'Odorico	*(H.T. 1-1)*	*Bellini 2, De Filippis*

Juventus: Bodoira, Foni, Rava, Depetrini, Menti, Varglien, Bellini, De Filippis, Gabetto, Tomasi, Borel.

Torino: Maina, Brunella, O.Ferrini, Cadario, Ellena, Neri, Bo, Vallone, Baldi, Bruscaglia, D'Adorico.

Coppa Italia Final (2nd Leg) (Torino – 08/05/38)

AC Torino (Torino)	1-2	FC JUVENTUS (TORINO)
Baldi	*(H.T. 1-2)*	*Gabetto 2*

Juventus: Bodoira, Foni, Rava, Depetrini, Menti, Varglien, Bellini, De Filippis, Gabetto, Tomasi, Borel.

Torino: Maina, Brunella, O.Ferrini, Cadario, Ellena, Neri, Bo, Vallone, Baldi, Bruscaglia, D'Adorico.

Semi-Finals

FC Juventus (Torino)	2-0	AS Ambrosiana "Inter" (Milano)
AC Milano (Milano)	2-2 (aet), 2-3 (aet)	AC Torino (Torino)

Quarter-Finals

AC Brescia (Brescia)	2-6	AC Torino (Torino)
FC Juventus (Torino)	6-0	Atalanta BC (Bergamo)
AC Milano (Milano)	2-0	Bologna FC (Bologna)
AC Napoli (Napoli)	0-2	AS Ambrosiana "Inter" (Milano)

1938-39

1938-1939 Serie "A"	Ambrosiana 'Inter'	US Bari	Bologna FC	Genova 1893 AC	FC Juventus	SS Lazio	AC Liguria	US Livorno	Lucchese Libertas	AC Milano	Modena FBC	AC Napoli	AC Novara	AS Roma	AC Torino	US Triestina
Ambrosiana 'Inter'		5-3	2-0	1-0	5-0	1-1	5-2	3-1	7-1	1-0	4-2	1-2	3-1	0-0	1-1	0-0
US Bari	4-1		2-2	0-0	1-1	2-1	2-1	2-0	1-1	2-1	1-0	1-1	1-0	3-1	0-0	0-0
Bologna FC	1-1	4-3		3-0	1-0	2-0	1-1	1-1	2-2	2-1	1-1	4-0	3-0	1-0	0-3	2-0
Genova 1893 AC	3-0	8-0	2-3		3-2	2-1	0-1	0-1	4-1	2-0	5-1	3-1	3-1	2-0	6-1	0-0
FC Juventus	0-0	3-0	1-0	1-1		1-0	2-1	2-1	2-1	2-2	1-1	1-0	1-0	0-0	1-1	2-1
SS Lazio	1-2	1-0	1-2	2-1	1-1		1-0	2-1	5-0	2-2	2-1	0-0	1-0	1-3	1-1	1-0
AC Liguria	1-0	1-0	1-2	1-0	1-1	0-1		3-3	1-1	0-1	1-0	2-0	3-1	3-2	2-1	2-2
US Livorno	2-2	3-0	3-1	2-2	1-0	2-3	0-1		1-0	0-2	1-0	2-0	0-2	3-1	1-1	1-0
Lucchese Libertas	1-1	0-0	1-1	0-1	1-0	2-1	3-1	2-1		1-2	3-1	2-2	0-1	1-4	1-1	1-0
AC Milano	3-1	3-1	0-1	1-2	0-0	3-0	0-0	2-2	1-0		2-0	0-2	2-1	0-1	0-0	2-4
Modena FBC	1-1	0-2	1-1	0-0	2-0	4-0	2-3	3-2	0-1	2-2		2-1	1-1	2-0	0-1	1-0
AC Napoli	1-0	1-1	1-6	2-0	4-1	0-0	0-0	3-1	3-1	1-0	0-1		2-1	1-0	0-0	2-0
AC Novara	0-1	2-0	1-3	0-0	0-0	2-0	1-0	2-1	1-1	2-1	0-0	0-0		5-0	0-1	1-0
AS Roma	2-3	2-0	0-1	3-1	1-0	0-2	1-0	4-1	3-0	1-0	0-1	2-2	3-0		2-0	1-2
AC Torino	2-1	2-1	1-1	0-1	3-2	3-1	1-0	3-2	5-1	3-2	4-2	3-0	1-1	0-1		1-0
US Triestina	1-2	1-0	1-1	1-1	1-1	2-0	0-2	2-0	2-1	0-1	0-0	0-0	0-0	0-1	3-1	

	Serie "A"	Pd	Wn	Dw	Ls	GF	GA	Pts	
1.	BOLOGNA FC (BOLOGNA)	30	16	10	4	53	31	42	
2.	AC Torino (Torino)	30	14	10	6	45	34	38	
3.	AS Ambrosiana "Inter" (Milano)	30	14	9	7	55	37	37	
4.	Genova 1893 AC (Genova)	30	14	7	9	53	30	35	
5.	AS Roma (Roma)	30	14	3	13	39	35	31	
6.	AC Liguria (Genova)	30	12	7	11	35	34	31	
7.	AC Napoli (Napoli)	30	10	11	9	30	35	31	
8.	FC Juventus (Torino)	30	8	13	9	28	34	29	
9.	AC Milano (Milano)	30	10	8	12	36	34	28	
10.	SS Lazio (Roma)	30	11	6	13	33	40	28	
11.	US Bari (Bari)	30	9	9	12	33	46	27	
12.	AC Novara (Novara)	30	9	8	13	27	32	26	
13.	Modena FBC (Modena)	30	8	9	13	32	40	25	
14.	US Triestina (Trieste)	30	7	10	13	23	28	24	
15.	US Livorno (Livorno)	30	9	6	15	40	49	24	R
16.	US Lucchese Libertas (Lucca)	30	7	10	13	31	54	24	R
		480	172	136	172	593	593	480	

Top goalscorers

	Player	Club	Goals
1)	Aldo BOFFI	(AC Milano)	19
	Ettore PURICELLI	(Bologna FC)	19
3)	LAZZARETTI	(Genova 1893 AC)	14
4)	Danilo MICHELINI	(AS Roma)	13

Note: AC Pistoia (Pistoia) changed their club name to US Pistoiese (Pistoia) for the next season.

	Serie "B"	Pd	Wn	Dw	Ls	GF	GA	Pts	
1.	AC Fiorentina (Firenze)	34	16	13	5	62	30	45	P
2.	AFC Venezia (Venezia)	34	16	11	7	39	23	43	P
3.	Atalanta BC (Bergamo)	34	15	13	6	43	26	43	
4.	AC Siena (Siena)	34	17	8	9	43	35	42	
5.	AC Verona (Verona)	34	16	8	10	46	36	40	
6.	US Pro Vercelli (Vercelli)	34	14	9	11	50	44	37	
7.	AC Palermo (Palermo)	34	13	10	11	35	34	36	
8.	US Alessandria (Alessandria)	34	14	7	13	57	43	35	
9.	AC Padova (Padova)	34	15	5	14	56	51	35	
10.	AC Fanfulla (Lido)	34	12	10	12	39	32	34	
11.	US Sanremese (San Remo)	34	14	6	14	41	45	34	
12.	US Anconitana Bianchi (Ancona)	34	13	7	14	50	44	33	
13.	AC Pisa (Pisa)	34	13	7	14	52	46	33	
14.	AC Vigevano (Vigevano)	34	11	11	12	43	48	33	
15.	Spezia FBC (La Spezia)	34	12	7	15	43	50	31	R
16.	S.P.A.L. (Ferrara)	34	10	6	18	37	55	26	R
17.	US Salernitana Fascista (Salerno)	34	10	3	21	40	58	23	R
18.	Casale FBC (Casale Monferrato)	34	2	5	27	12	88	9	R
		612	233	146	233	788	788	612	

Promoted to Serie "B": AC Brescia (Brescia), AC Catania (Catania), Molinella (Molinella) and AC Udinese.

Coppa Italia Final (Roma – 18/05/39)

AS AMBROSIANA "INTER" (MILANO) 2-1 AC Novara (Novara)

Ferraris, Frossi *(H.T. 2-0)* *Romano*

Ambrosiana: Sain, Bonocore, Setti, Locatelli, Olmi, Campatelli, Frossi, De Maria, Guarnieri, Meazza, Ferraris.

Novara: Caimo, Bonatti, Galimberti, Rigotti, Marnese, Galli, Borrini, Romano, Marchionneschi, Versaldi, Barberis.

Semi-Finals

Genova 1893 AC (Genova)	1-3 (aet)	AS Ambrosiana "Inter" (Milano)
AC Novara (Novara)	3-2	AC Milano (Milano)

Quarter-Finals

AS Ambrosiana "Inter" (Milano)	1-0	AS Roma (Roma)
AC Monza (Monza)	1-2	Genova 1893 AC (Genova)
AC Novara (Novara)	3-0	Modena FBC (Modena)
AFC Venezia (Venezia)	1-2	AC Milano (Milano)

1939-40

1939-1940 Serie "A"	Ambrosiana 'Inter'	US Bari	Bologna FC	AC Fiorentina	Genova 1893 AC	FC Juventus	SS Lazio	AC Liguria	AC Milano	Modena FBC	AC Napoli	AC Novara	AS Roma	AC Torino	US Triestina	AFC Venezia
Ambrosiana 'Inter'		0-0	1-0	3-0	2-1	4-0	4-0	1-0	0-3	2-1	4-0	1-0	3-0	5-1	5-1	2-1
US Bari	3-0		1-1	2-1	0-1	2-1	1-5	1-1	2-0	1-0	1-0	1-0	0-0	2-2	2-2	3-0
Bologna FC	0-0	3-1		3-2	5-3	1-0	3-1	2-0	1-0	1-0	1-1	3-0	1-0	3-1	2-0	2-0
AC Fiorentina	0-3	1-1	1-0		1-1	0-0	2-3	4-0	1-0	3-2	2-0	2-2	1-0	3-2	1-0	3-1
Genova 1893 AC	2-2	3-0	1-2	3-0		3-2	4-0	2-0	1-1	0-3	2-0	5-3	0-0	1-0	1-0	3-1
FC Juventus	1-0	6-2	1-0	3-2	3-1		3-1	4-0	2-2	1-0	2-1	1-0	1-1	1-1	2-6	1-0
SS Lazio	1-1	0-1	2-2	1-1	4-1	4-0		2-2	2-2	1-1	2-0	1-0	1-0	1-1	2-0	1-0
AC Liguria	0-2	1-0	1-1	2-1	2-1	0-2	0-0		0-2	1-1	2-0	1-0	1-0	2-1	1-1	0-0
AC Milano	1-3	4-0	0-2	3-1	2-2	1-2	0-2	1-1		4-0	3-0	0-2	3-0	1-3	0-0	2-1
Modena FBC	1-2	3-0	0-0	3-0	1-4	1-2	1-1	1-1	2-2		0-0	4-1	1-0	1-2	2-1	2-2
AC Napoli	0-1	1-1	1-1	2-1	3-1	0-0	1-1	3-2	1-4	1-0		2-1	0-1	3-1	3-1	2-0
AC Novara	1-0	1-0	0-0	2-1	3-1	1-0	0-0	1-0	1-0	1-0	0-1		1-0	0-1	2-1	2-0
AS Roma	1-2	4-1	2-0	0-0	2-0	3-1	1-0	2-2	3-1	1-0	1-0	3-1		0-0	1-0	0-2
AC Torino	0-1	2-2	2-1	2-1	3-1	1-2	0-1	3-0	2-1	4-3	1-0	1-0	4-0		3-1	0-0
US Triestina	2-1	1-0	0-2	2-1	0-1	1-0	2-3	3-1	1-1	4-1	2-0	2-0	1-0	2-2		0-0
AFC Venezia	2-1	2-1	1-1	2-0	2-6	1-1	2-1	2-1	0-2	0-4	2-0	3-1	2-2	2-1	3-1	

	Serie "A"	Pd	Wn	Dw	Ls	GF	GA	Pts	
1.	AS AMBROSIANA "INTER" (MILANO)	30	20	4	6	56	23	44	
2.	Bologna FC (Bologna)	30	16	9	5	44	23	41	
3.	FC Juventus (Torino)	30	15	6	9	45	40	36	
4.	SS Lazio (Roma)	30	12	11	7	44	36	35	
5.	Genova 1893 AC (Genova)	30	14	5	11	56	47	33	
6.	AC Torino (Torino)	30	13	7	10	47	41	33	
7.	AS Roma (Roma)	30	11	7	12	28	31	29	
8.	AC Milano (Milano)	30	10	8	12	46	38	28	
9.	AC Novara (Novara)	30	12	3	15	27	35	27	
10.	AFC Venezia (Venezia)	30	10	7	13	34	46	27	
11.	US Bari (Bari)	30	9	9	12	33	46	27	
12.	US Triestina (Trieste)	30	10	6	14	38	43	26	
13.	AC Fiorentina (Firenze)	30	9	6	15	37	48	24	
14.	AC Napoli (Napoli)	30	9	6	15	26	41	24	
15.	AC Liguria (Genova)	30	7	10	13	25	44	24	R
16.	Modena FBC (Modena)	30	7	8	15	39	43	22	R
		480	184	112	184	625	625	480	

Top goalscorers

1)	Aldo BOFFI	(AC Milano)	24
2)	GUARNIERI	(AS Ambrosiana)	15
	Ettore PURICELLI	(Bologna FC)	15
4)	CONTI	(Genova 1893 AC)	13
	Guglielmo GABETTO	(FC Juventus)	13
	Carlo REGUZZONI	(Bologna FC)	13

Note: S.P.A.L. (Ferrara) changed their club name to AC Ferrara (Ferrara) for the next season.

	Serie "B"	Pd	Wn	Dw	Ls	GF	GA	Pts	
1.	Atalanta BC (Bergamo)	34	19	9	6	62	31	47	P
2.	US Livorno (Livorno)	34	21	4	9	84	35	46	P
3.	US Lucchese Libertas (Lucca)	34	18	8	8	63	45	44	
4.	US Anconitana Bianchi (Ancona)	34	16	9	9	54	34	41	
5.	AC Siena (Siena)	34	15	10	9	49	34	40	
6.	AC Brescia (Brescia)	34	16	8	10	54	39	40	
7.	US Alessandria (Alessandria)	34	16	6	12	59	41	38	
8.	AC Padova (Padova)	34	15	7	12	69	57	37	
9.	US Pro Vercelli (Vercelli)	34	14	6	14	62	67	34	
10.	AC Udinese (Udine)	34	14	5	15	60	57	33	
11.	AC Fanfulla (Lido)	34	12	8	14	45	44	32	
12.	AC Pisa (Pisa)	34	11	9	14	54	62	31	
13.	AC Verona (Verona)	34	12	7	15	41	56	31	
14.	AC Palermo (Palermo)	34	11	7	16	39	69	29	#
15.	Molinella (Molinella)	34	10	6	18	42	62	26	R
16.	AC Vigevano (Vigevano)	34	9	5	20	44	70	23	R
17.	US Sanremese (San Remo)	34	6	9	19	27	60	21	R
18.	AC Catania (Catania)	34	3	13	18	24	69	19	R
		612	238	136	238	932	932	612	

\# AC Palermo (Palermo) were suspended from Serie "B" for the next season due to "financial irregularities".

Promoted to Serie "B": FBC Macerata (Macerata), AC Reggiana (Reggio Emilia), Savona FBC (Savona), Spezia FBC (La Spezia) and AC Vicenza (Vicenza).

Coppa Italia Final (Firenze – 15/06/40)

AC FIORENTINA (FIRENZE) 1-0 Genova 1893 AC (Genova)

Celoria *(H.T. 1-0)*

Fiorentina: Griffanti, De Costa, Piccardi, Ellena, Bigogno, Poggi, Menti, Morselli, Celoria, Baldini, Tagliasacchi.

Genova: Cerosoli, Marchi, Borelli, Genta, Sardelli, Michelini, Neri, Arcari, S.Bertoni, Gabardo, Garibaldi.

Semi-Finals

AC Fiorentina (Firenze) 3-0 FC Juventus (Torino)

Genova 1893 AC (Genova) 2-0 US Bari (Bari)

Quarter-Finals

US Bari (Bari) 3-0 AC Liguria (Genova)

AC Fiorentina (Firenze) 4-1 SS Lazio (Roma)

FC Juventus (Torino) 3-0 AC Brescia (Brescia)

Modena FBC (Modena) 1-2 (aet) Genova 1893 AC (Genova)

1940-41

1940-1941 Serie "A"	Ambrosiana 'Inter'	Atalanta BC	US Bari	Bologna FC	AC Fiorentina	Genova 1893 AC	FC Juventus	SS Lazio	US Livorno	AC Milano	AC Napoli	AC Novara	AS Roma	AC Torino	US Triestina	AFC Venezia
Ambrosiana 'Inter'		2-1	5-0	2-1	0-2	4-0	2-1	1-1	3-0	2-2	1-0	0-0	5-1	0-2	1-1	4-2
Atalanta BC	1-3		4-0	2-0	0-0	1-1	3-0	2-0	2-1	2-1	4-0	2-0	0-0	0-1	2-0	3-1
US Bari	0-0	2-2		1-0	1-0	1-1	3-5	1-2	1-1	1-3	0-4	1-2	2-2	1-0	0-3	3-2
Bologna FC	5-0	1-0	5-1		5-3	4-1	1-0	2-2	3-0	4-2	3-0	3-0	2-1	3-0	2-0	1-1
AC Fiorentina	2-1	1-1	4-0	3-0		4-3	5-0	2-1	5-2	2-3	1-2	2-2	1-1	2-1	6-3	2-1
Genova 1893 AC	2-0	2-0	6-1	0-1	0-1		2-0	2-2	3-0	1-1	1-2	1-1	0-0	4-0	2-1	1-0
FC Juventus	2-0	3-1	5-1	3-1	2-3	2-0		3-2	2-1	1-2	0-0	3-0	3-1	2-1	1-1	2-2
SS Lazio	2-4	1-1	2-2	2-4	4-1	0-1	2-2		1-0	0-0	1-1	0-0	2-0	0-2	2-1	4-1
US Livorno	1-1	3-1	1-0	2-2	1-1	2-2	1-0	2-1		1-0	1-1	1-1	6-1	0-1	2-1	3-1
AC Milano	0-1	0-3	5-0	5-1	3-1	1-1	2-2	3-0	5-0		4-0	2-0	1-3	1-1	1-1	0-0
AC Napoli	0-1	4-1	3-1	4-4	0-2	1-0	2-2	0-2	1-2	3-2		2-0	2-1	2-1	1-0	1-1
AC Novara	2-4	5-1	4-0	0-1	2-0	2-1	1-2	0-0	0-0	2-0	1-0		1-1	1-1	0-0	0-0
AS Roma	3-0	1-0	6-2	1-1	1-1	3-0	3-0	1-1	3-1	1-2	2-2	1-3		4-1	0-0	5-2
AC Torino	5-5	1-1	4-0	0-0	6-2	3-6	2-0	1-1	5-2	0-4	6-2	5-1	0-0		2-1	0-2
US Triestina	2-0	3-3	2-4	0-0	1-0	6-2	1-1	0-0	1-1	0-0	2-0	1-0	4-1	1-0		3-1
AFC Venezia	1-0	1-1	1-1	1-0	2-1	0-0	1-1	2-0	2-2	0-0	1-1	3-0	1-0	2-2	4-3	

	Serie "A"	Pd	Wn	Dw	Ls	GF	GA	Pts	
1.	BOLOGNA FC (BOLOGNA)	30	16	7	7	60	37	39	
2.	AS Ambrosiana "Inter" (Milano)	30	14	7	9	52	42	35	
3.	AC Milano (Milano)	30	12	10	8	55	34	34	
4.	AC Fiorentina (Firenze)	30	14	6	10	60	49	34	
5.	FC Juventus (Torino)	30	12	8	10	50	47	32	
6.	Atalanta BC (Bergamo)	30	11	9	10	45	38	31	
7.	AC Torino (Torino)	30	11	8	11	54	50	30	
8.	AC Napoli (Napoli)	30	11	8	11	41	48	30	
9.	US Triestina (Trieste)	30	9	11	10	43	39	29	
10.	Genova 1893 AC (Genova)	30	10	9	11	46	44	29	
11.	AS Roma (Roma)	30	9	11	10	48	46	29	
12.	AFC Venezia (Venezia)	30	8	13	9	39	44	29	
13.	US Livorno (Livorno)	30	9	10	11	40	51	28	
14.	SS Lazio (Roma)	30	7	13	10	38	42	27	
15.	AC Novara (Novara)	30	8	11	11	31	38	27	R
16.	US Bari (Bari)	30	5	7	18	31	84	17	R
		480	166	148	166	733	733	480	

Top goalscorers

1)	Ettore PURICELLI	(Bologna FC)	22
2)	Amadeo AMADEI	(AS Roma)	18
	Romeo MENTI	(AC Fiorentina)	18
4)	Carlo REGUZZONI	(Bologna FC)	17
5)	Aldo BOFFI	(AC Milano)	16
	Guglielmo GABETTO	(FC Juventus)	16

Note: AC Palermo (Palermo) merged with Juventina (Palermo) to become US Palermo-Juventina (Palermo).

	Serie "B"	Pd	Wn	Dw	Ls	GF	GA	Pts	
1.	AC Liguria (Liguria)	34	22	5	7	71	32	49	P
2.	Modena FBC (Modena)	34	21	6	7	74	33	48	P
3.	AC Brescia (Brescia)	34	20	6	8	67	32	46	
4.	Savona FBC (Savona)	34	17	10	7	48	23	44	
5.	AC Padova (Padova)	34	15	9	10	64	47	39	
6.	AC Vicenza (Vicenza)	34	15	8	11	66	58	38	
7.	US Alessandria (Alessandria)	34	12	11	11	58	54	35	
8.	AC Siena (Siena)	34	13	8	13	42	41	34	
9.	AC Reggiana (Reggio Emilia)	34	12	9	13	51	43	33	
10.	US Lucchese Libertas (Lucca)	34	12	9	13	42	47	33	
11.	AC Udinese (Udine)	34	9	13	12	45	50	31	
12.	Spezia FBC (La Spezia)	34	10	10	14	45	51	30	
13.	AC Fanfulla (Lodi)	34	11	8	15	48	61	30	
14.	AC Pisa (Pisa)	34	10	10	14	40	60	30	
15.	AC Verona (Verona)	34	11	4	19	47	76	26	R
16.	US Anconitana Bianchi (Ancona)	34	9	7	18	44	74	25	R
17.	FBC Macerata (Macerata)	34	9	3	22	35	78	21	R
18.	US Pro Vercelli (Vercelli)	34	6	8	20	42	69	20	R
		612	234	144	234	929	929	612	

Promoted to Serie "B": FBC Fiumana (Fiume), AS Pescara, Pro Patria et Libertate (Busto Arsizio) and AC Prato.

Coppa Italia Final (Roma – 08/06/41)

AS Roma (Roma) 3-3 (aet) AFC VENEZIA (VENEZIA)

Amadei 14', 16', 19' — *Mazzola 37', Diotalevi 63', Alberti 68'*

Venezia: Fioravanti, Piazza, Di Gennaro, Tortora, Puppo, Stefanini, Alberti, Loik, Diotalevi, Mazzola, Alberico.

Roma: Masetti, Brunella, Acerbi, Jacobini, Donati, Bonomi, Krieziu, Borsetti, Amadei, Coscia, Panto.

Final Replay (Venezia – 15/06/41)

AS Roma (Roma) 0-1 AFC VENEZIA (VENEZIA)

Loik 73'

Venezia: Fioravanti, Piazza, Di Gennaro, Tortora, Puppo, Stefanini, Alberti, Loik, Diotalevi, Mazzola, Alberico.

Roma: Masetti, Brunella, Acerbi, Jacobini, Donati, Bonomi, Krieziu, Borsetti, Amadei, Coscia, Panto.

Semi-Finals

AC Torino (Torino)	1-1 (aet), 0-1	AS Roma (Roma)
AFC Venezia (Venezia)	3-1	SS Lazio (Roma)

Quarter-Finals

Bologna FC (Bologna)	3-4	AFC Venezia (Venezia)
AC Padova (Padova)	1-3	AC Torino (Torino)
AS Roma (Roma)	4-1	AC Fiorentina (Firenze)
Spezia FBC (La Spezia)	2-5	SS Lazio (Roma)

1941-1942 Serie "A"	Ambrosiana 'Inter'	Atalanta BC	Bologna FC	AC Fiorentina	Genova 1893 AC	FC Juventus	SS Lazio	AC Liguria	US Livorno	AC Milano	Modena FBC	AC Napoli	AS Roma	AC Torino	US Triestina	AFC Venezia
Ambrosiana 'Inter'		0-0	0-1	0-1	1-1	4-1	0-1	2-1	1-1	2-2	1-0	5-1	0-2	2-3	1-1	1-1
Atalanta BC	1-1		0-2	2-1	0-0	2-3	3-0	1-1	4-0	0-2	3-0	5-1	2-2	1-3	1-1	1-0
Bologna FC	0-1	4-0		2-3	1-1	2-0	2-2	2-2	7-1	3-1	4-0	1-2	1-2	1-0	2-0	2-0
AC Fiorentina	4-1	0-1	2-5		2-0	1-1	3-1	4-1	2-0	4-3	8-0	0-1	2-2	2-1	2-1	1-3
Genova 1893 AC	6-1	1-0	3-2	4-0		1-4	1-2	1-1	3-1	1-1	6-0	3-0	2-0	4-3	0-0	1-0
FC Juventus	4-0	1-1	1-1	4-2	1-1		2-0	3-0	2-3	3-2	1-1	1-1	2-0	3-0	1-0	0-0
SS Lazio	2-2	2-1	5-1	1-1	1-1	2-1		4-0	3-0	2-2	2-1	1-0	1-1	4-1	5-0	2-1
AC Liguria	0-1	1-0	2-1	1-1	3-4	2-1	4-1		4-2	1-0	2-1	2-1	0-3	1-0	2-2	0-2
US Livorno	3-0	3-1	1-1	3-1	0-0	1-2	2-1	2-0		0-2	2-2	2-0	0-2	1-1	1-0	1-1
AC Milano	2-1	1-3	2-0	2-1	3-0	1-1	2-5	3-2	0-2		7-1	3-1	4-2	2-5	2-2	1-1
Modena FBC	1-1	2-0	1-0	1-1	2-3	0-2	1-0	1-1	3-0	1-0		1-0	0-0	0-3	0-1	0-1
AC Napoli	0-1	3-0	1-2	1-0	0-0	4-1	1-1	1-1	2-1	2-1	2-1		1-1	0-0	0-1	1-1
AS Roma	6-0	2-0	1-0	1-0	1-2	2-0	2-1	7-0	4-0	2-0	2-0	5-1		0-0	0-0	0-0
AC Torino	1-1	9-1	1-0	3-1	1-1	2-1	1-1	3-2	1-0	1-0	2-0	5-3	2-2		2-0	2-1
US Triestina	0-0	0-0	1-0	2-0	2-1	3-0	0-0	0-1	5-1	2-2	1-1	1-0	0-0	1-3		2-2
AFC Venezia	0-0	1-0	1-0	2-1	2-1	2-0	0-2	2-1	2-1	2-0	3-1	4-1	0-1	3-1	2-0	

	Serie "A"	Pd	Wn	Dw	Ls	GF	GA	Pts	
1.	AS ROMA (ROMA)	30	16	10	4	55	21	42	
2.	Ac Torino (Torino)	30	16	7	7	60	39	39	
3.	AFC Venezia (Venezia)	30	15	8	7	40	25	38	
4.	Genova 1893 AC (Genova)	30	13	11	6	53	35	37	
5.	SS Lazio (Roma)	30	14	9	7	55	37	37	
6.	FC Juventus (Torino)	30	12	8	10	47	41	32	
7.	Bologna FC (Bologna)	30	12	5	13	50	37	29	
8.	US Triestina (Trieste)	30	8	13	9	29	32	29	
9.	AC Fiorentina (Firenze)	30	11	5	14	51	50	27	
10.	AC Milano (Milano)	30	10	7	13	53	53	27	
11.	AC Liguria (Genova)	30	10	7	13	39	56	27	
12.	AS Ambrosiana "Inter" (Milano)	30	7	12	11	31	47	26	
13.	Atalanta BC (Bergamo)	30	8	8	14	34	47	24	
14.	US Livorno (Livorno)	30	9	6	15	35	57	24	
15.	AC Napoli (Napoli)	30	8	7	15	32	51	23	R
16.	Modena FBC (Modena)	30	6	7	17	23	59	19	R
		480	175	130	175	687	687	480	

Top goalscorers

1)	Aldo BOFFI	(AC Milano)	22
2)	Amadeo AMADEI	(AS Roma)	18
	Renato GEI	(AC Fiorentina)	18
	Silvio PIOLA	(SS Lazio)	18
5)	Bruno ISPIRO	(Genova 1893 AC)	17

The Goal-average system was abolished from the next season and teams level on points shared equal placing.

	Serie "B"	Pd	Wn	Dw	Ls	GF	GA	Pts	
1.	US Bari (Bari)	34	19	11	4	47	26	49	P
2.	AC Vicenza (Vicenza)	34	17	13	4	58	18	47	P
3.	AS Pescara (Pescara)	34	20	6	8	48	24	46	
4.	AC Padova (Padova)	34	19	7	8	61	26	45	
5.	AC Brescia (Brescia)	34	16	7	11	57	37	39	
6.	Spezia FBC (La Spezia)	34	16	6	12	66	40	38	
7.	AC Pisa (Pisa)	34	16	6	12	53	52	38	
8.	AC Novara (Novara)	34	14	8	12	47	36	36	
9.	AC Udinese (Udine)	34	15	6	13	43	42	36	
10.	US Alessandria (Alessandria)	34	14	6	14	38	47	34	
11.	Pro Patria et Libertate (Busto Arsizio)	34	12	8	14	49	41	32	
12.	AC Fanfulla (Lodi)	34	12	6	16	41	45	30	
13.	AC Siena (Siena)	34	11	7	16	34	46	29	
14.	Savona FBC (Savona)	34	11	6	17	43	47	28	
15.	FBC Fiumana (Fiume)	34	10	6	18	55	58	26	R
16.	AC Reggiana (Reggio Emilia)	34	7	11	16	25	59	25	R
17.	AC Prato (Prato)	34	7	9	18	30	71	23	R
18.	US Lucchese Libertas (Lucca)	34	4	3	27	24	104	11	R
		612	240	132	240	819	819	612	

Promoted to Serie "B": US Anconitana Bianchi (Ancona), US Cremonese (Cremona), Mater (Roma) and US Palermo-Juventina (Palermo).

Coppa Italia Final (Milano – 21/06/42)

AC Milano (Milano)	1-1	FC JUVENTUS (TORINO)
Cappello	*(H.T. 0-0)*	*Bellini*

Juventus: Perucchetti, Foni, Rava, Depetrini, Parola, Locatelli, Colaneri, Varglien, Lushta, Sentimenti, Bellini.

Milan: Rossetti, Boniforti, Guagneti, Antonini, Remondini, Troppan, Trapanelli, Todeschini, Boffi, Capello, Rosellini.

Final Replay (Torino – 28/06/42)

AC Milano (Milano)	1-4	FC JUVENTUS (TORINO)
Boffi	*(H.T. 0-2)*	*Lushta 3, Sentimenti pen*

Juventus: Perucchetti, Foni, Rava, Depetrini, Parola, Locatelli, Colaneri, Varglien, Lushta, Sentimenti, Bellini.

Milan: Rossetti, Boniforti, Guagneti, Antonini, Remondini, Troppan, Trapanelli, Todeschini, Boffi, Capello, Rosellini.

Semi-Finals

AC Milano (Milano)	2-1	AFC Venezia (Venezia)
FC Juventus (Torino)	4-1	Modena FBC (Modena)

Quarter-Finals

FC Juventus (Torino)	1-0	AC Padova (Padova)
AC Milano (Milano)	6-0	AC Reggiana (Reggio Emilia)
Modena FBC (Modena)	2-0	AC Novara (Novara)
AFC Venezia (Venezia)	2-0	Bologna FC (Bologna)

1942-43

1942-1943 Serie "A"	Ambrosiana 'Inter'	Atalanta BC	US Bari	Bologna FC	AC Fiorentina	Genova 1893 AC	FC Juventus	SS Lazio	AC Liguria	US Livorno	AC Milano	AS Roma	AC Torino	US Triestina	AFC Venezia	AC Vicenza
Ambrosiana 'Inter'		1-0	0-0	1-0	4-0	3-0	3-1	4-1	5-1	0-1	3-1	0-2	1-0	1-0	1-4	1-2
Atalanta BC	2-5		2-0	1-0	1-0	3-1	0-2	2-0	2-0	0-2	0-0	2-1	1-0	2-2	1-2	2-2
US Bari	1-0	0-0		0-1	4-2	0-0	2-3	2-1	2-0	1-1	2-0	2-2	0-1	1-0	2-1	0-0
Bologna FC	3-1	2-0	4-0		3-1	3-1	2-2	4-0	3-3	1-2	3-0	4-2	1-2	2-2	0-2	1-2
AC Fiorentina	2-0	2-0	1-0	0-1		3-2	3-4	1-1	5-1	4-3	3-0	3-0	2-3	2-2	2-1	4-2
Genova 1893 AC	1-0	1-0	3-2	3-1	0-2		1-2	6-5	3-0	5-2	4-2	0-2	3-3	1-1	5-1	6-1
FC Juventus	4-2	5-1	5-0	3-1	5-2	3-2		2-4	4-1	3-0	1-1	1-2	2-5	6-2	5-2	2-6
SS Lazio	3-1	3-2	0-0	2-1	3-3	1-1	5-3		5-1	0-1	4-2	3-1	2-3	3-1	1-1	2-1
AC Liguria	1-1	3-0	1-0	1-7	2-2	1-2	1-0	2-0		1-2	2-2	3-0	2-3	1-1	1-0	3-1
US Livorno	4-2	1-1	1-1	1-0	4-1	3-1	0-3	4-2	3-1		3-1	2-0	0-0	0-0	2-1	2-0
AC Milano	0-3	0-1	3-1	3-2	1-3	0-0	2-0	4-1	0-0	1-1		4-1	1-0	2-0	1-2	1-1
AS Roma	1-3	2-1	1-0	1-1	1-0	2-3	1-2	1-0	5-1	1-0	1-1		0-4	1-2	2-1	1-0
AC Torino	1-3	4-2	3-0	2-1	5-0	3-1	2-0	2-2	3-0	1-2	0-1	4-0		4-1	3-1	0-0
US Triestina	0-0	0-1	1-1	0-0	3-0	0-1	1-1	0-0	3-1	1-1	0-1	2-0	2-3		1-1	2-0
AFC Venezia	0-2	1-1	0-0	1-0	2-2	4-1	1-1	2-1	1-0	0-1	1-3	0-0	0-3	1-1		0-1
AC Vicenza	2-2	2-3	1-0	0-1	3-0	0-1	0-0	1-1	1-1	1-3	1-1	1-2	0-1	2-1	2-0	

	Serie "A"	Pd	Wn	Dw	Ls	GF	GA	Pts	
1.	AC TORINO (TORINO)	30	20	4	6	68	31	44	
2.	US Livorno (Livorno)	30	18	7	5	52	34	43	
3.	FC Juventus (Torino)	30	16	5	9	75	55	37	
4.	AS Ambrosiana "Inter" (Milano)	30	15	4	11	53	38	34	
5.	Genova 1893 AC (Genova)	30	14	5	11	59	53	33	
6.	Bologna FC (Bologna)	30	12	5	13	53	39	29	
6.	AC Fiorentina (Firenze)	30	12	5	13	55	61	29	
6.	AC Milano (Milano)	30	10	9	11	39	44	29	
9.	SS Lazio (Roma)	30	10	8	12	56	59	28	
9.	Atalanta BC (Bergamo)	30	11	6	13	34	44	28	
9.	AS Roma (Roma)	30	12	4	14	36	50	28	
12.	AC Vicenza (Vicenza)	30	8	9	13	36	44	25	
13.	US Triestina (Trieste)	30	5	14	11	32	40	24	PO
14.	AFC Venezia (Venezia)	30	8	8	14	34	46	24	PO
15.	US Bari (Bari)	30	7	10	13	24	38	24	R
16.	AC Liguria (Genova)	30	7	7	16	36	66	21	R
		480	185	110	185	742	742	480	

Top goalscorers

1)	Silvio PIOLA	(SS Lazio)	21
2)	Guglielmo TREVISAN	(Genova 1893 AC)	20
3)	SENTIMENTI	(FC Juventus)	19
4)	Riza LUSHTA	(FC Juventus)	17

Relegation Play-Offs

US Bari (Bari)	1-1	AC Venezia (Venezia)
US Triestina (Trieste)	2-0	AC Venezia (Venezia)
US Triestina (Trieste)	3-2	US Bari (Bari)

2nd Relegation Play-Off

AFC Venezia (Venezia)	3-0	US Bari (Bari)

All national competitions were suspended due to World War 2 and regional competitions were played during 1943-44 with the national competitions resuming for the 1945-46 season. Upon resumption, Serie "A" was divided into 2 sections (North with 14 clubs and South with 11 clubs) and Serie "B" was divided into three groups of 12 clubs.

	Serie "B"	Pd	Wn	Dw	Ls	GF	GA	Pts	
1.	Modena FBC (Modena)	32	19	7	6	65	31	45	P
2.	AC Brescia (Brescia)	32	18	7	7	53	30	43	P
3.	AC Napoli (Napoli)	32	16	9	7	46	27	41	
4.	Pro Patria et Libertate (Busto Arsizio)	32	13	11	8	39	25	37	
4.	AC Pisa (Pisa)	32	15	7	10	45	37	37	
6.	Spezia FBC (La Spezia)	32	12	11	9	55	34	35	
7.	US Cremonese (Cremona)	32	13	6	13	38	39	32	
8.	AC Fanfulla (Lodi)	32	12	7	13	60	46	31	
8.	AS Pescara (Pescara)	32	11	9	12	44	50	31	
10.	AC Padova (Padova)	32	12	6	14	48	42	30	
10.	US Anconitana Bianchi (Ancona)	32	12	6	14	45	58	30	
12.	US Alessandria (Alessandria)	32	11	6	15	37	55	28	
12.	Mater (Roma)	32	9	10	13	40	66	28	
14.	AC Siena (Siena)	32	13	1	18	49	68	27	
15.	AC Udinese (Udine)	32	10	6	16	50	53	26	
16.	AC Novara (Novara)	32	9	7	16	35	40	25	
17.	Savona FBC (Savona)	32	7	4	21	26	74	18	
---.	US Palermo-Juventina (Palermo)	24	6	5	13	18	33	17	#
		544	212	120	212	775	775	544	

US Palermo-Juventina (Palermo) withdrew from the league after 24 games as a result of the Allied landings in Sicilia. Their record was deleted and is not included in the above totals.

The following changes took place prior to the start of the 1945-46 season:
AS Ambrosiana "Inter" (Milano) changed their name to FC Internazionale (Milano).
US Anconitana Bianchi (Ancona) reverted to US Anconitana (Ancona).
US Bari (Bari) changed their name to AS Bari (Bari).
AC Ferrara (Ferrara) reverted to S.P.A.L. (Ferrara).
Genova 1893 AC (Genova) changed their name to Genoa Cricket & FBC (Genova).
Hellas (Verona) were founded as a new club with no connection to the earlier club of the same name.
Dopolavoro Interaziendale Italo Gambacciani (Empoli) reverted to Empoli FBC (Empoli).
FC Juventus (Torino) (Federazione Calcio) changed their name to Juventus FC (Torino) (Football Club).
AC Liguria (Genova) re-formed as SG Andrea Doria (Genova) and US Sampierdarenese (Genova).
US Livorno (Livorno) changed their name to US Pro Livorno (Livorno).
AC Milano (Milano) changed their name to Milan AC (Milano).
AS Messina (Messina) (dissolved in 1943) re-formed as AS Messina (Messina).
US Palermo-Juventina (Palermo) reverted to US Palermo (Palermo).
AC Pisa (Pisa) reverted to SC Pisa (Pisa).
AFC Venezia (Venezia) (Associazione Fascista Calcio) changed their name to AC Venezia (Venezia).

The 15 clubs from the 1942-43 championship (see AC Liguria above) together with the 2 promoted clubs plus the following clubs made up the two groups of Serie "A" for the 1945-46 season:
US Anconitana (Ancona), AC Napoli (Napoli), US Palermo (Palermo), AS Pescara (Pescara), US Salernitana (Salerno) and AC Siena (Siena).

SG Andrea Doria (Genova) and SG Sampierdarenese (Genova) formed out of AC Liguria (Genova) and were both accepted into the re-formed Serie "A" championship.

Coppa Italia Final (Milano – 30/05/43)

AC TORINO (TORINO)	4-0	AFC Venezia (Venezia)
Ossola, 2, Ferraris, Mazzola	*(H.T. 1-0)*	

Torino: Bodaira, Piacentini, O.Ferrini, Gallea, Ellena, Grezar, Ossola, Loik, Gabetto, Mazzola, Ferraris.

Venezia: Eberle, Tortora, Di Gennaro, Arienti, Puppo, Stefanini, Degli Esposti, Novello, Pernigo, Petron, Alberico.

Semi-Finals

AC Torino (Torino)	3-1	AS Roma (Roma)
(the match was abandoned after 88 minutes but the result stood)		
AFC Venezia (Venezia)	3-0	Genova 1893 AC (Genova)

Quarter-Finals

Bologna FC (Bologna)	2-5	Genova 1893 AC (Genova)
SS Lazio (Roma)	1-2	AS Roma (Roma)
AC Torino (Torino)	5-0	AC Milano (Milano)
AFC Venezia (Venezia)	3-2	AC Udinese (Udine)

1945-46

1945-1946 Serie "A" Final	AS Bari	FC Internazionale	Juventus FC	Milan AC	AC Napoli	US Pro Livorno	AS Roma	AC Torino
AS Bari		1-2	0-2	0-2	2-2	0-0	1-0	1-2
FC Internazionale	0-0		1-0	0-1	2-1	6-2	1-0	6-2
Juventus FC	6-1	1-0		3-1	6-0	5-1	2-1	1-0
Milan AC	8-0	3-2	1-1		2-3	1-0	2-0	2-0
AC Napoli	4-0	0-0	1-1	1-0		3-0	2-1	0-2
US Pro Livorno	3-0	1-0	0-3	1-0	2-1		1-1	0-3
AS Roma	1-0	3-0	0-0	2-2	2-0	3-1		0-7
AC Torino	3-0	1-0	1-0	3-0	7-1	9-1	3-2	

	Serie "A" Final	Pd	Wn	Dw	Ls	GF	GA	Pts	
1.	AC TORINO (TORINO)	14	11	-	3	43	14	22	
2.	Juventus FC (Torino)	14	9	3	2	31	8	21	
3.	Milan AC (Milano)	14	7	2	5	25	16	16	
4.	FC Internazionale (Milano)	14	6	2	6	20	16	14	
5.	AC Napoli (Napoli)	14	5	3	6	19	27	13	
6.	AS Roma (Roma)	14	4	3	7	16	22	11	
7.	US Pro Livorno (Livorno)	14	4	2	8	13	35	10	*
8.	AS Bari (Bari)	14	1	3	10	6	35	5	
		112	47	18	47	173	173	112	

Top goalscorers

1)	Eusebio CASTIGLIANI	(AC Torino)	13
2)	BARBIERI	(AC Napoli)	8
3)	Amadeo AMADEI	(FC Internazionale)	7
	Guglielmo GABETTO	(AC Torino)	7
5)	CANDIANI	(FC Internazionale)	6
	Silvio PIOLA	(Juventus FC)	6

1945-1946 Serie "A" North	SG Andrea Doria	Atalanta BC	Bologna FC	AC Brescia	Genoa Cricket & FBC	FC Internazionale	Juventus FC	Milan AC	Modena FBC	US Sampierdarenese	AC Torino	US Triestina	AC Venezia	AC Vicenza
SG Andrea Doria		1-0	0-0	1-1	0-1	1-1	1-1	1-2	1-1	0-1	2-3	0-0	2-0	3-2
Atalanta BC	0-3		0-1	0-0	2-2	2-1	1-1	0-2	0-1	3-0	1-0	2-1	1-0	2-2
Bologna FC	1-0	2-0		0-0	4-0	1-3	2-1	1-2	2-2	3-2	0-2	1-0	3-0	2-1
AC Brescia	2-0	1-1	2-1		3-1	1-2	2-1	2-0	1-0	1-0	1-3	1-1	3-1	4-1
Genoa Cricket & FBC	0-3	1-0	3-0	2-3		1-2	2-1	1-0	0-0	0-2	0-1	0-1	0-0	2-0
FC Internazionale	2-0	1-0	1-0	4-1	9-1		2-2	2-0	2-0	2-0	1-1	1-2	2-1	4-2
Juventus FC	6-1	2-0	1-0	3-1	4-1	0-0		2-2	1-0	6-0	2-1	1-1	5-0	2-1
Milan AC	1-2	2-1	2-2	3-1	1-0	1-3	1-1		1-0	3-0	2-3	2-0	2-1	2-4
Modena FBC	1-0	0-2	2-0	2-1	1-1	0-0	0-0	1-1		2-0	0-3	5-1	0-0	2-0
US Sampierdarenese	1-0	1-3	0-2	1-2	1-1	1-3	2-2	1-2	0-0		0-5	0-6	1-1	1-0
AC Torino	5-0	2-0	4-0	2-2	6-0	1-0	1-0	4-0	1-1	2-1		4-0	3-1	4-0
US Triestina	0-1	0-0	1-0	1-0	2-1	1-3	0-3	1-2	1-0	0-1	1-1		0-0	0-2
AC Venezia	2-2	0-0	1-2	1-2	0-0	0-1	0-2	0-0	2-3	3-1	2-1	1-1		1-0
AC Vicenza	1-0	1-0	3-0	1-0	0-0	1-0	1-2	2-2	1-0	1-1	1-2	0-1	0-1	

	Serie "A" (North)	Pd	Wn	Dw	Ls	GF	GA	Pts	
1.	AC Torino (Torino)	26	19	4	3	65	18	42	
2.	FC Internazionale (Milano)	26	17	5	4	52	21	39	
3.	Juventus FC (Torino)	26	13	9	4	52	23	35	
4.	Milan AC (Milano)	26	12	6	8	38	36	30	PO
—	—	—	—	—	—	—	—	—	—
4.	AC Brescia (Brescia)	26	12	6	8	38	33	30	PO
6.	Modena FBC (Modena)	26	8	10	8	24	22	26	
6.	Bologna FC (Bologna)	26	11	4	11	30	23	26	
8.	US Triestina (Trieste)	26	8	7	11	23	32	23	
9.	Atalanta BC (Bergamo)	26	7	7	12	21	28	21	
9.	SG Andrea Doria (Genova)	26	7	7	12	25	35	21	*
11.	AC Vicenza (Vicenza)	26	8	4	14	28	38	20	
12.	Genoa Cricket & FBC (Genova)	26	6	7	13	21	46	19	
13.	AC Venezia (Venezia)	26	4	9	13	19	37	17	
14.	US Sampierdarenese (Genova)	26	5	5	16	19	53	15	*
		364	137	90	137	455	455	364	

4th/5th Place Play-Off

Milan AC (Milan)	1-1, 2-1	AC Brescia (Brescia)

1945-1946 Serie "A" South-Centre	US Anconitana	AS Bari	AC Fiorentina	SS Lazio	AC Napoli	US Palermo	AS Pescara	US Pro Livorno	AS Roma	US Salernitana	AC Siena
US Anconitana		1-2	0-1	1-0	0-3	1-2	1-1	1-1	0-1	2-1	1-1
AS Bari	4-2		1-0	1-0	2-1	3-1	1-0	1-0	1-0	1-0	4-0
AC Fiorentina	5-0	2-0		4-3	0-1	2-0	3-1	2-1	2-0	4-0	5-0
SS Lazio	1-2	1-0	1-0		0-0	0-1	6-0	0-2	1-2	2-1	0-0
AC Napoli	2-0	2-1	1-0	0-0		2-0	1-0	1-0	1-1	1-0	6-1
US Palermo	3-0	0-2	0-0	0-1	0-0		1-0	1-0	1-3	1-0	2-2
AS Pescara	4-0	3-1	3-0	2-2	2-1	0-0		1-2	2-2	5-1	2-0
US Pro Livorno	4-0	4-1	1-1	1-0	1-0	4-2	1-0		1-1	3-0	0-0
AS Roma	3-0	1-1	1-0	0-1	0-0	2-1	0-0	2-2		4-2	1-0
US Salernitana	1-0	2-3	1-0	2-0	1-1	0-0	2-0	0-0	1-3		3-0
AC Siena	1-0	1-1	1-1	0-0	1-4	1-0	1-1	1-2	0-1	2-2	

	Serie "A" (South-Centre)	Pd	Wn	Dw	Ls	GF	GA	Pts	
1.	AC Napoli (Napoli)	20	11	6	3	28	10	28	
1.	AS Bari (Bari)	20	13	2	5	31	21	28	
3.	AS Roma (Roma)	20	10	7	3	28	17	27	
4.	US Pro Livorno (Livorno)	20	10	6	4	30	15	26	*
5.	AC Fiorentina (Firenze)	20	10	3	7	32	16	23	
6.	AS Pescara (Pescara)	20	6	6	8	27	26	18	R
7.	SS Lazio (Roma)	20	6	5	9	19	19	17	
7.	US Palermo (Palermo)	20	6	5	9	16	23	17	R
9.	US Salernitana (Salerno)	20	5	4	11	20	32	14	R
10.	AC Siena (Siena)	20	2	9	9	13	36	13	R
11.	US Anconitana (Ancona)	20	3	3	14	12	41	9	R
		220	82	56	82	256	256	220	

	Serie "B" (Final)	Pd	Wn	Dw	Ls	GF	GA	Pts	
1.	US Alessandria (Alessandria)	10	7	1	2	21	6	15	P
2.	Pro Patria et Libertate (Busto Arsizio)	10	4	3	3	10	6	11	
3.	AC Vigevano (Vigevano)	10	4	2	3	11	11	10	
4.	AC Reggiana (Reggio Emilia)	10	4	1	5	8	13	9	
5.	US Cremonese (Cremona)	10	3	2	5	7	12	8	
6.	AC Padova (Padova)	10	3	1	6	10	19	7	
		60	25	10	25	67	67	60	

	Serie "B" (Group "A")	Pd	Wn	Dw	Ls	GF	GA	Pts	
1.	US Alessandria (Alessandria)	22	13	4	5	42	19	30	
1.	AC Vigevano (Vigevano)	22	12	6	4	26	13	30	
3.	US Pro Vercelli (Vercelli)	22	11	5	6	32	23	27	
4.	Piacenza FC (Piacenza)	22	12	2	8	44	36	26	
5.	AC Novara (Novara)	22	9	6	7	23	15	24	
5.	Casale FBC (Casale Monferrato)	22	10	4	8	35	27	24	
7.	AC Biellese (Biella)	22	8	5	9	31	28	21	
7.	AC Vogherese (Voghera)	22	7	7	8	31	33	21	
9.	FS Sestrese (Sesto Fiorentino)	22	8	4	10	30	40	20	
10.	Savona FBC (Savona)	22	6	5	11	28	39	17	
11.	AC Cuneo (Cuneo)	22	4	4	14	18	43	12	R
12.	Ausonia (La Spezia)	22	3	6	13	14	38	12	
		264	103	58	103	354	354	264	

	Serie "B" (Group "B")	Pd	Wn	Dw	Ls	GF	GA	Pts	
1.	US Cremonese (Cremona)	22	12	9	1	39	11	33	
2.	Pro Patria et Libertate (Busto Arsizio)	22	10	8	4	34	21	28	
3.	AC Lecco (Lecco)	22	9	9	4	28	18	27	
4.	AC Legnano (Legnano)	22	9	8	5	36	28	26	
5.	AC Como (Como)	22	9	6	7	31	22	24	
6.	AC Crema 1908 (Crema)	22	8	7	7	32	25	23	
7.	AC Fanfulla (Lido)	22	8	5	8	28	37	21	
8.	AC Pro Sesto (Sesto San Giovanni)	22	6	7	9	20	21	19	
9.	Seregno FC (Seregno)	22	8	2	12	23	33	18	
10.	SG Gallaratese (Gallarate)	22	4	8	10	18	29	16	
10.	AC Mantova (Mantova)	22	6	4	12	22	42	16	
12.	AC Trento (Trento)	22	4	5	13	17	41	13	R
		264	93	78	93	328	328	264	

	Serie "B" (Group "C")	Pd	Wn	Dw	Ls	GF	GA	Pts	
1.	AC Padova (Padova)	22	11	7	4	35	18	29	
1.	AC Reggiana (Reggio Emilia)	22	11	7	4	32	19	29	
3.	Parma AS (Parma)	22	12	4	6	36	20	28	
3.	AC Verona (Verona)	22	11	6	5	34	22	28	
5.	Suzzara SC (Suzzara)	22	11	4	7	25	18	26	
6.	AC Treviso (Treviso)	22	9	5	8	30	28	23	
7.	AS Pro Gorizia (Gorizia)	22	7	8	7	26	24	22	
8.	AC Cesena (Cesena)	22	5	10	7	29	24	20	
8.	S.P.A.L. (Ferrara)	22	6	8	8	29	28	20	
10.	AC Udinese (Udine)	22	6	6	10	21	32	18	
11.	AC Forli (Forli)	22	4	5	13	21	48	13	
12.	Panigale (Bologna)	22	2	4	16	19	56	8	R
		264	95	74	95	337	337	264	

* SG Andrea Doria (Genova) merged with SG Sampierdarenese (Genova) to become UC Sampdoria (Genova). US Pro Livorno (Livorno) reverted to US Livorno (Livorno).

Serie "B" was extended to 3 groups of 22, 21 and 17 clubs respectively for the next season.

1946-47

1946-1947 Serie "A"	US Alessandria	Atalanta BC	AS Bari	Bologna FC	AC Brescia	AC Fiorentina	Genoa C & FBC	Internazionale	Juventus FC	SS Lazio	US Livorno	Milan AC	Modena FBC	AC Napoli	AS Roma	UC Sampdoria	AC Torino	US Triestina	AC Venezia	AC Vicenza
US Alessandria		1-1	1-0	0-1	2-2	1-1	2-2	1-0	2-0	2-1	4-1	4-1	1-3	5-0	1-0	0-1	2-0	5-0	1-1	0-2
Atalanta BC	1-0		3-0	2-1	2-0	1-1	1-0	0-3	1-3	1-1	3-1	1-3	1-1	2-1	0-0	1-1	0-3	1-1	3-2	1-1
AS Bari	2-2	2-0		1-0	0-0	1-0	2-0	1-2	0-1	1-3	2-1	0-3	0-0	1-0	2-0	2-1	0-0	2-0	1-0	1-0
Bologna FC	4-1	2-0	2-1		0-2	1-1	0-0	2-0	0-0	3-1	1-0	1-2	1-0	3-0	0-2	2-0	1-1	1-0	4-0	0-0
AC Brescia	0-3	4-1	0-0	0-1		1-0	5-1	2-2	1-1	2-0	0-1	1-1	0-1	2-1	3-0	2-1	0-1	2-2	0-2	0-2
AC Fiorentina	2-0	1-0	2-0	0-0	3-1		2-2	3-3	2-1	4-1	2-2	0-3	1-2	1-0	3-3	2-1	0-4	2-1	1-1	4-1
Genoa C & FBC	3-1	2-2	1-0	3-0	4-0	5-0		0-0	1-0	3-0	0-0	0-2	1-1	2-1	3-0	2-3	2-3	3-1	2-1	2-0
Internazionale	4-2	0-1	3-1	1-1	1-1	4-0	2-1		0-0	3-0	1-1	1-2	1-0	2-3	0-0	2-1	1-3	5-2	3-1	1-2
Juventus FC	3-1	4-1	6-0	2-0	1-0	3-1	2-1	4-1		3-3	2-1	1-2	1-0	1-0	4-0	2-1	0-1	4-0	7-3	1-2
SS Lazio	3-1	0-0	0-1	3-1	6-3	3-0	1-1	0-1	1-2		3-0	1-1	1-2	2-1	0-0	4-0	1-2	3-0	3-1	1-1
US Livorno	4-2	0-0	0-0	1-1	2-2	2-1	1-1	3-1	2-2	1-1		2-2	0-1	2-2	4-1	0-0	0-2	3-0	0-0	3-0
Milan AC	4-0	0-0	0-2	4-2	2-1	2-2	4-1	3-1	3-3	0-0	2-2		1-1	4-2	3-1	1-0	1-2	3-0	3-2	2-3
Modena FBC	0-0	0-0	0-1	1-0	1-1	3-0	2-1	1-0	1-0	2-1	1-0	2-1		6-1	1-0	1-0	2-4	0-1	2-0	1-0
AC Napoli	2-1	3-1	5-1	2-0	2-1	1-1	2-1	1-0	3-3	0-0	4-0	0-0	1-0		0-3	1-0	2-2	2-0	1-1	2-2
AS Roma	0-2	3-0	2-0	1-1	2-1	2-0	0-1	2-1	1-5	3-0	0-1	1-1	0-0	0-0		3-1	1-3	4-1	1-2	0-0
UC Sampdoria	1-1	1-1	6-1	0-1	2-2	1-0	3-0	1-5	0-3	1-1	2-1	2-1	0-2	0-1	4-0		3-1	4-1	3-1	2-1
AC Torino	4-1	5-3	2-1	4-0	4-0	7-2	6-0	5-2	0-0	5-1	3-2	6-2	1-1	2-1	4-0	1-1		1-1	2-0	6-0
US Triestina	1-3	1-3	0-1	3-1	0-1	1-1	0-0	0-0	1-5	2-2	0-3	1-2	0-1	3-0	0-2	1-1	0-1		2-0	2-0
AC Venezia	1-1	0-0	1-2	2-0	1-2	3-0	2-1	2-1	0-2	1-2	1-0	1-1	2-1	0-1	2-3	0-2	1-0	4-1		1-2
AC Vicenza	4-2	0-1	1-0	0-3	2-0	1-0	1-0	1-1	1-1	1-2	5-2	2-3	0-1	4-1	2-0	1-5	0-3	3-2	5-0	

	Serie "A"	Pd	Wn	Dw	Ls	GF	GA	Pts	
1.	AC TORINO (TORINO)	38	28	7	3	104	35	63	
2.	Juventus FC (Torino)	38	22	9	7	83	38	53	
3.	Modena FBC (Modena)	38	21	9	8	45	24	51	
4.	Milan AC (Milano)	38	19	12	7	75	52	50	
5.	Bologna FC (Bologna)	38	15	9	14	42	41	39	
5.	AC Vicenza (Vicenza)	38	16	7	15	53	57	39	
7.	AS Bari (Bari)	38	16	6	16	33	48	38	
8.	AC Napoli (Napoli)	38	14	9	15	50	59	37	
8.	Atalanta BC (Bergamo)	38	11	15	12	40	52	37	
10.	FC Internazionale (Milano)	38	13	10	15	59	54	36	
10.	UC Sampdoria (Genova)	38	14	8	16	56	52	36	
10.	Genoa Cricket & FBC (Genova)	38	13	10	15	53	53	36	
10.	SS Lazio (Roma)	38	12	12	14	56	56	36	
14.	US Alessandria (Alessandria)	38	13	9	16	59	60	35	
15.	US Livorno (Livorno)	38	9	15	14	49	55	33	
15.	AS Roma (Roma)	38	12	9	17	41	56	33	
17.	AC Fiorentina (Firenze)	38	10	12	16	46	69	32	
18.	AC Brescia (Brescia)	38	10	11	17	45	58	31	R
19.	AC Venezia (Venezia)	38	10	7	21	43	66	27	R
20.	US Triestina (Trieste)	38	5	8	25	32	79	18	*
		760	283	194	283	1064	1064	760	

Top goalscorers

1)	Valentino MAZZOLA	(AC Torino)	29
2)	Ettore PURICELLI	(Milan AC)	21
3)	Riccardo CARAPELLESE	(Milan AC)	20
4)	Guglielmo GABETTO	(AC Torino)	19
5)	Giuseppe BALDINI	(UC Sampdoria)	18

At a meeting held in Perugia, the F.I.G.C. decided that US Triestina (Trieste) should retain Serie "A" status in consideration of their "previous contributions to football" and in recognition of their difficult political situation. At the time Trieste was in Zone "A" of the "Free Territories" administered by the joint Anglo-American forces.

	Serie "B" (Group "A")	Pd	Wn	Dw	Ls	GF	GA	Pts	
1.	Pro Patria et Libertate (Busto Arsizio)	42	27	6	9	84	39	60	P
2.	AC Legnano (Legnano)	42	21	11	10	67	42	53	
3.	AC Novara (Novara)	42	18	12	12	47	34	48	
3.	Seregno FC (Seregno)	42	18	12	12	69	52	48	
3.	Spezia FC (La Spezia)	42	18	12	12	62	47	48	
3.	US Pistoiese (Pistoia)	42	21	6	15	86	70	48	
7.	AC Vigevano (Vigevano)	42	18	10	14	59	57	46	
8.	AC Como (Como)	42	16	10	16	61	59	42	
8.	US Pro Vercelli (Vercelli)	42	14	14	14	54	52	42	
8.	SG Gallaratese (Gallaratese)	42	13	16	13	31	40	42	
11.	AC Fanfulla (Lodi)	42	16	9	17	66	60	41	
11.	AC Crema 1908(Crema)	42	17	7	18	60	57	41	
11.	SU Carrarese (Carra)	42	15	11	16	51	53	41	
11.	AC Pro Sesto (Sesto San Giovanni)	42	17	7	18	49	56	41	
15.	ASC Viareggio (Viareggio)	42	16	8	18	72	70	40	
15.	FC Varese (Varese)	42	17	6	19	61	62	40	
17.	AC Vogherese (Voghera)	42	16	7	19	54	75	39	
17.	AC Biellese (Biella)	42	14	11	17	63	69	39	R
19.	FS Sestrese (Sesto Fiorentino)	42	12	13	17	61	69	37	R
20.	AC Lecco (Lecco)	42	12	10	20	50	67	34	R
21.	Savona FC (Savona)	42	13	6	23	49	78	32	R
22.	Casale FBC (Casale Monferrato)	42	7	8	27	47	95	22	R
		924	356	212	356	1303	1303	924	

Relegation Play-Off

AC Vogherese (Voghera)	3-1	AC Biellese (Biella)

	Serie "B" (Group "B")	Pd	Wn	Dw	Ls	GF	GA	Pts	
1.	US Lucchese Libertas (Lucca)	40	24	6	10	78	45	54	P
2.	AC Padova (Padova)	40	20	9	11	53	36	49	
3.	Empoli FBC (Empoli)	40	18	11	11	54	38	47	
4.	AC Treviso (Treviso)	40	19	8	13	56	41	46	
5.	AC Siena (Siena)	40	17	11	12	47	45	45	
6.	S.P.A.L. (Ferrara)	40	15	13	12	53	33	43	
6.	US Cremonese (Cremona)	40	17	9	14	65	47	43	
8.	AC Verona (Verona)	40	15	12	13	59	48	42	
8.	AC Mantova (Mantova)	40	16	10	14	48	51	42	
10.	Suzzara SC (Suzzara)	40	12	17	11	38	58	41	
11.	AC Udinese (Udine)	40	14	12	14	47	42	40	
12.	Piacenza FC (Piacenza)	40	15	9	16	37	44	39	*
12.	AC Reggiana (Reggio Emilia)	40	12	15	13	38	48	39	
14.	Parma AS (Parma)	40	14	10	16	41	45	38	
15.	AC Prato (Prato)	40	14	9	17	46	50	37	
16.	SC Pisa (Pisa)	40	12	12	16	38	44	36	
16.	US Anconitana (Ancona)	40	13	10	17	43	51	36	
18.	AC Mestrina (Mestre)	40	12	9	19	40	56	33	R
19.	AC Forli (Forli)	40	10	11	19	38	56	31	R
20.	AS Pro Gorizia (Gorizia)	40	9	12	19	38	57	30	
21.	AC Cesena (Cesena)	40	10	9	21	36	58	29	R
		840	308	224	308	993	993	840	

Relegation Play-Off

SC Pisa (Pisa) 2-1 US Anconitana (Ancona)

	Serie "B" (Group "C")	Pd	Wn	Dw	Ls	GF	GA	Pts	
1.	US Salernitana (Salerno)	32	16	12	4	59	23	44	P
2.	AC Ternana (Terni)	32	18	5	9	47	44	41	
3.	AS Pescara (Pescara)	32	15	7	10	61	35	37	
4.	US Lecce (Lecce)	32	15	5	12	56	33	35	
4.	Scafatese Calcio (Scafati)	32	14	7	11	34	36	35	
6.	Torrese	32	12	8	12	46	50	32	
6.	SC Rieti (Rieti)	32	13	6	13	36	41	32	
8.	US Palermo (Palermo)	32	11	9	12	36	35	31	
8.	Brindisi Sport (Brindisi)	32	10	11	11	34	42	31	
8.	Arsenal SC (Taranto)	32	11	9	12	38	49	31	
11.	AC Perugia (Perugia)	32	10	10	12	32	42	30	
12.	AS Cosenza (Cosenza)	32	7	15	10	39	33	29	
12.	AC Siracusa (Siracusa)	32	12	5	15	37	49	29	
14.	Alba Trastevere (Roma)	32	11	6	15	43	57	28	R
15.	AS Taranto (Taranto)	32	10	7	15	34	44	27	R
16.	US Catanzaro (Catanzaro)	32	11	4	17	37	36	26	R
16.	US Foggia (Foggia)	32	10	6	16	33	53	26	R
		544	206	132	206	702	702	544	

* Piacenza FC (Piacenza) changed their name to Piacenza Calcio (Piacenza) for the next season.

Promoted to Serie "B": AC Bolzano (Bolzano), US Cagliari (Cagliari), Centese Calcio (Cento), Gubbio Calcio (Gubbio), Magenta (Magenta) and Vita Nova (Ponte San Pietro).

Serie "B" was reduced to three groups of 18 clubs for the next season.

1947-1948 Serie "A"	US Alessandria	Atalanta BC	AS Bari	Bologna FC	AC Fiorentina	Genoa C & FBC	FC Internazion.	Juventus FC	SS Lazio	US Livorno	Lucchese Lib.	Milan AC	Modena FBC	AC Napoli	Pro Patria et Lib.	AS Roma	US Salernitana	UC Sampdoria	AC Torino	US Triestina	AC Vicenza
US Alessandria		0-1	1-0	0-2	1-0	0-0	1-0	1-3	2-2	1-0	4-2	2-2	0-0	2-2	2-5	4-0	3-0	1-1	2-2	1-1	4-0
Atalanta BC	0-0		3-1	1-0	1-0	2-1	1-1	0-0	5-0	3-1	5-0	1-0	2-1	2-1	2-2	1-1	0-0	2-0	1-0	3-1	2-0
AS Bari	1-0	3-0		1-1	1-0	0-2	2-1	2-1	2-1	3-0	1-0	1-0	1-1	2-1	1-3	2-1	0-0	0-2	1-0	0-0	1-0
Bologna FC	3-2	3-1	0-0		1-0	4-2	1-0	1-1	0-0	4-1	2-2	1-0	3-3	0-1	2-2	2-2	4-0	1-0	1-0	0-0	2-1
AC Fiorentina	2-1	2-0	2-0	1-1		4-0	1-0	2-4	4-1	1-1	2-0	2-1	4-2	1-0	1-0	1-0	1-0	4-3	1-2	2-1	1-2
Genoa C & FBC	3-0	1-1	2-2	7-2	1-2		2-1	2-3	3-1	0-0	1-1	3-1	2-0	3-2	4-1	2-4	3-1	2-1	1-2	2-1	4-0
FC Internazionale	6-0	0-3	4-1	2-1	4-1	1-0		4-2	1-1	1-0	6-0	0-2	1-1	1-0	4-0	3-2	2-1	2-4	0-1	1-1	2-0
Juventus FC	6-1	1-0	6-0	0-1	3-0	2-1	2-0		1-1	6-1	1-1	2-1	0-1	1-3	0-4	3-0	2-0	4-1	1-1	0-1	6-0
SS Lazio	1-0	1-1	3-3	2-1	5-0	3-0	1-0	0-0		4-1	1-0	1-2	1-0	0-0	1-0	0-1	3-1	3-3	0-0	3-1	2-1
US Livorno	1-0	2-0	1-1	2-0	2-2	1-1	3-2	0-0	0-0		2-0	1-1	1-1	1-0	2-2	2-1	3-0	1-1	1-3	2-1	2-0
Lucchese Libertas	2-1	1-1	1-0	1-0	1-0	0-3	1-1	2-2	2-1	2-2		0-0	2-0	2-1	2-0	2-2	1-0	2-1	2-2	1-1	1-1
Milan AC	1-3	1-0	8-1	2-1	2-1	2-0	3-2	5-0	5-2	2-0	1-2		2-1	3-0	4-2	2-2	2-0	1-0	3-2	1-1	3-2
Modena FBC	1-0	2-0	2-0	1-1	1-1	3-2	2-0	0-1	2-0	3-0	3-0	1-0		1-0	1-0	3-0	1-0	1-1	0-3	0-0	2-0
AC Napoli	1-2	1-1	1-0	1-1	3-0	3-0	3-0	0-0	0-0	3-0	5-0	0-2	5-1		1-0	1-2	0-0	3-1	0-0	1-0	1-1
Pro Patria et Libertate	3-2	2-0	2-0	1-0	1-0	3-2	2-0	2-3	1-1	2-0	5-1	2-3	0-1	3-1		2-2	1-0	1-0	0-2	3-1	2-0
AS Roma	4-1	4-1	0-0	0-2	0-1	3-0	2-3	2-3	0-2	1-0	4-2	1-4	0-0	1-0	1-1		1-0	2-0	1-7	1-3	2-0
US Salernitana	1-0	0-0	1-0	2-0	2-0	4-1	1-0	0-0	2-0	2-4	5-2	4-3	1-0	3-3	5-0	0-1		2-1	1-4	2-2	1-0
UC Sampdoria	4-0	1-0	0-1	2-0	0-0	1-1	1-4	5-2	2-1	1-1	4-1	0-0	0-0	2-1	5-3	2-1	6-3		0-1	2-2	6-1
AC Torino	10-0	4-0	5-1	5-1	5-0	2-1	5-0	1-1	4-3	5-2	6-0	2-1	5-2	4-0	4-1	4-1	7-1	3-2		6-0	2-0
US Triestina	2-1	1-1	1-1	1-0	1-0	1-0	4-3	1-0	2-1	1-1	4-1	2-0	1-0	1-0	4-1	2-0	0-0	2-0	0-0		1-0
AC Vicenza	0-3	1-0	3-1	2-1	1-2	0-3	1-4	0-1	2-1	1-0	1-3	0-0	0-0	2-1	1-0	1-1	2-0	3-2	0-4	1-1	

	Serie "A"	Pd	Wn	Dw	Ls	GF	GA	Pts	
1.	AC TORINO (TORINO)	40	29	7	4	125	33	65	
2.	Milan AC (Milano)	40	21	7	12	76	48	49	
2.	Juventus FC (Torino)	40	19	11	10	74	48	49	
2.	US Triestina (Trieste)	40	17	15	8	51	42	49	
5.	Atalanta BC (Bergamo)	40	16	12	12	48	41	44	
5.	Modena FBC (Modena)	40	16	12	12	45	40	44	
7.	AC Fiorentina (Firenze)	40	18	5	17	49	55	41	
8.	Pro Patria et Libertate (Busto Arsizio)	40	17	6	17	65	66	40	
8.	Bologna FC (Bologna)	40	14	12	14	51	52	40	
10.	SS Lazio (Roma)	40	13	13	14	54	55	39	
11.	AS Bari (Bari)	40	14	10	16	38	60	38	
12.	FC Internazionale (Milano)	40	16	5	19	67	60	37	
12.	Genoa Cricket & FBC (Genova)	40	15	7	18	68	65	37	
14.	UC Sampdoria (Genova)	40	13	10	17	68	63	36	
14.	US Livorno (Livorno)	40	11	14	15	45	62	36	
14.	US Lucchese Libertas (Lucca)	40	12	12	16	46	82	36	
17.	AS Roma (Roma)	40	13	9	18	54	69	35	
18	US Salernitana (Salerno)	40	13	8	19	46	63	34	R
19.	US Alessandria (Alessandria)	40	11	9	20	49	75	31	R
20.	AC Vicenza (Vicenza)	40	10	6	24	31	75	26	R
21.	AC Napoli (Napoli)	40	12	10	18	50	46	34	R#
		840	320	200	320	1200	1200	840	

Top goalscorers

1)	Giampiero BONIPERTI	(Juventus FC)	27
2)	Valentino MAZZOLA	(AC Torino)	25
3)	Guglielmo GABETTO	(AC Torino)	23
4)	Adriano BASSETTO	(UC Sampdoria)	21

AC Napoli (Napoli) were placed bottom of the table and relegated after an inquiry by the F.I.G.C. found the club guilty of "buying" the 1-0 away win over Bologna FC.

	Serie "B" (Group "A")	Pd	Wn	Dw	Ls	GF	GA	Pts	
1.	AC Novara (Novara)	34	19	8	7	54	26	46	P
2.	AC Brescia (Brescia)	34	15	12	7	42	26	42	
3.	AC Como (Como)	34	14	13	7	49	36	41	
4.	AC Legnano (Legnano)	34	17	6	11	62	45	40	
4.	Seregno FC (Seregno)	34	15	10	9	52	36	40	
4.	Spezia FC (La Spezia)	34	17	6	11	46	35	40	
7.	AC Pro Sesto (Sesto San Giovanni)	34	14	11	9	45	33	39	PO
7.	AC Crema 1908 (Crema)	34	14	11	9	44	34	39	R
9.	AC Vigevano (Vigevano)	34	15	7	12	45	36	37	R
10.	SG Gallatarese (Gallarate)	34	15	6	13	45	33	36	R
11.	AC Fanfulla (Lido)	34	14	7	13	48	46	35	R
11.	ASC Viareggio (Viareggio)	34	16	3	15	51	58	35	R
13.	US Pro Vercelli (Vercelli)	34	11	9	14	46	44	31	R
14.	FC Varese (Varese)	34	9	9	16	35	42	26	R-1
15.	Vita Nova (Ponte San Pietro)	34	10	5	19	42	69	25	R
16.	Magenta (Magenta)	34	9	4	21	31	54	22	R
17.	AC Vogherese (Voghera)	34	6	7	21	36	73	19	R
18.	US Cagliari (Cagliari)	34	7	4	23	32	79	18	R
		612	237	138	237	805	805	611	

Relegation Play-Off

AC Pro Sesto (Sesto San Giovanni)	2-1	AC Crema 1908 (Crema)

	Serie "B" (Group "B")	Pd	Wn	Dw	Ls	GF	GA	Pts	
1.	AC Padova (Padova)	34	21	9	4	71	29	51	P
2.	AC Verona (Verona)	34	18	10	6	50	25	46	
3.	S.P.A.L. (Ferrara)	34	18	7	9	56	32	43	
4.	AC Venezia (Venezia)	34	16	8	10	48	36	40	
5.	AC Reggiana (Reggio Emilia)	34	13	13	8	52	37	39	
6.	US Cremonese (Cremona)	34	15	8	11	52	28	38	
7.	Parma AS (Parma)	34	12	14	8	33	28	38	
7.	AC Prato (Prato)	34	14	10	101	49	41	38	R
9.	Piacenza Calcio (Piacenza)	34	15	6	13	47	55	36	R
9.	AC Mantova (Mantova)	34	13	10	11	46	40	36	R
11.	AC Udinese (Udine)	34	13	8	13	47	42	34	R
12.	AC Bolzano (Bolzano)	34	10	11	13	38	51	31	R
13.	AC Treviso (Treviso)	34	8	14	12	36	47	30	R
14.	US Pistoiese (Pistoia)	34	8	11	15	36	55	27	R
15.	AS Pro Gorizia (Gorizia)	34	8	7	19	38	64	23	R
16.	SU Carrarese (Carra)	34	6	10	18	32	65	22	R
17.	Suzzara SC (Suzzara)	34	7	6	21	29	57	20	R
17.	Centese Calcio (Cento)	34	5	10	19	28	56	20	R
		612	220	172	220	788	788	612	

AC Prato (Prato) were relegated after losing play-offs against US Cremonese (Cremona) and Parma AS (Parma).

	Serie "B" (Group "C")	Pd	Wn	Dw	Ls	GF	GA	Pts	
1.	US Palermo (Palermo)	34	19	8	7	66	30	46	P
2.	SC Pisa (Pisa)	34	19	7	8	62	34	45	
3.	US Lecce (Lecce)	34	18	7	9	70	36	43	
3.	Arsenal SC (Taranto)	34	17	9	8	65	39	43	
5.	Empoli FBC (Empoli)	34	17	6	11	50	36	40	
5.	AC Siracusa (Siracusa)	34	16	8	10	36	33	40	
7.	AS Pescara (Pescara)	34	16	6	12	49	42	38	
8.	AC Siena (Siena)	34	13	10	11	47	34	36	R
9.	US Anconitana (Ancona)	34	16	3	15	51	52	35	R
10.	AS Cosenza (Cosenza)	34	12	9	13	38	48	33	R
11.	AC Ternana (Terni)	34	11	9	14	54	63	31	R
12.	AC Nocerina (Nocera Inferiore)	34	13	4	17	39	42	30	R
12.	Torrese	34	11	8	15	48	59	30	R
12.	Scafatese Calcio (Scafati)	34	11	8	15	30	46	30	R
15.	SC Rieti (Rieti)	34	9	8	17	44	67	26	R
16.	AC Perugia (Perugia)	34	9	7	18	38	57	25	R
17.	Gubbio Calcio (Gubbio)	34	9	5	20	38	69	22	R-1
18.	Brindisi Sport (Briindisi)	34	5	8	21	21	59	18	R
		612	241	130	241	846	846	611	

Serie "B" was reduced to one division of 22 clubs for the next season.

1948-49

1948-1949 Serie "A"	Atalanta BC	AS Bari	Bologna FC	Fiorentina	Genoa C &	Internazion.	Juventus FC	SS Lazio	US Livorno	Lucchese	Milan AC	Modena FBC	AC Novara	AC Padova	US Palermo	Pro Patria	AS Roma	Sampdoria	AC Torino	US Triestina
Atalanta BC		0-2	1-1	2-1	0-0	1-2	2-4	1-1	4-2	1-1	1-1	2-0	3-1	0-1	2-1	0-1	3-0	1-5	3-2	0-1
AS Bari	0-2		3-0	0-0	0-0	1-2	2-1	0-0	3-0	0-0	0-2	0-1	2-0	1-0	2-1	1-0	0-4	1-2	1-1	1-1
Bologna FC	1-1	1-0		0-0	2-2	1-3	3-0	2-0	6-1	4-1	3-1	2-0	3-1	0-0	1-0	2-0	1-2	1-2	2-2	1-1
AC Fiorentina	2-0	0-2	1-0		2-1	0-2	0-0	4-0	3-2	1-0	4-2	1-1	2-0	0-0	0-3	3-1	3-1	1-0	0-0	5-3
Genoa C & FBC	2-0	2-1	0-0	4-2		4-1	2-1	1-0	3-2	0-0	1-0	1-0	0-4	7-1	1-1	0-2	1-0	0-0	3-0	5-1
Internazionale	4-0	9-1	2-2	7-1	2-1		1-1	1-0	3-1	4-0	4-4	2-0	5-0	1-1	0-0	2-1	1-0	4-2	0-0	1-1
Juventus FC	1-0	1-0	2-0	3-2	2-1	0-1		4-1	2-2	2-1	1-1	0-1	4-1	6-1	3-2	4-3	0-0	5-1	1-2	2-0
SS Lazio	1-1	1-1	8-2	2-1	5-1	2-2	0-4		2-0	2-1	2-3	5-1	2-1	1-1	5-1	2-5	0-0	2-0	2-2	4-0
US Livorno	0-2	1-0	1-1	1-1	2-2	0-2	1-3	1-1		0-0	2-1	1-0	1-0	2-2	0-2	2-0	2-1	1-0	0-2	1-0
Lucchese Libertas	0-1	1-1	1-1	4-0	0-0	0-0	2-1	2-1	0-1		2-2	1-0	5-1	4-0	6-2	1-0	5-1	3-1	1-1	3-1
Milan AC	3-0	4-1	2-2	3-1	2-2	0-2	1-1	3-0	2-0	4-0		5-1	4-1	2-0	2-1	3-2	3-0	3-2	1-0	3-1
Modena FBC	2-0	0-0	0-1	1-2	2-0	2-3	2-2	2-0	0-0	4-0	0-0		1-1	0-2	4-0	1-1	2-2	2-1	0-1	0-2
AC Novara	2-0	3-1	1-1	2-0	1-2	1-1	0-0	2-2	3-1	5-2	1-2	2-1		2-1	1-0	1-1	2-1	2-3	0-2	3-0
AC Padova	3-0	1-0	2-0	2-0	0-0	1-3	3-0	2-0	2-1	0-1	1-4	0-0	3-2		3-3	1-1	2-0	1-3	4-4	0-0
US Palermo	1-2	3-0	0-0	0-2	3-0	2-1	2-0	1-0	4-2	1-3	2-1	0-0	3-0	1-0		3-1	2-1	1-1	2-2	4-0
Pro Patria et Libertate	0-0	0-1	0-3	2-4	2-1	1-1	0-1	1-2	1-0	0-2	3-2	2-0	5-0	3-0	1-0		1-1	1-4	0-1	3-1
AS Roma	1-0	0-0	1-1	1-1	1-0	1-0	0-1	1-1	4-0	3-0	1-2	2-1	4-1	0-2	3-2	3-1		2-4	1-2	4-2
UC Sampdoria	4-2	2-1	1-1	2-1	5-1	0-4	2-0	2-2	3-0	5-0	2-1	1-1	1-3	0-0	2-2	4-4	2-0		2-3	1-1
AC Torino	2-0	2-0	1-0	2-0	4-0	4-2	3-1	1-0	1-0	2-1	4-0	3-1	4-0	3-1	3-0	4-1	4-0	2-1		1-1
US Triestina	1-1	2-0	1-1	4-0	0-0	2-0	1-0	4-1	5-4	1-0	1-3	1-2	1-1	9-1	3-1	0-0	2-0	3-1	1-1	

	Serie "A"	Pd	Wn	Dw	Ls	GF	GA	Pts	
1.	AC TORINO (TORINO)	38	25	10	3	78	34	60	*
2.	FC Internazionale (Milano)	38	22	11	5	85	39	55	
3.	Milan AC (Milano)	38	21	8	9	83	52	50	
4.	Juventus FC (Torino)	38	18	8	12	64	47	44	
5.	UC Sampdoria (Genova)	38	16	9	13	74	63	41	
5.	Bologna FC (Bologna)	38	12	17	9	53	46	41	
7.	Genoa Cricket & FBC (Genova)	38	14	12	12	51	51	40	
8.	US Lucchese Libertas (Lucca)	38	14	10	14	55	55	38	
8.	US Triestina (Trieste)	38	13	12	13	59	59	38	
8.	AC Fiorentina (Firenze)	38	15	8	15	51	60	38	
11.	US Palermo (Palermo)	38	14	8	16	57	58	36	
11.	AC Padova (Padova)	38	12	12	14	45	64	36	
13.	SS Lazio (Roma)	38	11	12	15	60	62	34	
14.	AS Roma (Roma)	38	12	8	18	47	57	32	
15.	AC Novara (Novara)	38	12	7	19	52	74	31	
15.	Atalanta BC (Bergamo)	38	11	9	18	40	58	31	
17.	Pro Patria et Libertate (Busto Arsizio)	38	11	8	19	51	61	30	
17.	AS Bari (Bari)	38	10	10	18	30	50	30	
19.	Modena FBC (Modena)	38	9	11	18	36	49	29	R
20.	US Livorno (Livorno)	38	9	8	21	39	71	26	R
		760	281	198	281	1110	1110	760	

Top goalscorers

1)	Stefano NYERS	(FC Internazionale)	26
2)	Amadeo AMADEI	(FC Internazionale)	22
3)	Istvan MAYER "MIKE"	(Bologna FC)	21
4)	STRADELLA	(US Livorno)	19
5)	Riccardo CARAPELLESE	(Milan AC)	18

* AC Torino (Torino) were nominated as champions with 4 games still to play at a special meeting of the F.I.G.C. on 6th May 1949. This meeting followed a plane crash on Superga Hill near Torino in which the entire First XI of the club were killed together with the coaching staff and other management whilst returning from a friendly match in Portugal versus Sport Lisboa e Benfica (Lisboa).

The remaining 4 games of the season were played by the club's youth team against the youth teams of their opponents.

	Serie "B"	Pd	Wn	Dw	Ls	GF	GA	Pts	
1.	AC Como (Como)	42	25	10	7	83	39	60	P
2.	AC Venezia (Venezia)	42	21	10	11	69	44	52	P
3.	AC Vicenza (Vicenza)	42	21	9	12	69	48	51	
4.	US Salernitana (Salerno)	42	21	5	16	75	64	47	
5.	AC Brescia (Brescia)	42	17	11	14	61	50	45	
5.	AC Napoli (Napoli)	42	17	11	14	43	40	45	
7.	AC Pro Sesto (Sesto San Giovanni)	42	18	8	16	61	51	44	
8.	AC Legnano (Legnano)	42	17	8	17	73	66	42	
8.	SC Pisa (Pisa)	42	17	8	17	63	58	42	
10.	S.P.A.L. (Ferrara)	42	16	9	17	72	57	41	
11.	US Alessandria (Alessandria)	42	17	6	19	70	54	40	
11.	AC Verona (Verona)	42	16	8	18	62	73	40	
11.	AC Siracusa (Siracusa)	42	17	6	19	55	70	40	
11.	Arsenal SC (Taranto)	42	18	4	20	56	72	40	
11.	US Cremonese (Cremona)	42	16	8	18	60	78	40	
16.	AC Reggiana (Reggio Emilia)	42	18	3	21	56	56	39	
17.	Empoli FBC (Empoli)	42	15	8	19	53	76	38	
18.	Spezia FC (La Spezia)	42	12	13	17	49	63	37	PO
18.	Parma AS (Parma)	42	12	13	17	42	59	37	R
20.	US Lecce (Lecce)	42	14	8	20	57	68	36	R
21.	Seregno FC (Seregno)	42	11	12	19	51	72	34	R
21.	AS Pescara (Pescara)	42	11	12	19	49	71	34	R
		924	367	190	367	1329	1329	924	

Relegation Play-Off

Spezia FC (La Spezia) 4-2 Parma AS (Parma)

Promoted to Serie "B": CC Catania (Catania), AC Fanfulla (Lodi), AC Prato (Prato) and UC Udinese (Udine).

Note: AS Messina (Messina) changed their club name to AC Messina (Messina)

1949-50

1949-1950 Serie "A"	Atalanta BC	AS Bari	Bologna FC	AC Como	AC Fiorentina	Genoa C & FBC	Internazionale	Juventus FC	SS Lazio	Lucchese Libertas	Milan AC	AC Novara	AC Padova	US Palermo	Pro Patria	AS Roma	UC Sampdoria	AC Torino	US Triestina	AC Venezia
Atalanta BC		2-1	1-1	0-2	3-2	4-0	2-1	2-2	1-0	1-1	5-2	0-2	4-0	3-0	2-1	3-2	3-1	0-0	0-1	3-1
AS Bari	1-0		3-2	1-0	1-0	2-0	2-3	0-0	2-1	2-1	2-0	0-0	1-0	1-2	1-1	1-1	3-1	1-5	1-1	4-0
Bologna FC	2-6	2-0		2-2	2-1	0-0	2-3	0-4	0-0	1-1	0-1	1-1	0-0	1-1	3-1	2-1	1-0	5-2	1-1	6-1
AC Como	4-0	4-1	2-2		4-1	0-0	1-5	2-6	1-0	4-0	1-4	2-2	1-2	1-0	1-0	0-0	3-1	1-3	3-1	0-0
AC Fiorentina	2-1	3-0	3-0	0-1		3-1	4-2	0-0	2-2	2-0	1-3	5-0	3-0	0-0	4-1	4-1	4-1	4-1	2-1	5-0
Genoa C & FBC	1-0	1-0	2-2	3-1	2-0		1-1	1-2	2-1	1-1	1-0	2-0	0-1	1-0	2-1	2-1	0-1	3-2	6-2	1-0
Internazionale	3-1	4-0	2-1	1-2	4-2	4-2		2-4	2-1	6-3	6-5	1-1	1-1	1-1	2-0	3-1	2-0	2-0	6-1	7-0
Juventus FC	2-0	4-0	3-2	2-2	5-2	6-1	3-2		1-2	1-2	1-7	1-1	4-0	6-2	3-1	3-0	1-0	4-3	3-0	1-0
SS Lazio	1-1	4-2	3-2	3-2	1-1	1-0	3-2	1-3		4-2	3-2	4-0	4-0	5-0	1-0	3-1	1-0	2-2	2-0	2-0
Lucchese Libertas	4-2	3-0	1-1	3-1	1-3	2-2	0-5	1-2	2-2		0-2	2-1	6-3	2-1	1-3	3-1	3-0	2-2	7-2	2-0
Milan AC	2-1	9-1	2-0	1-1	4-1	5-0	3-1	0-1	0-0	2-0		5-0	4-2	4-1	7-1	6-2	5-1	7-0	5-2	2-0
AC Novara	5-2	0-0	1-2	1-1	3-0	2-1	0-0	2-3	0-1	5-0	1-3		1-1	2-1	3-2	0-2	1-2	5-2	1-2	5-1
AC Padova	2-0	3-1	0-0	5-2	3-4	2-2	2-2	0-2	2-1	3-2	1-2	0-1		2-1	1-1	4-1	1-2	4-1	0-1	3-0
US Palermo	3-2	2-0	2-1	3-2	0-1	3-2	4-2	0-0	2-1	1-1	0-1	3-1	3-0		0-0	3-0	2-3	2-1	0-2	1-0
Pro Patria	1-2	2-1	3-3	0-0	3-0	2-0	0-3	0-3	1-0	2-2	2-4	1-0	2-1	2-0		2-1	1-1	6-1	0-0	1-0
AS Roma	1-3	6-0	3-1	0-1	1-1	3-0	1-3	1-0	0-0	2-2	1-0	2-1	0-1	2-1	2-0		2-1	3-1	0-0	3-2
UC Sampdoria	2-2	3-0	2-1	0-1	1-1	1-1	0-2	0-4	2-5	3-1	1-3	3-0	1-1	4-0	3-3	4-1		4-0	3-1	0-0
AC Torino	3-1	1-1	3-1	4-0	2-2	2-0	1-0	1-3	2-2	3-1	3-2	5-1	2-0	5-1	1-1	5-0	4-1		3-1	3-0
US Triestina	0-1	1-0	0-0	1-1	1-1	3-0	4-2	2-3	0-0	2-0	0-0	1-0	2-2	1-0	2-2	2-2	3-2	3-0		2-0
AC Venezia	1-2	2-1	1-1	1-2	1-2	3-1	1-1	1-4	1-0	1-0	1-4	0-1	0-8	1-1	0-0	2-1	3-7	0-1	0-1	

	Serie "A"	Pd	Wn	Dw	Ls	GF	GA	Pts	
1.	JUVENTUS FC (TORINO)	38	28	6	4	100	43	62	
2.	Milan AC (Milano)	38	27	3	8	118	45	57	
3.	FC Internazionale (Milano)	38	21	7	10	99	60	49	
4.	SS Lazio (Roma)	38	18	10	10	67	43	46	
5.	AC Fiorentina (Firenze)	38	18	8	12	76	57	44	
6.	AC Torino (Torino)	38	17	7	14	80	76	41	
6.	AC Como (Como)	38	15	11	12	59	59	41	
8.	Atalanta BC (Bergamo)	38	17	6	15	66	60	40	
8.	US Triestina (Trieste)	38	14	12	12	50	59	40	
10.	AC Padova (Padova)	38	13	9	16	61	65	35	
11.	Pro Patria et Libertate (Busto Arsizio)	38	11	12	15	50	61	34	
11.	Genoa Cricket & FBC (Genova)	38	13	8	17	45	64	34	
13.	UC Sampdoria (Genova)	38	13	7	18	62	70	33	
13.	US Palermo (Palermo)	38	13	7	18	47	64	33	
15.	Bologna FC (Bologna)	38	8	16	14	54	63	32	
15.	US Lucchese Libertas (Lucca)	38	11	10	17	65	79	32	
17.	AC Novara (Novara)	38	11	9	18	51	64	31	
17.	AS Roma (Roma)	38	12	7	19	52	70	31	
19.	AS Bari (Bari)	38	11	7	20	38	74	29	R
20.	AC Venezia (Venezia)	38	5	6	27	25	89	16	R
		760	296	168	296	1265	1265	760	

Top goalscorers

1)	Gunnar NORDAHL	(Milan AC)	35
2)	Stefano NYERS	(FC Internazionale)	30
3)	John HANSEN	(Juventus FC)	28
4)	Beniamino SANTOS	(AC Torino)	27
5)	Alberto GALASSI	(AC Fiorentina)	24

	Serie "B"	Pd	Wn	Dw	Ls	GF	GA	Pts	
1.	AC Napoli (Napoli)	42	27	7	8	76	34	61	P
2.	AC Udinese (Udine)	42	26	8	8	78	39	60	P
3.	AC Legnano (Legnano)	42	25	7	10	86	52	57	
4.	S.P.A.L. (Ferrara)	42	24	7	11	95	65	55	
5.	Modena FBC (Modena)	42	22	8	12	76	43	52	
6.	AC Brescia (Brescia)	42	17	14	11	81	64	48	
6.	Spezia FC (La Spezia)	42	21	6	15	69	55	48	
8.	US Livorno (Livorno)	42	19	8	15	61	59	46	
9.	SC Pisa (Pisa)	42	13	15	14	56	50	41	
9.	AC Verona (Verona)	42	17	7	18	68	68	41	
9.	AC Siracusa (Siracusa)	42	17	7	18	68	71	41	
12.	CC Catania (Catania)	42	15	10	17	54	61	40	
13.	US Salernitana (Salerno)	42	15	9	18	58	56	39	
13.	US Cremonese (Cremona)	42	14	11	17	56	57	39	
13.	AC Vicenza (Vicenza)	42	15	9	18	63	67	39	
16.	AC Fanfulla (Lodi)	42	16	6	20	63	71	38	
17.	AC Reggiana (Reggio Emilia)	42	15	7	20	56	64	37	
18.	US Alessandria (Alessandria)	42	15	6	21	70	74	36	R
19.	Empoli FBC (Empoli)	42	14	7	21	51	69	35	R
20.	Arsenal SC (Taranto)	42	15	2	25	56	96	32	R
21.	AC Prato (Prato)	42	8	10	24	55	97	26	R
21.	AC Pro Sesto (Sesto San Giovanni)	42	6	1	35	35	119	13	R
		924	376	172	376	1431	1431	924	

Promoted to Serie "B": US Anconitana (Ancona), AC Messina (Messina), Seregno FC (Seregno) and AC Treviso (Treviso).

1950-51

1950-1951 Serie "A"	Atalanta BC	Bologna FC	AC Como	AC Fiorentina	Genoa C & FBC	Internazionale	Juventus FC	SS Lazio	Lucchese Lib.	Milan AC	AC Napoli	AC Novara	AC Padova	US Palermo	Pro Patria et Lib.	AS Roma	UC Sampdoria	AC Torino	US Triestina	AC Udinese
Atalanta BC		2-0	2-1	0-2	2-1	3-3	1-5	1-0	0-5	4-7	2-2	3-0	3-1	3-2	1-0	0-0	0-0	1-1	1-0	0-0
Bologna FC	3-2		0-2	0-1	3-3	1-1	0-5	7-2	2-0	0-0	2-0	1-0	2-2	2-0	5-2	3-1	0-0	2-1	1-0	5-2
AC Como	1-0	2-1		1-0	3-2	3-1	1-0	2-1	5-0	2-2	1-2	2-1	1-0	2-1	2-1	1-0	2-0	4-2	3-1	0-2
AC Fiorentina	1-0	2-1	3-0		1-0	1-2	1-2	1-0	3-1	1-1	2-0	2-1	4-1	1-0	3-0	1-0	3-0	3-3	3-1	1-1
Genoa C & FBC	0-2	1-2	3-2	1-1		2-2	0-3	3-0	2-1	0-3	1-2	3-0	3-1	0-0	1-0	2-2	2-3	1-0	3-2	1-1
Internazionale	3-1	3-1	4-2	2-0	5-2		3-0	0-0	2-1	0-1	4-3	5-0	5-1	3-1	6-0	6-0	5-1	3-1	2-0	6-1
Juventus FC	6-2	1-1	0-3	5-0	4-1	0-2		1-1	1-0	1-1	3-2	4-0	5-1	4-1	2-1	7-2	7-2	4-1	2-2	1-1
SS Lazio	5-0	1-0	2-0	2-1	3-1	3-3	0-3		2-0	1-1	3-1	0-0	4-0	3-3	4-2	2-1	2-2	3-0	2-0	3-2
Lucchese Libertas	2-1	0-1	5-0	0-2	0-0	3-2	0-1	1-1		1-5	1-0	2-2	3-2	0-0	0-0	1-0	4-0	2-0	2-0	0-1
Milan AC	3-3	1-2	7-2	1-0	4-0	2-3	2-0	1-2	2-0		2-1	9-2	3-1	9-0	2-0	2-0	2-0	3-0	2-0	6-2
AC Napoli	0-0	4-1	7-0	3-2	1-1	0-4	1-1	0-0	1-0	3-5		3-0	1-0	3-0	1-1	0-0	4-0	1-1	2-1	2-1
AC Novara	1-1	1-2	1-1	0-1	1-0	0-1	3-1	4-2	3-3	1-3	6-0		2-1	3-0	3-0	1-0	3-0	3-2	4-1	2-0
AC Padova	0-0	0-2	3-1	3-0	4-0	2-3	0-1	2-0	2-1	1-2	2-0	1-2		1-0	3-1	3-1	2-1	2-2	2-0	1-1
US Palermo	2-0	1-1	3-0	1-0	4-1	0-3	1-5	2-1	1-0	0-2	0-1	3-2	3-1		8-0	3-0	4-1	1-1	6-0	1-0
Pro Patria et Libertate	2-0	2-0	1-0	2-1	5-2	2-0	0-7	1-0	2-2	0-0	1-3	2-1	1-0	2-1		3-1	1-1	4-3	2-2	2-1
AS Roma	3-3	2-2	2-0	3-0	0-1	0-1	3-0	0-1	0-1	2-1	0-0	0-0	5-0	1-2	2-0		5-0	1-0	5-0	4-1
UC Sampdoria	2-1	7-2	2-1	0-0	2-1	0-4	1-1	1-1	3-1	1-2	3-1	1-1	1-2	5-1	2-0	1-0		2-1	3-1	1-1
AC Torino	1-1	1-1	2-2	1-1	2-1	2-1	1-5	0-1	2-0	0-4	0-0	2-1	2-1	2-1	1-0	0-0	3-1		1-0	3-3
US Triestina	2-1	2-1	1-0	1-1	0-0	2-1	2-2	1-3	0-0	3-4	1-1	3-0	0-0	4-2	3-1	4-2	2-1	2-0		0-0
AC Udinese	2-1	2-1	1-1	2-2	1-0	1-3	0-3	2-3	2-1	0-0	0-1	2-1	2-0	0-0	0-3	1-0	3-0	3-1	1-1	

	Serie "A"	Pd	Wn	Dw	Ls	GF	GA	Pts	
1.	MILAN AC (MILANO)	38	26	8	4	107	39	60	
2.	FC Internazionale (Milano)	38	27	5	6	107	43	59	
3.	Juventus FC (Torino)	38	23	8	7	103	44	54	
4.	SS Lazio (Roma)	38	18	10	10	64	50	46	
5.	AC Fiorentina (Firenze)	38	18	8	12	52	42	44	
6.	AC Napoli (Napoli)	38	15	11	12	57	52	41	
6.	Bologna FC (Bologna)	38	16	9	13	61	59	41	
8.	AC Como (Como)	38	18	4	16	56	66	40	
9.	AC Udinese (Udine)	38	11	13	14	46	61	35	
10.	US Palermo (Palermo)	38	14	6	18	59	67	34	
10.	Pro Patria et Libertate (Busto Arsizio)	38	14	6	18	47	74	34	
12.	AC Novara (Novara)	38	13	7	18	56	67	33	
12.	UC Sampdoria (Genova)	38	12	9	17	51	76	33	
14.	Atalanta BC (Bergamo)	38	10	12	16	48	69	32	
15.	US Lucchese Libertas (Lucca)	38	11	8	19	44	53	30	
15.	US Triestina (Trieste)	38	10	10	18	45	67	30	
15.	AC Torino (Torino)	38	9	12	17	46	69	30	
18.	AC Padova (Padova)	38	12	5	21	49	68	29	
19.	AS Roma (Roma)	38	10	8	20	48	54	28	R
20.	Genoa Cricket & FBC (Genova)	38	9	9	20	46	72	27	R
		760	296	168	296	1192	1192	760	

Top goalscorers

1)	Gunnar NORDAHL	(Milan AC)	34
2)	Stefano NYERS	(FC Internazionale)	31
3)	Karl Aage HANSEN	(Juventus FC)	24
4)	WILKES	(FC Internazionale)	23
5)	Giampiero BONIPERTI	(Juventus FC)	22

	Serie "B"	Pd	Wn	Dw	Ls	GF	GA	Pts	
1.	S.P.A.L. (Ferrara)	40	25	8	7	74	37	58	P
2.	AC Legnano (Legnano)	40	24	6	10	89	47	54	P
3.	Modena FBC (Modena)	40	17	13	10	73	49	47	
3.	US Livorno (Livorno)	40	19	9	12	67	53	47	
5.	AC Siracusa (Siracusa)	40	18	8	14	62	47	44	
6.	AC Fanfulla (Lido)	40	18	6	16	69	61	42	
6.	CC Catania (Catania)	40	17	8	15	63	63	42.	
6.	AC Venezia (Venezia)	40	15	12	13	62	65	42	
9.	AC Brescia (Brescia)	40	18	5	17	69	49	41	
9.	AC Verona (Verona)	40	16	9	15	69	58	41	
9.	AC Vicenza (Vicenza)	40	17	7	16	65	58	41	
9.	SC Pisa (Pisa)	40	16	9	15	46	50	41	
13.	AC Reggiana (Reggio Emilia)	40	15	10	15	48	53	40	
13.	US Salernitana (Salerno)	40	15	10	15	57	65	40	
15.	AC Messina (Messina)	40	16	7	17	50	48	39	
15.	AC Treviso (Treviso)	40	15	9	16	56	55	39	
17.	Spezia FC (La Spezia)	40	14	8	18	44	61	36	R
18.	AS Bari (Bari)	40	9	13	18	51	75	31	R
19.	Seregno FC (Seregno)	40	10	10	20	42	67	30	R
20.	US Cremonese (Cremona)	40	8	12	20	36	68	28	R
21.	US Anconitana (Ancona)	40	4	9	27	32	95	17	R
		840	326	188	326	1224	1224	840	

Promoted to Serie "B": AC Monza (Monza), Marzotto, US Piombinese (Piombino Dese) and Stabia.

1951-52

1951-1952 Serie "A"	Atalanta BC	Bologna FC	AC Como	AC Fiorentina	Internazionale	Juventus FC	SS Lazio	AC Legnano	Lucchese Lib.	Milan AC	AC Napoli	AC Novara	AC Padova	US Palermo	Pro Patria et Lib.	UC Sampdoria	SPAL Ferrara	AC Torino	US Triestina	AC Udinese
Atalanta BC		1-2	1-0	1-0	0-2	0-1	0-2	2-0	1-2	1-0	2-4	2-0	1-1	2-2	1-1	2-1	1-0	5-0	7-1	3-0
Bologna FC	1-0		4-2	0-3	3-4	2-3	2-4	1-0	2-1	0-0	1-4	4-1	2-1	0-0	1-1	0-0	1-1	0-0	2-1	2-0
AC Como	2-1	1-0		0-2	2-1	2-0	2-2	3-0	1-1	1-2	2-4	2-2	3-2	4-0	0-1	2-1	1-3	1-0	2-0	5-0
AC Fiorentina	0-1	1-0	5-0		5-0	0-2	0-0	1-0	1-0	1-0	2-1	1-1	3-1	2-1	3-0	0-1	0-0	1-0	2-1	3-3
Internazionale	4-0	2-2	5-1	0-0		3-2	1-1	3-1	4-3	2-2	3-0	3-1	4-0	5-0	3-0	0-1	1-0	2-0	5-1	1-1
Juventus FC	7-1	1-1	0-0	4-0	3-2		5-3	6-1	2-0	3-1	1-1	3-1	3-0	4-0	5-1	2-1	1-1	6-0	2-1	5-1
SS Lazio	1-2	1-0	1-2	1-0	1-2	2-0		2-0	3-0	1-1	1-0	1-0	5-0	1-1	2-1	0-0	4-1	3-0	4-1	3-1
AC Legnano	2-2	0-2	1-2	1-0	0-4	0-3	1-1		0-2	2-1	2-4	2-3	2-2	2-2	1-2	1-2	3-3	2-2	1-3	0-0
Lucchese Libertas	2-0	0-0	1-2	0-0	1-0	0-0	4-0	4-2		0-5	0-0	1-1	0-1	1-0	2-0	1-1	2-0	3-0	1-2	1-1
Milan AC	4-4	4-0	2-0	3-1	2-1	1-1	1-1	4-1	4-0		3-2	6-2	3-0	4-0	5-1	2-1	1-1	4-1	2-0	0-0
AC Napoli	3-1	1-1	7-1	2-1	1-0	1-2	2-1	2-3	2-0	0-2		0-1	2-0	1-2	4-1	1-0	2-1	4-0	0-0	1-2
AC Novara	2-0	1-0	3-2	4-3	2-4	1-4	2-2	4-1	1-0	1-2	1-0		2-1	1-1	3-0	2-1	2-2	2-1	5-0	4-1
AC Padova	1-1	2-1	0-2	1-1	1-5	1-2	2-1	2-1	0-1	5-2	0-1	0-0		3-2	1-0	2-1	2-4	3-0	0-0	2-1
US Palermo	0-1	1-1	4-1	2-0	1-1	0-0	0-0	2-0	3-1	1-1	1-1	3-1	4-1		1-2	0-0	3-0	0-2	1-0	2-1
Pro Patria et Libertate	1-1	2-0	1-0	1-1	5-1	1-3	4-2	1-1	2-1	2-2	1-1	1-0	2-2	0-0		3-2	2-2	1-1	2-2	1-0
UC Sampdoria	3-2	2-1	3-1	1-1	1-3	2-1	4-0	3-0	1-1	1-1	2-1	3-1	1-1	1-1	1-0		0-1	1-0	3-1	1-0
SPAL Ferrara	2-1	2-1	1-0	1-2	1-1	0-1	4-0	3-1	1-0	1-2	2-1	2-1	1-1	3-0	2-2	0-1		1-1	1-1	2-3
AC Torino	1-1	3-2	4-0	2-0	1-0	0-0	1-1	0-1	1-1	0-6	0-2	0-1	4-1	2-0	2-0	2-0	1-0		5-2	0-0
US Triestina	3-1	4-1	2-0	2-3	1-3	0-3	1-1	1-1	3-1	1-1	0-0	2-2	2-1	2-0	3-0	1-0	2-1	0-1		0-0
AC Udinese	3-1	0-2	3-1	0-3	2-1	2-7	1-1	2-1	2-0	1-1	1-1	1-0	3-1	0-3	0-1	2-0	1-1	1-1	3-0	

	Serie "A"	Pd	Wn	Dw	Ls	GF	GA	Pts	
1.	JUVENTUS FC (TORINO)	38	26	8	4	98	34	60	
2.	Milan AC (Milano)	38	20	13	5	87	41	53	
3.	FC Internazionale (Milano)	38	21	7	10	86	49	49	
4.	AC Fiorentina (Firenze)	38	17	9	12	52	38	43	
4.	SS Lazio (Roma)	38	15	13	10	60	49	43	
6.	AC Napoli (Napoli)	38	17	8	13	64	44	42	
7.	UC Sampdoria (Genova)	38	16	9	13	48	40	41	
8.	AC Novara (Novara)	38	16	8	14	62	62	40	
9.	S.P.A.L. (Ferrara)	38	12	13	13	52	50	37	
9.	Pro Patria et Libertate (Busto Arsizio)	38	12	13	13	47	62	37	
11.	US Palermo (Palermo)	38	11	14	13	43	51	36	
12.	Atalanta BC (Bergamo)	38	13	8	17	54	61	34	
12.	AC Como (Como)	38	15	4	19	53	70	34	
12.	AC Udinese (Udine)	38	11	12	15	43	62	34	
12.	AC Torino (Torino)	38	12	10	16	39	58	34	
16.	Bologna FC (Bologna)	38	11	11	16	45	55	33	
17.	US Triestina (Trieste)	38	11	10	17	47	68	32	PO
17.	US Lucchese Libertas (Lucca)	38	11	10	17	39	49	32	R
19.	AC Padova (Padova)	38	10	9	19	45	73	29	R
20.	AC Legnano (Legnano)	38	4	9	25	37	85	17	R
		760	281	198	281	1101	1101	760	

Top goalscorers

1)	John HANSEN	(Juventus FC)	30
2)	Gunnar NORDAHL	(Milan AC)	26
3)	Stefano NYERS	(FC Internazionale)	23
4)	Renzo BURINI	(Milan AC)	22
	Hasse JEPPSON	(Atalanta BC)	22

Relegation Play-Off

US Triestina (Trieste) 3-3, 1-0 US Lucchese Libertas (Lucca)

Promotion/Relegation Play-Off

US Triestina (Trieste) 1-0 AC Brescia (Brescia)

(Triestina retained their Serie "A" status)

Serie "A" and Serie "B" were both reduced to 18 clubs for the next season.

	Serie "B"	Pd	Wn	Dw	Ls	GF	GA	Pts	
1.	AS Roma (Roma)	38	22	9	7	62	24	53	P
2.	AC Brescia (Brescia)	38	18	16	4	44	24	52	PO
3.	AC Messina (Messina)	38	16	13	9	37	23	45	
4.	CC Catania (Catania)	38	17	10	11	48	39	44	
5.	Genoa Cricket & FBC (Genova)	38	17	8	13	61	38	42	
6.	US Piombinese (Piombino Dese)	38	15	11	12	48	39	41	
6.	AC Treviso (Treviso)	38	14	13	11	44	38	41	
8.	Modena FBC (Modena)	38	12	15	11	51	46	39	
8.	US Salernitana (Salerno)	38	13	13	12	44	43	39	
10.	AC Vicenza (Vicenza)	38	13	12	13	47	40	38	
10.	AC Verona (Verona)	38	14	10	14	46	44	38	
12.	AC Fanfulla (Lido)	38	13	11	14	45	39	37	
12.	AC Siracusa (Siracusa)	38	14	9	15	39	56	37	
14.	Marzotto	38	12	12	14	48	47	36	
14.	AC Monza (Monza)	38	11	14	13	30	43	36	
16.	AC Venezia (Venezia)	38	10	14	14	38	47	34	R
16.	US Livorno (Livorno)	38	12	10	16	33	43	34	R
18.	SC Pisa (Pisa)	38	10	11	17	32	46	31	R
19.	AC Reggiana (Reggio Emilia)	38	8	8	22	38	70	24	R
20.	Stabia	38	5	9	24	35	81	18	R-1
		760	266	228	266	870	870	759	

Promoted to Serie "B": US Cagliari (Cagliari)

Note: AS Bari (Bari) changed their club name to FC Bari (Bari) for the next season.

1952-53

1952-1953 Serie "A"	Atalanta BC	Bologna FC	AC Como	AC Fiorentina	FC Internazionale	Juventus FC	SS Lazio	Milan AC	AC Napoli	AC Novara	US Palermo	Pro Patria et Libertate	AS Roma	UC Sampdoria	SPAL Ferrara	AC Torino	US Triestina	AC Udinese
Atalanta BC		2-0	1-1	1-2	0-1	1-5	0-0	1-1	1-1	1-0	0-0	3-2	1-5	4-0	0-1	1-3	5-2	5-0
Bologna FC	3-1		1-0	2-1	2-0	1-0	1-1	2-0	1-3	1-0	5-2	4-1	0-1	2-0	2-1	2-2	0-1	3-1
AC Como	2-1	1-0		2-1	0-1	0-1	0-1	3-1	2-1	0-0	3-1	4-1	2-1	1-0	1-0	0-1	2-0	0-0
AC Fiorentina	1-1	1-1	2-0		1-0	1-2	0-0	0-3	2-1	1-0	0-2	2-2	2-0	2-2	1-1	0-2	2-0	1-0
FC Internazionale	1-0	2-1	3-1	3-0		2-0	1-1	0-0	5-1	0-1	3-0	2-1	1-0	2-1	1-1	1-3	1-0	0-0
Juventus FC	1-1	1-2	2-1	8-0	2-1		5-0	0-3	1-1	1-1	2-1	2-0	3-2	3-0	2-2	4-1	3-2	4-0
SS Lazio	0-2	1-2	2-0	0-1	1-1	0-1		0-0	2-1	1-3	2-0	3-1	1-0	0-1	3-1	2-1	4-1	1-2
Milan AC	5-1	1-1	4-2	2-1	0-1	1-2	3-1		2-2	2-0	5-0	4-0	4-1	2-1	1-0	5-1	4-1	0-0
AC Napoli	2-0	4-1	1-0	0-0	0-1	3-2	3-0	4-2		2-3	0-0	1-0	0-0	2-1	1-0	3-0	1-1	4-2
AC Novara	1-1	2-2	2-1	1-2	1-2	0-6	2-2	2-1	0-1		3-4	2-2	3-1	2-0	0-0	2-0	1-0	3-1
US Palermo	4-2	4-1	2-0	0-0	0-3	1-1	3-1	0-1	0-0	2-1		2-0	1-1	3-0	2-2	1-1	0-0	3-2
Pro Patria et Libertate	0-3	3-0	2-0	0-0	2-2	3-3	1-0	0-1	1-1	2-3	2-1		0-1	0-1	2-0	3-0	3-2	2-3
AS Roma	2-2	2-1	3-0	1-0	1-3	3-0	0-2	2-1	5-2	4-1	1-0	0-0		0-0	0-0	2-1	2-2	2-2
UC Sampdoria	0-0	1-1	1-1	4-0	2-0	1-1	1-2	2-1	0-0	1-1	4-1	1-0	2-2		2-2	1-0	3-1	1-1
SPAL Ferrara	2-2	1-4	0-0	1-1	0-1	2-2	1-0	1-1	4-1	0-0	4-0	4-0	2-1	0-0		1-1	2-0	3-0
AC Torino	2-3	1-1	2-1	4-1	1-1	0-1	2-0	1-1	1-2	4-1	3-1	1-1	0-0	2-0	1-1		5-0	0-3
US Triestina	2-2	1-0	4-1	1-1	0-0	2-1	3-0	1-1	2-3	2-0	2-1	4-0	2-3	1-1	2-0	3-0		1-1
AC Udinese	1-3	0-2	1-0	0-1	0-0	1-1	0-4	0-1	1-1	2-1	1-1	7-3	3-1	3-2	2-0	1-0	1-1	

	Serie "A"	Pd	Wn	Dw	Ls	GF	GA	Pts	
1.	FC INTERNAZIONALE (MILANO)	34	19	9	6	46	24	47	
2.	Juventus FC (Torino)	34	18	9	7	73	40	45	
3.	Milan AC (Milano)	34	17	9	8	64	34	43	
4.	AC Napoli (Napoli)	34	15	11	8	53	43	41	
5.	Bologna FC (Bologna)	34	16	7	11	52	43	39	
6.	AS Roma (Roma)	34	13	10	11	50	44	36	
7.	AC Fiorentina (Firenze)	34	11	11	12	31	47	33	
8.	S.P.A.L. (Ferrara)	34	8	16	10	40	37	32	
8.	Atalanta BC (Bergamo)	34	10	12	12	52	53	32	
10.	AC Torino (Torino)	34	11	9	14	47	50	31	
10.	SS Lazio (Roma)	34	12	7	15	38	44	31	
10.	UC Sampdoria (Genova)	34	9	13	12	37	43	31	
10.	AC Novara (Novara)	34	11	9	14	43	52	31	
10.	AC Udinese (Udine)	34	10	11	13	42	55	31	
15.	US Triestina (Trieste)	34	10	10	14	47	54	30	
15.	US Palermo (Palermo)	34	10	10	14	43	56	30	
17.	AC Como (Como)	34	11	5	18	32	44	27	R
18.	Pro Patria et Libertate (Busto (Arsizio)	34	7	8	19	40	67	22	R
		612	218	176	218	830	830	760	

Top goalscorers

1)	Gunnar NORDAHL	(Milan AC)	26
2)	John HANSEN	(Juventus FC)	22
3)	Gian Carlo BACCI	(Bologna FC)	18
	Paul RASMUSSEN	(Atalanta BC)	18
5)	Pasquale VIVOLO	(Juventus FC)	16

* AC Vicenza (Vicenza) merged with Lanerossi Schio (Vicenza) to become AC Lanerossi (Vicenza).

	Serie "B"	Pd	Wn	Dw	Ls	GF	GA	Pts	
1.	Genoa Cricket & FBC (Genova)	34	16	12	6	38	23	44	P
2.	AC Legnano (Legnano)	34	17	7	10	52	32	41	P
2.	CC Catania (Catania)	34	16	9	9	40	28	41	PO
4.	AS Messina (Messina)	34	15	8	11	42	34	38	
4.	AC Brescia (Brescia)	34	13	12	9	33	28	38	
4.	US Cagliari (Cagliari)	34	14	10	10	51	44	38	
4.	AC Monza (Monza)	34	15	8	11	44	38	38	
8.	Marzotto	34	13	10	11	33	31	36	
9.	AC Treviso (Treviso)	34	12	11	11	33	34	35	
10.	Modena FBC (Modena)	34	12	10	12	34	33	34	
11.	US Salernitana (Salerno)	34	10	13	11	31	41	33	
12.	AC Vicenza (Vicenza)	34	10	12	12	38	43	32	*
13.	AC Verona (Verona)	34	12	7	15	41	47	31	
14.	AC Fanfulla (Lido)	34	10	10	14	47	46	30	
15.	US Piombinese (Piombino Dese)	34	8	12	14	33	40	28	
15.	AC Padova (Padova)	34	10	8	16	36	46	28	
17.	AC Siracusa (Siracusa)	34	8	11	15	30	42	27	R
18.	US Lucchese Libertas (Lucca)	34	5	10	19	27	53	2	R-18
		612	216	180	216	683	683	594	

US Lucchese Libertas (Lucca) had 18 points deducted by the F.I.G.C. Committee.

2nd/3rd Position Play-Off

AC Legnano (Legnano)	4-1	CC Catania (Catania)

Promoted to Serie "B": US Alessandria (Alessandria) and AC Pavia (Pavia).

1953-54

1953-1954 Serie "A"	Atalanta BC	Bologna FC	AC Fiorentina	Genoa C & FBC	FC Internazionale	Juventus FC	SS Lazio	AC Legnano	Milan AC	AC Napoli	AC Novara	US Palermo	AS Roma	UC Sampdoria	SPAL Ferrara	AC Torino	US Triestina	AC Udinese
Atalanta BC		1-3	1-1	1-0	0-2	3-2	1-0	4-1	31	1-1	1-1	0-1	1-1	1-1	0-1	1-1	4-2	6-0
Bologna FC	2-1		1-1	1-1	0-1	0-1	1-0	2-0	2-1	0-0	2-0	0-1	1-2	0-2	2-1	2-0	4-0	3-1
AC Fiorentina	3-0	1-3		1-0	1-1	1-1	0-1	4-0	0-0	1-0	2-0	3-1	2-0	2-0	1-1	2-2	1-0	0-0
Genoa C & FBC	1-0	3-3	1-3		1-3	1-3	3-1	2-1	2-2	1-1	2-0	1-0	1-0	0-1	1-0	1-1	1-0	4-1
FC Internazionale	3-1	3-2	2-1	1-0		6-0	2-0	2-2	3-0	2-0	3-1	4-0	1-1	2-1	4-2	2-0	4-2	0-2
Juventus FC	2-0	2-2	0-0	3-1	2-2		0-0	2-1	1-0	3-2	0-0	4-1	3-0	1-0	3-1	0-0	3-1	1-0
SS Lazio	2-2	1-1	2-3	3-0	0-1	2-1		1-1	1-1	0-4	2-1	3-0	1-2	3-0	2-1	0-1	5-1	0-1
AC Legnano	1-2	0-1	1-2	1-1	1-1	1-1	2-1		2-2	1-0	5-1	3-0	2-2	2-2	1-3	0-0	2-1	0-0
Milan AC	3-3	2-1	2-1	3-0	2-0	1-0	3-2	3-1		3-2	0-0	2-1	1-2	1-1	6-1	0-1	4-0	2-1
AC Napoli	6-3	2-1	0-0	0-2	2-1	1-2	2-1	1-0	0-1		5-1	3-0	1-0	1-1	3-1	2-2	1-0	2-1
AC Novara	0-4	1-0	0-0	2-0	2-3	0-1	2-1	0-0	1-1	1-1		3-0	2-0	3-0	4-2	1-1	2-0	0-0
US Palermo	0-0	3-1	0-1	2-1	2-2	1-3	2-0	3-3	1-4	2-2	1-1		1-3	2-1	1-0	1-1	1-1	4-0
AS Roma	0-0	1-3	1-2	4-0	1-1	1-1	1-1	5-3	1-2	0-0	3-0	3-1		3-1	3-0	2-2	3-1	3-0
UC Sampdoria	2-0	2-2	2-0	0-0	0-0	0-1	0-0	3-1	2-1	1-0	3-1	2-2	2-1		0-0	1-1	2-1	1-1
SPAL Ferrara	3-2	0-0	1-1	1-0	2-2	1-3	0-1	1-0	0-0	1-1	2-1	0-1	0-0	2-1		2-3	0-0	2-1
AC Torino	1-3	0-1	1-1	3-2	1-1	2-4	0-1	2-2	1-4	0-2	1-0	2-1	1-1	2-0	1-0		1-1	1-0
US Triestina	3-2	3-1	1-1	1-1	0-0	2-2	1-1	2-1	0-6	1-1	3-1	1-0	2-2	2-1	3-0	2-1		2-1
AC Udinese	2-2	3-2	1-2	3-1	0-2	0-2	1-1	1-2	2-2	3-3	1-1	1-0	2-1	1-2	1-1	3-0	4-2	

	Serie "A"	Pd	Wn	Dw	Ls	GF	GA	Pts	
1.	FC INTERNAZIONALE (MILANO)	34	20	11	3	67	32	51	
2.	Juventus FC (Torino)	34	20	10	4	58	34	50	
3.	Milan AC (Milano)	34	17	10	7	66	39	44	
3.	AC Fiorentina (Firenze)	34	15	14	5	45	27	44	
5.	AC Napoli (Napoli)	34	13	12	9	52	38	38	
6.	AS Roma (Roma)	34	12	12	10	53	42	36	
6.	Bologna FC (Bologna)	34	14	8	12	50	41	36	
8.	UC Sampdoria (Genova)	34	11	12	11	38	40	34	
9.	AC Torino (Torino)	34	9	15	10	37	46	33	
10.	Atalanta BC (Bergamo)	34	10	11	13	54	53	31	
11.	SS Lazio (Roma)	34	10	9	15	40	42	29	
12.	Genoa Cricket & FBC (Genova)	34	10	8	16	36	50	28	
12.	US Triestina (Trieste)	34	9	10	15	42	64	28	
14.	AC Novara (Novara)	34	8	11	15	34	50	27	
15.	AC Udinese (Udine)	34	8	10	16	39	57	26	PO
15.	S.P.A.L. (Ferrara)	34	8	10	16	33	53	26	PO
15.	US Palermo (Palermo)	34	9	8	17	37	59	26	R
18.	AC Legnano (Legnano)	34	6	13	15	44	58	25	R
		612	209	194	209	825	825	612	

Top goalscorers

1)	Gunnar NORDAHL	(Milan AC)	23
2)	Hasse JEPPSON	(AC Napoli)	20
3)	Adriano BASSETTO	(Atalanta BC)	17
	Eduardo RICAGNI	(Juventus FC)	17
5)	Paul RASMUSSEN	(Atalanta BC)	15
	L. Jørgen SØRENSEN	(Milan AC)	15

Relegation Play-Offs

AC Udinese (Udine)	2-0 (played in Milano)	SPAL (Ferrara)
SPAL (Ferrara)	2-1 (played in Roma)	US Palermo (Palermo)
US Palermo (Palermo)	1-1 (played in Firenze)	AC Udinese (Udine)

	Serie "B"	Pd	Wn	Dw	Ls	GF	GA	Pts	
1.	CC Catania (Catania)	34	16	11	7	54	31	43	P
2.	Pro Patria et Libertate (Busto Arsizio)	34	15	11	8	49	36	41	P
2.	US Cagliari (Cagliari)	34	16	9	9	42	30	41	PO
4.	AC Como (Como)	34	14	12	8	37	22	40	
5.	Marzotto	34	15	9	10	39	30	39	
6.	AC Lanerossi (Vicenza)	34	13	11	10	41	34	37	
7.	AC Verona (Verona)	34	12	12	10	44	37	36	
7.	AC Monza (Monza)	34	10	16	8	30	29	36	
9.	AC Brescia (Brescia)	34	11	11	12	33	38	33	
10.	Modena FBC (Modena)	34	9	12	13	35	37	30	
10.	AS Messina (Messina)	34	9	12	13	23	27	30	
10.	US Salernitana (Salerno)	34	10	10	14	31	46	30	
13.	AC Padova (Padova)	34	9	11	14	33	40	29	
13.	US Alessandria (Alessandria)	34	9	11	14	39	50	29	
13.	AC Pavia (Pavia)	34	9	11	14	39	51	29	
13.	AC Treviso (Treviso)	34	7	15	12	24	41	29	
17.	AC Fanfulla (Lodi)	34	11	11	12	37	34	28	R-5
18.	US Piombinese (Piombino Dese)	34	8	11	15	24	41	27	R
		612	203	206	203	654	654	607	

AC Fanfulla (Lodi) had 5 points deducted by the F.I.G.C. Committee.

2nd/3rd Place Play-Off

Pro Patria et Libertate (Busto Arsizio)	2-0	US Cagliari (Cagliari)

Promoted to Serie "B": Arsenal SC (Taranto) and Parma AS (Parma).

1954-55

1954-1955 Serie "A"	Atalanta BC	Bologna FC	CC Catania	AC Fiorentina	Genoa C & FBC	FC Internazionale	Juventus FC	SS Lazio	Milan AC	AC Napoli	AC Novara	Pro Patria et Libertate	AS Roma	UC Sampdoria	SPAL Ferrara	AC Torino	US Triestina	AC Udinese
Atalanta BC		0-1	4-0	5-1	0-2	1-1	2-1	3-2	1-1	1-1	4-0	1-2	1-1	1-1	0-0	2-0	0-0	0-2
Bologna FC	0-0		4-2	0-2	2-1	3-2	2-1	2-1	1-2	1-3	2-2	5-0	1-3	3-1	2-0	4-1	1-1	2-4
CC Catania	1-0	2-2		0-1	2-0	1-1	2-2	1-0	1-3	1-1	0-0	2-1	2-2	2-1	1-0	2-1	2-1	5-0
AC Fiorentina	2-1	0-2	2-1		2-2	3-3	0-0	0-1	0-2	0-0	1-0	1-0	1-1	1-0	1-0	2-2	4-1	3-1
Genoa C & FBC	1-0	1-2	0-0	0-0		2-0	2-0	2-0	0-8	1-1	0-0	1-3	1-0	1-1	1-1	2-0	0-0	1-1
FC Internazionale	3-0	2-2	3-0	3-5	0-1		1-2	2-1	1-1	1-4	3-0	2-0	1-2	1-0	1-0	1-1	4-1	2-2
Juventus FC	0-0	5-1	1-1	4-1	2-1	3-2		4-2	3-4	1-1	2-1	4-2	1-1	2-2	3-1	3-0	1-2	1-1
SS Lazio	1-0	0-0	1-0	2-1	2-1	3-2	2-1		2-4	2-1	1-1	2-0	1-1	1-3	0-0	0-2	1-1	0-2
Milan AC	3-1	0-0	2-0	4-0	2-2	1-1	3-1	3-0		1-1	3-0	2-0	0-2	1-3	6-0	4-1	4-0	2-2
AC Napoli	1-0	1-1	2-0	1-1	3-1	1-2	1-1	3-2	0-2		1-2	2-1	2-0	2-2	2-1	0-2	4-0	3-1
AC Novara	0-1	1-0	2-0	1-0	3-1	2-4	2-2	2-1	1-1	2-1		0-1	1-2	1-0	2-0	0-1	2-0	3-3
Pro Patria et Libertate	1-2	0-2	2-1	1-1	0-2	0-1	1-2	2-0	1-1	0-2	0-0		1-1	1-0	1-1	1-2	0-2	2-2
AS Roma	0-0	3-4	3-1	3-4	2-1	3-0	1-1	1-3	2-1	0-0	5-3	1-1		1-1	1-0	1-0	2-0	1-1
UC Sampdoria	2-1	2-0	1-1	3-3	2-2	1-1	5-1	0-0	0-3	5-2	6-2	3-0	1-1		1-0	1-1	2-0	2-0
SPAL Ferrara	0-0	1-1	1-3	1-3	1-0	2-0	0-0	2-2	0-0	1-1	2-1	1-1	2-5	2-0		1-1	1-0	1-4
AC Torino	1-1	1-2	1-0	0-1	0-0	1-1	2-2	3-1	1-2	1-0	3-2	3-1	1-1	1-0	1-0		5-1	1-1
US Triestina	3-1	0-0	1-1	1-1	1-1	0-1	4-2	1-3	4-3	0-2	1-0	1-0	0-0	3-1	1-1	2-1		0-0
AC Udinese	3-1	2-1	1-0	2-1	3-0	0-2	0-1	1-1	3-2	3-0	1-0	2-2	1-0	2-1	3-0	3-0	1-1	

	Serie "A"	Pd	Wn	Dw	Ls	GF	GA	Pts	
1.	MILAN AC (MILANO)	34	19	10	5	81	35	48	
2.	AC Udinese (Udine)	34	16	12	6	58	42	44	#
3.	AS Roma (Roma)	34	13	15	6	53	39	41	
4.	Bologna FC (Bologna)	34	15	10	9	56	47	40	
5.	AC Fiorentina (Firenze)	34	14	11	9	49	48	39	
6.	AC Napoli (Napoli)	34	13	12	9	50	40	38	
7.	Juventus FC (Torino)	34	12	13	9	60	53	37	
8.	FC Internazionale (Milano)	34	13	10	11	55	49	36	
9.	UC Sampdoria (Genova)	34	11	12	11	54	44	34	
9.	AC Torino (Torino)	34	12	10	12	42	45	34	
11.	Genoa Cricket & FBC (Genova)	34	9	13	12	34	44	31	
12.	CC Catania (Catania)	34	10	10	14	38	47	30	#
12.	SS Lazio (Roma)	34	11	8	15	41	52	30	
12.	US Triestina (Trieste)	34	9	12	13	34	52	30	
15.	Atalanta BC (Bergamo)	34	8	12	14	35	38	28	
15.	AC Novara (Novara)	34	10	8	16	39	53	28	
17.	S.P.A.L. (Ferrara)	34	5	13	16	24	49	23	#
18.	Pro Patria et Libertate (Busto Arsizio)	34	6	9	19	29	55	21	#
		612	206	200	206	832	832	612	

Top goalscorers

1)	Gunnar NORDAHL	(Milan AC)	27
2)	Lorenzo BETTINI	(AC Udinese)	20
3)	Gino PIVATELLI	(Bologna FC)	17
4)	Paul RASMUSSEN	(Atalanta BC)	16
5)	Gian Carlo BACCI	(AC Torino)	15
	John HANSEN	(SS Lazio)	15
	Juan Alberto SCHIAFFINO	(Milan AC)	15
	Giuseppe VIRGILI	(AC Fiorentina)	15

AC Udinese (Udine) were relegated by the F.I.G.C. after being found guilty of "buying" 2 games during this season and also 1 match during the 1953-54 season.
CC Catania (Catania) were relegated by the F.I.G.C. after being found guilty of "buying" a match during the 1953-54 season in order to gain promotion.
As a result of the above actions by the F.I.G.C. the relegated clubs S.P.A.L. (Ferrara) and Pro Patria et Libertate (Busto Arsizio) retained their places in Serie "A" for the next season.

Note: Vigor GS (Ascoli Piceno) changed their club name to AS del Duca (Ascoli Piceno) and then later to AC del Duca.

	Serie "B"	Pd	Wn	Dw	Ls	GF	GA	Pts	
1.	AC Lanerossi (Vicenza)	34	22	6	6	53	21	50	P
2.	AC Padova (Padova)	34	15	12	7	46	27	42	P
3.	Modena FBC (Modena)	34	13	14	7	42	30	40	
3.	AC Legnano (Legnano)	34	13	14	7	42	36	40	
5.	AC Brescia (Brescia)	34	15	7	12	44	36	37	
5.	AC Como (Como)	34	11	15	8	33	27	37	
7.	AS Messina (Messina)	34	11	14	9	46	43	36	
8.	Marzotto	34	14	7	13	55	45	35	
9.	US Cagliari (Cagliari)	34	10	13	11	33	35	33	
9.	Parma AS (Parma)	34	8	17	9	37	40	33	
11.	Arsenal SC (Taranto)	34	12	8	14	31	38	32	*
12.	US Salernitana (Salerno)	34	9	13	12	44	56	31	
13.	US Palermo (Palermo)	34	10	10	14	38	43	30	
13.	AC Monza (Monza)	34	8	14	12	34	43	30	*
15.	US Alessandria (Alessandria)	34	10	8	16	30	40	28	
15.	AC Verona (Verona)	34	10	8	16	35	50	28	
17.	AC Treviso (Treviso)	34	7	13	14	32	45	27	R
18.	AC Pavia (Pavia)	34	7	9	18	32	52	23	R
		612	205	202	205	707	707	612	

Promoted to Serie "B": FC Bari (Bari) and US Livorno (Livorno).

* Arsenal SC (Taranto) changed their club name to AS Taranto (Taranto).
AC Monza (Monza) changed their club name to Simmenthal (Monza).

1955-1956 Serie "A"	Atalanta BC	Bologna FC	AC Fiorentina	Genoa C & FBC	FC Internazionale	Juventus FC	AC Lanerossi	SS Lazio	Milan AC	AC Napoli	AC Novara	AC Padova	Pro Patria et Libertate	AS Roma	UC Sampdoria	SPAL Ferrara	AC Torino	UC Triestina
Atalanta BC		1-0	0-0	2-2	1-1	1-1	3-0	1-1	4-3	1-2	2-1	0-2	4-1	1-1	4-1	4-3	1-2	2-0
Bologna FC	1-0		0-2	4-1	2-3	0-1	1-1	0-2	2-1	3-1	3-2	3-1	6-1	1-0	5-2	2-2	6-1	3-1
AC Fiorentina	4-1	0-0		3-1	0-0	2-0	2-0	4-1	3-0	0-0	4-2	1-0	4-1	2-0	0-0	0-0	2-0	1-0
Genoa C & FBC	2-1	2-1	3-1		4-3	0-0	2-2	3-3	3-1	3-1	2-0	0-0	3-0	3-3	2-1	1-1	3-1	1-0
FC Internazionale	1-2	0-3	1-3	3-0		0-2	1-0	2-3	2-1	3-0	2-0	0-1	4-0	1-1	7-1	3-1	1-0	0-0
Juventus FC	2-1	2-2	0-4	1-0	1-0		0-0	1-0	0-0	0-1	2-2	3-0	3-1	0-0	2-2	2-2	0-2	0-1
AC Lanerossi	1-0	2-3	1-1	2-1	0-2	3-2		0-1	1-3	0-0	0-0	0-0	1-1	2-0	0-0	2-0	1-0	1-1
SS Lazio	2-2	2-2	2-2	2-0	2-2	2-0	1-3		2-3	1-1	2-0	3-1	2-0	1-0	1-2	3-0	0-1	1-1
Milan AC	4-1	3-0	0-2	3-2	1-2	3-1	0-0	1-3		0-0	4-2	4-1	3-3	4-1	6-1	2-0	3-1	1-0
AC Napoli	0-3	3-3	2-4	2-1	0-2	1-1	0-0	1-2	2-0		0-2	1-0	8-1	1-1	3-1	2-2	2-2	3-2
AC Novara	2-1	2-0	1-1	1-2	2-2	0-0	2-0	6-2	3-4	1-0		3-0	2-1	2-2	1-2	1-1	1-2	0-1
AC Padova	5-1	3-1	0-1	2-1	1-0	1-1	3-1	1-2	1-5	1-1	2-1		2-1	2-0	1-3	0-0	2-0	4-0
Pro Patria et Libertate	2-0	2-2	2-2	1-0	0-4	2-2	0-1	1-2	1-1	0-0	0-0	0-2		3-5	2-0	1-2	1-1	1-4
AS Roma	3-2	2-0	1-1	2-0	1-0	1-1	4-1	0-0	0-0	2-1	2-1	1-1	1-0		1-2	1-1	2-1	4-1
UC Sampdoria	4-0	2-5	0-0	0-0	3-2	2-0	1-3	1-1	2-2	3-0	1-1	0-1	7-0	1-0		3-1	0-0	1-0
SPAL Ferrara	0-0	2-1	0-1	1-0	0-1	0-0	5-0	1-0	0-0	1-2	2-0	2-0	2-1	1-0	1-1		1-2	4-0
AC Torino	1-3	1-0	0-1	2-2	0-2	0-0	0-0	2-2	1-1	1-4	2-1	2-0	6-0	2-1	2-1	0-0		5-0
US Triestina	0-0	1-3	1-1	2-0	0-0	1-1	0-2	1-0	1-3	2-1	0-0	1-0	1-0	0-0	0-0	3-1	1-0	

	Serie "A"	Pd	Wn	Dw	Ls	GF	GA	Pts	
1.	AC FIORENTINA (FIRENZE)	34	20	13	1	59	20	53	
2.	Milan AC (Milano)	34	16	9	9	70	48	41	
3.	FC Internazionale (Milano)	34	16	7	11	57	36	39	
3.	SS Lazio (Roma)	34	14	11	9	54	46	39	
5.	Bologna FC (Bologna)	34	15	7	12	68	52	37	
6.	AS Roma (Roma)	34	11	13	10	43	40	35	
6.	UC Sampdoria (Genova)	34	12	11	11	51	54	35	
8.	AC Padova (Padova)	34	14	6	14	41	43	34	
9.	S.P.A.L. (Ferrara)	34	10	13	11	40	39	33	
9.	Genoa Cricket & FBC (Genova)	34	12	9	13	50	52	33	
9.	AC Torino (Torino)	34	12	9	13	43	45	33	
9.	Juventus FC (Torino)	34	8	17	9	32	37	33	
9.	AC Lanerossi (Vicenza)	34	10	13	11	31	40	33	
14.	AC Napoli (Napoli)	34	10	12	12	46	49	32	
15.	Atalanta BC (Bergamo)	34	11	9	14	50	55	31	
16.	US Triestina (Trieste)	34	10	10	14	27	44	30	
17.	AC Novara (Novara)	34	8	10	16	45	51	26	R
18.	Pro Patria et Libertate (Busto Arsizio)	34	3	9	22	31	87	15	R
		612	212	188	212	838	838	612	

Top goalscorers

1)	Gino PIVATELLI	(Bologna FC)	29
2)	Gunnar NORDAHL	(Milan AC)	23
3)	Giuseppe VIRGILI	(AC Fiorentina)	21
4)	Adriano BASSETTO	(Atalanta BC)	18
5)	Eddie FIRMANI	(UC Sampdoria)	17

Note: AC Mantova (Mantova) changed their club name to Ozo Mantova (Mantova) for the next season.

	Serie "B"	Pd	Wn	Dw	Ls	GF	GA	Pts	
1.	AC Udinese (Udine)	34	21	7	6	66	31	49	P
2.	US Palermo (Palermo)	34	17	13	4	41	34	47	P
3.	AC Como (Como)	34	17	9	8	54	33	43	
3.	Simmenthal (Monza)	34	17	9	8	44	29	43	
5.	CC Catania (Catania)	34	14	12	8	42	28	40	
5.	US Cagliari (Cagliari)	34	15	10	9	51	45	40	
7.	AC Brescia (Brescia)	34	11	12	11	34	43	34	
8.	Modena FBC (Modena)	34	10	13	11	46	38	33	
9.	US Alessandria (Alessandria)	34	11	10	13	40	36	32	
9.	AC Verona (Verona)	34	12	8	14	45	49	32	
11.	FC Bari (Bari)	34	13	5	16	45	44	31	
11.	AS Messina (Messina)	34	11	9	14	41	45	31	
11.	AS Taranto (Taranto)	34	10	11	13	34	39	31	
14.	AC Legnano (Legnano)	34	10	10	14	40	47	30	
15.	Parma AS (Parma)	34	10	8	16	36	46	28	
16.	Marzotto	34	10	7	17	30	48	27	
17.	US Livorno (Livorno)	34	7	8	19	37	64	22	R
18.	US Salernitana (Salerno)	34	4	11	19	30	57	19	R
		612	220	172	220	756	756	612	

Promoted to Serie "B": Sambenedettese Calcio (San Benedetto del Tronto) and AC Venezia (Venezia).

1956-57

1956-1957 Serie "A"	Atalanta BC	Bologna FC	AC Fiorentina	Genoa C & FBC	FC Internazionale	Juventus FC	AC Lanerossi	SS Lazio	Milan AC	AC Napoli	AC Padova	UC Palermo	AS Roma	UC Sampdoria	SPAL Ferrara	AC Torino	UC Triestina	AC Udinese
Atalanta BC		3-2	1-1	0-1	2-1	0-0	1-1	0-1	2-2	2-0	0-0	1-0	4-1	3-3	1-0	0-1	3-1	1-1
Bologna FC	1-0		2-2	3-1	3-2	1-0	1-1	3-1	1-2	2-1	1-2	1-1	1-0	4-2	3-0	0-0	0-0	4-3
AC Fiorentina	0-1	2-1		1-0	3-1	2-2	2-1	0-0	0-3	4-0	3-0	3-1	2-2	3-0	2-0	1-0	3-0	2-1
Genoa C & FBC	2-1	5-2	1-2		0-0	1-1	0-0	1-1	0-1	1-0	1-1	2-2	1-1	1-1	2-1	1-0	0-1	1-1
FC Internazionale	2-2	2-2	2-1	2-0		1-1	3-1	0-1	1-1	3-1	2-0	1-0	3-2	6-1	2-0	3-0	1-0	2-3
Juventus FC	2-2	3-1	1-1	2-0	5-1		0-1	3-3	0-1	1-0	0-0	6-4	1-2	1-1	2-0	1-1	4-3	2-3
AC Lanerossi	2-0	2-1	4-0	0-1	2-1	1-1		1-1	3-1	0-0	0-0	4-1	1-0	3-2	4-1	1-2	3-1	1-1
SS Lazio	2-2	3-2	3-0	2-2	1-1	0-3	2-0		3-0	1-1	1-1	3-0	0-3	2-1	1-2	2-2	2-0	2-1
Milan AC	4-0	1-0	2-0	2-0	1-1	4-1	4-2	3-2		3-5	2-0	1-0	3-1	2-1	0-1	3-1	2-1	2-0
AC Napoli	2-0	0-0	1-1	1-2	1-1	1-2	1-0	0-0	2-2		1-0	4-1	1-2	2-0	0-1	2-1	2-1	2-1
AC Padova	0-0	1-1	2-2	2-0	3-2	2-1	1-1	0-1	2-0	1-1		1-0	0-1	2-6	1-2	1-3	1-1	4-1
US Palermo	3-1	2-1	0-1	1-0	1-1	0-2	3-1	2-6	1-2	0-0	1-1		1-0	1-1	0-0	1-0	2-1	0-1
AS Roma	1-0	2-3	0-2	1-1	0-0	2-3	2-2	2-2	0-0	1-3	2-2	2-1		5-1	5-1	0-2	3-1	6-1
UC Sampdoria	2-2	1-1	2-2	3-2	2-2	2-1	5-0	0-1	3-2	1-0	2-0	6-0	1-0		0-3	1-0	1-1	3-0
SPAL Ferrara	0-0	1-0	2-1	1-2	1-0	3-1	5-2	1-0	1-3	2-0	0-0	1-0	1-1	0-3		2-1	0-1	1-1
AC Torino	2-0	1-1	2-1	2-2	1-1	4-1	2-1	0-1	2-2	1-1	0-2	5-1	1-0	0-0	3-2		1-0	3-1
US Triestina	0-1	0-0	0-0	2-1	2-2	3-0	2-1	1-1	1-3	1-2	0-0	1-1	1-1	1-1	2-0	1-0		1-0
AC Udinese	3-0	1-5	2-5	5-1	1-0	3-0	3-2	2-0	2-1	2-1	0-0	2-0	2-2	3-0	3-2	5-1	0-1	

	Serie "A"	Pd	Wn	Dw	Ls	GF	GA	Pts	
1.	MILAN AC (MILANO)	34	21	6	7	65	40	48	
2.	AC Fiorentina (Firenze)	34	16	10	8	55	40	42	
3.	SS Lazio (Roma)	34	14	13	7	52	40	41	
4.	AC Udinese (Udine)	34	15	6	13	59	58	36	
5.	FC Internazionale (Milano)	34	11	13	10	53	45	35	
5.	Bologna FC (Bologna)	34	12	11	11	54	48	35	
5.	AC Torino (Torino)	34	13	9	12	45	42	35	
5.	UC Sampdoria (Genova)	34	12	11	11	59	56	35	
9.	Juventus FC (Torino)	34	11	11	12	54	54	33	
9.	S.P.A.L. (Ferrara)	34	14	5	15	38	47	33	
11.	AC Lanerossi (Vicenza)	34	11	10	13	49	51	32	
11.	AC Napoli (Napoli)	34	11	10	13	39	41	32	
11.	AC Padova (Padova)	34	8	16	10	33	39	32	
14.	AS Roma (Roma)	34	10	11	13	53	49	31	
14.	Atalanta BC (Bergamo)	34	9	13	12	36	44	31	
16.	Genoa Cricket & FBC (Genova)	34	9	12	13	36	46	30	
17.	US Triestina (Trieste)	34	9	11	14	33	42	29	R
18.	US Palermo (Palermo)	34	7	8	19	32	63	22	R
		612	213	186	213	845	845	612	

Top goalscorers

1)	Dino DA COSTA	(AS Roma)	22
2)	Giuseppe SECCHI	(AC Udinese)	18
	Luis VINICHIO	(AC Napoli)	18
4)	Gastone BEAN	(Milan AC)	17
5)	Adriano BASSETTO	(Atalanta BC)	15
	Bengt LINDSKOG	(AC Udinese)	15

* Modena FBC (Modena) changed their club name to Zenit (Modena) for the next season.

Note: US Foggia (Foggia) merged with GS Incedit (Foggia) to become US Foggia & Incedit (Foggia) for the next season.

	Serie "B"	Pd	Wn	Dw	Ls	GF	GA	Pts	
1.	AC Verona (Verona)	34	17	10	7	46	29	44	P
2.	US Alessandria (Alessandria)	34	17	9	8	57	36	43	P
2.	AC Brescia (Brescia)	34	19	5	10	42	29	43	PO
4.	CC Catania (Catania)	34	18	6	10	53	31	42	
5.	AC Venezia (Venezia)	34	15	11	8	46	27	41	
6.	AC Novara (Novara)	34	11	14	9	39	38	36	
6.	AC Como (Como)	34	13	10	11	37	38	36	
8.	Simmenthal (Monza)	34	14	6	14	44	44	34	
9.	Marzotto	34	10	13	11	38	40	33	
10.	US Cagliari (Cagliari)	34	11	10	13	30	34	32	
10.	FC Bari (Bari)	34	12	8	14	31	41	32	
12.	Parma AS (Parma)	34	9	13	12	33	38	31	
12.	Modena FBC (Modena)	34	11	9	14	32	37	31	*
14.	AS Messina (Messina)	34	9	11	14	28	35	29	
14.	Sambenedettese Calcio (San Benedetto del Tronto)	34	8	13	13	32	45	29	
16.	AS Taranto (Taranto)	34	10	8	16	35	47	28	
17.	Pro Patria et Libertate (Busto Arsizio)	34	7	11	16	35	49	25	R
18.	AC Legnano (Legnano)	34	7	9	18	31	51	23	R
		612	218	176	218	689	689	612	

2nd/3rd Place Play-Off

US Alessandria (Alessandria)	2-1	AC Brescia (Brescia)

Promoted to Serie "B": AC Lecco (Lecco) and AC Prato (Prato).

1957-58

1957-1958 Serie "A"	US Alessandria	Atalanta BC	Bologna FC	AC Fiorentina	Genoa	FC Internazion.	Juventus FC	AC Lanerossi	SS Lazio	Milan AC	AC Napoli	AC Padova	AS Roma	UC Sampdoria	SPAL Ferrara	AC Torino	AC Udinese	AC Verona
US Alessandria		0-0	2-0	1-0	3-1	2-1	1-2	2-1	4-0	0-0	0-0	0-0	1-3	2-0	0-0	0-0	1-2	3-1
Atalanta BC	1-1		1-1	0-0	1-1	1-0	0-0	2-4	1-1	1-0	2-4	1-1	0-0	1-0	0-0	0-1	1-1	2-1
Bologna FC	3-1	3-1		0-3	3-3	1-0	3-4	4-0	5-0	0-0	1-1	0-0	0-0	3-3	0-1	2-1	2-2	1-0
AC Fiorentina	0-0	2-2	2-1		2-0	0-0	2-1	2-1	2-0	4-3	4-1	6-1	2-0	1-1	3-0	2-1	2-0	1-1
Genoa C & FBC	0-2	1-2	0-0	1-3		0-0	1-3	1-0	5-2	1-1	2-1	1-4	4-2	3-1	0-0	1-1	1-0	4-1
FC Internazionale	1-1	1-1	0-2	0-1	1-0		2-2	1-0	5-2	1-0	0-1	0-0	1-1	2-2	4-0	0-0	0-1	1-0
Juventus FC	2-1	3-0	4-1	0-0	3-2	3-1		5-2	3-1	1-0	1-3	2-1	3-0	4-1	3-1	4-1	2-0	3-2
AC Lanerossi	4-0	2-0	3-2	3-0	3-3	2-0	2-1		1-0	1-1	4-0	1-2	3-1	2-4	2-0	1-1	0-0	1-1
SS Lazio	2-1	3-1	4-3	2-2	0-0	3-1	1-4	2-0		1-1	4-1	1-0	2-1	2-2	1-1	1-1	1-0	4-0
Milan AC	1-1	5-0	0-1	2-1	1-5	2-2	1-1	4-1	6-1		2-2	1-1	1-1	0-1	4-2	4-0	1-1	2-0
AC Napoli	4-1	2-2	0-1	3-1	4-0	1-0	4-3	3-1	1-1	1-0		4-0	0-0	0-1	2-0	3-0	3-2	6-0
AC Padova	2-1	0-3	3-1	3-2	6-3	0-0	1-1	1-0	3-1	3-2	3-0		3-0	2-0	3-0	3-0	0-0	2-0
AS Roma	2-1	0-0	2-0	0-0	2-1	0-1	4-1	1-1	3-0	3-3	0-2	3-1		5-1	1-1	2-0	3-3	2-1
UC Sampdoria	1-1	1-1	0-1	3-1	0-0	0-2	3-2	1-1	1-1	0-2	3-0	3-2	3-1		1-1	4-0	3-5	1-1
SPAL Ferrara	3-2	2-1	0-2	2-2	1-1	2-0	0-1	1-3	3-0	1-5	1-2	1-1	1-0	1-0		0-1	2-0	1-1
AC Torino	0-0	4-0	0-0	2-1	4-2	2-3	0-1	1-0	1-1	3-2	4-3	2-0	0-0	4-3	0-1		6-2	0-0
AC Udinese	2-0	1-0	1-0	1-1	2-2	1-1	0-1	0-1	1-0	1-1	7-0	1-2	1-2	3-3	5-0	1-1		2-0
AC Verona	3-0	3-0	1-0	0-1	1-3	2-4	2-3	1-0	1-0	4-3	4-3	1-1	0-1	5-3	1-2	2-0	3-2	

	Serie "A"	Pd	Wn	Dw	Ls	GF	GA	Pts	
1.	JUVENTUS FC (TORINO)	34	23	5	6	77	44	51	
2.	AC Fiorentina (Firenze)	34	16	11	7	56	36	43	
3.	AC Padova (Padova)	34	16	10	8	55	42	42	
4.	AC Napoli (Napoli)	34	17	6	11	65	55	40	
5.	AS Roma (Roma)	34	12	12	10	46	42	36	
6.	Bologna FC (Bologna)	34	12	10	12	47	43	34	
7.	AC Lanerossi (Vicenza)	34	13	7	14	51	48	33	
7.	AC Torino (Torino)	34	11	11	12	42	49	33	*
9.	Milan AC (Milano)	34	9	14	11	61	47	32	
9.	AC Udinese (Udine)	34	10	12	12	51	46	32	
9.	FC Internazionale (Milano)	34	10	12	12	36	36	32	
12.	Genoa Cricket & FBC (Genova)	34	9	12	13	53	60	30	
12.	UC Sampdoria (Genova)	34	9	12	13	54	62	30	
12.	US Alessandria (Alessandria)	34	9	12	13	36	42	30	
12.	SS Lazio (Roma)	34	10	10	14	45	65	30	
12.	S.P.A.L. (Ferrara)	34	10	10	14	32	52	30	
17.	Atalanta BC (Bergamo)	34	6	16	12	29	49	28	#
18.	AC Verona (Verona)	34	10	6	18	44	62	26	PO
		612	212	188	212	880	880	612	

Top goalscorers

1)	John CHARLES	(Juventus FC)	28
2)	Eddie FIRMANI	(UC Sampdoria)	23
3)	Omar SIVORI	(Juventus FC)	22
4)	Luis VINICIO	(AC Napoli)	21

Atalanta BC (Bergamo) were demoted to 18th place by the F.I.G.C. Committee of Enquiry and AC Verona (Verona) were placed 17th and entered a Promotion/Relegation play-off versus FC Bari (Bari). However, Atalanta BC were later re-instated in 17th place by the F.I.G.C. but only after the Promotion/Relegation matches had taken place and FC Bari had won promotion to Serie "A".

Promotion/Relegation Play-Off

AC Verona (Verona)	0-0, 0-2	FC Bari (Bari)

* AC Torino (Torino) changed their club name to Talmone Torino (Torino) for the next season.

	Serie "B"	Pd	Wn	Dw	Ls	GF	GA	Pts	
1.	US Triestina (Trieste)	34	20	7	7	64	29	47	P
2.	FC Bari (Bari)	34	17	11	6	47	28	45	PO
3.	AC Venezia (Venezia)	34	16	9	9	42	30	41	
4.	Marzotto	34	16	7	11	50	40	39	
4.	Simmenthal (Monza)	34	15	9	10	47	39	39	
6.	US Palermo (Palermo)	34	12	13	9	36	35	37	
7.	Zenit (Modena)	34	11	14	9	50	46	36	
8.	AC Brescia (Brescia)	34	14	7	13	46	36	35	
8.	AC Como (Como)	34	11	13	10	30	23	35	
10.	AC Prato (Prato)	34	12	10	12	34	40	34	
11.	AC Novara (Novara)	34	9	12	13	42	39	30	
11.	AS Taranto (Taranto)	34	10	10	14	25	31	30	
11.	CC Catania (Catania)	34	8	14	12	29	36	30	
14.	AC Lecco (Lecco)	34	8	13	13	28	44	29	
15.	Sambenedettese Calcio (San Benedetto del Tronto)	34	8	12	14	25	44	28	
16.	AS Messina (Messina)	34	8	11	15	23	41	27	
17.	US Cagliari (Cagliari)	34	8	10	16	31	44	26	
18.	Parma AS (Parma)	34	5	14	15	25	49	24	
		612	208	196	208	674	674	612	

Promoted to Serie "B": AC Reggiana (Reggio Emilia) and AC Vigevano (Vigevano).

Serie "B" was extended to 20 clubs for the next season.

Coppa Italia Final (Roma – 25/09/58)

SS LAZIO (ROMA)	1-0	AC Fiorentina (Firenze)
Prini	*(H.T. 1-0)*	

Lazio: Lovati, Lo Buono, Janich, Carradori, Pinardi, Pozzan, Bizzarri, Tagnin, Tozzi, Fumagalli, Prini.

Fiorentina: G.Sarti, Robotti, Castelletti, Chiappella, Cervato, Segato, Hamrin, Lojacono, Montuori, Gratton, Morosi.

Semi-Finals

AC Fiorentina (Firenze)	4-2	Bologna FC (Bologna)
SS Lazio (Roma)	2-0	Juventus FC (Torino)

Quarter-Finals

AC Fiorentina (Firenze)	2-1	AC Padova (Padova)
SS Lazio (Roma)	2-1	Marzotto
Milan AC (Milano)	2-4	Bologna FC (Bologna)
UC Sampdoria (Genova)	2-3 (aet)	Juventus FC (Torino)

1958-59

1958-1959 Serie "A"	Alessandria	FC Bari	Bologna FC	AC Fiorentina	Genoa	FC Internazion.	Juventus FC	AC Lanerossi	SS Lazio	Milan AC	AC Napoli	AC Padova	AS Roma	Sampdoria	SPAL Ferrara	Talm. Torino	UC Triestina	AC Udinese
US Alessandria		2-1	1-0	1-4	0-0	1-1	2-2	1-0	0-2	1-2	2-1	1-3	1-1	1-1	2-0	0-0	4-3	1-1
FC Bari	1-0		0-0	1-2	1-2	1-2	1-1	2-2	2-2	0-2	0-0	1-0	2-1	2-1	2-1	4-1	0-0	2-1
Bologna FC	4-0	1-1		0-4	2-1	2-2	4-1	1-0	1-1	1-1	1-1	2-0	1-0	1-2	3-2	0-0	0-2	2-0
AC Fiorentina	7-1	4-0	6-3		7-1	4-0	3-3	3-1	1-1	1-3	4-1	3-0	1-1	4-1	1-2	4-0	4-1	7-0
Genoa C & FBC	1-1	1-0	1-0	0-0		4-2	0-1	0-1	0-0	0-2	3-3	2-1	2-2	0-0	0-3	3-0	1-1	1-0
FC Internazionale	1-0	2-1	5-1	1-3	4-1		1-3	2-0	4-0	1-0	1-1	3-0	3-2	5-1	8-0	1-0	1-0	5-0
Juventus FC	2-2	2-2	2-2	3-2	4-3	3-2		2-3	6-1	4-5	2-0	2-1	2-0	1-0	1-1	4-3	4-0	3-0
AC Lanerossi	1-0	0-0	1-1	1-2	1-2	2-1	1-0		1-0	2-0	2-3	3-2	4-1	1-2	1-1	2-0	5-4	2-0
SS Lazio	0-2	3-2	2-1	0-0	2-4	1-2	1-0	0-1		0-0	0-0	1-1	1-3	1-0	4-0	2-0	3-1	1-1
Milan AC	5-1	4-2	4-3	2-0	4-2	1-1	1-1	0-0	5-0		6-1	4-1	4-1	4-1	0-0	5-1	2-0	7-0
AC Napoli	0-0	1-2	4-2	2-3	2-2	1-0	0-0	1-0	1-1	0-1		2-1	3-0	3-2	0-0	2-2	1-0	1-1
AC Padova	0-0	0-0	1-0	1-1	4-2	2-0	1-4	3-1	3-1	0-1	0-0		3-3	2-1	2-1	4-0	2-2	2-1
AS Roma	0-2	3-1	0-1	0-0	5-0	2-2	3-0	3-1	3-0	1-1	8-0	1-1		1-0	2-0	4-1	1-0	3-0
UC Sampdoria	3-1	3-0	2-1	1-1	2-1	2-4	3-2	2-0	1-2	0-0	0-0	3-0	0-0		1-1	3-0	2-0	3-1
SPAL Ferrara	1-1	0-1	0-1	0-0	1-5	0-1	0-0	0-0	0-3	1-1	2-1	0-2	1-0	1-2		3-0	4-0	0-1
Talmone Torino	6-1	2-2	2-2	0-6	0-0	0-5	3-2	1-1	1-0	3-3	1-2	3-1	2-2	1-2	1-0		1-0	0-1
US Triestina	2-0	0-0	3-2	1-3	2-1	1-1	0-3	0-0	3-0	2-2	0-0	2-4	1-0	1-2	0-1	1-1		1-1
AC Udinese	1-0	3-1	1-1	2-0	4-0	1-3	0-4	1-0	4-1	2-2	1-1	1-2	0-0	1-1	1-2	0-0	0-0	

	Serie "A"	Pd	Wn	Dw	Ls	GF	GA	Pts	
1.	MILAN AC (MILANO)	34	20	12	2	84	32	52	
2.	AC Fiorentina (Firenze)	34	20	9	5	95	35	49	
3.	FC Internazionale (Milano)	34	20	6	8	77	41	46	
4.	Juventus FC (Torino)	34	16	10	8	74	51	42	
5.	UC Sampdoria (Genova)	34	15	8	11	50	44	38	
6.	AS Roma (Roma)	34	12	11	11	57	41	35	
7.	AC Lanerossi (Vicenza)	34	13	8	13	41	41	34	
7.	AC Padova (Padova)	34	13	8	13	50	52	34	
7.	AC Napoli (Napoli)	34	9	16	9	39	50	34	
10.	Bologna FC (Bologna)	34	10	11	13	47	53	31	
11.	FC Bari (Bari)	34	9	12	13	38	49	30	
11.	Genoa Cricket & FBC (Genova)	34	10	10	14	44	62	30	
11.	SS Lazio (Roma)	34	10	10	14	37	54	30	
14.	US Alessandria (Alessandria)	34	8	12	14	33	57	28	
15.	AC Udinese (Udine)	34	8	11	15	32	59	27	
16.	S.P.A.L. (Ferrara)	34	8	10	16	29	48	26	
17.	US Triestina (Trieste)	34	6	11	17	34	56	23	R
17.	Talmone Torino (Torino)	34	6	11	17	36	72	23	R*
		612	213	186	213	897	897	612	

Top goalscorers

1)	Anton Valentin ANGELILLO	(FC Internazionale)	33
2)	José ALTAFINI	(Milan AC)	28
3)	Kurt HAMRIN	(AC Fiorentina)	26
4)	Miguel MONTUORI	(AC Fiorentina)	22

* Talmone Torino (Torino) reverted to AC Torino (Torino) for the next season.
AC Verona (Verona) merged with Hellas (Verona) to become Hellas-Verona AC (Verona) for the next season.
Zenit (Modena) changed their club name to Modena FC (Modena) for the next season.

	Serie "B"	Pd	Wn	Dw	Ls	GF	GA	Pts	
1.	Atalanta BC (Bergamo)	38	18	15	5	62	30	51	P
2.	US Palermo (Palermo)	38	18	13	7	52	28	49	P
3.	AC Lecco (Lecco)	38	16	13	9	50	42	45	
4.	AC Reggiana (Reggio Emilia)	38	17	9	12	45	36	43	
4.	US Cagliari (Cagliari)	38	15	13	10	48	48	43	
6.	AC Verona (Verona)	38	16	10	12	54	43	42	*
7.	AC Como (Como)	38	16	8	14	47	42	40	
7.	Simmenthal (Monza)	38	14	12	12	41	32	40	
9.	AC Venezia (Venezia)	38	14	11	13	45	41	39	
10.	AS Messina (Messina)	38	12	14	12	49	42	38	
10.	AC Novara (Novara)	38	14	10	14	45	48	38	
12.	AS Taranto (Taranto)	38	11	15	12	37	41	37	
13.	AC Brescia (Brescia)	38	10	16	12	47	46	36	
14.	Zenit (Modena)	38	10	14	14	34	45	34	*
14.	Marzotto	38	12	10	16	26	36	34	
16.	CC Catania (Catania)	38	9	15	14	37	42	33	
16.	Sambenedettese Calcio (San Benedetto del Tronto)	38	6	21	11	32	44	33	
18.	Parma AS (Parma)	38	10	12	16	41	64	32	
19.	AC Vigevano (Vigevano)	38	9	10	19	30	49	28	R
20.	AC Prato (Prato)	38	8	9	21	31	54	25	R
		760	255	250	255	853	853	760	

Promoted to Serie "B": US Catanzaro (Catanzaro) and Ozo Mantova (Mantova).

Coppa Italia Final (Milano – 10/06/59)

JUVENTUS FC (TORINO) 4-1 FC Internazionale (Milano)

Charles, Cervato 2 (1 pen), Sivori *(H.T. 2-1)* *Bicicli*

Juventus: Mattrel, Castano, Sarti, Emoli, Cervato, Colombo, Boniperti, Nicolé, Charles, Sivori, Stivanello.

Internazionale: Matteucci (Da Pozzo), Guarneri, Gatti, Masiero, Cardarelli, Bolchi, Bicicli, Firmani, Angelillo, Corso, Rizzolini.

Semi-Finals

FC Internazionale (Milano)	1-0	AC Venezia (Venezia)
Juventus FC (Torino)	3-1	Genoa Cricket & FBC (Genova)

Quarter-Finals

Bologna FC (Bologna)	1-2	Genoa Cricket & FBC (Genova)
Juventus FC (Torino)	3-1	AC Fiorentina (Firenze)
SS Lazio (Roma)	0-1	FC Internazionale (Milano)
AC Venezia (Venezia)	5-1	Talmone Torino (Torino)

1959-60

1959-1960 Serie "A"	US Alessandria	Atalanta BC	FC Bari	Bologna FC	AC Fiorentina	Genoa C & FBC	FC Internazion.	Juventus FC	AC Lanerossi	SS Lazio	Milan AC	AC Napoli	AC Padova	UC Palermo	AS Roma	UC Sampdoria	SPAL Ferrara	AC Udinese
US Alessandria		0-0	2-0	1-1	3-3	2-1	2-3	0-2	3-1	0-0	3-1	1-1	0-0	1-0	0-0	2-2	0-1	0-1
Atalanta BC	5-1		3-0	3-0	1-3	2-1	1-1	2-2	1-1	0-0	0-0	1-0	1-0	1-0	2-0	0-0	2-2	0-0
FC Bari	0-0	1-0		1-1	1-0	1-0	1-3	1-3	0-0	0-0	3-0	1-1	5-2	1-0	2-3	1-1	0-0	3-1
Bologna FC	2-1	5-0	2-0		3-1	3-1	1-0	3-2	0-1	1-1	0-3	4-1	2-2	3-1	3-1	0-1	2-3	2-0
AC Fiorentina	3-1	4-1	4-2	2-1		2-0	2-0	1-0	0-0	2-2	1-1	2-1	1-0	5-0	3-1	4-0	3-1	2-1
Genoa C & FBC	1-0	1-1	1-0	0-2	0-0		1-3	2-6	0-2	2-4	0-2	0-0	0-0	1-1	1-0	1-2	0-1	0-0
FC Internazionale	3-1	2-0	0-0	2-1	2-0	2-0		0-3	4-0	1-1	0-0	3-1	6-3	3-3	1-3	0-0	2-1	3-3
Juventus FC	7-0	0-1	2-0	3-0	3-1	2-0	1-0		4-1	2-0	3-1	4-2	5-1	2-1	4-0	2-2	3-1	4-3
AC Lanerossi	0-0	1-0	0-0	1-1	1-1	1-0	0-2	1-2		3-2	1-2	0-0	1-0	3-0	5-0	2-0	3-1	1-0
SS Lazio	2-0	1-1	1-1	1-3	0-5	0-0	0-2	0-2	2-1		0-1	2-1	2-0	2-1	0-1	3-1	3-1	2-1
Milan AC	3-1	2-1	2-0	2-2	0-0	2-1	5-3	0-2	2-0	1-0		3-1	3-2	0-0	1-1	4-0	3-1	3-1
AC Napoli	1-1	1-0	1-2	2-0	0-4	0-2	1-1	2-1	3-1	0-0	1-1		1-2	2-1	1-0	1-1	0-3	1-1
AC Padova	1-1	0-0	1-0	2-0	1-0	2-1	3-0	0-4	2-1	2-0	2-0	1-2		1-0	1-0	4-1	6-3	6-1
US Palermo	4-0	1-0	1-1	0-0	0-4	1-1	1-1	1-1	1-0	0-0	1-0	0-0	0-0		4-2	2-1	1-1	0-0
AS Roma	1-0	3-0	3-2	1-2	1-2	1-0	3-1	2-2	3-1	3-0	2-2	3-0	1-0	1-1		6-1	1-1	2-2
UC Sampdoria	0-0	4-0	1-0	1-0	2-1	3-0	0-0	0-2	2-2	4-0	2-1	0-2	1-1	0-0	3-0		0-2	3-1
SPAL Ferrara	0-0	1-0	3-1	0-0	1-0	0-0	0-0	3-6	2-1	1-1	0-3	2-2	1-1	1-0	2-1	1-1		2-1
AC Udinese	1-1	1-1	0-1	1-0	0-2	2-2	1-1	1-1	2-2	1-0	2-2	0-0	2-1	1-0	3-3	1-1	3-2	

	Serie "A"	Pd	Wn	Dw	Ls	GF	GA	Pts	
1.	JUVENTUS FC (TORINO)	34	25	5	4	92	33	55	
2.	AC Fiorentina (Firenze)	34	20	7	7	68	31	47	
3.	Milan AC (Milano)	34	17	10	7	56	37	44	
4.	FC Internazionale (Milano)	34	14	12	8	55	43	40	
5.	Bologna FC (Bologna)	34	14	8	12	50	42	36	
5.	AC Padova (Padova)	34	14	8	12	50	46	36	
5.	S.P.A.L. (Ferrara)	34	12	12	10	45	50	36	
8.	UC Sampdoria (Genova)	34	11	13	10	41	46	35	
9.	AS Roma (Roma)	34	13	8	13	53	53	34	
10.	AC Lanerossi (Vicenza)	34	11	10	13	39	42	32	
11.	Atalanta BC (Bergamo)	34	9	13	12	31	39	31	
12.	SS Lazio (Roma)	34	9	12	13	32	45	30	
13.	FC Bari (Bari)	34	9	11	14	32	42	29	
13.	AC Napoli (Napoli)	34	8	13	13	33	48	29	
15.	AC Udinese (Udine)	34	6	16	12	39	54	28	
16.	US Palermo (Palermo)	34	6	15	13	27	40	27	R
17.	US Alessandria (Alessandria)	34	5	15	14	28	51	25	R
18.	Genoa Cricket & FBC (Genova)	34	4	10	20	21	50	18	R#
		612	207	198	207	792	792	612	

Top goalscorers

1)	Omar SIVORI	(Juventus FC)	27
2)	Kurt HAMRIN	(AC Fiorentina)	26
3)	John CHARLES	(Juventus FC)	23
4)	Sergio BRIGHENTI	(AC Padova)	21

Genoa Cricket & FBC (Genova) had 28 points deducted by the F.I.G.C. Committee of Enquiry on 01/06/60. However, as they had only won 18 points this left the club with –10 points at the beginning of the next season, which was later reduced to –7 pts on appeal. This was deducted from their 1960-61 season total.

	Serie "B"	Pd	Wn	Dw	Ls	GF	GA	Pts	
1.	AC Torino (Torino)	38	16	19	3	44	21	51	P
2.	AC Lecco (Lecco)	38	17	16	5	51	28	50	P
3.	CC Catania (Catania)	38	14	19	5	55	38	47	P
4.	US Triestina (Trieste)	38	15	16	7	49	32	46	
5.	Ozo Mantova (Mantova)	38	15	9	14	42	38	39	
5.	Parma AS (Parma)	38	14	11	13	51	50	39	
7.	AC Reggiana (Reggio Emilia)	38	11	16	11	35	38	38	
8.	AC Brescia (Brescia)	38	12	13	13	49	45	37	
8.	Hellas-Verona AC (Verona)	38	14	9	15	51	48	37	
8.	AC Como (Como)	38	11	15	12	41	40	37	
8.	US Catanzaro (Catanzaro)	38	12	13	13	37	40	37	
8.	Marzotto	38	15	7	16	35	38	37	
13.	AS Messina (Messina)	38	13	9	16	38	40	35	
14.	AC Novara (Novara)	38	11	12	15	38	47	34	
14.	Sambenedettese Calcio (San Benedetto del Tronto)	38	9	16	13	38	50	34	
16.	Simmenthal (Monza)	38	11	11	16	46	53	33	PO
16.	AC Venezia (Venezia)	38	9	15	14	34	42	33	PO
16.	AS Taranto (Taranto)	38	12	9	17	33	48	33	R
19.	Modena FC (Modena)	38	9	14	15	38	51	32	R
20.	US Cagliari (Cagliari)	38	8	15	15	36	54	31	R
		760	248	264	284	841	841	760	

Relegation Play-Offs

Simmenthal (Monza)	2-0	AC Venezia (Venezia)
AC Venezia (Venezia)	4-2	AS Taranto (Taranto)
AS Taranto (Taranto)	0-0	Simmenthal (Monza)

Promoted to Serie "B": US Foggia & Incedit (Foggia), AC Prato (Prato), Pro Patria et Libertate (Busto Arsizio).

Coppa Italia Final (Milano – 18/09/60)

JUVENTUS FC (TORINO)	3-2 (aet)	AC Fiorentina (Firenze)
Charles 1-0, 2-2, Micheli 3-2 o.g.	*(H.T. 1-1 — 90 mins. 2-2)*	*Montuori 1-1, Da Costa 1-2*

Juventus: Vavassori, Burelli, Sarti, Emoli, Cervato, Colombo, Nicolé, Boniperti, Charles, Sivori, Stacchini.

Fiorentina: G.Sarti, Robotti, Castelletti, Micheli, Orzan, Marchesi, Hamrin, Montuori, Da Cosat, Milan, Petris.

Semi-Finals

AC Fiorentina (Firenze)	5-3	AC Torino (Torino)
Juventus FC (Torino)	3-0	SS Lazio (Roma)

Quarter-Finals

Atalanta BC (Bergamo)	2-2	Juventus FC (Torino)
	(Juventus qualified after the drawing of lots)	
Bologna FC (Bologna)	2-3 (aet)	SS Lazio (Roma)
AC Fiorentina (Firenze)	2-1	FC Internazionale (Milano)
AC Torino (Torino)	1-0	AC Venezia (Venezia)

1960-61

1960-1961 Serie "A"	Atalanta BC	FC Bari	Bologna FC	CC Catania	AC Fiorentina	FC Internazionale	Juventus FC	AC Lanerossi	SS Lazio	AC Lecco	Milan AC	AC Napoli	AC Padova	AS Roma	UC Sampdoria	SPAL Ferrara	AC Torino	AC Udinese
Atalanta BC		2-0	1-1	1-0	4-1	1-5	2-2	1-0	0-0	3-0	2-0	1-1	1-0	0-0	0-3	1-1	1-1	1-1
FC Bari	2-2		1-3	0-1	0-0	1-1	0-1	1-1	0-0	4-1	0-0	1-0	1-0	0-3	1-0	2-0	1-0	2-1
Bologna FC	3-1	0-0		1-2	3-3	2-1	2-4	1-1	1-1	0-0	0-2	0-2	2-1	2-0	4-4	3-1	3-1	1-1
CC Catania	3-1	3-1	1-0		1-1	2-0	1-2	4-0	0-1	2-0	4-3	1-0	2-0	1-1	3-0	1-1	0-0	3-0
AC Fiorentina	0-1	4-0	3-1	2-0		1-1	3-0	0-1	4-0	4-0	2-0	0-0	2-0	0-1	1-0	0-3	1-1	3-0
FC Internazionale	2-1	2-1	0-0	5-0	2-2		3-1	5-0	7-0	1-1	1-2	3-0	1-2	3-1	3-0	4-1	1-1	1-0
Juventus FC	3-2	1-1	3-0	4-1	3-0	9-1		2-0	3-1	4-2	3-4	2-2	2-1	3-0	3-2	1-0	1-0	5-1
AC Lanerossi	1-0	4-1	2-2	1-0	0-0	1-3	0-1		0-0	1-0	1-0	2-3	2-1	4-0	1-1	1-0	1-1	2-2
SS Lazio	1-2	0-1	1-3	2-2	1-2	0-0	1-4	1-1		0-1	0-1	1-1	1-2	0-4	0-1	4-0	1-0	0-1
AC Lecco	1-0	0-0	2-0	2-2	0-2	2-1	2-2	0-1	2-1		2-2	1-0	2-1	0-0	1-1	2-0	2-1	3-1
Milan AC	0-0	1-3	5-1	3-0	4-1	0-1	3-1	0-0	5-1	1-1		2-1	3-0	2-1	3-1	4-0	2-0	3-1
AC Napoli	0-0	1-0	1-2	0-1	1-0	0-0	0-4	0-0	2-5	3-1	1-2		1-2	3-2	1-0	0-2	1-1	2-2
AC Padova	3-0	1-1	2-1	2-1	0-0	2-1	1-0	2-1	2-1	3-1	4-1	2-0		0-0	3-0	1-1	5-1	1-0
AS Roma	0-0	1-0	1-0	4-1	1-3	0-2	2-1	6-3	1-2	1-0	2-2	2-0	3-1		3-2	2-1	2-1	6-1
UC Sampdoria	1-0	1-0	2-1	2-0	3-1	4-2	3-2	3-1	1-0	1-0	2-2	0-0	3-0	3-2		1-1	2-1	3-2
SPAL Ferrara	2-1	1-0	0-1	2-0	2-0	1-3	1-2	2-1	3-2	1-0	1-2	3-2	1-1	2-2	2-2		0-0	1-1
AC Torino	1-1	2-1	1-0	2-1	0-0	0-1	0-0	2-0	4-1	3-1	1-1	1-0	0-0	1-3	0-1	3-2		3-1
AC Udinese	2-1	0-0	0-0	0-1	0-0	0-6	0-1	1-0	2-0	2-0	0-0	1-1	3-1	2-1	7-1	0-0	3-0	

	Serie "A"	Pd	Wn	Dw	Ls	GF	GA	Pts	
1.	JUVENTUS FC (TORINO)	34	22	5	7	80	42	49	
2.	Milan AC (Milano)	34	18	9	7	65	39	45	
3.	FC Internazionale (Milano)	34	18	8	8	73	39	44	
4.	UC Sampdoria (Genova)	34	17	7	10	54	51	41	
5.	AS Roma (Roma)	34	16	7	11	58	46	39	
5.	AC Padova (Padova)	34	16	6	12	47	40	38	
7.	AC Fiorentina (Firenze)	34	13	11	10	46	34	37	
8.	CC Catania (Catania)	34	15	6	13	45	44	36	
9.	Bologna FC (Bologna)	34	10	11	13	44	51	31	
9.	Atalanta BC (Bergamo)	34	9	13	12	35	41	31	
9.	AC Lanerossi (Vicenza)	34	10	11	13	35	46	31	
12.	AC Torino (Torino)	34	9	12	13	34	41	30	
12.	S.P.A.L. (Ferrara)	34	10	10	14	39	50	30	
14.	AC Udinese (Udine)	34	9	11	14	39	53	29	PO
14.	AC Lecco (Lecco)	34	10	9	15	33	49	29	PO
14.	FC Bari (Bari)	34	9	11	14	27	38	29	R
17.	AC Napoli (Napoli)	34	7	11	16	30	47	25	R
18.	SS Lazio (Roma)	34	5	8	21	30	63	18	R
		612	223	166	223	814	814	612	

Top goalscorers

1)	Sergio BRIGHENTI	(UC Sampdoria)	27
2)	Omar SIVORI	(Juventus FC)	25
3)	José ALTAFINI	(Milan AC)	22
4)	Pedro MANFREDI	(AS Roma)	20

Relegation Play-Offs (Played in Bologna)

AC Lecco (Lecco)	4-2	FC Bari (Bari)
AC Udinese (Udine)	3-3	AC Lecco (Lecco)
FC Bari (Bari)	0-0	AC Udinese (Udine)

* Ozo Mantova (Mantova) reverted to AC Mantova (Mantova) for the next season.

	Serie "B"	Pd	Wn	Dw	Ls	GF	GA	Pts	
1.	AC Venezia (Venezia)	38	22	6	10	54	31	50	P
2.	Ozo Mantova (Mantova)	38	18	13	7	44	25	49	P *
3.	US Palermo (Palermo)	38	13	20	5	46	27	46	P
4.	AC Reggiana (Reggio Emilia)	38	16	11	11	63	55	43	
5.	Simmenthal (Monza)	38	14	14	10	36	26	42	
6.	AS Messina (Messina)	38	13	15	10	45	34	41	
7.	Pro Patria et Libertate (Busto Arsizio)	38	14	11	13	46	39	39	
7.	US Alessandria (Alessandria)	38	15	9	14	43	41	39	
7.	Sambenedettese Calcio (San Benedetto del Tronto)	38	15	9	14	35	42	39	
10.	US Catanzaro (Catanzaro)	38	15	8	15	46	42	38	
11.	AC Como (Como)	38	13	11	14	42	45	37	
11.	AC Prato (Prato)	38	14	9	15	35	41	37	
13.	Genoa Cricket & FBC (Genova)	38	14	14	10	47	42	35	-7
13.	Parma AS (Parma)	38	12	11	15	36	36	35	
15.	AC Brescia (Brescia)	38	12	10	16	44	38	34	
15.	Hellas-Verona AC (Verona)	38	11	12	15	31	44	34	
17.	AC Novara (Novara)	38	11	11	16	31	51	33	PO
18.	US Triestina (Trieste)	38	9	15	14	31	39	33	R
19.	US Foggia & Incedit (Foggia)	38	10	9	19	40	56	29	R
20.	Marzotto	38	5	10	38	28	69	20	R
		760	266	228	266	823	823	753	

Note: Genoa Cricket & FBC (Genova) started the season with –7 pts as a result of the F.I.G.C. committee ruling at the end of the 1959-60 season.

Relegation Play-Off

AC Novara (Novara)	2-1 (aet)	US Triestina (Trieste)

Promoted to Serie "B": AS Cosenza (Cosenza), US Lucchese Libertas (Lucca) and Modena FC (Modena).

Coppa Italia Final (Firenze – 11/06/61)

AC FIORENTINA (FIRENZE)	2-0	SS Lazio (Roma)
Petris 1-0, Milan 2-0	*(H.T. 1-0)*	

Fiorentina: Albertossi, Robotti, Castelletti, Gonfiantini, Orzan, Marchesi, Hamrin, Micheli, Da Costa, Milan, Petris.

Lazio: Cei, Molino, Eufumi, Carosi, Janich, Carradori, Mariani, Franzini, Rozzini, Prini, Mattei.

Semi-Finals

AC Fiorentina (Firenze)	3-1	Juventus FC (Torino)
SS Lazio (Roma)	1-1 (aet – 6-5 penalties)	AC Torino (Torino)

Quarter-Finals

FC Internazionale (Milano)	0-1	SS Lazio (Roma)
AC Padova (Padova)	0-1	AC Torino (Torino)
AS Roma (Roma)	4-6	AC Fiorentina (Firenze)
UC Sampdoria (Genova)	0-2	Juventus FC (Torino)

1961-62

1961-1962 Serie "A"	Atalanta BC	Bologna FC	CC Catania	AC Fiorentina	FC Internazionale	Juventus FC	AC Lanerossi	AC Lecco	AC Mantova	Milan AC	AC Padova	UC Palermo	AS Roma	UC Sampdoria	SPAL Ferrara	AC Torino	AC Udinese	AC Venezia
Atalanta BC		2-1	3-0	0-0	2-3	3-1	0-1	1-1	0-2	0-2	0-0	2-2	0-0	2-0	1-1	2-0	2-1	3-1
Bologna FC	0-0		3-1	0-3	0-2	2-2	2-0	1-0	3-0	1-0	4-1	1-0	3-1	2-1	2-0	2-1	2-1	1-1
CC Catania	2-1	1-1		3-1	0-2	2-0	2-0	1-0	2-1	1-3	0-0	0-0	1-1	2-0	0-0	0-1	2-0	1-1
AC Fiorentina	0-1	1-0	0-0		4-1	1-0	0-1	2-0	1-0	5-2	3-1	2-0	1-1	0-0	5-1	2-0	5-2	2-0
FC Internazionale	6-0	6-4	1-1	4-1		2-2	2-1	3-0	2-0	1-3	2-1	1-0	0-1	1-1	2-1	0-0	2-0	0-0
Juventus FC	1-1	2-3	1-0	0-0	2-4		2-0	2-2	1-1	2-4	4-0	2-4	1-0	0-1	2-1	0-1	2-3	1-0
AC Lanerossi	0-1	0-1	3-0	1-1	1-1	1-0		0-0	1-2	0-3	1-0	2-2	0-1	1-1	1-0	1-1	2-2	1-1
AC Lecco	0-1	2-2	3-1	3-2	0-1	2-2	0-3		1-0	2-2	0-0	2-1	0-1	1-1	0-0	1-1	2-1	4-1
AC Mantova	3-1	2-5	1-1	0-0	1-1	0-1	1-1	3-0		1-2	1-0	2-0	2-1	2-0	2-0	2-2	2-0	1-0
Milan AC	2-2	3-0	3-0	5-2	0-2	5-1	4-1	3-0	1-0		4-0	3-0	3-1	2-3	4-1	4-2	4-3	1-0
AC Padova	1-1	1-2	3-1	1-2	0-2	2-1	2-0	3-1	1-1	1-1		0-0	0-3	1-0	3-2	0-3	4-0	1-1
US Palermo	1-0	1-0	0-0	0-1	1-0	0-0	1-0	1-0	1-1	0-0	1-0		0-0	3-1	1-3	1-0	1-3	1-0
AS Roma	3-1	1-2	4-0	1-0	2-3	3-3	1-1	2-0	4-2	0-1	3-1	5-2		1-0	4-1	2-2	4-0	1-0
UC Sampdoria	1-1	0-2	4-1	1-3	0-0	2-3	3-0	2-1	1-0	1-3	1-0	0-2	1-0		0-0	2-0	2-2	0-2
SPAL Ferrara	0-1	1-2	1-0	1-1	1-0	0-3	1-0	0-0	2-1	0-3	2-1	0-2	1-2	1-1		1-0	2-1	1-1
AC Torino	1-1	2-1	1-1	0-2	0-0	1-3	3-3	2-1	2-1	1-1	1-0	3-0	1-1	0-0	1-0		1-2	4-2
AC Udinese	1-2	1-1	0-1	2-3	0-1	2-1	0-1	5-1	0-1	0-1	1-0	0-1	1-3	0-0	1-2	1-3		0-0
AC Venezia	0-1	1-1	2-2	0-1	1-1	3-0	2-0	2-0	4-3	2-1	0-0	1-0	1-3	1-1	2-2	0-1	2-1	

	Serie "A"	Pd	Wn	Dw	Ls	GF	GA	Pts	
1.	MILAN AC (MILANO)	34	24	5	5	83	36	53	
2.	FC Internazionale (Milano)	34	19	10	5	59	31	48	
3.	AC Fiorentina (Firenze)	34	19	8	7	57	32	46	
4.	Bologna FC (Bologna)	34	19	7	8	57	41	45	
5.	AS Roma (Roma)	34	18	8	8	61	35	44	
6.	Atalanta BC (Bergamo)	34	13	12	9	39	38	38	
7.	AC Torino (Torino)	34	12	12	10	42	40	36	
8.	US Palermo (Palermo)	34	13	9	12	30	35	35	
9.	AC Mantova (Mantova)	34	12	8	14	42	42	32	
10.	UC Sampdoria (Genova)	34	9	12	13	32	40	30	
10.	CC Catania (Catania)	34	9	12	13	30	45	30	
12.	AC Venezia (Venezia)	34	8	13	13	35	41	29	
12.	Juventus FC (Torino)	34	10	9	15	48	56	29	
14.	AC Lanerossi (Vicenza)	34	8	11	15	29	43	27	
14.	S.P.A.L. (Ferrara)	34	9	9	16	30	50	27	
16.	AC Padova (Padova)	34	7	9	18	29	49	23	R
16.	AC Lecco (Lecco)	34	6	11	17	30	53	23	R
18.	AC Udinese (Udine)	34	6	5	23	37	63	17	R
		612	221	170	221	770	770	612	

Top goalscorers

1)	José ALTAFINI	(Milan AC)	22
	Aurelio MILANI	(AC Fiorentina)	22
3)	Gerry HITCHINS	(FC Internazionale)	16
	Angelo Benedicto SORMANI	(AC Mantova)	16
5)	Kurt HAMRIN	(AC Fiorentina)	15

	Serie "B"	Pd	Wn	Dw	Ls	GF	GA	Pts	
1.	Genoa Cricket & FBC (Genova)	38	22	10	6	64	28	54	P
2.	AC Napoli (Napoli)	38	15	13	10	44	35	43	P
2.	Modena FC (Modena)	38	15	13	10	39	36	43	P
4.	SS Lazio (Roma)	38	14	14	10	50	28	42	
4.	Hellas-Verona AC (Verona)	38	14	14	10	39	27	42	
6.	Pro Patria et Libertate (Busto Arsizio)	38	15	11	12	43	38	41	
7.	AS Messina (Messina)	38	14	11	13	53	46	39	
8.	AC Brescia (Brescia)	38	14	9	15	37	36	37	
8.	Simmenthal (Monza)	38	13	11	14	37	44	37	
10.	US Alessandria (Alessandria)	38	13	10	15	45	46	36	
11.	AC Novara (Novara)	38	12	12	14	37	43	36	#
12.	FC Bari (Bari)	38	15	11	12	48	38	35	-6
12.	Parma AS (Parma)	38	9	17	12	25	33	35	
12.	Sambenedettese Calcio (San Benedetto del Tronto)	38	10	15	13	30	42	35	
15.	US Lucchese Libertas (Lucca)	38	13	8	17	46	54	34	
15.	AC Como (Como)	38	11	12	15	33	46	34	
15.	US Catanzaro (Catanzaro)	38	9	16	13	37	50	34	
18.	AS Cosenza (Cosenza)	38	11	11	16	29	46	33	#
19.	AC Reggiana (Reggio Emilia)	38	8	16	14	34	40	32	R
19.	AC Prato (Prato)	38	9	14	15	33	47	32	R
		760	256	248	256	803	803	754	

Note: FC Bari (Bari) had 6 points deducted by an F.I.G.C. Committee.

\# AC Novara (Novara) were relegated by the F.I.G.C. for a "breach of discipline". As a result of this decision AS Cosenza (Cosenza) retained their place in Serie "B" for the next season.

Promoted to Serie "B": US Cagliari (Cagliari), US Foggia & Incedit (Foggia) and US Triestina (Trieste).

Coppa Italia Final (Roma – 21/06/62)

AC NAPOLI (NAPOLI)	2-1	S.P.A.L. (Ferrara)
Corelli 1-0, Ronzon 2-1	*(H.T. 1-1)*	*Micheli 1-1*

Napoli: Pontel (Cuman), Molino, Gatti, Girardo, Rivellino, Corelli, Mariani, Ronzon, Tomeazzi, Fraschini, Tacchi.

SPAL: Patregnani, Muccini, Olivieri, Gori, Cervato, Riva, Dell'Omodarme, Massei, Mancacci, Micheli, Novelli.

Semi-Finals

AC Napoli (Napoli)	2-1	AC Mantova (Mantova)
S.P.A.L. (Ferrara)	4-1	Juventus FC (Torino)

Quarter-Finals

Juventus FC (Torino)	3-0	AC Lecco (Lecco)
AC Mantova (Mantova)	3-0	US Catanzaro (Catanzaro)
AS Roma (Roma)	0-1	AC Napoli (Napoli)
S.P.A.L. (Ferrara)	3-1	AC Novara (Novara)

1962-63

1962-1963 Serie "A"	Atalanta BC	Bologna FC	CC Catania	AC Fiorentina	Genoa C & FBC	FC Internazionale	Juventus FC	AC Lanerossi	AC Mantova	Milan AC	Modena FC	AC Napoli	UC Palermo	AS Roma	UC Sampdoria	SPAL Ferrara	AC Torino	AC Venezia
Atalanta BC		1-3	0-0	0-1	1-1	1-0	3-6	3-1	2-2	2-2	2-1	2-1	1-0	3-1	1-1	1-0	0-0	2-2
Bologna FC	1-0		5-0	2-1	1-1	0-4	1-2	2-1	2-2	1-2	7-1	4-2	4-0	0-0	4-1	4-1	1-0	0-0
CC Catania	2-0	1-1		0-1	3-1	1-0	1-5	1-0	1-1	1-0	3-2	1-0	0-0	0-0	0-1	0-0	3-0	3-2
AC Fiorentina	2-0	3-1	3-0		5-0	1-1	1-0	1-1	5-0	0-1	1-2	5-1	3-1	1-1	1-1	2-0	1-0	1-4
Genoa C & FBC	2-1	1-0	4-1	1-2		1-3	0-0	2-0	0-0	0-1	1-1	3-2	5-0	2-2	2-1	0-0	1-0	2-0
FC Internazionale	1-2	4-1	2-1	1-0	6-0		1-0	1-0	1-0	1-1	0-0	1-0	4-0	2-0	4-0	3-2	1-1	2-0
Juventus FC	2-3	3-1	0-1	0-0	2-0	0-1		2-0	2-0	1-0	2-1	1-0	2-1	2-0	3-0	2-2	0-1	2-1
AC Lanerossi	2-2	0-0	3-1	1-0	1-0	1-2	1-3		4-2	2-0	1-0	0-0	1-0	0-0	3-0	1-0	0-1	0-0
AC Mantova	0-1	0-1	3-1	1-1	2-0	0-0	0-0	0-0		1-3	3-0	2-1	1-0	1-0	3-1	0-1	1-1	2-0
Milan AC	0-0	3-1	0-0	0-0	1-0	1-1	0-0	6-1	2-2		4-0	0-1	2-0	0-1	1-1	4-0	2-1	3-3
Modena FC	0-2	0-1	4-1	3-0	1-1	0-0	0-0	0-0	0-0	2-2		4-0	2-0	1-3	1-0	1-0	1-0	2-1
AC Napoli	2-1	0-0	3-2	2-0	1-0	1-5	0-0	1-0	0-0	1-5	0-2		3-1	3-3	0-2	2-0	2-2	1-0
US Palermo	1-0	0-0	1-1	1-0	0-0	1-1	1-1	1-1	1-0	1-3	2-2	1-1		0-4	1-1	0-1	0-1	2-1
AS Roma	1-1	3-1	5-1	2-2	1-0	3-0	1-1	0-1	7-1	0-1	2-0	3-0	2-0		2-0	0-0	5-0	2-2
UC Sampdoria	2-0	2-3	4-0	1-0	3-1	0-0	2-1	1-3	2-2	2-1	1-1	3-0	2-0	0-0		0-1	1-3	3-1
SPAL Ferrara	2-5	0-1	2-2	3-1	4-0	0-0	0-2	1-1	1-1	0-0	1-0	4-2	1-0	3-0	1-0		2-0	1-1
AC Torino	1-0	0-1	1-1	0-4	2-0	1-1	0-1	1-2	1-0	0-0	2-0	1-1	3-0	2-2	4-2	2-1		1-0
AC Venezia	1-0	0-3	2-1	0-3	0-0	0-2	1-2	1-2	4-1	0-2	4-1	1-1	0-1	1-1	2-0	0-1	1-1	

Serie "A"		Pd	Wn	Dw	Ls	GF	GA	Pts	
1.	FC INTERNAZIONALE (MILANO)	34	19	11	4	56	20	49	
2.	Juventus FC (Torino)	34	18	9	7	50	25	45	
3.	Milan AC (Milano)	34	15	13	6	53	27	43	
4.	Bologna FC (Bologna)	34	17	8	9	58	39	42	
5.	AS Roma (Roma)	34	13	14	7	57	32	40	
6.	AC Fiorentina (Firenze)	34	15	8	11	52	32	38	
7.	AC Lanerossi (Vicenza)	34	13	10	11	35	35	36	
8.	Atalanta BC (Bergamo)	34	12	10	12	43	44	34	
8.	S.P.A.L. (Ferrara)	34	12	10	12	36	38	34	
8.	AC Torino (Torino)	34	12	10	12	34	38	34	
11.	UC Sampdoria (Genova)	34	11	8	15	41	50	30	
11.	Modena FC (Modena)	34	10	10	14	36	47	30	
11.	AC Mantova (Mantova)	34	8	14	12	34	46	30	
11.	CC Catania (Catania)	34	10	10	14	35	56	30	
15.	Genoa Cricket & FBC (Genova)	34	9	10	15	32	48	28	
16.	AC Napoli (Napoli)	34	9	9	16	35	59	27	R
17.	AC Venezia (Venezia)	34	6	10	18	36	51	22	R
18.	US Palermo (Palermo)	34	5	10	19	18	54	20	R
		612	214	184	214	741	741	612	

Top goalscorers

1)	Pedro MANFREDINI	(AS Roma)	19
	Harald NIELSEN	(Bologna FC)	19
3)	Omar SIVORI	(Juventus FC)	16
4)	Kurt HAMRIN	(AC Fiorentina)	14
	Enzio PASCUTTI	(Bologna FC)	14

Serie "B"		Pd	Wn	Dw	Ls	GF	GA	Pts	
1.	AS Messina (Messina)	38	18	14	6	50	31	50	P
2.	FC Bari (Bari)	38	15	18	5	47	26	48	P
2.	SS Lazio (Roma)	38	18	12	8	50	31	48	P
4.	AC Brescia (Brescia)	38	15	15	8	40	27	45	#
5.	US Foggia & Incedit (Foggia)	38	16	11	11	56	42	43	
6.	AC Lecco (Lecco)	38	14	14	10	45	36	42	
7.	Hellas-Verona AC (Verona)	38	15	11	12	41	34	41	
8.	AC Padova (Padova)	38	14	12	12	45	47	40	
9.	US Cagliari (Cagliari)	38	12	14	12	41	40	38	
9.	Pro Patria et Libertate (Busto Arsizio)	38	11	16	11	36	33	38	
9.	Simmenthal (Monza)	38	14	10	14	56	52	38	
12.	US Catanzaro (Catanzaro)	38	12	13	13	34	43	37	
13.	Parma AS (Parma)	38	12	11	15	32	44	35	
14.	US Alessandria (Alessandria)	38	11	12	15	32	34	34	
14.	AS Cosenza (Cosenza)	38	8	18	12	27	37	34	
14.	AC Udinese (Udine)	38	10	14	14	49	48	34	
17.	US Triestina (Trieste)	38	11	11	16	49	59	33	
18.	AC Como (Como)	38	9	13	16	38	51	31	R*
19.	Sambenedettese Calcio (San Benedetto del Tronto)	38	8	14	16	29	51	30	R
20.	US Lucchese Libertas (Lucca)	38	7	7	24	36	67	21	R
		760	250	260	250	833	833	760	

* The matches Como 4-1 Cosenza, Como 0-0 Catanzaro, Foggia 2-1 Como, Lazio 2-0 Como, Como 1-2 Padova, were all awarded by the F.I.G.C. to the opponents of AC Como with a 0-2 forfeit result being recorded.

AC Brescia (Brescia) were relegated to Serie "C" by the F.I.G.C. but this was later changed to a penalty of -7 points to be deducted from season 1963-64 in Serie "B".

Promoted to Serie "B": Potenza SC (Potenza), AC Prato (Prato) and FC Varese (Varese).

Coppa Italia Final (Milan – 02/06/63)

ATALANTA BC (BERGAMO)	3-1	AC Torino (Torino)
Domenghini 04', 49', 82'		*Ferrini 84'*

Atalanta: Pizzaballa, Pesenti, Nodari, Veneri, Gardoni, Colombo, Domenghini, F.Nielsen, Calvanese, Mereghetti, Magistrelli.

Torino: Vieri, Polletti, Buzzacchera, Bearzot, Lanciono, Rosato, Danova, Ferrini, Hitchens, Peirò, Crippa.

Semi-Finals

Atalanta BC (Bergamo)	1-0	FC Bari (Bari)
AC Torino (Torino)	2-1	Hellas-Verona AC (Verona)

Quarter-Finals

Atalanta BC (Bergamo)	2-0	AC Padova (Padova)
FC Bari (Bari)	2-1 (aet)	Genoa Cricket & FBC (Genova)
Juventus FC (Torino)	0-1	Hellas-Verona AC (Verona)
UC Sampdoria (Genova)	0-2	AC Torino (Torino)

1963-64

1963-1964 Serie "A"	Atalanta BC	FC Bari	Bologna FC	CC Catania	AC Fiorentina	Genoa C & FBC	FC Internazionale	Juventus FC	AC Lanerossi	SS Lazio	AC Mantova	AS Messina	Milan AC	Modena FC	AS Roma	UC Sampdoria	SPAL Ferrara	AC Torino
Atalanta BC		1-0	1-1	3-0	1-7	1-3	1-3	3-0	2-1	1-1	0-0	3-0	0-0	1-1	1-0	0-0	0-0	1-1
FC Bari	4-0		0-1	0-0	2-0	0-2	1-1	1-1	1-0	0-2	0-0	0-1	0-2	0-0	1-3	2-1	1-0	0-3
Bologna FC	2-0	3-1		1-0	2-0	1-1	1-2	2-1	3-0	1-0	2-1	2-0	2-2	0-0	4-0	1-0	2-1	4-1
CC Catania	0-0	1-0	1-3		2-0	5-3	1-2	2-0	0-1	1-0	0-0	2-0	0-1	1-0	0-0	1-5	0-0	1-0
AC Fiorentina	4-0	1-0	0-0	1-1		2-0	1-3	2-1	0-2	1-0	0-1	0-1	2-1	0-0	0-0	3-0	1-0	1-1
Genoa C & FBC	0-0	0-0	0-2	0-2	2-1		0-2	3-1	0-0	4-1	1-0	3-0	1-1	2-2	3-0	0-1	1-0	0-0
FC Internazionale	2-1	3-0	0-0	4-1	1-1	1-0		1-0	0-0	1-0	2-0	4-0	0-2	2-1	1-0	1-0	0-0	3-1
Juventus FC	0-0	4-0	0-0	4-2	1-1	0-0	4-1		4-1	0-3	2-2	2-1	1-2	0-0	3-1	1-0	3-1	3-1
AC Lanerossi	3-0	2-1	1-3	1-1	1-0	1-0	1-0	0-1		1-0	1-1	1-1	0-1	4-3	2-1	1-3	1-0	1-1
SS Lazio	0-1	1-0	1-2	0-0	1-1	1-0	0-0	0-2	0-1		2-0	0-0	1-1	1-0	1-1	0-0	0-0	0-0
AC Mantova	1-1	0-0	0-0	1-0	0-3	0-0	2-2	1-1	0-0	0-0		2-2	1-4	3-0	1-0	2-0	2-0	0-0
AS Messina	1-1	1-1	0-2	0-0	0-3	1-0	0-1	1-0	2-0	0-2	1-0		1-2	2-0	2-1	4-3	0-0	1-1
Milan AC	2-0	2-0	1-2	3-1	2-1	3-1	1-1	2-2	2-1	0-1	1-0	3-0		3-0	2-1	0-1	1-1	1-1
Modena FC	1-0	1-1	1-4	0-0	0-1	2-1	0-1	1-0	2-3	2-1	1-1	0-0	0-1		3-3	3-0	4-3	0-0
AS Roma	1-1	0-0	0-1	4-4	1-1	1-0	0-1	1-2	1-1	0-0	2-1	2-0	2-3	2-0		6-1	2-0	3-0
UC Sampdoria	1-1	2-0	2-0	4-1	0-1	0-1	1-5	0-2	1-1	1-0	1-1	3-1	1-2	1-1	0-2		3-1	0-0
SPAL Ferrara	0-0	3-1	0-0	3-1	0-0	0-0	0-1	1-3	1-0	0-1	5-2	1-1	2-4	0-0	2-0	3-1		0-1
AC Torino	3-0	1-2	0-0	0-0	0-3	2-1	0-2	0-0	0-0	2-0	5-2	1-0	0-0	0-0	2-2	2-1	2-0	

Championship Play-off (Roma – 07/06/64)

BOLOGNA FC (BOLOGNA) 2-0 FC Internazionale (Milano)

	Serie "A"	Pd	Wn	Dw	Ls	GF	GA	Pts	
1.	Bologna FC (Bologna)	34	22	10	2	54	18	54	
1.	FC Internazionale (Milano)	34	23	8	3	54	21	54	
3.	Milan AC (Milano)	34	21	9	4	58	28	51	
4.	AC Fiorentina (Firenze)	34	14	10	10	43	27	38	
4.	Juventus FC (Torino)	34	14	10	10	49	37	38	
6.	AC Lanerossi (Vicenza)	34	13	10	11	34	36	36	
7.	AC Torino (Torino)	34	9	17	8	32	32	35	
8.	Genoa Cricket & FBC (Genova)	34	10	10	14	33	34	30	
8.	SS Lazio (Roma)	34	9	12	13	21	24	30	
8.	CC Catania (Catania)	34	9	12	13	32	44	30	
8.	Atalanta BC (Bergamo)	34	7	16	11	26	43	30	
12.	AS Roma (Roma)	34	9	11	14	43	44	29	
12.	AC Mantova (Mantova)	34	6	17	11	28	39	29	
14.	AS Messina (Messina)	34	9	10	15	25	46	28	
15.	UC Sampdoria (Genova)	34	10	7	17	38	50	27	PO
15.	Modena FC (Modena)	34	6	15	13	29	42	27	R
17.	S.P.A.L. (Ferrara)	34	6	12	16	28	39	24	R
18.	FC Bari (Bari)	34	6	10	18	20	43	22	R
		612	203	206	203	647	647	612	

Top goalscorers

1)	Harald NIELSEN	(Bologna FC)	21
2)	Kurt HAMRIN	(AC Fiorentina)	19
3)	Luis VINICIO	(AC Lanerossi)	17
4)	José ALTAFINI	(Milan AC)	14
	AMARILDO Tavarés de Silveira	(Milan AC)	14

Relegation Play-Off

UC Sampdoria (Genova) 2-0 Modena FC (Modena)

Note: Bologna FC had 3 points deducted by the F.I.G.C. for alleged drug-taking by some players, however this decision was revoked on appeal.

Note: Monza Calcio (Monza) changed their name during the pre-season from AC Monza (Monza).

	Serie "B"	Pd	Wn	Dw	Ls	GF	GA	Pts	
1.	FC Varese (Varese)	38	17	17	4	44	19	51	P
2.	US Cagliari (Cagliari)	38	16	17	5	44	23	49	P
3.	US Foggia & Incedit (Foggia)	38	15	16	7	42	27	46	P
4.	AC Padova (Padova)	38	16	13	9	43	27	45	
5.	AC Lecco (Lecco)	38	15	14	9	36	29	44	
5.	Hellas-Verona AC (Verona)	38	15	14	9	44	31	44	
7.	AC Brescia (Brescia)	38	18	11	9	55	28	40	#
8.	AC Napoli (Napoli)	38	12	15	11	39	35	39	
9.	Potenza SC (Potenza)	38	10	18	10	31	28	38	
10.	US Catanzaro (Catanzaro)	38	13	11	14	38	47	37	
10.	US Triestina (Trieste)	38	11	15	12	28	33	37	
12.	US Palermo (Palermo)	38	9	17	12	25	28	35	
13.	Pro Patria et Libertate (Busto Arsizio)	38	9	15	14	35	42	33	
13.	AC Venezia (Venezia)	38	10	13	15	32	44	33	
15.	US Alessandria (Alessandria)	38	9	14	15	27	48	32	
15.	Parma AS (Parma)	38	8	16	14	31	43	32	
15.	Monza Calcio (Monza)	38	8	16	14	32	46	32	*
18.	AC Prato (Prato)	38	8	15	15	31	44	31	R
19.	AC Udinese (Udine)	38	9	11	18	28	40	29	R
20.	AS Cosenza (Cosenza)	38	8	10	20	23	46	26	R
		760	236	288	236	708	708	753	

AC Brescia started the season with -7 points as a result of the F.I.G.C. decision at the end of the 1962-63 season.

Promoted to Serie "B": US Livorno (Livorno), AC Reggiana (Reggio Emilia) and Polisportiva Trani (Trani).

Coppa Italia Final (Roma – 06/09/64)

AS ROMA (ROMA) 0-0 (aet) AC Torino (Torino)

Roma: Cudicini, Tomasin, Ardizzon, Carpanesi, Losi, Schnellinger, Leonardi, Tamborini, Nicolè, De Sisti. Francesconi.

Torino: Vieri, Poletti, Buzzacchera, Puia, Lancioni, Ferretti, Simoni, Ferrini, Hitchens, Cella, Meroni.

Final Replay (Torino – 01/11/64)

AS ROMA (ROMA) 1-0 AC Torino (Torino)

Nicolè 85'

Roma: Cudicini, Tomasin, Ardizzon, Carpanesi, Losi, Schnellinger, Leonardi, Tamborini, Nicolè, De Sisti. Francesconi.

Torino: Vieri, Poletti, Buzzacchera, Puia, Lancioni, Ferretti, Simoni, Ferrini, Hitchens, Cella, Meroni.

Semi-Finals

AS Roma (Roma)	1-1 (aet – 7-3 penalties)	AC Fiorentina (Firenze)
AC Torino (Torino)	2-0	Juventus FC (Torino)

Quarter-Finals

AC Fiorentina (Firenze)	1-0	Milan AC (Milan)
Juventus FC (Torino)	4-1	Bologna FC (Bologna)
AS Roma (Roma)	1-0	Atalanta BC (Bergamo)
AC Torino (Torino)	4-1	FC Internazionale (Milano)

1964-65

1964-1965 Serie "A"	Atalanta BC	Bologna FC	US Cagliari	CC Catania	AC Fiorentina	Foggia & Incedit	Genoa C & FBC	FC Internazionale	Juventus FC	AC Lanerossi	SS Lazio	AC Mantova	AS Messina	Milan AC	AS Roma	UC Sampdoria	AC Torino	FC Varese
Atalanta BC		2-0	0-1	0-0	2-1	1-0	0-2	1-3	0-0	1-0	1-1	2-1	0-1	1-1	1-0	0-0	0-0	0-0
Bologna FC	1-1		1-3	3-0	3-1	4-2	2-1	0-0	1-1	3-0	2-0	4-1	3-0	0-2	1-2	0-1	1-0	3-0
US Cagliari	0-1	0-0		2-0	1-1	0-1	2-1	0-2	1-0	2-1	3-0	2-1	2-1	2-1	1-0	1-1	0-1	1-1
CC Catania	4-1	4-0	2-1		0-2	1-0	3-2	2-3	3-1	2-0	3-0	1-1	4-2	1-1	4-0	1-0	1-1	0-0
AC Fiorentina	1-0	2-1	2-0	5-0		3-1	5-0	2-2	1-0	4-1	1-0	2-0	1-1	0-0	2-0	0-1	2-0	1-0
Foggia & Incedit	1-1	2-2	1-2	1-0	0-0		0-0	3-2	1-0	1-0	1-0	1-0	1-0	1-2	0-0	1-1	1-2	3-0
Genoa C & FBC	0-0	0-0	1-1	1-1	4-1	1-0		1-2	0-1	3-1	1-0	0-0	2-0	0-0	0-0	2-1	1-2	0-1
FC Internazionale	1-0	2-0	3-0	5-1	6-2	2-0	4-1		1-1	3-2	3-0	1-0	3-1	5-2	0-0	3-2	2-2	0-0
Juventus FC	0-0	1-0	0-0	4-1	1-0	1-0	7-0	0-2		3-1	0-0	1-0	1-0	2-2	1-0	2-0	1-1	3-2
AC Lanerossi	2-2	1-1	1-0	2-0	1-1	0-1	0-0	1-1	1-3		2-1	1-0	2-1	2-3	1-0	0-0	0-0	3-2
SS Lazio	0-0	1-1	1-0	2-2	0-1	2-1	1-1	1-1	0-2	0-0		2-0	2-1	0-0	0-0	2-0	1-1	3-1
AC Mantova	2-0	0-1	2-2	1-0	0-0	0-0	2-0	0-1	1-0	0-1	1-3		2-0	0-4	0-0	1-0	1-2	3-1
AS Messina	1-0	3-3	0-0	2-1	0-3	0-0	1-0	0-1	1-1	0-0	4-0	2-0		0-2	1-2	2-2	0-1	0-1
Milan AC	2-0	3-1	1-0	1-1	2-0	1-0	1-0	3-0	1-0	0-1	2-1	2-0	2-0		0-2	3-0	1-1	1-0
AS Roma	0-0	1-1	2-1	2-1	3-3	1-0	1-1	1-3	1-1	0-0	0-0	0-0	0-1	1-2		1-0	2-2	5-2
UC Sampdoria	1-0	0-0	1-0	0-1	3-0	1-1	0-1	0-1	1-0	0-3	0-0	1-0	0-0	0-2	1-0		0-0	0-0
AC Torino	1-1	5-0	4-0	2-1	3-1	0-0	4-1	0-0	0-3	3-0	2-0	2-0	1-0	1-2	3-1	0-1		1-0
FC Varese	0-0	0-0	0-2	3-0	1-1	0-0	2-2	0-0	1-1	3-2	0-1	1-0	1-0	0-0	1-1	2-0	2-0	

	Serie "A"	Pd	Wn	Dw	Ls	GF	GA	Pts	
1.	FC INTERNAZIONALE (MILANO)	34	22	10	2	68	29	54	
2.	Milan AC (Milano)	34	21	9	4	52	23	51	
3.	AC Torino (Torino)	34	16	12	6	48	27	44	
4.	AC Fiorentina (Firenze)	34	16	9	9	52	37	41	
4.	Juventus FC (Torino)	34	15	11	8	43	24	41	
6.	Bologna FC (Bologna)	34	11	12	11	43	42	34	
6.	US Cagliari (Cagliari)	34	13	8	13	33	35	34	
8.	CC Catania (Catania)	34	12	8	14	46	51	32	
9.	US Foggia & Incedit (Foggia)	34	10	11	13	26	30	31	
9.	AS Roma (Roma)	34	8	15	11	29	35	31	
11.	Atalanta BC (Bergamo)	34	7	16	11	19	28	30	
11.	AC Lanerossi (Vicenza)	34	10	10	14	33	44	30	
11.	FC Varese (Varese)	34	8	14	12	28	37	30	
14.	SS Lazio (Roma)	34	8	13	13	25	38	29	
14.	UC Sampdoria (Genova)	34	9	11	14	19	30	29	
16.	Genoa Cricket & FBC (Genova)	34	8	12	14	30	46	28	R
17.	AS Messina (Messina)	34	7	8	19	26	44	22	R
18.	AC Mantova (Mantova)	34	7	7	20	20	40	21	R
		612	208	196	208	640	640	612	

Top goalscorers

1)	Alessandro MAZZOLA	(FC Internazionale)	17
	Alberto ORLANDO	(AC Fiorentina)	17
3)	AMARILDO Tavarés de Silveira	(Milan AC)	14
4)	FACCHIN	(CC Catania)	13
	Harald NIELSEN	(Bologna FC)	13

	Serie "B"	Pd	Wn	Dw	Ls	GF	GA	Pts	
1.	AC Brescia (Brescia)	38	18	13	7	46	28	49	P
2.	AC Napoli (Napoli)	38	16	16	6	45	21	48	P
3.	S.P.A.L. (Ferrara)	38	17	13	8	40	27	47	P
4.	AC Lecco (Lecco)	38	16	14	8	50	23	46	
5.	Potenza SC (Potenza)	38	15	14	9	55	40	44	
6.	AC Padova (Padova)	38	14	14	10	32	23	42	
7.	Modena FC (Modena)	38	11	19	8	36	28	41	
8.	US Catanzaro (Catanzaro)	38	9	20	9	24	26	38	
9.	US Alessandria (Alessandria)	38	12	13	13	37	43	37	
9.	Pro Patria et Libertate (Busto Arsizio)	38	13	11	14	32	45	37	
11.	US Palermo (Palermo)	38	12	12	14	43	43	36	
11.	AC Reggiana (Reggio Emilia)	38	11	14	13	34	27	36	
11.	AC Venezia (Venezia)	38	9	18	11	30	33	36	
11.	Hellas-Verona AC (Verona)	38	10	16	12	38	44	36	
15.	Polisportiva Trani (Trani)	38	12	11	15	29	44	35	
16.	US Livorno (Livorno)	38	11	12	15	32	33	34	
17.	Monza Calcio (Monza)	38	9	16	13	32	45	34	
18.	FC Bari (Bari)	38	10	13	15	32	41	33	R
19.	US Triestina (Trieste)	38	8	12	18	26	48	28	R
20.	Parma AS (Parma)	38	7	9	22	23	54	23	R
		760	240	280	240	716	716	760	

Promoted to Serie "B": AC Novara (Novara), SC Pisa (Pisa) and AS Reggina (Reggio Calabria).

Coppa Italia Final (Roma - 29/08/65)

JUVENTUS FC (TORINO)	1-0	FC Internazionale (Milano)

Menichelli 14'

Juventus: Anzolin, Gori, Leoncini, Bercellino, Castano, Salvadore, Dell'Omodatme, Del Sol, Traspedini, Cinesinho, Menichelli.

Internazionale: Sarto, Burgnich, Facchetti, Bedin, Guarneri, Picchi, Jair, Mazzola, Peirò, Suarez, Corso.

Semi-Finals

Juventus FC (Torino)	1-0	AC Torino (Torino)
AS Roma (Roma)	2-2 (aet – 6-8 penalties)	FC Internazionale (Milano)

Quarter-Finals

Bologna FC (Bologna)	0-0 (aet)	Juventus FC (Torino)
	(Juventus FC (Torino) won on penalties)	
FC Internazionale (Milano)	6-3 (aet)	US Cagliari (Cagliari)
AC Napoli (Napoli)	1-2	AS Roma (Roma)
AC Torino (Torino)	2-0	Genoa Cricket & FBC (Genova)

1965-66

1965-1966 Serie "A"	Atalanta BC	Bologna FC	AC Brescia	US Cagliari	CC Catania	AC Fiorentina	Foggia & Incedit	FC Internazionale	Juventus FC	AC Lanerossi	SS Lazio	Milan AC	AC Napoli	AS Roma	UC Sampdoria	SPAL Ferrara	AC Torino	FC Varese
Atalanta BC		4-1	0-0	1-0	3-2	1-1	1-3	0-2	0-0	1-1	0-0	0-0	1-0	0-2	1-0	2-0	0-0	1-0
Bologna FC	3-0		2-1	1-0	2-0	3-2	1-1	2-1	0-1	1-3	3-1	4-1	0-1	3-1	2-1	1-3	2-0	3-1
AC Brescia	2-0	0-1		0-0	4-1	1-2	4-0	2-2	4-0	1-0	2-1	0-3	0-0	3-0	1-0	2-2	2-1	2-2
US Cagliari	0-0	1-3	1-0		3-1	0-1	1-0	0-1	2-1	3-0	3-0	1-2	0-2	4-0	1-1	3-0	3-2	1-1
CC Catania	0-0	1-1	1-1	2-1		0-3	0-0	1-0	1-1	1-3	0-0	1-1	0-0	1-0	2-3	0-0	0-2	3-0
AC Fiorentina	1-0	1-3	2-0	2-0	0-0		1-1	0-0	0-1	1-1	2-0	1-0	0-0	0-1	5-0	1-0	1-1	4-0
Foggia & Incedit	2-0	2-0	1-0	0-0	3-0	0-0		1-3	0-0	0-0	1-1	0-0	0-1	1-0	3-0	1-0	0-0	0-0
FC Internazionale	1-0	0-0	7-0	2-0	3-1	0-0	5-0		3-1	3-2	4-1	1-1	0-0	2-2	1-1	2-1	4-0	5-2
Juventus FC	1-1	0-0	3-1	0-0	1-0	3-0	1-0	0-0		4-1	0-0	3-0	0-0	0-0	2-1	3-0	2-0	3-1
AC Lanerossi	1-1	1-1	4-1	1-1	1-0	2-0	0-0	1-1	2-2		1-0	1-0	2-0	1-1	2-1	3-1	0-0	1-0
SS Lazio	0-1	1-1	0-3	3-1	1-1	0-0	2-0	1-3	0-1	2-1		0-0	2-1	0-0	0-0	2-2	1-0	2-1
Milan AC	1-0	1-1	2-1	2-2	6-1	1-2	1-0	1-2	2-1	1-1	0-2		4-1	3-1	2-0	1-1	0-0	3-1
AC Napoli	5-1	1-1	1-0	2-0	3-0	0-4	1-0	3-1	1-0	4-2	2-0	1-0		1-0	2-2	4-2	0-0	2-2
AS Roma	1-0	3-1	1-1	1-0	1-1	0-2	1-0	2-0	1-1	1-0	0-1	1-0	0-0		1-0	0-2	1-0	2-0
UC Sampdoria	2-0	0-2	0-2	1-1	1-0	0-3	2-1	0-5	0-0	0-0	2-1	1-2	1-0	0-1		1-0	1-1	2-0
SPAL Ferrara	3-1	0-3	0-2	3-0	3-0	1-2	2-1	0-1	2-2	0-0	2-0	1-1	1-2	2-1	1-1		0-0	2-0
AC Torino	2-1	2-4	2-0	0-0	4-0	1-0	2-0	1-2	0-0	1-3	2-2	0-1	1-1	1-1	1-0	1-0		2-0
FC Varese	0-2	1-4	2-0	1-3	1-2	1-1	0-0	1-3	0-0	0-2	1-1	0-0	0-2	0-0	1-2	1-1	2-1	

	Serie "A"	Pd	Wn	Dw	Ls	GF	GA	Pts	
1.	FC INTERNAZIONALE (MILANO)	34	20	10	4	70	28	50	
2.	Bologna FC (Bologna)	34	19	8	7	60	37	46	
3.	AC Napoli (Napoli)	34	17	11	6	44	27	45	
4.	AC Fiorentina (Firenze)	34	16	11	7	45	22	43	
5.	Juventus FC (Torino)	34	13	16	5	38	23	42	
6.	AC Lanerossi (Vicenza)	34	13	14	7	44	34	40	
7.	Milan AC (Milan)	34	13	12	9	43	33	38	
8.	AS Roma (Roma)	34	13	10	11	28	31	36	
9.	AC Brescia (Brescia)	34	12	8	14	43	44	32	
10.	AC Torino (Torino)	34	9	13	12	31	34	31	
11.	US Cagliari (Cagliari)	34	10	10	14	36	37	30	
12.	US Foggia & Incedit (Foggia)	34	8	13	13	22	30	29	
12.	SS Lazio (Roma)	34	8	13	13	28	41	29	
12.	Atalanta BC (Bergamo)	34	9	11	14	24	37	29	
15.	S.P.A.L. (Ferrara)	34	9	10	15	38	45	28	
16.	UC Sampdoria (Genova)	34	9	9	16	27	47	27	R
17.	CC Catania (Catania)	34	5	12	17	24	56	22	R*
18.	FC Varese (Varese)	34	2	11	21	23	62	15	R
		612	205	202	205	668	668	612	

Top goalscorers

1)	Luis VINICIO	(AC Lanerossi)	25
2)	Angelo Benedicto SORMANI	(Milan AC)	21
3)	Alessandro MAZZOLA	(FC Internazionale)	19
4)	José ALTAFINI	(AC Napoli)	14
5)	Virginio DEPAOLI	(AC Brescia)	13

* CC Catania (Catania) changed their club name to Catania Calcio (Catania) for the next season.
AS Messina (Messina) was dissolved but a new club ACR Messina (Messina) was formed immediately based on the remnants of the defunct club.

	Serie "B"	Pd	Wn	Dw	Ls	GF	GA	Pts	
1.	AC Venezia (Venezia)	38	18	13	7	53	34	49	P
2.	AC Lecco (Lecco)	38	17	14	7	43	26	48	P
3.	AC Mantova (Mantova)	38	14	18	6	45	26	46	P
4.	AS Reggina (Reggio Calabria)	38	16	13	9	46	32	45	
5.	Genoa Cricket & FBC (Genova)	38	15	14	9	44	35	44	
6.	Hellas-Verona AC (Verona)	38	11	18	9	35	32	40	
7.	US Livorno (Livorno)	38	12	14	12	33	32	38	
8.	AS Messina (Messina)	38	9	20	9	27	29	38	*
9.	AC Padova (Padova)	38	13	11	14	45	42	37	
10.	US Catanzaro (Catanzaro)	38	10	16	12	38	41	36	
10.	Potenza SC (Potenza)	38	13	10	15	37	40	36	
10.	AC Novara (Novara)	38	8	20	10	31	42	36	
13.	Modena FC (Modena)	38	6	23	9	32	32	35	
13.	US Alessandria (Alessandria)	38	10	15	13	27	37	35	
15.	US Palermo (Palermo)	38	9	16	13	34	34	34	
15.	SC Pisa (Pisa)	38	12	10	16	30	37	34	
15.	AC Reggiana (Reggio Emilia)	38	9	16	13	32	39	34	
18.	Pro Patria et Libertate (Busto Arsizio)	38	10	13	15	38	50	33	R
19.	Monza Calcio (Monza)	38	12	8	18	32	45	32	R
20.	Polisportiva Trani (Trani)	38	6	18	14	31	48	30	R
		760	230	300	230	733	733	760	

Promoted to Serie "B": US Arezzo (Arezzo), US Salernitana (Salerno) and Savona FC (Savona).

Coppa Italia Final (Roma – 19/05/66)

AC FIORENTINA (FIRENZE)	2-1 (aet)	US Catanzaro (Catanzaro)
Hamrin 1-0, Bertini 2-1	*(H.T. 1-0)*	*Marchioro 1-1*

Fiorentina: Albertosi, Pirovano, Rogora, Bertini, Ferrante, Brizi, Hamrin, Merlo, Brugnera, De Sisti, Chiarugi.

Catanzaro: Provasi, Marini, Lorenzini, Maccacaro, Tonani, Sardei, Vanini, Marchioro, Bui, Gasparini, Tribuzio.

Semi-Finals

AC Fiorentina (Firenze)	2-1	FC Internazionale (Milano)
Juventus FC (Torino)	1-2	US Catanzaro (Catanzaro)

Quarter-Finals

US Catanzaro (Catanzaro)	0-0 (aet)	AC Torino (Torino)
	(US Catanzaro (Catanzaro) won on penalties)	
Milan AC (Milano)	1-3	AC Fiorentina (Firenze)
S.P.A.L. (Ferrara)	1-4 (aet)	Juventus FC (Torino)
AC Lanerossi (Vicenza)	1-2	FC Internazionale (Milano)

1966-67

1966-1967 Serie "A"	Atalanta BC	Bologna FC	AC Brescia	US Cagliari	AC Fiorentina	Foggia & Incedit	FC Internazionale	Juventus FC	AC Lanerossi	SS Lazio	AC Lecco	AC Mantova	Milan AC	AC Napoli	AS Roma	SPAL Ferrara	AC Torino	AC Venezia
Atalanta BC	■	1-0	2-1	1-0	0-0	2-0	0-5	0-2	0-0	3-0	1-0	0-0	0-0	1-1	2-4	0-1	1-1	1-0
Bologna FC	2-1	■	2-0	1-1	1-1	5-0	3-2	2-0	2-0	1-0	2-0	1-1	2-0	1-0	2-0	2-0	2-1	0-0
AC Brescia	0-0	0-2	■	1-2	0-0	0-0	0-3	1-1	0-0	1-0	2-0	1-1	0-0	1-0	3-3	0-0	0-1	3-2
US Cagliari	3-1	4-0	2-0	■	1-0	0-0	1-1	0-0	0-0	1-0	3-1	0-0	0-0	0-0	2-1	1-1	2-0	4-0
AC Fiorentina	1-1	1-1	7-1	1-0	■	0-1	1-2	1-2	3-0	5-1	2-0	0-0	1-0	1-1	2-2	0-0	1-0	2-0
Foggia & Incedit	4-1	0-1	0-1	0-0	1-2	■	0-4	0-0	2-2	2-1	4-1	2-1	0-2	1-1	2-2	0-0	0-0	3-0
FC Internazionale	2-0	2-1	1-0	2-1	1-1	3-0	■	1-1	2-0	0-0	1-1	1-1	4-0	1-1	0-0	2-1	1-2	2-1
Juventus FC	0-0	2-1	0-0	1-0	4-1	3-0	1-0	■	2-0	2-1	3-0	1-1	1-1	2-0	2-0	2-1	0-0	2-1
AC Lanerossi	1-2	0-0	1-1	0-2	3-1	3-1	0-5	0-1	■	0-0	3-0	2-2	1-1	2-1	0-1	1-0	0-1	2-1
SS Lazio	1-3	2-1	0-2	0-1	0-0	2-1	1-0	0-0	0-0	■	2-0	1-0	0-0	0-0	0-1	1-1	0-0	1-1
AC Lecco	0-0	1-2	1-0	0-2	0-3	3-0	0-2	1-3	0-0	0-1	■	0-0	1-1	0-3	2-2	1-1	0-0	2-1
AC Mantova	0-0	1-1	0-0	0-0	0-0	0-1	1-0	1-1	2-0	0-0	1-1	■	1-0	0-2	1-0	1-0	0-0	2-1
Milan AC	0-0	1-1	0-1	2-1	0-2	3-1	0-1	3-1	2-0	2-2	1-1	2-2	■	1-0	3-1	2-0	1-1	2-1
AC Napoli	3-0	2-1	1-1	1-0	1-2	3-2	0-0	0-1	1-0	1-0	4-1	1-0	3-2	■	2-0	1-0	2-1	4-0
AS Roma	3-2	0-2	1-0	0-0	0-1	0-0	0-0	1-0	1-1	0-0	2-1	1-1	0-1	0-2	■	1-0	4-0	1-0
SPAL Ferrara	1-0	1-0	1-1	0-0	1-2	1-0	1-3	1-1	1-1	4-1	2-1	1-1	1-1	1-4	1-0	■	0-0	3-2
AC Torino	6-1	1-1	3-0	1-0	2-2	1-0	0-2	0-0	1-1	1-1	1-1	2-0	0-0	0-0	3-1	2-1	■	0-0
AC Venezia	1-1	1-2	3-0	1-1	2-6	1-0	2-3	0-2	0-2	1-1	2-0	0-0	1-2	0-0	1-2	1-0	1-1	■

	Serie "A"	Pd	Wn	Dw	Ls	GF	GA	Pts	
1.	JUVENTUS FC (TORINO)	34	18	13	3	44	19	49	
2.	FC Internazionale (Milano)	34	19	10	5	59	22	48	
3.	Bologna FC (Bologna)	34	18	9	7	48	27	45	
4.	AC Napoli (Napoli)	34	17	10	7	46	23	44	
5.	AC Fiorentina (Firenze)	34	15	13	6	53	29	43	
6.	US Cagliari (Cagliari)	34	13	14	7	35	17	40	
7.	AC Torino (Torino)	34	10	18	6	33	26	38	
8.	Milan AC (Milano)	34	11	15	8	36	32	37	
9.	AC Mantova (Mantova)	34	6	22	6	22	23	34	
10.	AS Roma (Roma)	34	11	11	12	35	39	33	
11.	Atalanta BC (Bergamo)	34	9	13	12	28	43	31	
12.	S.P.A.L. (Ferrara)	34	8	13	13	28	36	29	
13.	AC Lanerossi (Vicenza)	34	7	14	13	26	39	28	
13.	AC Brescia (Brescia)	34	7	14	13	22	40	28	
—	—	—	—	—	—	—	—	—	—
15.	SS Lazio (Roma)	34	6	15	13	20	35	27	R
16.	US Foggia & Incedit (Foggia)	34	7	10	17	28	49	24	R*
17.	AC Venezia (Venezia)	34	4	9	21	29	57	17	R.
17.	AC Lecco (Lecco)	34	3	11	20	21	57	17	R
		612	189	234	189	613	613	612	

Top goalscorers

1)	Luigi RIVA	(US Cagliari)	18
2)	Alessandro MAZZOLA	(FC Internazionale)	17
3)	José ALTAFINI	(AC Napoli)	16
	Kurt HAMRIN	(AC Fiorentina)	16
5)	BRUGNERA	(AC Fiorentina)	13

* US Foggia & Incedit (Foggia) changed their club name to US Foggia (Foggia) for the next season.
US Palermo (Palermo) changed their club name to SS Palermo (Palermo) for the next season.

Note: Parma AS (Parma) changed their club name to Parma FC (Parma).

Serie "A" was reduced to 16 clubs and Serie "B" extended to 21 clubs for the next season.

	Serie "B"	Pd	Wn	Dw	Ls	GF	GA	Pts	
1.	UC Sampdoria (Genova)	38	20	14	4	47	19	54	P
2.	FC Varese (Varese)	38	19	13	6	44	21	51	P
3.	US Catanzaro (Catanzaro)	38	14	14	10	44	42	42	
3.	Catania Calcio (Catania)	38	15	12	11	35	31	42	
3.	AC Reggiana (Reggio Emilia)	38	15	12	11	34	38	42	
6.	AC Padova (Padova)	38	11	17	10	37	33	39	
6.	Modena FC (Modena)	38	12	15	11	41	44	39	
6.	Potenza SC (Potenza)	38	13	13	12	35	38	39	
9.	US Palermo (Palermo)	38	12	14	12	34	26	38	*
9.	AS Reggina (Reggio Calabria)	38	11	16	11	35	33	38	
11.	ACR Messina (Messina)	38	11	15	12	36	40	37	
12.	Genoa Cricket & FBC (Genova)	38	12	12	14	39	33	36	
12.	Hellas-Verona AC (Verona)	38	12	12	14	33	36	36	
12.	SC Pisa (Pisa)	38	10	16	12	27	30	36	
12.	AC Novara (Novara)	38	13	10	15	31	35	36	
16.	US Livorno (Livorno)	38	12	11	15	32	39	35	
17.	Savona FC (Savona)	38	12	10	16	44	46	34	R
18.	US Arezzo (Arezzo)	38	11	10	17	38	43	32	R
19.	US Alessandria (Alessandria)	38	8	13	17	35	48	29	R
20.	US Salernitana (Salerno)	38	9	7	22	23	49	25	R
		760	252	256	252	724	724	760	

Promoted to Serie "B": FC Bari (Bari), Monza Calcio (Monza) and AC Perugia (Perugia).

Coppa Italia Final (Roma – 14/06/67)

MILAN AC (MILANO)	1-0	AC Padova (Padova)

Amarildo 49'

Milan: Belli, Anquilletti, Schnellinger, Maddé, Trapattoni, Baveni, Mora, Rivera, Amarildo, Lodetti, Fortunato.

Padova: Pontel, Cervato, Barbiero, Frezza, Barbolini, Sereni (Gatti 54'), Carminati, Morelli, Fraschini, Novelli.

Semi-Finals

Juventus FC (Torino)	1-2 (aet)	Milan AC (Milano)
AC Padova (Padova)	3-2	FC Internazionale (Milano)

Quarter-Finals

Bologna FC (Bologna)	1-1 (aet)	Juventus FC (Torino)
	(Juventus FC (Torino) won on penalties)	
FC Internazionale (Torino)	1-0	AC Fiorentina (Firenze)
AC Lecco (Lecco)	1-2	Milan AC (Milan)
AC Padova (Padova)	2-1 (aet)	AC Napoli (Napoli)

1967-68

1967-1968 Serie "A"	Atalanta BC	Bologna FC	AC Brescia	US Cagliari	AC Fiorentina	FC Internazionale	Juventus FC	AC Lanerossi	AC Mantova	Milan AC	AC Napoli	AS Roma	UC Sampdoria	SPAL Ferrara	AC Torino	FC Varese
Atalanta BC		1-0	1-3	2-1	0-3	3-1	0-0	1-0	2-0	0-3	1-0	2-1	1-0	1-0	1-1	4-0
Bologna FC	5-0		0-3	2-1	0-1	2-1	0-0	2-0	1-0	1-1	1-2	1-0	0-0	2-3	2-0	1-0
AC Brescia	2-1	0-0		2-1	1-1	2-0	0-1	0-0	0-1	1-2	0-0	1-0	1-2	0-1	0-5	0-1
US Cagliari	2-1	1-1	3-0		3-1	3-2	2-0	1-1	2-2	2-2	1-1	1-2	3-3	2-0	2-0	2-1
AC Fiorentina	1-0	1-0	0-1	1-0		1-1	2-0	3-1	2-0	0-2	3-0	0-0	0-0	2-0	1-1	3-1
FC Internazionale	3-0	1-0	3-0	0-2	3-1		0-0	1-0	3-0	1-1	1-2	1-1	2-0	2-0	1-0	1-0
Juventus FC	2-1	0-0	2-1	2-0	2-2	3-2		1-0	3-1	1-2	1-1	0-1	3-1	2-0	0-4	3-0
AC Lanerossi	4-1	1-1	0-1	3-1	1-0	2-1	0-2		2-0	2-2	0-1	0-0	0-0	1-0	1-0	1-0
AC Mantova	1-0	0-0	1-1	0-1	1-2	0-0	0-0	1-1		0-1	0-1	0-0	0-1	0-1	0-0	0-0
Milan AC	0-0	4-2	1-0	0-1	0-0	1-1	0-0	2-0	3-1		2-1	3-0	2-0	3-2	2-1	1-0
AC Napoli	1-0	0-0	0-0	1-0	1-0	2-1	1-2	1-1	0-0	1-1		2-0	1-1	1-0	2-2	5-0
AS Roma	1-1	0-0	2-0	2-3	2-1	2-6	0-0	0-0	2-2	1-1	2-1		1-1	1-1	0-2	1-0
UC Sampdoria	0-0	1-2	1-0	1-1	1-1	2-2	1-1	1-0	3-0	0-3	1-1	1-1		1-0	1-1	1-1
SPAL Ferrara	1-0	1-3	3-1	1-0	1-0	1-2	0-1	3-0	1-0	1-4	1-2	0-1	1-0		0-0	1-3
AC Torino	4-1	0-1	2-0	2-1	0-2	2-3	2-1	1-0	4-1	2-3	1-2	2-1	4-2	1-0		0-0
FC Varese	2-0	0-0	0-0	2-1	0-0	1-0	5-0	2-0	1-1	2-1	1-0	2-0	1-0	2-0	0-0	

	Serie "A"	Pd	Wn	Dw	Ls	GF	GA	Pts	
1.	MILAN AC (MILANO)	30	18	10	2	53	24	46	
2.	AC Napoli (Napoli)	30	13	11	6	34	24	37	*
3.	Juventus FC (Torino)	30	13	10	7	33	29	36	
4.	AC Fiorentina (Firenze)	30	13	9	8	35	23	35	
5.	FC Internazionale (Milano)	30	13	7	10	46	34	33	
5.	Bologna FC (Bologna)	30	11	11	8	30	23	33	
7.	AC Torino (Torino)	30	12	8	10	44	31	32	
7.	FC Varese (Varese)	30	12	8	10	28	27	32	
9.	US Cagliari (Cagliari)	30	12	7	11	44	38	31	
10.	UC Sampdoria (Genova)	30	6	15	9	27	34	27	
10.	AS Roma (Roma)	30	7	13	10	25	35	27	
12.	AC Lanerossi (Vicenza)	30	8	9	13	22	30	25	
12.	Atalanta BC (Bergamo)	30	10	5	15	26	42	25	
14.	S.P.A.L. (Ferrara)	30	10	2	18	24	38	22	R
14.	AC Brescia (Brescia)	30	8	6	16	20	35	22	R
16.	AC Mantova (Mantova)	30	3	11	16	13	37	17	R
		480	169	142	169	504	504	480	

Top goalscorers

1)	Pierino PRATO	(Milan AC)	15
2)	José ALTAFINI	(AC Napoli)	13
	Nestor COMBIN	(AC Torino)	13
	Luigi RIVA	(US Cagliari)	13
5)	MARASCHI	(AC Fiorentina)	12
	Giuseppe SAVOLDI	(Atalanta BC)	12

* AC Napoli (Napoli) changed their club name to SSC Napoli (Napoli) for the next season.
FC Bari (Bari) changed their club name to AS Bari (Bari) for the next season.

Note: Parma FC (Parma) changed their club name to Parma AC (Parma).
From the next season goal-difference was used to separate teams level on points.

	Serie "B"	Pd	Wn	Dw	Ls	GF	GA	Pts	
1.	SS Palermo (Palermo)	40	18	16	6	40	23	52	P
2.	Hellas-Verona AC (Verona)	40	17	14	9	41	27	48	P
2.	SC Pisa (Pisa)	40	17	14	9	48	32	48	P
4.	FC Bari (Bari)	40	18	11	11	55	41	47	*
4.	US Foggia (Foggia)	40	15	17	8	40	33	47	
6.	AC Reggiana (Reggio Emilia)	40	15	15	10	41	32	45	
7.	US Livorno (Livorno)	40	16	11	13	34	32	43	
8.	Monza Calcio (Monza)	40	12	18	10	49	45	42	
9.	AS Reggina (Reggio Calabria)	40	13	15	12	45	47	41	
10.	Catania Calcio (Catania)	40	14	12	14	41	38	40	
11.	SS Lazio (Roma)	40	10	18	12	27	33	38	
12.	Modena FC (Modena)	40	10	17	13	39	41	37	
12.	AC Padova (Padova)	40	12	13	15	31	33	37	
12.	US Catanzaro (Catanzaro)	40	9	19	12	26	32	37	
15.	Genoa Cricket & FBC (Genova)	40	9	18	13	36	31	36	PO
15.	AC Lecco (Lecco)	40	7	22	11	35	40	36	PO
15.	AC Perugia (Perugia)	40	10	16	14	38	45	36	PO
15.	AC Venezia (Venezia)	40	10	16	14	25	30	36	R
15.	ACR Messina (Messina)	40	10	16	14	21	37	36	R
20.	AC Novara (Novara)	40	8	19	13	31	40	35	R
21.	Potenza SC (Potenza)	40	4	15	21	24	55	23	R
		840	254	332	254	767	767	840	

1967-1968 Serie "B" Relegation Play-Offs Phase 1	Genoa Cricket	AC Venezia	AC Perugia	AC Lecco	ACR Messina
Genoa Cricket & FBC		2-0	1-1	0-1	3-0
AC Venezia			3-0	0-0	2-0
AC Perugia				2-1	3-0
AC Lecco					1-0
ACR Messina					

1967-1968 Serie "B" Relegation Play-Offs Phase 2	AC Perugia	AC Lecco	Genoa Cricket	AC Venezia
AC Perugia		0-0	2-0	2-1
AC Lecco			0-0	3-0
Genoa Cricket & FBC				2-1
AC Venezia				

	Relegation Play-Off (Phase 2)	Pd	Wn	Dw	Ls	GF	GA	Pts
1.	AC Perugia (Perugia)	3	2	1	-	4	1	5
2.	AC Lecco (Lecco)	3	1	2	-	3	-	4
3.	Genoa Cricket & FBC (Genova)	3	1	1	1	2	3	3
4.	AC Venezia (Venezia)	3	-	-	3	2	7	-
		12	4	4	4	11	11	12

	Relegation Play-Off (Phase 1)	Pd	Wn	Dw	Ls	GF	GA	Pts
1.	Genoa Cricket & FBC (Genova)	4	2	1	1	6	2	5
1.	AC Venezia (Venezia)	4	2	1	1	5	2	5
1.	AC Perugia (Perugia)	4	2	1	1	6	5	5
1.	AC Lecco (Lecco)	4	2	1	1	3	2	5
5.	ACR Messina (Messina)	4	-	-	4	-	9	-
		20	8	4	8	20	20	20

Promoted to Serie "B": AC Cesena (Cesena), AC Como (Como) and SS Ternana (Terni).

1967-1968 Coppa Italia Final	AC Torino	Milan AC	FC Internazionale	Bologna FC
AC Torino		0-0	1-0	4-0
Milan AC	1-1		4-2	2-1
FC Internazionale	0-2	0-0		3-3
Bologna FC	1-1	2-1	0-2	

	<u>Coppa Italia Final (13/06/68 – 30/06/68)</u>	<u>Pd</u>	<u>Wn</u>	<u>Dw</u>	<u>Ls</u>	<u>GF</u>	<u>GA</u>	<u>Pts</u>
1.	AC TORINO (TORINO)	6	3	3	-	9	2	9
2.	Milan AC (Milano)	6	2	3	1	8	6	7
3.	FC Internazionale (Milano)	6	1	2	3	7	10	4
3.	Bologna FC (Bologna)	6	1	2	3	7	13	4
		24	7	10	7	31	31	24

Quarter-Finals

FC Bari (Bari)	1-1, 1-4	Milan AC (Milano)
US Catanzaro (Catanzaro)	0-0, 0-2	AC Torino (Torino)
SC Pisa (Pisa)	1-1, 0-1	FC Internazionale (Milano)
AS Reggina (Reggio Calabria)	2-3, 0-4	Bologna FC (Bologna)

1968-69

1968-1969 Serie "A"	Atalanta BC	Bologna FC	US Cagliari	AC Fiorentina	Hellas Verona AC	FC Internazionale	Juventus FC	AC Lanerossi	Milan AC	SSC Napoli	SS Palermo	SC Pisa	AS Roma	UC Sampdoria	AC Torino	FC Varese
Atalanta BC		1-1	1-2	0-1	5-2	0-4	3-3	1-3	0-0	0-0	2-2	1-1	0-2	0-0	3-1	0-0
Bologna FC	1-0		2-2	0-0	1-1	1-2	1-1	3-0	1-0	2-1	2-0	1-0	0-0	0-0	2-0	1-0
US Cagliari	1-0	3-1		1-1	2-0	1-0	0-1	3-0	3-1	0-0	3-0	3-0	0-0	0-0	1-0	0-0
AC Fiorentina	2-1	1-3	1-1		1-0	1-0	2-1	3-0	0-0	2-1	1-0	3-1	0-0	1-0	0-0	3-1
Hellas-Verona AC	1-1	5-1	0-0	2-2		2-3	2-1	2-1	1-3	1-0	2-0	5-3	2-0	0-3	3-0	1-1
FC Internazionale	1-1	4-0	4-0	1-2	4-1		1-2	1-0	1-1	1-1	0-0	4-0	3-1	1-1	2-2	6-0
Juventus FC	1-0	1-0	1-2	0-2	1-0	1-0		1-0	0-1	2-0	0-0	2-0	2-2	1-1	0-0	2-0
AC Lanerossi	1-0	1-0	1-1	0-0	2-1	0-1	0-0		1-1	2-0	1-0	1-2	1-2	3-0	1-1	1-0
Milan AC	0-0	4-0	0-0	0-0	3-0	1-0	1-0	4-1		0-0	1-0	2-1	1-0	1-0	1-0	2-0
SSC Napoli	2-0	1-1	2-1	1-3	1-1	3-1	2-1	1-0	0-0		1-0	2-1	0-0	0-3	0-0	1-1
SS Palermo	5-1	2-0	0-0	0-0	0-0	1-1	1-1	2-1	0-0	0-2		1-0	0-3	1-0	1-0	1-1
SC Pisa	1-0	0-1	0-0	0-1	1-1	1-1	0-0	2-2	0-1	1-0	4-1		1-2	1-0	1-1	1-1
AS Roma	4-2	2-1	1-4	1-2	1-2	0-3	1-1	5-2	1-1	0-0	2-1	2-0		1-0	1-3	0-0
UC Sampdoria	0-0	0-0	0-1	1-1	3-2	0-3	1-1	1-0	1-1	0-2	0-1	1-2	0-0		1-1	4-0
AC Torino	3-1	3-0	0-0	0-0	4-0	2-1	1-2	0-0	1-0	0-0	3-1	1-0	2-0	2-0		2-1
FC Varese	1-2	1-1	1-6	2-2	1-0	0-1	0-2	1-0	0-0	1-2	0-0	3-1	2-1	0-0	1-0	

	Serie "A"	Pd	Wn	Dw	Ls	GF	GA	Pts	
1.	AC FIORENTINA (FIRENZE)	30	16	13	1	38	18	45	
2.	US Cagliari (Cagliari)	30	14	13	3	41	18	41	
3.	Milan AC (Milano)	30	14	13	3	31	12	41	
4.	FC Internazionale (Milano)	30	14	8	8	55	26	36	
5.	Juventus FC (Torino)	30	12	11	7	32	24	35	
6.	AC Torino (Torino)	30	11	11	8	33	24	33	
7.	SSC Napoli (Napoli)	30	10	12	8	26	25	32	
8.	AS Roma (Roma)	30	10	10	10	35	35	30	
9.	Bologna FC (Bologna)	30	10	9	11	27	36	29	
10.	Hellas-Verona AC (Verona)	30	9	8	13	40	49	26	
11.	SS Palermo (Palermo)	30	7	11	12	21	32	25	
12.	UC Sampdoria (Genova)	30	5	13	12	21	27	23	
13.	AC Lanerossi (Vicenza)	30	8	7	15	26	39	23	
14.	FC Varese (Varese)	30	5	12	13	20	43	22	R
15.	SC Pisa (Pisa)	30	6	8	16	26	44	20	R
16.	Atalanta BC (Bergamo)	30	4	11	15	25	45	19	R
		480	155	170	155	497	497	480	

Top goalscorers

1)	Luigi RIVA	(US Cagliari)	20
2)	BUI	(Hellas-Verona AC)	15
3)	Pietro ANASTASI	(Juventus FC)	14
	MARASCHI	(AC Fiorentina)	14
	Pierino PRATO	(Milan AC)	14

Note: Parma AC (Parma) merged with AC Parmense (Parma) to become Parma AC (Parma).

	Serie "B"	Pd	Wn	Dw	Ls	GF	GA	Pts	
1.	SS Lazio (Roma)	38	17	16	5	55	27	50	P
2.	AC Brescia (Brescia)	38	17	14	7	46	24	48	P
3.	AS Bari (Bari)	38	14	19	5	34	27	47	P
4.	AC Reggiana (Reggio Emilia)	38	17	12	9	36	23	46	
5.	AS Reggina (Reggio Calabria)	38	13	18	7	36	24	44	
6.	Genoa Cricket & FBC (Genova)	38	10	21	7	36	29	41	
7.	AC Como (Como)	38	14	13	11	33	28	41	
8.	AC Perugia (Perugia)	38	9	20	9	31	26	38	
9.	US Foggia (Foggia)	38	11	16	11	33	35	38	
10.	SS Ternana (Terni)	38	11	14	13	34	36	36	
11.	AC Mantova (Mantova)	38	10	15	13	30	30	35	
12.	US Livorno (Livorno)	38	11	13	14	29	35	35	
13.	Monza Calcio (Monza)	38	8	19	11	32	38	35	
14.	US Catanzaro (Catanzaro)	38	10	15	13	23	31	35	
15.	Catania Calcio (Catania)	38	10	15	13	19	28	35	
16.	AC Cesena (Cesena)	38	10	14	14	27	37	34	
17.	Modena FC (Modena)	38	9	14	15	26	34	32	
18.	S.P.A.L. (Ferrara)	38	8	15	15	30	38	31	R
19.	AC Lecco (Lecco)	38	7	16	15	26	38	30	R
20.	AC Padova (Padova)	38	8	13	17	25	53	29	R
		760	224	312	224	641	641	760	

Promoted to Serie "B": US Arezzo (Arezzo), Piacenza Calcio (Piacenza) and AS Taranto (Taranto).

1968-1969 Coppa Italia Final	AS Roma	US Cagliari	US Foggia	AC Torino
AS Roma		1-1	3-0	0-0
US Cagliari	1-2		2-3	2-0
US Foggia	1-3	1-1		2-2
AC Torino	2-2	1-2	2-2	

	Coppa Italia Final (30/04/69 – 28/06/69)	Pd	Wn	Dw	Ls	GF	GA	Pts
1.	AS ROMA (ROMA)	6	3	3	-	11	5	9
2.	US Cagliari (Cagliari)	6	2	2	2	9	8	6
3.	US Foggia (Foggia)	6	1	3	2	9	13	5
4.	AC Torino (Torino)	6	-	4	2	7	10	4
		24	6	12	6	36	36	24

Quarter-Finals

AC Brescia (Brescia)	1-0, 0-3	AS Roma (Roma)
US Cagliari (Cagliari)	1-0, 1-1	Juventus FC (Torino)
US Foggia (Foggia)	2-1, 2-0	SSC Napoli (Napoli)
AC Torino (Torino)	1-0, 1-0	Milan AC (Milan)

1969-70

1969-1970 Serie "A"	AS Bari	Bologna FC	AC Brescia	US Cagliari	AC Fiorentina	Hellas Verona AC	FC Internazionale	Juventus FC	AC Lanerossi	SS Lazio	Milan AC	SSC Napoli	SS Palermo	AS Roma	UC Sampdoria	AC Torino
AS Bari		0-2	2-0	0-0	1-1	0-2	0-1	2-1	0-0	0-0	0-5	0-0	1-0	1-0	0-0	0-1
Bologna FC	1-1		0-3	0-0	2-2	0-0	2-1	0-0	1-1	1-0	0-1	1-2	3-1	1-1	1-1	0-1
AC Brescia	0-0	1-1		0-2	1-2	0-0	1-1	0-1	1-1	0-0	1-4	1-2	4-2	0-1	0-0	0-1
US Cagliari	2-0	1-0	4-0		0-0	1-0	1-1	1-1	2-1	1-0	1-1	2-0	2-0	1-0	4-0	2-0
AC Fiorentina	3-0	0-1	0-1	0-1		1-0	2-0	2-0	2-1	2-0	4-2	1-2	3-1	2-2	1-0	0-0
Hellas-Verona AC	4-1	0-0	0-0	1-1	0-1		1-3	1-0	3-1	1-1	2-2	1-0	2-0	2-0	1-1	0-1
FC Internazionale	1-0	1-0	3-1	1-0	3-0	0-0		0-0	0-0	3-0	0-0	1-0	2-0	2-0	3-2	2-0
Juventus FC	1-0	1-1	1-0	2-2	2-0	3-0	2-1		4-0	2-1	3-0	0-0	4-1	1-1	2-0	1-2
AC Lanerossi	2-0	1-1	0-1	1-2	1-2	3-0	1-1	1-0		2-1	1-0	3-2	1-1	3-0	2-1	1-0
SS Lazio	4-1	1-0	1-0	0-2	5-1	0-1	3-1	2-0	1-0		1-0	0-2	4-0	1-1	1-0	1-1
Milan AC	1-0	0-0	1-1	0-0	4-2	2-0	0-1	0-2	1-0	3-0		1-0	1-0	2-3	0-0	3-0
SSC Napoli	1-0	0-0	0-0	0-2	0-1	2-1	0-0	1-0	1-0	1-1	1-1		0-0	0-0	0-2	4-0
SS Palermo	0-0	1-0	1-3	1-0	1-1	1-0	1-2	1-3	1-3	1-1	0-0	0-0		2-2	3-0	1-0
AS Roma	1-0	1-2	1-0	1-1	0-1	1-1	2-1	0-3	1-0	2-1	0-1	2-1	1-1		3-3	0-0
UC Sampdoria	1-0	0-0	2-0	0-0	1-3	2-1	0-5	0-0	0-1	0-2	1-1	0-0	1-0	2-0		1-1
AC Torino	0-1	1-1	1-0	0-4	1-0	2-1	0-0	0-3	1-0	3-0	0-1	0-2	1-1	0-0	2-1	

	Serie "A"	Pd	Wn	Dw	Ls	GF	GA	Pts	
1.	US CAGLIARI (CAGLIARI)	30	17	11	2	42	11	45	
2.	FC Internazionale (Milano)	30	16	9	5	41	19	41	
3.	Juventus FC (Torino)	30	15	8	7	43	20	38	
4.	Milan AC (Milano)	30	13	10	7	38	24	36	
5.	AC Fiorentina (Firenze)	30	15	6	9	40	33	36	
6.	SSC Napoli (Napoli)	30	10	11	9	24	21	31	
7.	AC Torino (Torino)	30	1	8	11	20	31	30	*
8.	SS Lazio (Roma)	30	11	7	12	33	32	29	
9.	AC Lanerossi (Vicenza)	30	11	7	12	32	31	29	*
10.	Bologna FC (Bologna)	30	6	16	8	22	24	28	
11.	AS Roma (Roma)	30	8	12	10	27	36	28	
12.	Hellas-Verona AC (Verona)	30	8	10	12	26	30	26	
13.	UC Sampdoria (Genova)	30	6	12	12	22	37	24	
—	—	—	—	—	—	—	—	—	—
14.	AC Brescia (Brescia)	30	5	10	15	20	35	20	R
15.	SS Palermo (Palermo)	30	5	10	15	23	45	20	R
16.	AS Bari (Bari)	30	5	9	16	11	35	19	R
		480	162	156	162	464	464	480	

Top goalscorers

1)	Luigi RIVA	(US Cagliari)	21
2)	VITALI	(AC Lanerossi)	17
3)	Pietro ANASTASI	(Juventus FC)	15
4)	Roberto BONINSEGNA	(FC Internazionale)	13

* AC Lanerossi (Vicenza) changed their club name to SS Lanerossi (Vicenza) for the next season.
Genoa Cricket & FBC (Genova) changed their club name to Genoa CFC (Genova) for the next season.
SS Ternana (Terni) changed their club name to AC Ternana (Terni) for the next season.
AC Torino (Torino) changed their club name to Torino Calcio (Torino) for the next season.
FC Varese (Varese) changed their club name to Varese Calcio (Varese) for the next season.

	Serie "B"	Pd	Wn	Dw	Ls	GF	GA	Pts	
1.	FC Varese (Varese)	38	16	17	5	41	21	49	P *
2.	US Foggia (Foggia)	38	16	16	6	42	25	48	P
3.	Catania Calcio (Calcio)	38	15	18	5	34	19	48	P
—	—	—	—	—	—	—	—	—	—
4.	AC Mantova (Mantova)	38	12	23	3	39	22	47	
5.	Monza Calcio (Monza)	38	15	15	8	30	19	45	
6.	AS Reggina (Reggio Calabria)	38	13	15	10	39	34	41	
7.	SC Pisa (Pisa)	38	11	17	10	31	29	39	
8.	SS Ternana (Terni)	38	10	19	9	30	31	39	*
9.	US Livorno (Livorno)	38	11	16	11	26	25	38	
10.	AC Perugia (Perugia)	38	10	15	13	25	25	35	
11.	AC Cesena (Cesena)	38	8	19	11	25	28	35	
12.	Modena FC (Modena)	38	9	17	12	24	30	35	
13.	AC Como (Como)	38	11	12	15	33	44	34	
14.	US Arezzo (Arezzo)	38	5	24	9	15	27	34	
15.	Atalanta BC (Bergamo)	38	8	17	13	30	29	33	
16.	US Catanzaro (Catanzaro)	38	7	19	12	23	30	33	
17.	AS Taranto (Taranto)	38	8	17	13	27	35	33	
—	—	—	—	—	—	—	—	—	—
18.	AC Reggiana (Reggio Emilia)	38	6	21	11	22	31	33	R
19.	Piacenza Calcio (Piacenza)	38	7	18	13	26	45	32	R
20.	Genoa Cricket & FBC (Genova)	38	6	17	15	19	32	29	R *
		760	204	352	204	581	581	760	

Promoted to Serie "B": Casertana Calcio (Casertana), AC Massese (Massa) and AC Novara (Novara).

1969-1970 Coppa Italia Final	Bologna FC	AC Torino	US Cagliari	FC Varese
Bologna FC		2-0	0-0	4-1
AC Torino	1-0		4-3	1-0
US Cagliari	0-4	1-0		0-0
FC Varese	0-1	0-3	1-1	

	Coppa Italia Final (07/05/70 – 10/06/70)	Pd	Wn	Dw	Ls	GF	GA	Pts
1.	BOLOGNA FC (BOLOGNA)	6	4	1	1	11	2	9
2.	AC Torino (Torino)	6	4	-	2	9	6	8
3.	US Cagliari (Cagliari)	6	1	3	2	5	9	5
4.	FC Varese (Varese)	6	-	2	4	2	10	2
		24	9	6	9	27	27	24

Quarter-Finals

AC Fiorentina (Firenze)	0-0, 0-0, 0-1	FC Varese (Varese)
FC Internazionale (Milano)	1-0, 0-1, 2-3	AC Torino (Torino)
Juventus FC (Torino)	0-0, 0-0, 0-1	Bologna FC (Bologna)
AS Roma (Roma)	0-1, 0-2	US Cagliari (Cagliari)

Play-off

Juventus FC (Torino)	2-1	US Foggia (Foggia)

1970-71

1970-1971 Serie "A"	Bologna FC	US Cagliari	Catania Calcio	AC Fiorentina	US Foggia	Hellas Verona AC	FC Internazionale	Juventus FC	lanerossi	SS Lazio	Milan AC	SSC Napoli	AS Roma	UC Sampdoria	Torino Calcio	Varese Calcio
Bologna FC		0-0	2-0	0-0	1-2	2-2	1-0	3-0	2-0	3-2	1-0	0-0	1-1	1-0	1-0	2-2
US Cagliari	2-1		1-1	2-0	1-1	4-1	0-0	1-1	1-1	2-1	0-4	1-1	0-1	2-1	0-0	1-1
Catania Calcio	0-0	1-1		0-0	2-0	0-1	0-1	0-1	1-1	3-1	0-0	1-0	1-2	1-3	1-0	0-0
AC Fiorentina	1-2	1-2	1-1		3-0	1-1	2-2	1-2	0-0	1-1	2-5	0-1	2-2	0-0	1-1	1-1
US Foggia	1-1	0-0	1-0	1-1		3-0	1-1	0-0	1-1	5-2	1-1	0-3	1-0	2-2	1-0	2-2
Hellas-Verona AC	0-0	2-0	1-1	1-1	1-1		1-2	0-0	1-0	1-0	1-3	0-2	1-0	3-1	1-0	1-1
FC Internazionale	1-0	1-3	3-2	2-1	5-0	1-0		2-0	2-1	1-1	2-0	2-1	0-0	3-1	2-0	3-2
Juventus FC	0-0	2-1	5-0	1-1	2-1	2-1	1-1		2-1	3-1	0-2	4-1	2-0	3-1	3-3	2-2
SS Lanerossi	0-0	1-1	0-0	0-1	1-0	0-0	1-2	1-1		1-0	1-1	0-1	0-0	0-0	1-1	3-1
SS Lazio	2-2	2-4	1-0	0-0	2-1	1-1	0-1	2-2	0-1		0-1	0-0	1-1	1-0	1-0	0-0
Milan AC	2-1	3-1	4-0	1-0	2-0	1-1	3-0	1-1	3-1	1-1		1-1	2-2	3-1	1-0	1-2
SSC Napoli	3-0	1-0	1-0	0-0	0-0	2-0	2-1	1-0	1-0	2-0	0-2		1-2	0-0	2-0	1-0
AS Roma	1-1	0-0	5-0	0-1	3-1	0-0	0-0	0-0	4-1	2-2	1-1	2-2		0-0	1-1	3-0
UC Sampdoria	1-2	0-0	2-0	2-2	2-0	3-0	0-2	2-0	1-2	2-3	1-1	0-1	0-0		0-0	2-1
Torino Calcio	1-0	2-1	1-1	1-1	1-1	1-0	0-2	2-1	2-3	1-1	1-1	1-1	4-0	0-0		3-1
Varese Calcio	0-0	4-1	0-1	0-0	3-0	2-0	1-3	0-0	0-0	2-1	1-1	1-1	0-0	1-1	0-0	

	Serie "A"	Pd	Wn	Dw	Ls	GF	GA	Pts	
1.	FC INTERNAZIONALE (MILANO)	30	19	8	3	50	26	46	
2.	Milan AC (Milano)	30	15	12	3	54	26	42	
3.	SSC Napoli (Napoli)	30	15	9	6	33	19	39	
4.	Juventus FC (Torino)	30	11	13	6	41	30	35	
5.	Bologna FC (Bologna)	30	10	14	6	30	24	34	
6.	AS Roma (Roma)	30	7	18	5	32	25	32	
7.	US Cagliari (Cagliari)	30	8	14	8	33	35	30	*
8.	Torino Calcio (Torino)	30	6	14	10	27	30	26	
9.	Varese Calcio (Varese)	30	5	16	9	29	33	26	
10.	SS Lanerossi (Vicenza)	30	6	14	10	23	31	26	
11.	Hellas-Verona AC (Verona)	30	7	12	11	23	35	26	
12.	UC Sampdoria (Genova)	30	6	13	11	30	34	25	
13.	AC Fiorentina (Firenze)	30	3	19	8	26	32	25	
14.	US Foggia (Foggia)	30	6	13	11	28	43	25	R
15.	SS Lazio (Roma)	30	5	12	13	28	43	22	R
16.	Catania Calcio (Catania)	30	5	11	14	18	39	21	R
		480	134	212	134	505	505	480	

Top goalscorers

1)	Roberto BONINSEGNA	(FC Internazionale)	24
2)	Pierino PRATI	(Milan AC)	19
3)	Giuseppe SAVOLDI	(Bologna FC)	15
4)	Roberto BETTEGA	(Juventus FC)	13

* US Cagliari (Cagliari) changed their club name to Cagliari Calcio (Cagliari) for the next season.

	Serie "B"	Pd	Wn	Dw	Ls	GF	GA	Pts	
1.	AC Mantova (Mantova)	38	17	14	7	40	24	48	P
2.	Atalanta BC (Bergamo)	38	15	17	6	41	25	47	P
3.	US Catanzaro (Catanzaro)	38	17	13	8	37	27	47	P
4.	AS Bari (Bari)	38	19	9	10	43	24	47	
5.	AC Brescia (Brescia)	38	15	16	7	39	27	46	
6.	AC Perugia (Perugia)	38	15	12	11	36	28	42	
7.	US Arezzo (Arezzo)	38	13	13	12	40	33	39	
8.	AS Reggina (Reggio Calabria)	38	12	14	12	24	28	38	
9.	Modena FC (Modena)	38	12	14	12	31	37	38	
10.	AC Como (Como)	38	12	14	12	35	43	38	
11.	AC Novara (Novara)	38	11	15	12	37	34	37	
12.	AC Ternana (Terni)	38	11	15	12	35	32	37	
13.	SS Palermo (Palermo)	38	8	21	9	33	33	37	
14.	US Livorno (Livorno)	38	10	16	12	21	25	36	
15.	Monza Calcio (Monza)	38	9	17	12	31	38	35	
16.	AC Cesena (Cesena)	38	10	15	13	25	29	33	-2
17.	AS Taranto (Taranto)	38	6	20	12	27	34	32	
18.	SC Pisa (Pisa)	38	9	14	15	31	44	32	R
19.	Casertana Calcio (Casertana)	38	6	15	17	32	50	27	R
20.	AC Massese (Massa)	38	4	14	20	20	43	22	R
		760	231	298	231	658	658	758	

Note: AC Cesena (Cesena) had 2 points deducted by the F.I.G.C. Committee for "irregularities".

Promotion Play-Offs

Atalanta BC (Bergamo)	1-0	US Catanzaro (Catanzaro)
Atalanta BC (Bergamo)	2-0	AS Bari (Bari)
US Catanzaro (Catanzaro)	1-0	AS Bari (Bari)

The Atalanta vs Bari match was abandoned after 69 minutes then later awarded 2-0 to Atalanta by the F.I.G.C..

Promoted to Serie "B": Genoa CFC (Genova), AC Reggiana (Reggio Emilia) and SS Sorrento (Sorrento).

Coppa Italia Final Play-off (Genova – 27/06/71)

TORINO CALCIO (TORINO) 0-0 (aet – 5-3 penalties) Milan AC (Milano)

Torino: Castellini, Poletti, Fossati, Puia, Cereser, Agroppi, Rampanti, Ferrini, Petrini (Maddè 77'), C.Sala, Luppi.

Milan: Belli, Anquilletti, Zignoli, Rosato, Schnellinger, Trapattoni, Zazzaro, Biasiolo, Combin, Rivera, Rognoni (Paina 79').

1970-1971 Coppa Italia Final	Milan AC	Torino Calcio	AC Fiorentina	SSC Napoli
Milan AC		3-2	1-0	2-2
Torino Calcio	1-0		1-1	2-0
AC Fiorentina	1-2	4-0		2-0
SSC Napoli	3-2	1-3	1-1	

	Coppa Italia Final (30/05/71 – 23/06/71)	Pd	Wn	Dw	Ls	GF	GA	Pts
1.	Milan AC (Milano)	6	3	1	2	10	9	7
2.	Torino Calcio (Torino)	6	3	1	2	9	9	7
3.	AC Fiorentina (Firenze)	6	2	2	2	9	5	6
4.	SSC Napoli (Napoli)	6	1	2	3	7	12	4
		24	9	6	9	35	35	24

Quarter-Finals

AC Fiorentina (Firenze)	2-1, 2-0	Monza Calcio (Monza)
Milan AC (Milano)	2-0, 4-0	US Livorno (Livorno)
SSC Napoli (Napoli)	1-0, +:-	AC Cesena (Cesena)
	(the 2nd leg was awarded as a forfeit win to Napoli)	
Torino Calcio (Torino)	1-0, 1-0	AS Roma (Roma)

Play-off

Monza Calcio (Monza)	0-0 (aet)	AC Novara (Novara)
	(Monza Calcio (Monza) won on penalties)	

1971-72

1971-1972 Serie "A"	Atalanta BC	Bologna FC	Cagliari Calcio	US Catanzaro	AC Fiorentina	Hellas Verona AC	FC Internazionale	Juventus FC	lanerossi	AC Mantova	Milan AC	SSC Napoli	AS Roma	UC Sampdoria	Torino Calcio	Varese Calcio
Atalanta BC		0-0	2-1	1-0	3-1	0-0	1-0	0-0	1-3	2-0	0-1	3-1	1-1	0-0	0-0	1-0
Bologna FC	1-1		2-1	2-1	1-1	1-0	0-3	1-2	2-1	1-1	0-2	2-2	2-2	1-0	2-3	1-0
Cagliari Calcio	2-0	2-1		0-0	0-0	3-1	2-1	2-1	3-0	1-0	2-1	2-1	1-0	3-1	1-2	1-1
US Catanzaro	1-1	1-0	2-2		0-2	0-0	0-1	1-0	1-1	1-1	0-0	0-0	1-1	1-0	1-3	1-1
AC Fiorentina	2-0	2-1	0-1	1-0		2-1	0-0	1-1	2-1	0-1	2-0	2-1	2-0	0-0	1-1	1-0
Hellas-Verona AC	1-2	0-0	0-2	0-0	0-0		2-1	1-0	2-2	1-0	1-1	1-1	1-1	3-2	0-0	1-1
FC Internazionale	2-0	1-1	0-0	1-0	1-1	4-1		0-0	2-1	2-0	2-3	2-0	2-2	4-4	2-0	2-0
Juventus FC	1-0	2-1	2-1	4-2	1-0	4-0	3-0		2-0	2-1	1-1	2-2	2-1	3-1	2-1	1-0
SS Lanerossi	1-0	2-3	0-1	2-0	0-1	2-1	0-4	1-3		1-0	0-2	6-2	0-1	1-0	0-0	0-4
AC Mantova	1-0	1-1	2-1	1-1	1-2	1-0	1-6	1-1	0-1		0-0	0-0	0-2	1-2	1-2	2-2
Milan AC	1-0	1-0	0-0	1-0	2-0	2-0	1-1	1-4	1-1	0-1		3-0	3-0	0-0	1-0	3-1
SSC Napoli	2-1	0-0	0-0	0-0	0-0	1-1	0-0	1-1	1-1	1-0	0-0		4-0	0-0	1-1	3-0
AS Roma	1-0	1-0	2-2	4-0	0-0	1-0	3-1	1-1	1-0	3-1	1-2	1-0		1-0	3-1	0-0
UC Sampdoria	1-0	2-1	0-0	1-1	0-0	1-0	0-0	0-0	1-1	0-0	0-2	1-2	1-0		2-1	2-0
Torino Calcio	1-0	1-0	1-0	1-0	2-1	2-2	2-1	2-1	2-1	1-0	0-0	1-0	2-0	2-0		2-0
Varese Calcio	0-1	0-0	0-2	1-1	1-1	0-0	0-3	0-1	0-0	2-4	0-1	0-1	1-3	0-1	2-2	

	Serie "A"	Pd	Wn	Dw	Ls	GF	GA	Pts	
1.	JUVENTUS FC (TORINO)	30	17	9	4	48	24	43	
2.	Milan AC (Milano)	30	16	10	4	36	17	42	
3.	Torino Calcio (Torino)	30	17	8	5	39	25	42	
4.	Cagliari Calcio (Cagliari)	30	15	9	6	39	23	39	
5.	FC Internazionale (Milano)	30	13	10	7	49	28	36	
6.	AC Fiorentina (Firenze)	30	12	12	6	28	20	36	
7.	AS Roma (Roma)	30	13	9	8	37	31	35	
8.	SSC Napoli (Napoli)	30	6	16	8	27	31	28	
9.	UC Sampdoria (Genova)	30	8	12	10	23	28	28	
10.	Atalanta BC (Bergamo)	30	9	8	13	21	26	26	
11.	Bologna FC (Bologna)	30	7	11	12	28	36	25	
12.	SS Lanerossi (Vicenza)	30	8	7	15	30	43	23	
13.	Hellas-Verona AC (Verona)	30	4	14	12	21	36	22	
14.	AC Mantova (Mantova)	30	6	9	15	23	39	21	R
15.	US Catanzaro (Catanzaro)	30	3	15	12	17	34	21	R
16.	Varese Calcio (Varese)	30	1	11	18	17	42	13	R
		480	155	170	155	483	483	480	

Top goalscorers

1)	Roberto BONINSEGNA	(FC Internazionale)	22
2)	Luigi RIVA	(Cagliari Calcio)	21
3)	Albertino BIGON	(Milan AC)	14
4)	Pietro ANASTASI	(Juventus FC)	11
	MARASCHI	(SS Lanerossi)	11
	Giuseppe SAVOLDI	(Bologna FC)	11

* AC del Duca (Ascoli Piceno) changed their club name to Ascoli Calcio (Ascoli Piceno) for the next season.
AC Lecco (Lecco) changed their club name to Lecco Calcio (Lecco) for the next season.

Note: Casale FBC (Casale Monferrato) merged with FC Juniorcasale (Casale Monferrato) to become AC Juniorcasale (Casale Monferrato) for the next season.

	Serie "B"	Pd	Wn	Dw	Ls	GF	GA	Pts	
1.	AC Ternana (Terni)	38	18	14	6	43	28	50	P
2.	SS Lazio (Roma)	38	18	13	7	48	28	49	P
3.	SS Palermo (Palermo)	38	17	14	7	35	22	48	P
4.	AC Como (Como)	38	14	18	6	35	24	46	
5.	AC Reggiana (Reggio Emilia)	38	14	17	7	42	23	45	
6.	AC Cesena (Cesena)	38	13	17	8	36	25	43	
7.	AC Perugia (Perugia)	38	15	13	10	35	29	43	
8.	Catania Calcio (Catania)	38	14	13	11	34	27	41	
9.	US Foggia (Foggia)	38	13	15	10	39	33	41	
10.	Genoa CFC (Genova)	38	14	13	11	35	34	41	
11.	AS Bari (Bari)	38	12	16	10	36	31	40	
12.	AC Brescia (Brescia)	38	11	16	11	29	25	38	
13.	AS Taranto (Taranto)	38	11	14	13	29	31	36	
14.	AC Novara (Novara)	38	14	8	16	40	45	36	
15.	US Arezzo (Arezzo)	38	8	17	13	28	37	33	
16.	AS Reggina (Reggio Calabria)	38	8	13	17	23	41	29	
17.	Monza Calcio (Monza)	38	6	16	16	20	37	28	
18.	US Livorno (Livorno)	38	7	12	19	21	42	26	R
19.	SS Sorrento (Sorrento)	38	8	9	21	23	42	25	R
20.	Modena FC (Modena)	38	5	12	21	22	49	22	R
		760	240	280	240	653	653	760	

Promoted to Serie "B": AC del Duca (Ascoli Piceno), Brindisi Sport (Brindisi) and AS Lecco (Lecco).

Coppa Italia Final (Roma – 05/07/72)

MILAN AC (MILANO) 2-0 SSC Napoli (Napoli)

Panzanato 49' o.g., Rosato 78'

Milan: Cudicini, Sabadini, Zignoli, Anquilletti, Schnellinger, Rosato, Golin (Magherini 46', A.Maldera 75'), Biasiolo, Bigon, Rivera, Prati.

Napoli: Zoff, Pogliana, Vianello, Zurlini, Panzanato, M.Perego, Pincelli (A.Esposito 56'), Juliano, Sormani, Improta, Macchi.

1971-1972 Coppa Italia Semi-Finals Group "A"	Milan AC	Torino Calcio	FC Internazionale	Juventus FC
Milan AC		1-1	1-0	3-2
Torino Calcio	0-0		1-0	2-1
FC Internazionale	0-1	3-0		3-1
Juventus FC	0-1	2-1	2-1	

Semi-Finals (Group "A")		Pd	Wn	Dw	Ls	GF	GA	Pts
1.	Milan AC (Milano)	6	4	2	-	7	3	10
2.	Torino Calcio (Torino)	6	2	2	2	5	7	6
3.	FC Internazionale (Milano)	6	2	-	4	7	6	4
4.	Juventus FC (Torino)	6	2	-	4	8	11	4
		24	10	4	10	27	27	24

1971-1972 Coppa Italia Semi-Finals Group "B"	SSC Napoli	AC Fiorentina	Bologna FC	SS Lazio
SSC Napoli		1-1	2-1	5-1
AC Fiorentina	1-1		0-0	1-1
Bologna FC	2-2	0-2		2-1
SS Lazio	3-0	1-0	0-1	

Semi-Finals (Group "B")		Pd	Wn	Dw	Ls	GF	GA	Pts
1.	SSC Napoli (Napoli)	6	2	3	1	11	9	7
2.	AC Fiorentina (Firenze)	6	1	4	1	5	4	6
3.	Bologna FC (Bologna)	6	2	2	2	6	7	6
4.	SS Lazio (Roma)	6	2	1	3	7	9	5
		24	7	10	7	29	29	24

1972-73

1972-1973 Serie "A"	Atalanta BC	Bologna FC	Cagliari Calcio	AC Fiorentina	Hellas Verona AC	FC Internazionale	Juventus FC	lanerossi	SS Lazio	Milan AC	SSC Napoli	SS Palermo	AS Roma	UC Sampdoria	AC Ternana	Torino Calcio
Atalanta BC		1-0	0-0	1-1	0-1	0-0	0-2	0-1	1-1	1-1	0-0	1-0	1-0	0-2	0-0	1-0
Bologna FC	1-0		4-2	2-0	4-1	1-0	0-2	0-0	1-1	3-2	2-0	3-0	1-2	1-1	3-0	1-0
Cagliari Calcio	0-0	1-0		2-2	1-1	2-3	0-1	3-0	0-1	0-1	1-0	2-0	2-2	1-0	1-0	1-0
AC Fiorentina	4-0	3-0	3-0		2-0	1-2	2-1	1-0	0-1	3-1	1-0	3-0	2-1	2-0	2-1	0-0
Hellas-Verona AC	1-1	0-0	1-1	1-2		0-1	0-0	0-0	1-1	5-3	0-0	1-1	2-2	1-1	1-0	0-0
FC Internazionale	0-0	0-0	1-0	1-0	1-0		0-2	1-2	1-1	0-2	2-0	3-1	0-0	0-0	4-0	2-0
Juventus FC	0-0	2-0	2-0	2-1	1-1	2-1		3-2	1-0	2-2	0-0	4-1	1-0	1-1	2-0	0-2
SS Lanerossi	1-1	0-0	1-0	0-1	2-2	0-1	0-2		1-2	0-3	1-0	1-1	0-0	0-0	1-0	1-0
SS Lazio	2-1	0-0	2-1	0-0	2-1	0-0	1-1	1-0		2-1	3-0	2-0	2-0	1-0	2-1	0-0
Milan AC	9-3	3-1	1-1	2-0	2-1	3-2	2-2	2-0	3-1		1-0	4-0	3-1	3-1	3-1	1-0
SSC Napoli	1-0	1-1	1-1	3-0	1-1	2-0	1-1	2-0	1-0	0-0		1-1	1-0	0-0	1-0	1-1
SS Palermo	1-2	1-1	0-1	1-0	0-0	0-2	0-1	0-1	0-2	0-1	1-0		1-1	0-0	1-1	2-1
AS Roma	2-0	0-1	0-0	1-1	0-1	0-2	1-2	0-0	0-1	0-0	1-0	0-0		3-1	0-0	1-0
UC Sampdoria	0-0	2-1	0-1	0-1	0-1	0-1	0-1	0-0	0-0	1-4	1-1	0-0	0-0		0-0	2-1
AC Ternana	0-0	2-1	1-1	0-1	2-1	0-1	2-3	2-0	0-1	0-0	0-0	0-0	1-4	0-2		0-0
Torino Calcio	2-1	3-1	0-0	3-0	3-2	4-0	2-1	3-0	0-0	2-2	0-0	2-0	2-0	0-1	2-0	

	Serie "A"	Pd	Wn	Dw	Ls	GF	GA	Pts	
1.	JUVENTUS FC (TORINO)	30	18	9	3	45	22	45	
2.	Milan AC (Milano)	30	18	8	4	65	33	44	
3.	SS Lazio (Roma)	30	16	11	3	33	16	43	
4.	AC Fiorentina (Firenze)	30	16	5	9	39	26	37	
5.	FC Internazionale (Milano)	30	15	7	8	32	23	37	
6.	Torino Calcio (Torino)	30	11	9	10	33	21	31	
7.	Bologna FC (Bologna)	30	11	9	10	33	31	31	
8.	Cagliari Calcio (Cagliari)	30	9	11	10	26	28	29	
9.	SSC Napoli (Napoli)	30	7	14	9	18	20	28	
10.	Hellas-Verona AC (Verona)	30	5	16	9	28	34	26	
11.	AS Roma (Roma)	30	6	12	12	23	28	24	
12.	UC Sampdoria (Genova)	30	5	14	11	16	25	24	
13.	SS Lanerossi (Vicenza)	30	7	10	13	15	31	24	
14.	Atalanta BC (Bergamo)	30	5	14	11	16	33	24	R
15.	SS Palermo (Palermo)	30	3	11	16	13	41	17	R
16.	AC Ternana (Terni)	30	3	10	14	14	37	16	R *
		480	155	170	155	449	449	480	

Top goalscorers

1)	Paolino PULICI	(Torino Calcio)	17
	Gianni RIVERA	(Milan AC)	17
	Giuseppe SAVOLDI	(Bologna FC)	17
4)	Roberto BONINSEGNA	(FC Internazionale)	12
	Luciano CHIARUGI	(Milan AC)	12
	Luigi RIVA	(Cagliari Calcio)	12

* AC Ternana (Terni) changed their club name to Ternana Calcio (Terni) for the next season.

	Serie "B"	Pd	Wn	Dw	Ls	GF	GA	Pts	
1.	Genoa CFC (Genova)	38	20	13	5	47	26	53	P
2.	AC Cesena (Cesena)	38	17	15	6	36	21	49	P
3.	US Foggia (Foggia)	38	19	11	8	37	25	49	P
4.	Ascoli Calcio (Ascoli Piceno)	38	20	8	10	45	31	48	
5.	Catania Calcio (Catania)	38	14	15	9	29	20	43	
6.	Varese Calcio (Varese)	38	13	16	9	30	26	42	
7.	Brindisi Sport (Brindisi)	38	12	17	9	32	24	41	
8.	US Catanzaro (Catanzaro)	38	12	15	11	38	27	39	
9.	AC Novara (Novara)	38	13	12	13	37	37	38	
10.	AC Reggiana (Reggio Emilia)	38	11	15	12	31	31	37	
11.	AC Como (Como)	38	11	14	13	31	33	36	
12.	AS Bari (Bari)	38	10	16	12	29	33	36	
13.	US Arezzo (Arezzo)	38	9	16	13	24	29	34	
14.	AC Perugia (Perugia)	38	11	11	16	29	34	33	
15.	AS Taranto (Taranto)	38	8	17	13	29	39	33	
16.	AS Reggina (Reggio Calabria)	38	6	19	13	18	26	31	
17.	AC Brescia (Brescia)	38	7	17	14	26	37	31	
18.	AC Mantova (Mantova)	38	8	15	15	19	32	31	R
19.	Monza Calcio (Monza)	38	8	15	15	24	39	31	R
20.	Lecco Calcio (Lecco)	38	5	15	18	19	40	25	R
		760	234	292	234	610	610	760	

Promoted to Serie "B": US Avellino (Avellino), Parma AC (Parma) and S.P.A.L. (Ferrara).

Coppa Italia Final (Roma - 01/07/73)

MILAN AC (MILANO) 1-1 (aet – 5-2 penalties) Juventus FC (Torino)

Benetti 50' pen *Bettega 15'*

Milan: Vecchi, Anquilletti (Casone 95'), Zignoli, Dolci, Schnellinger, Rosato (Magherini 76'), Sabadini, Benetti, Bigon, Biasiolo, Chiarugi.

Juventus: Zoff, Spinosi, Marchetti, Cuccureddu, Longobucco (Furino 64'), Salvadore, Causio, Haller (GL Savoldi 98'), Anastasi, Capello, Bettega.

1972-1973 Coppa Italia Semi-Finals Group "A"	Juventus FC	FC Internazionale	Bologna FC	AC Reggiana
Juventus FC		4-2	4-3	1-1
FC Internazionale	1-1		3-0	1-0
Bologna FC	0-0	1-0		2-2
AC Reggiana	1-2	0-2	0-1	

	Semi-Finals (Group "A")	Pd	Wn	Dw	Ls	GF	GA	Pts
1.	Juventus FC (Torino)	6	3	3	-	12	8	9
2.	FC Internazionale (Milano)	6	3	1	2	9	6	7
3.	Bologna FC (Bologna)	6	2	2	2	7	9	6
4.	AC Reggiana (Reggio Emilia)	6	-	2	4	4	9	2
		24	8	8	8	32	32	24

AC Reggiana 0-2 FC Internazionale was awarded as forfeit win.

1972-1973 Coppa Italia Semi-Finals Group "B"	Milan AC	Atalanta BC	SSC Napoli	Cagliari Calcio
Milan AC		1-0	2-0	0-1
Atalanta BC	0-2		1-1	2-1
SSC Napoli	0-2	0-2		1-0
Cagliari Calcio	0-1	1-2	1-1	

	Semi-Finals (Group "B")	Pd	Wn	Dw	Ls	GF	GA	Pts
1.	Milan AC (Milano)	6	5	-	1	8	1	10
2.	Atalanta BC (Bergamo)	6	3	1	2	7	6	7
3.	SSC Napoli (Napoli)	6	1	2	3	3	8	4
4.	Cagliari Calcio (Cagliari)	6	1	1	4	4	7	3
		24	10	4	10	22	22	24

1973-74

1973-1974 Serie "A"	Bologna FC	Cagliari Calcio	AC Cesena	AC Fiorentina	US Foggia	Genoa CFC	Hellas Verona AC	FC Internazionale	Juventus FC	SS Lanerossi	SS Lazio	Milan AC	SSC Napoli	AS Roma	UC Sampdoria	Torino Calcio
Bologna FC		3-1	1-1	1-1	0-0	2-0	1-2	3-0	0-0	4-0	2-2	3-2	2-2	0-0	2-1	2-2
Cagliari Calcio	0-0		0-0	1-0	1-0	0-1	1-1	1-1	2-1	2-0	0-1	0-1	0-0	1-1	2-1	1-1
AC Cesena	3-0	1-1		0-0	2-0	1-1	1-0	0-1	0-2	2-2	0-0	1-0	1-1	1-1	2-1	0-0
AC Fiorentina	1-1	4-1	0-0		0-1	0-0	2-1	1-0	2-0	0-1	1-1	3-2	1-1	1-0	1-1	3-1
US Foggia	1-1	1-1	1-1	2-1		1-0	1-1	1-2	0-0	2-1	0-1	0-0	1-0	1-0	2-2	1-1
Genoa CFC	1-1	1-1	1-2	0-1	2-1		1-0	1-1	0-1	1-1	1-2	0-1	1-2	2-1	0-2	0-2
Hellas-Verona AC	1-1	2-0	2-1	1-1	3-0	2-0		1-3	0-0	1-1	0-1	2-1	1-0	0-1	1-0	0-1
FC Internazionale	1-1	0-1	3-1	1-1	5-1	0-0	0-0		0-2	2-0	3-1	2-1	2-2	2-0	2-1	3-0
Juventus FC	1-1	1-1	2-2	3-1	2-1	3-0	5-1	2-0		0-0	3-1	2-0	4-1	2-1	2-0	1-1
SS Lanerossi	2-1	1-1	0-0	2-1	1-0	1-1	1-1	1-0	0-3		0-3	1-1	2-1	0-1	0-0	0-0
SS Lazio	4-0	2-0	2-0	0-0	1-0	1-0	4-2	1-1	3-1	3-0		1-0	1-0	2-1	1-0	0-1
Milan AC	1-1	2-2	1-0	1-1	1-0	2-0	2-1	1-5	2-2	1-2	0-0		0-0	2-0	2-1	1-0
SSC Napoli	2-0	1-0	1-0	2-1	1-1	1-0	2-0	2-1	2-0	2-1	3-3	1-2		1-1	1-0	1-1
AS Roma	2-1	2-0	1-0	0-0	3-0	2-0	1-0	3-3	3-2	0-0	1-2	1-2	0-1		2-1	0-0
UC Sampdoria	0-0	1-1	1-1	1-2	0-0	1-1	2-1	1-1	1-2	2-1	1-0	3-2	0-0	0-0		1-1
Torino Calcio	2-0	1-2	2-1	0-1	0-0	1-0	0-0	2-2	0-1	1-0	2-1	1-0	1-1	1-0	1-1	

	Serie "A"	Pd	Wn	Dw	Ls	GF	GA	Pts	
1.	SS LAZIO (ROMA)	30	18	7	5	45	23	43	
2.	Juventus FC (Torino)	30	16	9	5	50	26	41	
3.	SSC Napoli (Napoli)	30	12	12	6	35	28	36	
4.	FC Internazionale (Milano)	30	12	11	7	47	33	35	
5.	Torino Calcio (Torino)	30	10	14	6	27	24	34	
6.	AC Fiorentina (Firenze)	30	10	13	7	32	26	33	
7.	Milan AC (Milano)	30	11	8	11	34	36	30	
8.	AS Roma (Roma)	30	10	9	11	29	28	29	
9.	Bologna FC (Bologna)	30	6	17	7	35	36	29	
10.	Cagliari Calcio (Cagliari)	30	7	14	9	25	32	28	
11.	AC Cesena (Cesena)	30	6	15	9	25	28	27	
12.	SS Lanerossi (Vicenza)	30	7	12	11	22	37	26	
13.	UC Sampdoria (Genova)	30	5	13	12	27	34	20	-3
14.	US Foggia (Foggia)	30	6	12	12	20	34	18	R -6
15.	Genoa CFC (Genova)	30	4	9	17	16	37	17	R
16.	Hellas-Verona AC (Verona)	30	8	9	13	28	35	25	R #
		480	148	184	148	497	497	471	

Top goalscorers

1)	Giorgio CHINAGLIA	(SS Lazio)	24
2)	Roberto BONINSEGNA	(FC Internazionale)	23
3)	Pietro ANASTASI	(Juventus FC)	16
4)	Sergio CLERICI	(SSC Napoli)	15
	Luigi RIVA	(Cagliari Calcio)	15

Hellas-Verona AC (Verona) were placed bottom of the table by the F.I.G.C. investigation committee after being found guilty of "fixing" the result of their away match versus US Foggia (Foggia).
US Foggia (Foggia) had 6 points deducted by the F.I.G.C. investigation committee.
UC Sampdoria (Genova) had 3 points deducted by the F.I.G.C. investigation committee after being found guilty of "bribing" opponents during the 1972-73 season.

Note: AS Pescara (Pescara) changed their club name to Pescara Calcio (Pescara) for the next season.

	Serie "B"	Pd	Wn	Dw	Ls	GF	GA	Pts	
1.	Varese Calcio (Varese)	38	18	15	5	51	28	51	P
2.	Ascoli Calcio (Ascoli Piceno)	38	16	19	3	41	22	51	P
3.	Ternana Calcio (Terni)	38	18	14	6	46	20	50	P
4.	AC Como (Como)	38	15	16	7	37	27	46	
5.	Parma AC (Parma)	38	10	19	9	39	32	39	
6.	AS Taranto (Taranto)	38	11	17	10	27	26	39	
7.	SS Palermo (Palermo)	38	9	21	8	35	42	39	
8.	AC Novara (Novara)	38	12	14	12	33	34	38	
9.	S.P.A.L. (Ferrara)	38	11	16	11	29	32	38	
10.	US Arezzo (Arezzo)	38	12	13	13	42	41	37	
11.	Atalanta BC (Bergamo)	38	11	14	13	24	24	36	
12.	AC Brescia (Brescia)	38	10	16	12	35	36	36	
13.	US Catanzaro (Catanzaro)	38	11	13	14	31	37	35	
14.	US Avellino (Avellino)	38	11	13	14	34	39	35	
15.	AC Perugia (Perugia)	38	10	14	14	30	31	34	
16.	AC Reggiana (Reggio Emilia)	38	9	16	13	30	37	34	
17.	Brindisi Sport (Brindisi)	38	8	18	12	27	37	34	
18.	AS Reggina (Reggio Calabria)	38	10	14	14	20	34	34	R
19.	AS Bari (Bari)	38	9	10	19	12	26	28	R
20.	Catania Calcio (Catania)	38	5	16	17	21	39	26	R
		760	226	308	226	644	644	760	

Promoted to Serie "B": US Alessandria (Alessandria), Pescara Calcio (Pescara) and Sambenedettese Calcio (San Benedetto del Tronto).

Coppa Italia Final (Roma – 23/05/74)

BOLOGNA FC (BOLOGNA) 0-0 (aet – 5-4 penalties) SS Palermo (Palermo)

Bologna: Buso, Roversi, Rimbano (Pecci 76'), Battisodo, Cresci, Gregori (Novellini 46'), Ghetti, Bulgarelli, G.Savoldi, Vieri, F.Landini (Barbara 46').

Palermo: Girardi, Zanin, Cerantola, Arcaleo, Pighin, Barlassina, Favalli, Ballabio (Vullo 61'), Magistrelli, Vanello, La Rosa.

1973-1974 Coppa Italia Semi-Finals Group "A"	Bologna FC	FC Internazionale	Milan AC	Atalanta BC
Bologna FC		2-0	1-0	3-1
FC Internazionale	2-1		2-1	2-0
Milan AC	1-1	0-1		2-1
Atalanta BC	1-2	1-0	2-4	

Semi-Finals (Group "A")

		Pd	Wn	Dw	Ls	GF	GA	Pts
1.	Bologna FC (Bologna)	6	4	1	1	10	5	9
2.	FC Internazionale (Milano)	6	4	-	2	7	5	8
3.	Milan AC (Milano)	6	2	1	3	8	8	5
4.	Atalanta BC (Bergamo)	6	1	-	5	6	13	2
		24	11	2	11	31	31	24

1973-1974 Coppa Italia Semi-Finals Group "B"	SS Palermo	Juventus FC	AC Cesena	SS Lazio
SS Palermo		2-0	2-0	2-0
Juventus FC	1-1		1-1	3-0
AC Cesena	1-1	0-1		2-1
SS Lazio	1-0	0-0	1-1	

Semi-Finals (Group "B")

		Pd	Wn	Dw	Ls	GF	GA	Pts
1.	SS Palermo (Palermo)	6	3	2	1	8	3	8
2.	Juventus FC (Torino)	6	2	3	1	6	4	7
3.	AC Cesena (Cesena)	6	1	3	2	5	7	5
4.	SS Lazio (Roma)	6	1	2	3	3	8	4
		24	7	10	7	22	22	24

1974-75

1974-1975 Serie "A"	Ascoli Calcio	Bologna FC	Cagliari Calcio	AC Cesena	AC Fiorentina	FC Internazionale	Juventus FC	SS Lanerossi	SS Lazio	Milan AC	SSC Napoli	AS Roma	UC Sampdoria	Ternana Calcio	Torino Calcio	Varese Calcio
Ascoli Calcio		1-3	0-0	0-0	0-1	0-0	0-0	1-0	1-0	1-1	1-1	0-0	1-0	1-0	1-1	2-0
Bologna FC	1-1		2-0	3-2	1-0	2-1	2-1	1-1	1-2	0-0	1-0	1-0	2-2	1-1	1-3	1-1
Cagliari Calcio	2-0	1-1		2-2	2-1	0-1	1-1	0-0	1-1	0-0	1-1	1-2	1-0	2-0	0-0	1-1
AC Cesena	0-0	2-2	2-1		1-1	0-0	0-1	3-1	0-0	1-0	0-0	0-0	1-1	2-1	1-1	1-1
AC Fiorentina	0-0	1-0	2-1	2-2		1-1	4-1	0-0	1-1	1-1	1-1	0-0	0-2	2-0	2-2	2-0
FC Internazionale	0-1	1-1	4-1	0-1	1-0		0-1	0-0	3-1	0-0	0-0	0-2	0-0	1-0	1-0	1-0
Juventus FC	4-0	0-0	1-0	1-0	0-0	1-0		5-0	4-0	2-1	2-1	1-0	1-1	2-0	0-0	3-0
SS Lanerossi	1-0	0-1	0-0	2-0	0-1	1-3	1-2		1-2	2-0	2-2	0-2	1-1	1-0	1-0	1-1
SS Lazio	1-0	1-0	1-0	2-1	1-0	1-2	1-0	1-0		3-0	1-1	0-1	3-0	0-0	1-5	2-0
Milan AC	2-0	3-0	0-0	3-0	1-1	3-0	0-2	1-0	1-1		0-0	1-1	0-0	3-1	2-0	4-0
SSC Napoli	3-1	1-0	5-0	4-0	1-0	3-2	2-6	2-0	1-1	2-0		2-0	2-0	7-1	1-0	3-0
AS Roma	1-0	2-1	1-1	2-0	1-0	1-0	1-0	1-0	1-0	0-1	0-0		1-0	4-2	0-1	1-0
UC Sampdoria	0-0	1-0	0-0	0-0	3-4	1-1	1-3	1-1	0-2	2-4	1-1	0-0		1-0	0-0	1-0
Ternana Calcio	1-0	0-0	0-2	1-0	0-1	0-0	0-2	0-0	1-1	1-3	0-0	2-2	1-1		2-1	2-0
Torino Calcio	1-0	3-3	1-0	2-0	2-1	2-3	3-2	2-1	2-2	1-1	1-1	1-0	1-1	1-1		3-1
Varese Calcio	3-1	1-4	0-1	1-1	1-1	2-0	0-0	1-1	0-1	0-1	0-2	0-0	4-0	1-1	0-0	

	Serie "A"	Pd	Wn	Dw	Ls	GF	GA	Pts	
1.	JUVENTUS FC (TORINO)	30	18	7	5	49	19	43	
2.	SSC Napoli (Napoli)	30	14	13	3	50	22	41	
3.	AS Roma (Roma)	30	15	9	6	27	15	39	
4.	SS Lazio (Roma)	30	14	9	7	34	28	37	
5.	Milan AC (Milano)	30	12	12	6	37	22	36	
6.	Torino Calcio (Torino)	30	11	13	6	40	30	35	
7.	Bologna FC (Bologna)	30	10	12	8	36	33	32	
8.	AC Fiorentina (Firenze)	30	9	13	8	31	27	31	
9.	FC Internazionale (Milano)	30	10	10	10	26	26	30	
10.	Cagliari Calcio (Cagliari)	30	6	14	10	22	30	26	
11.	AC Cesena (Cesena)	30	5	15	10	23	35	25	
12.	Ascoli Calcio (Ascoli Piceno)	30	6	12	12	14	27	24	
13.	UC Sampdoria (Genova)	30	4	16	10	21	35	24	
14.	SS Lanerossi (Vicenza)	30	5	11	14	19	34	21	R
15.	Ternana Calcio (Terni)	30	4	11	15	19	42	19	R
16.	Varese Calcio (Varese)	30	3	11	16	19	42	17	R
		480	146	188	146	467	467	480	

Top goalscorers

1)	Paolino PULICI	(Torino Calcio)	18
2)	Giuseppe SAVOLDI	(Bologna FC)	15
3)	Giorgio CHINAGLIA	(SS Lazio)	14
	Sergio CLERICI	(SSC Napoli)	14
	Pierino PRATI	(AS Roma)	14

* US Alessandria changed their club name to US Alessandria Calcio (Alessandria) for the next season.
AC Como (Como) changed their club name to Como Calcio (Como) for the next season.
AC Novara (Novara) changed their club name to Novara Calcio (Novara) for the next season.

	Serie "B"	Pd	Wn	Dw	Ls	GF	GA	Pts	
1.	AC Perugia (Perugia)	38	17	15	6	44	27	49	P
2.	AC Como (Como)	38	18	10	10	40	23	46	P *
3.	Hellas-Verona AC (Verona)	38	16	13	9	39	30	45	P
4.	US Catanzaro (Catanzaro)	38	13	19	6	27	18	45	PO
5.	SS Palermo (Palermo)	38	13	17	8	31	25	43	
6.	Atalanta BC (Bergamo)	38	14	11	13	37	36	39	
7.	Genoa CFC (Genova)	38	14	10	14	31	33	38	
8.	US Foggia (Foggia)	38	10	18	10	31	35	38	
9.	AC Brescia (Brescia)	38	10	17	11	24	28	37	
10.	Pescara Calcio (Pescara)	38	9	18	11	37	38	36	
11.	Sambenedettese Calcio (San Benedetto del Tronto)	38	13	10	15	36	43	36	
12.	AC Novara (Novara)	38	10	15	13	30	33	35	*
13.	S.P.A.L. (Ferrara)	38	13	9	16	38	42	35	
14.	Brindisi Sport (Brindisi)	38	11	13	14	32	38	35	
15.	AS Taranto (Taranto)	38	10	15	13	24	34	35	
16.	US Avellino (Avellino)	38	11	12	15	33	29	34	
17.	AC Reggiana (Reggio Emilia)	38	9	16	13	33	36	34	PO
18.	US Alessandria (Alessandria)	38	9	16	13	35	38	34	R *
19.	US Arezzo (Arezzo)	38	9	15	14	35	44	33	R
20.	Parma AC (Parma)	38	9	15	14	30	37	30	R -3
		760	238	284	238	667	667	757	

Note: Parma AC (Parma) had 3 points deducted by the F.I.G.C. Committee.

Promotion Play-Off

Hellas-Verona AC (Verona)	1-0	US Catanzaro (Catanzaro)

Relegation Play-Off

AC Reggiana (Reggio Emilia)	2-1	US Alessandria (Alessandria)

Promoted to Serie "B": Catania Calcio (Catania), Modena FC (Modena) and Piacenza Calcio (Piacenza).

Coppa Italia Final (Roma – 28/06/75)

AC FIORENTINA (FIRENZE)	3-2	Milan AC (Milano)
Casarsa 14' pen., Guerini 54', Rosi 67'		*Bigon 20', Chiarugi 65'*

Fiorentina: Superchi, Beatrice (Lelj 46', Rosi 47'), Roggi, Guerini, Pellegrini, Della Martira, Caso, Merlo, Casarsa, Antognoni, Desolati.

Milan: Albertosi, Sabadini (Biasiolo 60'), Zecchini, Turone, Bet, A.Maldera, D.Gorin, Benetti, Calloni, Bigon, Chiarugi.

1974-1975 Coppa Italia Semi-Finals Group "A"	AC Fiorentina	Torino Calcio	AS Roma	SSC Napoli
AC Fiorentina		3-1	2-1	3-1
Torino Calcio	1-0		3-0	2-1
AS Roma	2-2	0-0		0-0
SSC Napoli	1-0	1-0	0-2	

	Semi-Finals (Group "A")	Pd	Wn	Dw	Ls	GF	GA	Pts
1.	AC Fiorentina (Firenze)	6	3	1	2	10	7	7
2.	Torino Calcio (Torino)	6	3	1	2	7	5	7
3.	AS Roma (Roma)	6	1	3	2	5	7	5
4.	SSC Napoli (Napoli)	6	2	1	3	4	7	5
		24	9	6	9	26	26	24

1974-1975 Coppa Italia Semi-Finals Group "B"	Milan AC	Juventus FC	FC Internazionale	Bologna FC
Milan AC		1-0	0-0	1-0
Juventus FC	2-1		1-2	1-0
FC Internazionale	0-1	2-6		0-1
Bologna FC	1-4	0-5	0-0	

	Semi-Finals (Group "B")	Pd	Wn	Dw	Ls	GF	GA	Pts
1.	Milan AC (Milano)	6	4	1	1	8	3	9
2.	Juventus FC (Torino)	6	4	-	2	15	6	8
3.	FC Internazionale (Milano)	6	1	2	3	4	9	4
4.	Bologna FC (Bologna)	6	1	1	4	2	11	3
		24	10	4	10	29	29	24

1975-76

1975-1976 Serie "A"	Ascoli Calcio	Bologna FC	Cagliari Calcio	AC Cesena	Como Calcio	AC Fiorentina	Hellas Verona AC	FC Internazionale	Juventus FC	SS Lazio	Milan AC	SSC Napoli	AC Perugia	AS Roma	UC Sampdoria	Torino Calcio
Ascoli Calcio		0-0	1-1	0-0	1-1	1-0	2-0	2-0	0-3	2-1	0-1	0-0	1-2	0-0	1-1	1-1
Bologna FC	1-1		0-0	5-3	1-1	1-1	0-0	1-2	1-4	1-0	1-1	2-0	1-1	2-1	1-0	1-0
Cagliari Calcio	0-0	1-2		1-2	1-0	2-1	0-2	0-0	0-1	2-1	1-3	1-1	0-0	1-5	5-3	0-0
AC Cesena	3-1	0-0	0-0		2-0	1-1	3-0	2-3	2-1	0-0	2-1	0-1	2-1	2-0	1-1	1-1
Como Calcio	0-0	2-1	3-0	0-0		0-1	2-1	3-0	2-2	2-2	1-4	0-1	0-0	0-0	0-0	0-1
AC Fiorentina	0-0	1-2	3-0	3-1	0-2		2-2	0-0	1-1	4-3	0-1	1-1	3-1	2-0	0-1	0-1
Hellas-Verona AC	1-0	1-0	2-1	2-2	3-2	1-2		1-1	1-2	2-2	2-2	2-4	3-1	0-1	4-1	0-0
FC Internazionale	3-0	1-1	1-0	0-0	2-1	1-0	3-0		1-0	1-0	0-1	2-1	2-2	2-0	2-1	1-0
Juventus FC	2-1	1-0	1-0	3-3	1-1	4-2	2-1	2-0		2-0	1-1	2-1	1-0	1-1	2-0	0-2
SS Lazio	3-1	1-1	3-0	2-2	3-2	1-2	1-1	1-1	1-2		4-0	0-1	1-0	1-1	1-1	1-1
Milan AC	4-0	3-1	2-3	2-1	2-2	2-1	1-0	2-1	0-1	3-0		1-1	0-0	1-0	1-0	1-2
SSC Napoli	0-0	2-2	3-1	2-0	1-0	1-2	0-1	3-1	1-1	1-0	1-0		4-0	2-1	0-0	0-0
AC Perugia	1-1	1-1	4-1	1-0	2-0	2-1	1-0	1-1	1-0	2-0	0-0	2-2		0-1	0-0	2-1
AS Roma	1-1	0-0	1-1	2-2	2-1	2-2	2-0	1-1	0-1	0-0	0-0	0-3	1-2		1-0	1-1
UC Sampdoria	1-0	0-1	2-1	0-1	1-0	0-0	2-0	0-2	0-2	0-1	0-1	2-1	3-1	1-0		0-0
Torino Calcio	3-1	3-1	5-1	1-1	1-0	4-3	4-2	2-1	2-0	2-1	2-1	3-1	3-0	1-0	2-0	

	Serie "A"	Pd	Wn	Dw	Ls	GF	GA	Pts	
1.	TORINO CALCIO (TORINO)	30	18	9	3	49	22	45	
2.	Juventus FC (Torino)	30	18	7	5	46	26	43	
3.	Milan AC (Milano)	30	15	8	7	42	28	38	
4.	FC Internazionale (Milano)	30	14	9	7	36	28	37	
5.	SSC Napoli (Napoli)	30	13	10	7	40	27	36	
6.	AC Cesena (Cesena)	30	9	14	7	39	35	32	
7.	Bologna FC (Bologna)	30	9	14	7	32	32	32	
8.	AC Perugia (Perugia)	30	10	11	9	31	34	31	
9.	AC Fiorentina (Firenze)	30	9	9	12	39	39	27	
10.	AS Roma (Roma)	30	6	13	11	25	31	25	
11.	Hellas-Verona AC (Verona)	30	8	8	14	35	46	24	
12.	UC Sampdoria (Genova)	30	8	8	14	21	32	24	
13.	SS Lazio (Roma)	30	6	11	13	35	40	23	
14.	Ascoli Calcio (Ascoli Piceno)	30	4	15	11	19	34	23	R
15.	Como Calcio (Como)	30	5	11	14	28	36	21	R
16.	Cagliari Calcio (Cagliari)	30	5	9	16	25	52	19	R
		480	157	166	157	542	542	480	

Top goalscorers

1)	Paolino PULICI	(Torino Calcio)	21
2)	Roberto BETTEGA	(Juventus FC)	15
	Francesco GRAZIANI	(Torino Calcio)	15
4)	Giuseppe SAVOLDI	(SSC Napoli)	14
5)	Egidio CALLONI	(Milan AC)	13

* AC Brescia (Brescia) changed their club name to Brescia Calcio (Brescia) for the next season.

Note: US Livorno (Livorno) changed their club name to US Livorno Calcio (Livorno) for the next season.

	Serie "B"	Pd	Wn	Dw	Ls	GF	GA	Pts	
1.	Genoa CFC (Genova)	38	14	17	7	57	33	45	P
2.	US Catanzaro (Catanzaro)	38	16	13	9	36	23	45	P
3.	US Foggia (Foggia)	38	15	15	8	28	23	45	P
4.	Varese Calcio (Varese)	38	15	14	9	50	37	44	
5.	AC Brescia (Brescia)	38	13	17	8	42	37	43	*
6.	Novara Calcio (Novara)	38	10	21	7	31	29	41	
7.	S.P.A.L. (Ferrara)	38	14	12	12	40	36	40	
8.	Modena FC (Modena)	38	13	13	12	30	34	39	
9.	US Avellino (Avellino)	38	15	8	15	38	34	38	
10.	Atalanta BC (Bergamo)	38	13	12	13	26	24	38	
11.	SS Palermo (Palermo)	38	11	16	11	34	35	38	
12.	AS Taranto (Taranto)	38	11	16	11	28	31	38	
13.	Sambenedettese Calcio (San Benedetto del Tronto)	38	11	16	11	26	30	38	
14.	Pescara Calcio (Pescara)	38	12	14	12	25	32	38	
15.	Ternana Calcio (Terni)	38	11	15	12	30	33	37	
16.	SS Lanerossi (Vicenza)	38	9	17	12	36	35	35	
17.	Catania Calcio (Catania)	38	9	17	12	27	30	35	
18.	Piacenza Calcio (Piacenza)	38	10	12	16	42	50	32	R
19.	Brindisi Sport (Brindisi)	38	7	13	18	20	41	27	R
20.	AC Reggiana (Reggio Emilia)	38	5	14	19	31	50	24	R
		760	234	292	234	677	677	760	

Promoted to Serie "B": US Lecce (Lecce), Monza Calcio (Monza) and Rimini Calcio (Rimini).

Coppa Italia Final (Roma – 29/06/76)

SSC NAPOLI (NAPOLI) 4-0 Hellas-Verona AC (Verona)

Ginulfi 76' o.g., Braglia 78', Savoldi 79', 86'

Napoli: Carmignani, Bruscolotti, La Palma, Burgnich, Vavassori, Orlandini, Massa, Juliano, G.Savoldi, Esposito, Braglia.

Hellas: Ginulfi, Bachlechner, Sirena, Guidolin (Vriz 77'), Catellani, Nanni, Franzot, Mascetti, Luppi (Macchi 67'), A.Moro, Zigoni.

1975-1976 Coppa Italia Semi-Finals Group "A"	Hellas-Verona AC	FC Internazionale	SS Lazio	Genoa CFC
Hellas-Verona AC		2-0	3-0	1-0
FC Internazionale	3-1		3-2	1-0
SS Lazio	0-0	1-0		1-0
Genoa CFC	1-1	1-3	0-3	

Semi-Finals (Group "A")		Pd	Wn	Dw	Ls	GF	GA	Pts
1.	Hellas-Verona AC (Verona)	6	3	2	1	8	4	8
2.	FC Internazionale (Milano)	6	4	-	2	10	7	8
3.	SS Lazio (Roma)	6	3	1	2	7	6	7
4.	Genoa CFC (Genova)	6	-	1	5	2	10	1
		24	10	4	10	27	27	24

1975-1976 Coppa Italia Semi-Finals Group "B"	SSC Napoli	AC Fiorentina	Milan AC	UC Sampdoria
SSC Napoli		0-0	2-1	2-1
AC Fiorentina	1-1		2-2	3-1
Milan AC	0-2	1-1		3-1
UC Sampdoria	2-2	3-3	0-2	

Semi-Finals (Group "B")		Pd	Wn	Dw	Ls	GF	GA	Pts
1.	SSC Napoli (Napoli)	6	3	3	-	9	5	9
2.	AC Fiorentina (Firenze)	6	1	5	-	10	8	7
3.	Milan AC (Milano)	6	2	2	2	9	8	6
4.	UC Sampdoria (Genova)	6	-	2	4	8	15	2
		24	6	12	6	36	36	24

1976-77

1976-1977 Serie "A"	Bologna FC	US Catanzaro	AC Cesena	AC Fiorentina	US Foggia	Genoa CFC	Hellas Verona AC	FC Internazionale	Juventus FC	SS Lazio	Milan AC	SSC Napoli	AC Perugia	AS Roma	UC Sampdoria	Torino Calcio
Bologna FC		0-0	0-0	2-0	0-0	0-0	0-0	1-5	0-1	1-0	2-2	0-1	1-0	2-0	4-1	0-3
US Catanzaro	1-2		4-2	0-1	3-1	2-1	2-1	1-3	0-2	1-2	1-0	0-0	1-1	1-1	1-0	0-4
AC Cesena	0-0	1-0		1-2	2-3	1-1	0-1	0-0	1-1	0-0	0-2	0-2	0-3	4-0	1-1	0-3
AC Fiorentina	3-0	1-1	2-1		4-1	1-2	2-1	3-0	1-3	0-1	1-1	2-1	1-0	1-1	1-1	0-1
US Foggia	1-0	1-0	0-2	2-3		2-3	4-1	0-0	0-1	1-0	2-1	2-2	2-1	1-0	2-0	0-1
Genoa CFC	0-2	2-0	4-1	1-1	1-2		1-0	2-2	2-2	3-1	1-0	2-3	0-0	2-2	1-1	1-1
Hellas-Verona AC	3-3	0-0	2-1	1-2	2-1	3-2		1-0	0-0	0-0	0-0	1-0	2-0	1-1	2-2	0-0
FC Internazionale	0-0	2-1	1-1	1-1	1-1	1-0	0-0		0-2	1-1	0-0	3-2	1-1	3-0	0-0	0-1
Juventus FC	2-1	3-0	3-2	0-0	1-0	1-0	2-1	2-0		2-0	2-1	2-1	1-0	1-0	3-0	0-2
SS Lazio	3-0	0-1	3-0	4-1	0-0	4-1	1-1	2-1	2-3		1-2	0-0	1-0	1-0	1-0	0-0
Milan AC	1-1	3-2	0-0	0-0	0-0	2-2	0-0	1-1	2-3	2-2		1-1	2-1	1-1	3-0	0-0
SSC Napoli	1-2	1-0	3-1	0-2	3-2	1-1	3-0	0-3	0-2	1-1	3-1		1-1	1-0	1-1	0-0
AC Perugia	1-0	1-1	1-0	0-0	1-0	2-1	1-1	0-1	1-1	2-0	3-1	4-2		3-0	0-0	1-1
AS Roma	1-0	1-0	2-0	0-0	3-1	1-0	0-0	2-3	3-1	1-0	1-1	0-0	2-2		3-0	1-0
UC Sampdoria	0-0	3-1	2-1	2-2	2-1	1-2	3-1	0-1	0-2	0-0	0-0	2-2	2-0	1-0		2-3
Torino Calcio	1-0	3-1	2-0	2-0	1-0	5-1	1-0	1-0	1-1	3-3	2-0	2-1	2-1	2-0	3-1	

	Serie "A"	Pd	Wn	Dw	Ls	GF	GA	Pts	
1.	JUVENTUS FC (TORINO)	30	23	5	2	50	20	51	
2.	Torino Calcio (Torino)	30	21	8	1	51	14	50	
3.	AC Fiorentina (Firenze)	30	12	11	7	38	31	35	
4.	FC Internazionale (Milano)	30	10	13	7	34	27	33	
5.	SS Lazio (Roma)	30	10	11	9	34	28	31	
6.	AC Perugia (Perugia)	30	9	11	10	32	28	29	
7.	SSC Napoli (Napoli)	30	9	11	10	37	38	28	-1
8.	AS Roma (Roma)	30	9	10	11	27	33	28	
9.	Hellas-Verona AC (Verona)	30	7	14	9	26	32	28	
10.	Milan AC (Milano)	30	5	17	8	30	33	27	
11.	Genoa CFC (Genova)	30	8	11	11	40	45	27	
12.	Bologna FC (Bologna)	30	8	11	11	24	31	27	
13.	US Foggia (Foggia)	30	10	6	14	33	39	26	
14.	UC Sampdoria (Genova)	30	6	12	12	28	42	24	R
15.	US Catanzaro (Catanzaro)	30	7	7	16	26	43	21	R
16.	AC Cesena (Cesena)	30	3	8	19	22	48	14	R
		480	157	166	157	532	532	480	

Top goalscorers

1)	Francesco GRAZIANI	(Torino Calcio)	21
2)	Roberto PRUZZO	(Genoa CFC)	18
3)	Roberto BETTEGA	(Juventus FC)	17
4)	Paolino PULICI	(Torino Calcio)	16
	Giuseppe SAVOLDI	(SSC Napoli)	16

* Novara Calcio (Novara) changed their club name to AC Novara (Novara) for the next season.
SS Palermo (Palermo) changed their club name to SSC Palermo (Palermo) for the next season.

Note: US Livorno Calcio (Livorno) changed their club name to UC Livorno (Livorno) for the next season.
AC Padova (Padova) changed their club name to Padova Calcio (Padova) for the next season.

	Serie "B"	Pd	Wn	Dw	Ls	GF	GA	Pts	
1.	SS Lanerossi (Vicenza)	38	18	15	5	47	29	51	P
2.	Pescara Calcio (Pescara)	38	17	15	6	48	29	49	P
3.	Atalanta BC (Bergamo)	38	19	11	8	44	26	49	P
4.	Cagliari Calcio (Cagliari)	38	17	15	6	45	32	49	PO
5.	Monza Calcio (Monza)	38	17	14	7	46	27	48	
6.	Como Calcio (Como)	38	12	17	9	35	27	41	
7.	US Lecce (Lecce)	38	13	13	12	33	32	39	
8.	Varese Calcio (Varese)	38	12	14	12	41	37	38	
9.	AS Taranto (Taranto)	38	12	13	13	32	31	37	
10.	Ascoli Calcio (Ascoli Piceno)	38	12	13	13	41	43	37	
11.	Sambenedettese Calcio (San Benedetto del Tronto)	38	9	19	10	27	31	37	
12.	Rimini Calcio (Rimini)	38	9	15	14	25	27	33	
13.	SS Palermo (Palermo)	38	8	17	13	29	41	33	*
14.	Modena FC (Modena)	38	10	12	16	28	35	32	
15.	US Avellino (Avellino)	38	10	12	16	27	37	32	
16.	Brescia Calcio (Brescia)	38	9	14	15	35	46	32	
17.	Ternana Calcio (Terni)	38	11	10	17	32	45	32	
18.	S.P.A.L. (Ferrara)	38	6	19	13	29	37	31	R
19.	Catania Calcio (Catania)	38	6	19	13	26	44	31	R
20.	Novara Calcio (Novara)	38	7	15	16	34	48	29	R *
		760	234	292	234	704	704	760	

Promotion Play-Offs

Atalanta BC (Bergamo)	0-0	Pescara Calcio (Pescara)
Atalanta BC (Bergamo)	2-1	Cagliari Calcio (Cagliari)
Pescara Calcio (Pescara)	0-0	Cagliari Calcio (Cagliari)

Promoted to Serie "B": AS Bari (Bari), US Cremonese (Cremona) and US Pistoiese (Pistoia).

Coppa Italia Final (Milano – 03/07/77)

MILAN AC (MILANO)	2-0	FC Internazionale (Milano)

Maldera 64', Braglia 89'

Milan: Albertosi, Sabadini, A.Maldera, G.Morini (Boldini 12'), Bet, Turone, Bigon, Biasiolo, Calloni, Rivera, G.Braglia.

Internazionale: Bordon, Canuti (Guida 70'), Fedele, Oriali, Gasparini, Facchetti, Pavone, Merlo (Grosselli 76'), Anastasi, Mazzola, Marini.

1976-1977 Coppa Italia Semi-Finals Group "A"	Milan AC	Bologna FC	SSC Napoli	S.P.A.L.
Milan AC		5-0	3-1	2-0
Bologna FC	1-1		0-0	3-0
SSC Napoli	1-2	1-0		0-0
S.P.A.L.	0-2	0-2	0-1	

	Semi-Finals (Group "A")	Pd	Wn	Dw	Ls	GF	GA	Pts
1.	Milan AC (Milano)	6	5	1	-	15	3	11
2.	Bologna FC (Bologna)	6	2	2	2	6	7	6
3.	SSC Napoli (Napoli)	6	2	2	2	4	5	6
4.	S.P.A.L. (Ferrara)	6	-	1	5	-	10	1
		24	9	6	9	25	25	24

1976-1977 Coppa Italia Semi-Finals Group "B"	FC Internazionale	Juventus FC	SS Lanerossi	US Lecce
FC Internazionale		1-0	1-1	0-0
Juventus FC	0-1		2-1	1-1
SS Lanerossi	0-3	2-4		3-0
US Lecce	1-1	1-1	1-2	

	Semi-Finals (Group "B")	Pd	Wn	Dw	Ls	GF	GA	Pts
1.	FC Internazionale (Milano)	6	3	3	-	7	2	9
2.	Juventus FC (Torino)	6	2	2	2	8	7	6
3.	SS Lanerossi (Vicenza)	6	2	1	3	9	11	5
4.	US Lecce (Lecce)	6	-	4	2	4	8	4
		24	7	10	7	28	28	24

1977-78

1977-1978 Serie "A"	Atalanta BC	Bologna FC	AC Fiorentina	US Foggia	Genoa CFC	Hellas Verona AC	FC Internazionale	Juventus FC	SS Lanerossi	SS Lazio	Milan AC	SSC Napoli	AC Perugia	Pescara Calcio	AS Roma	Torino Calcio
Atalanta BC		0-0	0-0	1-2	1-1	1-0	0-1	0-2	2-4	1-1	1-1	1-1	1-1	2-0	0-1	0-0
Bologna FC	0-0		0-1	2-1	2-1	0-3	2-1	1-1	3-2	2-1	0-0	0-0	2-3	1-1	0-0	1-3
AC Fiorentina	2-2	0-0		1-1	0-0	1-2	0-2	1-1	1-3	0-1	1-1	1-0	2-1	3-0	2-0	2-0
US Foggia	1-0	1-0	1-1		1-1	4-0	0-2	0-0	1-1	3-1	1-2	1-1	0-1	2-0	0-0	1-0
Genoa CFC	0-1	0-0	2-1	0-0		2-2	1-1	2-2	1-2	2-1	1-1	1-1	2-0	1-0	1-0	1-2
Hellas-Verona AC	1-2	1-1	0-0	3-1	2-0		0-0	0-0	0-0	2-2	1-2	0-1	0-0	1-0	0-0	0-0
FC Internazionale	1-0	0-1	2-1	2-1	2-0	0-0		0-1	2-0	1-1	1-3	1-0	2-0	0-0	4-2	0-0
Juventus FC	1-1	1-0	5-1	6-0	4-0	1-0	2-2		3-2	3-0	1-1	1-0	2-0	2-0	2-0	0-0
SS Lanerossi	2-2	3-0	1-0	2-0	1-0	1-0	1-2	0-0		2-1	1-1	0-0	3-1	1-1	4-3	0-0
SS Lazio	0-2	0-1	1-0	1-1	0-0	1-1	1-0	3-0	1-3		2-0	1-1	2-0	2-1	1-1	1-1
Milan AC	0-1	1-0	5-1	2-0	2-2	1-1	0-0	0-0	3-1	0-2		0-1	2-2	2-0	1-0	1-1
SSC Napoli	2-2	0-0	0-0	5-0	0-0	3-0	2-2	1-2	1-4	4-3	1-1		3-2	1-1	2-0	1-3
AC Perugia	1-1	2-0	2-1	3-1	0-0	0-1	1-1	0-0	1-1	4-0	0-1	2-0		2-1	3-2	2-0
Pescara Calcio	0-0	2-1	1-2	1-2	0-0	2-2	2-1	1-2	1-2	1-0	0-2	1-3	1-1		1-1	2-1
AS Roma	3-1	1-1	2-2	1-0	1-0	2-1	1-2	1-1	1-1	0-0	1-2	0-0	2-0	2-0		2-1
Torino Calcio	3-2	2-0	1-0	3-1	3-1	2-1	1-0	0-0	2-2	1-0	1-0	1-0	1-1	2-0	1-1	

	Serie "A"	Pd	Wn	Dw	Ls	GF	GA	Pts	
1.	JUVENTUS FC (TORINO)	30	15	14	1	46	17	44	
2.	SS Lanerossi (Vicenza)	30	14	11	5	50	34	39	
3.	Torino Calcio (Torino)	30	14	11	5	36	23	39	
4.	Milan AC (Milano)	30	12	13	5	38	25	37	
5.	FC Internazionale (Milano)	30	13	10	7	35	24	36	
6.	SSC Napoli (Napoli)	30	8	14	8	35	31	30	
7.	AC Perugia (Perugia)	30	10	10	10	36	35	30	
8.	AS Roma (Roma)	30	8	12	10	31	34	28	
9.	Atalanta BC (Bergamo)	30	6	15	9	28	32	27	
10.	Hellas-Verona AC (Verona)	30	6	14	10	25	30	26	
11.	SS Lazio (Roma)	30	8	10	12	30	38	26	
12.	Bologna FC (Bologna)	30	7	12	11	21	32	26	
13.	AC Fiorentina (Firenze)	30	7	11	12	28	37	25	
14.	Genoa CFC (Genova)	30	5	15	10	23	33	25	R
15.	US Foggia (Foggia)	30	8	9	13	28	43	25	R
16.	Pescara Calcio (Pescara)	30	4	9	17	22	44	17	R
		480	145	190	145	512	512	480	

Top goalscorers

1)	Paolo ROSSI	(SS Lanerossi)	24
2)	Giuseppe SAVOLDI	(SSC Napoli)	16
3)	Bruno GIORDANO	(SS Lazio)	12
	Paolino PULICI	(Torino Calcio)	12

* AC Udinese (Udine) changed their club name to Udinese Calcio (Udine) for the next season.

	Serie "B"	Pd	Wn	Dw	Ls	GF	GA	Pts	
1.	Ascoli Calcio (Ascoli Piceno)	38	26	9	3	73	30	61	P
2.	US Catanzaro (Catanzaro)	38	16	12	10	50	41	44	P
3.	US Avellino (Avellino)	38	15	14	9	34	29	44	P
4.	Monza Calcio (Monza)	38	14	14	10	36	29	42	
5.	Ternana Calcio (Terni)	38	14	14	10	34	27	42	
6.	SSC Palermo (Palermo)	38	12	16	10	42	36	40	
7.	US Lecce (Lecce)	38	12	15	11	27	26	39	
8.	UC Sampdoria (Genova)	38	12	14	12	41	37	38	
9.	AC Cesena (Cesena)	38	11	16	11	36	33	38	
10.	Sambenedettese Calcio (San Benedetto del Tronto)	38	11	16	11	30	28	38	
11.	AS Taranto (Taranto)	38	10	18	10	31	38	38	
12.	Cagliari Calcio (Cagliari)	38	12	13	13	52	47	37	
13.	AS Bari (Bari)	38	12	13	13	38	42	37	
14.	Brescia Calcio (Brescia)	38	9	17	12	35	40	35	
15.	Varese Calcio (Varese)	38	10	15	13	34	44	35	
16.	US Pistoiese (Pistoia)	38	12	10	16	33	40	34	
17.	Rimini Calcio (Rimini)	38	9	16	13	31	39	34	
18.	US Cremonese (Cremona)	38	9	15	14	34	38	33	R
19.	Como Calcio (Como)	38	8	15	15	25	37	31	R
20.	Modena FC (Modena)	38	6	8	24	24	59	20	R
		760	240	280	240	740	740	760	

Promoted to Serie "B": AC Nocerina (Nocera Inferiore), S.P.A.L. (Ferrara) and AC Udinese (Udine).

Coppa Italia Final (Roma – 08/06/78)

FC INTERNAZIONALE (MILANO) 2-1 SSC Napoli (Napoli)

Altobelli 18', Bini 87' *Restelli 06'*

Internazionale: Cipollini, Canuti, Fedele (Chierico 58'), G.Baresi, Gasperini, Bini, Scanziani, Oriali, Altobelli, Marini, Muraro (Anastasi 89').

Napoli: Mattolini, Bruscolotti, La Palma, Restelli, Ferrario, Stanzione, Vinazzani, Juliano, G.Savoldi, Valente (Mocellin 62'), Chiarugi.

1977-1978 Coppa Italia Semi-Finals Group "A"	FC Internazionale	AC Fiorentina	Torino Calcio	Monza Calcio
FC Internazionale		2-2	1-0	3-0
AC Fiorentina	0-0		2-0	2-0
Torino Calcio	0-0	0-0		1-1
Monza Calcio	0-2	3-2	1-3	

Semi-Finals (Group "A")

		Pd	Wn	Dw	Ls	GF	GA	Pts
1.	FC Internazionale (Milano)	6	3	3	-	8	2	9
2.	AC Fiorentina (Firenze)	6	2	3	1	8	5	7
3.	Torino Calcio (Torino)	6	1	3	2	4	5	5
4.	Monza Calcio (Monza)	6	1	1	4	5	13	3
		24	7	10	7	25	25	24

1977-1978 Coppa Italia Semi-Finals Group "B"	SSC Napoli	Milan AC	Juventus FC	AS Taranto
SSC Napoli		1-0	5-0	3-0
Milan AC	1-1		4-2	2-0
Juventus FC	1-0	0-3		3-1
AS Taranto	0-0	1-1	1-1	

Semi-Finals (Group "B")

		Pd	Wn	Dw	Ls	GF	GA	Pts
1.	SSC Napoli (Napoli)	6	3	2	1	10	2	8
2.	Milan AC (Milano)	6	3	2	1	11	5	8
3.	Juventus FC (Torino)	6	2	1	3	7	14	5
4.	AS Taranto (Taranto)	6	-	3	3	3	10	3
		24	8	8	8	31	31	24

1978-79

1978-1979 Serie "A"	Ascoli Calcio	Atalanta BC	AC Avellino	Bologna FC	US Catanzaro	AC Fiorentina	Hellas Verona AC	FC Internazionale	Juventus FC	SS Lanerossi	SS Lazio	Milan AC	SSC Napoli	AC Perugia	AS Roma	Torino Calcio
Ascoli Calcio		1-0	2-0	2-2	1-1	2-1	1-0	1-2	1-0	0-0	0-0	0-1	0-0	0-0	0-0	3-0
Atalanta BC	3-2		0-0	0-0	0-2	0-0	1-0	0-1	0-1	2-0	0-0	1-3	2-1	0-2	2-0	0-1
US Avellino	3-1	0-0		0-0	0-0	1-1	2-0	1-0	0-0	2-1	1-3	1-0	1-1	0-1	0-0	1-1
Bologna FC	0-0	1-0	0-0		1-1	0-0	1-0	0-1	0-0	5-2	2-1	0-1	1-1	2-2	1-2	1-1
US Catanzaro	1-1	0-0	0-0	0-0		0-0	1-1	1-1	0-0	2-0	3-1	1-3	0-0	1-1	1-0	2-1
AC Fiorentina	1-0	0-1	1-0	1-0	1-1		1-0	1-2	0-1	0-0	3-0	2-3	2-1	1-1	2-0	0-0
Hellas-Verona AC	2-3	1-1	0-1	1-0	0-0	0-1		0-0	0-3	0-0	2-0	1-3	0-0	1-1	1-1	0-1
FC Internazionale	1-1	2-2	2-0	0-0	0-0	1-2	4-0		2-1	0-0	4-0	2-2	2-0	1-1	1-2	0-0
Juventus FC	1-0	3-0	3-3	1-1	3-1	1-1	6-2	1-1		1-2	2-1	1-0	1-0	1-2	4-1	1-1
SS Lanerossi	1-1	1-1	2-1	2-2	2-0	0-1	0-0	0-1	1-1		4-1	2-3	0-0	1-1	1-0	2-2
SS Lazio	3-1	1-1	0-0	1-0	3-1	4-0	1-0	1-1	2-2	4-3		1-1	1-2	0-0	0-0	0-0
Milan AC	0-0	1-1	1-0	0-0	4-0	4-1	2-1	1-0	0-0	0-0	2-0		0-1	1-1	1-0	1-0
SSC Napoli	2-1	2-0	3-0	2-1	1-0	0-0	1-0	0-0	0-0	2-2	0-2	1-1		1-1	1-0	0-1
AC Perugia	2-0	2-0	0-0	3-1	1-0	1-0	1-1	2-2	0-0	2-0	2-0	1-1	2-0		1-1	0-0
AS Roma	1-0	2-2	2-1	2-0	1-3	1-1	2-0	1-1	1-0	3-0	1-2	0-3	0-0	0-0		0-2
Torino Calcio	3-1	3-0	1-0	3-1	3-0	1-1	0-0	3-3	0-1	4-0	2-2	0-3	0-0	0-0	1-0	

	Serie "A"	Pd	Wn	Dw	Ls	GF	GA	Pts	
1.	MILAN AC (MILANO)	30	17	10	3	46	19	44	
2.	AC Perugia (Perugia)	30	11	19	-	34	16	41	
3.	Juventus FC (Torino)	30	12	13	5	40	23	37	
4.	FC Internazionale (Milano)	30	10	16	4	38	24	36	
5.	Torino Calcio (Torino)	30	11	14	5	35	23	36	
6.	SSC Napoli (Napoli)	30	9	14	7	23	21	32	
7.	AC Fiorentina (Firenze)	30	10	12	8	26	26	32	
8.	SS Lazio (Roma)	30	9	11	10	35	40	29	
9.	US Catanzaro (Catanzaro)	30	6	16	8	23	30	28	
10.	Ascoli Calcio (Ascoli Piceno)	30	7	12	11	26	31	26	
11.	US Avellino (Avellino)	30	6	14	10	19	26	26	
12.	AS Roma (Roma)	30	8	10	12	24	32	26	
13.	Bologna FC (Bologna)	30	4	16	10	23	30	24	
14.	Atalanta BC (Bergamo)	30	6	12	12	20	33	24	R
15.	SS Lanerossi (Vicenza)	30	5	14	11	29	42	24	R
16.	Hellas-Verona AC (Verona)	30	2	11	17	14	39	15	R
		480	133	214	133	455	455	480	

Top goalscorers

1)	Bruno GIORDANO	(SS Lazio)	19
2)	Paolo ROSSI	(SS Lanerossi)	15
3)	Albertino BIGON	(Milan AC)	12
4)	Alessandro ALTOBELLI	(FC Internazionale)	11
	Carlo MURARO	(FC Internazionale)	11

Note: AC Juniorcasale (Casale Monferrato) changed their name to AS Casale (Casale Monferrato) for next season.
US Pro Vercelli (Vercelli) changed their club name to AS Pro Vercelli (Vercelli) for the next season.
US Salernitana (Salerno) changed their club name to Salernitana Sport (Salerno) for the next season.

	Serie "B"	Pd	Wn	Dw	Ls	GF	GA	Pts	
1.	Udinese Calcio (Udine)	38	21	13	4	52	22	55	P
2.	Cagliari Calcio (Cagliari)	38	16	17	5	46	24	49	P
3.	Pescara Calcio (Pescara)	38	16	16	6	44	27	48	P
4.	Monza Calcio (Monza)	38	16	16	6	39	20	48	PO
5.	US Pistoiese (Pistoia)	38	15	14	9	38	28	44	
6.	US Lecce (Lecce)	38	14	15	9	33	33	43	
7.	SSC Palermo (Palermo)	38	11	19	8	38	34	41	
8.	Brescia Calcio (Brescia)	38	11	17	10	41	41	39	
9.	UC Sampdoria (Genova)	38	9	18	11	37	39	36	
10.	Ternana Calcio (Terni)	38	8	20	10	33	39	36	
11.	Sambenedettese Calcio (San Benedetto del Tronto)	38	9	18	11	35	42	36	
12.	Genoa CFC (Genova)	38	11	13	14	34	35	35	
13.	AC Cesena (Cesena)	38	9	17	12	27	29	35	
14.	S.P.A.L. (Ferrara)	38	9	17	12	34	37	35	
15.	AS Taranto (Taranto)	38	7	21	10	25	30	35	
16.	AS Bari (Bari)	38	6	23	9	29	36	35	
17.	US Foggia (Foggia)	38	8	17	13	39	45	33	R
18.	AC Nocerina (Nocera Inferiore)	38	8	13	17	24	39	29	R
19.	Rimini Calcio (Rimini)	38	3	18	17	17	39	24	R
20.	Varese Calcio (Varese)	38	6	12	20	29	55	24	R
		760	213	334	213	694	694	760	

Relegation Play-Off

Pescara Calcio (Pescara)	2-0	Monza Calcio (Monza)

Promoted to Serie "B": Como Calcio (Como), Parma AC (Parma), SC Pisa (Pisa) and Matera FC (Matera).

Coppa Italia Final (Napoli – 20/06/79)

JUVENTUS FC (TORINO)	2-1 (aet)	SSC Palermo (Palermo)
Brio 83', Causio 117'		*Chimenti 01'*

Juventus: Zoff, Gentile, Cabrini, Furino, F.Morini (Brio 49'), Scirea, Causio, Tardelli, Virdis (Boninsegna 49'), Benetti, Bettega.

Palermo: Frison, Gregorio, Citterio, Brignani, Di Cicco, Silipo, Maritozzi, Borsellino (I.Arcoleo 76'), V.Chimenti (Osellame 46'), Magherini, Conte.

Semi-Finals

US Catanzaro (Catanzaro)	1-1, 2-4	Juventus FC (Torino)
SSC Palermo (Palermo)	0-0, 2-1	SSC Napoli (Napoli)

Quarter-Finals

Cagliari Calcio (Cagliari)	2-2, 0-1	US Catanzaro (Catanzaro)
Juventus FC (Torino)	3-1, 0-1	FC Internazionale (Milano)
SSC Napoli (Napoli)	2-1, 0-0	AC Perugia (Perugia)
SSC Palermo (Palermo)	0-0, 0-0 (aet)	SS Lazio (Roma)

(SS Lazio (Roma) won on penalties)

1979-80

1979-1980 Serie "A"	Ascoli Calcio	AC Avellino	Bologna FC	Cagliari Calcio	US Catanzaro	AC Fiorentina	FC Internazionale	Juventus FC	SS Lazio	Milan AC	SSC Napoli	AC Perugia	Pescara Calcio	AS Roma	Torino Calcio	Udinese Calcio
Ascoli Calcio		0-0	2-0	1-0	2-2	1-0	1-1	2-3	1-1	0-0	0-0	1-0	3-1	3-0	1-0	3-0
US Avellino	2-2		1-0	2-2	2-0	0-2	0-0	1-0	0-0	1-0	2-3	2-2	2-0	0-1	0-2	0-0
Bologna FC	0-0	1-0		0-1	4-1	2-1	1-2	1-1	1-0	0-1	0-0	1-1	0-0	1-1	1-2	2-1
Cagliari Calcio	1-1	1-1	1-0		1-0	2-1	1-1	2-1	1-1	0-0	1-0	1-2	1-0	1-3	0-0	3-1
US Catanzaro	1-1	0-0	0-0	1-0		0-1	0-0	0-1	2-1	0-3	2-0	2-1	1-1	2-2	0-0	1-1
AC Fiorentina	3-1	3-0	0-0	1-1	3-0		0-2	2-1	0-0	1-1	0-0	0-0	2-0	3-1	1-0	1-1
FC Internazionale	2-4	3-0	0-0	3-3	3-1	0-0		4-0	2-1	2-0	1-0	3-2	2-0	2-2	1-1	2-1
Juventus FC	2-3	2-0	1-1	1-0	1-0	3-0	2-0		0-0	2-1	1-0	3-0	3-0	2-0	0-0	1-1
SS Lazio	0-1	1-1	0-1	1-1	2-0	2-0	0-0	1-0		0-2	1-1	1-1	2-0	1-2	2-1	0-0
Milan AC	3-0	1-0	4-0	2-0	0-0	2-0	0-1	2-1	2-1		1-2	1-0	3-1	0-0	0-2	0-0
SSC Napoli	1-0	0-1	1-1	0-0	1-1	0-0	3-4	0-0	0-0	0-1		1-1	2-0	3-0	1-0	1-0
AC Perugia	0-0	2-1	1-1	1-0	0-0	1-2	0-0	1-0	0-0	1-1	1-0		1-0	3-1	0-2	2-0
Pescara Calcio	0-0	1-1	0-0	2-0	1-1	1-2	0-2	0-2	2-0	2-1	1-0	1-1		2-3	0-2	1-1
AS Roma	1-0	1-1	1-2	1-1	1-0	2-1	1-0	1-3	1-1	0-0	0-0	4-0	2-0		1-1	1-1
Torino Calcio	1-0	2-2	0-0	0-0	0-0	1-1	0-0	1-2	1-0	0-1	0-0	2-0	2-0	1-0		1-1
Udinese Calcio	3-1	0-1	0-2	1-1	1-2	2-2	1-1	1-3	1-1	2-1	0-0	1-2	2-1	0-0	0-1	

	Serie "A"	Pd	Wn	Dw	Ls	GF	GA	Pts	
1.	FC INTERNAZIONALE (MILANO)	30	14	13	3	44	25	41	
2.	Juventus FC (Torino)	30	16	6	8	42	25	38	
3.	Milan AC (Milano)	30	14	8	8	34	19	36	R
4.	Torino Calcio (Torino)	30	11	13	6	26	15	35	
5.	Ascoli Calcio (Ascoli Piceno)	30	11	12	7	35	28	34	
6.	AC Fiorentina (Firenze)	30	11	11	8	33	27	33	
7.	AS Roma (Roma)	30	10	12	8	34	35	32	
8.	Bologna FC (Bologna)	30	8	14	8	23	24	30	
9.	Cagliari Calcio (Cagliari)	30	8	14	8	27	29	30	
10.	AC Perugia (Perugia)	30	9	12	9	27	32	30	
11.	SSC Napoli (Napoli)	30	7	14	9	20	20	28	
12.	US Avellino (Avellino)	30	7	13	10	24	32	27	
13.	SS Lazio (Roma)	30	5	15	10	21	25	25	R
14.	US Catanzaro (Catanzaro)	30	5	14	11	20	34	24	#
15.	Udinese Calcio (Udine)	30	3	15	12	24	38	21	#
16.	Pescara Calcio (Pescara)	30	4	8	18	18	44	16	R
		480	143	194	143	452	452	480	

Top goalscorers

1)	Roberto BETTEGA	(Juventus FC)	16
2)	Alessandro ALTOBELLI	(FC Internazionale)	15
3)	Paolo ROSSI	(AC Perugia)	13
4)	Francesco GRAZIANI	(Torino Calcio)	12
	Roberto PRUZZO	(AS Roma)	12
	Franco SELVAGGI	(Cagliari Calcio)	12

Milan AC (Milano) and SS Lazio (Roma) were relegated by the F.I.G.C. after being found guilty of trying to "fix" match results for the purpose of winning on the football pools. Some players/officials of both clubs were suspended from football for varying periods of time. As a result of this action US Catanzaro (Catanzaro) and Udinese Calcio (Udine) retained their places in Serie "A" for the next season.

	Serie "B"	Pd	Wn	Dw	Ls	GF	GA	Pts	
1.	Como Calcio (Como)	38	16	16	6	33	17	48	P
2.	US Pistoiese (Pistoia)	38	12	22	4	36	23	46	P
3.	Brescia Calcio (Brescia)	38	17	11	10	39	27	45	P
4.	AC Cesena (Cesena)	38	12	19	7	39	32	43	
5.	SS Lanerossi (Vicenza)	38	13	16	9	49	37	42	
6.	Monza Calcio (Monza)	38	15	12	11	40	38	42	
7.	UC Sampdoria (Genova)	38	10	21	7	33	27	41	
8.	S.P.A.L. (Ferrara)	38	10	19	9	33	32	39	
9.	Atalanta BC (Bergamo)	38	11	16	11	29	24	38	
10.	SSC Palermo (Palermo)	38	12	14	12	35	32	38	
11.	Genoa CFC (Genova)	38	11	16	11	33	34	38	*
12.	AS Bari (Bari)	38	9	20	9	26	30	38	
13.	Hellas-Verona AC (Verona)	38	12	13	13	25	27	37	
14.	SC Pisa (Pisa)	38	12	12	14	25	24	36	
15.	US Lecce (Lecce)	38	10	16	12	27	30	36	
16.	AS Taranto (Taranto)	38	12	11	15	24	29	35	
17.	Sambenedettese Calcio (San Benedetto del Tronto)	38	11	12	15	23	31	34	R
18.	Ternana Calcio (Terni)	38	10	11	17	26	36	31	R
19.	Parma AC (Parma)	38	7	13	18	27	49	27	R
20.	Matera FC (Matera)	38	8	10	20	20	43	26	R
		760	230	300	230	622	622	760	

Promoted to Serie "B": Catania Calcio (Catania), US Foggia (Foggia), Rimini Calcio (Rimini) and Varese Calcio.

* US Triestina (Trieste) changed their club name to US Triestina Calcio (Trieste) for the next season.

Coppa Italia Final (Roma – 17/05/80)

AS ROMA (ROMA) 0-0 (aet – 3-2 penalties) Torino Calcio (Torino)

Roma: Tancredi, Maggiora, De Nadai, Benedetti (Di Bartolomei 91'), Turone, Santarini, B.Conti, P.Giovanelli, Pruzzo, Ancelotti, Amenta (Scarnecchia 75').

Torino: Terraneo, Volpati, Vullo (Mandorlini 62'), P.Sala, Danova, Masi, Greco, Pecci, Graziani, Zaccarelli, Pulici (Mariani 96').

Semi-Finals

Juventus FC (Torino)	0-0, 0-0 (aet – 2-4 penalties)	Torino Calcio (Torino)
Ternana Calcio (Terni)	1-1, 0-2	AS Roma (Roma)

Quarter-Finals

FC Internazionale (Milano)	1-2, 0-0	Juventus FC (Torino)
Milan AC (Milano)	0-4, 2-2	AS Roma (Roma)
SSC Napoli (Napoli)	2-1, 0-1	Ternana Calcio (Terni)
	(Ternana Calcio (Terni) won on the away goals rule)	
Torino Calcio (Torino)	0-0, 0-0 (aet)	SS Lazio (Roma)
	(Torino Calcio (Torino) won on penalties)	

1980-81

1980-1981 Serie "A"	Ascoli Calcio	AC Avellino	Bologna FC	Brescia Calcio	Cagliari Calcio	US Catanzaro	Como Calcio	AC Fiorentina	FC Internazionale	Juventus FC	SSC Napoli	AC Perugia	US Pistoiese	AS Roma	Torino Calcio	Udinese Calcio
Ascoli Calcio		1-1	1-1	0-0	0-0	1-2	2-1	1-0	0-1	0-0	3-2	0-3	0-0	0-0	0-0	1-0
US Avellino	4-2		2-0	1-0	2-1	1-0	2-1	2-3	1-3	1-1	0-0	2-1	3-0	1-1	3-0	0-0
Bologna FC	1-0	0-0		0-1	2-1	0-0	1-1	2-1	2-1	1-5	1-1	4-0	2-0	1-1	1-0	1-0
Brescia Calcio	0-1	1-2	0-0		1-0	1-1	1-0	0-0	0-0	1-1	1-2	1-1	2-2	1-2	1-1	1-1
Cagliari Calcio	2-0	1-0	0-0	1-2		2-1	1-1	0-0	1-1	1-1	0-0	2-1	2-0	1-0	1-1	1-1
US Catanzaro	2-0	1-1	2-2	0-0	0-0		2-0	2-2	0-0	0-0	0-0	0-1	1-3	1-1	1-0	2-1
Como Calcio	0-0	2-0	2-1	2-2	3-1	0-0		2-1	1-0	1-2	0-1	1-0	1-0	0-1	0-2	2-0
AC Fiorentina	2-1	2-1	2-1	1-0	0-0	1-1	1-1		0-0	0-1	0-1	1-0	1-2	1-1	2-0	1-1
FC Internazionale	1-2	0-0	1-0	0-0	4-1	2-2	2-1	1-2		1-0	3-0	3-1	2-0	2-4	1-1	2-0
Juventus FC	3-0	1-0	0-1	2-0	1-1	3-0	2-0	1-0	2-1		1-1	2-1	4-1	0-0	1-2	4-0
SSC Napoli	1-0	1-0	2-1	1-1	2-0	1-1	2-0	1-1	1-0	0-1		0-1	1-0	4-0	1-3	1-0
AC Perugia	0-0	0-0	0-0	0-0	1-1	0-0	0-0	0-0	0-2	0-0	0-0		3-0	1-1	1-0	1-2
US Pistoiese	0-1	2-1	0-2	1-0	1-3	0-1	2-0	0-1	1-2	1-3	0-1	1-0		0-4	1-1	1-1
AS Roma	4-1	1-1	1-1	1-0	1-0	0-0	1-1	1-1	1-0	0-0	1-1	5-0	1-0		2-0	3-1
Torino Calcio	3-0	2-0	1-2	1-1	1-2	2-0	1-1	1-1	0-1	0-2	0-1	2-0	1-0	0-2		0-0
Udinese Calcio	0-0	5-4	1-1	0-0	2-2	2-1	2-0	0-0	0-4	0-2	2-1	1-1	1-0	0-2	0-0	

	Serie "A"	Pd	Wn	Dw	Ls	GF	GA	Pts	
1.	JUVENTUS FC (TORINO)	30	17	10	3	46	15	44	
2.	AS Roma (Roma)	30	14	14	2	43	20	42	
3.	SSC Napoli (Napoli)	30	14	10	6	31	21	38	
4.	FC Internazionale (Milano)	30	14	8	8	41	24	36	
5.	AC Fiorentina (Firenze)	30	9	14	7	28	25	32	
6.	Cagliari Calcio (Cagliari)	30	8	14	8	29	30	30	
7.	Bologna FC (Bologna)	30	11	12	7	32	27	29	-5
8.	US Catanzaro (Catanzaro)	30	6	17	7	24	27	29	
9.	Torino Calcio (Torino)	30	8	10	12	26	29	26	
10.	US Avellino (Avellino)	30	10	10	10	36	33	25	-5
11.	Ascoli Calcio (Ascoli Piceno)	30	7	11	12	18	34	25	
12.	Udinese Calcio (Udine)	30	6	13	11	24	39	25	
13.	Como Calcio (Como)	30	8	9	13	25	33	25	
14.	Brescia Calcio (Brescia)	30	4	17	9	19	25	25	R
15.	AC Perugia (Perugia)	30	5	13	12	18	31	18	R -5
16.	US Pistoiese (Pistoia)	30	6	4	20	19	46	16	R
		480	147	186	147	459	459	465	

Top goalscorers

1) Roberto PRUZZO (AS Roma) 18
2) Massimo PALANCA (US Catanzaro) 13
3) Alessandro ALTOBELLI (FC Internazionale) 12

Note: US Avellino (Avellino), Bologna FC (Bologna) and AC Perugia (Perugia) each had 5 points deducted by the F.I.G.C. as a result of the 1979-80 season football pools inquiry.

Positions 10 to 14 were decided on the results of the clubs' mutual matches (mini-league) to decide relegation.

Note: AC Novara (Novara) changed their club name to Novara Calcio (Novara) for the next season.

	Serie "B"	Pd	Wn	Dw	Ls	GF	GA	Pts	
1.	Milan AC (Milano)	38	18	14	6	49	29	50	P
2.	Genoa CFC (Genova)	38	17	14	7	47	29	48	P
3.	AC Cesena (Cesena)	38	16	16	6	44	26	48	P
4.	SS Lazio (Roma)	38	13	20	5	50	32	46	
5.	UC Sampdoria (Genova)	38	11	21	6	39	33	43	
6.	Pescara Calcio (Pescara)	38	14	13	11	35	38	41	
7.	SC Pisa (Pisa)	38	10	19	9	35	37	39	
8.	AS Bari (Bari)	38	13	11	14	40	41	37	
9.	Rimini Calcio (Rimini)	38	10	16	12	40	42	36	
10.	US Foggia (Foggia)	38	8	20	10	32	38	36	
11.	US Lecce (Lecce)	38	11	14	13	33	40	36	
12.	S.P.A.L. (Ferrara)	38	10	15	13	45	46	35	
13.	Catania Calcio (Catania)	38	11	13	14	38	50	35	
14.	SSC Palermo (Palermo)	38	9	21	8	35	33	34	-5
15.	Varese Calcio (Varese)	38	11	12	15	41	43	34	
16.	Hellas-Verona AC (Verona)	38	6	22	10	24	28	34	
17.	SS Lanerossi (Vicenza)	38	8	17	13	34	40	33	R
18.	AS Taranto (Taranto)	38	10	15	13	29	32	30	R -5
19.	Atalanta BC (Bergamo)	38	9	12	17	28	40	30	R
20.	Monza Calcio (Monza)	38	4	17	17	24	45	25	R
		760	219	322	219	742	742	750	

SSC Palermo (Palermo) and AS Taranto (Taranto) each had 5 points deducted by the F.I.G.C. as a result of the 1979-80 season football pools bribery inquiry.

Promoted to Serie "B": SS Cavese (Cava dei Tirreni), US Cremonese (Cremona), AC Reggiana (Reggio Emilia) and Sambenedettese Calcio (San Benedetto del Tronto).

Coppa Italia Final (1st leg) (Roma – 13/06/81)

AS ROMA (ROMA)	1-1	Torino Calcio (Torino)
Ancelotti 31'		*Santarini 59' o.g.*

Roma: Tancredi, V.Romano, Maggiora, Turone, Falcao, Santarini, B.Conti, Di Bartolomei, Faccini, Ancelotti, Scarnecchia.

Torino: Terraneo, Cuttone, Salvadori, Volpati, Danova, Zaccarelli (Davin 28'), Bertoneri, Pecci, Graziani, Sclosa, Pulici (D'Amico 67').

Coppa Italia Final (2nd leg) (Torino – 17/06/81)

AS ROMA (ROMA)	1-1 (aet – 5-3 penalties)	Torino Calcio (Torino)
Di Bartolomei 62'	*Cuttone 37'*	

Torino: Terraneo, Cuttone, Volpati, P.Sala, Danova, Zaccarelli (Davin 98'), Bertoneri, Pecci, Graziani, Sclosa, Pulici (Salvadori 75').

Roma: Tandredi, V.Romano, Maggiora, Turone (Santarini 20'), Falcao, Bonetti, B.Conti, Di Bartolomei, Pruzzo (Birigozzi 46'), Ancelotti, Scarnecchia.

Semi-Finals

Bologna FC (Bologna)	2-2, 2-3 (aet)	Torino Calcio (Torino)
Juventus FC (Torino)	0-1, 1-1	AS Roma (Roma)

Quarter-Finals

US Avellino (Avellino)	1-3, 2-3	Juventus FC (Torino)
AC Fiorentina (Firenze)	0-1, 0-0	AS Roma (Roma)
SS Lazio (Roma)	0-2, 0-2	Bologna FC (Bologna)
S.P.A.L. (Ferrara)	1-0, 0-4	Torino Calcio (Torino)

1981-82

1981-1982 Serie "A"	Ascoli Calcio	AC Avellino	Bologna FC	Cagliari Calcio	US Catanzaro	AC Cesena	Como Calcio	AC Fiorentina	Genoa CFC	FC Internazionale	Juventus FC	Milan AC	SSC Napoli	AS Roma	Torino Calcio	Udinese Calcio
Ascoli Calcio		1-1	2-1	2-1	2-1	1-0	1-1	0-0	1-1	2-2	1-0	1-0	0-0	0-1	0-0	3-0
US Avellino	1-0		0-1	1-4	1-0	2-0	1-1	1-2	0-0	0-1	0-1	2-0	3-0	1-0	0-0	0-1
Bologna FC	2-1	1-0		1-1	0-0	0-0	1-0	0-2	1-1	3-1	0-0	0-0	2-2	2-0	0-0	0-2
Cagliari Calcio	1-0	0-0	2-2		2-1	1-1	2-0	0-0	2-1	1-1	0-1	1-1	1-1	2-4	1-0	1-1
US Catanzaro	1-0	0-0	1-0	1-0		3-0	0-0	0-2	1-0	0-0	0-1	3-0	0-1	1-1	1-0	0-0
AC Cesena	1-1	2-0	4-1	2-1	4-1		1-1	2-1	1-1	1-3	1-1	2-3	1-3	1-1	0-0	2-1
Como Calcio	1-2	0-1	2-2	2-1	1-1	2-1		1-1	1-1	1-1	0-2	2-0	0-4	0-1	0-1	0-2
AC Fiorentina	0-0	1-0	1-0	1-1	1-0	1-0	1-0		3-2	4-2	0-0	1-0	2-1	1-0	2-1	3-0
Genoa CFC	0-0	0-2	1-0	1-1	2-0	0-0	1-0	0-0		1-1	2-1	1-2	2-0	0-1	0-1	2-1
FC Internazionale	0-0	2-1	2-1	1-3	1-1	3-2	4-0	1-1	0-0		0-0	2-1	1-1	3-2	1-0	1-1
Juventus FC	1-1	4-0	2-0	1-0	4-1	6-1	3-1	0-0	1-0	1-0		3-2	0-0	0-1	4-2	1-0
Milan AC	0-0	2-1	2-1	1-0	0-1	1-0	1-1	0-0	0-0	0-1	0-1		1-1	1-2	0-0	0-1
SSC Napoli	0-0	0-0	2-0	1-0	1-1	2-2	2-0	0-1	2-2	2-0	0-0	0-1		1-0	2-0	0-0
AS Roma	2-1	0-0	3-1	2-1	2-2	0-1	2-0	2-0	1-0	3-2	0-3	1-1	1-1		3-0	1-1
Torino Calcio	2-1	1-1	1-0	4-2	1-2	0-0	0-0	2-2	2-0	0-1	0-1	2-1	0-0	2-2		1-0
Udinese Calcio	0-2	1-2	2-2	1-0	2-1	0-1	1-0	1-2	3-2	1-1	1-5	0-0	0-1	0-1	3-2	

	Serie "A"	Pd	Wn	Dw	Ls	GF	GA	Pts	
1.	JUVENTUS FC (TORINO)	30	19	8	3	48	14	46	
2.	AC Fiorentina (Firenze)	30	17	11	2	36	17	45	
3.	AS Roma (Roma)	30	15	8	7	40	29	38	
4.	SSC Napoli (Napoli)	30	10	15	5	31	21	35	
5.	FC Internazionale (Milano)	30	11	13	6	39	33	35	
6.	Ascoli Calcio (Ascoli (Piceno)	30	9	14	7	26	21	32	
7.	US Catanzaro (Catanzaro)	30	9	10	11	25	29	28	
8.	Torino Calcio (Torino)	30	8	11	11	25	30	27	
9.	US Avellino (Avellino)	30	9	9	12	21	26	27	
10.	AC Cesena (Cesena)	30	8	11	11	34	41	27	
11.	Udinese Calcio (Udine)	30	9	8	13	27	37	26	
12.	Cagliari Calcio (Cagliari)	30	7	11	12	33	36	25	
13.	Genoa CFC (Genova)	30	6	13	11	24	29	25	
14.	Milan AC (Milano)	30	7	10	13	21	31	24	R
15.	Bologna FC (Bologna)	30	6	11	13	25	37	23	R
16.	Como Calcio (Como)	30	3	11	16	18	42	17	R
		480	153	174	153	473	473	480	

Top goalscorers

1) Roberto PRUZZO (AS Roma) 15
2) Edy BIVI (US Catanzaro) 12
3) Claudio PELLEGRINI (SSC Napoli) 11

Note: US Anconitana (Ancona) changed their club name to Ancona Calcio (Ancona) for the next season.
UC Livorno (Livorno) changed their club name to US Livorno (Livorno) for the next season.

	Serie "B"	Pd	Wn	Dw	Ls	GF	GA	Pts	
1.	Hellas-Verona AC (Verona)	38	17	14	7	49	31	48	P
2.	SC Pisa (Pisa)	38	12	23	3	47	26	47	P
3.	UC Sampdoria (Genova)	38	17	13	8	41	25	47	P
4.	AS Bari (Bari)	38	15	15	8	47	33	45	
5.	Varese Calcio (Varese)	38	15	15	8	42	30	45	
6.	AC Perugia (Perugia)	38	16	10	12	37	26	42	
7.	SSC Palermo (Palermo)	38	15	12	11	52	42	42	
8.	Sambenedettese Calcio (San Benedetto del Tronto)	38	11	16	11	38	33	38	
9.	Catania Calcio (Catania)	38	11	16	11	38	41	38	
10.	SS Lazio (Roma)	38	11	15	12	38	35	37	
11.	US Cremonese (Cremona)	38	11	15	12	36	39	37	
12.	AC Reggiana (Reggio Emilia)	38	8	21	9	31	36	37	
13.	US Lecce (Lecce)	38	10	17	11	30	35	37	
14.	US Foggia (Foggia)	38	11	14	13	30	37	36	
15.	SS Cavese (Cava dei Tirreni)	38	11	14	13	28	35	36	
16.	US Pistoiese (Pistoia)	38	9	18	11	31	38	36	
17.	Rimini Calcio (Rimini)	38	11	14	13	39	45	36	R
18.	Brescia Calcio (Brescia)	38	8	15	15	27	40	31	R
19.	S.P.A.L. (Ferrara)	38	6	16	16	26	43	28	R
20.	Pescara Calcio (Pescara)	38	4	9	25	20	57	17	R
		760	229	302	229	727	727	760	

Promoted to Serie "B": US Arezzo (Arezzo), Atalanta BC (Bergamo), SS Campobasso, Monza Calcio.

Coppa Italia Final (1st leg) (Milano – 08/05/82)

FC INTERNAZIONALE (MILANO) 1-0 Torino Calcio (Torino)

Serena 40'

Internazionale: Bordon, G.Baresi, Oriali, G.Marini, Bergomi, Bini, Bagni (Centi 86'), Prohaska, Altobelli, Beccalossi, Serena.

Torino: Terraneo (Copparoni 72'), Cuttone, Danova, Van de Korput, Zaccarelli, Beruatto, Bertoneri, Ermini, Dossena, G.Ferri, Polici (Bonesso 76').

Coppa Italia Final (2nd leg) (Torino – 20/05/82)

FC INTERNAZIONALE (MILANO) 1-1 Torino Calcio (Torino)

Altobelli 23' *Cuttone 13'*

Torino: Copparoni, Cuttone, Danova, G.Ferri, Van de Korput, Beruatto, Bonesso, Bertoneri, Dossena, Ermini (Sclosa 84'), Mariani (Zennaro 73').

Internazionale: Bordon, Bergomi, G.Baresi, Marini, Canuti, Bini, Bagni, Prohaska, Altobelli, Beccalossi (Serena 79'), Oriali.

Semi-Finals

FC Internazionale (Milano) 2-1, 2-3 (aet) US Catanzaro (Catanzaro)
FC Internazionale (Milano) won on the away goals rule

UC Sampdoria (Genova) 2-1, 0-1 Torino Calcio (Torino)
Torino Calcio (Torino) won on the away goals rule

Quarter-Finals

US Catanzaro (Catanzaro) 0-1, 2-1 SSC Napoli (Napoli)
US Catanzaro (Catanzaro) won on the away goals rule

AC Reggiana (Reggio Emilia)	1-0, 0-1 (aet)	UC Sampdoria (Genova)
	UC Sampdoria (Genova) won on penalties	
AS Roma (Roma)	4-1, 0-3	FC Internazionale (Milano)
	FC Internazionale (Milano) won on the away goals rule	
Torino Calcio (Torino)	0-0, 1-1	AC Fiorentina (Firenze)
	Torino Calcio (Torino) won on the away goals rule	

1982-83

1982-1983 Serie "A"	Ascoli Calcio	US Avellino	Cagliari Calcio	US Catanzaro	AC Cesena	AC Fiorentina	Genoa CFC	Hellas-Verona	FC Internazion.	Juventus FC	SSC Napoli	SC Pisa	AS Roma	UC Sampdoria	Torino Calcio	Udinese Calcio
Ascoli Calcio		2-1	2-0	3-2	1-1	1-0	0-0	2-3	0-0	2-0	2-1	2-2	1-1	2-0	2-0	3-0
US Avellino	2-0		0-0	4-0	1-0	2-0	2-0	3-0	1-2	1-1	0-0	1-0	1-1	0-0	2-0	1-1
Cagliari Calcio	3-1	1-1		1-0	0-0	0-0	1-1	2-1	0-2	1-2	1-0	1-1	1-3	1-0	0-0	0-0
US Catanzaro	1-0	1-1	1-2		1-1	0-1	2-2	2-1	1-2	1-2	1-2	0-2	0-0	1-1	0-0	1-1
AC Cesena	1-1	2-0	0-0	0-0		3-3	0-1	1-2	2-2	2-2	0-0	0-0	1-1	0-2	2-0	1-0
AC Fiorentina	1-0	3-0	3-1	4-0	4-0		2-1	1-1	0-0	0-1	1-0	2-1	2-2	3-1	0-0	1-2
Genoa CFC	0-0	1-1	3-0	4-1	2-1	0-3		0-1	2-3	1-0	0-0	1-0	1-1	1-1	1-1	2-3
Hellas-Verona AC	2-1	3-0	2-2	3-1	1-1	0-1	2-2		1-2	2-1	0-0	2-1	1-1	1-1	1-0	0-0
FC Internazionale	2-0	2-0	2-0	5-0	3-1	0-0	2-1	1-1		0-0	2-2	0-1	0-0	1-2	1-3	1-1
Juventus FC	5-0	4-1	1-1	3-1	2-0	3-0	4-2	0-0	0-2		3-0	3-2	2-1	1-1	1-0	4-0
SSC Napoli	0-0	1-1	1-0	2-0	1-0	1-0	1-1	1-2	1-1	0-0		2-1	1-3	0-1	1-0	0-0
SC Pisa	2-1	2-0	0-0	0-0	1-0	0-0	0-0	0-1	1-1	0-0	2-0		1-2	3-2	0-1	0-0
AS Roma	2-1	2-0	1-0	2-0	1-0	3-1	2-0	1-0	2-1	1-2	5-2	3-1		1-0	3-1	0-0
UC Sampdoria	1-1	0-0	1-1	4-2	0-0	0-0	2-2	2-2	0-0	1-0	1-1	1-0	1-0		0-0	1-3
Torino Calcio	2-0	4-1	3-2	1-0	0-1	2-0	1-1	1-1	0-0	3-2	1-1	0-2	1-1	3-0		0-0
Udinese Calcio	2-1	1-1	1-1	2-1	3-1	0-0	1-1	0-0	0-0	0-0	0-0	1-1	1-1	0-4	2-2	

	Serie "A"	Pd	Wn	Dw	Ls	GF	GA	Pts	
1.	AS ROMA (ROMA)	30	16	11	3	47	24	43	
2.	Juventus FC (Torino)	30	15	9	6	49	26	39	
3.	FC Internazionale (Milano)	30	12	14	4	40	24	38	
4.	Hellas-Verona AC (Verona)	30	11	13	6	37	31	35	
5.	AC Fiorentina (Firenze)	30	12	10	8	36	25	34	
6.	Udinese Calcio (Udine)	30	6	20	4	25	28	32	
7.	UC Sampdoria (Genova)	30	8	15	7	31	30	31	
8.	Torino Calcio (Torino)	30	9	12	9	30	28	30	
9.	US Avellino (Avellino)	30	8	12	10	29	34	28	
10.	SSC Napoli (Napoli)	30	7	14	9	22	29	28	
11.	SC Pisa (Pisa)	30	8	11	11	27	27	27	
12.	Genoa CFC (Genova)	30	6	15	9	34	38	27	
13.	Ascoli Calcio (Ascoli Piceno)	30	9	9	12	32	37	27	
14.	Cagliari Calcio (Cagliari)	30	6	14	10	23	33	26	R
15.	AC Cesena (Cesena)	30	4	14	12	22	35	22	R
16.	US Catanzaro (Catanzaro)	30	2	9	19	21	56	13	R
		480	139	202	139	505	505	480	

Top goalscorers

1)	Michel PLATINI	(Juventus FC)	16
2)	Alessandro ALTOBELLI	(FC Internazionale)	15
	Domenico PENZO	(Hellas-Verona AC)	15
4)	Roberto PRUZZO	(AS Roma)	12

* Empoli FBC (Empoli) changed their club name to Empoli FC (Empoli) for the next season.
AC Mantova (Mantova) changed their club name to NAC Mantova (Mantova) for the next season.
Pro Patria et Libertate (Busto Arsizio) changed their club name to Pro Patria et Libertate Calcio (Busto Arsizio)
AC Venezia (Venezia) changed their club name to Venezia Calcio (Venezia) for the next season.

	Serie "B"	Pd	Wn	Dw	Ls	GF	GA	Pts	
1.	Milan AC (Milano)	38	19	16	3	77	36	54	P
2.	SS Lazio (Roma)	38	14	18	6	44	32	46	P
3.	Catania Calcio (Catania)	38	14	17	7	37	21	45	P
4.	US Cremonese (Cremona)	38	13	19	6	42	28	45	PO
5.	Como Calcio (Como)	38	13	19	6	36	24	45	PO
6.	SS Cavese (Cava dei Tirreni)	38	12	18	8	38	37	42	
7.	Monza Calcio (Monza)	38	13	12	13	40	42	38	
8.	Atalanta BC (Bergamo)	38	10	17	11	30	27	37	
9.	Sambenedettese Calcio (San Benedetto del Tronto)	38	10	17	11	33	32	37	
10.	Varese Calcio (Varese)	38	9	19	10	31	37	37	
11.	AC Perugia (Perugia)	38	11	14	13	36	37	36	
12.	US Arezzo (Arezzo)	38	10	16	12	30	38	36	
13.	SS Campobasso (Campobasso)	38	9	18	11	26	34	36	
14.	US Pistoiese (Pistoia)	38	7	20	11	33	34	34	
15.	SSC Palermo (Palermo)	38	11	12	15	36	46	34	
16.	US Lecce (Lecce)	38	10	14	14	33	44	34	
17.	AC Reggiana (Reggio Emilia)	38	6	20	12	39	49	32	R
18.	Bologna FC (Bologna)	38	9	14	15	31	47	32	R
19.	US Foggia (Foggia)	38	8	14	16	24	35	30	R
20.	AS Bari (Bari)	38	9	12	17	30	46	30	R
		760	217	326	217	726	726	760	

Promotion Play-Offs

Catania Calcio (Catania)	0-0	US Cremonese (Cremona)
Catania Calcio (Catania)	1-0	Como Calcio (Como)
US Cremonese (Cremona)	0-0	Como Calcio (como)

Promoted: Empoli FBC (Empoli), Padova Calcio (Padova), Pescara Calcio (Pescara), US Triestina Calcio (Trieste).

Coppa Italia Final (1st leg) (Verona – 19/06/83)

Hellas-Verona AC (Verona) 2-0 JUVENTUS FC (TORINO)

Penzo 44', Volpati 51'

Hellas: Garella, E.Oddi, L.Marangon, Volpati, Guidetti, Tricella, Fanna (Sella 76'), Sacchetti, Di Gennaro, Dirceu (Fedele 89'), Penzo (Manueli 87').

Juventus: Bodini, Gentile, Prandelli (Storgato 74'), Bonini, Brio, Scirea, Galderisi, Tardelli, Rossi, Platini, Boniek.

Coppa Italia Final (2nd leg) (Torino - 22/-6/83)

Hellas-Verona AC (Verona) 0-3 (aet) JUVENTUS FC (TORINO)

Rossi 08', Platini 81', 119'

Juventus: Bodini, Gentile, Cabrini, Bonini, Brio (Storgato 75'), Scirea, Marocchinini (Furino 60'), Tardelli, Rossi, Platini, Boniek.

Hellas: Garella, E.Oddi, L.Marangoni, Volpati, Guidetti, Tricella, Fanna, Sacchetti, Di Gennaro, Dirceu, Penzo.

Semi-Finals

Hellas-Verona AC (Verona) 0-1, 2-1 Torino Calcio (Torino)

(Hellas-Verona AC (Verona) won on the away goals rule)

Juventus FC (Torino) 2-1, 0-0 FC Internazionale (Milano)

Quarter-Finals

Hellas-Verona AC (Verona) 2-2, 3-3 Milan AC (Milano)

(Hellas-Verona AC (Verona) won on the away goals rule)

FC Internazionale (Milano) 3-2, 0-0 SC Pisa (Pisa)

Juventus FC (Torino) 3-0, 2-0 AS Roma (Roma)

Torino Calcio (Torino) 2-0, 0-0 SSC Napoli (Napoli)

1983-84

1983-1984 Serie "A"	Ascoli Calcio	AC Avellino	Catania Calcio	AC Fiorentina	Genoa CFC	Hellas Verona AC	FC Internazionale	Juventus FC	SS Lazio	Milan AC	SSC Napoli	SC Pisa	AS Roma	UC Sampdoria	Torino Calcio	Udinese Calcio
Ascoli Calcio		4-1	2-1	1-2	0-0	2-1	1-0	0-0	2-0	2-4	2-2	3-2	0-0	0-1	0-0	1-0
US Avellino	2-1		0-0	0-0	3-1	1-0	1-1	1-2	3-0	4-0	1-0	1-1	2-2	0-2	0-0	2-1
Catania Calcio	1-1	1-1		0-2	1-2	0-1	0-0	0-2	1-1	1-1	0-0	2-0	2-2	1-1	0-0	0-2
AC Fiorentina	2-1	1-0	5-0		0-0	2-0	1-1	3-3	3-2	2-2	5-1	0-0	0-0	3-0	4-1	0-0
Genoa CFC	1-0	0-2	3-0	2-2		1-1	1-1	2-1	0-0	2-0	0-0	0-0	0-2	0-0	2-1	0-5
Hellas-Verona AC	3-1	3-0	3-1	3-1	0-0		1-2	2-1	4-2	1-1	1-1	2-0	1-0	1-0	2-2	2-1
FC Internazionale	0-0	3-0	6-0	2-1	1-1	1-0		1-2	1-1	2-0	1-0	3-0	1-0	1-2	0-0	2-0
Juventus FC	7-0	1-1	2-0	1-0	4-2	3-1	2-0		2-1	2-1	2-0	3-1	2-2	1-2	2-1	3-2
SS Lazio	2-1	2-1	3-0	1-2	2-1	1-1	3-0	0-1		0-0	3-2	0-1	0-2	2-1	1-0	2-2
Milan AC	0-0	1-0	2-1	2-2	1-0	4-2	0-0	0-3	4-1		0-2	2-1	1-1	2-1	0-1	3-3
SSC Napoli	1-0	2-0	3-0	0-0	0-0	1-0	0-2	1-1	3-0	0-0		0-0	1-2	1-1	0-0	2-1
SC Pisa	0-1	1-0	2-0	1-1	1-1	0-3	0-0	0-0	2-2	0-0	1-1		1-1	0-0	1-1	1-1
AS Roma	1-1	3-2	1-0	2-1	1-0	3-2	1-0	0-0	2-2	3-1	5-1	2-0		1-1	2-1	4-1
UC Sampdoria	1-2	0-1	2-0	1-2	2-0	1-0	0-2	1-1	1-1	1-1	4-1	1-0	1-2		2-1	2-1
Torino Calcio	0-0	4-2	2-0	1-0	2-1	1-1	3-1	2-1	4-0	1-2	2-1	2-2	2-1	2-1		0-1
Udinese Calcio	0-0	2-1	3-1	3-1	3-1	1-1	2-2	2-2	2-0	1-2	4-1	2-1	1-0	0-3	0-0	

	Serie "A"	Pd	Wn	Dw	Ls	GF	GA	Pts	
1.	JUVENTUS FC (TORINO)	30	17	9	4	57	29	43	
2.	AS Roma (Roma)	30	15	11	4	48	28	41	
3.	AC Fiorentina (Firenze)	30	12	12	6	48	31	36	
4.	FC Internazionale (Milano)	30	12	11	7	37	23	35	
5.	Torino Calcio (Torino)	30	11	11	8	37	30	33	
6.	Hellas-Verona AC (Verona)	30	12	8	10	43	35	32	
7.	UC Sampdoria (Genova)	30	12	8	10	36	30	32	
8.	Milan AC (Milano)	30	10	12	8	37	40	32	
9.	Udinese Calcio (Udine)	30	11	9	10	47	40	31	
10.	Ascoli Calcio (Ascoli Piceno)	30	9	11	10	29	35	29	
11.	US Avellino (Avellino)	30	9	8	13	33	39	26	
12.	SSC Napoli (Napoli)	30	7	12	11	28	38	26	
13.	SS Lazio (Roma)	30	8	9	13	35	49	25	
14.	Genoa CFC (Genova)	30	6	13	11	24	36	25	R
15.	SC Pisa (Pisa)	30	3	16	11	20	35	22	R
16.	Catania Calcio (Catania)	30	1	10	19	14	55	12	R
		480	155	170	155	573	573	480	

Top goalscorers

1)	Michel PLATINI	(Juventus FC)	20
2)	Artur ZICCO	(Udinese Calcio)	19
3)	Maurizio IORIO	(Hellas-Verona AC)	14
4)	Paolo ROSSI	(Juventus FC)	13

US Foggia (Foggia) changed their club name to Foggia Calcio (Foggia) for the next season.
US Lucchese Libertas (Lucca) changed their club name to AS Lucchese Libertas (Lucca) for the next season.
AS Pro Vercelli (Vercelli) changed their club name to US Pro Vercelli Calcio (Vercelli) for the next season.

	Serie "B"	Pd	Wn	Dw	Ls	GF	GA	Pts	
1.	Atalanta BC (Bergamo)	38	16	17	5	49	28	49	P
2.	Como Calcio (Como)	38	17	14	7	41	26	48	P
3.	US Cremonese (Cremona)	38	15	15	8	44	29	45	P
4.	US Lecce (Lecce)	38	13	16	9	33	28	42	
5.	Padova Calcio (Padova)	38	11	18	9	34	28	40	
6.	US Arezzo (Arezzo)	38	12	16	10	34	33	40	
7.	SS Campobasso (Campobasso)	38	13	14	11	31	31	40	
8.	AC Perugia (Perugia)	38	9	20	9	33	30	38	
9.	US Triestina Calcio (Trieste)	38	11	16	11	37	40	38	
10.	Varese Calcio (Varese)	38	11	15	12	30	38	37	
11.	Cagliari Calcio (Cagliari)	38	10	16	12	31	32	36	
12.	Pescara Calcio (Pescara)	38	13	10	15	41	48	36	
13.	AC Cesena (Cesena)	38	10	15	13	31	33	35	
14.	Sambenedettese Calcio (San Benedetto del Tronto)	38	9	17	12	30	35	35	
15.	Monza Calcio (Monza)	38	11	13	14	29	34	35	
16.	Empoli FC (Empoli)	38	8	19	11	27	34	35	
17.	SSC Palermo (Palermo)	38	9	16	13	30	32	34	R
18.	US Pistoiese (Pistoia)	38	12	10	16	27	34	34	R
19.	SS Cavese (Cava dei Tirreni)	38	8	17	13	25	33	33	R
20.	US Catanzaro (Catanzaro)	38	10	10	18	34	45	30	R
		760	228	304	228	671	671	760	

Promoted to Serie "B": AS Bari (Bari), Bologna FC (Bologna), Parma AC (Parma) and AS Taranto (Taranto).

Coppa Italia Final (1st leg) (Verona – 21/06/84)

Hellas-Verona AC (Verona)	1-1	AS ROMA (ROMA)
Storgato 72'		*Cerezo 49'*

Hellas: Garella, M.Ferroni, L.Marangon, Volpati, Fontolan, Tricella, Bruni (Jordan 88'), Storgato, Jorio, Di Gennaro, Galderisi.

Roma: Tancredi, Nappi, E.Oddi, Nela, Falcao, A.Maldera, B.Conti, Cerezo, Pruzzo (Chierico 88'), Di Bartolomei, Graziani.

Coppa Italia Final (2nd leg) (Roma – 26/06/84)

Hellas-Verona AC (Verona)	0-1	AS ROMA (ROMA)
		Ferroni 27' o.g.

Roma: Tancredi, Nappi, Nela, Di Bartolomei, Falcao, A.Maldera, B.Conti (Strukelj 18', Giannini 62'), Cerezo, Pruzzo (F.Vincenzi 80'), Chierico, Graziani.

Hellas: Garella, M.Ferroni, L.Marangon (Bruni 54'), Volpati, Fontolan, Tricella, Fanna, Storgato (Guidetti 83'), Lorio, Di Gennaro, Galderisi (Jordan 70').

Semi-Finals

AS Bari (Bari)	1-2, 1-3	Hellas-Verona AC (Verona)
Torino Calcio (Torino)	1-3, 0-1	AS Roma (Roma)

Quarter-Finals

AS Bari (Bari)	2-1, 2-1	AC Fiorentina (Firenze)
AS Roma (Roma)	1-1, 2-1 (aet)	Milan AC (Milano)(aet)
UC Sampdoria (Genova)	1-1, 0-0	Torino Calcio (Torino)
	Torino Calcio (Torino) won on the away goals rule	
Udinese Calcio (Udine)	2-1, 0-1	Hellas-Verona AC (Verona)
	Hellas-Verona AC (Verona) won on the away goals rule	

1984-85

1984-1985 Serie "A"	Ascoli Calcio	Atalanta BC	AC Avellino	Como Calcio	US Cremonese	AC Fiorentina	Hellas Verona	FC Internazion.	Juventus FC	SS Lazio	Milan AC	SSC Napoli	AS Roma	UC Sampdoria	Torino Calcio	Udinese Calcio
Ascoli Calcio		0-0	2-2	1-0	3-2	2-1	1-3	1-1	1-1	0-0	0-1	1-1	0-0	2-0	2-2	2-0
Atalanta BC	0-0		3-3	1-0	1-0	2-2	1-1	1-1	1-1	1-0	1-0	1-0	0-0	0-0	0-0	0-1
US Avellino	2-0	1-1		1-1	2-0	0-0	2-1	0-0	0-0	1-0	0-0	0-1	0-0	2-1	1-3	4-1
Como Calcio	1-0	0-0	2-1		1-0	0-0	0-0	0-0	0-0	1-0	0-0	1-1	0-0	0-0	0-0	2-1
US Cremonese	2-0	0-0	0-0	2-0		1-1	0-2	1-2	1-3	1-1	0-1	1-1	0-5	1-1	2-1	2-0
AC Fiorentina	1-1	5-0	1-0	2-1	1-1		1-3	1-1	0-0	3-0	0-0	0-1	1-0	0-3	0-0	3-1
Hellas-Verona AC	2-0	1-1	4-2	0-0	3-0	2-1		1-1	2-0	1-0	0-0	3-1	1-0	0-0	1-2	1-0
FC Internazionale	5-1	1-0	2-1	1-0	2-0	1-0	0-0		4-0	1-0	2-2	2-1	0-0	2-0	1-1	1-0
Juventus FC	2-2	5-1	2-1	2-0	5-1	1-2	1-1	3-1		1-0	1-1	2-0	1-1	1-1	1-2	3-2
SS Lazio	0-0	1-1	0-1	3-2	2-1	0-1	0-1	1-1	3-3		0-1	1-1	1-1	0-3	0-0	1-4
Milan AC	2-1	2-2	2-0	0-2	2-1	1-1	0-0	2-1	3-2	2-0		2-1	2-1	0-1	0-1	2-2
SSC Napoli	1-1	1-0	0-0	3-0	1-0	1-0	0-0	3-1	0-0	4-0	0-0		1-2	1-1	2-1	4-3
AS Roma	3-1	1-1	1-0	1-1	3-2	2-1	0-0	4-3	1-1	0-0	0-1	1-1		1-1	1-0	2-1
UC Sampdoria	2-0	3-0	1-0	1-0	1-0	2-0	1-1	1-2	1-1	2-2	2-1	0-0	3-0		2-2	1-0
Torino Calcio	1-0	0-0	2-0	3-1	1-0	2-2	1-2	1-1	0-2	1-0	2-0	3-0	1-0	1-1		1-0
Udinese Calcio	1-1	2-0	2-0	4-1	2-0	2-2	3-5	2-1	0-3	5-0	1-1	2-2	0-2	1-0	0-1	

	Serie "A"	Pd	Wn	Dw	Ls	GF	GA	Pts	
1.	HELLAS-VERONA AC (VERONA)	30	15	13	2	42	19	43	
2.	Torino Calcio (Torino)	30	14	11	5	36	22	39	
3.	FC Internazionale (Milano)	30	13	12	5	42	28	38	
4.	UC Sampdoria (Genova)	30	12	13	5	36	21	37	
5.	Juventus FC (Torino)	30	11	14	5	48	33	36	
6.	Milan AC (Milano)	30	12	12	6	31	25	36	
7.	AS Roma (Roma)	30	10	14	6	33	25	34	
8.	SSC Napoli (Napoli)	30	10	13	7	34	29	33	
9.	AC Fiorentina (Firenze)	30	8	13	9	33	31	29	
10.	Atalanta BC (Bergamo)	30	5	18	7	20	32	28	
11.	Udinese Calcio (Udine)	30	10	5	15	43	46	25	
12.	US Avellino (Avellino)	30	7	11	12	27	33	25	
13.	Como Calcio (Como)	30	6	13	11	17	27	25	
14.	Ascoli Calcio (Ascoli Piceno)	30	4	14	12	24	40	22	R
15.	US Cremonese (Cremona)	30	4	7	19	22	48	15	R
16.	SS Lazio (Roma)	30	2	11	17	16	45	15	R
		480	143	194	143	504	504	480	

Top goalscorers

1)	Michel PLATINI	(Juventus FC)	18
2)	Alessandro ALTOBELLI	(FC Internazionale)	17
3)	Diego MARADONA	(SSC Napoli)	14
4)	Massimo BRIASCHI	(Juventus FC)	12

	Serie "B"	Pd	Wn	Dw	Ls	GF	GA	Pts	
1.	SC Pisa (Pisa)	38	17	16	5	52	27	50	P
2.	US Lecce (Lecce)	38	16	18	4	40	26	50	P
3.	AS Bari (Bari)	38	18	13	7	42	25	49	P
4.	AC Perugia (Perugia)	38	11	26	11	38	25	48	
5.	US Triestina Calcio (Trieste)	38	16	15	7	39	27	47	
6.	Genoa CFC (Genova)	38	13	14	11	38	32	40	
7.	Pescara Calcio (Pescara)	38	12	14	12	38	35	38	
8.	Empoli FC (Empoli)	38	8	21	9	22	28	37	
9.	Bologna FC (Bologna)	38	9	18	11	25	31	36	
10.	Monza Calcio (Monza)	38	10	16	12	26	28	36	
11.	Sambenedettese Calcio (San Benedetto del Tronto)	38	9	18	11	27	29	36	
12.	AC Cesena (Cesena)	38	9	18	11	35	34	36	
13.	SS Campobasso (Campobasso)	38	12	12	14	29	32	36	
14.	Padova Calcio (Padova)	38	8	19	11	31	34	35	R #
15.	Catania Calcio (Catania)	38	7	21	10	33	38	35	
16.	US Arezzo (Arezzo)	38	10	15	13	25	33	35	
17.	Cagliari Calcio (Cagliari)	38	12	10	16	29	32	34	#
18.	Varese Calcio (Varese)	38	9	15	14	37	42	33	R
19.	Parma AC (Parma)	38	6	14	18	25	47	26	R
20.	AS Taranto (Taranto)	38	6	11	21	25	51	23	R
		760	218	324	218	656	656	760	

Padova Calcio (Padova) were relegated by the F.I.G.C. and as a result of this action Cagliari Calcio (Cagliari) retained their place in Serie "B" for the next season.

Promoted to Serie "B": Brescia Calcio (Brescia), US Catanzaro (Catanzaro), SS Lanerossi (Vicenza), SSC Palermo.

Coppa Italia Final (1st leg) (Milano - 30/06/85)

Milan AC (Milano) 0-1 UC Sampdoria (GENOVA)

Souness 24'

Milan: Terraneo, F.Baresi, Tassotti, Icardi, Battistini, Evani, Verza, Wilkins, Hateley, Scarnecchia (L.Russo 46'), Virdis.

Sampdoria: Bordon, Paganin, Galia, Pari, Vierchowod, L.Pellegrini, Scanziani, Souness, Francis (Mancini 63'), Salsano (Renica 87'), Vialli.

Coppa Italia Final (2nd leg) (Genova - 03/07/85)

Milan AC (Milano) 1-2 UC Sampdoria (GENOVA)

Virdis 66' — *Mancini 41' pen., Vialli 61'*

Sampdoria: Bordon, Paganin, Renica, Pari, Vierchowod, L.Pellegrini, Scanziani, Souness, Mancini, Salsano (Casagrande 88'), Vialli.

Milan: Terraneo, F.Baresi (Evani 77'), L.Russo (Scarnexxhia 46'), Icardi, Di Bartolomei, Tassotti, Incocciati, Wilkins, Hateley, Battistini, Virdis.

Semi-Finals

AC Fiorentina (Firenze)	0-0, 1-3	UC Sampdoria (Genova)
FC Internazionale (Milano)	1-2, 1-1	Milan AC (Milano)

Quarter-Finals

Hellas-Verona AC (Verona)	3-0, 1-5 (aet)	FC Internazionale (Milano)
Milan AC (Milano)	0-0, 1-0	Juventus FC (Torino)
Parma AC (Parma)	1-0, 0-3	AC Fiorentina (Firenze)
Torino Calcio (Torino)	0-0, 2-4	UC Sampdoria (Genova)

1985-86

1985-1986 Serie "A"	Atalanta BC	AC Avellino	AS Bari	Como Calcio	AC Fiorentina	Hellas Verona AC	FC Internazionale	Juventus FC	US Lecce	Milan AC	SSC Napoli	SC Pisa	AS Roma	UC Sampdoria	Torino Calcio	Udinese Calcio
Atalanta BC		2-0	0-0	1-1	0-0	0-0	2-1	0-0	3-1	1-1	0-0	1-2	1-2	2-1	2-2	1-1
US Avellino	1-0		0-0	1-4	3-1	3-1	1-0	0-0	2-0	1-1	0-1	1-1	1-0	2-1	0-0	2-2
AS Bari	0-0	0-1		1-1	0-1	3-1	1-3	0-3	2-0	0-1	1-2	0-0	2-0	0-0	1-0	1-0
Como Calcio	0-2	1-1	1-1		0-0	1-0	1-0	0-1	2-0	1-1	1-1	1-1	1-0	2-2	1-1	0-0
AC Fiorentina	0-0	1-0	0-0	1-0		0-0	3-0	2-0	3-1	2-0	0-0	1-1	1-1	1-0	0-0	1-0
Hellas-Verona AC	0-3	2-0	2-0	3-0	2-2		0-0	0-1	2-2	1-0	2-2	3-0	3-2	2-1	1-0	1-1
FC Internazionale	1-3	3-1	1-0	3-2	2-0	0-0		1-1	3-0	1-0	1-1	3-1	2-1	1-0	3-3	2-1
Juventus FC	2-0	1-0	4-0	0-0	1-0	3-0	2-0		4-0	1-0	1-1	3-1	3-1	1-0	1-1	2-1
US Lecce	2-1	2-2	1-1	1-4	2-1	1-0	0-1	2-3		0-2	0-0	1-1	0-3	0-1	0-0	2-0
Milan AC	1-1	3-0	0-0	1-0	1-0	1-1	2-2	0-0	1-0		1-2	1-0	0-1	2-2	1-0	2-0
SSC Napoli	1-0	1-0	1-0	2-1	0-0	5-0	1-0	1-0	1-0	2-0		0-1	1-1	3-0	3-1	1-1
SC Pisa	1-1	1-1	1-1	4-1	1-2	0-1	1-0	1-1	3-0	0-1	1-1		2-4	0-2	0-0	0-0
AS Roma	4-0	5-1	2-1	0-0	2-1	2-1	3-1	3-0	2-3	2-1	2-0	1-0		1-0	2-0	1-0
UC Sampdoria	0-0	0-2	2-0	0-0	2-2	0-0	0-0	0-0	2-0	1-1	2-0	3-0	1-0		0-0	3-0
Torino Calcio	0-0	1-0	1-0	1-3	2-1	2-1	1-0	1-2	3-1	2-0	2-1	4-1	0-1	1-0		2-0
Udinese Calcio	1-0	3-1	2-2	2-2	2-2	5-1	1-1	1-2	2-1	0-0	2-0	1-1	0-2	2-1	0-0	

	Serie "A"	Pd	Wn	Dw	Ls	GF	GA	Pts	
1.	JUVENTUS FC (TORINO)	30	18	9	3	43	17	45	
2.	AS Roma (Roma)	30	19	3	8	51	27	41	
3.	SSC Napoli (Napoli)	30	14	11	5	35	21	39	
4.	AC Fiorentina (Firenze)	30	10	13	7	29	23	33	
5.	Torino Calcio (Torino)	30	11	11	8	31	26	33	
6.	FC Internazionale (Milano)	30	12	8	10	36	33	32	
7.	Milan AC (Milano)	30	10	11	9	26	24	31	
8.	Atalanta BC (Bergamo)	30	7	15	8	27	26	29	
9.	Como Calcio (Como)	30	7	15	8	32	32	29	
10.	Hellas-Verona AC (Verona)	30	9	10	11	31	40	28	
11.	UC Sampdoria (Genova)	30	8	11	11	27	25	27	
12.	US Avellino (Avellino)	30	9	9	12	28	38	27	
13.	Udinese Calcio (Udinese)	30	6	13	11	31	37	25	#
14.	SC Pisa (Pisa)	30	5	13	12	27	40	23	R
15.	AS Bari (Bari)	30	5	12	13	18	31	22	R
16.	US Lecce (Lecce)	30	5	6	19	23	55	16	R
		480	155	170	155	495	495	480	

Top goalscorers

1)	Roberto PRUZZO	(AS Roma)	19
2)	Karl-Heinz RUMMENIGGE	(FC Internazionale)	13
3)	Michel PLATINI	(Juventus FC)	12
4)	Diego MARADONA	(SSC Napoli)	11
	Daniel PASSARELLA	(AC Fiorentina)	11
	Aldo SERENA	(Juventus FC)	11

Udinese Calcio (Udine) were relegated to Serie "B" by the F.I.G.C. after an inquiry into bribery allegations, but on appeal they were allowed to remain in Serie "A" with a -9 point penalty for the next season.

As a result of the above bribery inquiry Cagliari Calcio (Cagliari), SS Lazio (Roma), SSC Palermo (Palermo) and AC Perugia (Perugia) were all relegated to Serie "C", however after appeal SS Lazio were allowed to remain in Serie "B" with a -9 point penalty and Cagliari Calcio (Cagliari) with – 5 point penalty for the next season. Promoted club SS Lanerossi (Vicenza) were ordered to remain in Serie "B" for the next season with Empoli FC (Empoli) being promoted in their place. Pescara Calcio (Pescara) retained Serie "B" status as a result of SSC Palermo (Palermo) being relegated.

	Serie "B"	Pd	Wn	Dw	Ls	GF	GA	Pts	
1.	Ascoli Calcio (Ascoli Piceno)	38	17	16	5	56	33	50	P
2.	Brescia Calcio (Brescia)	38	17	13	8	41	28	47	P
3.	SS Lanerossi (Vicenza)	38	16	14	8	48	33	46	#
4.	Empoli FC (Empoli)	38	13	19	6	32	28	45	P #
5.	US Triestina Calcio (Trieste)	38	15	15	8	40	30	44	-1
6.	Bologna FC (Bologna)	38	15	11	12	37	29	41	
7.	Genoa CFC (Genova)	38	14	12	12	35	31	40	
8.	AC Cesena (Cesena)	38	12	15	11	42	38	39	
9.	US Cremonese (Cremona)	38	10	17	11	35	31	37	
10.	SS Campobasso (Campobasso)	38	9	19	10	30	36	37	
11.	US Arezzo (Arezzo)	38	9	18	11	37	40	36	
12.	SS Lazio (Roma)	38	11	14	13	38	42	36	#
13.	Catania Calcio (Catania)	38	12	12	14	30	37	36	
14.	Sambenedettese Calcio (San Benedetto del Tronto)	38	10	15	13	26	26	35	
15.	Cagliari Calcio (Cagliari)	38	13	9	16	27	38	35	#
16.	SSC Palermo (Palermo)	38	7	20	11	27	35	34	R #
17.	Pescara Calcio (Pescara)	38	10	13	15	33	37	33	#
18.	AC Perugia (Perugia)	38	8	16	14	29	39	32	R
19.	US Catanzaro (Catanzaro)	38	9	12	17	33	45	30	R
20.	Monza Calcio (Monza)	38	6	14	18	25	45	26	R
		760	233	294	233	701	701	759	

** US Triestina Calcio (Trieste) had 1 point deducted by the F.I.G.C. committee.

Promoted to Serie "B": ACR Messina (Messina), Modena FC (Modena), Parma AC (Parma) and AS Taranto.

Coppa Italia Final (1st leg) (Genova – 07/06/86)

UC Sampdoria (Genova) 2-1 AS ROMA (ROMA)

Mancini 19', Galia 67' *Tovalieri 45'*

Sampdoria: Bordon, Mannini, Galia, Pari, Paganin, L.Pellegrini, Lorenzo (Fiondella 74'), Salsano, Francis, Matteoli, Mancini.

Roma: Gregori, Oddi, Gerolin, Desideri, Lucci, Righetti, Graziani, Giannini, Tovalieri, Di Carlo, Impallomeni.

Coppa Italia Final (2nd leg) (Roma – 14/06/86)

UC Sampdoria (Genova) 0-2 AS ROMA (ROMA)

Desideri 43', Cerezo 89' pen.

Roma: Gregori, Oddi, Gerolin, Desideri, Lucci, Righetti, Graziani, Giannini, Pruzzo (Impallomeni 83'), Di Carlo, Tovalieri (Cerezo 85').

Sampdoria: Bordon, Mannini, Galia, Pari, Paganin, L.Pellegrini, Fiondella (Lorenzo 56'), Salsano, Francis, Matteoli, Mancini.

Semi-Finals

AS Roma (Roma)	2-0, 1-1	AC Fiorentina (Firenze)
UC Sampdoria (Genova)	1-1, 1-2	Como Calcio (Como)

(the result of the 2nd leg was later changed to 2-0 by the F.I.G.C.)

Quarter-Finals

Empoli FC (Empoli)	3-2, 0-3	AC Fiorentina (Firenze)
Hellas-Verona AC (Verona)	2-1, 1-3	Como Calcio (Como)
AS Roma (Roma)	2-0, 1-2	FC Internazionale (Milano)
UC Sampdoria (Genova)	2-0, 4-3	Torino Calcio (Torino)

1986-87

1986-1987 Serie "A"	Ascoli Calcio	Atalanta BC	AC Avellino	Brescia Calcio	Como Calcio	Empoli FC	AC Fiorentina	Hellas Verona AC	FC Internazionale	Juventus FC	Milan AC	SSC Napoli	AS Roma	UC Sampdoria	Torino Calcio	Udinese Calcio
Ascoli Calcio		2-1	0-1	0-0	0-0	0-1	0-1	0-1	1-0	0-5	1-0	1-1	1-1	0-1	1-1	1-0
Atalanta BC	0-0		1-1	1-0	0-0	1-0	2-0	1-0	1-0	0-0	1-2	0-1	0-1	1-0	0-2	4-2
US Avellino	0-0	2-1		0-0	1-1	0-1	2-1	1-1	0-1	1-1	2-1	0-0	2-1	3-1	0-0	1-1
Brescia Calcio	1-2	1-0	2-0		2-0	3-0	0-0	1-1	0-1	0-0	1-0	0-1	1-1	0-1	2-0	1-0
Como Calcio	0-0	2-1	1-2	1-0		0-1	0-0	1-1	1-1	0-0	0-1	1-1	0-0	0-0	1-1	3-1
Empoli FC	1-0	0-0	0-1	0-0	0-0		1-0	1-0	1-0	0-1	0-3	0-0	1-3	0-0	2-0	0-0
AC Fiorentina	2-1	1-0	2-0	4-3	1-2	1-1		0-1	0-1	1-1	2-2	3-1	2-1	2-0	0-0	0-1
Hellas-Verona AC	2-1	2-1	2-2	4-1	1-0	1-0	2-2		2-1	1-1	1-0	3-0	0-1	1-1	2-1	3-1
FC Internazionale	3-0	1-0	0-0	4-0	1-0	2-1	1-0	0-0		2-1	1-2	1-0	4-1	1-0	2-1	2-0
Juventus FC	2-2	2-0	3-0	3-2	1-0	3-0	1-0	2-1	1-1		0-0	1-3	2-0	2-1	1-0	2-1
Milan AC	0-1	2-1	2-0	2-0	0-0	1-0	3-0	1-0	0-0	1-1		0-0	4-1	0-2	1-0	0-0
SSC Napoli	3-0	2-2	3-0	2-1	2-1	4-0	1-1	0-0	0-0	2-1	2-1		0-0	1-1	3-1	1-1
AS Roma	1-1	4-2	3-0	2-1	0-0	2-1	1-1	0-0	1-0	3-0	1-2	0-1		0-3	1-0	4-0
UC Sampdoria	1-0	1-0	2-2	2-0	0-1	3-0	3-1	0-0	3-1	4-1	3-0	1-2	0-0		3-0	0-0
Torino Calcio	0-2	0-0	4-1	2-2	1-0	1-0	2-1	2-1	0-0	1-1	0-0	0-1	0-2	2-0		3-1
Udinese Calcio	3-0	1-0	2-6	1-0	0-0	3-0	1-1	2-2	0-0	0-2	0-0	0-3	2-1	0-0	1-1	

	Serie "A"	Pd	Wn	Dw	Ls	GF	GA	Pts	
1.	SSC NAPOLI (NAPOLI)	30	15	12	3	41	21	42	
2.	Juventus FC (Torino)	30	14	11	5	42	27	39	
3.	FC Internazionale (Milano)	30	15	8	7	32	17	38	
4.	Hellas-Verona AC (Verona)	30	12	12	6	36	25	36	*
5.	Milan AC (Milano)	30	13	9	8	31	21	35	PO
6.	UC Sampdoria (Genova)	30	13	9	8	37	21	35	PO
7.	AS Roma (Roma)	30	12	9	9	37	31	33	
8.	US Avellino (Avellino)	30	9	12	9	31	38	30	
9.	Como Calcio (Como)	30	5	16	9	16	20	26	
10.	AC Fiorentina (Firenze)	30	8	10	12	30	35	26	
11.	Torino Calcio (Torino)	30	8	10	12	26	32	26	
12.	Ascoli Calcio (Ascoli (Piceno)	30	7	10	13	18	33	24	
13.	Empoli FC (Empoli)	30	8	7	15	13	33	23	
14.	Brescia Calcio (Brescia)	30	7	8	15	25	35	22	R
15.	Atalanta BC (Bergamo)	30	7	7	16	22	32	21	R
16.	Udinese Calcio (Udine)	30	6	12	12	25	41	15	R -9
		480	159	162	159	462	462	471	

Top goalscorers

1)	Pietro Paulo VIRDIS	(Milan AC)	17
2)	Gianluca VIALLI	(UC Sampdoria)	12
3)	Alessandro ALTOBELLI	(FC Internazionale)	11
4)	Ramon DIAZ	(AC Fiorentina)	10
	Diego MARADONA	(SSC Napoli)	10
	Aldo SERENA	(Juventus FC)	10

Udinese Calcio (Udine) started the season with –9 points as a result of the 1985-86 bribery inquiry.

5th/6th Position Play-Off

Milan AC (Milano)	1-0	UC Sampdoria (Genova)

(played in Torino to determine place in UEFA Cup for the next season)

* Hellas-Verona AC (Verona) changed their club name to Hellas-Verona (Verona) for the next season.
SSC Palermo (Palermo) dissolved and re-formed as US Città di Palermo (Palermo) for the next season.
US Pistoiese (Pistoia) changed their club name to Pistoiese Calcio (Pistoia) for the next season.
Venezia Calcio (Venezia) merged with AC Mestre 1929 (Venezia) as Venezia-Mestre Calcio (Venezia)

	Serie "B"	Pd	Wn	Dw	Ls	GF	GA	Pts	
1.	Pescara Calcio (Pescara)	38	16	12	10	43	33	44	P
2.	SC Pisa (Pisa)	38	16	12	10	42	32	44	P
3.	AC Cesena (Cesena)	38	15	13	10	38	29	43	P
4.	US Lecce (Lecce)	38	15	13	10	38	32	43	PO
5.	US Cremonese (Cremona)	38	14	15	9	35	29	43	PO
6.	Genoa CFC (Genova)	38	12	18	8	44	39	42	
7.	Parma AC (Parma)	38	11	18	9	30	26	40	
8.	ACR Messina (Messina)	38	12	16	10	29	28	40	
9.	AS Bari (Bari)	38	11	17	10	33	32	39	
10.	Bologna FC (Bologna)	38	10	16	12	40	38	36	
11.	US Triestina Calcio (Trieste)	38	10	19	9	31	26	35	-4
12.	US Arezzo (Arezzo)	38	7	21	10	30	33	35	
13.	Modena FC (Modena)	38	10	15	13	32	50	35	
14.	Sambenedettese Calcio (San Benedetto del Tronto)	38	11	12	15	33	37	34	
15.	SS Lazio (Roma)	38	14	14	10	35	28	33	PO -9
16.	AS Taranto (Taranto)	38	10	13	15	37	40	33	PO
17.	SS Campobasso (Campobasso)	38	9	15	14	34	35	33	R
18.	SS Lanerossi (Vicenza)	38	9	14	15	31	40	32	R
19.	Catania Calcio (Catania)	38	8	16	14	25	38	32	R
20.	Cagliari Calcio (Cagliari)	38	9	13	16	32	47	26	R -5
		760	229	302	229	692	692	742	

Cagliari Calcio (Cagliari) started the season with -5 points as a result of the 1985-86 bribery inquiry.
SS Lazio (Roma) started the season with -9 points as a result of the 1985-86 bribery inquiry.
US Triestina Calcio (Trieste) had 4 points deducted by the F.I.G.C. committee.

2nd Promotion Play-Off

AC Cesena (Cesena)	2-1	US Lecce (Lecce)

Promotion Play-Offs

US Lecce (Lecce)	0-0	AS Cesena (Cesena)
US Lecce (Lecce)	4-1	US Cremonese (Cremona)
AC Cesena (Cesena)	1-0	US Cremonese (Cremona)

Relegation Play-Offs

AS Taranto (Taranto)	1-0	SS Lazio (Roma)
AS Taranto (Taranto)	1-1	SS Campobasso (Campobasso)
SS Lazio (Roma)	1-0	SS Campobasso (Campobasso)

Promoted to Serie "B": SS Barletta (Barletta), US Catanzaro (Catanzaro), Padova Calcio (Padova), Piacenza Calcio (Piacenza).

Coppa Italia Final (1st leg) (Napoli - 07/06/87)

SSC NAPOLI (NAPOLI)	3-0	Atalanta BC (Bergamo)

Renica 67', Muro 71', Bagni 77'

Napoli: Garella, Ferrara, Volpecina (Bigliardi 88'), Bagni, Ferrario, Renica, Sola (Muro 59'), F.Romano, Giordano, Maradona, Carnevale (Caffarelli 81').

Atalanta: Piotto, G.Rosi (Cantarutti 81'), Ca.Gentile, Prandelli, Barcella, Progna, Stromberg, Bonacina, Incocciati (Pasciullo 84'), Magrin, Compagna (Limido 52').

Coppa Italia Final (2nd leg) (Bergamo - 13/06/87)

SSC NAPOLI (NAPOLI)	1-0	Atalanta BC (Bergamo)

Giordano 85'

Napoli: Garella, Ferrara, Volpecina (Bruscolotti 46'), Bagni, Bigliardi, Ferrario, Carnevale (Muro 60'), De Napoli (Cafferelli 75'), Giordano, Maradona, F. Romano.

Atalanta: Piotto, G.Rosi (Perico 75'), C.Gentile, Icardi, Barcellone, Progna, Stromberg, Bonacina, Compagno, Magrin, Limido (Cantarutti 54').

Semi-Finals

Atalanta BC (Bergamo)	2-0, 0-0	US Cremonese (Cremona)
Cagliari Calcio (Cagliari)	0-1, 1-4	SSC Napoli (Napoli)

Quarter-Finals

Atalanta BC (Bergamo)	1-0, 0-0	Parma AC (Parma)
Cagliari Calcio (Cagliari)	1-1, 2-2	Juventus FC (Torino)
US Cremonese (Cremona)	1-1, 1-1 (aet)	FC Internazionale (Milano)
	(US Cremonese (Cremona) won on penalties)	
SSC Napoli (Napoli)	3-0, 4-2	Bologna FC (Bologna)

1987-88

1987-1988 Serie "A"	Ascoli Calcio	AC Avellino	AC Cesena	Como Calcio	Empoli FC	AC Fiorentina	Hellas Verona	FC Internazionale	Juventus FC	Milan AC	AC Napoli	Pescara Calcio	SC Pisa	AS Roma	UC Sampdoria	Torino Calcio
Ascoli Calcio		2-0	0-0	0-0	2-0	3-0	1-1	2-1	1-1	1-1	1-3	2-1	2-2	1-1	1-1	3-0
US Avellino	1-1		1-1	1-1	1-0	1-1	1-0	1-3	1-0	0-0	0-1	1-1	1-0	2-3	1-2	2-1
AC Cesena	1-0	1-1		3-0	1-1	1-0	1-0	2-2	0-0	0-0	0-1	0-1	1-1	0-0	2-0	0-0
Como Calcio	3-1	0-0	2-0		3-2	1-0	1-1	1-2	1-1	1-1	0-0	2-1	0-0	0-1	0-1	0-0
Empoli FC	2-0	0-0	2-2	1-1		0-0	1-0	1-1	1-0	0-0	0-0	3-2	0-1	2-1	2-2	0-0
AC Fiorentina	1-0	2-1	3-1	1-1	0-0		0-0	1-2	1-1	1-1	3-2	4-0	0-0	1-0	1-1	1-0
Hellas-Verona	2-1	4-1	0-1	0-1	1-0	1-0		1-1	2-1	0-1	1-1	2-0	0-0	0-1	3-1	0-2
FC Internazionale	2-2	1-1	2-0	1-0	2-0	3-0	1-1		2-1	0-1	1-1	0-2	2-1	4-2	3-1	0-1
Juventus FC	1-0	3-0	0-2	1-0	4-0	1-2	0-0	1-0		0-1	3-1	3-1	2-1	1-0	1-1	2-1
Milan AC	2-0	3-0	3-0	5-0	1-0	0-2	0-0	2-0	0-0		4-1	2-0	1-0	0-2	2-1	0-0
SSC Napoli	2-1	4-0	2-0	3-0	2-1	4-0	4-1	1-0	2-1	2-3		6-0	2-1	1-2	1-2	3-1
Pescara Calcio	0-0	2-0	1-0	2-0	0-0	1-1	3-0	1-1	2-0	0-2	0-1		2-1	0-0	0-0	2-2
SC Pisa	1-1	0-0	1-0	1-1	0-0	2-1	0-0	2-1	1-2	1-3	0-2	2-0		1-1	0-1	2-0
AS Roma	3-0	0-0	2-0	3-1	1-0	2-1	1-0	3-2	2-0	0-2	1-1	5-1	1-0		0-2	1-1
UC Sampdoria	2-0	2-0	4-1	3-0	2-0	1-0	3-1	1-1	2-1	1-1	0-1	2-1	0-0	0-0		1-1
Torino Calcio	2-1	0-0	2-2	1-1	0-1	2-1	1-1	1-1	2-2	1-1	0-0	2-0	3-1	2-0	4-1	

	Serie "A"	Pd	Wn	Dw	Ls	GF	GA	Pts	
1.	MILAN AC (MILANO)	30	17	11	2	43	14	45	
2.	SSC Napoli (Napoli)	30	18	6	6	55	27	42	
3.	AS Roma (Roma)	30	15	8	7	39	26	38	
4.	UC Sampdoria (Genova)	30	13	11	6	41	30	37	
5.	FC Internazionale (Milano)	30	11	10	9	42	35	32	
6.	Juventus FC (Torino)	30	11	9	10	35	30	31	PO
7.	Torino Calcio (Torino)	30	8	15	7	33	30	31	PO
8.	AC Fiorentina (Firenze)	30	9	10	11	29	33	28	
9.	AC Cesena (Cesena)	30	7	12	11	23	32	26	
10.	Hellas-Verona (Verona)	30	7	11	12	23	30	25	
11.	Como Calcio (Como)	30	6	13	11	22	37	25	
12.	Ascoli Calcio (Ascoli Piceno)	30	6	12	12	30	37	24	
13.	SC Pisa (Pisa)	30	6	12	12	23	30	24	
14.	Pescara Calcio (Pescara)	30	8	8	14	27	44	24	
15.	US Avellino (Avellino)	30	5	13	12	19	39	23	R
16.	Empoli FC (Empoli)	30	6	13	11	20	30	20	R -5
		480	153	174	153	504	504	475	

Top goalscorers

1)	Diego MARADONA	(SSC Napoli)	15
2)	Antonio CARECA	(SSC Napoli)	13
3)	Giuseppe GIANNINI	(AS Roma)	11
	Pietro Paolo VIRDIS	(Milan AC)	11
5)	Gianluca VIALLI	(UC Sampdoria)	10

SC Pisa 1-0 SSC Napoli was awarded 0-2 after Napoli player Renica was hit by a coin thrown from the crowd.
Juventus 2-1 AC Cesena was awarded 0-2 after Cesena player was struck by a firework and had to leave field.
Milan AC 1-0 AS Roma was awarded 0-2 after a Roma player was hit by fireworks thrown from the crowd.

Note: Empoli FC (Empoli) had 5 points deducted by the F.I.G.C. committee.

6th/7th Place Play-Off

Juventus FC (Torino) 0-0 (aet – 4-2 penalties) Torino Calcio (Torino)
(played to determine place in UEFA Cup for the next season)

US Livorno (Livorno) changed their club name to Pro Livorno Calcio (Livorno) for the next season.
Pistoiese Calcio (Pistoia) dissolved and re-formed as AC Pistoiese (Pistoia) for the next season.
Ternana Calcio (Terni) changed their club name to Polisportiva Ternana Calcio (Terni) for the next season.
Varese Calcio (Varese) changed their club name to FC Varese (Varese) for the next season.

	Serie "B"	Pd	Wn	Dw	Ls	GF	GA	Pts	
1.	Bologna FC (Bologna)	38	17	17	4	62	37	51	P
2.	US Lecce (Lecce)	38	17	15	6	42	26	49	P
3.	SS Lazio (Roma)	38	14	19	5	50	34	47	P
4.	Atalanta BC (Bergamo)	38	14	19	5	50	34	47	P
5.	US Catanzaro (Catanzaro)	38	14	18	6	36	24	46	
6.	US Cremonese (Cremona)	38	10	21	7	26	18	41	
7.	AS Bari (Bari)	38	12	17	9	30	27	41	
8.	Brescia Calcio (Brescia)	38	11	17	10	30	26	39	
9.	Padova Calcio (Padova)	38	13	13	12	38	41	39	
10.	Udinese Calcio (Udine)	38	12	14	12	37	35	38	
11.	Parma AC (Parma)	38	9	20	9	33	33	38	
12.	ACR Messina (Messina)	38	12	11	15	36	38	35	
13.	Piacenza Calcio (Piacenza)	38	9	15	14	26	42	33	
14.	Genoa CFC (Genova)	38	9	14	15	25	32	32	
15.	Sambenedettese Calcio San Benedetto del Tronto)	38	5	22	11	26	37	32	
16.	AS Taranto (Taranto)	38	9	14	15	40	54	32	
17.	SS Barletta (Barletta)	38	7	17	14	27	37	31	
18.	Modena FC (Modena)	38	7	16	15	30	46	30	R
19.	US Triestina Calcio (Trieste)	38	11	11	16	32	40	28	R -5
20.	US Arezzo (Arezzo)	38	4	18	16	22	38	26	R
		760	217	326	217	690	690	755	

Note: US Triestina Calcio (Trieste) had 5 points deducted by the F.I.G.C. committee.

Promoted to Serie "B": Ancona Calcio (Ancona), AS Cosenza (Cosenza), Polisportiva Licata (Licata), Monza Calcio (Monza) and AS Reggina (Reggio Calabria).

Serie "A" was extended to 18 clubs for the next season.

Coppa Italia Final (1st leg) (Genova - 05/05/88)

UC Sampdoria (GENOVA) 2-0 Torino Calcio (Torino)

Briegel 10', Vialli 33'

Sampdoria: Pagliuca, Briegel, Mannini, Fusi (Salsano 87'), Vierchowod, Pellegrini, Pari, Cerezo, Bonomi, Mancini (Ganz 82'), Vialli (Branca 78').

Torino: Lorieri, Corradini (Benedetti 46'), Ferri, Crippa, Rossi, Cravero, Berggreen (Lentini 68'), Sabato, Polster, Comi, Gritti (Bresciani 46').

Coppa Italia Final (2nd leg) (Torino - 19/05/88)

UC Sampdoria (GENOVA) 1-2 (aet) Torino Calcio (Torino)

Salsano 112' *Vierchowod 05' o.g., Paganin 35' o.g.*

Torino: Lorieri, Corradini, G.Ferri, Crippa, Benedetti, Cravero, E.Rossi, Sabato (Fuser 89'), Polster, Comi (Di Bindal 105'), Gritti (Bresciani 108').

Sampdoria: Pagliuca, Briegel (Paganin 26'), Mannini, Fusi, Vierchowod, Pellegrini (Salsano 28'), Pari, Cerezo, Bonomi, Mancini (Branca 114'), Vialli.

Semi-Finals

FC Internazionale (Milano)	0-0, 0-1	UC Sampdoria (Genova)
Juventus FC (Torino)	0-2, 2-1	Torino Calcio (Torino)

Quarter-Finals

US Avellino (Avellino)	1-1, 0-1	Juventus FC (Torino)
FC Internazionale (Milano)	2-1, 1-0	Empoli FC (Empoli)
UC Sampdoria (Genova)	4-2, 1-1	Ascoli Calcio (Ascoli Piceno)
Torino Calcio (Torino)	1-1, 3-2	SSC Napoli (Napoli)

1988-89

1988-1989 Serie "A"	Ascoli Calcio	Atalanta BC	Bologna FC	AC Cesena	Como Calcio	AC Fiorentina	Hellas Verona	FC Internazion.	Juventus FC	SS Lazio	US Lecce	Milan AC	SSC Napoli	Pescara Calcio	SC Pisa	AS Roma	UC Sampdoria	Torino Calcio
Ascoli Calcio		3-1	1-0	1-1	2-0	1-1	3-0	1-3	1-1	0-0	1-1	0-2	2-0	0-1	0-1	0-3	2-2	1-0
Atalanta BC	1-0		2-0	5-1	1-1	0-1	2-2	1-1	0-0	3-1	0-0	1-2	1-1	0-0	1-0	2-2	1-0	1-0
Bologna FC	1-0	1-1		2-2	1-0	1-0	0-0	0-6	3-4	0-0	2-1	1-4	1-1	1-0	1-0	0-1	0-0	2-0
AC Cesena	2-1	0-0	2-0		1-0	0-3	0-0	1-2	1-2	0-0	3-2	1-0	0-1	1-0	1-0	1-1	0-0	3-2
Como Calcio	0-1	1-0	1-0	0-0		3-2	1-1	1-2	0-3	2-1	2-1	1-1	0-1	1-0	1-1	0-1	0-2	2-3
AC Fiorentina	2-1	1-1	0-0	4-1	3-1		1-1	4-3	2-1	3-0	1-1	0-2	1-3	3-2	3-0	2-2	0-2	2-1
Hellas-Verona	0-1	1-0	0-0	0-0	0-0	2-1		0-0	2-0	0-0	2-1	1-2	0-1	0-0	1-0	0-0	1-1	0-0
FC Internazionale	3-1	4-2	1-0	1-0	4-0	2-0	1-0		1-1	1-0	2-0	0-0	2-1	2-1	4-1	2-0	1-0	2-0
Juventus FC	2-0	0-1	2-0	2-2	0-0	1-1	3-0	1-1		4-2	1-0	0-0	3-5	1-1	3-1	2-1	0-0	1-0
SS Lazio	0-0	0-1	0-0	0-0	1-1	1-0	3-1	1-3	0-0		0-0	1-1	1-1	2-2	1-0	1-0	1-0	1-1
US Lecce	1-2	2-1	1-1	0-0	0-0	0-0	0-0	0-3	2-0	1-0		1-1	1-0	1-0	1-0	0-0	1-0	3-1
Milan AC	5-1	1-2	1-1	0-0	4-0	4-0	1-1	0-1	4-0	0-0	2-0		0-0	6-1	0-0	4-1	0-0	2-1
SSC Napoli	4-1	1-0	3-1	1-0	3-2	2-0	1-0	0-0	2-4	1-1	4-0	4-1		8-2	0-0	1-1	1-1	4-1
Pescara Calcio	0-0	1-1	3-1	3-0	1-1	0-0	0-0	0-2	0-0	0-0	1-1	1-3	0-0		0-0	0-0	0-1	2-0
SC Pisa	0-0	0-1	0-2	1-0	3-1	0-0	1-0	0-3	1-4	1-1	1-1	0-2	0-1	1-1		1-0	1-1	1-0
AS Roma	1-1	2-1	1-1	1-0	1-0	2-1	0-0	0-3	1-3	0-0	1-1	1-3	1-0	1-3	2-1		1-0	1-3
UC Sampdoria	1-0	1-1	4-1	2-0	2-0	1-2	2-1	0-1	1-2	1-0	3-0	1-1	0-0	4-1	2-0	0-2		5-1
Torino Calcio	1-1	1-1	1-1	2-0	2-1	1-0	1-1	2-0	0-0	4-3	0-0	2-2	0-1	1-1	0-0	3-1	2-3	

	Serie "A"	Pd	Wn	Dw	Ls	GF	GA	Pts	
1.	FC INTERNAZIONALE (MILANO)	34	26	6	2	67	19	58	
2.	SSC Napoli (Napoli)	34	18	11	5	57	28	47	
3.	Milan AC (Milano)	34	16	14	4	61	25	46	
4.	Juventus FC (Torino)	34	15	13	6	51	36	43	
5.	UC Sampdoria (Genova)	34	14	11	9	43	25	39	
6.	Atalanta BC (Bergamo)	34	11	14	9	37	32	36	
7.	AC Fiorentina (Firenze)	34	12	10	12	44	43	34	PO
8.	AS Roma (Roma)	34	11	12	11	33	40	34	PO
9.	US Lecce (Lecce)	34	8	15	11	25	35	31	
10.	SS Lazio (Roma)	34	5	19	10	23	32	29	
11.	Hellas-Verona (Verona)	34	5	19	10	18	27	29	
12.	Ascoli Calcio (Ascoli Piceno)	34	9	11	14	30	41	29	
13.	AC Cesena (Cesena)	34	8	13	13	24	39	29	
14.	Bologna FC (Bologna)	34	8	13	13	26	43	29	
15.	Torino Calcio (Torino)	34	8	11	15	37	49	27	R
16.	Pescara Calcio (Pescara)	34	5	17	12	28	43	27	R
17.	SC Pisa (Pisa)	34	6	11	17	17	39	23	R
18.	Como Calcio (Como)	34	6	10	18	24	49	22	R
		612	191	230	191	645	645	612	

Top goalscorers

1)	Aldo SERENA	(FC Internazionale)	22
2)	Antonio CARECA	(SSC Napoli)	19
	Marco VAN BASTEN	(Milan AC)	19
4)	Roberto BAGGIO	(AC Fiorentina)	16
5)	Stefano BORGONOVO	(AC Fiorentina)	14
	Gianluca VIALLI	(UC Sampdoria)	14

7th/8th Place Play-Off

AC Fiorentina (Firenze) 1-0 AS Roma (Roma)

(played in Perugia to determine a UEFA Cup place for the next season)

Ascoli Calcio (Ascoli Piceno) changed their club name to Ascoli Calcio 1898 (Ascoli Piceno) for the next season.
Venezia-Mestre Calcio (Venezia) changed their club name to AC Venezia (Venezia) for the next season.

	Serie "B"	Pd	Wn	Dw	Ls	GF	GA	Pts	
1.	Genoa CFC (Genova)	38	16	19	3	35	13	51	P
2.	AS Bari (Bari)	38	16	19	3	38	21	51	P
3.	Udinese Calcio (Udine)	38	13	19	6	37	24	45	P
4.	US Cremonese (Cremona)	38	13	18	7	40	30	44	P
5.	AS Reggina (Reggio Calabria)	38	13	18	7	33	31	44	PO
6.	AS Cosenza (Cosenza)	38	17	10	11	35	29	44	
7.	US Avellino (Avellino)	38	11	19	8	31	29	41	
8.	ACR Messina (Messina)	38	13	12	13	46	42	38	
9.	Polisportiva Licata (Licata)	38	11	15	12	39	40	37	
10.	Parma AC (Parma)	38	8	21	9	29	31	37	
11.	US Catanzaro (Catanzaro)	38	8	19	11	24	26	35	
12.	SS Barletta (Barletta)	38	8	19	11	40	43	35	
13.	Ancona Calcio (Ancona)	38	6	23	9	28	35	35	
14.	Padova Calcio (Padova)	38	10	15	13	27	35	35	
15.	Monza Calcio (Monza)	38	7	20	11	31	32	34	
16.	Brescia Calcio (Brescia)	38	9	16	13	27	29	34	PO
17.	Empoli FC (Empoli)	38	8	18	12	29	33	34	R
18.	Sambenedettese Calcio (San Benedetto del Tronto)	38	7	17	14	21	30	31	R
19.	AS Taranto (Taranto)	38	8	13	17	24	40	29	R
20.	Piacenza Calcio (Piacenza)	38	7	12	19	20	41	26	R
		760	209	342	209	634	634	760	

Promotion Play-Off

US Cremonese (Cremona) 0-0 (aet – 4-3 penalties) AS Reggina (Reggio Calabria)

Relegation Play-Off

Brescia Calcio (Brescia) 0-0 (aet – 3-0 penalties) Empoli FC (Empoli)

Promoted to Serie "B": Cagliari Calcio (Cagliari), Foggia Calcio (Foggia), AC Reggiana (Reggio Emilia) and US Triestina Calcio.

Coppa Italia Final (1st leg) (Napoli – 07/06/89)

SSC Napoli (Napoli) 1-0 UC Sampdoria (GENOVA)

Renica 55'

Napoli: Giuliana, Corradini, Francini, Fusi (Neri 49'), Alemao, Renica, Carannante, Crippa, Careca, Maradona, Carnevale.

Sampdoria: Pagliuca, Lanna, Carboni, Pari, Vierchowod, L.Pellegrini, Victor (Salsano 78'), Cerezo, Vialli, Mancini, Dossena (Bonomi 71').

Coppa Italia Final (2nd leg) (Cremona – 28/06/89)

SSC Napoli (Napoli) 0-4 UC Sampdoria (GENOVA)

Vialli 32', Cerezo 38', Vierchowod 47', Mancini 59' pen.

Sampdoria: Pagliuca, Lanna, Carboni, Pari, Vierchowod, L.Pellegrini, Victor (Bonomi 87'), Cerezo, Vialli (Salsano 83'), Mancini, Dossena.

Napoli: Giuliana, Corradini, Francini, Fusi (Bigliadi 80'), Alemao, Renica, Crippa, De Napoli, Careca, Maradona, Carannante (Neri 51').

Semi-Finals

Atalanta BC (Bergamo)	2-3, 1-3	UC Sampdoria (Genova)
SC Pisa (Pisa)	0-2, 0-1	SSC Napoli (Napoli)

Quarter-Finals

Atalanta BC (Bergamo)	2-0, 2-3	SS Lazio (Roma)
Hellas-Verona (Verona)	2-1, 0-1	SC Pisa (Pisa)
SSC Napoli (Napoli)	3-0, 1-3	Ascoli Calcio (Ascoli (Piceno)
UC Sampdoria (Genova)	3-0, 1-1	AC Fiorentina (Firenze)

1989-90

1989-1990 Serie "A"	Ascoli Calcio 1898	Atalanta BC	AS Bari	Bologna FC	AC Cesena	US Cremonese	AC Fiorentina	Genoa CFC	Hellas Verona	FC Internazionale	Juventus FC	SS Lazio	US Lecce	Milan AC	SSC Napoli	AS Roma	UC Sampdoria	Udinese Calcio
Ascoli Calcio 1898		1-1	1-1	1-1	0-0	0-1	2-1	0-0	1-1	0-1	1-2	0-0	0-2	1-0	0-1	1-1	2-1	1-0
Atalanta BC	1-0		0-0	0-0	1-0	2-0	0-0	1-0	1-0	2-1	1-2	4-0	2-1	0-1	0-2	3-0	2-2	1-0
AS Bari	2-2	4-0		0-0	2-0	2-0	1-1	0-0	2-1	0-0	1-1	0-0	0-1	0-1	1-1	1-2	0-2	3-1
Bologna FC	2-1	0-0	3-1		1-0	1-1	1-0	1-0	1-0	2-2	1-1	1-1	2-1	0-0	2-4	1-1	1-0	0-0
AC Cesena	1-0	0-0	2-2	0-0		1-1	1-1	1-1	1-0	2-3	1-1	0-0	4-0	0-3	0-0	0-0	1-2	1-1
US Cremonese	2-1	1-1	0-2	2-1	1-2		1-2	0-1	1-1	0-1	2-2	2-1	1-1	1-0	1-1	0-1	0-3	2-2
AC Fiorentina	5-1	4-1	2-2	0-1	0-0	0-0		0-0	3-1	2-2	2-2	1-0	3-0	2-3	0-1	1-2	3-1	1-2
Genoa CFC	2-0	2-2	0-0	0-0	2-3	1-0	1-1		0-1	0-0	2-3	2-2	1-0	1-1	1-1	0-2	1-2	0-0
Hellas-Verona	0-0	1-1	1-1	3-2	0-2	1-1	1-0	1-1		0-3	1-4	1-1	0-0	2-1	1-2	2-2	1-0	2-0
FC Internazionale	0-0	7-2	1-1	3-0	1-1	2-1	2-0	1-0	0-0		2-1	3-0	2-1	0-3	3-1	3-0	2-0	2-0
Juventus FC	3-1	0-1	1-0	1-1	1-1	4-0	3-1	1-1	2-1	1-0		1-0	3-0	3-0	1-1	1-1	1-0	1-1
SS Lazio	3-0	1-2	2-2	3-0	4-0	1-1	1-1	0-0	0-0	2-1	1-1		3-0	1-3	3-0	0-1	0-2	0-0
US Lecce	1-1	2-1	1-1	1-0	2-1	2-1	1-0	2-1	1-0	0-0	2-3	0-0		1-2	1-1	0-2	0-0	1-0
Milan AC	2-1	3-1	4-0	1-0	3-0	2-1	1-1	1-0	0-0	1-3	3-2	0-1	2-0		3-0	1-0	1-0	3-1
SSC Napoli	1-0	3-1	3-0	2-0	1-0	3-0	3-2	2-1	2-0	2-0	3-1	1-0	3-2	3-0		3-1	1-1	1-0
AS Roma	0-0	4-1	1-0	2-2	1-0	3-2	0-0	0-1	5-2	1-1	1-0	1-1	2-1	0-4	1-1		1-1	3-1
UC Sampdoria	2-0	1-0	0-0	3-0	0-0	1-1	3-0	0-0	1-0	2-0	0-0	2-0	1-0	1-1	2-1	4-2		3-1
Udinese Calcio	2-0	0-0	2-2	1-1	1-0	1-1	1-1	2-4	2-1	4-3	2-2	0-2	3-1	0-2	2-2	1-1	3-3	

	Serie "A"	Pd	Wn	Dw	Ls	GF	GA	Pts	
1.	SSC NAPOLI (NAPOLI)	34	21	9	4	57	31	51	
2.	Milan AC (Milano)	34	22	5	7	56	27	49	
3.	FC Internazionale (Milano)	34	17	10	7	55	32	44	
4.	Juventus FC (Torino)	34	15	14	5	56	36	44	
5.	UC Sampdoria (Genova)	34	16	11	7	46	26	43	
6.	AS Roma (Roma)	34	14	13	7	45	40	41	
7.	Atalanta BC (Bergamo)	34	12	11	11	36	43	35	
8.	Bologna FC (Bologna)	34	9	16	9	29	36	34	
9.	SS Lazio (Roma)	34	8	15	11	34	33	31	
10.	AS Bari (Bari)	34	6	19	9	34	37	31	
11.	Genoa CFC (Genova)	34	6	17	11	27	31	29	
12.	AC Fiorentina (Firenze)	34	7	14	13	41	42	28	
13.	AC Cesena (Cesena)	34	6	16	12	26	36	28	
14.	US Lecce (Lecce)	34	10	8	16	29	46	28	
15.	Udinese Calcio (Udine)	34	6	15	13	37	51	27	R
16.	Hellas-Verona (Verona)	34	6	13	15	27	44	25	R
17.	US Cremonese (Cremona)	34	5	13	16	29	50	23	R
18.	Ascoli Calcio 1898 (Ascoli Piceno)	34	4	13	17	20	43	21	R *
		612	190	232	190	684	684	612	

Top goalscorers

1)	Marco VAN BASTEN	(Milan AC)	19
2)	Roberto BAGGIO	(AC Fiorentina)	17
3)	Diego MARADONA	(SSC Napoli)	16
4)	Salvatore SCHILLACI	(Juventus FC)	15
5)	Rudi VÖLLER	(AS Roma)	14

Atalanta BC 0-0 SSC Napoli was awarded 0-2 after Napoli player Alamao was hit by a coin thrown from the crowd after 80' and was forced to leave the field of play.

	Serie "B"	Pd	Wn	Dw	Ls	GF	GA	Pts	
1.	Torino Calcio (Torino)	38	19	15	4	63	24	53	P
2.	SC Pisa (Pisa)	38	16	19	3	51	23	51	P
3.	Cagliari Calcio (Cagliari)	38	17	13	8	39	22	47	P
4.	Parma AC (Parma)	38	16	14	8	49	30	46	P
5.	Ancona Calcio (Ancona)	38	13	17	8	46	34	43	
6.	AS Reggina (Reggio Calabria)	38	13	16	9	32	27	42	
7.	AC Reggiana (Reggio Emilia)	38	11	18	9	33	31	40	
8.	Foggia Calcio (Foggia)	38	15	9	14	45	38	39	
9.	Pescara Calcio (Pescara)	38	14	11	13	34	39	39	
10.	Brescia Calcio (Brescia)	38	10	17	11	31	34	37	
11.	Padova Calcio (Padova)	38	12	13	13	26	33	37	
12.	US Avellino (Avellino)	38	12	11	15	33	35	35	
13.	US Triestina Calcio (Trieste)	38	9	17	12	33	41	35	
14.	AS Cosenza (Cosenza)	38	9	16	13	27	40	34	
15.	SS Barletta (Barletta)	38	9	16	13	24	37	34	
16.	ACR Messina (Messina)	38	11	12	15	28	44	34	PO
17.	Monza Calcio (Monza)	38	11	12	15	26	37	34	R
18.	Polisportiva Licata (Licata)	38	6	16	16	22	38	28	R
19.	Como Calcio (Como)	38	7	13	18	16	32	27	R
20.	US Catanzaro (Catanzaro)	38	3	19	16	16	35	25	R
		760	233	294	233	674	674	760	

Relegation Play-Off

ACR Messina (Messina)	1-0	Monza Calcio (Monza)

Promoted to Serie "B": AS Lucchese Libertas (Lucca), Modena FC (Modena), Salernitana Sport (Salerno), AS Taranto (Taranto)

SS Lanerossi (Vicenza) changed their club name to Vicenza Calcio (Vicenza) for the next season.
Pro Livorno Calcio (Livorno) changed their club name to UC Livorno (Livorno) for the next season.

Coppa Italia Final (1st leg) (Torino – 29/02/90)

JUVENTUS FC (TORINO)	0-0	Milan AC (Milano)

Juventus: Tacconi, Galia, De Agostini, Alessio, Bonetti, Tricella (Brio 79'), Aleynikov, Rui Barros, Casiraghi, Marocchi, Schillaci.

Milan: G.Galli, Tassotti, Maldini, Fuser (Stroppa 76'), F.Galli, Baresi, Massaro, Rijkaard, Van Basten, Ancelotti, Evani (Salvatori 87').

Coppa Italia Final (2nd leg) (Milano – 25/04/90)

JUVENTUS FC (TORINO)	1-0	Milan AC (Milano)

Galia 17'

Milan: G.Galli, Tassotti, Costacurta, Colomo (Salvatori 66'), F.Galli, Baresi, Donadoni, Rijkaard, Van Basten, Evani, Massaro (Borgonovo 46').

Juventus: Tacconi, Napoli, De Agostini, Galia, Bruno, D.Bonetti, Aleynikov, Rui Barros, Casiraghi, Marocchi, Schillaci (Alesio 74').

Semi-Finals

Juventus FC (Torino)	2-0, 2-3	AS Roma (Roma)
Milan AC (Milano)	0-0, 3-1	SSC Napoli (Napoli)

The Quarter-Finals were played in four groups of three teams each.

1990-91

1990-1991 Serie "A"	Atalanta BC	AS Bari	Bologna FC	Cagliari Calcio	AC Cesena	AC Fiorentina	Genoa CFC	FC Internazionale	Juventus FC	SS Lazio	US Lecce	Milan AC	SSC Napoli	Parma AC	SC Pisa	AS Roma	UC Sampdoria	Torino Calcio
Atalanta BC		2-0	4-0	2-1	3-0	2-1	0-0	1-1	0-0	4-1	2-1	0-2	0-0	0-0	1-0	2-2	1-1	0-1
AS Bari	4-1		4-0	4-1	1-0	0-0	4-0	1-1	3-0	0-0	1-1	2-1	0-0	2-2	2-0	0-1	1-1	2-1
Bologna FC	1-1	3-0		1-2	0-1	1-1	0-3	0-0	0-1	1-2	1-1	1-1	1-0	1-3	0-1	2-3	0-3	1-0
Cagliari Calcio	1-1	1-1	0-0		0-0	1-1	1-0	0-3	0-0	0-1	2-0	1-1	1-1	2-1	2-1	0-0	0-0	1-2
AC Cesena	0-1	4-2	3-2	3-0		0-4	1-1	1-5	1-1	1-1	3-1	0-1	0-0	0-1	1-1	1-1	0-1	2-2
AC Fiorentina	3-1	1-1	1-0	4-1	2-0		2-2	0-0	1-0	1-1	0-0	0-0	0-0	2-3	4-0	1-1	0-0	0-0
Genoa CFC	2-0	3-1	0-0	2-2	4-1	3-2		3-0	2-0	3-1	0-0	1-1	1-1	2-1	4-2	3-0	0-0	0-0
FC Internazionale	3-1	5-1	1-0	1-1	2-0	1-1	2-1		2-0	2-0	5-0	0-1	2-1	2-1	6-3	2-1	0-2	1-0
Juventus FC	1-1	3-1	1-1	2-2	3-0	2-1	0-1	4-2		0-0	0-0	0-3	1-0	5-0	4-2	5-0	0-0	1-2
SS Lazio	2-2	1-1	3-1	1-1	1-1	2-1	1-1	0-0	1-0		2-0	1-1	0-2	0-0	0-0	1-1	3-3	2-1
US Lecce	0-0	1-1	1-3	2-0	2-0	2-0	0-3	0-2	0-1	1-0		0-3	0-0	1-0	1-1	1-1	1-0	1-1
Milan AC	0-1	2-0	6-0	2-0	2-0	2-1	1-0	0-1	2-0	3-1	1-0		4-1	0-0	1-0	1-1	0-1	1-0
SSC Napoli	2-0	1-0	3-2	1-2	1-0	1-0	1-0	1-1	1-1	2-1	2-2	1-1		4-2	2-1	1-1	1-4	2-1
Parma AC	1-0	1-0	1-1	2-0	2-0	1-0	2-1	0-0	1-2	0-0	0-0	2-0	1-0		2-3	2-1	0-0	0-0
SC Pisa	0-2	1-0	2-2	1-0	3-2	0-4	0-0	0-1	1-5	0-1	4-0	0-1	1-1	0-2		0-1	0-3	2-0
AS Roma	2-1	1-0	4-1	0-0	4-1	4-0	3-1	1-1	0-1	1-1	3-0	0-0	1-1	1-1	0-2		0-1	2-0
UC Sampdoria	4-1	3-2	2-1	2-2	1-0	1-0	1-2	3-1	1-0	1-1	3-0	2-0	4-1	1-0	4-2	2-1		1-2
Torino Calcio	0-0	4-0	4-1	1-1	2-1	1-1	5-2	2-0	1-1	0-0	2-0	1-1	1-1	0-0	1-0	1-0	1-1	

	Serie "A"	Pd	Wn	Dw	Ls	GF	GA	Pts	
1.	UC Sampdoria (GENOVA)	34	20	11	3	57	24	51	
2.	Milan AC (Milano)	34	18	10	6	46	19	46	
3.	FC Internazionale (Milano)	34	18	10	6	56	31	46	
4.	Genoa CFC (Genova)	34	14	12	8	51	36	40	
5.	Torino Calcio (Torino)	34	12	14	8	40	29	38	
6.	Parma AC (Parma)	34	13	12	9	35	31	38	
7.	Juventus FC (Torino)	34	13	11	10	45	32	37	
8.	SSC Napoli (Napoli)	34	11	15	8	37	37	37	
9.	AS Roma (Roma)	34	11	14	9	43	37	36	
10.	Atalanta BC (Bergamo)	34	11	13	10	38	37	35	
11.	SS Lazio (Roma)	34	8	19	7	33	36	35	
12.	AC Fiorentina (Firenze)	34	8	15	11	40	34	31	
13.	AS Bari (Bari)	34	9	11	14	41	47	29	
14.	Cagliari Calcio (Cagliari)	34	6	17	11	29	44	29	
15.	US Lecce (Lecce)	34	6	13	15	20	47	25	R
16.	SC Pisa (Pisa)	34	8	6	20	34	60	22	R
17.	AC Cesena (Cesena)	34	5	9	20	28	58	19	R
18.	Bologna FC (Bologna)	34	4	10	20	29	63	18	R
		612	195	222	195	702	702	612	

Top goalscorers

1)	Gianluca VIALLI	(UC Sampdoria)	19
2)	Lothar MATTHAUS	(FC Internazionale)	16
3)	Carlos AGUILERA	(Genoa CFC)	15
	Tomas SKUHRAVY	(Genoa CFC)	15
5)	Roberto BAGGIO	(Juventus FC)	14
	Massimo CIOCCI	(AC Cesena)	14
	Jürgen KLINSMANN	(FC Internazionale)	14

* Hellas-Verona (Verona) dissolved and re-formed as Hellas Verona FC (Verona) for the next season.

	Serie "B"	Pd	Wn	Dw	Ls	GF	GA	Pts	
1.	Foggia Calcio (Foggia)	38	21	9	8	67	36	51	P
2.	Hellas-Verona (Verona)	38	15	15	8	42	29	45	P *
3.	US Cremonese (Cremona)	38	12	19	7	28	21	43	P
4.	Ascoli Calcio 1898 (Ascoli Piceno)	38	13	16	9	48	34	42	P
5.	Padova Calcio (Padova)	38	13	15	10	41	36	41	
6.	AS Lucchese Libertas (Lucca)	38	10	20	8	29	30	40	
7.	AC Reggiana (Reggio Emilia)	38	12	15	11	52	45	39	
8.	Udinese Calcio (Udine)	38	13	17	8	53	43	38	-5
9.	Brescia Calcio (Brescia)	38	9	19	10	29	32	37	
10.	Ancona Calcio (Ancona)	38	11	15	12	38	43	37	
11.	AS Taranto (Taranto)	38	10	17	11	28	33	37	
12.	ACR Messina (Messina)	38	9	19	10	34	45	37	
13.	Modena FC (Modena)	38	10	16	12	35	35	36	
14.	Pescara Calcio (Pescara)	38	9	18	11	36	32	36	
15.	US Avellino (Avellino)	38	11	14	13	27	36	36	
16.	AS Cosenza (Cosenza)	38	11	14	13	38	50	36	PO
17.	Salernitana Sport (Salerno)	38	7	22	9	29	38	36	R
18.	AS Reggina (Reggio Calabria)	38	7	16	15	29	37	30	R
19.	US Triestina Calcio (Trieste)	38	7	16	15	33	43	30	R
20.	SS Barletta (Barletta)	38	8	12	18	29	47	28	R
		760	218	324	218	745	745	755	

Note: Udinese Calcio (Udine) had 5 points deducted by the F.I.G.C. committee.

Relegation Play-Off

AS Cosenza (Cosenza) 1-0 (aet) Salernitana Sport (Salerno)

Promoted to Serie "B": Casertana Calcio (Caserta), US Città di Palermo (Palermo), Piacenza Calcio (Piacenza) and AC Venezia (Venezia).

Coppa Italia Final (1st leg) (Roma – 30/05/91)

AS ROMA (ROMA) 3-1 UC Sampdoria (Genova)

Pellegrini 13' o.g., Berthold 35', Völler 41' pen. *Katanec 29'*

Roma: Cervone, S.Pellegrini, Carboni, Berthold, Aldair, Nela, Desideri, Di Mauro, Völler, Giannini (Gerolin 84'), Rizitelli (Muzzi 76').

Sampdoria: Pagliuca, Mannini, Katanec (Bonetti 84'), Pari, Vierchowod, L.Pellegrini, Lombardo (Invernizzi 84'), Cerezo, Vialli, Mancini, Dossena.

Coppa Italia Final (2nd leg) (Genova - 09/06/91)

AS ROMA (ROMA)	1-1	UC Sampdoria (Genova)
Völler 56' pen.		*Aldair 79' o.g.*

Sampdoria: Pagliuca, Mannini, Katanec, Pari, Vierchowod, Lanna (Branca 62'), Lombardo, Cerezo, Vialli, Mancini, Invernizzi (Mikhailichenko 56').

Roma: Cervone, S.Pellegrini, Carboni, Gerolin, Aldair, Nela, Desideri, Di Mauro, Völler (Salsano 84'), Giannini (Tempestilli 67'), Rizzitelli.

Semi-Finals

Milan AC (Milano)	0-0, 0-1	AS Roma (Roma)
SSC Napoli (Napoli)	1-0, 0-2	UC Sampdoria (Genova)

Quarter-Finals

AS Bari (Bari)	0-1, 0-0	Milan AC (Milano)
SSC Napoli (Napoli)	0-1, 3-1	Bologna FC (Bologna)
AS Roma (Roma)	1-1, 2-0	Juventus FC (Torino)
Torino Calcio (Torino)	1-0, 0-1 (aet – 3-1 penalties)	UC Sampdoria (Genova)

1991-92

1991-1992 Serie "A"	Ascoli Calcio	Atalanta BC	AS Bari	Cagliari Calcio	US Cremonese	AC Fiorentina	Foggia Calcio	Genoa CFC	Hellas Verona FC	FC Internazionale	Juventus FC	SS Lazio	Milan AC	SSC Napoli	Parma AC	AS Roma	UC Sampdoria	Torino Calcio
Ascoli Calcio		1-0	2-2	1-3	1-0	0-0	2-1	0-2	1-1	1-2	0-2	1-4	0-1	1-4	2-3	1-1	0-1	0-4
Atalanta BC	1-1		2-1	0-1	1-1	1-0	4-4	1-0	0-0	1-0	0-0	1-0	0-2	1-1	0-1	0-1	0-0	1-3
AS Bari	2-1	0-0		1-0	0-0	1-0	1-3	1-2	2-1	0-2	0-0	1-2	0-1	1-3	1-1	2-1	1-1	1-1
Cagliari Calcio	2-0	0-0	0-0		0-0	4-0	2-2	1-1	4-0	1-1	1-1	0-1	1-4	0-0	0-0	0-1	3-2	0-1
US Cremonese	3-1	1-2	1-1	0-1		1-3	0-2	2-1	3-0	0-1	0-2	2-0	1-1	0-0	0-1	1-2	0-1	0-2
AC Fiorentina	1-2	3-0	2-0	1-0	1-1		1-2	3-1	4-1	1-1	2-0	1-1	0-0	4-2	1-1	0-1	1-2	0-0
Foggia Calcio	1-0	2-3	4-1	3-1	2-0	3-3		1-0	5-0	2-2	0-1	2-1	2-8	1-0	1-1	1-2	0-0	1-1
Genoa CFC	1-0	0-2	1-3	2-2	2-0	3-2	0-2		1-0	1-2	2-1	1-0	0-0	3-4	2-0	1-1	0-0	1-1
Hellas Verona FC	1-0	1-3	2-1	2-0	2-2	2-3	1-0	2-1		1-0	3-3	0-2	0-1	0-1	1-0	0-1	0-0	1-2
FC Internazionale	2-1	0-0	1-0	0-0	0-2	1-1	1-1	2-2	2-0		1-3	1-0	1-1	0-0	0-0	0-0	0-0	0-0
Juventus FC	1-0	2-1	2-0	0-0	2-0	1-0	4-1	3-0	2-0	2-1		1-1	1-1	3-1	1-0	2-1	0-0	1-0
SS Lazio	1-1	1-1	3-1	2-1	3-2	1-1	5-2	1-1	2-0	0-1	1-1		1-1	3-3	1-1	1-1	1-2	2-1
Milan AC	4-1	3-1	2-0	1-0	3-1	1-1	3-1	1-1	4-0	1-0	1-1	2-0		5-0	2-0	4-1	5-1	2-0
SSC Napoli	5-1	1-0	1-0	4-0	3-0	1-0	3-3	1-0	3-1	1-1	0-1	3-0	1-1		2-2	3-2	2-1	0-1
Parma AC	2-0	0-0	1-0	1-1	1-1	1-1	2-0	2-0	1-1	1-1	0-0	1-0	1-3	2-1		3-1	2-1	0-0
AS Roma	1-0	1-1	2-0	0-0	3-0	1-3	1-1	0-0	1-0	0-1	1-1	1-1	1-1	1-1	1-0		2-0	1-0
UC Sampdoria	4-0	0-2	1-1	1-1	2-2	2-0	1-1	2-2	2-0	4-0	1-0	1-0	0-2	1-1	2-0	1-1		0-0
Torino Calcio	5-2	1-1	1-0	1-0	2-0	2-0	3-1	4-0	0-0	0-0	2-0	0-1	2-2	0-0	0-0	1-1	1-1	

	Serie "A"	Pd	Wn	Dw	Ls	GF	GA	Pts	
1.	MILAN AC (MILANO)	34	22	12	-	74	21	56	
2.	Juventus FC (Torino)	34	18	12	4	45	22	48	
3.	Torino Calcio (Torino)	34	14	15	5	42	20	43	
4.	SSC Napoli (Napoli)	34	15	12	7	56	40	42	
5.	AS Roma (Roma)	34	13	14	7	37	31	40	
6.	UC Sampdoria (Genova)	34	11	16	7	38	31	38	
7.	Parma AC (Parma)	34	11	16	7	32	28	38	
8.	FC Internazionale (Milano)	34	10	17	7	28	28	37	
9.	Foggia Calcio (Foggia)	34	12	11	11	58	58	35	
10.	SS Lazio (Roma)	34	11	12	11	43	40	34	
11.	Atalanta BC (Bergamo)	34	10	14	10	31	33	34	
12.	AC Fiorentina (Firenze)	34	10	12	12	44	41	32	
13.	Cagliari Calcio (Cagliari)	34	7	15	12	30	34	29	
14.	Genoa CFC (Genova)	34	9	11	14	35	47	29	
15.	AS Bari (Bari)	34	6	10	18	26	47	22	R
16.	Hellas Verona FC (Verona)	34	7	7	20	24	57	21	R
17.	US Cremonese (Cremona)	34	5	10	19	27	49	20	R
18.	Ascoli Calcio 1898 (Ascoli Piceno)	34	4	6	24	25	68	14	R
		612	195	222	195	695	695	612	

Top goalscorers

1)	Marco VAN BASTEN	(Milan AC)	25
2)	Roberto BAGGIO	(Juventus FC)	18
3)	Francesco BAIANO	(Foggia Calcio)	16
4)	Antonio CARECA	(SSC Napoli)	15
5)	Rubén SOSA	(SS Lazio)	14

FC Varese (Varese) dissolved and re-formed as Varese FC (Varese) for the next season.

	Serie "B"	Pd	Wn	Dw	Ls	GF	GA	Pts	
1.	Brescia Calcio (Brescia)	38	14	21	3	54	31	49	P
2.	Pescara Calcio (Pescara)	38	15	16	7	58	43	46	P
3.	Ancona Calcio (Ancona)	38	12	21	5	36	27	45	P
4.	Udinese Calcio (Udine)	38	13	18	7	41	33	44	P
5.	AS Cosenza (Cosenza)	38	13	16	9	39	36	42	
6.	SC Pisa (Pisa)	38	12	15	11	40	36	39	
7.	AC Reggiana (Reggio Emilia)	38	11	16	11	33	32	38	
8.	AC Cesena (Cesena)	38	10	17	11	38	33	37	
9.	AS Lucchese Libertas (Lucca)	38	8	21	9	34	34	37	
10.	US Lecce (Lecce)	38	12	13	13	35	38	37	
11.	Piacenza Calcio (Piacenza)	38	11	14	13	37	39	36	
12.	Padova Calcio (Padova)	38	8	20	10	30	32	36	
13.	Bologna FC (Bologna)	38	12	12	14	37	41	36	
14.	Modena FC (Modena)	38	11	14	13	33	41	36	
15.	AC Venezia (Venezia)	38	7	21	10	33	36	35	
16.	AS Taranto (Taranto)	38	9	17	12	26	34	35	PO
17.	Casertana Calcio (Caserta)	38	8	19	11	31	40	35	R
18.	US Città di Palermo (Palermo)	38	11	13	14	41	43	35	R
19.	ACR Messina (Messina)	38	10	13	15	31	38	33	R
20.	US Avellino (Avellino)	38	8	13	17	33	53	29	R
		760	215	230	215	740	740	760	

Relegation Play-Off

AS Taranto (Taranto)	2-1 (aet)	Casertana Calcio (Caserta)

Promoted to Serie "B": AS Fidelis Andria (Andria), Monza Calcio (Monza), S.P.A.L. (Ferrara) and Ternana Calcio (Terni).

Coppa Italia Final (1st leg) (Torino - 07/05/92)

Juventus FC (Torino)	1-0	PARMA AC (PARMA)
Baggio 23' pen		

Juventus: Peruzzi, Luppi, Marocchi, Conte (De Agostini 58'), Carrera, Julio César, Galia, Reuter, Schillaci (Corini 64'), Baggio, Di Canio.

Parma: Ballotta, Benarrivo, Di Chiara, Minotti, Apolloni, Grün, Melli (Agostini 84'), Zoratto (Catanese 68'), Osio, Cuoghi, Brolin.

Coppa Italia Final (2nd leg) (Parma - 14/05/92)

Juventus FC (Torino)	0-2	PARMA AC (PARMA)
		Melli 45', Osio 61'

Parma: Ballotta, Benarrivo, Di Chiara, Minotti, Apolloni, Grün, Melli (Agostini 85'), Zoratto, Osio (Pulga 83'), Cuoghi, Brolin.

Juventus: Peruzzi, Luppi, Marocchi, De Agostini (Conte 73'), Köhler Carrera (Di Canio 66'), Galia, Reuter, Schillachi, Baggio, Casiraghi.

Semi-Finals

Milan AC (Milano)	0-0, 0-1	Juventus FC (Torino)
Parma AC (Parma)	1-0, 2-2 (aet)	UC Sampdoria (Genova)

Quarter-Finals

Juventus FC (Torino)	1-0, 2-1	FC Internazionale (Milano)
Milan AC (Milano)	2-0, 1-1	Torino Calcio (Torino)
Parma AC (Parma)	2-0, 2-1	Genoa CFC (Genova)
UC Sampdoria (Genova)	1-0, 1-1	AS Roma (Roma)

1992-93

1992-1993 Serie "A"	Ancona Calcio	Atalanta BC	Brescia Calcio	Cagliari Calcio	AC Fiorentina	Foggia Calcio	Genoa CFC	FC Internazionale	Juventus FC	SS Lazio	Milan AC	SSC Napoli	Parma AC	Pescara Calcio	AS Roma	UC Sampdoria	Torino Calcio	Udinese Calcio
Ancona Calcio		0-2	5-1	0-1	2-1	3-0	0-0	3-0	0-1	0-3	1-3	1-1	1-1	5-3	1-1	2-3	0-1	1-0
Atalanta BC	2-1		1-1	2-1	2-1	2-1	1-2	1-1	2-1	2-2	1-1	3-2	2-1	2-1	3-1	1-2	0-0	2-0
Brescia Calcio	1-1	2-0		0-2	1-1	4-1	2-2	1-3	2-0	2-0	0-1	2-1	0-1	1-0	0-2	3-1	0-0	2-1
Cagliari Calcio	3-0	2-1	3-1		2-1	1-1	3-0	0-0	0-0	1-1	1-1	1-0	0-1	4-0	1-0	0-2	0-0	1-1
AC Fiorentina	7-1	0-1	2-2	2-1		6-2	1-1	2-2	2-0	0-2	3-7	1-1	1-1	2-0	2-1	4-0	0-0	2-2
Foggia Calcio	1-0	1-0	0-0	1-1	1-0		2-2	1-3	2-1	2-1	2-2	2-4	1-0	1-0	0-0	1-0	0-0	1-0
Genoa CFC	4-4	1-0	1-1	2-3	2-2	0-0		1-1	2-2	2-3	2-2	2-1	1-1	4-3	0-0	0-0	2-1	1-0
FC Internazionale	3-0	1-0	2-1	3-1	2-2	1-1	4-0		3-1	2-0	1-1	0-0	2-1	2-0	1-1	0-0	3-0	2-2
Juventus FC	5-1	4-1	0-0	2-1	3-0	4-2	1-0	0-2		4-1	0-1	4-3	2-2	2-1	1-1	1-1	2-1	5-1
SS Lazio	5-0	3-0	2-0	1-2	2-2	1-1	1-1	3-1	1-1		2-2	4-3	5-2	2-1	1-1	2-1	1-2	4-0
Milan AC	2-0	2-0	1-1	1-0	2-0	1-0	1-0	1-1	1-3	5-3		2-2	0-1	4-0	0-0	4-0	0-0	1-1
SSC Napoli	0-0	1-0	0-0	1-0	4-1	2-0	2-2	1-2	2-3	3-1	1-5		1-1	2-0	2-1	1-1	1-1	3-0
Parma AC	3-0	0-0	2-0	3-1	1-1	4-0	1-0	2-0	2-1	2-1	0-2	1-1		1-0	3-1	1-0	2-2	3-1
Pescara Calcio	4-3	2-0	2-0	0-1	0-2	2-4	1-2	1-4	5-1	2-3	4-5	3-0	0-2		1-1	2-2	2-2	2-2
AS Roma	2-1	2-2	2-3	1-1	1-1	3-1	3-0	4-1	2-1	0-0	0-1	1-1	1-0	0-1		0-0	4-5	1-1
UC Sampdoria	3-1	2-3	1-0	2-0	2-0	3-3	4-1	1-3	1-1	3-3	1-2	3-1	2-1	1-1	2-2		0-1	2-0
Torino Calcio	4-1	1-1	1-0	0-5	1-1	1-1	1-1	1-2	1-2	1-1	1-1	0-1	3-0	3-1	0-0	2-2		1-0
Udinese Calcio	2-0	1-2	2-2	2-1	4-0	3-2	3-0	2-1	0-0	0-0	0-0	2-0	1-0	5-2	1-2	1-2	1-0	

	Serie "A"	Pd	Wn	Dw	Ls	GF	GA	Pts	
1.	MILAN AC (MILANO)	34	18	14	2	65	32	50	
2.	FC Internazionale (Milano)	34	17	12	5	59	36	46	
3.	Parma AC (Parma)	34	16	9	9	47	34	41	
4.	Juventus FC (Torino)	34	15	9	10	49	47	39	
5.	SS Lazio (Roma)	34	13	12	9	65	51	38	
6.	Cagliari Calcio (Cagliari)	34	14	9	11	45	33	37	
7.	UC Sampdoria (Genova)	34	12	12	10	50	48	36	
8.	Atalanta BC (Bergamo)	34	14	8	12	42	44	36	
9.	Torino Calcio (Torino)	34	9	17	8	38	38	35	
10.	AS Roma (Roma)	34	8	17	9	42	39	33	
11.	SSC Napoli (Napoli)	34	10	12	12	49	50	32	
12.	Foggia Calcio (Foggia)	34	10	12	12	39	55	32	
13.	Genoa CFC (Genova)	34	7	17	10	41	55	31	
14.	Udinese Calcio (Udine)	34	10	10	14	42	48	30	PO
15.	Brescia Calcio (Brescia)	34	9	12	13	36	44	30	R
16.	AC Fiorentina (Firenze)	34	8	14	12	53	56	30	R
17.	Ancona Calcio (Ancona)	34	6	7	21	39	73	19	R
18.	Pescara Calcio (Pescara)	34	6	5	23	47	75	17	R
		612	202	208	202	858	858	612	

Top goalscorers

1)	Giuseppe SIGNORI	(SS Lazio)	26
2)	Roberto BAGGIO	(Juventus FC)	21
	Abel BALBO	(Udinese Calcio)	21
4)	Rubén SOSA	(FC Internazionale)	20
5)	Gabriel BATISTUTA	(AC Fiorentina)	16
	Daniel FONSECA	(SSC Napoli)	16

Relegation Play-Off

Udinese Calcio (Udine) 3-1 Brescia Calcio (Brescia)

	Serie "B"	Pd	Wn	Dw	Ls	GF	GA	Pts	
1.	AC Reggiana (Reggio Emilia)	38	18	17	3	41	16	53	P
2.	US Cremonese (Cremona)	38	19	13	6	63	35	51	P
3.	Piacenza Calcio (Piacenza)	38	17	14	7	42	26	48	P
4.	US Lecce (Lecce)	38	15	18	5	45	38	48	P
5.	Padova Calcio (Padova)	38	17	13	8	45	35	47	
6.	Ascoli Calcio 1898 (Ascoli Piceno)	38	16	14	8	57	35	46	
7.	AS Cosenza (Cosenza)	38	14	15	9	37	27	43	
8.	SC Pisa (Pisa)	38	13	14	11	25	26	40	
9.	AC Cesena (Cesena)	38	12	14	12	37	35	38	
10.	AS Bari (Bari)	38	14	10	14	43	44	38	
11.	AC Venezia (Venezia)	38	11	14	13	41	41	36	
12.	Hellas Verona FC (Verona)	38	10	15	13	30	34	35	
13.	AS Lucchese Libertas (Lucca)	38	6	21	11	35	38	33	
14.	Monza Calcio (Monza)	38	6	21	11	24	31	33	
15.	Modena FC (Modena)	38	10	13	15	34	43	33	
16.	AS Fidelis Andria (Andria)	38	6	20	12	27	34	32	
17.	S.P.A.L. (Ferrara)	38	8	15	15	30	42	21	R
18.	Bologna FC (Bologna)	38	9	12	17	38	55	30	R
19.	AS Taranto (Taranto)	38	6	15	17	30	51	27	R
20.	Ternana Calcio (Terni)	38	4	10	24	25	63	18	R
		760	231	298	231	749	749	760	

Promoted to Serie "B": AS Acireale (Acireale), US Città di Palermo (Palermo), US Ravenna (Ravenna), Vicenza Calcio (Vicenza).

Coppa Italia Final (1st leg) (Torino - 12/06/93)

TORINO CALCIO (TORINO) 3-0 AS Roma (Roma)

Benedetti 17' o.g. Cois 53', Fortunato 83'

Torino: Marchegiani, Bruno, Mussi, D.Fortunato, Annoni (Cois 46'), Fusi, Sordo (Sergio 77'), Venturin, Aguilera, Scifo, Silenzi.

Roma: Fimiani, Garzja, Petruzzi (Muzzi 46'), Bonacina, Benedetti, Aldair (Comi 64'), Mihajlovic, Hässler, Piacentini, Giannin, Rizzitelli.

Coppa Italia Final (2nd leg) (Roma – 19/06/93)

TORINO CALCIO (TORINO)	2-5	AS Roma (Roma)
Silenzi 48', 53'		*Giannini 22' pen., 50' pen., 55' pen., Rizzitelli 47', Mihajlovic 65'*

AS Roma (Roma) won on the away goals rule.

Roma: Fimiani, Garzja, Piacentini (Salsano 90'), Bonacina (Muzzi 89'), Benedetti, Comi, Mihajlovic, Hässler, Carnevale, Giannini, Rizitelli.

Torino: Marchegiani, Bruno, Mussi, D.Fortunato, Cois, Fusi, Sordo (Falcone 89'), Venturin, Aguilera (Casagrande 77'), Scifo, Silenzi.

Semi-Finals

AS Roma (Roma)	2-0, 0-1	Milan AC (Milano)
Torino Calcio (Torino)	1-1, 2-2	Juventus FC (Torino)

Torino Calcio (Torino) won on the away goals rule.

Quarter-Finals

Juventus FC (Torino)	2-1, 1-1	Parma AC (Parma)
SS Lazio (Roma)	2-2, 2-3	Torino Calcio (Torino)
Milan AC (Milano)	0-0, 3-0	FC Internazionale (Milano)
SSC Napoli (Napoli)	0-0, 0-2	AS Roma (Roma)

1993-94

1993-1994 Serie "A"	Atalanta BC	Cagliari Calcio	US Cremonese	Foggia Calcio	Genoa CFC	FC Internazionale	Juventus FC	SS Lazio	US Lecce	Milan AC	SSC Napoli	Parma AC	Piacenza Calcio	AC Reggiana	AS Roma	UC Sampdoria	Torino Calcio	Udinese Calcio
Atalanta BC		5-2	0-0	1-1	2-1	2-1	1-3	1-1	3-4	0-1	1-1	0-2	0-0	2-1	1-1	1-4	2-2	1-1
Cagliari Calcio	1-1		0-0	1-1	0-0	1-0	0-1	4-1	2-1	0-0	1-2	0-4	2-0	3-0	1-1	0-0	2-1	1-2
US Cremonese	2-0	3-1		2-0	1-1	1-4	1-1	1-0	2-1	0-2	2-0	0-0	4-0	1-1	1-1	0-0	1-1	1-1
Foggia Calcio	1-1	0-1	1-1		3-0	1-1	1-1	4-1	5-0	1-1	0-1	3-2	1-0	1-0	1-1	1-2	1-0	2-2
Genoa CFC	2-1	1-1	1-0	1-4		1-0	1-1	1-1	2-0	0-0	0-0	0-4	0-1	0-0	2-0	1-1	1-1	3-0
FC Internazionale	1-2	3-3	2-1	3-1	1-3		2-2	1-2	4-1	1-2	0-0	3-2	2-0	2-1	2-2	3-0	0-0	1-0
Juventus FC	2-1	1-1	1-0	2-0	4-0	1-0		6-1	5-1	0-1	1-0	4-0	2-0	4-0	0-0	3-1	3-2	1-0
SS Lazio	3-1	4-0	4-2	0-0	4-0	0-0	3-1		3-0	0-1	3-0	2-1	1-0	2-0	1-0	1-1	1-2	2-1
US Lecce	5-1	0-1	2-4	0-2	0-0	1-3	1-1	1-2		0-1	0-1	1-1	1-1	2-4	0-2	0-3	1-2	1-0
Milan AC	2-0	2-1	1-0	2-1	1-0	2-1	1-1	0-0	0-0		2-1	1-1	2-0	0-1	2-0	1-0	1-0	2-2
SSC Napoli	4-0	1-2	2-1	1-1	1-1	0-0	0-0	1-2	3-1	1-0		2-0	0-0	5-0	1-1	1-2	0-0	2-1
Parma AC	2-1	3-1	2-1	3-0	2-1	4-1	2-0	2-0	1-0	0-0	1-3		0-0	1-0	0-2	2-1	3-0	0-1
Piacenza Calcio	4-0	1-1	1-1	5-4	1-1	2-1	0-0	1-2	2-1	0-0	1-1	1-1		3-2	1-0	2-0	0-3	0-0
AC Reggiana	3-0	3-1	2-0	0-0	1-1	1-0	0-0	0-0	1-0	0-1	1-0	2-0	1-1		0-0	1-1	1-0	1-1
AS Roma	2-1	2-0	1-2	0-0	1-1	1-1	2-1	1-1	3-0	0-2	2-3	2-0	3-1	0-0		0-1	2-0	0-2
UC Sampdoria	3-1	1-2	3-1	6-0	1-1	3-1	1-1	3-4	2-1	3-2	4-1	1-1	2-1	1-0	0-1		1-0	6-2
Torino Calcio	2-1	2-1	1-1	1-4	2-0	2-0	1-1	1-1	3-0	0-0	1-1	1-2	1-0	2-0	1-1	2-3		1-0
Udinese Calcio	0-0	1-1	3-3	3-0	0-4	0-1	0-3	2-2	2-1	0-0	3-1	0-1	2-2	2-1	0-0	0-2	1-1	

	Serie "A"	Pd	Wn	Dw	Ls	GF	GA	Pts	
1.	MILAN AC (MILANO)	34	19	12	3	36	15	50	
2.	Juventus FC (Torino)	34	17	13	4	58	25	47	
3.	UC Sampdoria (Genova)	34	18	8	8	64	39	44	
4.	SS Lazio (Roma)	34	17	10	7	55	40	44	
5.	Parma AC (Parma)	34	17	7	10	50	35	41	
6.	SSC Napoli (Napoli)	34	12	12	10	41	35	36	
7.	AS Roma (Roma)	34	10	15	9	35	30	35	
8.	Torino Calcio (Torino)	34	11	12	11	39	37	34	
9.	Foggia Calcio (Foggia)	34	10	13	11	46	46	33	
10.	US Cremonese (Cremona)	34	9	14	11	41	41	32	
11.	Genoa CFC (Genova)	34	8	16	10	32	40	32	
12.	Cagliari Calcio (Cagliari)	34	10	12	12	39	48	32	
13.	FC Internazionale (Milano)	34	11	9	14	46	45	31	
14.	AC Reggiana (Reggio Emilia)	34	10	11	13	29	37	31	
15.	Piacenza Calcio (Piacenza)	34	8	14	12	32	43	30	R
16.	Udinese Calcio (Udine)	34	7	14	13	35	48	28	R
17.	Atalanta BC (Bergamo)	34	5	11	18	35	65	21	R
18.	US Lecce (Lecce)	34	3	5	26	28	72	11	R
		612	202	208	202	741	741	612	

Top goalscorers

1)	Giuseppe SIGNORI	(SS Lazio)	23
2)	Gianfranco ZOLA	(Parma AC)	18
3)	Roberto BAGGIO	(Juventus FC)	17
	Andrea SILENZI	(Torino Calcio)	17
5)	Rubén SOSA	(FC Internazionale)	16

NAC Mantova (Mantova) changed their club name to Mantova 1994 Calcio (Mantova) for the next season.

	Serie "B"	Pd	Wn	Dw	Ls	GF	GA	Pts	
1.	AC Fiorentina (Firenze)	38	17	16	5	53	19	50	P
2.	AS Bari (Bari)	38	14	17	7	49	27	45	P
3.	Brescia Calcio (Brescia)	38	15	14	9	67	53	44	P
4.	Padova Calcio (Padova)	38	11	21	6	37	28	43	P
5.	AC Cesena (Cesena)	38	17	9	12	49	48	43	PO
6.	AC Venezia (Venezia)	38	13	14	11	43	40	40	
7.	Ascoli Calcio 1898 (Ascoli Piceno)	38	13	14	11	38	38	40	
8.	Ancona Calcio (Ancona)	38	11	17	10	46	43	39	
9.	AS Fidelis Andria (Andria)	38	8	23	7	28	28	39	
10.	AS Lucchese Libertas (Lucca)	38	8	21	9	34	35	37	
11.	Vicenza Calcio (Vicenza)	38	9	19	10	30	33	37	
12.	Hellas Verona FC (Verona)	38	11	15	12	36	42	37	
13.	AS Cosenza (Cosenza)	38	10	17	11	30	38	37	
14.	US Città di Palermo (Palermo)	38	12	12	14	32	38	36	
15.	Pescara Calcio (Pescara)	38	12	14	12	50	54	35	-3
16.	AS Acireale (Acireale)	38	8	19	11	32	39	35	PO
17.	SC Pisa (Pisa)	38	10	15	13	36	40	35	R
18.	US Ravenna (Ravenna)	38	8	15	15	36	47	31	R
19.	Modena FC (Modena)	38	8	15	15	29	45	31	R
20.	Monza Calcio (Monza)	38	5	13	20	27	47	23	R
		760	220	320	220	782	782	757	

Note: Pescara Calcio (Pescara) had 3 points deducted by the F.I.G.C. committee.

Promotion Play-Off

Padova Calcio (Padova)	2-1	AC Cesena (Cesena)

Relegation Play-Off

AS Acireale (Acireale)	0-0 (aet – 4-3 penalties)	SC Pisa (Pisa)

Promoted to Serie "B": AC Chievo (Verona), Como Calcio (Como), AC Perugia (Perugia) and Salernitana Sport (Salerno).

Coppa Italia Final (1st leg) (Ancona – 06/04/94)

Ancona Calcio (Ancona)	0-0	UC Sampdoria (GENOVA)

Ancona: Armellini, Sogliano, Centofanti, Pecoraro, Mazzarano, Glonek, Lupo, Bruniera (Caccia 49'), Agostini, De Angelis, Vecchiola.

Sampdoria: Pagliuca, Dall'Igna, Serena, Gullit, Vierchowod, Sacchetti, Lombardo, Jugovic (Invernizzi 70'), Platt, Mancini, Evani.

Coppa Italia Final (2nd leg) (Genova – 20/04/94)

Ancona Calcio (Ancona)	1-6	UC Sampdoria (GENOVA)
Lupo 71'		*Vecchiola 50' o.g., Lombardo 57', 75', Vierchowod 66', Bertarelli 80' pen., Evani 85' pen*

Sampdoria: Pagliuca, Invernizzi, Serena, Gullit, Vierchowod, Sacchetti (Manini 87'), Lombardo, Jugovic, Platt, Bertarelli (Salsano 87'), Evani.

Ancona: Nista, Fontana, Sogliano, Pecoraro, Mazzarano, Glonek, Lupo, Gadda (Caccia 59'), Agostini, De Angelis (Bruniera 68'), Vecchiola.

Semi-Finals

Ancona Calcio (Ancona)	1-0, 0-0	Torino Calcio (Torino)
UC Sampdoria (Genova)	2-1, 1-0	Parma AC (Parma)

Quarter-Finals

Foggia Calcio (Foggia)	0-3, 1-6	Parma AC (Parma)
Piacenza Calcio (Piacenza)	2-2, 1-2	Torino Calcio (Torino)
UC Sampdoria (Genova)	1-0, 1-1	FC Internazionale (Milano)
AC Venezia (Venezia)	0-0, 0-2	Ancona Calcio (Ancona)

1994-95

1994-1995 Serie "A"	AS Bari	Brescia Calcio	Cagliari Calcio	US Cremonses	AC Fiorentina	Foggia Calcio	Genoa CFC	FC Internazionale	Juventus FC	SS Lazio	Milan AC	SSC Napoli	Padova Calcio	Parma AC	AC Reggiana	AS Roma	UC Sampdoria	Torino Calcio
AS Bari		3-0	0-0	2-0	2-2	2-1	4-1	0-1	0-2	0-1	3-5	1-1	0-1	1-2	1-0	2-2	1-2	3-1
Brescia Calcio	1-2		2-3	1-2	2-4	1-0	1-2	0-0	1-1	0-1	0-5	1-2	1-3	1-2	1-0	0-0	0-0	1-4
Cagliari Calcio	2-1	2-0		1-0	2-0	2-1	1-0	1-1	3-0	1-1	1-1	0-1	2-0	2-0	4-2	0-1	0-2	1-0
US Cremonese	0-0	0-0	2-0		0-0	1-3	4-1	0-1	1-2	0-0	1-0	2-0	3-0	1-1	2-1	2-5	2-0	3-0
AC Fiorentina	2-0	4-0	2-1	3-1		1-1	3-1	2-2	1-4	1-1	1-2	4-0	4-1	1-1	1-1	1-0	2-2	6-3
Foggia Calcio	2-2	3-1	2-0	0-1	2-1		2-1	0-0	2-0	0-1	1-3	1-1	4-1	0-0	1-0	0-1	1-1	0-2
Genoa CFC	1-1	1-0	1-1	0-1	1-1	3-0		2-1	0-4	1-2	1-1	3-3	2-1	0-0	3-1	1-0	2-1	1-0
FC Internazionale	1-2	1-0	1-2	0-0	3-1	3-0	2-0		0-0	0-2	3-1	0-2	2-1	1-1	1-0	0-1	2-0	2-1
Juventus FC	2-0	2-1	3-1	1-0	3-2	2-0	1-1	0-0		0-3	1-0	1-0	0-1	4-0	3-1	3-0	1-0	1-2
SS Lazio	1-2	1-0	0-0	1-0	8-2	7-1	4-0	4-1	3-4		4-0	5-1	5-1	2-2	2-0	0-3	1-0	3-0
Milan AC	0-1	1-0	1-1	3-1	2-0	3-0	1-0	1-1	0-2	2-1		1-1	1-0	1-1	2-1	1-0	0-0	5-1
SSC Napoli	3-0	1-1	1-1	1-0	2-5	2-1	1-0	1-3	0-2	3-2	1-0		3-3	1-0	1-0	0-0	2-0	1-1
Padova Calcio	0-2	2-0	2-1	3-2	0-1	0-0	1-1	1-0	1-2	2-0	2-0	2-0		0-3	3-0	0-0	1-4	4-2
Parma AC	1-0	4-0	2-1	2-0	3-0	2-0	0-0	3-0	1-3	2-0	2-3	2-0	1-0		2-1	1-0	3-2	2-0
AC Reggiana	0-1	2-0	0-0	2-0	1-1	1-1	0-1	0-1	1-2	0-0	0-4	1-2	3-0	2-2		1-4	0-2	1-0
AS Roma	2-0	3-0	1-1	1-1	2-0	1-1	3-0	3-1	3-0	0-2	0-0	1-1	2-0	1-0	2-0		1-0	1-1
UC Sampdoria	1-1	2-1	5-0	2-1	2-2	1-1	3-2	2-2	0-1	3-1	0-3	0-0	5-0	3-1	2-1	3-0		1-1
Torino Calcio	2-0	2-0	3-2	1-1	1-0	2-0	0-0	0-2	3-2	2-0	0-0	1-1	2-0	0-2	4-0	2-2	0-0	

	Serie "A"	Pd	Wn	Dw	Ls	GF	GA	Pts	
1.	JUVENTUS FC (TORINO)	34	23	4	7	59	32	73	
2.	SS Lazio (Roma)	34	19	6	9	69	34	63	
3.	Parma AC (Parma)	34	18	9	7	51	31	63	
4.	Milan AC (Milano)	34	17	9	8	53	32	60	
5.	AS Roma (Roma)	34	16	11	7	46	25	59	
6.	FC Internazionale (Milano)	34	14	10	10	39	34	52	
7.	SSC Napoli (Napoli)	34	13	12	9	40	45	51	
8.	UC Sampdoria (Genova)	34	13	11	10	51	37	50	
9.	Cagliari Calcio (Cagliari)	34	13	10	11	40	39	49	
10.	AC Fiorentina (Firenze)	34	12	11	11	61	57	47	
11.	Torino Calcio (Torino)	34	12	9	13	44	48	45	
12.	AS Bari (Bari)	34	12	8	14	40	43	44	
13.	US Cremonese (Cremona)	34	11	8	15	35	38	41	
14.	Padova Calcio (Padova)	34	12	4	18	37	58	40	PO
15.	Genoa CFC (Genova)	34	10	10	14	34	49	40	R
16.	Foggia Calcio (Foggia)	34	8	10	16	32	50	34	R
17.	AC Reggiana (Reggio Emilia)	34	4	6	24	24	56	18	R
18.	Brescia Calcio (Brescia)	34	2	6	26	18	65	12	R
		612	229	154	229	773	773	841	

Top goalscorers

1)	Gabriel BATISTUTA	(AC Fiorentina)	26
2)	Abel BALBO	(AS Roma)	22
3)	Ruggiero RIZZITELLI	(Torino Calcio)	19
	Gianfranco ZOLA	(Parma AC)	19
5)	Giuseppe SIGNORI	(SS Lazio)	17
	Sandro TOVALIERI	(AS Bari)	17

Relegation Play-Off

Genoa CFC (Genova) 1-1 (aet – 4-5 penalties) Padova Calcio (Padova)

	Serie "B"	Pd	Wn	Dw	Ls	GF	GA	Pts	
1.	Piacenza Calcio (Piacenza)	38	19	14	5	55	27	71	P
2.	Udinese Calcio (Udine)	38	19	13	6	63	35	70	P
3.	Vicenza Calcio (Vicenza)	38	17	17	4	54	26	68	P
4.	Atalanta BC (Bergamo)	38	17	15	6	49	36	66	P
5.	Salernitana Sport (Salerno)	38	16	13	9	57	40	61	
6.	Ancona Calcio (Ancona)	38	16	10	12	55	50	58	
7.	AC Perugia (Perugia)	38	12	18	8	47	35	54	
8.	AC Cesena (Cesena)	38	12	15	11	44	43	51	
9.	AC Venezia (Venezia)	38	14	8	16	46	44	50	
10.	Hellas Verona FC (Verona)	38	11	15	12	40	40	48	
11.	Pescara Calcio (Pescara)	38	11	13	14	50	63	46	
12.	AS Fidelis Andria (Andria)	38	8	20	10	36	41	44	
13.	AC Chievo (Verona)	38	10	14	14	35	38	44	
14.	US Città di Palermo (Palermo)	38	10	14	14	33	35	44	
15.	AS Lucchese Libertas (Lucca)	38	8	18	12	49	54	42	
16.	AS Cosenza (Cosenza)	38	11	18	9	38	35	42	-9
17.	AS Acireale (Acireale)	38	10	11	17	27	42	41	R
18.	Ascoli Calcio 1898 (Ascoli Piceno)	38	7	13	18	27	57	34	R
19.	Como Calcio (Como)	38	7	12	19	25	58	33	R
20.	US Lecce (Lecce)	38	5	9	14	36	67	24	R
		760	240	280	240	866	866	991	

Note: AC Chievo (Verona) had 9 points deducted by the F.I.G.C. committee.

Promoted to Serie "B": US Avellino (Avellino), Bologna FC (Bologna), AC Pistoiese (Pistoia), AS Reggina (Reggio Calabria).

Coppa Italia Final (1st leg) (Torino – 07/06/95)

JUVENTUS FC (TORINO) 1-0 Parma AC (Parma)

Porrini 10'

Juventus: Rampulla (Squizzi 70'), Ferrara, Al.Orlando, Torricelli, Porrini, Paulo Sousa (Fusi 78'), Di Livio, Deschamps (Marocchi 60'), Vialli, Del Piero, Ravanelli.

Parma: Bucci, Mussi, Di Chiara, Minotti, Apolloni, Fernando, F. Couto, Branca, D.Baggio (Asprilla 82'), Crippa, Zola, Pin (Fiore 75').

Coppa Italia Final (2nd leg) (Parma - 10/06/95)

JUVENTUS FC (TORINO)	2-0	Parma AC (Parma)

Porrini 26', Ravanelli 54'

Parma: Bucci, Mussi, Di Chiara, Minotti, Apolloni, F.Couto (Asprilla 46'), Branca, D.Baggio, Crippa, Zola, Fiore (Sensini 55').

Juventus: Rampulla, Ferrara, Torricelli, Tacchinardi, Porrini, Marocchi (Conte 67'), Di Livio, Deschamps, Vialli (A.Orlando 74'), Del Piero, Ravanelli.

Semi-Finals

Foggia Calcio (Foggia)	1-1, 1-3	Parma AC (Parma)
SS Lazio (Roma)	0-1, 1-2	Juventus FC (Torino)

Quarter-Finals

FC Internazionale (Milano)	1-0, 0-2	Foggia Calcio (Foggia)
Juventus FC (Torino)	3-0, 1-3	AS Roma (Roma)
SS Lazio (Roma)	1-0, 2-1	SSC Napoli (Napoli)
Parma AC (Parma)	2-0, 2-1	AC Fiorentina (Firenze)

1995-96

1995-1996 Serie "A"	Atalanta BC	AS Bari	Cagliari Calcio	US Cremonese	AC Fiorentina	FC Internazionale	Juventus FC	SS Lazio	Milan AC	SSC Napoli	Padova Calcio	Parma AC	Piacenza Calcio	AS Roma	UC Sampdoria	Torino Calcio	Udinese Calcio	Vicenza Calcio
Atalanta BC		1-2	3-0	1-1	1-3	1-1	0-1	1-3	0-1	1-3	3-0	1-1	2-0	2-1	3-2	1-0	0-0	3-1
AS Bari	1-3		3-0	2-1	1-1	4-1	2-2	3-3	1-0	1-1	2-1	1-1	0-0	1-2	1-3	2-2	4-2	0-2
Cagliari Calcio	2-0	4-2		1-0	0-0	0-0	0-0	0-1	1-2	2-0	0-1	2-0	0-0	0-2	3-0	1-0	4-1	2-0
US Cremonese	1-1	7-1	3-1		0-0	2-4	3-3	2-1	0-0	1-1	2-1	0-2	0-0	0-1	0-0	1-1	2-2	1-1
AC Fiorentina	1-0	3-2	3-1	3-2		1-1	0-1	2-0	2-2	3-0	6-4	1-0	2-1	1-4	2-2	2-0	3-0	1-1
FC Internazionale	1-0	3-0	4-0	2-0	1-1		1-2	0-0	1-1	4-0	8-2	1-1	0-0	2-0	0-2	4-0	2-1	1-0
Juventus FC	1-0	1-1	4-1	4-1	1-0	1-0		4-2	1-1	1-1	3-1	1-0	2-0	0-2	0-3	5-0	2-1	1-0
SS Lazio	5-1	4-3	4-0	2-1	4-0	0-1	4-0		0-1	1-0	2-0	2-1	4-1	1-0	6-3	1-1	2-2	3-0
Milan AC	3-0	3-2	3-2	7-1	3-1	0-1	2-1	0-0		0-0	1-0	3-0	3-0	3-1	3-0	1-1	2-1	4-0
SSC Napoli	2-0	1-0	0-0	0-0	0-2	2-1	0-1	1-0	0-1		2-0	1-1	0-0	0-2	1-0	1-0	2-1	1-1
Padova Calcio	3-2	3-0	2-1	1-2	0-1	2-1	0-5	1-3	1-2	4-2		1-3	1-1	1-2	1-1	1-1	2-3	3-2
Parma AC	2-0	3-1	4-0	2-0	3-0	2-1	1-1	2-1	0-0	1-0	2-1		3-2	1-1	1-0	1-0	1-0	0-1
Piacenza Calcio	2-2	3-2	1-1	2-1	0-1	1-0	0-4	2-1	0-2	0-1	4-0	2-1		1-0	3-2	1-0	0-2	0-1
AS Roma	0-1	2-1	1-1	3-0	2-2	1-0	2-2	0-0	1-2	4-1	2-0	1-1	2-1		3-1	1-0	2-1	1-1
UC Sampdoria	2-3	2-0	1-2	2-0	2-1	0-0	2-0	3-3	3-0	2-2	3-1	3-0	3-0	1-1		1-0	1-0	2-2
Torino Calcio	0-1	3-1	1-1	1-0	0-3	0-1	1-2	0-2	1-1	0-0	2-0	2-2	4-2	2-2	1-1		2-0	1-0
Udinese Calcio	3-0	1-2	1-0	3-2	1-0	1-2	1-0	1-1	0-2	3-2	3-1	0-0	0-0	1-1	2-4	1-0		1-1
Vicenza Calcio	1-0	2-0	0-1	1-0	1-0	1-1	2-1	1-0	1-1	3-0	2-1	0-1	1-1	2-1	2-2	2-1	0-1	

	Serie "A"	Pd	Wn	Dw	Ls	GF	GA	Pts	
1.	MILAN AC (MILANO)	34	21	10	3	60	24	73	
2.	Juventus FC (Torino)	34	19	8	7	58	35	65	
3.	SS Lazio (Roma)	34	17	8	9	66	38	59	
4.	AC Fiorentina (Firenze)	34	17	8	9	53	41	59	
5.	AS Roma (Roma)	34	16	10	8	51	34	58	
6.	Parma AC (Parma)	34	16	10	8	44	31	58	
7.	FC Internazionale (Milano)	34	15	9	10	51	30	54	
8.	UC Sampdoria (Genova)	34	14	10	10	59	47	52	
9.	Vicenza Calcio (Vicenza)	34	13	10	11	36	37	49	
10.	Cagliari Calcio (Cagliari)	34	11	8	15	34	47	41	
11.	Udinese Calcio (Udine)	34	11	8	15	41	49	41	
12.	SSC Napoli (Napoli)	34	10	11	13	28	41	41	
13.	Atalanta BC (Bergamo)	34	11	6	17	38	50	39	
14.	FC Piacenza (Piacenza)	34	9	10	15	31	48	37	*
15.	AS Bari (Bari)	34	8	8	18	49	71	32	R
16.	Torino Calcio (Torino)	34	6	11	17	28	46	29	R
17.	US Cremonese (Cremona)	34	5	12	17	37	57	27	R
18.	Padova Calcio (Padova)	34	7	3	24	41	79	24	R
		612	226	160	226	805	805	838	

Top goalscorers

1)	Igor PROTTI	(AS Bari)	24	
	Giuseppe SIGNORI	(SS Lazio)	24	
3)	Enrico CHIESA	(UC Sampdoria)	22	
4)	Gabriel BATISTUTA	(AC Fiorentina)	19	
	Marco BRANCO	(AS Roma/FC Internazionale)	19	(17/2)

* FC Piacenza (Piacenza) changed their club name in July 1995 from Piacenza Calcio (Piacenza).

	Serie "B"	Pd	Wn	Dw	Ls	GF	GA	Pts	
1.	Bologna FC 1909 (Bologna)	38	16	17	5	42	23	65	P*
2.	Hellas Verona FC (Verona)	38	17	12	9	50	33	63	P
3.	AC Perugia (Perugia)	38	16	13	9	52	42	61	P
4.	AC Reggiana (Reggio Emilia)	38	16	13	9	42	32	61	P
5.	Salernitana Sport (Salerno)	38	15	13	10	46	32	58	
6.	AS Lucchese Libertas (Lucca)	38	13	15	10	45	43	54	
7.	Genoa CFC (Genova)	38	14	10	14	56	52	52	
8.	US Città di Palermo (Palermo)	38	12	16	10	36	35	52	
9.	Pescara Calcio (Pescara)	38	13	11	14	47	50	50	
10.	AC Cesena (Cesena)	38	13	10	15	50	49	49	
11.	Foggia Calcio (Foggia)	38	13	9	16	31	50	48	
12.	Cosenza Calcio (Cosenza)	38	11	15	12	47	51	48	*
13.	AC Venezia (Venezia)	38	11	15	12	34	39	48	
14.	Reggina Calcio (Reggio Calabria)	38	11	14	13	38	46	47	*
15.	AC Chievo (Verona)	38	9	20	9	37	30	47	
16.	Brescia Calcio (Brescia)	38	12	10	16	48	49	46	
17.	AS Fidelis Andria (Andria)	38	10	15	13	42	45	45	R
18.	US Avellino (Avellino)	38	11	10	17	39	54	43	R
19.	Ancona Calcio (Ancona)	38	11	9	18	42	51	42	R
20.	AC Pistoiese (Pistoia)	38	7	11	20	35	53	32	R
		760	251	258	251	859	859	1011	

* Bologna FC 1909 (Bologna) changed their club name pre-season from Bologna FC (Bologna).
Cosenza Calcio (Cosenza) changed their club name pre-season from AS Cosenza (Cosenza).
Reggina Calcio (Reggio Calabria) changed their club name pre-season from AS Reggina (Reggio Calabria).

Promoted to Serie "B": Castel di Sangro Calcio (Castel di Sangro), Empoli FC (Empoli), US Lecce (Lecce) and US Ravenna (Ravenna).

Coppa Italia Final (1st leg) (Firenze – 01/05/96 – 40,000)

AC FIORENTINA (FIRENZE)	1-0	Atalanta BC (Bergamo)

Batistuta 52'

Fiorentina: Toldo, Carnasciali, Padalino, Sottil (Bigica 86'), Amoruso, Piacentini, Rui Costa, Schwarz, M.Orlando (Banchelli 46'), Batistuta, Robbiati.

Atalanta: Ferron, Pavone (Salvatori 78'), Valentini, Montero, Herrera, Paganin, Bonacina, Fortunato, Gallo (Sgrò 78'), Morfeo, Tovalieri (Pisani 84').

Coppa Italia Final (2nd leg) (Bergamo – 18/05/96 – 25,000)

AC FIORENTINA (FIRENZE)	2-0	Atalanta BC (Bergamo)

Amoruso 48', Batistuta 61'

Atalanta: Ferron, Herrera, Valentini, Montero, Paganin (Rotella 50'), Pavone (Temelin 59'), Bonacina, Fortunato, Gallo (Salvatori 68'), Tovalieri, Morfeo.

Fiorentina: Toldo (Mareggini 89'), Carnasciali, Padalino, Malusci, Amoruso, Cois, Piacentini, Bigica, Rui Costa, Batistuta, Flachi (Robbiati 63', M.Orlando 89').

Semi-Finals

Bologna FC 1909 (Bologna)	1-1, 0-2	Atalanta BC (Bergamo)
AC Fiorentina (Firenze)	3-1, 1-0	FC Internazionale (Milano)

Quarter-Finals

Bologna FC 1909 (Bologna)	1-1, 1-1 (aet – 7-6 penalties)	Milan AC (Milano)
Cagliari Calcio (Cagliari)	1-0, 2-4	Atalanta BC (Bergamo)
AC Fiorentina (Firenze)	1-0, 2-1	US Palermo (Palermo)
FC Internazionale (Milano)	1-1, 1-0	SS Lazio (Roma)

1996-97

1996-1997 Serie "A"	Atalanta BC	Bologna 1909 FC	Cagliari Calcio	AC Fiorentina	Hellas Verona FC	FC Internazionale	Juventus FC	SS Lazio	Milan AC	SSC Napoli	Parma AC	AC Perugia	Piacenza Calcio	AC Reggiana	AS Roma	UC Sampdoria	Udinese Calcio	Vicenza Calcio
Atalanta BC		1-1	4-1	2-2	1-0	1-1	1-1	2-1	0-2	2-2	1-2	2-2	4-0	1-0	0-4	4-0	1-0	3-1
Bologna FC 1909	3-1		3-0	0-2	6-1	2-2	0-1	1-0	1-2	2-1	0-1	0-0	1-1	3-2	3-2	2-1	0-0	0-0
Cagliari Calcio	2-0	2-2		4-1	3-2	1-2	0-0	0-0	1-1	1-1	0-1	2-1	1-0	1-1	2-1	3-4	1-2	2-1
AC Fiorentina	0-0	3-2	2-0		2-0	0-0	1-1	0-0	1-0	3-0	1-0	4-1	1-1	3-0	2-1	1-1	2-3	2-4
Hellas Verona FC	1-1	0-2	2-2	2-1		0-1	0-2	1-1	3-1	2-0	1-2	2-0	0-0	2-4	2-1	1-1	3-2	2-2
FC Internazionale	2-0	0-2	2-2	2-2	2-1		0-0	1-1	3-1	3-2	3-1	1-0	2-0	3-1	3-1	3-4	1-1	0-1
Juventus FC	0-0	1-0	2-1	1-0	3-2	2-0		2-2	0-0	1-1	1-1	2-1	4-1	3-1	3-0	0-0	0-3	2-0
SS Lazio	3-2	1-2	2-1	1-0	4-1	2-2	0-2		3-0	3-2	2-1	4-1	2-0	6-1	0-0	1-1	0-1	0-2
Milan AC	1-1	2-0	0-1	2-0	4-1	1-1	1-6	2-2		3-1	0-1	3-0	0-0	3-1	1-1	2-3	2-1	1-0
SSC Napoli	0-1	3-2	1-1	2-2	1-0	1-2	0-0	1-0	0-0		2-1	4-2	1-1	1-0	1-0	1-1	1-1	1-0
Parma AC	0-0	1-0	3-2	0-0	1-0	1-0	1-0	2-0	1-1	3-0		1-2	1-0	3-2	0-0	3-0	0-2	3-0
AC Perugia	3-1	5-1	3-2	1-1	3-1	0-0	1-2	1-2	1-0	1-1	1-2		1-1	1-3	2-0	1-0	2-1	1-1
Piacenza Calcio	3-1	1-1	1-1	1-1	2-0	0-3	1-1	1-3	3-2	1-0	0-0	2-1		3-0	0-0	2-2	0-0	1-0
AC Reggiana	0-3	1-3	0-3	0-0	2-2	1-1	1-1	0-2	0-3	1-1	0-0	1-4	0-0		1-1	1-1	0-0	0-0
AS Roma	0-2	1-1	3-1	3-3	4-3	1-1	1-1	1-1	3-0	1-0	0-1	4-1	3-1	2-2		1-4	0-3	2-0
UC Sampdoria	2-0	1-2	4-1	1-1	0-0	1-2	0-1	1-0	2-1	0-1	1-1	5-2	3-0	3-0	1-2		4-0	2-1
Udinese Calcio	2-0	2-2	1-0	2-0	3-0	0-1	1-4	2-3	1-1	2-2	3-1	2-1	4-0	2-1	1-0	4-5		1-1
Vicenza Calcio	4-1	2-0	2-0	3-2	0-0	1-1	2-1	0-2	2-0	2-2	1-1	4-1	1-1	2-0	0-2	1-1	2-0	

	Serie "A"	Pd	Wn	Dw	Ls	GF	GA	Pts	
1.	JUVENTUS FC (TORINO)	34	17	14	3	51	24	65	
2.	Parma AC (Parma)	34	18	9	7	41	26	63	
3.	FC Internazionale (Milano)	34	15	14	5	51	35	49	
4.	SS Lazio (Roma)	34	15	10	9	54	37	55	
5.	Udinese Calcio (Udine)	34	15	9	10	53	41	54	
6.	UC Sampdoria (Genova)	34	14	11	9	60	46	53	
7.	Bologna FC 1909 (Bologna)	34	13	10	11	50	44	49	
8.	Vicenza Calcio (Vicenza)	34	12	11	11	43	38	47	
9.	AC Fiorentina (Firenze)	34	10	15	9	46	41	45	
10.	Atalanta BC (Bergamo)	34	11	11	12	44	46	44	
11.	Milan AC (Milano)	34	11	10	13	43	45	43	
12.	AS Roma (Roma)	34	10	11	13	46	47	41	
13.	SSC Napoli (Napoli)	34	9	14	11	38	45	41	
14.	FC Piacenza (Piacenza)	34	7	16	11	29	45	37	PO
15.	Cagliari Calcio (Cagliari)	34	9	10	15	45	55	37	R
16.	AC Perugia (Perugia)	34	10	7	17	48	62	37	R
17.	Hellas Verona FC (Verona)	34	6	9	19	38	64	27	R
18.	AC Reggiana (Reggio Emilia)	34	2	13	19	28	67	19	R
		612	204	204	204	808	808	816	

Top goalscorers

1)	Filippo INZAGHI	(Atalanta BC)	24
2)	Vincenzo MONTELLA	(UC Sampdoria)	22
3)	Abel BALBO	(AS Roma)	17
4)	Sandro TOVALIERI	(AC Reggiana/Cagliari Calcio)	16 (4/12)
5)	Roberto MANCINI	(UC Sampdoria)	15
	Marco NEGRI	(AC Perugia)	15
	Giuseppe SIGNORI	(SS Lazio)	15

Relegation Play-Off

Piacenza Calcio (Piacenza)	3-1	Cagliari Calcio (Cagliari)

	Serie "B"	Pd	Wn	Dw	Ls	GF	GA	Pts	
1.	Brescia Calcio (Brescia)	38	18	12	8	49	34	66	P
2.	Empoli FC (Empoli)	38	17	13	7	45	34	64	P
3.	US Lecce (Lecce)	38	16	15	7	52	39	63	P
4.	AS Bari (Bari)	38	15	17	6	52	35	62	P
5.	Genoa CFC (Genova)	38	15	16	7	58	31	61	
6.	Pescara Calcio (Pescara)	38	14	12	12	50	38	54	
7.	AC Chievo (Verona)	38	12	18	8	44	40	54	
8.	US Ravenna (Ravenna)	38	14	13	11	43	35	52	-3
9.	Torino Calcio (Torino)	38	13	11	14	45	48	50	
10.	Reggina Calcio (Reggio Calabria)	38	12	13	13	40	43	49	
11.	Foggia Calcio (Foggia)	38	11	15	12	40	40	48	
12.	Padova Calcio (Padova)	38	11	15	12	41	43	48	
13.	AC Venezia (Venezia)	38	10	16	12	47	49	46	
14.	AS Lucchese Libertas (Lucca)	38	10	15	13	36	44	45	
15.	Salernitana Sport (Salerno)	38	10	14	14	31	44	44	
16.	Castel di Sangro Calcio (Castel di Sangro)	38	12	8	18	29	45	44	
17.	Cosenza Calcio (Cosenza)	38	9	14	15	44	55	41	R
18.	AC Cesena (Cesena)	38	9	13	16	36	45	40	R
19.	US Città di Palermo (Palermo)	38	6	17	15	40	55	35	R
20.	US Cremonese (Cremona)	38	7	11	20	30	55	32	R
		760	241	278	241	852	852	998	

Note: US Ravenna (Ravenna) had 3 points deducted by the F.I.G.C. committee.

Promoted to Serie "B": Ancona Calcio (Ancona), AS Fidelis Andria (Andria), Monza Calcio (Monza), Treviso FBC (Treviso).

Coppa Italia Final (1st leg) (Napoli – 08/05/97 – 65,932)

SSC Napoli (Napoli)	1-0	VICENZA CALCIO (VICENZA)

Peccia 21'

Napoli: Taglialatela, Baldini, Colonnese, Ayala, Milanese, Bordin, Pecchia, R.Longo, Cruz (Altomare 90'), Esposito (Boghossian 78'), Caccia (Aglietti 90').

Vicenza: Brivio, Mendez, Belotti, Viviani, D'Ignazio (Gentilini 51'), Beghetto, Otero (M.Rossi 33'), Di Carlo, Maini, Ambrosetti, Cornacchini (Murgita 87').

Coppa Italia Final (2nd leg) (Vicenza – 29/05/97 – 21,000)

SSC Napoli (Napoli)	0-3 (aet)	VICENZA CALCIO (VICENZA)
		Maini 20', Rossi 103', Ianuzzi 106'

Vicenza: Brivio, Viviani, Sartor, Lopez, Beghetto, Gentilini (M.Rossi 98'), Di Carlo, Maini, Ambrosetti (Ianuzzi 18'), Murgita, Cornacchini (D'Ignazio 72').

Napoli: Taglialatela, Crasson (Panarelli 98'), Baldini, Boghossian, Ayala, Milanese, Esposito, Bordin (Aglietti 62'), Longo (Altomare 72'), Pecchia, Caccia.

Semi-Finals

FC Internazionale (Milano)	1-1, 1-1 (aet – 3-5 penalties)	SSC Napoli (Napoli)
Vicenza Calcio (Vicenza)	1-0, 1-1	Bologna FC 1909 (Bologna)

Quarter-Finals

US Cremonese (Cremona)	1-3, 1-2	Bologna FC 1909 (Bologna)
Juventus FC (Torino)	0-3, 1-1	FC Internazionale (Milano)
Milan AC (Milano)	1-1, 0-0	Vicenza Calcio (Vicenza)
	Vicenza Calcio (Vicenza) won on the away goals rule	
SSC Napoli (Napoli)	1-0, 1-1	SS Lazio (Roma)

1997-98

1997-1998 Serie "A"	Atalanta BC	AS Bari	Bologna 1909 FC	Brescia Calcio	Empoli FC	AC Fiorentina	FC Internazionale	Juventus FC	SS Lazio	US Lecce	Milan AC	SSC Napoli	Parma AC	FC Piacenza	AS Roma	UC Sampdoria	Udinese Calcio	Vicenza Calcio
Atalanta BC		2-0	4-2	0-1	1-0	1-0	1-2	1-1	0-0	0-0	1-2	1-0	0-0	2-2	0-1	0-2	1-1	1-3
AS Bari	0-0		0-0	2-1	2-0	0-1	2-1	0-5	0-2	2-2	1-0	2-0	0-2	0-0	1-3	0-1	0-0	0-0
Bologna FC 1909	0-0	4-2		2-1	2-2	2-2	2-4	1-3	2-1	2-0	3-0	5-1	1-2	3-0	0-0	2-2	2-0	3-1
Brescia Calcio	2-2	1-1	1-3		3-1	1-3	0-1	1-1	1-1	3-2	2-2	2-1	2-1	2-0	1-1	3-3	0-4	4-0
Empoli FC	1-0	2-3	0-0	3-1		1-1	1-1	0-1	1-0	5-1	0-1	5-0	2-0	2-3	1-3	4-1	1-0	3-2
AC Fiorentina	5-0	3-1	1-1	5-1	1-2		1-1	3-0	1-3	5-0	2-0	4-0	1-1	1-1	0-0	1-1	1-0	1-1
FC Internazionale	4-0	0-1	0-1	2-1	4-1	3-2		1-0	1-1	5-0	2-2	2-0	1-0	0-0	3-0	3-0	2-0	2-1
Juventus FC	3-1	1-0	3-2	4-0	5-2	2-1	1-0		2-1	2-0	4-1	2-2	2-2	2-0	3-1	3-0	4-1	2-0
SS Lazio	0-2	3-2	1-0	1-0	3-1	1-4	3-0	0-1		4-0	2-1	2-0	1-2	0-0	2-0	3-0	2-3	4-0
US Lecce	1-1	0-1	1-1	2-0	2-2	1-1	1-5	0-2	1-0		0-0	2-0	0-2	1-3	1-3	1-3	1-2	0-1
Milan AC	3-0	2-0	0-0	2-1	3-1	0-2	0-3	1-1	1-1	1-2		0-0	1-1	1-0	0-0	1-0	0-0	0-1
SSC Napoli	0-1	2-2	0-0	0-3	2-1	1-1	0-2	1-2	0-0	2-4	1-2		0-4	1-2	0-2	0-2	1-3	2-0
Parma AC	2-2	1-0	2-0	1-3	2-0	1-2	1-0	2-2	1-1	2-1	3-1	3-1		1-1	0-2	2-2	4-0	2-1
FC Piacenza	3-0	0-1	0-0	0-0	0-0	0-0	0-1	1-1	0-0	1-0	1-1	1-0	1-3		3-3	1-0	0-2	1-1
AS Roma	3-0	2-1	2-1	5-0	4-3	4-1	1-2	0-0	1-3	3-1	5-0	6-2	2-2	1-1		2-0	1-2	2-2
UC Sampdoria	2-0	1-0	2-3	2-1	3-0	2-1	1-1	1-1	0-4	1-1	0-3	6-3	5-2	3-1	1-1		0-3	2-1
Udinese Calcio	1-0	2-0	4-3	3-1	2-2	2-3	1-0	1-1	0-2	6-0	2-1	1-1	1-1	2-0	4-2	3-2		3-0
Vicenza Calcio	1-0	1-2	3-2	2-1	1-0	1-5	1-3	0-0	2-1	1-3	1-4	1-1	0-0	3-2	1-1	1-1	1-3	

	Serie "A"	Pd	Wn	Dw	Ls	GF	GA	Pts	
1.	JUVENTUS FC (TORINO)	34	21	11	2	67	28	74	
2.	FC Internazionale (Milano)	34	21	6	7	62	27	69	
3.	Udinese Calcio (Udine)	34	19	7	8	62	40	64	
4.	AS Roma (Roma)	34	16	11	7	67	42	59	
5.	AC Fiorentina (Firenze)	34	15	12	7	65	36	57	
6.	Parma AC (Parma)	34	15	12	7	55	39	57	
7.	SS Lazio (Roma)	34	16	8	10	53	30	56	
8.	Bologna FC 1909 (Bologna)	34	12	12	10	55	46	48	
9.	UC Sampdoria (Genova)	34	13	9	12	52	55	48	
10.	Milan AC (Milano)	34	11	11	12	37	43	44	
11.	AS Bari (Bari)	34	10	8	16	30	45	38	
12.	Empoli FC (Empoli)	34	10	7	17	50	58	37	
13.	FC Piacenza (Piacenza)	34	7	16	11	29	38	37	
14.	Vicenza Calcio (Vicenza)	34	9	9	16	36	61	36	
15.	Brescia Calcio (Brescia)	34	9	8	17	45	63	35	R
16.	Atalanta BC (Bergamo)	34	7	11	16	25	48	32	R
17.	US Lecce (Lecce)	34	6	8	20	32	72	26	R
18.	SSC Napoli (Napoli)	34	2	8	24	25	76	14	R
		612	219	174	219	847	847	831	

Top goalscorers

1)	Oliver BIERHOFF	(Udinese Calcio)	27
2)	RONALDO	(FC Internazionale)	25
3)	Roberto BAGGIO	(Bologna FC 1909)	22
4)	Gabriel BATISTUTA	(AC Fiorentina)	21
	Alessandro DEL PIERO	(Juventus FC)	21

	Serie "B"	Pd	Wn	Dw	Ls	GF	GA	Pts	
1.	Salernitana Sport (Salerno)	38	19	15	4	65	32	72	P
2.	AC Venezia (Venezia)	38	17	13	8	51	31	64	P
3.	Cagliari Calcio (Cagliari)	38	15	18	5	53	36	63	P
4.	AC Perugia (Perugia)	38	16	14	8	46	37	62	P
5.	Torino Calcio (Torino)	38	17	11	10	50	40	62	PO
6.	Hellas Verona FC (Verona)	38	15	8	15	51	38	53	
7.	Reggina Calcio (Reggio Calabria)	38	13	14	11	37	41	53	
8.	Treviso FBC (Treviso)	38	12	16	10	43	42	52	
9.	Genoa CFC (Genova)	38	14	9	15	50	53	51	
10.	AC Reggiana (Reggio Emilia)	38	13	11	14	36	35	50	
11.	AC Chievo (Verona)	38	12	14	12	43	46	50	
12.	AS Fidelis Andria (Andria)	38	11	15	12	42	43	48	
13.	Pescara Calcio (Pescara)	38	12	11	15	41	48	47	
14.	US Ravenna (Ravenna)	38	11	12	15	41	43	45	
15.	Monza Calcio (Monza)	38	9	17	12	48	56	44	
16.	AS Lucchese Libertas (Lucca)	38	11	11	16	35	47	44	
17.	Foggia Calcio (Foggia)	38	9	14	15	48	55	41	R
18.	Ancona Calcio (Ancona)	38	8	16	14	49	61	40	R
19.	Padova Calcio (Padova)	38	8	12	18	30	49	36	R
20.	Castel di Sangro Calcio (Castel di Sangro)	38	5	15	18	38	64	30	R
		760	247	266	247	897	897	1007	

Promotion Play-Off

AC Perugia (Perugia)	1-1 (aet – 5-4 penalties)	Torino Calcio (Torino)

Promoted to Serie "B": AC Cesena (Cesena), Cosenza Calcio (Cosenza), US Cremonese (Cremona), Ternana Calcio (Terni).

Coppa Italia Final (1st leg) (Milano – 08/04/98)

Milan AC (Milano)	1-0	SS LAZIO (ROMA)
Weah 90'		

Milan: Rossi, Nilsen, Smoje, Costacurta, Maldini, Savicevic (Ba 60', Leonardo 76'), Albertini, Desailly, Donadoni, Weah, Ganz (Maniero 60').

Lazio: Marchegiani, Chamot (Grandoni 74'), Nesta, Negro, Favalli, Fuser, Venturin, Jugovic, Nedved, Casiraghi, Mancini (Gottardi 85').

Coppa Italia Final (2nd leg) (Roma – 29/04/98)

Milan AC (Milano)	1-3	SS LAZIO (ROMA)
Albertini 47'		*Gottardi 56', Jugovic 59' pen., Nesta 65'*

Lazio: Marchegiani, Grandoni (Gottardi 51'), Nesta, Negro, Favalli, Fuser, Venturin, Jugovic, Nedved (Marcolin 90'), Casiraghi, Mancini (Lopez 85').

Milan: Rossi, Daino, Costacurta, Desailly, Maldini, Ba (Ganz 65'), Albertini, Donadoni, Ziege, Savicevic (Kluivert 31', Maini 51'), Weah.

Semi-Finals

Juventus FC (Torino)	0-1, 2-2	SS Lazio (Roma)
Milan AC (Milano)	0-0, 2-2	Parma AC (Parma)

Milan AC (Milano) won on the away goals rule.

Quarter-Finals

AC Fiorentina (Firenze)	2-2, 0-0	Juventus FC (Torino)
AC Fiorentina (Firenze) won on the away goals rule.		
SS Lazio (Roma)	4-1, 2-1	AS Roma (Roma)
Milan AC (Milano)	5-0, 0-1	FC Internazionale (Milano)
Parma AC (Parma)	1-0, 1-1	Atalanta BC (Bergamo)

1998-99

1998-1999 Serie "A"	AS Bari	Bologna 1909 FC	Cagliari Calcio	Empoli FC	AC Fiorentina	FC Internazionale	Juventus FC	SS Lazio	Milan AC	Parma AC	AC Perugia	FC Piacenza	AS Roma	Salernitana Sport	UC Sampdoria	Udinese Calcio	AC Venezia	Vicenza Calcio
AS Bari		0-0	1-1	2-1	0-0	1-0	0-1	1-3	0-0	1-1	2-1	3-1	1-4	0-0	3-1	1-1	1-0	0-0
Bologna FC 1909	3-1		1-3	2-0	3-0	2-0	3-0	0-1	2-3	0-0	1-1	3-1	1-1	1-1	2-2	1-3	2-1	4-2
Cagliari Calcio	3-3	0-1		5-1	1-1	2-2	1-0	0-0	1-0	1-0	2-2	3-2	4-3	3-1	5-0	1-2	0-1	1-0
Empoli FC	0-2	0-0	2-1		0-3	1-2	1-0	0-0	1-1	3-5	2-0	1-2	0-0	2-3	0-1	1-3	2-2	1-0
AC Fiorentina	2-2	1-0	4-2	2-0		3-1	1-0	1-1	0-0	2-1	5-1	2-1	0-0	4-0	1-0	1-0	4-1	3-0
FC Internazionale	2-3	3-1	5-1	5-1	2-0		0-0	3-5	2-2	1-3	2-0	1-0	4-1	2-1	3-0	1-3	6-2	1-1
Juventus FC	1-1	2-2	1-0	0-0	2-1	1-0		0-1	0-2	2-4	2-1	1-0	1-1	3-0	2-0	2-1	3-2	2-0
SS Lazio	0-0	2-0	2-0	4-1	2-0	1-0	1-3		0-0	2-1	3-0	4-1	3-3	6-1	5-2	3-1	2-0	1-1
Milan AC	2-2	3-0	1-0	4-0	1-3	2-2	1-1	1-0		2-1	2-1	1-0	3-2	3-2	3-2	3-0	2-1	1-0
Parma AC	2-1	1-1	1-1	1-0	2-0	1-0	1-0	1-3	4-0		3-1	0-1	1-1	2-0	1-1	4-1	2-2	0-0
AC Perugia	0-1	0-0	2-1	3-1	2-2	2-1	3-4	2-2	1-2	2-1		2-0	3-2	1-0	2-0	1-3	1-0	3-1
FC Piacenza	3-2	5-0	2-0	0-0	4-2	0-0	0-2	1-1	1-1	3-6	2-0		2-0	1-1	4-1	4-3	0-1	2-0
AS Roma	1-1	3-1	3-1	1-1	2-1	4-5	2-0	3-1	1-0	1-0	5-1	2-2		3-1	3-1	4-0	2-0	3-0
Salernitana Sport	2-2	4-0	1-3	1-1	1-1	2-0	1-0	1-0	1-2	1-2	2-0	1-1	2-1		2-0	1-2	1-0	2-1
UC Sampdoria	1-0	1-1	0-0	3-0	3-2	4-0	1-2	0-1	2-2	0-2	1-1	3-2	2-1	1-0		1-1	2-1	0-0
Udinese Calcio	4-0	2-0	2-1	0-0	1-0	0-1	2-2	0-3	1-5	2-1	1-2	1-0	2-1	2-0	2-2		1-1	2-1
AC Venezia	2-1	0-2	1-0	3-2	4-1	3-1	1-1	2-0	0-2	0-0	2-1	0-0	3-1	0-0	0-0	1-0		1-2
Vicenza Calcio	1-0	0-4	2-1	2-0	1-2	1-1	1-1	1-2	0-2	0-0	3-0	1-0	1-4	1-0	1-0	2-3	0-0	

	Serie "A"	Pd	Wn	Dw	Ls	GF	GA	Pts	
1.	MILAN AC (MILANO)	34	20	10	4	59	34	70	
2.	SS Lazio (Roma)	34	20	9	5	65	31	69	
3.	AC Fiorentina (Firenze)	34	16	8	10	55	41	56	
4.	Parma AC (Parma)	34	15	10	9	55	36	55	
5.	AS Roma (Roma)	34	15	9	10	69	49	54	
6.	Juventus FC (Torino)	34	15	9	10	42	36	54	
7.	Udinese Calcio (Udine)	34	16	6	12	52	52	54	
8.	FC Internazionale (Milano)	34	13	7	14	59	54	46	
9.	Bologna FC 1909 (Bologna)	34	11	11	12	44	47	44	
10.	AS Bari (Bari)	34	9	15	10	39	44	42	
11.	AC Venezia (Venezia)	34	11	9	14	38	45	42	
12.	Cagliari Calcio (Cagliari)	34	11	8	15	49	50	41	
13.	FC Piacenza (Piacenza)	34	11	8	15	48	49	41	
14.	AC Perugia (Perugia)	34	11	6	17	43	61	39	
15.	Salernitana Sport (Salerno)	34	10	8	16	37	51	38	R
16.	UC Sampdoria (Genova)	34	9	10	15	38	55	37	R
17.	Vicenza Calcio (Vicenza)	34	8	9	17	27	47	33	R
18.	Empoli FC (Empoli)	34	4	10	20	26	63	20	R -2
		612	225	162	225	845	845	835	

Top goalscorers

1)	Marcio AMOROSO	(Udinese Calcio)	22
2)	Gabriel BATISTUTA	(AC Fiorentina)	21
3)	Oliver BIERHOFF	(Milan AC)	20
4)	Marco DELVECCHIO	(AS Roma)	18
5)	Hernán CRESPO	(Parma AC)	16
	Roberto MUZZI	(Cagliari Calcio)	16

Note: Empoli FC (Empoli) had 2 points deducted by the F.I.G.C. committee for alleged "attempted match-fixing".

UEFA Cup Play-Offs

Udinese Calcio (Udine) 0-0, 1-1 Juventus FC (Torino)

(Juventus FC (Torino) qualified on the away goals rule)

FC Internazionale (Milano) 1-2, 1-2 Bologna FC 1909 (Bologna)

(played between losing Semi-Finalists in Coppa Italia)

	Serie "B"	Pd	Wn	Dw	Ls	GF	GA	Pts	
1.	Hellas Verona FC (Verona)	38	18	12	8	60	38	66	P
2.	Torino Calcio (Torino)	38	19	8	11	58	36	65	P
3.	Reggina Calcio (Reggio Calabria)	38	16	16	6	45	32	64	P
4.	US Lecce (Lecce)	38	18	10	10	47	39	64	P
5.	Pescara Calcio (Pescara)	38	18	9	11	50	42	63	
6.	Atalanta BC (Bergamo)	38	14	19	5	44	27	61	
7.	Brescia Calcio (Brescia)	38	14	14	10	44	33	56	
8.	Treviso FBC (Treviso)	38	14	14	10	52	42	56	
9.	SSC Napoli (Napoli)	38	12	15	11	41	38	51	
10.	US Ravenna (Ravenna)	38	13	12	13	47	51	51	
11.	AC Chievo (Verona)	38	11	15	12	37	40	48	
12.	Genoa CFC (Genova)	38	10	16	12	53	53	46	
13.	AC Cesena (Cesena)	38	10	15	13	37	41	45	
14.	Monza Calcio (Monza)	38	10	15	13	32	38	45	
15.	Ternana Calcio (Terni)	38	10	15	13	39	50	45	
16.	Cosenza Calcio (Cosenza)	38	11	10	17	41	53	43	
17.	AC Reggiana (Reggio Emilia)	38	9	14	15	40	49	41	R
18.	AS Fidelis Andria (Andria)	38	9	13	16	33	49	40	R
19.	AS Lucchese Libertas (Lucca)	38	8	13	17	35	45	37	R
20.	US Cremonese (Cremona)	38	3	11	24	30	69	20	R
		760	247	266	247	865	865	1007	

Promoted to Serie "B": FC Alzano Virescit (Alzano Lombardo), Fermana Calcio (Fermo), AC Pistoiese (Pistoia) and Savoia 1908 AC (Torre Annunziata).

Coppa Italia Final (1st leg) (Parma – 14/04/99 – 21,038)

PARMA AC (PARMA) 1-1 AC Fiorentina (Firenze)

Crespo 15' *Batistuta 81'*

Parma: Buffon, Thuram, Sensini, Cannavaro, Stanic, Fuser, D.Baggio, Vanoli, Veron, Crespo (Balbo 80'), Chiesa (Mussi 69').

Fiorentina: Toldo, Padalino, Falcone, Repka, Torricelli, Cois, Rui Costa, Amoroso, Heinrich, Batistuta, Edmundo.

Coppa Italia Final (2nd leg) (Firenze – 05/05/99 – 39,070)

PARMA AC (PARMA)	2-2	AC Fiorentina (Firenze)
Crespo 44', Vanoli 71'		*Repka 48', Cois 62'*

Parma AC (Parma) won on the away goals rule.

Fiorentina: Toldo, Padalino, Falcone, Repka, Torricelli, Cois (Oliviera 79'), Rui Costa, Amoroso, Heinrich, Edmundo, Batistuta.

Parma: Buffon, Thuram, Sensini, Cannavaro, Stanic (Fiore 64'), Fuser, Boghossian, Vanoli, Veron (Mussi 79'),Chiesa, Crespo (Balbo 85').

Semi-Finals

Bologna FC 1909 (Bologna)	0-2, 2-2	AC Fiorentina (Firenze)
FC Internazionale (Firenze)	0-2, 1-2	Parma AC (Parma)

Quarter-Finals

Atalanta BC (Bergamo)	3-2, 0-1	AC Fiorentina (Firenze)
Juventus FC (Torino)	1-2, 1-0	Bologna FC 1909 (Bologna)
	Bologna FC 1909 (Bologna) won on the away goals rule	
SS Lazio (Roma)	2-1, 2-5	FC Internazionale (Milano)
Udinese Calcio (Udine)	3-2, 0-4	Parma AC (Parma)

1999-2000

1999-2000 Serie "A"	AS Bari	Bologna 1909 FC	Cagliari Calcio	AC Fiorentina	Hellas Verona FC	FC Internazionale	Juventus FC	SS Lazio	US Lecce	Milan AC	Parma AC	AC Perugia	FC Piacenza	Reggina Calcio	AS Roma	Torino Calcio	Udinese Calcio	AC Venezia
AS Bari		1-1	1-0	1-0	1-1	2-1	1-1	0-0	3-1	1-1	0-1	0-2	3-2	1-1	0-0	1-1	1-1	3-0
Bologna FC 1909	1-0		1-0	0-0	0-0	3-0	0-2	2-3	2-0	2-3	1-0	2-1	0-0	0-1	1-0	0-0	2-1	1-1
Cagliari Calcio	2-3	2-2		1-1	0-1	0-2	0-1	0-0	0-0	0-0	2-3	2-1	3-0	0-1	1-0	1-1	0-3	1-1
AC Fiorentina	1-0	2-2	2-0		4-1	2-1	1-1	3-3	3-0	2-1	0-2	1-0	2-1	1-0	1-3	1-1	1-1	3-0
Hellas Verona FC	0-1	0-0	2-0	2-2		1-2	2-0	1-0	2-0	0-0	4-3	2-0	1-0	1-1	2-1	0-1	2-2	1-0
FC Internazionale	3-0	1-1	2-1	0-4	3-0		1-2	1-1	6-0	1-2	5-1	5-0	2-1	1-1	2-1	1-1	3-0	3-0
Juventus FC	2-0	2-0	1-1	1-0	1-0	1-0		0-1	1-0	3-1	1-0	3-0	1-0	1-1	2-1	3-2	4-1	1-0
SS Lazio	3-1	3-1	2-1	2-0	4-0	2-2	0-0		4-2	4-4	0-0	1-0	2-0	3-0	2-1	3-0	2-1	3-2
US Lecce	1-0	1-1	2-1	0-0	2-1	1-0	2-0	0-1		2-2	0-0	0-1	0-1	2-1	0-0	2-1	1-0	2-1
Milan AC	4-1	4-0	2-2	1-1	3-3	1-2	2-0	2-1	2-2		2-1	3-1	1-0	2-2	2-2	2-0	4-0	3-0
Parma AC	2-1	1-1	3-1	0-4	3-0	1-1	1-1	1-2	4-1	1-0		1-2	1-0	3-0	2-0	4-1	0-0	3-1
AC Perugia	1-2	3-2	3-0	1-2	0-0	1-2	1-0	0-2	2-2	0-3	1-1		2-0	2-1	2-2	1-0	0-5	2-1
FC Piacenza	2-1	0-0	1-1	2-0	1-0	1-3	0-2	0-2	1-1	0-1	1-2	0-0		0-0	1-1	0-2	0-1	2-2
Reggina Calcio	1-0	1-0	1-1	2-2	1-1	0-1	0-2	0-0	2-1	1-2	2-2	1-1	1-0		0-4	2-1	0-0	1-0
AS Roma	3-1	2-0	2-2	4-0	3-1	0-0	0-1	4-1	3-2	1-1	0-0	3-1	2-1	0-2		1-0	1-1	5-0
Torino Calcio	3-1	2-1	1-1	1-0	0-3	0-1	0-0	2-4	1-2	2-2	2-2	0-1	2-1	2-1	1-1		0-1	2-1
Udinese Calcio	5-1	2-1	5-2	1-1	3-3	3-0	1-1	0-3	2-1	1-2	0-1	2-1	3-0	3-2	0-2	0-0		5-2
AC Venezia	0-1	0-1	3-0	2-1	2-2	1-0	0-4	2-0	0-0	1-0	0-2	1-2	0-0	2-0	1-3	2-2	1-1	

	Serie "A"	Pd	Wn	Dw	Ls	GF	GA	Pts	
1.	SS LAZIO (ROMA)	34	21	9	4	64	33	72	
2.	Juventus FC (Torino)	34	21	8	5	46	20	71	
3.	Milan AC (Milano)	34	16	13	5	65	40	61	
4.	FC Internazionale (Milano)	34	17	7	10	58	36	58	PO
5.	Parma AC (Parma)	34	16	10	8	52	37	58	PO
6.	AS Roma (Roma)	34	14	12	8	57	34	54	
7.	AC Fiorentina (Firenze)	34	13	12	9	48	38	51	
8.	Udinese Calcio (Udine)	34	13	11	10	55	45	50	
9.	Hellas Verona FC (Verona)	34	10	13	11	40	45	43	
10.	AC Perugia (Perugia)	34	12	6	16	36	52	42	
11.	Bologna FC 1909 (Bologna)	34	9	13	12	32	39	40	
12.	Reggina Calcio (Reggio Calabria)	34	9	13	12	31	42	40	
13.	US Lecce (Lecce)	34	10	10	14	33	49	40	
14.	AS Bari (Bari)	34	10	9	15	34	48	39	
15.	Torino Calcio (Torino)	34	8	12	14	35	47	36	R
16.	AC Venezia (Venezia)	34	6	8	20	30	60	26	R
17.	Cagliari Calcio (Cagliari)	34	3	13	18	29	54	22	R
18.	FC Piacenza (Piacenza)	34	4	9	21	19	45	21	R
		612	212	188	212	764	764	824	

Top goalscorers

1)	Andriy SHEVCHENKO	(Milan AC)	24
2)	Gabriel BATISTUTA	(AC Fiorentina)	23
3)	Hernán CRESPO	(Parma AC)	22
4)	Marco FERRANTE	(Torino Calcio)	18
	Vincenzo MONTELLA	(AS Roma)	18

Champions League Qualification Play-Off (played in Verona)

Parma AC (Parma) 1-3 FC Internazionale (Milano)

	Serie "B"	Pd	Wn	Dw	Ls	GF	GA	Pts	
1.	Vicenza Calcio (Vicenza)	38	20	7	11	69	45	67	P
2.	Atalanta BC (Bergamo)	38	17	12	9	51	34	63	P
3.	Brescia Calcio (Brescia)	38	16	15	7	54	38	63	P
4.	SSC Napoli (Napoli)	38	17	12	9	55	44	63	P
5.	UC Sampdoria (Genova)	38	17	11	10	45	40	62	
6.	Genoa CFC (Genova)	38	16	9	13	51	42	57	
7.	Salernitana Sport (Salerno)	38	14	10	14	55	61	52	
8.	Treviso FBC (Treviso)	38	13	12	13	56	48	51	
9.	Empoli FC (Empoli)	38	13	12	13	42	52	51	
10.	Ternana Calcio (Terni)	38	11	16	11	45	47	49	
11.	US Ravenna (Ravenna)	38	11	15	12	41	39	48	
12.	Cosenza Calcio (Cosenza)	38	11	15	12	36	41	48	
13.	Pescara Calcio (Pescara)	38	10	17	11	62	55	47	
14.	Monza Calcio (Monza)	38	9	20	9	45	46	47	
15.	AC Chievo (Verona)	38	11	14	13	48	53	47	
16.	AC Pistoiese (Pistoia)	38	13	10	15	39	43	45	-4
17.	AC Cesena (Cesena)	38	8	21	9	47	45	45	R
18.	FC Alzano Virescit (Alzano Lombardo)	38	10	12	16	39	51	42	R
19.	Savoia 1908 AC (Torre Annunziata)	38	6	11	21	36	62	29	R
20.	Fermana Calcio (Fermo)	38	6	11	21	36	66	29	R
		760	249	262	249	952	952	1005	

Note: AC Pistoiese (Pistoia) had 4 points deducted by the F.I.G.C. committee.

Relegation Play-Off

AC Pistoiese (Pistoia)	+:-	AC Cesena (Cesena)

The match was awarded as a forfeit win to AC Pistoiese (Pistoia)

Promoted to Serie "B": Ancona Calcio (Ancona), AC Cittadella (Cittadella), FC Crotone (Crotone) and AC Siena (Siena).

Coppa Italia Final (1st leg) (Roma - 12/04/2000 - 40,000)

SS LAZIO (ROMA)	2-1	FC Internazionale (Milano)
Nedved 40', Simeone 52'		*Seedorf 08'*

Lazio: Ballotta, Gottardi, Fernando Couto, Mihajlovic, Pancaro, Sérgio Conceição, Sensini, Stankovic (Mancini 53'), Simeone (Almeyda 80'), Nedved, Inzaghi (Salas 76').

Internazionale: Peruzzi, Panucci, Blanc, Córdoba, Moriero (Di Baggio 46'), Zanetti, Seedorf, Cauet, Serena, Baggio (Zamorano 58'), Mutu (Ronaldo 58').

Coppa Italia Final (2nd leg) (Milano - 18/05/2000 - 53,406)

SS LAZIO (ROMA)	0-0	FC Internazionale (Milano)

Internazionale: Peruzzi, Serena (Georgatos 67'), Córdoba, Blanc, Domoraud, Zanetti, Di Baggio, Cauet, Seedorf, Baggio (Recoba 61'), Zamorano (Vieri 46').

Lazio: Ballotta, Pancaro (Fernando Couto 87'), Nesta, Negro, Favalli, Sérgio Conceição, Sensini, Verón, Simeone, Mancini (Ravanelli 46'), Inzaghi (Salas 46').

Semi-Finals

Cagliari Calcio (Cagliari)	1-3, 2-1	FC Internazionale (Milano)
SS Lazio (Roma)	5-0, 2-2	AC Venezia (Venezia)

Quarter-Finals

Juventus FC (Torino)	3-2, 1-2	SS Lazio (Roma)
SS Lazio (Roma) won on the away goals rule.		
Milan AC (Milano)	2-3, 1-1	FC Internazionale (Milano)
AS Roma (Roma)	0-1, 0-1	Cagliari Calcio (Cagliari)
AC Venezia (Venezia)	0-0, 1-1	AC Fiorentina (Firenze)
AC Venezia (Venezia) won on the away goals rule.		

2000-2001

2000-2001 Serie "A"	Atalanta BC	AS Bari	Bologna 1909 FC	Brescia Calcio	AC Fiorentina	Hellas Verona FC	FC Internazionale	Juventus FC	SS Lazio	US Lecce	Milan AC	SSC Napoli	Parma AC	AC Perugia	Reggina Calcio	AS Roma	Udinese Calcio	Vicenza Calcio
Atalanta BC		0-0	2-2	2-0	0-0	3-0	0-1	2-1	2-2	1-0	1-1	1-1	0-1	0-0	1-1	0-2	0-1	1-1
AS Bari	0-2		2-0	1-3	2-1	1-1	1-2	0-1	1-2	3-2	1-3	0-1	0-1	3-4	2-1	1-4	2-1	2-2
Bologna FC 1909	0-1	4-2		1-0	1-1	1-0	0-3	1-4	2-0	2-2	2-1	2-1	2-1	3-2	2-0	1-2	1-1	1-1
Brescia Calcio	0-3	3-1	0-0		1-1	1-0	1-0	0-0	0-1	2-2	1-1	1-1	0-0	1-0	4-0	2-4	3-1	2-1
AC Fiorentina	1-1	2-2	1-1	2-2		2-0	2-0	1-3	1-4	2-0	4-0	1-2	0-1	3-4	2-1	3-1	2-1	3-2
Hellas Verona FC	2-1	3-2	5-4	2-1	2-1		2-2	0-1	2-0	0-0	1-1	2-1	0-2	2-1	0-3	1-4	1-1	1-0
FC Internazionale	3-0	1-0	2-1	0-0	4-2	2-0		2-1	1-1	0-1	0-6	3-1	1-1	2-1	1-1	2-0	2-1	1-1
Juventus FC	2-1	2-0	1-0	1-1	3-3	2-1	3-1		1-1	1-1	3-0	3-0	1-0	1-0	1-0	2-2	1-2	4-0
SS Lazio	0-0	2-0	2-0	2-1	3-0	5-3	2-0	4-1		3-2	1-1	1-2	1-0	3-0	2-0	0-1	3-1	2-1
US Lecce	0-2	2-0	0-0	0-3	1-1	4-2	1-2	1-4	2-1		3-3	1-1	1-2	2-2	2-1	0-4	2-1	3-1
Milan AC	3-3	4-0	3-3	1-1	1-2	1-0	2-2	2-2	1-0	4-1		1-0	2-2	1-2	1-0	3-2	3-0	2-0
SSC Napoli	0-0	1-0	1-5	1-1	1-0	2-0	1-0	1-2	2-4	1-1	0-0		2-2	0-0	6-2	2-2	0-1	1-2
Parma AC	2-0	4-0	0-0	3-0	2-2	1-2	3-1	0-0	2-0	1-1	2-0	4-0		5-0	0-2	1-2	2-0	0-2
AC Perugia	2-2	4-1	1-3	2-2	2-2	1-0	2-3	0-1	1-0	1-1	2-1	1-1	3-1		1-1	0-0	3-1	1-0
Reggina Calcio	1-0	1-0	2-1	0-3	1-1	1-1	2-1	0-2	0-2	0-1	2-1	3-1	2-0	0-2		0-0	1-1	1-0
AS Roma	1-0	1-1	2-0	3-1	1-0	3-1	3-2	0-0	2-2	1-0	1-1	3-0	3-1	2-2	2-1		2-1	3-1
Udinese Calcio	2-4	2-0	3-1	4-2	1-3	2-1	3-0	0-2	3-4	2-0	0-1	0-0	1-3	3-3	3-0	1-3		2-3
Vicenza Calcio	1-2	1-0	4-2	1-1	1-1	2-2	0-0	0-3	1-4	0-0	2-0	2-0	0-1	1-0	2-1	0-2	1-2	

	Serie "A"	Pd	Wn	Dw	Ls	GF	GA	Pts	
1.	AS ROMA (ROMA)	34	22	9	3	68	33	75	
2.	Juventus FC (Torino)	34	21	10	3	61	27	73	
3.	SS Lazio (Roma)	34	21	6	7	65	36	69	
4.	Parma AC (Parma)	34	16	8	10	51	31	56	
5.	FC Internazionale (Milano)	34	14	9	11	47	47	51	
6.	Milan AC (Milano)	34	12	13	9	56	46	49	
7.	Atalanta BC (Bergamo)	34	10	14	10	38	34	44	
8.	Brescia Calcio (Brescia)	34	10	14	10	44	42	44	
9.	AC Fiorentina (Firenze)	34	10	13	11	53	52	43	
10.	Bologna FC 1909 (Bologna)	34	11	10	13	49	53	43	
11.	AC Perugia (Perugia)	34	10	12	12	49	53	42	
12.	Udinese Calcio (Udine)	34	11	5	18	49	59	38	
13.	US Lecce (Lecce)	34	8	13	13	40	54	37	
14.	Reggina Calcio (Reggio Calabria)	34	10	7	17	32	49	37	PO
15.	Hellas Verona FC (Verona)	34	10	7	17	40	59	37	R
16.	Vicenza Calcio (Vicenza)	34	9	9	16	37	51	36	R
17.	SSC Napoli (Napoli)	34	8	12	14	35	51	36	R
18.	AS Bari (Bari)	34	5	5	24	31	68	20	R
		612	218	176	218	845	845	830	

Top goalscorers

1)	Hernán CRESPO	(SS Lazio)	26
2)	Andriy SHEVCHENKO	(Milan AC)	24
3)	Enrico CHIESA	(AC Fiorentina)	22
4)	Gabriel BATISTUTA	(AS Roma)	20
5)	Christian VIERI	(FC Internazionale)	18

Relegation Play-Off

Hellas Verona FC (Verona) 1-0, 1-2 Reggina Calcio (Reggio Calabria)

(Reggina won on results of the mutual matches in league)

	Serie "B"	Pd	Wn	Dw	Ls	GF	GA	Pts	
1.	Torino Calcio (Torino)	38	22	7	9	48	33	73	P
2.	FC Piacenza (Piacenza)	38	20	10	8	48	26	70	P
3.	AC Chievo (Verona)	38	19	13	6	54	34	70	P
4.	AC Venezia (Venezia)	38	19	12	7	62	43	69	P
5.	UC Sampdoria (Genova)	38	16	16	6	60	38	64	
6.	Empoli FC (Empoli)	38	18	10	10	52	43	64	
7.	Ternana Calcio (Terni)	38	16	14	8	59	38	62	
8.	Cosenza Calcio (Cosenza)	38	17	9	12	49	46	60	
9.	FC Crotone (Crotone)	38	15	8	15	47	53	53	
10.	Ancona Calcio (Ancona)	38	14	9	15	56	58	51	
11.	Cagliari Calcio (Cagliari)	38	12	14	12	53	45	50	
12.	Genoa CFC (Genova)	38	10	17	11	44	39	47	
13.	AC Siena (Siena)	38	10	17	11	38	43	47	
14.	AC Cittadella (Cittadella)	38	10	15	13	40	52	45	
15.	Salernitana Sport (Salerno)	38	11	10	17	37	42	43	
16.	AC Pistoiese (Pistoia)	38	10	11	17	46	51	41	
17.	Treviso FBC (Treviso)	38	8	12	18	40	56	36	R
18.	Monza Calcio (Monza)	38	9	4	25	41	77	31	R
19.	US Ravenna (Ravenna)	38	4	13	21	33	64	25	R
20.	Pescara Calcio (Pescara)	38	3	13	22	30	56	22	R
		760	263	234	263	937	937	1023	

Promoted to Serie "B": Como Calcio (Como), ACR Messina (Messina), Modena FC (Modena), US Città di Palermo (Palermo).

Coppa Italia Final (1st leg) (Parma - 24/05/2001 - 17,685)

Parma AC (Parma) 0-1 AC FIORENTINA (FIRENZE)

Vanoli 87'

Parma: Guardalben, Thuram, Sensini, Cannavaro, Sartor (Sérgio Conceição 73'), Lamouchi, Almeyda, Júnior, Micoud, Milosevic (Mboma 80'), Di Vaio (Amoroso 62').

Fiorentina: Toldo, Repka, Adani, Pierini, Moretti, Rossi (Bressan 71'), Amaral, Di Livio, Vanoli, Rui Costa, Chiesa.

Coppa Italia Final (2nd leg) (Firenze – 13/06/2001 – 40,000)

Parma AC (Parma) 1-1 AC FIORENTINA (FIRENZE)

Milosevi 38' *Nuno Gomes 65'*

Fiorentina: Toldo, Repka, Adani, Pierini, Moretti (Nuno Gomes 46'), Rossi, Amaral, Di Livio, Vanoli (Bressan 76'), Rui Costa, Chiesa (Lasisi 89').

Parma: Guardalben, Sartor (Fuser 76'), Thuram, Cannavaro, Júnior, Almeyda (Appiah 82'), Sensini, Lamouchi, Micoud (Mboma 85'), Milosevic, Di Vaio.

Semi-Finals

Milan AC (Milano)	2-2, 0-2	AC Fiorentina (Firenze)
Udinese Calcio (Udine)	2-1, 0-1	Parma AC (Parma)

Parma AC (Parma) won on the away goals rule.

Quarter-Finals

AC Fiorentina (Firenze)	6-0, 1-3	Brescia Calcio (Brescia)
SS Lazio (Roma)	2-1, 1-4	Udinese Calcio (Udine)
Milan AC (Milano)	4-2, 1-2	Atalanta BC (Bergamo)
Parma AC (Parma)	6-1, 0-0	FC Internazionale (Milano)

2001-2002

2001-2002 Serie "A"	Atalanta BC	Bologna 1909 FC	Juventus FCbrescia	AS Chievo	AC Fiorentina	Hellas Verona FC	FC Internazionale	Juventus FC	SS Lazio	US Lecce	Milan AC	Parma AC	AC Perugia	FC Piacenza	AS Roma	Torino Calcio	Udinese Calcio	AC Venezia
Atalanta BC		2-2	0-0	1-2	2-0	1-0	2-4	0-2	0-1	2-1	1-1	4-1	2-1	1-1	1-1	1-1	1-5	1-0
Bologna FC 1909	1-0		2-1	3-1	3-2	2-1	2-1	0-0	2-0	4-3	2-0	1-0	2-1	1-2	1-3	1-0	0-1	1-1
Brescia Calcio	3-3	3-0		2-2	3-0	0-0	1-3	0-4	1-1	1-1	2-2	1-4	3-0	2-2	0-0	1-2	2-0	3-2
AS Chievo	2-1	2-0	1-1		2-2	2-1	2-2	1-3	3-1	2-1	1-1	1-0	2-0	4-2	0-3	3-0	1-2	1-1
AC Fiorentina	3-1	1-1	1-0	0-2		0-2	0-1	1-1	0-1	1-2	1-1	1-2	1-3	1-3	2-2	0-0	0-0	3-1
Hellas Verona FC	3-1	0-1	2-0	3-2	1-2		0-3	2-2	3-1	2-1	1-2	1-0	1-1	1-0	1-1	0-1	1-0	1-0
FC Internazionale	1-2	1-0	2-1	1-2	2-0	3-0		2-2	0-0	2-0	2-4	2-0	4-1	3-1	3-1	0-0	3-2	2-1
Juventus FC	3-0	2-1	5-0	3-2	2-1	1-0	0-0		1-1	3-0	1-0	3-1	2-0	2-0	0-2	3-3	3-0	4-0
SS Lazio	2-0	2-2	5-0	1-1	3-0	5-4	4-2	1-0		1-0	1-1	0-0	5-0	1-1	1-5	0-0	2-0	4-2
US Lecce	0-2	1-0	1-3	2-3	4-1	1-1	1-2	0-0	1-2		0-1	1-1	2-3	0-0	1-1	1-1	1-2	2-1
Milan AC	0-0	0-0	0-0	3-2	5-2	2-1	0-1	1-1	2-0	3-0		3-1	1-1	0-0	0-0	2-1	2-3	1-1
Parma AC	1-1	2-1	1-0	0-0	2-0	2-2	2-2	1-0	1-0	1-1	0-1		2-1	2-2	1-2	0-1	2-0	2-1
AC Perugia	2-0	1-0	1-1	2-2	2-0	3-1	0-2	0-4	0-0	2-1	3-1	2-1		1-0	0-0	2-0	1-2	2-0
FC Piacenza	1-2	2-0	0-1	2-2	3-0	3-0	2-3	0-1	1-0	1-2	0-1	2-3	2-0		2-0	3-1	1-2	5-0
AS Roma	3-1	3-1	0-0	5-0	2-1	3-2	0-0	0-0	2-0	5-1	1-0	3-0	1-0	2-0		1-0	1-1	1-0
Torino Calcio	1-2	1-1	1-3	2-2	1-0	5-1	0-1	2-2	1-0	1-1	1-0	1-0	1-0	1-1	0-1		3-1	1-2
Udinese Calcio	1-2	0-1	3-2	1-2	1-2	2-1	1-1	0-2	1-4	0-1	1-2	3-2	0-0	1-1	1-1	2-2		1-0
AC Venezia	0-1	0-1	1-2	0-0	2-0	0-1	1-1	1-2	0-0	1-1	1-4	3-4	0-2	2-3	2-2	1-1	2-1	

	Serie "A"	Pd	Wn	Dw	Ls	GF	GA	Pts	
1.	JUVENTUS FC (TORINO)	34	20	11	3	64	23	71	
2.	AS Roma (Roma)	34	19	13	2	58	24	70	
3.	FC Internazionale (Milano)	34	20	9	5	62	35	69	
4.	Milan AC (Milano)	34	14	13	7	47	33	55	
5.	AC Chievo (Verona)	34	14	12	8	57	52	54	
6.	SS Lazio (Roma)	34	14	11	9	50	37	53	
7.	Bologna FC 1909 (Bologna)	34	15	7	12	40	40	52	
8.	AC Perugia (Perugia)	34	13	7	14	38	46	46	
9.	Atalanta BC (Bergamo)	34	12	9	13	41	50	45	
10.	Parma AC (Parma)	34	12	8	14	43	47	44	
11.	Torino Calcio (Torino)	34	10	13	11	37	39	43	
12.	FC Piacenza (Piacenza)	34	11	9	14	49	43	42	
13.	Brescia Calcio (Brescia)	34	9	13	12	43	52	40	
14.	Udinese Calcio (Udine)	34	11	7	16	41	52	40	
15.	Hellas Verona FC (Verona)	34	11	6	17	41	53	39	R
16.	US Lecce (Lecce)	34	6	10	18	36	56	28	R
17.	AC Fiorentina (Firenze)	34	5	7	22	29	63	22	R #
18.	AC Venezia (Venezia)	34	3	9	22	30	61	18	R
		612	219	174	219	806	806	831	

Top goalscorers

1)	Dario HUBNER	(FC Piacenza)	24
	David TREZEGUET	(Juventus FC)	24
3)	Christian VIERI	(FC Internazionale)	22
4)	Marco DI VAIO	(Parma AC)	20
5)	Filippo MANIERO	(AC Venezia)	18

AC Fiorentina (Firenze) were relegated to Serie "C-2" due to the club going into liquidation and being re-formed as Fiorentina 1926 Florentia (Firenze).

	Serie "B"	Pd	Wn	Dw	Ls	GF	GA	Pts	
1.	Como Calcio (Como)	38	22	8	8	53	35	74	P
2.	Modena FC (Modena)	38	20	12	6	58	23	72	P
3.	Reggina Calcio (Reggio Calabria)	38	19	11	8	50	33	68	P
4.	Empoli FC (Empoli)	38	19	10	0	60	35	67	P
5.	SSC Napoli (Napoli)	38	16	13	9	48	39	61	
6.	Salernitana Sport (Salerno)	38	14	11	13	57	59	53	
7.	AS Bari (Bari)	38	14	11	13	44	51	53	
8.	Ancona Calcio (Ancona)	38	14	8	16	43	52	50	
9.	Vicenza Calcio (Vicenza)	38	12	13	13	50	52	49	
10.	UC Sampdoria (Genova)	38	12	12	14	42	46	48	
11.	US Città di Palermo (Palermo)	38	12	12	14	47	54	48	
12.	Genoa CFC (Genova)	38	10	17	11	43	40	47	
13.	Cagliari Calcio (Cagliari)	38	10	17	11	39	39	47	
14.	ACR Messina (Messina)	38	11	14	13	41	42	47	
15.	AC Siena (Siena)	38	12	11	15	35	44	47	
16.	Cosenza Calcio (Cosenza)	38	13	8	17	47	57	47	
17.	Ternana Calcio (Terni)	38	9	18	11	46	49	45	**
18.	AC Cittadella (Cittadella)	38	9	10	19	49	63	37	R
19.	AC Pistoiese (Pistoia)	38	8	12	18	38	51	36	R
20.	FC Crotone (Crotone)	38	5	10	23	44	70	25	R
		760	261	238	261	934	934	1021	

** As a result of AC Fiorentina (Firenze) being relegated to Serie "C-2", Ternana Calcio (Terni) retained their place in Serie "B" for the next season.

Promoted to Serie "B": Ascoli Calcio 1898 (Ascoli Piceno), Catania Calcio (Catania), Pro Livorno Calcio (Livorno) and US Triestina Calcio (Trieste).

Coppa Italia Final (1st leg) (Torino -25/04/2002 - 35,874)

Juventus FC (Torino)	2-1	PARMA AC (PARMA)
Amoruso 04' pen, Zalayeta 56'		*Nakata 90'*

Juventus: Carini, Birindelli, Thuram, Tudor (Montero 46'), Paramatti, Zenoni, Conte, Davids (Tacchinardi 58'), Nedved (Zambrotta 46'), Zalayeta, Amoruso.

Parma: Taffarel, Djetou (Gurenko 46'), Boghossian, Benarrivo, Sartor, Appiah (Nakata 74'), Lamouchi, Diana, Marchionni, Micoud, Hakan (Bonazzoli 58').

Coppa Italia Final (2nd leg) (Parma - 10/05/2002 - 26,864)

Juventus FC (Torino)	0-1	PARMA AC (PARMA)
		Júnior 04'

Parma AC (Parma) won on the away goals rule.

Parma: Taffarel, Sartor (Ferrari 88'), Sensini, Benarrivo, Diana, Almeyda, Lamouchi, Júnior, Nakata (Appiah 86'), Micoud (Bonazzoli 83'), Di Vaio.

Juventus: Carini,Birindelli(DelPiero46'),Ferrara,Montero,Paramatti,Zenoni,Conte,Tacchinardi,Zambrotta,Amoruso (Trezeguet 56'), Zalayeta (Salas 72').

Semi-Finals

Milan AC (Milano)	1-2, 1-1	Juventus FC (Torino)
Parma AC (Parma)	2-0, 1-2	Brescia Calcio (Brescia)

Quarter-Finals

Juventus CF (Torino)	4-2, 1-2	Atalanta BC (Bergamo)
Milan AC (Milano)	2-1, 3-2	SS Lazio (Roma)
AS Roma (Roma)	0-1, 0-3	Brescia Calcio (Brescia)
Udinese Calcio (Udine)	1-1, 0-0	Parma AC (Parma)

Parma AC (Parma) won on the away goals rule.

2002-2003

2002-2003 Serie "A"	Atalanta BC	Bologna 1909 FC	Brescia Calcio	AS Chievo	Como Calcio	Empoli FC	FC Internazionale	Juventus FC	SS Lazio	Milan AC	Modena FC	Parma AC	AC Perugia	FC Piacenza	Reggina Calcio	AS Roma	Torino Calcio	Udinese Calcio
Atalanta BC		2-2	2-0	1-0	2-1	2-2	1-1	1-1	0-1	1-4	1-3	0-0	0-2	2-0	1-1	2-1	2-2	0-0
Bologna 1909 FC	2-3		3-0	1-1	1-0	2-0	1-2	2-2	0-2	0-2	3-0	2-1	2-1	1-0	0-2	2-1	2-2	1-0
Brescia Calcio	3-0	0-0		0-0	1-1	0-2	0-1	2-0	0-0	1-0	2-2	1-1	3-1	1-2	2-1	2-3	1-0	1-1
AS Chievo	4-1	0-0	1-2		2-0	1-0	2-1	1-4	1-1	3-2	2-0	0-4	3-0	3-1	2-1	0-0	3-2	3-0
Como Calcio	1-1	5-0	1-1	2-4		0-2	0-2	1-3	1-3	1-2	0-0	2-2	1-1	1-1	1-1	2-0	1-0	0-2
Empoli FC	0-0	0-0	0-0	2-1	0-0		3-4	0-2	1-2	1-1	1-0	0-2	1-1	3-1	4-2	1-3	1-1	1-1
FC Internazionale	1-0	2-0	4-0	2-1	4-0	3-0		1-1	1-1	0-1	2-0	1-1	2-2	3-1	3-0	3-3	1-0	1-2
Juventus FC	3-0	1-1	2-1	4-3	1-1	1-0	3-0		1-2	2-1	3-0	2-2	2-2	2-0	5-0	2-1	2-0	1-0
SS Lazio	0-0	1-1	3-1	2-3	3-0	4-1	3-3	0-0		1-1	4-0	0-0	3-0	2-1	0-1	2-2	1-1	2-1
Milan AC	3-3	3-1	0-0	0-0	2-0	0-1	1-0	2-1	2-2		2-1	2-1	3-0	2-1	2-0	1-0	6-0	1-0
Modena FC	0-2	3-2	0-0	1-0	1-1	1-1	0-2	0-1	0-0	0-3		2-1	1-1	1-0	2-1	1-1	2-1	0-1
Parma AC	2-1	1-2	4-3	0-1	2-0	2-0	1-2	1-2	2-1	1-0	1-1		2-2	3-2	2-0	3-0	1-0	3-2
AC Perugia	1-0	1-1	0-0	1-0	3-0	1-3	4-1	0-1	2-2	1-0	2-0	1-2		0-0	2-0	1-0	2-1	0-2
FC Piacenza	2-0	3-1	1-4	0-3	0-1	1-2	1-4	0-1	2-3	4-2	3-3	1-1	5-1		2-2	1-1	1-0	2-0
Reggina Calcio	1-1	1-0	2-2	1-1	4-1	1-0	1-2	2-1	0-3	0-0	0-1	0-0	3-1	3-1		2-3	2-1	3-2
AS Roma	1-2	3-1	0-0	0-1	2-1	3-1	2-2	2-2	1-1	2-1	1-2	2-1	2-2	3-0	3-0		3-1	4-1
Torino Calcio	1-1	2-1	0-2	1-0	0-0	1-1	0-2	0-4	0-1	0-3	1-1	0-4	2-1	1-3	1-0	0-1		0-1
Udinese Calcio	1-0	0-0	0-0	2-1	3-2	2-1	2-1	0-1	2-1	1-0	2-1	1-1	0-0	2-1	1-0	2-1	1-1	

	Serie "A"	Pd	Wn	Dw	Ls	GF	GA	Pts	
1.	JUVENTUS FC (TORINO)	34	21	9	4	64	29	72	
2.	FC Internazionale (Milano)	34	19	8	7	64	38	65	
3.	Milan AC (Milano)	34	18	7	9	55	30	61	
4.	SS Lazio (Roma)	34	15	15	4	57	32	60	
5.	Parma AC (Parma)	34	15	11	8	55	36	56	
6.	Udinese Calcio (Udine)	34	16	8	10	38	35	56	
7.	AC Chievo (Verona)	34	16	7	11	51	39	55	
8.	AS Roma (Roma)	34	13	10	11	55	46	49	
9.	Brescia Calcio (Brescia)	34	9	15	10	36	38	42	
10.	AC Perugia (Perugia)	34	10	12	12	40	48	42	
11.	Bologna FC 1909 (Bologna)	34	10	11	13	39	47	41	
12.	Modena FC (Modena)	34	9	11	14	30	48	38	
13.	Empoli FC (Empoli)	34	9	11	14	36	46	38	
14.	Reggina Calcio (Reggio Calabria)	34	10	8	16	38	53	38	PO
15.	Atalanta BC (Bergamo)	34	8	14	12	35	47	38	R
16.	FC Piacenza (Piacenza)	34	8	6	20	44	62	30	R
17.	Como Calcio (Como)	34	4	12	18	29	57	24	R
18.	Torino Calcio (Torino)	32	4	9	21	23	58	21	R
		612	214	184	214	789	789	826	

Top goalscorers

1)	Christian VIERI	(FC Internazionale)	24
2)	Adrian MUTU	(Parma AC)	18
3)	Filippo INZAGHI	(Milan AC)	17
4)	Alessandro DEL PIERO	(Juventus FC)	16
5)	ADRIANO	(Parma AC)	15
	Claudio Javier LOPEZ	(SS Lazio)	15

Como Calcio 0-1 Udinese Calcio on 18/12/02 was abandoned after 81 minutes due to crowd trouble and was later awarded 0-2.

Torino Calcio 0-3 Milan AC on 23/02/03 was abandoned after 64 minutes due to a pitch invasion by the crowd and was later awarded 0-3.

Relegation Play-Off

Reggina Calcio (Reggio Calabria)	0-0, 2-1	Atalanta BC (Bergamo)

	Serie "B"	Pd	Wn	Dw	Ls	GF	GA	Pts	
1.	AC Siena (Siena)	38	17	17	4	47	25	68	P
2.	UC Sampdoria (Genova)	38	17	16	5	53	31	67	P
3.	US Lecce (Lecce)	38	15	18	5	46	33	63	P
4.	Ancona Calcio (Ancona)	38	16	13	9	53	40	61	P
5.	US Triestina Calcio (Trieste)	38	16	10	12	54	46	58	
6.	US Città di Palermo (Palermo)	38	15	13	10	45	42	58	
7.	Ternana Calcio (Terni)	38	14	13	11	45	37	55	
8.	Vicenza Calcio (Vicenza)	38	13	15	10	55	50	54	
9.	Cagliari Calcio (Cagliari)	38	14	12	12	47	46	54	
10.	Pro Livorno Calcio (Livorno)	38	12	13	13	48	43	49	
11.	AS Bari (Bari)	38	10	19	9	38	37	49	
12.	Ascoli Calcio 1898 (Ascoli Piceno)	38	13	9	16	46	52	48	
13.	Hellas Verona FC (Verona)	38	10	16	12	42	42	46	
14.	ACR Messina (Messina)	38	10	16	12	51	54	46	
15.	SSC Napoli (Napoli)	38	10	15	13	42	49	45	
16.	AC Venezia (Venezia)	38	11	12	15	39	49	45	
17.	Catania Calcio (Catania)	38	12	8	18	46	59	44	**
18.	Genoa CFC (Genova)	38	9	12	17	47	51	39	**
19.	Cosenza Calcio (Cosenza)	38	10	6	22	29	52	36	R
20.	Salernitana Sport (Salerno)	38	4	11	23	28	63	23	**
		760	248	264	248	901	901	1008	

Due to the F.I.G.C. decision to extend Serie "B" to 24 clubs for the next season Catania Calcio (Catania), Genoa CFC (Genova) and Salernitana Sport (Salerno) retained their places in Serie "B" for the next season.

Promoted to Serie "B": UC Albinoleffe (Albino), US Avellino (Avellino), Fiorentina 1926 Florentia (Firenze) *, Pescara Calcio (Pescara) and Treviso FBC (Treviso).

* Fiorentina 1926 Florentia (Firenze) changed to AC Fiorentina (Firenze) after winning promotion from Serie "C-2" to Serie "C-1" but were then further promoted by the F.I.G.C. to Serie "B".

Coppa Italia Final (1st leg) (Roma - 20/05/2003)

AS Roma (Roma)	1-4	MILAN AC (MILANO)
Totti 28'		*Serginho 62' pen.,73', Ambrosini 70', Shevchenko 89'*

Roma: I. Pelizzoli, J. Zebina, W. Samuel, C. Panucci, M. Cafu (G. Guigou 86'), D. Tommasi, F. Emerson (D. De Rossi 80'), O. Dacourt, V. Candela, F. Totti, A. Cassano (M. Delvecchio 75').

Milan: C. Abbiati, D. Simic (K. Kaladze 69'), M. Laursen, J. Roque Junior, T. Helveg, C. Brocchi, F. Redondo, M. Ambrosini, S. Serginho (S. Dalla Bona 86'), V. Rivaldo, J. Tomasson (A. Shevchenko 71').

Coppa Italia Final (2nd leg) (Milano - 31/05/2003 - 76,000)

AS Roma (Roma)	2-2	MILAN AC (MILANO)
Totti 56', 64'		*Rivaldo 65', Inzaghi 90'*

Milan: C. Abbiati, D. Simic (T. Helveg 83'), A. Nesta, M. Laursen, P. Maldini, G. Gattuso (K. Kaladze 89'), F. Redondo, C. Seedorf (Rui Costa 61'), V. Rivaldo, S. Serginho, F. Inzaghi.

Roma: I. Pelizzoli, J. Zebina, W. Samuel, C. Panucci, V. Candela (D. Fuser 84'), D. Tommasi (M. Delvecchio 54'), F. Emerson, O. Dacourt (D. De Rossi 78'), F. Lima, F. Totti, A. Cassano.

Semi-Finals

SS Lazio (Roma)	1-2, 0-1	AS Roma (Roma)
AC Perugia (Perugia)	0-0, 1-2	Milan AC (Milano)

Quarter-Finals

Juventus FC (Torino)	1-2, 0-2	AC Perugia (Perugia)
SS Lazio (Roma)	2-1, 0-0	AS Bari (Bari)
Milan AC (Milano)	0-0, 5-2	AS Chievo (Verona)
Vicenza Calcio (Vicenza)	1-2, 3-6	AS Roma (Roma)

2003-04

2003-2004 Serie "A"	Ancona	Bologna	Brescia	Chievo	Empoli	Inter	Juventus	Lazio	Lecce	Milan	Modena	Parma	Perugia	Reggina	Roma	Sampdoria	Siena	Udinese
Ancona Calcio		3-2	1-1	0-2	2-1	0-2	2-3	0-1	0-2	0-2	1-1	0-2	0-0	1-1	0-0	0-1	0-0	0-3
Bologna FC 1909	3-2		3-0	3-1	2-1	0-2	0-1	2-1	1-1	0-2	1-1	2-2	2-2	2-2	0-4	0-1	3-1	2-0
Brescia Calcio	5-2	0-0		1-1	2-0	2-2	2-3	2-1	1-2	0-1	0-0	2-3	1-1	4-4	1-0	1-1	4-2	1-2
AC Chievo	1-0	2-1	3-1		0-0	0-2	1-2	0-0	2-3	0-2	2-0	0-2	4-1	0-0	0-3	1-1	1-1	0-0
Empoli FC	2-0	2-0	1-1	0-1		2-3	3-3	2-2	0-0	0-1	0-3	1-0	1-0	1-1	0-2	1-1	1-0	2-0
FC Internazionale	3-0	4-2	1-3	0-0	0-1		3-2	0-0	3-1	1-3	2-0	1-0	2-0	6-0	0-0	0-0	4-0	1-2
Juventus FC	3-0	2-1	2-0	1-0	5-1	1-3		1-0	3-4	1-3	3-1	4-0	1-0	1-0	2-2	2-0	4-2	4-1
SS Lazio	4-2	2-1	0-1	1-0	3-0	2-1	2-0		4-1	0-1	2-1	2-3	3-1	1-1	1-1	1-1	5-2	2-2
US Lecce	3-1	1-2	1-4	1-2	2-1	2-1	1-1	0-1		1-1	1-0	1-2	1-2	2-1	0-3	0-0	0-0	2-1
Milan AC	5-0	2-1	4-2	2-2	1-0	3-2	1-1	1-0	3-0		2-0	3-1	2-1	3-1	1-0	3-1	2-1	1-2
Modena FC	2-1	2-0	1-1	0-3	1-1	1-1	0-2	1-1	2-0	1-1		2-2	1-0	1-2	0-1	1-0	1-3	0-1
Parma AC	3-1	0-0	2-2	3-1	4-0	1-0	2-2	0-3	3-1	0-0	3-0		3-0	1-2	1-4	1-0	1-1	4-3
AC Perugia	1-0	4-2	2-2	0-2	1-1	2-3	1-0	1-2	2-2	1-1	1-1	2-2		0-0	0-1	3-3	2-2	3-3
Reggina Calcio	0-0	0-0	0-0	0-0	2-0	0-2	0-2	2-1	1-3	2-1	1-1	1-1	1-2		0-0	2-2	2-1	0-1
AS Roma	3-0	1-2	5-0	3-1	3-0	4-1	4-0	2-0	3-1	1-2	1-0	2-0	1-3	2-0		3-1	6-0	1-1
UC Sampdoria	2-0	3-2	2-1	1-0	2-0	2-2	1-2	1-2	2-2	0-3	1-1	1-2	3-2	2-0	0-0		2-1	1-3
AC Siena	3-2	0-0	0-1	1-2	4-0	0-1	1-3	3-0	2-1	1-2	4-0	1-2	2-1	0-0	0-0	0-0		1-0
Udinese Calcio	3-0	1-3	4-3	1-1	2-0	0-0	0-0	1-2	1-0	0-0	1-0	1-1	1-1	1-0	1-2	0-1	1-1	

Serie "A"		Pd	Wn	Dw	Ls	GF	GA	Pts	
1.	MILAN AC (MILANO)	34	25	7	2	65	24	82	
2.	AS Roma (Roma)	34	21	8	5	68	19	71	
3.	Juventus FC (Torino)	34	21	6	7	67	42	69	
4.	FC Internazionale (Milano)	34	17	8	9	59	37	59	
5.	Parma AC (Parma)	34	16	10	8	57	46	58	
6.	SS Lazio (Roma)	34	16	8	10	52	38	56	
7.	Udinese Calcio (Udine)	34	13	11	10	44	40	50	
8.	UC Sampdoria (Genova)	34	11	13	10	40	42	46	
9.	AC Chievo (Verona)	34	11	11	12	36	37	44	
10.	US Lecce (Lecce)	34	11	8	15	43	56	41	
11.	Brescia Calcio (Brescia)	34	9	13	12	52	57	40	
12.	Bologna FC 1909 (Bologna)	34	10	9	15	45	53	39	
13.	AC Siena (Siena)	34	8	10	16	41	54	34	
14.	Reggina Calcio (Reggio Calabria)	34	6	16	12	29	45	34	
15.	AC Perugia (Perugia)	34	6	14	14	44	56	32	PO
16.	Modena FC (Modena)	34	6	12	16	27	46	30	R
17.	Empoli FC (Empoli)	34	7	9	18	26	54	30	R
18.	Ancona Calcio (Ancona)	34	2	7	25	21	70	13	R #
		612	216	180	216	816	816	826	

Ancona Calcio (Ancona) were relegated to Serie "C" for financial reasons.

The Lazio vs Roma match played on 21/03/04 was abandoned due to crowd trouble after 49 minutes with the score at 0-0. The match was replayed on 21/04/04 with a final result of 1-1.

AS Roma home games versus AC Chievo, Empoli FC and AC Perugia were played in Palermo.

Top goalscorers

1)	Andriy SHEVCHENKO	(Milan AC)	24
2)	Alberto GILARDINO	(Parma AC)	23
3)	Francesco TOTTI	(AS Roma)	20
4)	Javier CHEVANTON	(US Lecce)	19
5)	ADRIANO	(Parma AC/FC Internazionale)	17

Promotion/Relegation Play-Off

AC Perugia (Perugia) 0-1, 1-1 AC Fiorentina (Firenze)

Serie "B"	Pd	Wn	Dw	Ls	GF	GA	Pts	
1. US Città di Palermo (Palermo)	46	22	17	7	75	39	83	P
2. Cagliari Calcio (Cagliari)	46	23	14	9	80	51	83	P
3. Pro Livorno Calcio (Livorno)	46	20	19	7	75	45	79	P
4. Messina PFC (Messina)	46	21	16	9	71	45	79	P
5. Atalanta BC (Bergamo)	46	19	20	7	59	36	77	P
6. AC Fiorentina (Firenze)	46	19	16	11	53	48	73	POP
7. Ternana Calcio (Terni)	46	18	15	13	64	52	69	
8. FC Piacenza (Piacenza)	46	17	17	12	50	47	68	
9. Catania Calcio (Catania)	46	18	13	15	53	53	67	
10. US Triestina Calcio (Trieste)	46	15	19	12	50	50	64	
11. Ascoli Calcio 1898 (Ascoli)	46	14	18	14	54	54	60	
12. Torino Calcio (Torino)	46	14	17	15	57	54	59	
13. Vicenza Calcio (Vicenza)	46	12	20	14	48	51	56	
14. SSC Napoli (Napoli)	46	10	26	10	35	43	56	#
15. Treviso FBC (Treviso)	46	12	19	15	48	51	55	
16. Genoa CFC (Genova)	46	13	16	17	57	62	55	
17. Salernitana Sport (Salerno)	46	14	13	19	36	53	55	
18. UC Albinoleffe (Albino)	46	13	15	18	47	59	54	
19. Hellas Verona FC (Verona)	46	13	14	19	54	65	53	
20. AC Venezia (Venezia)	46	12	15	19	40	57	51	PO
21. AS Bari (Bari)	46	13	11	22	50	63	50	POR
22. Pescara Calcio (Pescara)	46	11	13	22	46	69	46	R
23. US Avellino (Avellino)	46	8	13	25	51	69	37	R
24. Como Calcio (Como)	46	7	12	27	34	71	33	R
	1104	358	388	358	1287	1287	1462	

SSC Napoli (Napoli) were relegated to Serie "C" for financial reasons.

Relegation Play-Off

AS Bari (Bari) 1-0, 0-2 AC Venezia (Venezia)

(A play-off was required as the teams in 20th and 21st position were separated by less than 6 points)

Promoted to Serie "B": US Arezzo (Arezzo), US Catanzaro (Catanzaro), AC Cesena (Cesena), FC Crotone (Crotone)

As a result of the forced relegation of Ancona Calcio and SSC Napoli, AS Bari (Bari) and Pescara Calcio (Pescara) retained their places in Serie "B" for the next season.

Coppa Italia Final (1st leg) (Roma – 17/03/2004 – 62,204)

SS LAZIO (ROMA) 2-0 Juventus FC (Torino)

Fiore 57', 80'

Lazio: Sereni, Oddo, Stam, Couto, Favalli, Fiore, Giannichedda, Livorno (Dabio 81'), Cesar (Zauri 88'), Corradi, Muzzi (S. Inzaghi 46').

Juventus: Chimenti, Thuram, Legrottaglie, Tudor, Pessoto, Camoranesi (Bartolucci 73'), Tacchinardi, Nedved, Conte (Maresca 73'), Appiah, Divaio (Palladino 66').

Coppa Italia Final (2nd leg) (Torino - 12/05/2004 - 38,849)

SS LAZIO (ROMA)	2-2	Juventus FC (Torino)
Corradi 69', Fiore 86'		*Trezeguet 20', Del Piero 46'*

Juventus: Buffon, Ferrara, Thuram, Legrottaglie, Birindelli, Zambrotta, Maresca (Di Vaio 75'), Nedved, Pessotto (Appiah 46'), Trezeguet, Del Piero (Miccoli 78').

Lazio: Peruzzi, Oddo, Mihajlovic, Stam, Favalli, Fiore, Liverani (Albertini 75'), Giannichedda, César, Corradi (Negro 86'), Muzzi (S. Inzaghi 60').

Semi-finals

Juventus FC (Torino)	2-2, 2-2 (aet)	FC Internazionale (Milano)
Juventus won 5-4 on penalties		
Milan AC (Milano)	1-2, 0-4	SS Lazio (Roma)

Quarter-finals

SS Lazio (Roma)	2-0, 1-1	Parma AC (Parma)
Milan AC (Milano)	2-1, 2-1	AS Roma (Roma)
AC Perugia (Perugia)	1-2, 0-1	Juventus FC (Torino)
Udinese Calcio (Udine)	0-0, 1-3	FC Internazionale (Milano)

2004-05

2004-2005 Serie "A"	Atalanta	Bologna	Brescia	Cagliari	Chievo	Fiorentina	Inter	Juventus	Lazio	Lecce	Livorno	Messina	Milan	Palermo	Parma	Reggina	Roma	Sampdoria	Siena	Udinese
Atalanta BC		2-0	0-0	2-2	3-0	1-0	2-3	1-2	1-1	2-2	1-0	2-1	1-2	1-0	1-0	0-1	0-1	0-0	1-1	0-1
Bologna FC 1909	2-1		1-2	1-0	3-1	0-0	0-1	0-1	1-2	0-0	0-0	2-2	0-2	1-1	3-1	2-0	3-1	0-0	1-1	0-1
Brescia Calcio	1-0	1-1		2-0	1-0	1-1	0-3	0-3	0-2	0-1	2-3	2-1	0-0	0-2	3-1	2-0	0-1	0-1	0-1	0-1
Cagliari Calcio	3-3	1-0	2-1		4-2	1-0	3-3	1-1	1-1	3-1	0-0	2-1	0-1	0-0	2-1	1-1	3-0	0-0	2-0	1-1
AC Chievo	1-0	1-0	3-1	1-1		1-2	2-2	0-1	0-1	2-1	1-0	1-0	0-1	2-1	2-0	0-0	2-2	0-2	1-3	0-0
AC Fiorentina	0-0	1-0	3-0	2-1	2-0		1-1	3-3	2-3	4-0	1-1	1-1	1-2	1-2	2-1	2-1	1-2	0-2	0-0	2-2
FC Internazionale	1-0	2-2	1-0	2-0	1-1	3-2		2-2	1-1	2-1	1-0	5-0	0-1	1-1	2-2	0-0	2-0	3-2	2-0	3-1
Juventus FC	2-0	2-1	2-0	4-2	3-0	1-0	0-1		2-1	5-2	4-2	2-1	0-0	1-1	2-0	1-0	2-0	0-1	3-0	2-1
SS Lazio	2-1	2-1	0-0	2-3	0-1	1-1	1-1	0-1		3-3	3-1	2-0	1-2	1-3	2-0	1-1	3-1	1-2	1-1	0-1
US Lecce	1-0	1-1	4-1	3-1	3-0	2-2	2-2	0-1	5-3		3-2	1-0	2-2	2-0	3-3	1-1	1-1	1-4	2-2	3-4
Pro Livorno Calcio	1-1	1-0	2-1	3-3	1-2	2-0	0-2	2-2	1-0	1-0		3-1	1-0	2-2	2-0	1-1	0-2	1-0	3-6	1-2
Messina PCF	1-0	0-0	2-0	2-1	0-0	1-1	2-1	0-0	1-0	1-4	1-1		1-4	0-0	1-0	2-1	4-3	2-2	4-1	1-0
Milan AC	3-0	0-1	1-1	1-0	1-0	6-0	0-0	0-1	2-1	5-2	2-2	1-2		3-3	3-0	3-1	1-1	1-0	2-1	3-1
US Città di Palermo	1-0	1-0	3-3	3-0	2-2	0-0	0-2	1-0	3-3	3-2	1-2	2-1	0-0		1-1	1-1	2-0	2-0	1-0	1-5
Parma AC	2-2	1-2	2-1	3-2	2-2	0-0	2-2	1-1	3-1	2-1	6-4	0-0	1-2	3-3		1-0	2-1	1-1	0-0	1-0
Reggina Calcio	0-0	1-1	1-3	3-2	1-0	1-2	0-0	2-1	2-1	2-2	2-1	0-2	0-1	1-0	1-3		1-0	0-1	3-3	0-0
AS Roma	2-1	1-1	2-2	5-1	0-0	1-0	3-3	1-2	0-0	2-2	3-0	3-2	0-2	1-1	5-1	1-2		1-1	0-2	0-3
UC Sampdoria	1-2	0-0	0-1	0-0	1-0	3-0	0-1	0-3	0-1	3-0	2-0	1-0	0-1	1-0	1-0	3-2	2-1		1-1	2-0
AC Siena	2-1	1-1	2-3	2-2	0-1	1-0	2-2	0-3	1-0	1-1	1-1	2-2	2-1	0-0	0-1	0-0	0-4	2-1		2-3
Udinese Calcio	2-1	0-1	1-2	2-0	3-0	2-2	1-1	0-1	3-0	2-1	1-1	1-1	1-1	1-0	4-0	0-2	3-3	1-1	1-0	

Serie "A"		Pd	Wn	Dw	Ls	GF	GA	Pts	
1.	JUVENTUS FC (TORINO)	38	26	8	4	67	27	86	
2.	Milan AC (Milano)	38	23	10	5	63	28	79	
3.	FC Internazionale (Milano)	38	18	18	2	65	37	72	
4.	Udinese Calcio (Udine)	38	17	11	10	56	40	62	
5.	UC Sampdoria (Genova)	38	17	10	11	42	29	61	
6.	US Città di Palermo (Palermo)	38	12	17	9	48	44	53	
7.	Messina PFC (Messina)	38	12	12	14	44	52	48	
8.	AS Roma (Roma)	38	11	12	15	55	58	45	
9.	Livorno Calcio (Livorno)	38	11	12	15	49	60	45	
10.	SS Lazio (Roma)	38	11	11	16	48	53	44	
11.	US Lecce (Lecce)	38	10	14	14	66	73	44	
12.	Cagliari Calcio (Cagliari)	38	10	14	14	51	60	44	
13.	Reggina Calcio (Reggio Calabria)	38	10	14	14	36	45	44	
14.	AC Siena (Siena)	38	9	16	13	44	55	43	
15.	AC Chievo (Verona)	38	11	10	17	32	49	43	
16.	AC Fiorentina (Firenze)	38	9	15	14	42	50	42	
17.	Parma AC (Parma)	38	10	12	16	48	65	42	PO
18.	Bologna FC 1909 (Bologna)	38	9	15	14	33	36	42	POR
19.	Brescia Calcio (Brescia)	38	11	8	19	37	54	41	R
20.	Atalanta BC (Bergamo)	38	8	11	19	34	45	35	R
		760	255	250	255	960	960	1015	

Messina 1-0 Atalanta on 19/12/04 was abandoned after 23 minutes due to heavy rain. The match was replayed in its entirety on 19/01/05 with a final result of 1-0.

Top goalscorers

1)	Cristiano LUCARELLI	(Livorno Calcio)	24
2)	Alberto GILARDINO	(Parma AC)	23
3)	Vincenzo MONTELLA	(AS Roma)	21
4)	Luca TONI	(US Città di Palermo)	20
5)	VUCINIC	(US Lecce)	19

Relegation Play-Off

Bologna FC 1909 (Bologna) 0-2, 1-0 Parma AC (Parma)

Serie "B"	Pd	Wn	Dw	Ls	GF	GA	Pts	
1. Genoa CFC (Genova)	42	19	19	4	72	44	76	P
2. Empoli FC (Empoli)	42	19	17	6	58	36	74	P
3. Torino Calcio (Torino)	42	21	11	10	49	31	74	POP
4. AC Perugia (Perugia)	42	21	11	10	56	34	74	PO
5. Treviso FBC (Treviso)	42	18	10	14	58	48	64	PO
6. Ascoli Calcio 1898 (Ascoli)	42	17	11	14	51	52	62	PO
7. Hellas Verona FC (Verona)	42	15	16	11	60	47	61	
8. Modena FC (Modena)	42	16	14	12	47	37	61	-1
9. Ternana Calcio (Terni)	42	14	15	13	51	54	57	
10. FC Piacenza (Piacenza)	42	16	8	18	44	46	56	
11. AS Bari (Bari)	42	13	17	12	41	37	55	-1
12. UC Albinoleffe (Albino)	42	14	13	15	55	51	55	
13. Catania Calcio (Catania)	42	13	16	13	42	44	55	
14. Salernitana Sport (Salerno)	42	12	15	15	50	57	51	
15. US Arezzo (Arezzo)	42	12	15	15	51	52	51	
16. AC Cesena (Cesena)	42	12	14	16	47	61	50	
17. FC Crotone (Crotone)	42	13	14	15	48	45	50	-3
18. Vicenza Calcio (Vicenza)	42	12	13	17	59	67	49	POR
19. US Triestina Calcio (Trieste)	42	12	12	18	43	54	48	PO
20. Pescara Calcio (Pescara)	42	10	16	16	43	61	46	R
21. AC Venezia (Venezia)	42	7	14	21	33	58	35	R
22. US Catanzaro (Catanzaro)	42	5	11	26	40	82	26	R
	924	311	302	311	1098	1098	1230	

Note: US Catanzaro had 5 points deducted for involvement in a betting scandal during 2003-04, but this penalty was later revoked.

Modena FC had 4 points deducted for involvement in a betting scandal during 2003-04, but this penalty was later reduced to a 1 point deduction.

AS Bari had 1 point deducted for crowd trouble during the away match versus AC Cesena.

FC Crotone had 3 points deducted for crowd trouble during their home match versus AC Venezia.

Promotion Play-Offs

AC Perugia (Perugia)	1-1, 0-2	Torino Calcio (Torino)
Ascoli Calcio 1898 (Ascoli)	0-1, 1-2	Torino Calcio (Torino)
Treviso FBC (Treviso)	0-1, 0-2	AC Perugia (Perugia)

Relegation Play-Off

US Triestina Calcio (Trieste)	2-0	Vicenza Calcio (Vicenza)

Promoted to Serie "B": US Avellino (Avellino), US Cremonese (Cremona), AC Mantova (Mantova) and Rimini Calcio FC (Rimini).

Coppa Italia Final (1st leg) (Roma - 12/06/2005 - 73,437)

AS Roma (Roma)	0-2	FC INTERNAZIONALE (MILANO)
		Adriano 30', 35'

Roma: Curci, Panucci, Ferrari, Chivu, Cufré (Scurto 82'), Virga (Montella 58'), Dacourt, Perrotta, Totti, Mancini (Greco 72'), Cassano.

Inter: Toldo, Zanetti, Materazzi, Mihajlovic, Favalli, Stankovic, Cambiasso, Zé María, Gonzalez (Van der Meyde 86'), Adriano, Martins (Julió Cruz 76').

Coppa Italia Final (2nd leg) (Milano - 15/06/2005 - 72,034)

AS Roma (Roma)	0-1	FC INTERNAZIONALE (MILANO)
		Mihajlovic 52'

Inter: Toldo, Cordoba, Materazzi, Mihajlovic, Favalli (Gamarra 88'), Zé María (Veron 86'), C. Zanetti, Stankovic (Biava 90'), Gonzalez, Martins, Julió Cruz.

Roma: Curci, Panucci, Mexes, Chivu (Ferrari 79'), Cufré, Perrotta, Dacourt (Montella 46', Corvia 72'), De Rossi, Mancini, Totti, Cassano.

Semi-finals

Cagliari Calcio (Cagliari)	1-1, 1-3	FC Internazionale (Milano)
AS Roma (Roma)	1-1, 2-1	Udinese Calcio (Udine)

Quarter-finals

Atalanta BC (Bergamo)	0-1, 0-3	FC Internazionale (Milano)
Cagliari Calcio (Cagliari)	2-0, 2-3	UC Sampdoria (Genova)
Milan AC (Milano)	3-2, 1-4	Udinese Calcio (Udine)
AS Roma (Roma)	1-0, 0-1 (aet)	AC Fiorentina (Firenze)

AS Roma won 7-6 on penalties

2005-06

2005-06 Serie "A"	Ascoli	Cagliari	Chievo	Empoli	Fiorentina	Inter	Juventus	Lazio	Lecce	Livorno	Messina	Milan	Palermo	Parma	Reggina	Roma	Sampdoria	Siena	Treviso	Udinese
Ascoli Calcio 1898		2-2	2-2	3-1	0-2	1-2	1-3	1-4	2-0	0-0	1-0	1-1	1-1	3-1	1-1	3-2	2-1	1-1	1-0	1-1
Cagliari Calcio	2-1		2-2	4-1	0-0	2-2	1-1	1-1	0-0	1-1	1-1	0-2	1-1	3-1	0-2	0-0	2-0	1-0	0-0	2-1
AC Chievo	1-1	2-1		2-2	0-2	0-1	1-1	2-2	3-1	2-1	2-0	2-1	0-0	1-0	4-0	4-4	1-1	4-1	0-0	2-0
Empoli FC	1-2	3-1	2-1		1-1	1-0	0-4	2-3	1-0	2-1	1-3	1-3	0-1	1-2	3-0	1-0	2-1	2-1	1-1	1-1
AC Fiorentina	3-1	2-1	2-1	2-1		2-1	1-2	1-2	1-0	3-2	2-0	3-1	1-0	4-1	5-2	1-1	2-1	2-1	1-0	4-2
FC Internazionale	1-0	3-2	1-0	4-1	1-0		1-2	3-1	3-0	5-0	3-0	3-2	3-0	2-0	4-0	2-3	1-0	1-1	3-0	3-1
Juventus FC	2-1	4-0	1-0	2-1	1-1	2-0		1-1	3-1	3-0	1-0	0-0	2-1	1-1	1-0	1-1	2-0	2-0	3-1	1-0
SS Lazio	4-1	1-1	2-2	3-3	1-0	0-0	1-1		1-0	3-1	1-0	0-0	4-2	1-0	3-1	0-2	2-0	3-2	3-1	1-1
US Lecce	0-0	3-0	0-0	1-2	1-3	0-2	0-3	0-0		0-0	0-2	1-0	2-0	1-2	0-0	2-2	0-3	3-0	1-1	1-2
AS Livorno Calcio	2-0	0-1	0-0	2-0	2-0	0-0	1-3	2-1	2-1		2-2	0-3	3-1	2-0	1-0	0-0	0-0	2-2	1-1	0-2
Messina PFC	1-1	1-0	2-0	0-3	2-2	1-2	2-2	1-1	2-1	0-0		1-3	0-0	0-1	1-1	0-2	1-4	0-0	3-1	1-1
Milan AC	1-0	1-0	4-1	3-0	3-1	1-0	3-1	2-0	2-1	2-0	4-0		2-1	4-3	2-1	2-1	1-1	3-1	5-0	5-1
US Citta di Palermo	1-1	2-2	2-2	2-2	1-0	3-2	1-2	3-1	3-0	0-2	1-0	0-2		4-2	1-0	3-3	0-2	1-3	1-0	2-0
Parma AC	0-0	1-0	2-1	1-0	2-4	1-0	1-2	1-1	2-0	2-1	1-1	2-3	1-1		4-0	0-3	1-1	1-1	1-1	1-2
Reggina Calcio	2-0	3-1	1-3	0-2	1-1	0-4	0-2	1-0	2-0	1-1	3-0	1-4	2-2	2-1		0-3	2-1	1-1	1-2	2-0
AS Roma	2-1	4-3	4-0	1-0	1-1	1-1	1-4	1-1	3-1	3-0	2-1	1-0	1-2	4-1	3-1		0-0	2-3	1-0	0-1
UC Sampdoria	1-2	1-1	1-2	2-0	3-1	2-2	0-1	2-0	1-3	0-2	4-2	2-1	0-2	1-2	3-2	1-1		3-3	1-1	1-1
AC Siena	1-1	2-1	0-1	1-0	0-2	0-0	0-3	2-3	1-2	0-0	4-2	0-3	1-2	2-2	0-0	0-2	1-0		1-0	2-3
Treviso FBC 1993	2-2	1-2	1-2	1-2	1-3	0-1	0-0	0-1	2-1	0-1	0-0	0-2	2-2	0-1	0-1	0-1	0-2	0-1		2-1
Udinese Calcio	1-1	2-0	1-1	1-0	0-0	0-1	0-1	3-0	1-2	0-2	1-0	0-4	0-0	2-0	1-2	1-4	2-0	1-2	2-2	

	Serie "A"	Pd	Wn	Dw	Ls	GF	GA	Pts	
1.	FC INTERNAZIONALE (MILANO)	38	23	7	8	68	30	76	
2.	AS Roma (Roma)	38	19	12	7	70	42	69	
3.	Milan AC (Milano)	38	28	4	6	85	31	58	-30
4.	AC Chievo (Verona)	38	13	15	10	54	49	54	
5.	US Cìtta di Palermo (Palermo)	38	13	13	12	50	52	52	
6.	AS Livorno Calcio (Livorno)	38	12	13	13	37	44	49	
7.	Empoli FC (Empoli)	38	13	6	19	47	61	45	
8.	Parma FC (Parma)	38	12	9	17	46	60	45	
9.	AC Fiorentina (Firenze)	38	22	8	8	66	41	44	-30
10.	Ascoli Calcio 1898 (Ascoli)	38	9	16	13	43	53	43	
11.	Udinese Calcio (Udine)	38	11	10	17	40	54	43	
12.	UC Sampdoria (Genova)	38	10	11	17	47	51	41	
13.	Reggina Calcio (Reggio Calabria)	38	11	8	19	39	65	41	
14.	Cagliari Calcio (Cagliari)	38	8	15	15	42	55	39	
15.	AC Siena (Siena)	38	9	12	17	42	60	39	
16.	SS Lazio (Roma)	38	16	14	8	57	47	32	-30
17.	Messina PFC (Messina)	38	6	13	19	33	59	31	
18.	US Lecce (Lecce)	38	7	8	23	30	57	29	R
19.	Treviso FBC 1993 (Treviso)	38	3	12	23	24	56	21	R
20.	Juventus FC (Torino)	38	27	10	1	71	24	91	R ##
		760	272	216	272	991	991	942	(-90)

As a result of the "match-fixing" inquiry Juventus FC (Torino) were stripped of the 2004-05 title, were placed 20th and therefore relegated for 2005-06 and began the 2006-07 season in Serie "B" with –17 points.

FC Internazionale (Milano) were subsequently declared 2005-06 champions on 26th July 2006.

As a result of the above inquiry Milan AC (Milano), AC Fiorentina (Firenze) and SS Lazio (Roma) each had 30 points deducted with Milan AC to start 2006-07 with –8 points, AC Fiorentina to start 2006-07 with –19 points and SS Lazio to start 2006-07 with –11 points. Reggina Calcio started 2006-07 with –15 points.

Messina PFC vs Empoli FC on 7th May 2006 was abandoned after 89 minutes when the score stood at 1-2. The game was later awarded to Empoli with a 3-0 scoreline.

Treviso played their 'home' games versus Empoli, Livorno, Milan and Sampdoria in Padova.

Top goalscorers

1)	Luca TONI	(AC Fiorentina)	31
2)	David TREZEGUET	(Juventus FC)	23
3)	David SUAZO	(Cagliari Calcio)	22
4)	Cristiano LUCARELLI	(AS Livorno Calcio)	19
	Andriy SHEVCHENKO	(Milan AC)	19
	Francesco TAVANO	(Empoli FC)	19

	Serie "B"	Pd	Wn	Dw	Ls	GF	GA	Pts	
1.	Atalanta BC (Bergamo)	42	24	9	9	61	39	81	P
2.	Catania Calcio (Catania)	42	22	12	8	67	42	78	P
3.	Torino FC (Torino)	42	21	13	8	51	31	76	POP
4.	AC Mantova (Mantova)	42	18	15	9	46	35	69	PO
5.	Modena FC (Modena)	42	17	16	9	59	41	67	PO
6.	AC Cesena (Cesena)	42	18	12	12	66	54	66	PO
7.	US Arezzo (Arezzo)	42	17	15	10	45	34	66	
8.	Bologna FC 1909 (Bologna)	42	16	16	10	55	42	64	
9.	FC Crotone Calcio (Crotone)	42	18	9	15	56	48	63	
10.	Brescia Calcio (Brescia)	42	15	15	12	54	44	60	
11.	Pescara Calcio (Pescara)	42	14	12	16	41	50	54	
12.	FC Piacenza (Piacenza)	42	13	15	14	56	52	54	
13.	AS Bari (Bari)	42	11	18	13	43	47	51	
14.	US Triestina Calcio (Trieste)	42	12	15	15	44	51	51	
15.	Hellas Verona FC (Verona)	42	10	19	13	42	41	49	
16.	Vicenza Calcio (Vicenza)	42	13	10	19	38	49	49	
17.	Rimini Calcio FC (Rimini)	42	11	15	16	42	49	48	
18.	UC AlbinoLeffe (Albino)	42	10	16	16	38	52	46	PO
19.	US Avellino (Avellino)	42	11	13	18	42	62	46	R
20.	Ternana Calcio (Terni)	42	7	18	17	36	58	39	R
21.	US Cremonese (Cremona)	42	6	12	24	36	60	30	R
22.	US Catanzaro (Catanzaro)	42	7	7	28	26	63	28	R
		924	311	302	311	1044	1044	1235	

Promotion Play-offs

AC Mantova (Mantova)	4-2, 1-3 (aet)	Torino FC (Torino)
	(Torino FC won promotion due to their better league record)	
AC Cesena (Cesena)	1-1, 0-1	Torino FC (Torino)
Modena FC (Modena)	0-0, 1-1	AC Mantova (Mantova)

Relegation Play-off

US Avellino (Avellino)	0-2, 3-2	UC AlbinoLeffe (Albino)

Promoted to Serie "B": Genoa Cricket & FC (Genova), Frosinone Calcio (Frosinone), SSC Napoli (Napoli) and Spezia Calcio 1906 (La Spezia).

Coppa Italia Final (1st leg) (Roma – 03/05/2006 – 70,000)

AS Roma (Roma)	1-1	FC INTERNAZIONALE (MILANO)
Mancini 55'		*Julio Cruz 07'*

Roma: Marangon "Doni", Panucci, Mexes, Chivu (Bovo 46'), Cufrè, Tommasi (Chuka 80'), De Rossi, Perrotta, Kharja, Mancini (Alvarez 85'), Taddei.

Internazionale: De Espindola, Zanetti, Cordoba, Samuel (Burdisso 70'), Favalli, Caeiro "Figo", Pizarro, Cambiasso, Stankovic (Aparecido 73'), Ribeiro "Adriano" (Martins 80'), Julio Cruz.

Coppa Italia Final (2nd leg) (Milano 11/05/2006 – 49,557)

AS Roma (Roma)	1-3	FC INTERNAZIONALE (MILANO)
Nonda 80'		*Cambiasso 06', Julio Cruz 45', Martins 78'*

Internazionale: De Espindola, Zanetti, Materazzi, Samuel, Favalli, Caeiro "Figo" (Kily Gonzalez 81'), Pizarro, Cambiasso, Stankovic (Solari 58'), Ribeiro "Adriano" (Martins 67'), Julio Cruz.

Roma: Marangon "Doni", Panucci, Chivu (Kuffour 13'), Bovo, Cufrè, Kharja (Nonda 76'), Dacourt, De Rossi, Tommasi, Mancini, Chuka (Totti 54').

Semi-finals

FC Internazionale (Milano)	1-0, 2-2	Udinese Calcio (Udine)
US Citta di Palermo (Palermo)	2-1, 0-1	AS Roma (Roma)
	(Aggregate 2-2. AS Roma won on the away goals rule)	

Quarter-finals

Juventus FC (Torino)	2-3, 1-0	AS Roma (Roma)
	(Aggregate 3-3. AS Roma won on the away goals rule)	
SS Lazio (Roma)	1-1, 0-1	FC Internazionale (Milano)
Milan AC (Milano)	1-0, 0-3	US Cìtta di Palermo (Palermo)
Udinese Calcio (Udine)	1-1, 2-2	UC Sampdoria (Genova)
	(Aggregate 3-3. Udinese Calcio won on the away goals rule)	

2006-07

2006-07 Serie "A"	Ascoli	Atalanta	Cagliari	Catania	Chievo	Empoli	Fiorentina	Inter	Lazio	Livorno	Messina	Milan	Palermo	Parma	Reggina	Roma	Sampdoria	Siena	Torino	Udinese
Ascoli Calcio 1898		1-3	2-1	2-2	3-0	0-1	1-1	1-2	2-2	0-2	1-1	2-5	3-2	0-0	2-3	1-1	1-1	0-1	0-2	2-2
Atalanta BC	3-1		3-3	1-1	1-0	0-0	2-2	1-1	0-0	5-1	3-2	2-0	1-1	1-1	1-1	2-1	3-2	3-1	1-2	1-2
Cagliari Calcio	1-0	2-0		0-1	0-2	0-0	0-2	1-1	0-2	2-2	2-0	2-2	1-0	0-0	0-2	3-2	1-0	2-2	0-0	2-1
Catania Calcio	3-3	0-0	0-1		2-0	1-1	0-1	2-5	3-1	3-2	2-2	1-1	1-2	2-0	1-4	0-2	4-2	1-1	1-1	1-0
AC Chievo	1-0	2-2	0-0	2-1		0-0	0-1	0-2	0-1	2-1	1-1	0-1	0-1	1-0	3-2	2-2	1-1	1-2	3-0	2-0
Empoli FC	4-1	2-0	1-0	2-1	1-1		1-2	0-3	1-1	2-2	3-1	0-0	2-0	2-0	3-3	1-0	2-0	1-0	0-0	1-1
AC Fiorentina	4-0	3-1	1-0	3-0	1-0	2-0		2-3	1-0	2-1	4-0	2-2	2-3	1-0	3-0	0-0	5-1	1-0	5-1	2-0
FC Internazionale	2-0	2-1	1-0	2-1	4-3	3-1	3-1		4-3	4-1	2-0	2-1	2-2	2-0	1-0	1-3	1-1	2-0	3-0	1-1
SS Lazio	3-1	1-0	0-0	3-1	0-0	3-1	0-1	0-2		1-0	1-0	0-0	1-2	0-0	0-0	3-1	1-0	1-1	2-0	5-0
AS Livorno Calcio	0-0	4-2	2-1	4-1	0-2	0-0	1-0	1-2	1-1		2-1	0-0	1-2	3-0	1-1	1-1	1-0	0-0	1-1	1-0
Messina PFC	1-2	0-0	2-2	1-1	2-1	2-2	2-2	0-1	1-4	0-1		1-3	2-0	1-1	2-0	1-1	0-2	1-0	0-3	1-0
Milan AC	1-0	1-0	3-1	3-0	3-1	3-1	0-0	3-4	2-1	2-1	1-0		0-2	1-0	3-1	1-2	1-0	0-0	0-0	2-3
US Citta di Palermo	4-0	2-3	1-3	5-3	1-1	0-1	1-1	1-2	0-3	3-0	2-1	0-0		3-4	4-3	1-2	2-0	2-1	3-0	2-0
Parma AC	1-0	3-1	2-1	1-1	2-2	3-1	2-0	1-2	1-3	1-0	4-1	0-2	0-0		2-2	0-4	0-1	1-0	1-0	0-3
Reggina Calcio	2-1	1-1	2-1	0-1	1-1	4-1	1-1	0-0	2-3	2-2	3-1	2-0	0-0	3-2		1-0	0-1	0-1	1-1	1-1
AS Roma	2-2	2-1	2-0	7-0	1-1	1-0	3-1	0-1	0-0	2-0	4-3	1-1	4-0	3-0	3-0		4-0	1-0	0-1	3-1
UC Sampdoria	2-0	2-1	1-1	1-0	3-0	1-2	0-0	0-2	2-0	4-1	3-1	1-1	1-1	3-2	0-0	2-4		0-0	1-0	3-3
AC Siena	0-1	1-1	0-0	1-1	2-1	2-0	1-1	1-2	2-1	0-0	3-1	3-4	1-1	2-2	0-1	1-3	0-2		1-0	2-2
Torino FC	1-0	1-2	1-0	1-0	1-0	1-0	0-1	1-3	0-4	0-0	1-1	0-1	0-0	1-1	1-2	1-2	1-0	1-2		2-3
Udinese Calcio	0-0	2-3	3-1	0-1	2-1	0-1	1-0	0-0	2-4	4-0	1-0	0-3	1-2	3-3	1-1	0-1	1-0	3-0	2-0	

	Serie "A"	Pd	Wn	Dw	Ls	GF	GA	Pts	
1.	FC INTERNAZIONALE (MILANO)	38	30	7	1	80	34	97	
2.	AS Roma (Roma)	38	22	9	7	74	34	75	
3.	SS Lazio (Roma)	38	18	11	9	59	33	62	-3
4.	Milan AC (Milano)	38	19	12	7	57	36	61	-8
5.	AC Fiorentina (Firenze)	38	21	10	7	62	31	58	-15
6.	US Citta di Palermo (Palermo)	38	16	10	12	58	51	58	
7.	Empoli FC (Empoli)	38	14	12	12	42	43	54	
8.	Atalanta BC (Bergamo)	38	12	14	12	56	54	50	
9.	UC Sampdoria (Genova)	38	13	10	15	44	48	49	
10.	Udinese Calcio (Udine)	38	12	10	16	49	55	46	
11.	AS Livorno Calcio (Livorno)	38	10	13	15	41	54	43	
12.	Parma FC (Parma)	38	10	12	16	41	56	42	
13.	Catania Calcio (Catania)	38	10	11	17	46	68	41	
14.	Reggina Calcio (Reggio Calabria)	38	12	15	11	52	50	40	-11
15.	AC Siena (Siena)	38	9	14	15	35	45	40	-1
16.	Cagliari Calcio (Cagliari)	38	9	13	16	35	46	40	
17.	Torino FC (Torino)	38	10	10	18	27	47	40	
18.	AC Chievo (Verona)	38	9	12	17	38	48	39	R
19.	Ascoli Calcio 1898 (Ascoli)	38	5	12	21	36	67	27	R
20.	Messina PFC (Messina)	38	5	11	22	37	69	26	R
		760	266	228	266	969	969	988	(-38)

Matches underlined were played behind "closed doors" due to new security rules following crowd trouble at the Calcio vs Palermo Round 22 match.

Catania 'home' games versus Fiorentina, Reggina and Siena were played in Rimini, matches versus Lazio and Roma were played in Lecce and the match versus Internazionale was played in Cesena.

AC Siena (Siena) had 1 point deducted for late payment of "social security".

All points deductions shown above were as a result of the 2004-05 and 2005-06 investigations into bribery.

Top goalscorers

1)	Francesco TOTTI	(AS Roma)	26
2)	Cristiano LUCARELLI	(AS Livorno Calcio)	20
3)	Christian RIGANÒ	(Messina PFC)	19
4)	Rolando BIANCHI	(Reggina Calcio)	18
5)	Nicola AMORUSO	(Reggina Calcio)	17
	Gionatha SPINESI	(Catania Calcio)	17

	Serie "B"	Pd	Wn	Dw	Ls	GF	GA	Pts	
1.	Juventus FC (Torino)	42	28	10	4	83	30	85	P -9
2.	SSC Napoli (Napoli)	42	21	16	5	52	29	79	P
3.	Genoa Cricket & FC (Genova)	42	23	9	10	68	44	78	P
4.	FC Piacenza (Piacenza)	42	20	8	14	57	50	68	
5.	Rimini Calcio FC (Rimini)	42	17	16	9	55	38	67	
6.	Brescia Calcio (Brescia)	42	19	10	13	51	43	67	
7.	Bologna FC 1909 (Bologna)	42	18	11	13	52	43	65	
8.	AC Mantova (Mantova)	42	15	19	8	47	36	64	
9.	US Lecce (Lecce)	42	17	7	18	56	53	58	
10.	UC AlbinoLeffe (Albino)	42	11	20	11	46	48	53	
11.	Vicenza Calcio (Vicenza)	42	12	14	16	42	43	50	
12.	Treviso FBC 1993 (Treviso)	42	11	17	14	44	47	50	
13.	AS Bari (Bari)	42	12	14	16	40	46	50	
14.	Frosinone Calcio (Frosinone)	42	12	14	16	44	54	50	
15.	Modena FC (Modena)	42	12	13	17	38	46	49	
16.	AC Cesena (Cesena)	42	12	13	17	51	66	49	
17.	US Triestina Calcio (Trieste)	42	11	16	15	37	48	48	-1
18.	Hellas Verona FC (Verona)	42	12	12	18	34	46	48	POR
19.	Spezia Calcio 1906 (La Spezia)	42	11	13	18	50	61	46	PO
20.	US Arezzo (Arezzo)	42	12	15	15	42	46	45	R -6
21.	FC Crotone Calcio (Crotone)	42	7	11	24	36	67	32	R
22.	Pescara Calcio (Pescara)	42	5	10	27	36	77	24	R -1
		924	318	298	318	1061	1061	1225	(-17)

All points deductions shown above were as a result of the 2004-05 and 2005-06 investigations into bribery.

Relegation Play-off

Spezia Calcio 1906 (La Spezia) 2-1, 0-0 Hellas Verona FC (Verona)

Promoted to Serie "B": US Avellino (Avellino), US Grosseto (Grosseto), Pisa Calcio (Pisa) and Ravenna Calcio (Ravenna).

Coppa Italia Final (1st leg) (Stadio Olimpico, Roma - 09/05/2007 - 39,095)

AS ROMA (ROMA)	6-2	FC Internazionale (Milano)
Totti 01', De Rossi 05', Perrotta 15', Mancini 30', Panucci 55', 90'		*Crespo 20', 56'*

Roma: Doni, Panucci, Mexès (Cassetti 47'), Ferrari, Chivu, De Rossi, Pizarro (Tonetto 87'), Taddei (Aquilani 77'), Perrotta, Mancini, Totti.

Internazionale: Toldo, Maicon, Materazzi, Córdoba, Maxwell (Grosso 68'), Zanetti, Cambiasso, Dacourt, Figo (Vieira 52'), Adriano (Recoba 58'), Crespo.

Coppa Italia Final (2nd leg) (Stadio Giuseppe Meazza, Milano - 17/05/2007 - 26,606)

AS ROMA (ROMA)	1-2	FC Internazionale (Milano)
Perrotta 83'		*Crespo 50', Cruz 56'*

Internazionale: Toldo, Maicon, Burdisso, Córdoba, Ranetti, Vieira (Cruz 27'), Cambiasso, Stankovic, Figo (Maxwell 86'), González (Recoba 58'), Crespo.

Roma: Doni, Panucci, Mexès, Ferrari, Chivu, De Rossi, Aquilani (Pizarro 62'), Taddei, Perrotta, Mancini (Tonetto 83'), Totti.

Semi-finals

Milan AC (Milano)	2-2, 1-3	AS Roma (Roma)
UC Sampdoria (Genova)	0-3, 0-0	FC Internazionale (Milano)

Quarter-finals

Empoli FC (Empoli)	0-2, 0-2	FC Internazionale (Milano)
Milan AC (Milano)	2-0, 0-1	US Arezzo (Arezzo)
AS Roma (Roma)	2-1, 2-2	Parma FC (Parma)
UC Sampdoria (Genova)	1-0, 2-1	AC Chievo (Verona)

2007-08

2007-08 Serie "A"	Atalanta	Cagliari	Catania	Empoli	Fiorentina	Genoa	Inter	Juventus	Lazio	Livorno	Milan	Napoli	Palermo	Parma	Reggina	Roma	Sampdoria	Siena	Torino	Udinese
Atalanta BC		2-2	0-0	4-1	2-2	2-0	0-2	0-4	2-1	3-2	2-1	5-1	1-3	2-0	2-2	1-2	4-1	2-2	2-2	0-0
Cagliari Calcio	1-0		1-1	2-0	2-1	2-1	0-2	2-3	1-0	0-0	1-2	2-1	0-1	1-1	2-2	1-1	0-3	1-0	3-0	0-1
Catania Calcio	1-2	2-1		1-0	0-1	0-0	0-2	1-1	1-0	1-0	1-1	3-0	3-1	0-0	1-2	1-1	2-0	0-0	1-2	2-0
Empoli FC	0-1	4-1	2-0		0-2	1-1	0-2	0-0	1-0	2-1	1-3	0-0	3-1	1-1	1-1	2-2	0-2	0-2	0-0	0-1
AC Fiorentina	2-2	5-1	2-1	3-1		3-1	0-2	1-1	1-0	1-0	0-1	1-0	1-0	3-1	2-0	2-2	2-2	3-0	2-1	1-2
Genoa Cricket & FC	2-1	2-0	2-1	0-1	0-0		1-1	0-2	0-2	1-1	0-3	2-0	3-3	1-0	2-0	0-1	0-1	1-3	3-0	3-2
FC Internazionale	2-1	2-1	2-0	1-0	2-0	4-1		1-2	3-0	2-0	2-1	2-1	2-1	3-2	2-0	1-1	3-0	2-2	4-0	1-1
Juventus FC	1-0	1-1	1-1	3-0	2-3	1-0	1-1		5-2	5-1	3-2	1-0	5-0	3-0	4-0	1-0	0-0	2-0	0-0	0-1
SS Lazio	3-0	3-1	2-0	0-0	0-1	1-2	1-1	2-3		2-0	1-5	2-1	1-2	1-0	1-0	3-2	2-1	1-1	2-2	0-1
AS Livorno Calcio	1-1	1-2	1-0	1-0	0-3	1-1	2-2	1-3	0-1		1-4	1-2	2-4	1-1	1-1	1-1	3-1	0-0	0-1	0-0
Milan AC	1-2	3-1	1-1	0-1	1-1	2-0	2-1	0-0	1-1	1-1		5-2	2-1	1-1	5-1	0-1	1-2	1-0	0-0	4-1
SSC Napoli	2-0	0-2	2-0	1-3	2-0	1-2	1-0	3-1	2-2	1-0	3-1		1-0	1-0	1-1	0-2	2-0	0-0	1-1	3-1
US Citta di Palermo	0-0	2-1	1-0	2-0	2-0	2-3	0-0	3-2	2-2	1-0	2-1	2-1		1-1	1-1	0-2	0-2	2-3	1-1	1-1
Parma AC	2-3	1-1	2-2	1-0	1-2	1-0	0-2	2-2	2-2	3-2	0-0	1-2	2-1		3-0	0-3	1-2	2-2	2-0	2-0
Reggina Calcio	1-1	2-0	3-1	2-0	0-0	2-0	0-1	2-1	1-1	1-3	0-1	1-1	0-0	2-1		0-2	1-0	4-0	1-3	1-3
AS Roma	2-1	2-0	2-0	2-1	1-0	3-2	1-4	2-2	3-2	1-1	2-1	4-4	1-0	4-0	2-0		2-0	3-0	4-1	2-1
UC Sampdoria	3-0	1-1	3-1	3-0	2-2	0-0	1-1	3-3	0-0	2-0	0-5	2-0	3-0	3-0	3-0	0-3		1-0	2-2	3-0
AC Siena	1-1	1-0	1-1	3-0	1-0	0-1	2-3	1-0	1-1	2-3	1-1	1-1	2-2	2-0	0-0	3-0	1-2		0-0	1-1
Torino FC	1-0	2-0	1-1	0-1	0-1	1-1	0-1	0-1	0-0	1-2	0-1	2-1	3-1	4-4	2-2	0-0	1-0	1-1		0-1
Udinese Calcio	2-0	0-2	2-1	2-2	3-1	3-5	0-0	1-2	2-2	2-0	0-1	0-5	1-1	2-1	2-0	1-3	3-2	2-0	2-1	

	Serie "A"	Pd	Wn	Dw	Ls	GF	GA	Pts	
1.	FC INTERNAZIONALE (MILANO)	38	25	10	3	69	26	85	
2.	AS Roma (Roma)	38	24	10	4	72	37	82	
3.	Juventus FC (Torino)	38	20	12	6	72	37	72	
4.	AC Fiorentina (Firenze)	38	19	9	10	55	39	66	
5.	Milan AC (Milano)	38	18	10	10	66	38	64	
6.	UC Sampdoria (Genova)	38	17	9	12	56	46	60	
7.	Udinese Calcio (Udine)	38	16	9	13	48	53	57	
8.	SSC Napoli (Napoli)	38	14	8	16	50	53	50	
9.	Atalanta BC (Bergamo)	38	12	12	14	52	56	48	
10.	Genoa Cricket & FC (Genova)	38	13	9	16	44	52	48	
11.	US Citta di Palermo (Palermo)	38	12	11	15	47	57	47	
12.	SS Lazio (Roma)	38	11	13	14	47	51	46	
13.	AC Siena (Siena)	38	9	17	12	40	45	44	
14.	Cagliari Calcio (Cagliari)	38	11	9	18	40	56	42	
15.	Torino FC (Torino)	38	8	16	14	36	49	40	
16.	Reggina Calcio (Reggio Calabria)	38	9	13	16	37	56	40	
17.	Catania Calcio (Catania)	38	8	13	17	33	45	37	
18.	Empoli FC (Empoli)	38	9	9	20	29	52	36	R
19.	Parma FC (Parma)	38	7	13	18	42	62	34	R
20.	AS Livorno Calcio (Livorno)	38	6	12	20	35	60	30	R
		760	268	224	268	970	970	1028	

Atalanta BC vs Milan AC played on 11th November 2007 was abandoned after 7 minutes due to crowd trouble with the game goalless. The match was replayed in full on 23rd January 2008.

Top goalscorers

1)	Alessandro DEL PIERO	(Juventus FC)	21
2)	David TREZEGUET	(Juventus FC)	20
3)	Marco BORRIELLO	(Genoa Cricket & FC)	19
4)	Zlatan IBRAHIMOVIC	(FC Internazionale)	17
	Adrian MUTU	(AC Fiorentina)	17
	Antonio DI NATALE	(Udinese Calcio)	17

	Serie "B"	Pd	Wn	Dw	Ls	GF	GA	Pts	
1.	AC Chievo (Verona)	42	24	13	5	77	43	85	P
2.	Bologna FC 1909 (Bologna)	42	24	12	6	58	29	84	P
3.	US Lecce (Lecce)	42	23	14	5	70	29	83	POP
4.	UC AlbinoLeffe (Albino)	42	23	9	10	67	48	78	PO
5.	Brescia Calcio (Brescia)	42	20	12	10	59	40	72	PO
6.	Pisa Calcio (Pisa)	42	19	14	9	61	44	71	PO
7.	Rimini Calcio FC (Rimini)	42	20	9	13	68	46	69	
8.	Ascoli Calcio 1898 (Ascoli)	42	16	14	12	64	49	62	
9.	AC Mantova (Mantova)	42	16	12	14	56	49	60	
10.	Frosinone Calcio (Frosinone)	42	15	11	16	63	67	56	
11.	AS Bari (Bari)	42	13	16	13	50	55	55	
12.	US Triestina Calcio (Trieste)	42	13	12	17	55	67	51	
13.	US Grosseto (Grosseto)	42	10	19	13	47	54	49	
14.	Messina PFC (Messina)	42	13	10	19	38	62	49	##
15.	FC Piacenza (Piacenza)	42	13	8	21	43	59	47	
16.	Modena FC (Modena)	42	10	16	16	57	65	46	
17.	Treviso FC 1993 (Treviso)	42	11	12	19	41	52	45	
18.	Vicenza Calcio (Vicenza)	42	10	15	17	43	60	45	
19.	US Avellino (Avellino)	42	8	12	22	42	64	36	##
20.	Ravenna Calcio (Ravenna)	42	8	11	23	48	75	35	R
21.	Spezia Calcio 1906 (La Spezia)	42	6	16	20	45	66	33	R
22.	AC Cesena (Cesena)	42	5	17	20	37	66	32	R
		924	320	284	320	1189	1189	1244	

Messina PFC (Messina) were relegated. As a result, US Avellino (Avellino) retained their Serie "B" status.

Promoted to Serie "B": AC Ancona (Ancona), AC Cittadella (Cittadella), Salernitana Calcio 1919 (Salerno) and US Sassuolo Calcio (Sassuolo)

Coppa Italia Final (Stadio Olimpico, Roma – 24/05/2008 – 50,000)

AS ROMA (ROMA) 2-1 FC Internazionale (Milano)

Mexès 36', Perrotta 54' *Pelé 60'*

Roma: Doni, Cassetti, Mexès, Juan, Tonetto, De Rossi, Pizarro, Aquilani (Panucci 90'), Perrotta (Brighi 72'), Giuly (Cicinho 66'), Vucinic.

Internazionale: Toldo. Maicon, Chivu, Burdisso, Maxwell, Zannetti (Crespo 90'), Vieira, Stankovic (Pelé 46'), César (Jimenez 62'), Suazo, Balotelli.

Semi-finals

FC Internazionale (Milano) 0-0, 2-0 SS Lazio (Roma)
AS Roma (Roma) 1-0, 1-1 Catania Calcio (Catania)

Quarter-finals

FC Internazionale (Milano) 2-2, 3-2 Juventus FC (Torino)
SS Lazio (Roma) 2-1, 2-1 AC Fiorentina (Firenze)
UC Sampdoria (Genova) 1-1, 0-1 AS Roma (Roma)
Udinese Calcio (Udine) 3-2, 1-2 Catania Calcio (Catania)

(Aggregate 4-4. Catania Calcio won on the away goals rule)

2008-09

2008-09 Serie "A"	Atalanta	Bologna	Cagliari	Catania	Chievo	Fiorentina	Genoa	Inter	Juventus	Lazio	Lecce	Milan	Napoli	Palermo	Reggina	Roma	Sampdoria	Siena	Torino	Udinese
Atalanta BC		0-1	1-0	1-0	0-2	1-2	1-1	3-1	1-3	2-0	0-0	0-1	3-1	2-2	0-1	3-0	4-2	1-0	2-0	3-0
Bologna FC 1909	0-1		0-1	3-1	1-1	1-3	2-0	1-2	1-2	3-1	2-1	1-4	0-1	1-1	1-2	1-1	3-0	1-4	5-2	0-3
Cagliari Calcio	0-1	5-1		1-0	2-0	1-0	0-1	2-1	0-1	1-4	2-0	0-0	2-0	1-0	1-1	2-2	1-0	1-0	0-0	2-0
Catania Calcio	1-0	1-2	2-1		1-0	0-2	1-0	0-2	1-2	1-1	1-1	0-2	3-1	2-0	2-0	3-2	2-0	0-3	3-2	0-2
AC Chievo	1-1	0-0	1-1	1-1		0-2	0-1	2-2	0-2	1-2	1-1	0-1	2-1	1-0	2-1	0-1	1-1	0-2	1-1	1-2
AC Fiorentina	2-1	1-0	2-1	2-0	2-1		1-0	0-0	1-1	1-0	1-2	0-2	2-1	0-2	3-0	4-1	1-0	1-0	1-0	4-2
Genoa Cricket & FC	1-1	1-1	2-1	1-1	2-2	3-3		0-2	3-2	0-1	4-1	2-0	3-2	1-0	4-0	3-1	3-1	1-0	3-0	2-0
FC Internazionale	4-3	2-1	1-1	2-1	4-2	2-0	0-0		1-0	2-0	1-0	2-1	2-1	2-2	3-0	3-3	1-0	3-0	1-1	1-0
Juventus FC	2-2	4-1	2-3	1-1	3-3	1-0	4-1	1-1		2-0	2-2	4-2	1-0	1-2	4-0	2-0	1-1	1-0	1-0	1-0
SS Lazio	0-1	2-0	1-4	1-0	0-3	3-0	1-1	0-3	1-1		1-1	0-3	0-1	1-0	1-0	4-2	2-0	3-0	1-1	1-3
US Lecce	2-2	0-0	2-0	2-1	2-0	1-1	0-2	0-3	1-2	0-2		1-1	1-1	1-1	0-0	0-3	1-3	1-1	3-3	2-2
Milan AC	3-0	1-2	1-0	1-0	1-0	1-0	1-1	1-0	1-1	4-1	2-0		1-0	3-0	1-1	2-3	3-0	2-1	5-1	5-1
SSC Napoli	0-0	1-1	2-2	1-0	3-0	2-1	0-1	1-0	2-1	0-2	3-0	0-0		2-1	3-0	0-3	2-0	2-0	1-2	2-2
US Citta di Palermo	3-2	4-1	5-1	0-4	3-0	1-3	2-1	0-2	0-2	2-0	5-2	3-1	2-1		1-0	3-1	2-2	2-0	1-0	3-2
Reggina Calcio	3-1	2-2	2-1	1-1	0-1	1-1	0-1	2-3	2-2	2-3	2-0	1-2	1-1	0-0		2-2	0-2	1-1	2-1	0-2
AS Roma	2-0	2-1	3-2	4-3	0-0	1-0	3-0	0-4	1-4	1-0	3-2	2-2	1-1	2-1	3-0		2-0	1-0	3-2	1-1
UC Sampdoria	1-0	2-0	3-3	3-0	1-1	0-1	0-1	1-1	0-0	3-1	3-2	2-1	2-2	0-2	5-0	2-2		2-2	1-0	2-2
AC Siena	1-0	1-1	2-0	1-1	0-2	1-0	0-0	1-2	0-3	2-0	1-2	1-5	2-1	1-0	1-0	1-0	0-0		1-0	1-1
Torino FC	2-1	1-1	0-1	2-1	1-0	1-4	2-3	1-3	0-1	1-3	3-0	2-2	1-0	1-0	0-0	0-1	1-3	1-0		1-0
Udinese Calcio	3-0	1-0	6-2	1-1	0-1	3-1	2-2	0-1	2-1	3-3	2-0	2-1	0-0	3-1	0-1	3-1	1-1	2-1	2-0	

	Serie "A"	Pd	Wn	Dw	Ls	GF	GA	Pts	
1.	FC INTERNAZIONALE (MILANO)	38	25	9	4	70	32	84	
2.	Juventus FC (Torino)	38	21	11	6	69	37	74	
3.	Milan AC (Milano)	38	22	8	8	70	35	74	
4.	AC Fiorentina (Firenze)	38	21	5	12	53	38	68	
5.	Genoa Cricket & FC (Genova)	38	19	11	8	56	39	68	
6.	AS Roma (Roma)	38	18	9	11	64	61	63	
7.	Udinese Calcio (Udine)	38	16	10	12	61	50	58	
8.	US Citta di Palermo (Palermo)	38	17	6	15	57	50	57	
9.	Cagliari Calcio (Cagliari)	38	15	8	15	49	50	53	
10.	SS Lazio (Roma)	38	15	5	18	46	55	50	
11.	Atalanta BC (Bergamo)	38	13	8	17	45	48	47	
12.	SSC Napoli (Napoli)	38	12	10	16	43	45	46	
13.	UC Sampdoria (Genova)	38	11	13	14	49	52	46	
14.	AC Siena (Siena)	38	12	8	18	33	44	44	
15.	Catania Calcio (Catania)	38	12	7	19	41	51	43	
16.	AC Chievo (Verona)	38	8	14	16	35	49	38	
17.	Bologna FC 1909 (Bologna)	38	9	10	19	43	62	37	
18.	Torino FC (Torino)	38	8	10	20	37	61	34	R
19.	Reggina Calcio (Reggio Calabria)	38	6	13	19	30	62	31	R
20.	US Lecce (Lecce)	38	5	15	18	37	67	30	R
		760	285	190	285	988	988	1045	

Roma vs Sampdoria played on 29th October 2008 was abandoned after 6 minutes due to heavy rain with the game goalless. The remaining 84 minutes was played on 14th January 2009 and finished with a 2-0 scoreline.

Top goalscorers

1)	Zlatan IBRAHIMOVIC	(FC Internazionale)	25
2)	Diego Alberto MILITO	(Genoa Cricket & FC)	24
	Marci DI VAIO	(Bologna FC 1909)	24
4)	Alberto GILARDINO	(AC Fiorentina)	19
5)	"KAKÁ" (Ricardo Izecson Santos Leite)	(Milan AC)	16

	Serie "B"	Pd	Wn	Dw	Ls	GF	GA	Pts	
1.	AS Bari (Bari)	42	22	14	6	65	35	80	P
2.	Parma FC (Parma)	42	19	19	4	65	34	76	P
3.	AS Livorno Calcio (Livorno)	42	16	20	6	64	40	68	POP
4.	Brescia Calcio (Brescia)	42	18	13	11	54	40	67	PO
5.	Empoli FC (Empoli)	42	18	13	11	53	44	67	PO
6.	US Grosseto (Grosseto)	42	18	10	14	64	66	64	PO
7.	US Sassuolo Calcio (Sassuolo)	42	15	15	12	57	50	60	
8.	US Triestina Calcio (Trieste)	42	16	11	15	52	47	59	
9.	UC AlbinoLeffe (Albino)	42	15	13	14	49	49	58	
10.	FC Piacenza (Piacenza)	42	14	13	15	48	48	55	
11.	Frosinone Calcio (Frosinone)	42	13	14	15	48	53	53	
12.	Vicenza Calcio (Vicenza)	42	13	13	16	44	41	52	
13.	AC Mantova (Mantova)	42	12	16	14	41	46	52	
14.	Modena FC (Modena)	42	13	12	17	54	63	51	
15.	Salernitana Calcio 1919 (Salerno)	42	14	9	19	46	56	51	
16.	Ascoli Calcio 1898 (Ascoli)	42	14	10	18	37	48	51	-1
17.	AC Cittadella (Cittadella)	42	11	17	14	42	43	50	
18.	Rimini Calcio FC (Rimini)	42	13	11	18	43	56	50	POR
19.	AC Ancona (Ancona)	42	14	7	21	54	66	49	PO
20.	Pisa Calcio (Pisa)	42	12	12	18	45	55	48	R
21.	US Avellino (Avellino)	42	9	15	18	41	61	40	R-2
22.	Treviso FC 1993 (Treviso)	42	7	15	20	37	62	35	R-1
		924	316	292	316	1103	1103	1236	(-4)

Ascoli Calcio 1898 (Ascoli) and Treviso FC 1993 (Treviso) each had 1 point deducted for "financial irregularities".

US Avellino (Avellino) had 2 points deducted for "financial irregularities".

Promotion Play-Offs

Brescia Calcio (Brescia)	2-2, 0-3	AS Livorno Calcio (Livorno)
Empoli FC (Empoli)	1-1, 0-3	Brescia Calcio (Brescia)
US Grosseto (Grosseto)	2-0, 1-4	AS Livorno Calcio (Livorno)

Relegation Play-off

AC Ancona (Ancona)	1-1, 1-0	Rimini Calcio (Rimini)

Promoted to Serie "B": AC Cesena (Cesena), FC Crotone Calcio (Crotone), Gallipoli Calcio (Gallipoli) and Padova Calcio (Padova).

Coppa Italia Final (Stadio Olimpico, Roma – 13/05/2009 – 68,000)

SS LAZIO (ROMA) 1-1 (aet) UC Sampdoria (Genova)

Zárate 04' *(SS Lazio won 6-5 on penalties)* *Pazzini 31'*

Lazio: Muslera, Lichsteiner, Siviglia, Rozehnal, Kolarov, Brocchi (de Silvestri 103'), Dabo, Ledesma, Foggia (del Nero 80'), Zárate, Pandev (Rocchi 73').

Sampdoria: Castellazzi, Campanaro, Lucchini (Gastaldello 96'), Accardi, Stankevicius, Sammarco (Dessena 90'), Palombo, Franceschini (Delvecchio 88'), Pieri, Pazzini, Cassano.

Semi-finals

SS Lazio Roma) 2-1, 2-1 Juventus FC (Torino)
UC Sampdoria (Genova) 3-0, 0-1 FC Internazionale (Milano)

Quarter-finals

FC Internazionale (Milano) 2-1 AS Roma (Roma)
Juventus FC (Torino) 0-0 (aet) SSC Napoli (Napoli)
(Juventus FC won 4-3 on penalties)
SS Lazio (Roma) 3-1 Torino FC (Torino)
Udinese Calcio (Udine) 1-1 UC Sampdoria (Genova)

2009-10

2009-10 Serie "A"	Atalanta	Bari	Bologna	Cagliari	Catania	Chievo	Fiorentina	Genoa	Inter	Juventus	Lazio	Livorno	Milan	Napoli	Palermo	Parma	Roma	Sampdoria	Siena	Udinese
Atalanta BC		1-0	1-1	3-1	0-0	0-1	2-1	0-1	1-1	2-5	3-0	3-0	1-1	0-2	1-2	3-1	1-2	0-1	2-0	0-0
Bari FC	4-1		0-0	0-1	0-0	1-0	2-0	3-0	2-2	3-1	2-0	1-0	0-2	1-2	4-2	1-1	0-1	2-1	2-1	2-0
Bologna FC 1909	2-2	2-1		0-1	1-1	0-2	1-1	1-3	1-3	1-2	2-3	2-0	0-0	2-1	3-1	2-1	0-2	1-1	2-1	2-1
Cagliari Calcio	3-0	3-1	1-1		2-2	1-2	2-2	3-2	1-2	2-0	0-2	3-0	2-3	3-3	2-0	2-2	2-2	2-0	1-3	2-2
Catania Calcio	0-0	4-0	1-0	2-1		1-2	1-0	1-0	3-1	1-1	1-1	0-1	0-2	0-0	2-0	3-0	1-1	1-2	2-2	1-1
AC Chievo	1-1	1-2	1-1	2-1	1-1		2-1	3-1	0-1	1-0	1-2	2-0	1-2	1-2	1-0	0-0	0-2	1-2	0-1	1-1
AC Fiorentina	2-0	2-1	1-2	1-0	3-1	0-2		3-0	2-2	1-2	0-0	2-1	1-2	0-1	1-0	2-3	0-1	2-0	1-1	4-1
Genoa Cricket & FC	2-0	1-1	3-4	5-3	2-0	1-0	2-1		0-5	2-2	1-2	1-1	1-0	4-1	2-2	2-2	3-2	3-0	4-2	3-0
FC Internazionale	3-1	1-1	3-0	3-0	2-1	4-3	1-0	0-0		2-0	1-0	3-0	2-0	3-1	5-3	2-0	1-1	0-0	4-3	2-1
Juventus FC	2-1	3-0	1-1	1-0	1-2	1-0	1-1	3-2	2-1		1-1	2-0	0-3	2-3	0-2	2-3	1-2	5-1	3-3	1-0
SS Lazio	1-0	0-2	0-0	0-1	0-1	1-1	1-1	1-0	0-2	0-2		4-1	1-2	1-1	1-1	1-2	1-2	1-1	2-0	3-1
AS Livorno Calcio	1-0	1-1	0-1	0-0	3-1	0-2	0-1	2-1	0-2	1-1	1-2		0-0	0-2	1-2	2-1	3-3	3-1	1-2	0-2
Milan AC	3-1	0-0	1-0	4-3	2-2	1-0	1-0	5-2	0-4	3-0	1-1	1-1		1-1	0-2	2-0	2-1	3-0	4-0	3-2
SSC Napoli	2-0	3-2	2-1	0-0	1-0	2-0	1-3	0-0	0-0	3-1	0-0	3-1	2-2		0-0	2-3	2-2	1-0	2-1	0-0
US Citta di Palermo	1-0	1-1	3-1	2-1	1-1	3-1	3-0	0-0	1-1	2-0	3-1	1-0	3-1	2-1		2-1	3-3	1-1	1-0	1-0
Parma FC	1-0	2-0	2-1	0-2	2-1	2-0	1-1	2-3	1-1	1-2	0-2	4-1	1-0	1-1	1-0		1-2	1-0	1-0	0-0
AS Roma	2-1	3-1	2-1	2-1	1-0	1-0	3-1	3-0	2-1	1-3	1-0	0-1	0-0	2-1	4-1	2-0		1-2	2-1	4-2
UC Sampdoria	2-0	0-0	4-1	1-1	1-1	2-1	2-0	1-0	1-0	1-0	2-1	2-0	2-1	1-0	1-1	1-1	0-0		4-1	3-1
AC Siena	0-2	3-2	1-0	1-1	3-2	0-0	1-5	0-0	0-1	0-1	1-1	0-0	1-2	0-0	1-2	1-1	1-2	1-2		2-1
Udinese Calcio	1-3	3-3	1-1	2-1	4-2	0-0	0-1	2-0	2-3	3-0	1-1	2-0	1-0	3-1	3-2	2-2	2-1	2-3	4-1	

	Serie "A"	Pd	Wn	Dw	Ls	GF	GA	Pts	
1.	FC INTERNAZIONALE (MILANO)	38	24	10	4	75	34	82	
2.	AS Roma (Roma)	38	24	8	6	68	41	80	
3.	Milan AC (Milano)	38	20	10	8	60	39	70	
4.	UC Sampdoria (Genova)	38	19	10	9	49	41	67	
5.	US Citta di Palermo (Palermo)	38	18	11	9	59	47	65	
6.	SSC Napoli (Napoli)	38	15	14	9	50	43	59	
7.	Juventus FC (Torino)	38	16	7	15	55	56	55	
8.	Parma FC (Parma)	38	14	10	14	46	51	52	
9.	Genoa Cricket & FC (Genova)	38	14	9	15	57	61	51	
10.	AS Bari (Bari)	38	13	11	14	49	49	50	
11.	AC Fiorentina (Firenze)	38	13	8	17	48	47	47	
12.	SS Lazio (Roma)	38	11	13	14	39	43	46	
13.	Catania Calcio (Catania)	38	10	15	13	44	45	45	
14.	Cagliari Calcio (Cagliari)	38	11	11	16	56	58	44	
15.	Udinese Calcio (Udine)	38	11	11	16	54	59	44	
16.	AC Chievo (Verona)	38	12	8	18	37	42	44	
17.	Bologna FC 1909 (Bologna)	38	10	12	16	42	55	42	
18.	Atalanta BC (Bergamo)	38	9	8	21	37	53	35	R
19.	AC Siena (Siena)	38	7	10	21	40	67	31	R
20.	AS Livorno Calcio (Livorno)	38	7	8	23	27	61	29	R
		760	278	204	278	992	992	1038	

Top goalscorers

1)	Antonio DI NATALE	(Udinese Calcio)	29
2)	Diego Alberto MILITO	(FC Internazionale)	22
3)	Fabrizio MICCOLI	(US Citta di Palermo)	19
	Giampaolo PAZZINI	(UC Sampdoria)	19
5)	Alberto GILARDINO	(AC Fiorentina)	15

	Serie "B"	Pd	Wn	Dw	Ls	GF	GA	Pts	
1.	US Lecce (Lecce)	42	20	15	7	66	47	75	P
2.	AC Cesena (Cesena)	42	20	14	8	55	29	74	P
3.	Brescia Calcio (Brescia)	42	21	9	12	60	44	72	POP
4.	US Sassuolo Calcio (Sassuolo)	42	18	15	9	60	42	69	PO
5.	Torino FC (Torino)	42	19	11	12	53	36	68	PO
6.	AC Cittadella (Cittadella)	42	18	12	12	62	43	66	PO
7.	US Grosseto (Grosseto)	42	14	19	9	66	63	61	
8.	FC Crotone Calcio (Crotone)	42	17	11	14	53	50	60	-2
9.	Ascoli Calcio 1898 (Ascoli)	42	15	12	15	57	57	57	
10.	Empoli FC (Empoli)	42	15	11	16	66	56	56	
11.	UC AlbinoLeffe (Albino)	42	14	13	15	59	56	55	
12.	Modena FC (Modena)	42	14	12	16	39	47	54	
13.	Reggina Calcio (Reggio Calabria)	42	15	9	18	51	56	54	
14.	Vicenza Calcio (Vicenza)	42	12	17	13	40	41	53	
15.	FC Piacenza (Piacenza)	42	13	14	15	40	45	53	
16.	Frosinone Calcio (Frosinone)	42	15	8	19	50	67	53	
17.	AC Ancona (Ancona)	42	15	9	18	55	56	52	-2
18.	US Triestina Calcio (Trieste)	42	13	12	17	41	51	51	PO
19.	Padova Calcio (Padova)	42	12	15	15	44	48	51	PO
20.	AC Mantova (Mantova)	42	10	18	14	46	58	48	R
21.	Gallipoli Calcio (Gallipoli)	42	10	10	22	43	74	40	R
22.	Salernitana Calcio 1919 (Salerno)	42	5	8	29	40	80	17	R-6
		924	325	274	325	1146	1146	1239	(-10)

FC Crotone Calcio had 2 points deducted due to financial irregularities.

AC Ancona had 2 points deducted due to financial irregularities and were subsequently excluded from all football leagues after entering bankruptcy. The club were duly relegated to the Eccellenza (sixth level of Italian football) as US Ancona 1905. As a result of this relegation, US Triestina Calcio retained their Serie "B" status.

Salernitana Calcio 1919 (Salerno) had 6 points deducted due to their involvement in match-fixing during the 2007-08 Serie C1 season.

AC Mantova entered bankruptcy and were relegated to Serie "D"

Gallipoli Calcio entered bankruptcy and were relegated to the Promozione (seventh level of Italian football).

Promotion Play-offs

Torino FC (Torino)	0-0, 1-2	Brescia Calcio (Brescia)
Torino FC (Torino)	1-1, 2-1	US Sassuolo Calcio (Sassuolo)
AC Cittadella (Cittadella)	0-1, 1-0	Brescia Calcio (Brescia)

(Brescia Calcio qualified for the Play-off final due to their higher final league position)

Relegation Play-off

Padova Calcio (Padova)	0-0, 3-0	US Triestina Calcio (Trieste)

Promoted to Serie "B": Delfino Pescara 1936 (Pescara), Novara Calcio (Novara), AS Varese 1910 (Varese) and Calcio Portogruaro Summaga (Portogruaro).

Coppa Italia Final (Stadio Olimpico, Roma – 05/05/2010 – 55,000)

FC INTERNAZIONALE (MILANO)	1-0	AS Roma (Roma)

Milito 39'

Internazionale: Júlio César, Maicon, Córdoba (Samuel), Materazzi, Chivu, Zanetti, Cambiasso, Motta, Sneijder (Balotelli 05'), Eto'o, Milito.

Roma: Júlio Sérgio, Burdisso (Motta 46'), Juan, Mexès, Riise, Taddei, Perrotta, Pizarro (Totti 46'), de Rossi, Vucinic, Toni (Menez 63').

Semi-finals

FC Internazionale (Milano)	1-0, 1-0	AC Fiorentina (Firenze)
AS Roma (Roma)	2-0, 0-1	Udinese Calcio (Udine)

Quarter-finals

AC Fiorentina (Firenze)	3-2	SS Lazio (Roma)
FC Internazionale (Milano)	2-1	Juventus FC (Torino)
Milan AC (Milano)	0-1	Udinese Calcio (Udine)
AS Roma (Roma)	1-0	Catania Calcio (Catania)

2010-11

2010-11 Serie "A"	Bari	Bologna	Brescia	Cagliari	Catania	Cesena	Chievo	Fiorentina	Genoa	Internazionale	Juventus	Lazio	Lecce	Milan	Napoli	Palermo	Parma	Roma	Sampdoria	Udinese
AS Bari		0-2	2-1	0-0	1-1	1-1	1-2	1-1	0-0	0-3	1-0	0-2	0-2	2-3	0-2	1-1	0-1	2-3	0-1	0-2
Bologna FC 1909	0-4		1-0	2-2	1-0	0-2	2-1	1-1	1-1	0-0	0-0	3-1	2-0	0-3	0-2	1-0	0-0	0-1	1-1	2-1
Brescia Calcio	2-0	3-1		1-2	1-2	1-2	0-3	2-2	0-0	1-1	1-1	0-2	2-2	0-1	0-1	3-2	2-0	2-1	1-0	0-1
Cagliari Calcio	2-1	2-0	1-1		3-0	0-2	4-1	1-2	0-1	0-1	1-3	1-0	3-2	0-1	0-1	3-1	1-1	5-1	0-0	0-4
Catania Calcio	1-0	1-1	1-0	2-0		2-0	1-1	0-0	2-1	1-2	1-3	1-4	3-2	0-2	1-1	4-0	2-1	2-1	1-0	1-0
AC Cesena	1-0	0-2	1-0	1-0	1-1		1-0	2-2	0-0	1-2	2-2	1-0	1-0	2-0	1-4	1-2	1-1	0-1	0-1	0-3
AC Chievo	0-0	2-0	0-1	0-0	2-1	2-1		0-1	0-0	2-1	1-1	0-1	1-0	1-2	2-0	0-0	0-0	2-2	0-0	0-2
AC Fiorentina	2-1	1-1	3-2	1-0	3-0	1-0	1-0		1-0	1-2	0-0	1-2	1-1	1-2	1-1	1-2	2-0	2-2	0-0	5-2
Genoa CFC	2-1	1-0	3-0	0-1	1-0	3-2	1-3	1-1		0-1	0-2	0-0	4-2	1-1	0-1	1-0	3-1	4-3	2-1	2-4
FC Internazionale	4-0	4-1	1-1	1-0	3-1	3-2	2-0	3-1	5-2		0-0	2-1	1-0	0-1	3-1	3-2	5-2	5-3	1-1	2-1
Juventus FC	2-1	0-2	2-1	4-2	2-2	3-1	2-2	1-1	3-2	1-0		2-1	4-0	0-1	2-2	1-3	1-4	1-1	3-3	1-2
SS Lazio	1-0	3-1	1-0	2-1	1-1	1-0	1-1	2-0	4-2	3-1	0-1		1-2	1-1	2-0	2-0	2-0	0-2	1-0	3-2
US Lecce	0-1	0-1	2-1	3-3	1-0	1-1	3-2	1-0	1-3	1-1	2-0	2-4		1-1	2-1	2-4	1-1	1-2	2-3	2-0
Milan AC	1-1	1-0	3-0	4-1	1-1	2-0	3-1	1-0	1-0	3-0	1-2	0-0	4-0		3-0	3-1	4-0	0-1	3-0	4-4
SSC Napoli	2-2	4-1	0-0	2-1	1-0	2-0	1-3	0-0	1-0	1-1	3-0	4-3	1-0	1-2		1-0	2-0	2-0	4-0	1-2
US Città di Palermo	2-1	4-1	1-0	0-0	3-1	2-2	1-3	2-4	1-0	1-2	2-1	0-1	2-2	1-0	2-1		3-1	3-1	3-0	0-7
Parma AC	1-2	0-0	2-0	1-2	2-0	2-2	0-0	1-1	1-1	2-0	1-0	1-1	0-1	0-1	1-3	3-1		0-0	1-0	2-1
AS Roma	1-0	2-2	1-1	3-0	4-2	0-0	1-0	3-2	2-1	1-0	0-2	2-0	2-0	0-0	0-2	2-3	2-2		3-1	2-0
UC Sampdoria	3-0	3-1	3-3	0-1	0-0	2-3	0-0	2-1	0-1	0-2	0-0	2-0	1-2	1-1	1-2	1-2	0-1	2-1		0-0
Udinese Calcio	1-0	1-1	0-0	1-1	2-0	1-0	2-0	2-1	0-1	3-1	0-4	2-1	4-0	0-0	3-1	2-1	0-2	1-2	2-0	

	Serie "A"	Pd	Wn	Dw	Ls	GF	GA	Pts	
1	MILAN AC (MILANO)	38	24	10	4	65	24	82	
2	FC Internazionale (Milano)	38	23	7	8	69	42	76	
3	SSC Napoli (Napoli)	38	21	7	10	59	39	70	
4	Udinese Calcio (Udine)	38	20	6	12	65	43	66	
5	SS Lazio (Roma)	38	20	6	12	55	39	66	
6	AS Roma (Roma)	38	18	9	11	59	52	63	
7	Juventus FC (Torino)	38	15	13	10	57	47	58	
8	US Città di Palermo (Palermo)	38	17	5	16	58	63	56	
9	AC Fiorentina (Firenze)	38	12	15	11	49	44	51	
10	Genoa CFC (Genova)	38	14	9	15	45	47	51	
11	AC Chievo (Verona)	38	11	13	14	38	40	46	
12	Parma AC (Parma)	38	11	13	14	39	47	46	
13	Catania Calcio (Catania)	38	12	10	16	40	52	46	
14	Cagliari Calcio (Cagliari)	38	12	9	17	44	51	45	
15	AC Cesena (Cesena)	38	11	10	17	38	50	43	
16	Bologna FC 1909 (Bologna)	38	11	12	15	35	52	42	-3
17	US Lecce (Lecce)	38	11	8	19	46	66	41	
18	US Sampdoria (Genova)	38	8	12	18	33	49	36	R
19	Brescia Calcio (Brescia)	38	7	11	20	34	52	32	R
20	AS Bari (Bari)	38	5	9	24	27	56	24	R
		760	283	194	283	955	955	1040	(-3)

Bologna FC 1909 (Bologna) had a total of 3 points deducted. 1 point was deducted due to unpaid taxes and 2 points were deducted due to unpaid wages.

Top goalscorers

1)	Antonio DI NATALE	(Udinese Calcio)	28
2)	Edinson CAVANI	(SSC Napoli)	26
3)	Samuel ETO'O	(FC Internazionale)	21
4)	Alessandro MATRI	(Cagliari Calcio/Juventus FC)	20
5	Marco DI VAIO	(Bologna FC 1909)	19

	Serie "B"	Pd	Wn	Dw	Ls	GF	GA	Pts	
1	Atalanta FC (Bergamo)	42	22	13	7	61	35	79	P
2	AC Siena (Siena)	42	21	14	7	67	35	77	P
3	Novara Calcio (Novara)	42	18	16	8	63	38	70	POP
4	AS Varese 1910 (Varese)	42	16	20	6	51	34	68	PO
5	Calcio Padova (Padova)	42	15	17	10	63	48	62	PO
6	Reggina Calcio (Reggio Calabria)	42	15	16	11	46	40	61	PO
7	Livorno Calcio (Livorno)	42	15	14	13	49	46	59	
8	Torino Calcio (Torino)	42	15	13	14	49	48	58	
9	Empoli FC (Empoli)	42	13	18	11	46	39	57	
10	Modena FC (Modena)	42	12	19	11	46	51	55	
11	FC Crotone (Crotone)	42	13	15	14	45	50	54	
12	Vicenza Calcio (Vicenza)	42	15	9	18	44	54	54	
13	Pescara Calcio (Pescara)	42	14	11	17	44	48	53	
14	AS Cittadella (Cittadella)	42	12	15	15	50	54	51	
15	US Grosseto FC (Grosseto)	42	12	15	15	43	50	51	
16	US Sassuolo Calcio (Sassuolo)	42	13	12	17	42	46	51	
17	Ascoli Calcio 1898 (Ascoli Piceno)	42	14	14	14	44	48	50	-6
18	UC AlbinoLeffe (Albino)	42	13	10	19	55	66	49	PO
19	FC Piacenza (Piacenza)	42	11	13	18	50	63	46	POR
20	US Triestina Calcio (Trieste)	42	8	16	18	34	57	40	R
21	Calcio Portogruaro Summaga (Portgruaro)	42	10	10	22	39	63	40	R
22	Frosinone Calcio (Frosinone)	42	8	14	20	46	64	38	R
		924	305	314	305	1077	1077	1223	(-6)

Ascoli Calcio 1898 (Ascoli) had 6 points deducted.

Promotion Play-offs

Calcio Padova (Padova)	0-0, 0-2	Novara Calcio (Novara)
Reggina Calcio (Reggio Calabria)	0-0, 2-2	Novara Calcio (Novara)

(Novara Calcio qualified for the Play-off final due to their higher final league position)

Calcio Padova (Padova)	1-0, 3-3	AS Varese 1910 (Varese)

Relegation Play-off

FC Piacenza (Piacenza)	0-0, 2-2	UC AlbinoLeffe (Albino)

(FC Piacenza were relegated due to their lower final league position)

Promoted to Serie "B": AS Gubbio 1910 (Gubbio), SS Juve Stabia (Castellammare di Stabia), ASG Nocerina (Nocera Inferiore) and Hellas Verona FC (Verona).

Coppa Italia Final (Stadio Olimpico, Roma - 29/05/2011 - 70,000)

FC INTERNAZIONALE (MILANO) 3-1 US Città di Palermo (Palermo)

Eto'o 26', 76', Milito 90+2' *Mu-oz 88'*

Internazionale: César, Nagatomo, Lúcio, Ranocchia, Chivu, Stankovic, Zanetti, Sneijder (Milito 87'), Motta (Mariga 83'), Pazzini (Pandev), Eto'o.

Palermo: Sirigu, Cassani, Mu-oz, Goian (Carrozzieri 24'), Balzaretti, Migliaccio, Acquah (Miccoli 55'), Nocerino, Ilicic, Pastore, Hernández (Pinilla 79').

Semi-finals

AS Roma (Roma) 0-1, 1-1 FC Internazionale (Milano)
Milan AC (Milano) 2-2, 1-2 US Città di Palermo (Palermo)

Quarter-finals

US Città di Palermo (Palermo) 0-0 (aet) Parma AC (Parma)
(Palermo won 5-4 on penalties)
US Sampdoria (Genova) 1-2 AC Milan (Milano)
SSC Napoli (Napoli) 0-0 (aet) FC Internazionale (Milano)
(FC Internazionale won 5-4 on penalties)
Juventus FC (Torino) 0-2 AS Roma (Roma)

2011-12

2011-12 Serie "A"	Atalanta	Bologna	Cagliari	Catania	Cesena	Chievo	Fiorentina	Genoa	Internazionale	Juventus	Lazio	Lecce	Milan	Napoli	Novara	Palermo	Parma	Roma	Siena	Udinese
Atalanta BC		2-0	1-0	1-1	4-1	1-0	2-0	1-0	1-1	0-2	0-2	0-0	0-2	1-1	2-1	1-0	1-1	4-1	1-2	0-0
Bologna FC 1909	3-1		1-0	2-0	0-1	2-2	2-0	3-2	1-3	1-1	0-2	0-2	2-2	2-0	1-0	1-3	0-0	0-2	1-0	1-3
Cagliari Calcio	2-0	1-1		3-0	3-0	0-0	0-0	3-0	2-2	0-2	0-3	1-2	0-2	0-0	2-1	2-1	0-0	4-2	0-0	0-0
Catania Calcio	2-0	0-1	0-1		1-0	1-2	1-0	4-0	2-1	1-1	1-0	1-2	1-1	2-1	3-1	2-0	1-1	1-1	0-0	0-2
AC Cesena	0-1	0-0	1-1	0-0		0-0	0-0	2-0	0-1	0-1	1-2	0-1	1-3	1-3	3-1	2-2	2-2	2-3	0-2	0-1
AC Chievo	0-0	0-1	2-0	3-2	1-0		1-0	2-1	0-2	0-0	0-3	1-0	0-1	1-0	2-2	1-0	1-2	0-0	1-1	0-0
AC Fiorentina	2-2	2-0	0-0	2-2	2-0	1-2		1-0	0-0	0-5	1-2	0-1	0-0	0-3	2-2	0-0	3-0	3-0	2-1	3-2
Genoa CFC	2-2	2-1	2-1	3-0	1-1	0-1	2-2		0-1	0-0	3-2	0-0	0-2	3-2	1-0	2-0	2-2	2-1	1-4	3-2
FC Internazionale	0-0	0-3	2-1	2-2	2-1	1-0	2-0	5-4		1-2	2-1	4-1	4-2	0-3	0-1	4-4	5-0	0-0	2-1	0-1
Juventus FC	3-1	1-1	1-1	3-1	2-0	1-1	2-1	2-2	2-0		2-1	1-1	2-0	3-0	2-0	3-0	4-1	4-0	0-0	2-1
SS Lazio	2-0	1-3	1-0	1-1	3-2	0-0	1-0	1-2	3-1	0-1		1-1	2-0	3-1	3-0	0-0	1-0	2-1	1-1	2-2
US Lecce	1-2	0-0	0-2	0-1	0-0	2-2	0-1	2-2	1-0	0-1	2-3		3-4	0-2	1-1	1-1	1-2	4-2	4-1	0-2
Milan AC	2-0	1-1	3-0	4-0	1-0	4-0	1-2	1-0	0-1	1-1	2-2	2-0		0-0	2-1	3-0	4-1	2-1	2-0	1-1
SSC Napoli	1-3	1-1	6-3	2-2	0-0	2-0	0-0	6-1	1-0	3-3	0-0	4-2	3-1		2-0	2-0	1-2	1-3	2-1	2-0
Novara Calcio	0-0	0-2	0-0	3-3	3-0	1-2	0-3	1-1	3-1	0-4	2-1	0-0	0-3	1-1		2-2	2-1	0-2	1-1	1-0
US Città di Palermo	2-1	3-1	3-2	1-1	0-1	4-4	2-0	5-3	4-3	0-2	5-1	2-0	0-4	1-3	2-0		1-2	0-1	2-0	1-1
Parma AC	1-2	1-0	3-0	3-3	2-0	2-1	2-2	3-1	3-1	0-0	3-1	3-3	0-2	1-2	2-0	0-0		0-1	3-1	2-0
AS Roma	3-1	1-1	1-2	2-2	5-1	2-0	1-2	1-0	4-0	1-1	1-2	2-1	2-3	2-2	5-2	1-0	1-0		1-1	3-1
AC Siena	2-2	1-1	3-0	0-1	2-0	4-1	0-0	0-2	0-1	0-1	4-0	3-0	1-4	1-1	0-2	4-1	0-2	1-0		1-0
Udinese Calcio	0-0	2-0	0-0	2-1	4-1	2-1	2-0	2-0	1-3	0-0	2-0	2-1	1-2	2-2	3-0	1-0	3-1	2-0	2-1	

	Serie "A"	Pd	Wn	Dw	Ls	GF	GA	Pts	
1	JUVENTUS FC (TORINO)	38	23	15	0	68	20	84	
2	Milan AC (Milano)	38	24	8	6	74	33	80	
3	Udinese Calcio (Udine)	38	18	10	10	52	35	64	
4	SS Lazio (Roma)	38	18	8	12	56	47	62	
5	SSC Napoli (Napoli)	38	16	13	9	66	46	61	
6	FC Internazionale (Milano)	38	17	7	14	58	55	58	
7	AS Roma (Roma)	38	16	8	14	60	54	56	
8	Parma AC (Parma)	38	15	11	12	54	53	56	
9	Bologna FC 1909 (Bologna)	38	13	12	13	41	43	51	
10	AC Chievo (Verona)	38	12	13	13	35	45	49	
11	Catania Calcio (Catania)	38	11	15	12	47	52	48	
12	Atalanta BC (Bergamo)	38	13	13	12	41	43	46	-6
13	AC Fiorentina (Firenze)	38	11	13	14	37	43	46	
14	AC Siena (Siena)	38	11	11	16	45	45	44	
15	Cagliari Calcio (Cagliari)	38	10	13	15	37	46	43	
16	US Città di Palermo (Palermo)	38	11	10	17	52	62	43	
17	Genoa CFC (Genova)	38	11	9	18	50	69	42	
18	US Lecce (Lecce)	38	8	12	18	40	56	36	R
19	Novara Calcio (Novara)	38	7	11	20	35	65	32	R
20	AC Cesena (Cesena)	38	4	10	24	24	60	22	R
		760	269	222	269	972	972	1023	(-6)

Atalanta BC had 6 points deducted due to their involvement in the 2011-12 Italian football scandal.

US Lecce were initially relegated to Serie "B", but were then further relegated into the Lega Pro Prima Divisione due to their involvement in the 2011-12 Italian football scandal.

Top goalscorers

1)	Zlatan IBRAHIMOVIC	(Milan AC)	28
2)	Diego MILITO	(FC Internazionale)	24
3)	Edinson CAVANI	(SSC Napoli)	23
	Antonio DI NATALE	(Udinese Calcio)	23
5)	Rodrigo PALACIO	(Genoa CFC)	19

	Serie "B"	Pd	Wn	Dw	Ls	GF	GA	Pts	
1	Pescara Calcio (Pescara)	42	26	5	11	90	55	83	P
2	Torino Calcio (Torino)	42	24	11	7	57	28	83	P
3	US Sassuolo Calcio (Sassuolo)	42	22	14	6	57	33	80	PO
4	Hellas Verona FC (Verona)	42	23	9	10	60	41	78	PO
5	AS Varese 1910 (Varese)	42	20	11	11	57	41	71	PO
6	UC Sampdoria (Genova)	42	17	16	9	53	34	67	POP
7	Calcio Padova (Padova)	42	18	9	15	56	58	63	
8	Brescia Calcio (Brescia)	42	15	12	15	48	50	57	
9	SS Juve Stabia (Castellammare di Stabia)	42	16	13	13	53	49	57	-4
10	Reggina Calcio (Reggio Calabria)	42	14	13	15	63	59	55	
11	FC Crotone (Crotone)	42	13	15	14	60	58	52	-2
12	Modena FC (Modena)	42	12	16	14	50	58	52	
13	AS Bari (Bari)	42	14	14	14	47	48	50	-6
14	US Grosseto FC (Grosseto)	42	11	16	15	47	60	49	
15	Ascoli Calcio 1898 (Ascoli)	42	15	11	16	47	50	49	-7
16	AS Cittadella (Cittadella)	42	13	9	20	51	64	48	
17	Livorno Calcio (Livorno)	42	12	12	18	49	49	48	
18	Empoli FC (Empoli)	42	12	11	19	48	59	47	PO
19	Vicenza Calcio (Vicenza)	42	10	14	18	43	61	44	POR
20	ASG Nocerina (Nocera Inferiore)	42	10	10	22	52	71	40	R
21	AS Gubbio 1910 (Gubbio)	42	7	11	24	37	69	32	R
22	UC AlbinoLeffe (Albino)	42	6	12	24	39	69	30	R
		924	330	264	330	1164	1164	1235	(-19)

SS Juve Stabia had a total of 4 points deducted. 1 point was deducted due to financial irregularities and 3 points were deducted for match fixing with Sorrento. The initial match-fixing penalty was 5 points but this was reduced to 3 points on appeal.

AS Bari had 6 points deducted due to financial irregularities.

FC Crotone had 2 points deducted due to financial irregularities.

Ascoli Calcio 1898 had 7 points deducted, 4 points were deducted due to financial irregularities and 3 points were deducted due to the the club's involvement in the 2011-12 Italian football scandal. The initial penalty for this was 6 points, but this was reduced to 3 point on appeal.

Vicenza Calcio remained in Serie "B" following the relegation of US Lecce due to their relegation into the Lega Pro Prima Divisione following the 2011-12 Italian football scandal.

Promotion Play-offs

UC Sampdoria (Genova)	3-2, 1-0	AS Varese 1910 (Varese)
UC Sampdoria (Genova)	2-1, 1-1	US Sassuolo Calcio (Sassuolo)
AS Varese 1910 (Varese)	2-0, 1-1	Hellas Verona FC (Verona)

Relegation Play-off

Vicenza (Calcio)	0-0, 2-3	Empoli FC (Empoli)

Promoted to Serie "B": FC Pro Vercelli 1892 (Vercelli), Ternana Calcio (Terni), Spezia Calcio (La Spezia) and SS Virtus Lanciano 1924 (Lanciano).